Fundamentals of Jewish Conflict Resolution

Traditional Jewish Perspectives on Resolving Interpersonal Conflicts

Studies in Orthodox Judaism

Series Editor
Marc B. Shapiro (University of Scranton, Scranton, Pennsylvania)

Editorial Board
Alan Brill (Seton Hall University, South Orange, New Jersey)
Benjamin Brown (Hebrew University, Jerusalem)
David Ellenson (Hebrew Union College, New York)
Adam S. Ferziger (Bar-Ilan University, Ramat Gan)
Miri Freud-Kandel (University of Oxford, Oxford)
Jeffrey Gurock (Yeshiva University, New York)
Shlomo Tikoshinski (Jerusalem Institute for Israel Studies, Jerusalem)

ACADEMIC STUDIES PRESS

Fundamentals of Jewish Conflict Resolution

Traditional Jewish Perspectives on Resolving Interpersonal Conflicts

HOWARD KAMINSKY

Boston
2017

Library of Congress Cataloging-in-Publication Data

Names: Kaminsky, Howard, author.

Title: Fundamentals of Jewish conflict resolution: traditional Jewish perspectives on resolving interpersonal conflicts/Howard Kaminsky.

Description: Brighton, MA: Academic Studies Press, [2017]

Series: Studies in Orthodox Judaism

Identifiers: LCCN 2016057230 (print) | LCCN 2017020578 (ebook) | ISBN 9781618115645 (e-book) | ISBN 9781618115638 (hardcover)

Subjects: LCSH: Conflict management—Religious aspects—Judaism. | Interpersonal relations—Religious aspects—Judaism. | Jewish ethics.

Classification: LCC BJ1286.C65 (ebook) | LCC BJ1286.C65 K36 2017 (print) | DDC 296.3/6—dc23

LC record available at https://lccn.loc.gov/2016057230

ISBN 978-1-61811-563-8 (hardback); ISBN 978-1-61811-845-5 (paper)
ISBN 978-1-61811-564-5 (electronic)

Book design by Kryon Publishing Services (P) Ltd.
www.kryonpublishing.com

Published by Academic Studies Press
28 Montfern Avenue
Brighton, MA 02135, USA
press@academicstudiespress.com
www.academicstudiespress.com

לעילוי נשמת אבי מורי
ר' ישראל ב"ר משה קמינסקי ז"ל
נלב"ע ט"ו תמוז תשע"א
ת'נ'צ'ב'ה

In loving memory of my father
Israel Kaminsky ז"ל

Contents

Detailed Table of Contents viii
Acknowledgments xvi
Preface xix

PART I—INTRODUCTORY ESSAY

Chapter 1: Contemporary Conflict Resolution: An Overview of the Field and the Core Components of its Educational Programs 2

PART II—FOUNDATIONAL VALUES AND CONCEPTS

Chapter 2: Pursuing Peace and Refraining from Destructive Conflict 36

Chapter 3: Rabbinic Perspectives on Constructive Conflict: A "Dispute for the Sake of Heaven" 74

PART III—FOUNDATIONAL COMMANDMENTS AND LAWS

Chapter 4: Basic Interpersonal Obligations and Prohibitions 110

PART IV—BASIC COMMANDMENTS AND LAWS OF INTERPERSONAL CONFLICT RESOLUTION

Chapter 5: Judging People Favorably: Countering Negative Judgmental Biases 190

The Nature and the Extent of the Obligation of Promoting Interpersonal Peace 49
The Principle of "Positive Peace" 53
Maḥaloket (Conflict) in the Traditional Sources 56
Defining the Primary Hebrew Terms for Conflict 56
General Talmudic and Midrashic Perspectives on Conflict 59
The Halakhic Obligation of Refraining from Conflict 62
Summary 66
Similarities and Differences between Contemporary Conflict Resolution and Traditional Jewish Approaches in Respect to the Fundamental Value of Promoting Peace 68

Chapter 3: Rabbinic Perspectives on Constructive Conflict: A "Dispute for the Sake of Heaven" 74
Introduction 74
The Literal-Primary Sense of the Mishnah 77
A Conceptual Analysis of the Mishnah 77
The Evidence from the Mishnah and the Tosefta 80
Interpretations of the *Rishonim* and *Aḥaronim* 87
Motif A: The Positive Aspects of Conflict 87
Motif B: Ascription of Positive Attributes to Hillel and Shammai and Negative Attributes to Korah 90
Motif C: Recognition of Ulterior Motives 97
Summary 100
Similarities and Differences between Contemporary Conflict Resolution and Traditional Jewish Approaches in Respect to Fundamental, Underlying Concepts about Constructive/Destructive Conflict 102

Constructive Conflict as Understood in Contemporary Conflict Resolution and a Dispute for the Sake of Heaven in Traditional Jewish Approaches 102

PART III—FOUNDATIONAL COMMANDMENTS AND LAWS

Chapter 4: Basic Interpersonal Obligations and Prohibitions **110**

"You Shall Love Your Neighbor as Yourself" 111

Rabbinic Formulations of "You Shall Love Your Neighbor as Yourself" 112

Ahavat ha-Beriyot, Love for All Humanity 121

"You Shall Not Hate Your Brother in Your Heart" 134

Rabbinic Formulations of "You Shall Not Hate Your Brother in Your Heart" 135

Two Approaches to Dealing with Hatred 142

The Commandment Prohibiting Physical Violence 145

Commandments Prohibiting Verbal Abuse—The Prohibitions against Saying Things That Are Hurtful/Embarrassing and Cursing Someone 150

The Rabbinic Stance toward Verbal Abuse 152

Ona'at Devarim—The Prohibition against Saying Things That Are Hurtful 155

The Prohibition against Embarrassing Someone 158

Comparing and Contrasting the Two Commandments 162

The Prohibition against Cursing Someone 164

Summary 168

Similarities and Differences between Contemporary Conflict Resolution and Traditional Jewish Approaches in Respect to

Underlying Values and Behavioral Guidelines of the Basic Interpersonal Obligations and Prohibitions 169
The Value of Loving One's Neighbor as Opposed to Cooperation 172
Basic Interpersonal Behavioral Guidelines and Rules of Conduct 174
The Value of Character Development 184

PART IV—BASIC COMMANDMENTS AND LAWS OF INTERPERSONAL CONFLICT RESOLUTION

Chapter 5: Judging People Favorably: Countering Negative Judgmental Biases **190**
The Commandment of "In Righteousness You Shall Judge Your Friend" 192
The Basic Halakhic Parameters of Judging Someone Favorably 195
The Ḥafets Ḥayim on Judging "Towards the Scale of Merit" 197
Related Concepts 205
"Respect Him and Suspect Him" 205
"Vindicating the Wicked" 206
"Do Not Judge Your Friend until You Are in His Place" 207
Summary 209
Similarities and Differences between Contemporary Conflict Resolution and Traditional Jewish Approaches in Respect to Judging People Favorably 211
Research on Negative Judgmental Biases 212
Countering Negative Judgmental Biases 215
Comparing Contemporary Conflict Resolution's and Traditional Jewish Approaches' Respective Methods 218

Chapter 6: *Tokhaḥah*: Judaism's Basic Approach to Resolving Interpersonal Conflict through Dialogue 223
The Biblical Source 225
Maimonides on *Tokhaḥah* 228
Hilkhot De'ot (Laws of Dispositions), Subsection 6:6 229
Hilkhot De'ot, Subsection 6:7 235
Hilkhot De'ot, Subsection 6:8 240
Hilkhot De'ot, Subsection 6:9 242
The Dialogic Component 247
Summary 250
Similarities and Differences between Contemporary Conflict Resolution and Traditional Jewish Approaches in Respect to Their Methods for Resolving Interpersonal Conflict through Dialogue 255

Chapter 7: Retaliation and Resentment: Not Taking Revenge and Not Bearing a Grudge 261
Underlying Reasons for the Commandments 263
Sa'adia Gaon's Explanation 263
Maimonides' Explanation 266
The Sefer ha-Ḥinukh's Explanation 269
An Essential Cognitive Component 274
The Practical Halakhic Discourse 277
Tsa'ara de-Gufa, "Personal Suffering" 280
Responding to Insults and Ridicule during the Initial Verbal Exchange 286
The Relationship between Tokhaḥah and the Commandment against Bearing a Grudge 290
Summary 292
Similarities and Differences between Contemporary Conflict Resolution and Traditional Jewish Approaches in Respect to Retaliation and Resentment 293

Chapter 8: Apologies: The Asking and Granting of Forgiveness **299**

The Obligations of the One Who Asks for Forgiveness 300

The Talmudic Sources 300

Asking for Forgiveness on the Day before Yom Kippur 303

The Obligation of Personally Going to Ask for Forgiveness 312

Specifying the Offense Committed 316

The Obligation to Ask for Forgiveness Three Times 323

The Requirement of Appeasement 330

The Obligations of the One Who Forgives 335

The Primary Sources for the Obligation to Forgive Someone 335

How Readily Must One Grant Forgiveness? 339

When One Is and Is Not Obligated to Forgive 341

How Sincere Must One's Forgiveness Be? 350

Summary 360

Similarities and Differences between Contemporary Conflict Resolution and Traditional Jewish Approaches in Respect to Apologies and Forgiveness 363

Theories and Research on Apologies 364

Comparing Contemporary Approaches to Apologies and the Obligations of the One Who Asks for Forgiveness 379

Contemporary Models of Forgiveness 383

Comparing Contemporary Models of Forgiveness and the Obligations of the One Who Forgives 398

Apologies and Forgiveness in Contemporary Conflict Resolution 401

Comparing Contemporary Conflict Resolution and Traditional Jewish Approaches in Respect to Apologies and Forgiveness 404

PART V—THE AFFECTIVE COMPONENT—ANGER MANAGEMENT

Chapter 9: Jewish Anger Management **408**

Orekh Apayim and *Ma'aneh Rakh* 410

How R. Jelen and R. Levinson Describe Their Works 410

Some of the Stylistic Differences between Orekh Apayim and Ma'aneh Rakh 412

Significant Similarities between *Orekh Apayim* and *Ma'aneh Rakh* 413

Underlying Assumptions and Fundamental Principles 413

Behavioral and Cognitive Strategies 417

Significant Differences between *Orekh Apayim* and *Ma'aneh Rakh* 422

Unique Features of Orekh Apayim 422

Unique Features of Ma'aneh Rakh 427

Summary 431

Similarities and Differences between Contemporary Conflict Resolution and Traditional Jewish Approaches in Respect to Anger Management 434

Foundational Elements of Contemporary Anger Management 434

Contemporary Anger Management, Traditional Jewish Approaches, and Contemporary Conflict Resolution 446

Conclusion **453**

Summary 453

The Nature of Jewish Conflict Resolution 455

Gopin's and Steinberg's Characterizations 455

Practical Applications for Jewish Education 458

Similarities and Differences between Contemporary Conflict Resolution and Traditional Jewish Approaches 461
Suggestions for Contemporary Conflict Resolution 465
A Proposal for Future Research 465
Some Practical Applications for Contemporary Conflict Resolution 465

Glossary 468
Bibliography 474
Index 543

Acknowledgments

There are innumerable people who have contributed to this book in one way or another, and, unfortunately, I'm not able to list and thank them all. I would, however, like to mention the following:

I would like to express my deep gratitude to my friend and colleague Rabbi Dr. Daniel Roth, who is the director of the Pardes Center for Judaism and Conflict Resolution (PCJCR). Without Rabbi Roth's strong support and encouragement and the sponsorship of the PCJCR, this book, in all likelihood, would never have been published. I extend to him my most sincere thanks and wish him continued success with the wonderful programs that he runs through the PCJCR.

I would also like to express my deep gratitude and appreciation to all of the editors and staff at Academic Studies Press who have helped in the publication of this book. Particularly, I would like to thank Rabbi Dr. Marc Shapiro for deciding to include my work in the "Studies in Orthodox Judaism" series; Dr. Gregg Stern and Dr. David Michelson, who patiently and professionally guided me through the entire process and offered many valuable suggestions to improve my manuscript; and Ms. Eileen Wolfberg, who was my copy editor and did an outstanding job of catching mistakes and improving the overall quality of my material.

This book is a revised version of my doctoral dissertation. In the preparation and writing of my dissertation, I had the very good fortune to work under a number of outstanding scholars. These include Dr. John Kuentzel, the past coordinator of the program in religion and education, Teachers College, Columbia University, who was my dissertation sponsor; Dr. Douglas Sloan, who headed the program in religion and education before Dr. Kuentzel; Rabbi Dr. Yitzchak Handel, who was my dissertation advisor; and Dr. Peter Coleman, the director of the International Center for Cooperation and Conflict Resolution, who was my teacher and served on my dissertation defense committee. I am indebted to them all and sincerely thank them for their guidance and encouragement during my time at Teachers College.

My *rebbeim* (teachers of Torah), who showed me caring concern, inspired and guided me, and opened up for me the worlds of Torah and *musar* (Jewish ethics)—I simply cannot thank them enough. Two such wonderful *rebbeim*, who are no longer with us, and are sorely missed, were Rabbi A. Henach Leibowitz, *zt"l*, who was the *Rosh Yeshiva* of Yeshivas Rabbeinu Yisrael Meir ha-Kohen (the Rabbinical Seminary of America, "Yeshiva Chofetz Chaim" in Queens, New York) and Rabbi Michel Barenbaum, *zt"l*, who was the *mashgiaḥ ruḥani* (spiritual overseer) of Mesivtha Tifereth Jerusalem.

The overwhelming majority of material in this book is based on classic Jewish sources and the earlier works of great Torah scholars. A number of important but, unfortunately, somewhat lesser-known scholars and their works played a major role in the development of certain chapters in this book. These include Rabbi Joseph D. Epstein, *zt"l*, whose theories regarding the Jewish perspective on peace are highlighted in Chapter 2; Rabbi Zvi Weinberger and Rabbi Baruch Heifetz, whose research on *tokhaḥah* for interpersonal offenses and the laws of taking revenge and bearing a grudge was invaluable in the writing of Chapters 6 and 7; and Rabbi Yitzchak Isaac Silver, whose summary of the laws of judging people favorably is presented in Chapter 5. I am indebted to these *talmide ḥakhamim* (rabbinic scholars), and I want to acknowledge the very important contribution that they have made to this book. I am particularly grateful to Rabbi Silver, who has given me his kind permission to reproduce the chart that appears on page 200, which originally appeared in his work *Mishpete ha-Shalom: Hilkhot ben Adam la-Ḥavero* (Jerusalem: n.p., 2005).

My love and appreciation for family goes far beyond words. My mother, Tillie Kaminsky, whom I cherish and love dearly, has shown an inexhaustible amount of support, caring concern, and love for her children over the years. I pray that God will bless her with good health and happiness in the years to come. For my brother Marvin, who is my dearest friend, I have the greatest respect and love. And to all of my other relatives, I take this opportunity to express to them how much they all mean to me and my love for them all.

As far as my friends are concerned, I feel that the *Ribono shel Olam* (the Master of the Universe) has blessed me with an array of dedicated friends who possess the most beautiful character traits, incredible *sekhel* (common sense), and remarkably deep insights, all of which I have gained from in more ways than they could ever imagine.

This book was written in loving memory of my father, Israel Kaminsky, *z"l*. Born in Chmielnik, Poland in 1919, my father was a Holocaust survivor, an ardent Zionist, a devoted and loving parent, an extremely bright individual, who possessed many outstanding qualities, and he was my best friend. Without his influence, staunch and unwavering support, and encouragement, this book would certainly never have been written.

Preface

Conflict resolution theorists, who have developed their paradigmatic models of conflict resolution based on Western cultural values and principles of social psychology, have expressed concern about the cultural specificity of their approaches. Their concern is that, in developing their models of conflict resolution, they may have overlooked alternative orientations and perspectives that offer valuable contributions to conflict resolution theory and practice.[1] One of the clearest indications of this is that their models of conflict resolution often fail dismally in addressing the needs of religious communities whose ideologies and values differ significantly from those of Western culture. This realization has sparked a movement that has attempted to integrate conflict resolution theory and religious ethics. Professor Marc Gopin of George Mason University, who is at the forefront of this movement, has forcefully argued that through an understanding of religious approaches to resolving conflict, conflict resolution theorists may not only formulate models of conflict resolution that appeal to even the most traditionally religious groups, they may also come to broaden their own perspectives and incorporate key missing ingredients in the work that they do.[2]

---

1 See Morton Deutsch, introduction to *The Handbook of Conflict Resolution: Theory and Practice*, ed. Morton Deutsch and Peter T. Coleman (San Francisco: Jossey-Bass, 2000), 16; and Peter T. Coleman, concluding overview to *The Handbook of Conflict Resolution: Theory and Practice*, ed. Morton Deutsch and Peter T. Coleman (San Francisco: Jossey-Bass, 2000), 595–97.

2 Marc Gopin, *Between Eden and Armageddon: The Future of World Religions, Violence, and Peacemaking* (New York: Oxford University Press, 2000), 152–54, 167–95. See also S. Ayse Kadayifci-Orellana, "Ethno-Religious Conflicts: Exploring the Role of Religion in Conflict Resolution," in *The SAGE Handbook of Conflict Resolution*, ed. Jacob Bercovitch, Victor Kremenyuk, and I. William Zartman (Los Angeles: Sage

Gopin has specifically bemoaned the fact that there is as of yet no "serious investigation of Jewish tradition" that explicates "a Jewish philosophy of conflict resolution."[3] Even though there exists a diverse and impressive body of literature in Hebrew that offers in-depth analyses of specific aspects of the traditional Jewish approach towards promoting peace and resolving conflict, and there are even a number of more extensive works that cover multiple topics, there is currently no scholarly work that presents in English an in-depth, systematic study of the major components of traditional Judaism's perspective on conflict resolution. This book will attempt to take a small first step in trying to fill this void by explicating a Jewish paradigm of interpersonal conflict resolution.

The Focal Topic

Conflict resolution theorists, researchers, and practitioners differentiate between and categorize conflicts in a variety of ways. One of the primary ways that they categorize conflicts is to classify them as being either "interpersonal" (a conflict that takes place between two people, e.g., a husband and wife; two friends, neighbors, or coworkers; or two total strangers who meet in the street, and so on) or as being "intergroup" (a conflict that takes place between any two groups, e.g., conflicts between religious factions; social, ethnic, or racial groups; management and labor, and so on). My focus in this work will be on interpersonal conflicts (although for certain chapters one may find multiple applications to intergroup conflicts as well).[4] Specifically, I will focus on the common, everyday interpersonal

---

Publications, 2009), 274–78; and Rachel Goldberg and Brian Blancke, "God in the Process: Is There a Place for Religion in Conflict Resolution?" *Conflict Resolution Quarterly* 28, no. 4 (2011): 386, 392.

3 Gopin, *Between Eden and Armageddon*, 194–95. See also Gerald Steinberg, "Jewish Sources on Conflict Management: Realism and Human Nature," in *Conflict and Conflict Management in Jewish Sources*, ed. Michal Rones (Ramat Gan, Israel: Program on Conflict Management and Negotiation, Bar-Ilan University, 2008), 10.

4 Social psychologists have highlighted an array of phenomena that interpersonal and intergroup conflicts share. For example, both levels of conflict may accurately be described in terms of their underlying motivations, misunderstandings between the

conflict, and I will attempt to present what I believe to be the essential substance of traditional Jewish thought that relates to the prevention, amelioration, and resolution of such conflicts.[5]

It should be understood that all religious traditions have their own unique perspectives on peace and conflict.[6] Judaism, with its

---

parties, breakdowns in communication, parties' tendencies to judge themselves favorably and the other party negatively, abilities to restrain emotional responses, competencies to reconcile differences in a rational and judicious manner, and their capacities to forgive each other (see Morton Deutsch, *The Resolution of Conflict: Constructive and Destructive Processes* [New Haven: Yale University Press, 1973], 7; and Deutsch, *Handbook of Conflict Resolution*, 6–9). Despite the similarities, there are very significant differences that exist between the dynamics of interpersonal conflicts and those of intergroup conflicts. For example, in intergroup conflicts, the parties exhibit a greater degree of difficulty in empathizing with and taking the other party's perspective, they act more irrationally and aggressively, and conflict escalates faster and to a higher degree than in interpersonal conflicts (see Amelie Mummendey and Sabine Otten, "Aggression: Interaction between Individuals and Social Groups," in *Aggression and Violence: Social Interactionist Perspectives*, ed. Richard B. Felson and James T. Tedeschi [Washington, DC: American Psychological Association, 1993], 145–67; and Joseph M. Mikolic, John C. Parker, and Dean G. Pruitt, "Escalation in Response to Persistent Annoyance: Groups Versus Individuals and Gender Effects," *Journal of Personality and Social Psychology*, vol. 72, no. 1 [1997]: 151–63). Therefore, one would be well advised to not indiscriminately extrapolate from the interpersonal realm to that of the intergroup.

5 Even though a good percentage of what I will be discussing could very well be designated as "conflict prevention" or as "conflict management" (a term that is often used in relation to cases in which conflict cannot be totally resolved, but its destructive effects are ameliorated; see, for example, Berghof Foundation, ed., "Conflict Prevention, Management, Resolution," in *Berghof Glossary on Conflict Transformation* [Berlin, Germany: Berghof Foundation, 2012], 18), I will be employing the terminology "conflict resolution." This reflects the standard usage of the term *conflict resolution*, which in many contexts encompasses the prevention and management of conflicts as well as their resolution (e.g., "conflict resolution" education teaches skills that are not only meant to resolve conflicts after they have developed but are also supposed to help prevent conflicts from developing and ameliorate the destructive effects of conflicts that cannot be resolved). For discussions of conflict terminology that lend support to the usage of the term *conflict resolution* as an umbrella term that encompasses the prevention, amelioration, and resolution of conflict, see Oliver Ramsbotham, Tom Woodhouse, Hugh Miall, *Contemporary Conflict Resolution*, 3rd ed. (Cambridge: Polity Press, 2011), 9–10; Berghof Foundation, "Conflict Prevention, Management, Resolution," 18; and Karin Aggestam, "Conflict Prevention: Old Wine in New Bottles?" *International Peacekeeping* 10, no. 1 (2003): 20.

6 For an overview of works on Jewish perspectives, see Daniel Roth, "*Masoret Aharon Rodef Shalom ben Ish le-Ish ke-Model Rabani le-Fiyus*" [The Tradition of Aaron Pursuer of Peace between People as a Rabbinic Model of Reconciliation] (PhD diss., Bar-Ilan University, 2012), 1–9. For examples of Christian perspectives, see Ronald G. Musto,

unique halakhic (see Glossary) emphasis on normative standards of behavior, has developed a *sui generis* set of principles and procedures for averting and responding to conflict. Within the vast corpus of traditional Jewish literature, there exists what may be viewed as various complex paradigms (conceptual and methodological models) of conflict resolution. Using the standard classifications of conflict resolution theorists, we may differentiate between Jewish paradigms of conflict resolution that relate to interpersonal conflicts and those that relate to intergroup conflicts, in which each individual paradigm encompasses a set of underlying values, fundamental concepts, prescriptive rules, and guidelines for addressing its specific form of conflict. I intend to traverse the spectrum of traditional Jewish texts and cull from Scripture, Mishnah, Talmud, Midrash, halakhic and ethical literature to elucidate a Jewish paradigm of interpersonal conflict resolution.

The Catholic Peace Tradition (New York: Peace Books, 2002); Ken Sende, *The Peacemaker: A Biblical Guide to Resolving Personal Conflict* (Grand Rapids, MI: Baker Books, 2004); and Catherine Morris, "Conflict Transformation and Peacebuilding: A Selected Bibliography—Christian Perspectives on Conflict Transformation, Nonviolence and Reconciliation," Peacemakers Trust, accessed November 4, 2016, http://www.peacemakers.ca/bibliography/bib40christian.html. For Islamic perspectives, see Abdul Aziz Said, Nathan C. Funk, and Ayse S. Kadayifci, *Peace and Conflict Resolution in Islam: Precept and Practice* (Lanham, MD: University Press of America, 2001); Mohammed Abu-Nimer, *Nonviolence and Peace Building in Islam: Theory and Practice* (Gainesville, FL: University Press of Florida, 2003); and Elias Jabbour, *Sulha: Palestinian Traditional Peacemaking Process* (Montreat, NC: House of Hope Publications, 1996). For Buddhist perspectives, John Ferguson, "Buddhism," in *War and Peace in the World's Religions* (NY: Oxford University Press, 1978); David W. Chappell, *Buddhist Peacework* (Somerville, MA: Wisdom Publications, 1999); and Thich Nhat Hanh, *Being Peace* (Berkeley, CA: Parallax Press, 1987). For Hinduism, see Rajmohan Ghandi, "Hinduism and Peacebuilding," in *Religion and Peacebuilding*, eds. Harold Coward and Gordon S. Smith (Albany: State University of New York Press, 2004), 45–68; and Dawn Hibbard, "Conflict Resolution and Hinduism," accessed September 11, 2016, https://www.kettering.edu/news/conflict-resolution-and-hinduism. Some good general works include Gopin, *Between Eden and Armageddon*; Harold Coward and Gordon S. Smith, eds., *Religion and Peacebuilding* (Albany: State University of New York Press, 2004); and R. Scott Appleby, *The Ambivalence of the Sacred: Religion, Violence, and Reconciliation* (Lanham, MD: Rowman and Littlefield, 2000).

For the most part, I will not be addressing disputes that have escalated to the point that they would appropriately be adjudicated or handled through the traditional Jewish judicial procedures (e.g., *din Torah* [a legal procedure based on the strict letter of the law] or *pesharah* ["compromise," the parties agree to resolve their issues based on standards of equity, as perceived by a court or arbitral body]) and institutions (e.g., Jewish courts, arbitral bodies, or lay tribunals). Such disputes have their own unique sets of rules and guidelines in Jewish tradition, and thus rightly deserve a separate, extensive, and detailed analysis. I will be dealing with the types of commonplace interpersonal provocations, arguments, and conflicts that every human being faces (for many people on a regular, or even daily, basis), which are the source of so much heartache and anguish, and when not dealt with properly all too often escalate and threaten to shatter people's lives. The approaches to conflict resolution presented in this work (with a small number of exceptions) are meant to serve as ways in which two individuals who are involved in a conflict may potentially resolve their issues on their own without the assistance of any type of third party (*see footnote*).[7] (This, however, does not mean to exclude the possible applicability or use of these approaches in the context of third-party interventions, e.g., counseling or mediation.)

The Choice and Organization of Subtopics

In order to explain how this work is organized, I first have to explain why I chose to focus on specific subtopics and the research that lead up to this. In 1997, I enrolled in a doctoral program in religion and education at Teachers College, Columbia University. Teachers College is home to one of the premier centers of conflict resolution education and research—the International Center for

7 When actually dealing with real-life, potentially destructive conflict in one's personal life, the reader will, hopefully, be able to recognize when he or she needs the assistance of a third party. In such situations, I would strongly encourage the reader to seek whatever help he or she may need.

Cooperation and Conflict Resolution (ICCCR).[8] From the fall of 1998 through the spring of 2001, I attended the ICCCR and studied the theoretical foundations of negotiation, mediation, and arbitration, took their practicums in conflict resolution, and under their auspices did internships in community mediation and school-based conflict resolution education. From 2001 through 2004, I continued to do a considerable amount of independent research into conflict resolution curricula for my doctoral dissertation. Throughout this period, as part of my course work and doctoral research, I was exposed to a wide variety of models of interpersonal conflict resolution. As I was studying these models, I began to identify certain common denominators that they all seemed to share. I found five very broad and basic components[9] that were present in veritably all models of interpersonal conflict resolution: (1) they all had certain *fundamental, underlying values* on which they were based; (2) they were also all based on certain *fundamental, underlying theoretical concepts about conflict* (which are closely related to, but distinguishable from, the first category of underlying values); (3) they all included certain practical *behavioral guidelines and rules of conduct* that the disputing parties should follow in the process of resolving their differences; (4) they all asked the parties to engage in certain internal *cognitive processes;* and (5) they all had an *affective component,* that is, they all at some point dealt with the constructive expression of emotions and addressed the issue of anger management.[10] (It should be noted that these are not totally separate and discrete categories, and that there is some overlap between them.) The first two components together serve

8 The ICCCR was founded by—and between 1986 and 1998 ran under the directorship of—Morton Deutsch, who for over fifty years was one of the leading figures in the field of conflict resolution. Peter T. Coleman, a renowned scholar and practitioner in the field, took over its directorship in 1998.

9 There are a multitude of other common denominators that these models share. My emphasis here is on fundamental, overarching commonalities.

10 For further elaboration on these five elements, see pp. 30–34.

as the foundation of any given model, and components three through five constitute the model's applied behavioral, cognitive, and affective components. After identifying these five essential components, I proceeded with my research into the traditional Jewish perspective on these elements of interpersonal conflict resolution.

Underlying Values and Concepts of Jewish Conflict Resolution. Having determined that any functional and effective model of interpersonal conflict resolution is invariably grounded in certain fundamental core values and theoretical concepts about conflict, the first thing I did in formulating what I believed to be a Jewish paradigm of interpersonal conflict resolution was to mine the traditional Jewish sources and search for comparable underlying values and concepts.[11] Working with the premise that many of Judaism's foundational values and concepts about conflict and conflict resolution were embodied within its "peace ethos" (i.e., its distinctive guiding values, beliefs, and attitudes that relate to peace, and conflict), I began to explore rabbinic perspectives on peace and conflict. The first step that I took in my research was to obtain and go through all the anthological compilations and major studies on Jewish perspectives on peace and conflict that I could find. I quickly discovered that there exist some very significant works on these topics.[12] After studying these works, I still felt compelled to do my

---

11 It should be understood that the underlying theoretical concepts of contemporary conflict resolution are "theoretical" in the sense that they constitute the theory behind its applied practices and procedures. Even though this definition is applicable to traditional Jewish conflict resolution's "theoretical" concepts, there are other connotations to the word "theory" that are not applicable. I will therefore generally avoid using the term *theoretical* when discussing Jewish conflict resolution's underlying concepts.

12 Some of the noteworthy works that discuss Jewish perspectives on peace and conflict include Marcus Wald, *Shalom: Jewish Teaching on Peace* (New York: Bloch Publishing Company, 1944); Joseph D. Epstein, *Mitzvot ha-Shalom: The Commandments on Peace; A Guide to the Jewish Understanding of Peace and Harmony in Interpersonal and Communal Life in Light of Torah* [in Hebrew] (Brooklyn: Torath HaAdam Institute Inc., 1987); Shmuel D. Eisenblatt, *Ḥayim shel Shalom: Hilkhot Isure Maḥaloket*

own personal research. I therefore proceeded, starting from scratch, with basic searches of databases of rabbinic literature, using the search terms *shalom*, "peace," and *maḥaloket*, "conflict."[13] After going through the painstaking process of looking up the original sources, figuring out what they were saying, and then attempting to analyze and categorize them, I sat down and formulated what I believed were classic rabbinic perspectives on peace and conflict. These would serve as the underlying values and primary concepts of the paradigm I was formulating. Salient highlights of the material that I compiled, analyzed, and categorized, in conjunction with what I gleaned from other works, are presented in Chapter 2, "Pursuing Peace and Refraining from Destructive Conflict."

The sources that I treat in Chapter 2 encompass many but far from all of the underlying values and concepts of Jewish conflict resolution. I was well aware that there are many other sources and topics that deal with other basic values and concepts that directly relate to Jewish perspectives on conflict resolution and deserve my attention. One of these was clearly the mishnah in *Pirke Avot* (*Chapters of the Fathers*) that discusses the concept of "a dispute for the sake of Heaven," which is one of the most well-known rabbinic sources that relates to conflict, and conflict resolution. In this mishnah, the Jewish sages established a basic typology of conflicts that sets forth standards by which one may identify and classify a conflict as being either constructive or destructive. The concepts set forth in this mishnah were subsequently expounded on by countless rabbinic scholars down through the centuries. I therefore decided that I would go through all of the major commentaries on *Pirke Avot* and search for exegetical motifs, or reoccurring expository themes, that relate to this mishnah and the concept of constructive/destructive conflict. An analysis of this mishnah in *Avot* and

(Jerusalem: n.p., 1989); and Avraham Meshi Zahav, *Dover Shalom* (Jerusalem: Shmuel Dov Eisenblatt, 1980).

13 In the *Taklitor ha-Torani* (*The Torah CD-ROM Library*) (Jerusalem: Disc Book Systems Ltd, 1999), CD-ROM, ver. 7.5, which as I started off my research was the only database of rabbinic literature that I had at my disposal, in talmudic literature alone (i.e., Tosefta, Jerusalem Talmud, Babylonian Talmud, and Minor Tractates), the word *shalom* appeared 1070 times and the word *maḥaloket*, "conflict," appeared 705 times.

a presentation of prominent exegetical motifs, in conjunction with some of my own conclusions about traditional perspectives on constructive conflict based on this material, are presented in Chapter 3, "Rabbinic Perspectives on Constructive Conflict: A 'Dispute for the Sake of Heaven.'"

Behavioral Guidelines and Rules of Conduct. All models of interpersonal conflict resolution contain certain behavioral guidelines and rules of conduct. The purpose of these guidelines and rules is to steer the disputing parties through the arduous process of resolving their issues in the most effective way possible, as perceived through the eyes of the formulators of the model, and in consonance with the model's underlying values and theoretical concepts. In Judaism, prescriptive norms and standards of proper conduct for veritably all realms of life—whether personal, religious, or social—are embodied within Halakhah (Jewish law; see Glossary). It therefore follows that any type of serious exploration of Jewish ethics and principles of human duty logically necessitates an in-depth study of Halakhah (see footnote).[14] The *halakhot* (laws) that govern interpersonal conflict encompass manifold normative elements, or guidelines and rules. According to the Talmud (*Gittin* 59b), "the entire Torah[15] is for the sake of *darkhe shalom* (literally: "paths of peace," i.e., promoting

14 A succinct and eloquent explanation of the central role that in-depth halakhic analyses play in defining an authentic Jewish ethic is offered by Eugene B. Borowitz, who writes that "Jewish teachers have long insisted that one finds the authoritative delineation of Jewish duty in the halakhah (rabbinic law). If so any ethics that claims to be authentically 'Jewish' ought to validate itself by Jewish standards, that is, by serious attention to the dialectical working out of the halakhah over the centuries" (Eugene B. Borowitz, *Exploring Jewish Ethics: Papers on Covenant Responsibility* [Detroit: Wayne University Press, 1990], 33). In addition to this, observance of Halakhah has historically formed the foundation of the Jewish religious experience (see Abraham J. Heschel, "Religion and Law," in *Between God and Man: An Interpretation of Judaism*, ed. Fritz A. Rothschild [New York: The Free Press, 1959], 155–61), and the halakhic value system was not subjected to the same "foreign" influences of other "Jewish" *Weltanschauungen* (see Joseph B. Soloveitchik, *The Halakhic Mind: An Essay on Jewish Tradition and Modern Thought* [New York: Seth Press, 1986], 100–102).

15 This may be understood literally—that the goal of all 613 commandments is the perfection of the human being (see *Genesis Rabbah* 44:1), which in turn should ultimately promote peaceful coexistence; see Joseph D. Epstein, *Torat ha-Adam*, vol. 2 (New York: Balshon, 1977), 9. Alternatively, when the Talmud uses the expression

harmonious and peaceful coexistence between people)," the implication being that the 613 *mitsvot* (commandments)[16] and countless rabbinic enactments form a complex system of laws that are supposed to work together in order to promote peaceful coexistence. The question that I had to deal with, first and foremost, was which *mitsvot* and *halakhot* are directly related to interpersonal conflict resolution, which I would have to subsequently research in depth.[17] Further complicating matters was the fact that from a traditional perspective, beyond the *halakhot*, which take the form of established rules of conduct and are binding in nature, there exists an entirely separate area of behaviors, character traits, and virtues that either are not viewed as technically being mandatory or for which neither the Torah nor the Rabbis set down definitive rules regarding their application. These elements have been traditionally categorized as *midot ḥasidut* (pious character traits) and *midot tovot* (good, or desirable, character traits).[18] Many of these (e.g., the traits of thinking before speaking, humility, remaining silent in the face of insults, patience, and so forth) seem to play an integral role in, and to a certain extent are inseparable from, the *halakhot* of interpersonal conflict resolution.

"the whole Torah," it may simply be referring to the majority of commandments (for a similar usage, see Rashi, *Shabbat* 31a, s.v. *de-alakh sene*).

16 According to the Talmud, there are 613 biblical commandments in the Pentateuch; see *Makkot* 23b.

17 I fondly recall the first time I met Rabbi Dr. Daniel Roth, who is the director of the Pardes Center for Judaism and Conflict Resolution. Rabbi Roth had contacted me and wanted to discuss my doctoral dissertation, "Traditional Jewish Perspectives on Peace and Interpersonal Conflict Resolution." One of the first questions he asked me was, considering the multitude of topics that relate to interpersonal conflict resolution, how did I decide to focus on the specific subtopics that make up my dissertation.

18 To be totally clear in regard to *midot tovot,* from a traditional Jewish perspective, good character traits are absolutely essential to one's personal development as a human being and as a Jew. However, when it comes to the exact application or implementation of *midot tovot,* neither the Torah nor the Rabbis have established definitive binding rules that are applicable to all Jews in all circumstances (i.e., in all normal circumstances) in regard to these traits, as they have when it comes to *halakhot* (see Vidal Yom Tov of Tolosa, *Magid Mishneh*, in *Mishneh Torah* [Jerusalem: Shabse Frankel, 2002], *Hilkhot Shekhenim* 14:5; and see Elijah ben Solomon, *Be'ur ha-Gera: Megilat Ester* [Jerusalem: Mossad Harav Kook, 2010] 10:3, p. 142).

After surveying the pertinent literature, I decided to distinguish between normative halakhic obligations and the aforementioned *midot*, putting the primary emphasis on halakhic obligations. This decision was primarily based on the premise that the binding and definitive nature of halakhic obligations reflects Judaism's view that these actions are essential, basic requirements that normally fall within the functional range of behavior of the average person (i.e., the average person is capable of performing them) and, as a general rule, they are applicable to the overwhelming majority of times, places, and situations. This is as opposed to those things that are nonobligatory in nature or are not formulated as established rules of conduct, which may be considered praiseworthy and actions that one should normally aspire to, but which the average person may often find excessively difficult to put into practice or may be highly variable in their applicability and implementation.[19]

In deciding on which *mitsvot* and *halakhot* I would focus on, I utilized R. Shmuel Eisenblatt's list of thirty-eight *mitsvot* that directly relate to conflict[20] as my starting point. I proceeded to narrow my focus to those things that I perceived as being fundamental features of Judaism's approach to the promotion of social harmony and peace, and constructive interpersonal conflict resolution. Going through R. Eisenblatt's list of commandments, I first chose six *mitsvot* that I believed to play pivotal roles in the prevention of destructive conflict and that serve major functions throughout the entire process of interpersonal conflict resolution. These include the foundational commandments that deal with love and hate (which embody some of the most basic interpersonal values and concepts of Judaism, and could therefore also arguably have been categorized as underlying values and concepts of Jewish conflict resolution), physical violence, and verbal abuse.[21] The primary

---

19 I also emphasized halakhic obligations because of certain practical pedagogical concerns; see pp. 458–59. See also above, footnote 14.

20 Eisenblatt, *Ḥayim shel Shalom*, 17–56.

21 In addition to these six *mitsvot*, and those that are discussed in the following paragraphs in the text, interspersed throughout this work I will also touch on other fundamental commandments and laws that are highly pertinent to interpersonal

sources and pertinent normative obligations of these six *mitsvot* are elucidated in Chapter 4, "Basic Interpersonal Obligations and Prohibitions."

By far the most basic and essential element of Jewish interpersonal conflict resolution (that does not require a third-party intervention), which in my mind is the centerpiece of the paradigm I present, is the halakhic obligation of *tokhaḥah* (literally "reproof") *for interpersonal offenses. Tokhaḥah* for interpersonal offenses, which in halakhic literature is classified as a biblical commandment with definitive guidelines and rules, basically requires one to respond to an interpersonal provocation by going over to the person who committed the offense and discussing the matter with the offender in a respectful manner. Having extensively researched the primary and secondary sources that deal with this topic, I present the major highlights of my research in Chapter 6, "*Tokhaḥah*: Judaism's Basic Approach to Resolving Interpersonal Conflict through Dialogue."

Viewing *tokhaḥah* as the primary halakhic response to an interpersonal provocation, that means to say, how one preferably *should* respond, the next logical element to explore would be how one should *not* respond. How according to Halakhah one should not respond could theoretically encompass a number of different *mitsvot,* but clearly two of the most prominent are the biblical commandments against taking revenge and bearing a grudge. Aside from the all-important behavioral aspects of these prohibitions in relation to conflict, the discussions in the traditional Jewish sources revolving around taking revenge and bearing a grudge also encompass what I believe to be an important cognitive component. The traditional sources that discuss taking revenge and bearing a grudge are not only replete with prescriptive standards of conduct that are inherently behavioral in nature, they

conflict (e.g., the prohibition of "holding on to a quarrel" [*Sanhedrin* 110a], which serves as the general prohibition against engaging in destructive conflict, and the commandment of *ve-halakhta bi-drakhav,* "And you shall walk in His ways" [Deut. 28:9], which requires that one emulate God's attributes of being compassionate, gracious, slow to anger, and so on).

also offer various reasons for these injunctions. These explanations, which were offered by rabbinic authorities down through the ages, are not only of theoretical interest; they also provide ideas and concepts that, when thought about and contemplated, may assist in cognitively restructuring the way a person perceives and feels about an interpersonal provocation. They may thereby incorporate a significant part of the requisite cognitive component of interpersonal conflict resolution as well (see below, under "Cognitive Processes"). This is all to be elaborated on in Chapter 7, "Retaliation and Resentment: Not Taking Revenge (*Nekamah*) and Not Bearing a Grudge (*Netirah*)."

The next topic that I felt was of vital importance and deserved an in-depth treatment was forgiveness—that is, the halakhic requirements of asking and granting forgiveness for interpersonal offenses. Aside from the empirical research that stresses the integral role of apologies and forgiveness in conflict resolution,[22] there were other compelling reasons to focus on forgiveness. First, it was clear from the traditional sources that forgiveness is an absolutely indispensable part of the reconciliation process, and, remarkably, there were relatively few in-depth halakhic studies on forgiveness. Even those few studies, as extremely valuable as they were, did not cover what I considered to be certain very basic concepts. Such disregard of a practical and fundamental requirement by contemporary authors was not only hard to fathom, but heightened the need for this topic to be researched and elucidated at length.[23] My analysis of the

22 For a sampling of this research, see the sources cited on pp. 401–2, nn. 264–72.

23 For me, this called to mind something R. Aryeh Leib Poupko wrote in the name of his father, the "*Ḥafets Ḥayim*," R. Israel Meir ha-Kohen (Kagan, 1838–1933): "[For my father] when it came to those commandments that people would show disrespect for, he would emphasize them to a greater extent. On a number of occasions, he cited the words of the *Sefer Ḥasidim* [authored by R. Judah of Regensburg, 1150–1217] that a mitzvah which people neglect, is comparable to a *met mitsvah* [an "abandoned corpse," which according to Halakhah one is required to attend to and whose needs override other religious obligations], which gives it precedence over everything else." Aryeh Leib ha-Kohen Poupko, *Dugma mi-Darkhe Avi*, in *Kol Kitve Ḥafets Ḥayim ha-Shalem*, vol. 3 (New York: Avraham Yitsḥak Friedman, n.d.), subsection 67, p. 9.

halakhot of asking and granting forgiveness for interpersonal offenses is presented in Chapter 8, "Apologies: The Asking and Granting of Forgiveness."

Cognitive Processes. As I pointed out earlier, all full-fledged models of interpersonal conflict resolution contain behavioral, affective, and cognitive components. In other words, in addition to promoting certain ways of acting (the behavioral component) and certain ways of dealing with a person's natural emotional responses to conflict (the affective component), they also ask the parties to engage in certain mental processes, and offer various things for the parties to think about and contemplate, that means to say, a cognitive component.[24] All of these components, taken in conjunction with each other, are supposed to facilitate effective conflict resolution. From among the *mitsvot* that relate to conflict resolution, there is one that clearly stands out as being cognitive in nature—the commandment to judge others favorably. In order to adequately understand Judaism's perspective on judging others favorably, one needs to be familiar with the halakhic guidelines of this mitzvah, and a number of related perspective-taking concepts (such as, "Do not judge your friend until you are in his place" [*Avot* 2:4]; *kabdehu ve-ḥashdehu,* "You should respect him and suspect him" [based on *Kallah Rabbati,* chap. 9]; and others). Chapter 5,[25] "Judging People Favorably: Countering Negative Judgmental Biases," will present an overview of the commandment, its requirements, and related concepts.

---

24 See pp. 31, 297, and 450–51.

25 The placement and order of the chapters in this work were based on a number of factors. One factor was that I wanted to follow the (logical) order in which the topics appear in the Pentateuch (i.e., the mitzvah of judging people favorably is based on Lev. 19:15, then there is the mitzvah of *tokhaḥah,* Lev. 19:17, and then the commandments regarding revenge and bearing a grudge, Lev. 19:18). Having Chapter 5 deal with judging people favorably, which begins the fourth section of the book, Basic Commandments and Laws of Interpersonal Conflict Resolution, also reflects the vital role that judging people favorably plays throughout the process of interpersonal conflict resolution, starting from even before one attempts to engage in dialogue with the other party.

The Affective Component—Anger Management. An essential part of any type of viable model of interpersonal conflict resolution is its system of anger management. In traditional Jewish sources, there exists a wealth of material that discusses the deleterious effects of anger and offers an array of strategies for controlling it. A number of contemporary authors have compiled some very impressive anthologies on the topic of anger in traditional Jewish sources.[26] In examining these works, I realized that the majority of the strategies and suggestions for controlling anger that appear in them can be found in one form or another in the two seminal monographs on the topic of anger in traditional Jewish sources—R. Abraham Jelen's *Orekh Apayim,* which was first published in 1906, and R. Moshe Levinson's *Ma'aneh Rakh,* which was first published in 1911. *Orekh Apayim* and *Ma'aneh Rakh* were not only the first Jewish anthologies that specifically focused on anger, they also offered fully developed, detailed systems of anger management. I therefore decided to analyze R. Jelen's and R. Levinson's works (which, for some reason, have never received the attention that they most assuredly deserve) and to highlight the major behavioral, cognitive, and affective elements for dealing with anger that they offer. In focusing on these works, I believe that I have been able to encapsulate most (if not all) of the principal approaches for controlling anger that appear in the traditional literature. This material is presented in Chapter 9, "Jewish Anger Management."

The First Chapter and the Conclusion. This book, which is a revised version of my doctoral dissertation, is based on approximately eight years of research into the modern theory and practice of conflict resolution and Jewish approaches to conflict resolution. In studying contemporary conflict resolution and comparing it with traditional Jewish approaches, I became acutely aware of the fact that despite the many similarities between the two, there also exist fundamental differences between them, which I felt needed to be discussed. Therefore, as an introduction to this work, the first

26 See p. 409, n. 4.

chapter presents an overview of the field of contemporary conflict resolution. This chapter introduces many of the basic concepts of conflict resolution and will help facilitate comparisons and contrasts between contemporary and Jewish approaches, which appear at the end of each chapter and are summarized in the conclusion.[27] Also, in order to facilitate informed and accurate comparisons and contrasts between contemporary and Jewish approaches in relation to apologies, forgiveness, and anger management, I have included relatively lengthy summaries of contemporary theories and research on apologies and forgiveness, and contemporary approaches to anger management at the end of the respective chapters that address these topics.

I believe that some fair warning is called for regarding the sections in which I compare and contrast contemporary approaches with the traditional Jewish approaches. Even though I have tried to present this interdisciplinary material in as clear and accessible a manner as possible, a good percentage of these sections consist of some highly involved discussions that may possibly confuse the average reader who is not familiar with the specific areas of contemporary conflict resolution that are discussed and the traditional Jewish literature that deals with interpersonal relations. For those who may be confused by, or are not interested in, these discussions, I have made sure to present these sections as stand-alone units that may be readily skipped without any serious loss in the understanding of the traditional Jewish approaches, which are the primary focus of this book.

My interest in contemporary conflict resolution and Jewish approaches to conflict resolution has stemmed from my desire to teach about conflict resolution, specifically those aspects that people can actually put to good use in real-life situations. As a result, throughout my research, I have always tried to focus on

27 In studying contemporary conflict resolution and traditional Jewish approaches, one may find a remarkable amount of similarities and differences. I have attempted to highlight only a select number of elements that I believe to be of major import and are clearly discernible from the material I have researched.

those elements that have real-world, practical applicability, and that could be used in curriculum development and teaching (*see footnote*).[28] This is clearly reflected in this book. The first chapter's overview of contemporary conflict resolution emphasizes school-based conflict resolution education, which, as a general rule, focuses on interpersonal conflict resolution that does not necessitate the intervention of a third party; and in the conclusion, I touch on various issues that relate to conflict resolution education.

The chapters of this book are divided into six sections: Part I—Introductory Essay (Chapter 1); Part II—Foundational Values and Concepts (Chapters 2 and 3); Part III—Foundational Commandments and Laws (Chapter 4); Part IV—Basic Commandments and Laws of Interpersonal Conflict Resolution (Chapters 5, 6, 7, and 8); Part V—The Affective Component—Anger Management (Chapter 9); and the Conclusion.

In engaging in a work such as this, one faces multiple analytical and expositional challenges. As with all types of research, fundamental questions of objectivity and accuracy must be raised. The interpretation of traditional Jewish texts is particularly susceptible to all sorts of distortions, fanciful assumptions, superficial readings, inaccurate translations, judgmental bias, and so forth. When explicating any intricate and complex topic, one must constantly struggle with reductionist tendencies, search for clear and concise definitions, and conceptualize and present the subject matter in a coherent, systematic, and well-organized fashion. Even though it is my intention to do justice to the topics that I cover by providing clear and accurate explanations, I am quite aware of the difficulties in discerning the shortcomings of one's own work, for "Who can discern [his own] errors" (Psalms 19:13). Therefore, if while reading through this work one comes across any mistakes,

28 However, it should be self-evident that this book is not in any way meant to serve as a practical halakhic guide.

I would be indebted if the reader would inform me about them. I would also greatly appreciate any comments, feedback, and pertinent sources that relate to the subject matter that I discuss. I can be contacted at HGK10@aol.com.

This work employs a system of Hebrew transliteration that is similar to the one used by the American Library Association and the Library of Congress (which can be used for searches in the OCLC WorldCat network of library catalogs).[29]

29 For a simplified description of the system I have used, see Paul E. Maher, *Hebraica Cataloging: A Guide to ALA/LC Romanization and Descriptive Cataloging* (Washington, DC: Cataloging Distribution Service, Library of Congress, 1987), 71.

PART I

Introductory Essay

CHAPTER 1

Contemporary Conflict Resolution: An Overview of the Field and the Core Components of Its Educational Programs

Conflict resolution is an exceptionally broad and highly complex field. Conflict resolution scholars and professionals have developed an intricate and sophisticated network of theory, research, and practice that encompasses a remarkably diverse spectrum of views and orientations. To be able to fully grasp the nature of the field of conflict resolution, one has to be familiar with an enormous amount of information that would go far beyond the scope of what could possibly be presented in this introductory essay. What I intend to do here is to present a basic overview of the field that will hopefully give the reader a rudimentary understanding of its fundamental concepts and will be useful for comparisons to Jewish approaches that will be discussed later on in this work. We will begin with a simple definition of the term "conflict resolution" and by delineating the three major fields of study that are associated with it.

Conflict Resolution: The Different Fields of Study

There is considerable disagreement among conflict resolution theorists, researchers, and practitioners about many of the basic definitions and concepts of conflict resolution, including what exactly is meant by the expression "conflict resolution." *The Encyclopedia of Conflict*

Resolution offers a definition of conflict resolution that understands it in the broadest possible terms:

> The term *conflict resolution* is used broadly to refer to any process that is used to end a conflict or dispute in a peaceful way . . . Used in this way, *conflict resolution* refers to all judicial processes and alternative dispute resolution techniques—negotiation, mediation, arbitration—as well as consensus building, diplomacy, analytical problem solving, and peacemaking. In short, it involves all nonviolent means of solving interpersonal, intergroup, interorganizational, or international problems.[1]

In contrast to this definition, there is a more nuanced one that appears in the scholarly literature, which differentiates between the fields of "peace studies" and "alternative dispute resolution," each with its own unique orientation and emphasis, and conflict resolution, which incorporates elements from peace studies and alternative dispute resolution, but is considered a distinct field in and of itself. John Stephens, a professor at the University of North Carolina, offers a conceptual framework that may be very helpful in explaining all of this.

Stephens suggests that we may conceive of the three fields—peace studies, alternative dispute resolution, and conflict resolution—as being spread across a continuum of "social change" and "system maintenance," that is, whether they challenge and/or perpetuate certain values of the present social order:[2]

---

1 Heidi Burgess and Guy M. Burgess, eds., *Encyclopedia of Conflict Resolution* (Santa Barbara: ABC-CLIO, 1997), s.v. "Conflict Resolution, Conflict Management, and Dispute Settlement."

2 John B. Stephens, "'Gender Conflict': Connecting Feminist Theory and Conflict Resolution Theory and Practice," in *Conflict and Gender,* ed. A. Taylor and J. Beinstein Miller (Cresskill, NJ: Hampton Press, 1994), 217–35; cited in Peter T. Coleman and Morton Deutsch, "Introducing Cooperation and Conflict Resolution into Schools: A Systems Approach," in *Peace, Conflict and Violence: Peace Psychology for the 21st Century,* ed. Daniel J. Christie, Richard V. Wagner, and Deborah Du Nann Winter (Upper Saddle River, NJ: Prentice Hall, 2001), 224–25.

PEACE/CONFLICT FIELDS OF STUDY:

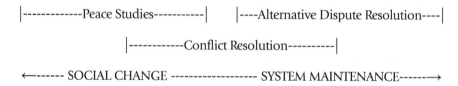

|------------Peace Studies----------| |----Alternative Dispute Resolution----|

|-----------Conflict Resolution---------|

←------ SOCIAL CHANGE ----------------- SYSTEM MAINTENANCE------→

Fig. 1. Diagram situating the fields of Peace Studies, Alternative Dispute Resolution, and Conflict Resolution along a continuum of social change and system maintenance. Adapted from Stephens, "Gender Conflict," figure 10.1 (permission granted by publisher).

Using Stephens's framework, I will briefly discuss the fields of peace studies and alternative dispute resolution. I will then focus and elaborate on the field of conflict resolution.

Peace Studies

At one extreme (appropriately situated to the left of the diagram) is the field of peace studies, which is seen as challenging many of the values of the present social order. This field of study, its programs of education, and its associated areas of activism generally deal with a wide range of global concerns.[3] Peace theorists, educators, and activists attempt to promote ideas such as the peaceful resolution of conflicts, social justice, the inherent dignity and worth of all human beings, universal human rights, human interdependence, global consciousness, and planetary stewardship. In practical terms, these

3 For a comprehensive introduction to the field of peace studies, see David P. Barash and Charles P. Webel, *Peace and Conflict Studies* (Thousand Oaks, CA: Sage Publications, 2002); and Ho-Won Jeong, *Peace and Conflict Studies: An Introduction* (Burlington, VT: Ashgate Publishing, 2000). For a general overview of the field and an excellent introduction to peace education, see Betty A. Reardon, *Comprehensive Peace Education: Educating for Global Responsibility* (New York: Teachers College Press, 1988); for an encyclopedic exposition of the field, see Javier Perez de Cuellar and Young Seek Choue, eds., *World Encyclopedia of Peace,* 2nd ed., 8 vols. (Dobbs Ferry, NY: Oceana Publications, 1999).

are translated into the abolishment of war and armed conflicts and the minimization of all forms of violence, including "structural violence." Structural violence is a key concept that was formulated by Johan Galtung (see p. 13) and is used within this field to identify the consequences of those social, political, and economic structures that lower the quality of life of particular groups or classes of people.[4] With a focus on structural violence, peace advocates encourage initiatives that will eliminate poverty, hunger, disease, oppression, and discrimination. (Some peace theorists have also expanded the concept of peace to encompass humankind's interactions with the "living earth" and its ecosystem, which explains the work that they do for the protection of the environment and its resources.)[5]

It is primarily in relation to peaceful coexistence—that means to say, resolving conflicts using peaceful means, repudiating all types of violence, and the cultivation of positive human relationships—that the fields of peace studies and conflict resolution (which will be defined below) intersect. Writing in 1988, Betty Reardon (who is one of the pioneering figures of peace education) pointed out that, even though a clear distinction must be drawn between the fields of peace studies and conflict resolution, some peace educators are inclined to give particular prominence to the area of conflict resolution. Reardon also pointed out that there was a growing convergence between the two fields, particularly at the university level, where many programs combine the two fields under the title "peace and conflict studies."[6]

---

4 Johan Galtung, "Violence, Peace, and Peace Research," *Journal of Peace Research* 6, no. 3 (1969): 167–91.

5 Loreta N. Castro, "Peace and Peace Education: A Holistic View," in *World Encyclopedia of Peace*, ed. Javier Perez de Cuellar and Young Seek Choue, 2nd ed., vol. 4 (Dobbs Ferry, NY: Oceana Publications, 1999), 166, 168; Jeong, *Peace and Conflict Studies*, 8, 29; Reardon, *Comprehensive Peace Education*, 29–32, 43, 59, 61; and Charles W. Kegley, Jr. and Geoffrey G. Kegley, "Global Environment and Peace," in *World Encyclopedia of Peace*, ed. Javier Perez de Cuellar and Young Seek Choue, 2nd ed., vol. 2 (Dobbs Ferry, NY: Oceana Publications, 1999), 320.

6 Reardon, *Comprehensive Peace Education*, 15. Evidence of this trend can be clearly seen in the *Global Directory of Peace Studies and Conflict Resolution Programs*, which profiles over 450 undergraduate, master's, and doctoral programs in forty countries. (Peace and Justice Studies Association and International Peace Research Association Foundation, *Global*

Alternative Dispute Resolution

At the other extreme of the Peace/Conflict Fields of Study continuum is the field of alternative dispute resolution (ADR). ADR is an umbrella term that refers to the resolution of potential legal disputes through various methods that do not involve litigation (i.e., the process of carrying on a lawsuit). The three primary processes of ADR are negotiation, mediation, and arbitration.[7]

The term *negotiation*, in the context of ADR, carries with it a somewhat specific denotation. According to *Black's Law Dictionary*, negotiation is "a consensual bargaining process in which the parties attempt to reach agreement on a disputed or potentially disputed matter."[8] Negotiation differs from the other two primary processes of ADR, of mediation and arbitration, in that in negotiation the parties involved maintain complete autonomy and attempt to resolve their dispute without the intervention of any type of third party.[9] An extensive and in-depth body of literature surrounding the topic of negotiation theory and practice has developed over the past fifty years.[10] According to Stephen Ware, a well-known legal scholar

---

Directory of Peace Studies and Conflict Resolution Programs, accessed January 21, 2012, http://www.peacejusticestudies.org/globaldirectory [site discontinued].)

7 Stephen B. Goldberg, Frank E. A. Sander, and Nancy H. Rogers, *Dispute Resolution: Negotiation, Mediation, and Other Processes*, 2nd ed. (Boston: Little, Brown and Company, 1992), 3. For a concise general introduction to ADR, see Jacqueline M. Nolan-Haley, *Alternative Dispute Resolution in a Nutshell*, 3rd ed. (St. Paul, MN: Thomson/West Publishing, 2008); for a more extensive treatment, see Stephen J. Ware, *Alternative Dispute Resolution* (St. Paul, MN: West Group, 2001); and for a comprehensive treatment, see Edward A. Dauer, *Manual of Dispute Resolution: ADR Law and Practice*, 2 vols. (Deerfield, IL: Clark, Boardman, Callaghan, 1995); and Joey Gillan, ed., *Corporate Counsel's Guide to Alternative Dispute Resolution Techniques* 64 (2002).

8 Bryan A. Garner, ed., *Black's Law Dictionary*, 7th ed. (St. Paul, MN: West Group, 1999), s.v. "negotiation."

9 Ibid; see also Nolan-Haley, *Alternative Dispute Resolution*, 16–17.

10 For an introduction to negotiation theory and practice, see Roger Fisher, William Ury, and Bruce Patton, *Getting to Yes: Negotiating Agreement without Giving In*, 2nd ed. (New York: Penguin Books, 1991); Roy J. Lewicki, David M. Saunders, and John W. Minton, *Essentials of Negotiation* (Boston: Irwin/McGraw-Hill, 1997); J. William Breslin and Jeffrey Z. Rubin, eds., *Negotiation Theory and Practice* (Cambridge, MA: Program on Negotiation Books, 1991); and Gary Goodpaster,

whose expertise is in ADR, "approaches to negotiation are as varied as negotiators themselves."[11] As a result of the diversity of theories and approaches that exist, it is somewhat difficult to make any type of ironclad generalization regarding the modern practice of negotiation. One predominant framework that is used to classify the diverse principles and procedures of negotiation differentiates between approaches that are "competitive" and those that are "cooperative." In conflict resolution literature, numerous appellations for these two very different approaches can be found:[12]

Competitive	Cooperative
Adversarial	Problem-Solving
Positional	Interest-Based
Distributive	Integrative
Distributional	Principled
Win–Lose	Win–Win

Fig. 2. Diagram of common terms that are often used synonymously to differentiate between competitive and cooperative approaches to negotiation. Adapted from Ware, *Alternative Dispute Resolution,* Diagram 3–5 (reprinted with permission of West Academic).

In negotiation that is "competitive," the attainment of the goals of the parties in conflict are seen as being mutually exclusive and the parties are generally arguing in a manner that is combative and oppositional. In negotiation that is "cooperative," the respective goals of the parties are seen as being potentially compatible and the parties are attempting to work together to find a mutually agreeable resolution. Cooperative negotiation is one of the prominent features of the field of conflict resolution, and will be discussed later (see pp. 27–28).

A Guide to Negotiation and Mediation (Irvington-on Hudson, NY: Transnational Publishers, 1997).

11 Ware, *Alternative Dispute Resolution,* 146.

12 Ibid., 146–47.

The second primary process of ADR, mediation, is basically facilitated negotiation.[13] It uses an impartial third-party mediator who assists the disputants through the negotiation process. A mediator has no power to impose a decision on the parties involved and is supposed to remain neutral throughout the proceedings.[14] Just as there is an extensive body of literature that discusses the theory and practice of negotiation, there exists an equally extensive body of literature that discusses the theory and practice of mediation.[15] Two of the most prominent approaches to mediation, and correspondingly negotiation, are known as the "problem-solving approach" and the "transformative approach" (see the explanations on pp. 27–29).

In arbitration (also known as "binding arbitration"), the third primary process of ADR, a claimant and respondent present their dispute in front of a neutral third party who has been empowered to render and impose a decision regarding their case. Arbitration is markedly different from the other two primary processes of ADR, and similar to litigation in that it is categorized as a form of "adjudication," in which somebody (an adjudicator) is empowered to decide how the dispute will be resolved.[16] It should be noted that, in addition to the primary processes of negotiation, mediation, and

---

13 Ibid., 201.

14 Ibid.; Gillan, ed., *Guide to Alternative Dispute Resolution,* 1.005; cf. Goldberg, Sander, and Rogers, *Dispute Resolution,* 103–4.

15 See the reference sections of Jay Folberg and Alison Taylor, *Mediation: A Comprehensive Guide to Resolving Conflicts without Litigation* (San Francisco: Jossey-Bass, 1984); Christopher W. Moore, *The Mediation Process: Practical Strategies for Resolving Conflict* (San Francisco: Jossey-Bass, 1984); and Karen G. Duffy, James W. Grosch, and Paul V. Olczak, eds., *Community Mediation: A Handbook for Practitioners and Researchers* (New York: Guilford Press, 1991).

16 Ware, *Alternative Dispute Resolution,* 5 n. 12, 19; cf. Gerry W. Beyer and Kenneth R. Redden, *Modern Dictionary for the Legal Profession,* ed. Margaret M. Beyer, 2nd ed., (Buffalo, NY: William S. Hein & Co., 1996), s.v. "alternative dispute resolution," who explain alternative dispute resolution as "dispute resolution by peaceable processes *other than adjudication* [emphasis mine]." They, as various other authors, are evidently using the term adjudication as a synonym for litigation. Bryan A. Garner, *A Dictionary of Modern Legal Usage* (New York: Oxford University Press, 1987), s.v. "adjudication," quotes Leff, who asserts that the terms *adjudication* and *litigation* are synonymous. In Garner's opinion, this is a "slipshod extension [that] should be eschewed."

arbitration, there are also many innovative "hybrid" ADR processes, which combine these three processes in various ways.[17]

In Stephens's view, ADR supports system maintenance for three reasons: it generally does not challenge the "adversarial, legal mechanism," it has a tendency to focus only on the surface manifestations of what may be deeply rooted conflicts, and it does not stress the potentially educative-transformational role of conflict.[18] The overlap between the fields of ADR and "conflict resolution," as we will see later (p. 26), is primarily in the areas of negotiation and mediation.

The Field of Conflict Resolution

Conflict resolution (understood as a distinct field in and of itself) is an extremely complex field that is difficult to readily sum up and fully grasp. This is particularly true when taking into consideration the overlap and differences between conflict resolution, peace

17 Goldberg, Sander, and Rogers, *Dispute Resolution*, 3. Some of the most popular hybrid processes include "Med-Arb" (a combination of mediation and arbitration, in which, if the parties cannot resolve their dispute through mediation, they then resort to arbitration), "Non-Binding Arbitration" (the parties have the option of rejecting the arbitrator's decision and requesting that the case be adjudicated through regular litigation), "Ombudsmanship" ("[a]n ombudsperson is a neutral individual employed by a company to assist employees in resolving workplace deputes . . . these individuals hear complaints, engage in fact finding, and generally promote the resolution of disputes through informal methods such as mediation and counseling" [Nolan-Haley, *Alternative Dispute Resolution*, 259]), "Mini-Trials" (a mini-trial does not resemble any sort of actual trial; according to Dauer, it is "a blended procedure, incorporating elements of advocacy and persuasion, adjudication, evaluation, negotiation, mediation, and information management all in one" [Dauer, *Manual of Dispute Resolution*, 11.17; cf. Ware, *Alternative Dispute Resolution*, 268; Nolan-Haley, *Alternative Dispute Resolution*, 146–47]), and "Conciliation" (according to Garner, *Black's Law Dictionary*, 7th ed., s.v. "mediation," "the distinction between mediation and conciliation is widely debated").

18 Stephens, "'Gender Conflict,'" 218, 220–21, 223. Stephens's perspective reflects the views of John Burton (1915–2010), who was at the forefront of the field of conflict resolution for over forty years. See Howard G. Kaminsky, "Traditional Jewish Perspectives on Peace and Interpersonal Conflict Resolution" (Ed.D. dissertation, Teachers College, Columbia University, 2005), 33–34, ProQuest (document ID 305013218).

studies, and ADR, and that conflict resolution is an interdisciplinary field,[19] which, together with its own original insights and perspectives, has synthesized a multiplicity of concepts, theories, terminologies, and methodologies from a wide and diverse spectrum of disciplines (e.g., international diplomacy, law, religion, anthropology, sociology, communications, history, philosophy, and all branches of psychology). In order to attain a decent basic understanding of the field of conflict resolution, one would be well advised to be somewhat familiar with a number of these interdisciplinary elements. Therefore, I will begin by highlighting some of the major historical contributions of other disciplines that have helped to shape the field, and aided in its enormous growth and influence.

Contributions from Other Disciplines

Organizational Psychology. Violent labor conflicts in the 1920s and 1930s precipitated an early and major strand of conflict resolution theory and practice. The pioneering work of Mary Parker Follet (1868–1933) in the field of organizational psychology (which deals with workplace-related issues, such as labor–management relations) laid the groundwork for what modern conflict resolution characterizes as "constructive conflict." From 1924 to 1933, Follet became a featured speaker at some of the most important business conferences of that period. Her proposed theories of business management advocated what is today referred to as an "integrative problem-solving approach," which basically means, a mutual-gains approach that seeks win–win solutions. Follet was extremely influential—her theories have been adopted by an overwhelming percentage of contemporary conflict resolution theorists and practitioners.[20]

---

19 See Jacob Bercovitch, Victor Kremenyuk, and I. William Zartman, introduction to *The SAGE Handbook of Conflict Resolution* (Los Angeles: Sage Publications, 2009), 1.

20 See Mary Parker Follett, *Dynamic Administration: The Collected Papers of Mary Parker Follett,* ed. Henry C. Metcalf and L. Urwick (New York: Harper and Brothers, n.d.), 16–17, 30–49; Albie M. Davis, "An Interview with Mary Parker Follet," in *Negotiation Theory and Practice,* ed. J. William Breslin and Jeffrey Z. Rubin (Cambridge, MA: Program on Negotiation Books, 1993), 13–25; Alan C. Tidwell, *Conflict Resolved: A Critical Assessment*

The Field of International Relations. In the early part of the twentieth century, responding to World War I, scholars began to apply scientific methods in the investigation of the causes and processes of conflict in an attempt to develop ways to avoid its escalation and potential devastating results.[21] The field of international relations continued throughout the last century, and will no doubt continue for the foreseeable future, to be a major impetus for the academic study of alternative methods for preventing and resolving conflicts. From within this field emerged the Research Exchange on the Prevention of War, in the early 1950s, which was headed by Herbert C. Kelman (1927–), Kenneth Boulding (1910–1993), and Anatol Rapoport (1911–2007), who were to become three of the leading figures in the field of conflict resolution in the twentieth century.[22] In 1957, in collaboration with scholars from various disciplines, Kelman, Boulding, and Rapoport began to publish the *Journal of Conflict Resolution*, which, since its inception, has been one of the premier sources of conflict resolution theory and research.[23] In the 1960s, Kelman, together with John Burton (1915–2010), developed analytic problem-solving workshops to deal with deep-rooted international conflicts.[24] These workshops proposed that the key to resolving serious conflicts was to focus in on and address underlying and often unspoken "needs," of the sort put forth by Paul Sites's "control theory" and Abraham Maslow's "hierarchy of needs," which hypothesized that, beyond basic survival and security needs, there are other universal needs, such as recognition, justice, and self-actualization.[25] This fundamental concept of focusing on

of Conflict Resolution (New York: Pinter, 1999), 10–11; Burgess and Burgess, *Encyclopedia of Conflict Resolution*, vii, s.v. "Mary Parker Follet"; and Oliver Ramsbothom, Tom Woodhouse, and Hugh Miall, *Contemporary Conflict Resolution*, 3rd ed. (Cambridge: Polity Press, 2011), 38, 47

21 Burgess and Burgess, *Encyclopedia of Conflict Resolution*, vii.

22 Herbert C. Kelman, "Reflections on the History and Status of Peace Research," *Conflict Management and Peace Science* 5, no. 2 (1981): 95–98.

23 Ibid.

24 Tidwell, *Conflict Resolved*, 12–15.

25 John Burton, *Conflict: Resolution and Provention* (New York: St. Martin's Press, 1990), 36, 92–98; John Burton, ed., *Conflict: Human Needs Theory* (New York: St. Martin's

underlying needs in resolving conflicts is applicable to all levels of conflict (i.e., interpersonal, intergroup, and international); it is mentioned frequently in conflict resolution literature; and it plays a crucial role in cooperative negotiation (see p. 28).

Social Psychology. Theories of personality, group dynamics, cooperation and competition have had a lasting and far-reaching impact on the field of conflict resolution. The work of Kurt Lewin (1890–1947), one of the pioneers of modern social psychology, laid the groundwork for the theories and research of Morton Deutsch (1920–2017).[26] Deutsch's insights and work on "social interdependence," which analyzes the factors that promote competition or cooperation, have supplied a considerable amount of the theoretical basis for modern conflict resolution.[27] Over the past fifty years, Deutsch's theories have been continuously quoted, argued, refined, and enriched by hundreds (if not thousands) of scholars. In conjunction with this strand of theory, there was also the integral contribution of "game theory" (the mathematical study of conflict strategies), which has allowed social scientists to formulate, quantify, and study situations of cooperation/competition in concrete and even mathematical terms.[28]

The Civil Rights and Peace Movements. In the 1960s, the civil rights and peace movements not only provided important

---

Press, 1990), viii; and Joseph A. Scimecca, "Self-Reflexivity and Freedom," in Burton, *Conflict: Human Needs Theory*, 206.

26 Specifically, Lewin's "field theory," which attempts to analyze the interaction of interdependent factors that affect a person's behavior. See Kurt Lewin, *Field Theory in Social Science; Selected Theoretical Papers* (New York: Harper and Row, 1951), 240; Morton Deutsch, "Field Theory in Social Psychology," in *The Handbook of Social Psychology*, vol. 1, 2nd ed., ed. Gardner Lindzey and Elliot Aronson (Reading, MA: Addison-Wesley Publishing, 1968), 412–87; and Morton Deutsch, "A Theory of Cooperation and Competition," *Human Relations* 2, no. 2 (1949): 129–52.

27 Morton Deutsch, "A Personal History of Social Interdependence—Theory, Research, and Practice," accessed November 7, 2016, http://www.tc.columbia.edu/i/a/document/9450_APersonalHistoryofSocialInterdependence_TheoryResearchandPractice.pdf; and David W. Johnson and Roger T. Johnson, "New Developments in Social Interdependence Theory," *Genetic, Social, and General Psychology Monographs* 131, no. 4 (2005): 285–358.

28 Morton Deutsch, "Sixty Years of Conflict," *The International Journal of Conflict Management* 1, no. 3 (1990): 237–263; and David W. Johnson and Roger T. Johnson, *Cooperation and Competition: Theory and Research* (Edina, MN: Interaction Book Co., 1989), 7–8.

conceptual insights into conflict and spurred the development of new approaches to conflict resolution, but they also served the vital functions of raising public awareness about conflict and inspiring a new societal mind-set about inalienable human rights.[29] Johan Galtung (1930–; one of the leading theorists in the field of peace and conflict studies in the twentieth century)[30] relates how, after studying the situation in Rhodesia in 1965, he came to expand the concept of "violence" from simple physical violence to include unintentional social injustices, which he termed "structural violence."[31] This new way of looking at violence led to his development of the constructs of "negative peace" (absence of physical violence) and "positive peace" (promulgation of social justice):

> An extended concept of violence leads to an extended concept of peace . . . peace also has two sides: absence of personal [physical] violence, and absence of structural. We shall refer to them as *negative peace* and *positive peace* respectively."[32]

Galtung's reconceptualizations of violence and peace have become some of the most often cited and influential concepts in peace and conflict studies.

---

29 Burgess and Burgess, *Encyclopedia of Conflict Resolution*, vii; and Tidwell, *Conflict Resolved*, 12–15.

30 It should be noted that Galtung's standing and reputation as a peace scholar has suffered greatly due to apparently anti-Semitic views that he has expressed. See Benjamin Weinthal, "Swiss Group Suspends 'Anti-Semitic' Norway Scholar," *Jerusalem Post*, August 9, 2012, http://www.jpost.com/International/Article.aspx?id=280726; and Ofer Aderet, "Pioneer of Global Peace Studies Hints at Link between Norway Massacre and Mossad," *Haaretz*, April 30, 2012, http://www.haaretz.com/news/diplomacy-defense/pioneer-of-global-peace-studies-hints-at-link-between-norway-massacre-and-mossad-1.427385. Cf. "TRANSCEND International's Statement Concerning the Label of Anti-Semitism against Johan Galtung," accessed March 3, 2013, https://www.transcend.org/galtung/statement-may-2012.

31 Johan Galtung, "Twenty-Five Years of Peace Research: Ten Challenges and Some Responses," *Journal of Peace Research* 22, no. 2 (1985): 145; Galtung, "Violence, Peace, and Peace Research," 171.

32 Galtung, "Violence, Peace, and Peace Research," 183.

The American Judicial System. Starting in the 1960s, an overburdened American judicial system precipitated the development and promotion of alternative dispute resolution procedures.[33] A considerable percentage of conflict resolution theory and practice has developed from, and is based in, this context. In 1979, the Harvard Negotiation Project (HNP) was started at Harvard Law School. The HNP is perhaps best known for its development of "principled negotiation," as described in the international bestseller *Getting to Yes: Negotiating Agreement Without Giving In*, by Roger Fisher, Bill Ury, and Bruce Patton. First published in 1981, *Getting to Yes* has been translated into twenty-five languages and has become the singular most popular work of modern conflict resolution. The often-cited methods advocated by the HNP center around four major elements of negotiation: separating the people from the problem, focusing on underlying interests and not the stated positions, coming up with inventive options for mutual gain, and insisting on the use of objective criteria in resolving disputes.[34]

Religion. In 1972, thanks to the efforts of a group of teachers who were members of the Religious Society of Friends (the Quakers, one of the historic "peace churches"), the Creative Response to Conflict program (CRC, originally called the Children's Creative Response to Conflict program) was founded. The CRC was one of the pioneer organizations of conflict resolution education. The conceptual base for this program was grounded in Christian pacifism and the teachings of the Quakers, who at the time provided nonviolence training to various constituencies.[35] Since then, the CRC's handbook, *The Friendly Classroom for a Small Planet*,[36] has attained the status of one of the classic texts of

---

33 Burgess and Burgess, *Encyclopedia of Conflict Resolution*, vii; and Dauer, *Manual of Dispute Resolution*, 2.02.

34 See Fisher, Ury, and Patton, *Getting to Yes*; and the Harvard Negotiation Project's website, accessed November 9, 2016, http://www.pon.harvard.edu/research_projects/harvard-negotiation-project/hnp/.

35 Richard J. Bodine and Donna K. Crawford, *The Handbook of Conflict Resolution Education: A Guide to Building Quality Programs in Schools* (San Francisco: Jossey-Bass, 1998), 89–91.

36 Priscilla Prutzman et al., *The Friendly Classroom for a Small Planet: A Handbook on Creative Approaches to Living and Problem Solving for Children* (Gabriola Island, BC, Canada: New Society Publishers, 1988). Originally published in 1974.

conflict resolution education. The original overarching themes that the CRC emphasized were cooperation, communication, affirmation (recognizing and appreciating the positive qualities in oneself and others), and creative conflict resolution. As the field of conflict resolution expanded, several subthemes, such as bias awareness and creative problem solving, emerged as requisite areas of study.[37] It should be noted that even though the CRC's program was originally geared towards elementary schools, the developers of this program had made a concerted effort to emphasize experiential learning and develop highly stimulating educational material and activities. As a result of this, a good amount of this material has been used in conflict resolution training for teenagers and adults, even at the graduate school level.[38] Another noteworthy and more recent strand of conflict resolution that is grounded in religious teachings is an approach called "conflict transformation." Conflict transformation, which was developed by John Paul Lederach and is based on principles of the Anabaptist-Mennonite tradition, emphasizes the potentially positive aspects of conflict and the need to focus on the parties' underlying relationship patterns in order to achieve long-term positive outcomes.[39]

The Core Components of Conflict Resolution's Educational Programs

It is no simple matter to accurately identify contemporary conflict resolution's core components. There is a vast array of elements that can be seen as being absolutely vital to the constructive

37 Priscilla Prutzman, Judith M. Johnson, and Susan Fountain, *CCRC's Friendly Classrooms and Communities for Young Children: A Manual for Conflict Resolution Activities and Resources* (Nyack, NY: Creative Response to Conflict Inc., 1998); and Bodine and Crawford, *Handbook of Conflict Resolution Education*, xxv, 89–91.

38 A number of these activities are used by Teachers College, Columbia University's International Center for Cooperation and Conflict Resolution in their Basic Practicum in Conflict Resolution and Mediation.

39 John Paul Lederach, *The Little Book of Conflict Transformation* (Intercourse, PA: Good Books, 2003); and Marc Gopin, "Conflict Resolution as a Religious Experience: Contemporary Mennonite Peacemaking," in *Between Eden and Armageddon: The Future of World Religions, Violence, and Peacemaking* (New York: Oxford University Press, 2000), 139–66.

resolution of conflicts based on contemporary conflict resolution theory and what is being practiced in the field. I would by no means be so presumptuous as to offer my own personal opinion as to what those elements are. However, I would argue that some of the best resources to help identify these core components are the popular conflict resolution education programs and their curricula, particularly the top-rated ones that are heavily grounded in theory and research, and incorporate the best practices from the field. Some of these programs have been around since the 1960s and 1970s, and have been continuously evolving. They have taught conflict resolution skills to millions of students, and may serve as an excellent indicator of what is being emphasized by theorists, researchers, and practitioners of conflict resolution. This is especially true when it comes to the skills of interpersonal conflict resolution that does not involve an intermediary, which is a main focus of these educational programs.

When one surveys the major conflict resolution education programs and curricula, one becomes aware that there are many commonalities in their themes and content. In the following section, I will highlight the main themes and core content of these programs and curricula, and offer examples of how they attempt to teach the foundational skills of conflict resolution.

Conflict Resolution Education

Most of the major conflict resolution education programs and curricula were developed for teaching conflict resolution skills in a school-based setting, and thus are geared for elementary and secondary school students, ranging from kindergarten to twelfth grade. The overall goal of these programs is to impart to young people the theoretical understanding and the practical experience necessary to constructively deal with conflict in their lives.[40] As such, conflict resolution programs form

40 Bodine and Crawford, *Handbook of Conflict Resolution Education*, 13; cf. William L. Carruthers et al., "Conflict Resolution as Curriculum: A Definition, Description, and

a significant part of the larger field of "social and emotional learning," which teaches life skills, social competencies, and values that help promote physical and mental well-being and facilitate positive interpersonal relationships.[41] In reviewing conflict resolution programs,[42]

Process for Integration in Core Curricula," *The School Counselor* 43, no. 5 (May 1996): 353.

41 See Maurice J. Elias et al., *Promoting Social and Emotional Learning: Guidelines for Educators* (Alexandria, VA: Association for Supervision and Curriculum Development, 1997). Many social and emotional learning programs, and conflict resolution programs, in developing the themes and methodologies of their curricula, have been guided or influenced by the recommendations of John Mayer of the University of New Hampshire and Peter Salovey of Yale University. Mayer and Salovey have designated the following three intrapersonal and two interpersonal competencies as absolutely essential to one's social and emotional development: (1) *self-awareness* (i.e., the recognition of one's emotions and understanding the underlying reasons for why one feels as one does); (2) *self-regulation of emotion* (this refers to the controlling of negative impulses such as aggression, coping with anxiety and depressive tendencies, and the mobilization of positive feelings such as self-esteem); (3) *self-motivation* (which focuses on such capacities as being able to set realistic short- and long-term goals, the ability to draw on untapped resources of optimism, and the marshaling of the requisite emotions when confronted by setbacks; Elias et al. group self-motivation with *self-monitoring*, which refers to the modification of one's performance in light of feedback); (4) *empathy and perspective taking* (these basically require one to be a good listener and to understand, and to be sensitive to, others' points of view and feelings); and (5) *the effective handling of relationships* (included in this category is the constructive expression of emotions, the development of effective communication skills, the ability to cooperate when faced with diverse feelings and viewpoints, and responding to difficult situations using constructive decision-making and problem-solving skills). Elias et al., *Promoting Social and Emotional Learning*, 27–30; Daniel Goleman, *Emotional Intelligence* (New York: Bantam Books, 1995), 42–44; and Peter Salovey, Christopher, K. Hsee, and John D. Mayer, "Emotional Intelligence and the Self-Regulation of Affect," in *Handbook of Mental Control*, ed. Daniel M. Wegner and James W. Pennebaker (Englewood Cliffs, NJ: Prentice Hall, 1993), 258–77. For a slightly different, revamped version of these core competencies, see Collaborative for Academic, Social, and Emotional Learning, http://casel.org/why-it-matters/what-is-sel.

42 I have reviewed numerous conflict resolution programs, and I have decided to focus on the following influential and popular programs and source material: (1) the Teaching Students to Be Peacemakers Program, as described in David W. Johnson and Roger T. Johnson, *Teaching Students to Be Peacemakers*, 4th ed. (Edina, MN: Interaction Book Co., 2005). This program was originally developed in the mid-1960s at the University of Minnesota; it is *heavily* grounded in theory and research, and has served as the prototype for many conflict resolution programs. It has been reviewed and is highly rated by the United States government's

I have found seven prominent themes that they focus on: (1) cooperation, (2) communication, (3) perspective taking, (4) anger management, (5) decision making and problem solving, (6) "principles of conflict resolution," and (7) bias awareness.[43]

Substance Abuse and Mental Health Services Administration's National Registry of Evidence-Based Programs and Practices, and it is estimated that more than one and a half million students have been taught conflict resolution skills through this program; see http://legacy.nreppadmin.net/ViewIntervention.aspx?id=64, accessed October 6, 2012. (2) The Resolving Conflict Creatively Program (RCCP), which is one of the largest and longest-running school-based programs focusing on conflict resolution and has been used in over 400 schools (see Educators for Social Responsibility, accessed September 6, 2012, http://esrnational.org/professional-services/elementary-school/prevention/resolving-conflict-creatively-program-rccp/[site discontinued]). Their approach is described in Linda Lantieri and Janet Patti, *Waging Peace in Our Schools* (New York: Beacon Press, 1996). RCCP's curricula is, to a great extent, based on the works of William J. Kreidler, which include William J. Kreidler, *Creative Conflict Resolution: More Than 200 Activities for Keeping Peace in the Classroom* (Glenview, IL: Good Year Books, 1984); and William J. Kreidler, *Conflict Resolution in the Middle School* (Cambridge, MA: Educators for Social Responsibility, 1997). (3) Creative Response to Conflict's "handbook," *The Friendly Classroom for a Small Planet,* and their "manual of conflict resolution activities and resources," *CCRC's Friendly Classrooms and Communities for Young Children* (see above, pages 14–15, and nn. 36–37) (4) The school-based program that was developed by the Community Boards of San Francisco, and is delineated in Gail Sadalla et al., *Conflict Resolution: A Middle School and High School Curriculum* (San Francisco, CA: Community Boards, 1998). The Community Boards of San Francisco is one of America's leading conflict resolution organizations. Their program is outlined in Bodine and Crawford's *The Handbook of Conflict Resolution Education,* 73–74, in which it is listed under "Exemplary Programs." I have also used the following works that present general overviews of school-based programs: Bodine and Crawford, *The Handbook of Conflict Resolution Education;* American School Counselor Association's special two-part issue on conflict resolution education, *The School Counselor,* vol. 43, no. 5 (May 1996), and vol. 44, no. 1 (Sept. 1996); and Kathryn Girard and Susan J. Koch, *Conflict Resolution in the Schools: A Manual for Educators* (San Francisco: Jossey-Bass, 1996).

43 The programs that I reviewed use different names for the same basic themes. For example, some refer to their anger management component as "expressing feelings" or "emotions and conflict," or their bias awareness component is referred to as "appreciation of diversity," "teaching tolerance," or some similar expression. It should also be noted that some programs stress certain components over others. One finds this to be the case when it comes to the Community Boards of San Francisco's program, which only touches on the theme of bias awareness in their section that deals with communication, and the Teaching Students to be Peace

Cooperation. For many programs, cooperation is *the* underlying theme of their curricula, and is seen as the foundation of all conflict resolution. The ability to interact with and work together with others in a collaborative fashion is the basic competency that these programs attempt to nurture. In helping to develop this ability, some form of "cooperative learning" is often employed. Cooperative learning is a generic term referring to various teaching methodologies that have students working together in small groups towards a common goal in a manner that fosters interdependence.[44] As with many of the components of the conflict resolution curricula, cooperative learning takes fundamental theoretical concepts of conflict resolution and creatively translates them into active, experiential learning activities ("learning through doing").

There are various models of cooperative learning,[45] but the one developed by David W. Johnson and Roger T. Johnson, who are two of the leading researchers in the field and have developed the highly acclaimed conflict resolution program "Teaching Students to Be Peacemakers," has become particularly popular. This model emphasizes the development of "positive interdependence," which is defined by Johnson and Johnson as "the perception that one is linked with others in a way so that one cannot succeed unless they do."[46] It also focuses on the acquisition of social skills that are

---

Makers program, which never directly addresses bias awareness. Another example of this would be the curricula material from the Creative Response to Conflict's program, which never explicitly addresses the topic of anger (however, it does deal with it implicitly, with its emphasis on being "friendly"). Also, every program has a different approach to teaching each of these core themes; therefore, it should be understood that not all of the educational techniques that I will offer as illustrations of how the themes are taught are necessarily used by all of the programs.

44 Janet Ward Schofield, "Cooperative Learning," in *Encyclopedia of Child Behavior and Development*, ed. Sam Goldstein and Jack A. Naglieri (New York: Springer, 2011), 415–16, doi: 10.1007/978-0-387-79061-9_693.

45 See Robert E. Slavin, *Cooperative Learning: Theory, Research, and Practice* (Englewood Cliffs, NJ: Prentice-Hall, 1990), 10–12, 93–115; and Shlomo Sharan, "Differentiating Methods of Cooperative Learning in Research and Practice," *Asia Pacific Journal of Education* 22, no. 1 (2002): 106–16.

46 Johnson and Johnson, *Cooperation and Competition*, 24, 29. Positive interdependence is seen as one of the basic elements, if not the most basic, of cooperative learning and

necessary for collaborative interactions,[47] and it has students self-monitor, reflect upon, and discuss how well they are cooperating and functioning as a group.[48]

Communication. The importance of good communication to constructive conflict resolution cannot be overstated. The verbal exchange of ideas, perspectives, and feelings is the vehicle through which conflicts are resolved, and as a general rule the quality of that exchange determines if the parties will reach a resolution and the quality of the resolution.[49] As such, communication skills play a crucial role in conflict resolution programs.

The program activities that focus on communication skills are designed to train students in effectively conveying what they are thinking and feeling, as well as to listen to and understand what the other party is thinking and feeling. The skills that relate to the conveying of thoughts and feelings primarily focus on how to

---

cooperation in general. In conjunction with positive interdependence, Johnson and Johnson emphasize "face-to-face promotive interaction," which has been described as "positive interdependence [expressed] in behavior"; see Morton Deutsch, "Educating for a Peaceful World," *American Psychologist* 48, no. 5 (1993): 510. Face-to-face promotive interaction requires the students to physically sit in close proximity, interact with each other, and to try to help facilitate each other's efforts. It is "characterized by mutual help and assistance . . . the exchange of needed resources, interpersonal feedback . . . [through which the students] get to know each other as persons" (Johnson and Johnson, *Cooperation and Competition*, 29).

47 Examples of this would include the abilities of getting to know, respect, and trust each other; clarify goals; communicate effectively; initiate and use appropriate decision-making procedures; and avoiding behaviors that are disruptive or counterproductive.

48 Cooperative learning takes place in groups, and it provides students opportunities to self-monitor, reflect upon, and discuss how their groups are functioning. In these groups, they discuss whether they are achieving their goals, functioning properly, and what can be done to improve their work. To facilitate this process, the groups list the member behaviors that were helpful, those that were not helpful, and possible behaviors that could enhance the group performance. Teachers also monitor the groups and provide feedback on how well they are functioning.

49 See Burgess and Burgess, *Encyclopedia of Conflict Resolution*, s.v. communication; Deborah Borisoff and David A. Victor, *Conflict Management: A Communication Skills Approach* (Englewood Cliffs, NJ: Prentice Hall, 1989), 28–83; Robert M. Krauss and Ezequiel Morsella, "Communication and Conflict," in *The Handbook of Conflict Resolution: Theory and Practice*, ed. Morton Deutsch and Peter T. Coleman (San Francisco: Jossey-Bass, 2000), 131–43.

maintain a balance between openly expressing one's ideas, needs, and emotions while at the same time showing sensitivity towards the other person. This requires such things as expressing oneself accurately and with clarity; not interrupting when the other person is speaking; avoiding insulting, blaming, patronizing, and threatening the other party; being careful with the choice of one's words; and regulating one's verbal tone and volume. As far as listening skills are concerned, there is an emphasis on Rogerian "active" or "empathic" listening techniques,[50] which require listening carefully to what the other person is saying, asking clarifying questions, and restating, paraphrasing, and summarizing what the other individual is trying to communicate and is feeling, and to do all of this in a calm, nonconfrontational manner.

One example of a very popular communication technique that is taught in many programs is the use of "I-messages." An I-message is a statement that describes a negative emotion one experiences, the actions of the other person that have elicited that emotion, and offers an explanation of why one is feeling the way one does. They are generally formulated as "I feel ___ when (you) ___ because ___." I-messages, which were originally developed by Thomas Gordon in the early 1960s, have been shown to be much less provocative than accusative "You-messages" (e.g., "You did ___" or "You are ___"), which often trigger anger and cause people to become defensive.[51]

Perspective Taking. Perspective taking (also referred to as social perspective taking), that is, the ability to put oneself in someone

---

50 See Carl R. Rogers and Richard E. Farson, "Active Listening," http://www.go-get.org/pdf/Rogers_Farson.pdf; and Carl R. Rogers, "Empathic: An Unappreciated Way of Being," in *A Way of Being* (New York: Houghton Mifflin, 1995), 137–63, http://www.sageofasheville.com/pub_downloads/EMPATHIC_AN_UNAPPRECIATED_WAY_OF_BEING.pdf; see also Nancy H. Rogers and Richard A. Salem, *A Student's Guide to Mediation and the Law* (New York: Matthew Bender, 1987), 12–13.

51 Lantieri and Patti, *Waging Peace in Our Schools*, 74–79. For a study that supports the use of I-messages, see Edward S. Kubany et al., "Verbalized Anger and Accusatory 'You' Messages as Cues for Anger and Antagonism among Adolescents," *Adolescence* 27, no. 107 (1992): 505–16. For a study that questions the effectiveness of I-messages, see Amy M. Bippus and Stacy L. Young, "Owning Your Emotions: Reactions to Expressions of Self- versus Other-Attributed Positive and Negative Emotions," *Journal of Applied Communication Research* 33, no. 1 (2005): 26–45.

else's place and see things from the other person's perspective, plays a key role in constructive conflict resolution.[52] Various methods are employed in promoting this ability. "Role reversal"—a form of role-playing in which the participants take on the other party's role and present the other's perspective as if it were their own—is no doubt the most popular technique that is used in teaching perspective taking.[53]

An example of how perspective taking is taught to younger students is through Leif Fearn's revised version of the tale of "Little Red Riding Hood," entitled "The Maligned Wolf," in which the wolf gets to tell his side of the story.[54] Students read and discuss the story, or it is presented/performed in the form of a dialogue between "Wolf" and "Red," in which the students are taken step by step through a typical negotiation/mediation process (see pp. 27–28).[55]

Something that deserves to be underscored is that with activities such as these, conflict resolution education programs are not only attempting to help their students develop a cognitive awareness of

52 See Adam D. Galinsky, Debra Gilin, and William W. Maddux, "Using Both Your Head and Your Heart: The Role of Perspective Taking and Empathy in Resolving Social Conflict," in *The Psychology of Social Conflict and Aggression*, ed. Joseph P. Forgas, Arie W. Kruglanski, and Kipling D. Williams (New York: Psychology Press, 2011), 103–18; Adam D. Galinsky, William W. Maddux, Debra Gilin, and Judith B. White, "Why It Pays to Get Inside the Head of Your Opponent: The Differential Effects of Perspective Taking and Empathy in Negotiations," *Psychological Science*, 19, no. 4 (2008): 378–84; Hunter Gehlbach, "A New Perspective on Perspective Taking: A Multidimensional Approach to Conceptualizing an Aptitude," *Educational Psychology Review* 16, no. 3 (2004): 207–34; Deborah R. Richardson et al., "Empathy as a Cognitive Inhibitor of Interpersonal Aggression," *Aggressive Behavior* 20, no. 4 (1994): 275–89; and Deborah R. Richardson, Laura R. Green, and Tania Lago, "The Relationship between Perspective-Taking and Nonaggressive Responding in the Face of an Attack," *Journal of Personality* 66, no. 2 (1998): 235–56.

53 See, for example, David W. Johnson and Roger T. Johnson, *Reducing School Violence through Conflict Resolution* (Alexandria, Va.: Association for Supervision and Curriculum Development, 1995): 64, 85–86; Johnson and Johnson, *Teaching Students to Be Peacemakers*, 5:20; Kreidler, *Creative Conflict Resolution*, 27–28; and Prutzman et al., *The Friendly Classroom*, 62.

54 The story can be found online at http://www.mediate.com/articles/LenskiTbl20110523.cfm.

55 Lantieri and Patti, *Waging Peace in Our Schools*, 32; Bodine and Crawford, *Conflict Resolution Education*, xvii–xxiii.

the other person's point of view, they are also trying to train them to be sensitive to and identify with the feelings and emotions of others. In other words, they are trying to nurture empathy and teach "empathic understanding."

In addition to focusing on the ability to understand the thoughts, views, attitudes, motivations, and emotions of another individual, conflict resolution curricula also train students in a correlative of perspective taking—the ability to explore complex issues and to maintain and synthesize several diverse points of view. For older students, one of the most popular approaches to help develop this ability is the use of a technique known as "structured academic controversy," which was developed by Karl Smith, David Johnson, and Roger Johnson."[56] Similar to cooperative learning (see p. 19), this technique takes fundamental conflict resolution concepts and gives them concrete form through active, experiential learning. The process of academic controversy, without going into all of the details, has students first develop and present opinions about a given topic. They then discuss and debate the topic with students who have opposing viewpoints.[57] Subsequently, they adopt the opposite viewpoint and present it as their own. They conclude the activity by synthesizing the different perspectives, whereby the best evidence and reasoning from both sides are integrated into a coherent and cogent presentation. The theoretical basis that underlies structured academic controversy proposes that constructive conflict is much more likely to occur when the participants in a conflict are able to

---

56 According to Smith, it was probably David Johnson who coined this term. Smith believes that the first time "structured academic controversy" appeared in an article was in Karl A. Smith, David W. Johnson, and Roger T. Johnson, "Can Conflict be Constructive? Controversy versus Concurrence Seeking in Learning Groups," *Journal of Educational Psychology* 73, no. 5 (1981): 651–63. Karl A. Smith, e-mail message to the author, February 2003.

57 At this stage, the participants challenge each other's conclusions, differentiate between the positions, and try to refute the opposing position through logical analysis of supporting evidence, all of which is done while following a set of rules that helps them criticize ideas and not the people who are promoting the ideas.

attain an understanding of alternative perspectives, and subsequently modify their own perspective as a result of doing so.[58]

Anger Management. There is more than ample evidence that anger can be an extremely destructive emotion that contributes in a major way to the perpetuation and escalation of conflicts. Anger is probably the most prominent and pervasive emotion that is experienced in conflict,[59] and research has shown that it negatively affects a wide range of mental processes. Anger may promote biased perceptions and attributions, a lack of understanding and empathy, shallower information processing, and poorer judgment and problem-solving ability. It also tends to elicit reciprocal feelings of anger, aggression, revenge, and hostility from the other party, which can readily precipitate a vicious cycle of conflict.[60] Therefore, as one would expect, anger management is a prominent component of interpersonal conflict resolution and conflict resolution education programs.

The regulation of anger, and the appropriate expression of feelings, is generally dealt with in conflict resolution education programs by initially discussing the negative effects of anger and encouraging self-reflection on one's "anger triggers" (the external and internal stimuli that precipitate one's anger) and on how one expresses one's anger. The programs then offer various approaches for controlling and constructively expressing anger. Strategies for controlling anger include the use of "cooling off" techniques (e.g., waiting out the emotional surge of anger, distracting oneself, or the use of progressive muscle relaxation techniques) and encouraging

58 Johnson and Johnson, *Reducing School Violence,* 104–11; and Deutsch, "Educating for a Peaceful World," 515–16.

59 See Gerben A. Van Kleef, "Don't Worry, Be Angry? Effects of Anger on Feelings, Thoughts, and Actions in Conflict and Negotiation," in *International Handbook of Anger: Constituent and Concomitant Biological, Psychological, and Social Processes,* ed. Michael Potegal, Gerhard Stemmler and Charles Spielberger (New York: Springer, 2010), 545–59, doi: 10.1007/978-0-387-89676-2_3; and Benoit Bediou et al., "Effects of Outcomes and Random Arbitration on Emotions in a Competitive Gambling Task," *Frontiers in Psychology* 2, article 213 (2011): 8, doi: 10.3389/fpsyg.2011.00213.

60 See Van Kleef, "Effects of Anger on Feelings, Thoughts, and Actions," 545–58; Jeffrey Z. Rubin, Dean G. Pruitt, and Sung Hee Kim, *Social Conflict: Escalation, Stalemate, and Settlement,* 2nd ed. (New York: McGraw Hill, 1994), 76–80; and Raymond W. Novaco, "Anger," in *Encyclopedia of Psychology,* vol. 1, ed. Alan E. Kazdin (Washington, DC: American Psychological Association, 2000) 170–74.

the person to challenge his or her irrational assumptions and appraisals that promote anger. It is noteworthy that some curricula also recommend some form of venting (see footnote).[61] A direct, thoughtful, and constructive conversation with the individual who has provoked the person's anger is generally seen as the best possible approach for constructively expressing anger.

Decision Making and Problem Solving. An overwhelming percentage of conflict resolution education programs employ some form of multi-step heuristic for decision making and problem solving, which can be invaluable in resolving conflicts (and can be applied to a wide variety of other real-life problems).[62] Most of these problem-solving models are based on "normative decision theory." Normative decision theory basically prescribes that a decision-maker: (*a*) clearly define the problem that needs to be resolved; (*b*) generate possible options; (*c*) identify the possible consequences of each option; (*d*) evaluate the desirability of each consequence; (*e*) assess the likelihood of each consequence; and, finally, (*f*) choose the most prudent course of

---

61 For example, see Gail Sadalla et al., *Conflict Resolution: A Middle and High School Curriculum*, 3–34; and Johnson and Johnson, *Teaching Students to Be Peacemakers*, 6:6. Cf. Arnold P. Goldstein, Barry Glick, and John C. Gibbs, *Aggression Replacement Training: A Comprehensive Intervention for Youth* (Champaign, IL: Research Press, 1998), 22–25. That there are some programs that still recommend some form of venting as an approach to dealing with anger—which contemporary, mainstream research has found to be counterproductive (or is at least a highly questionable approach) for controlling anger—may serve as an indicative example that in certain areas there does seem to exist some disparity, or a slight lag, between contemporary research and what is actually being advocated by and taught in conflict resolution programs. For research on venting and catharsis theory, see Brad J. Bushman, "Does Venting Anger Feed or Extinguish the Flame? Catharsis, Rumination, Distraction, Anger, and Aggressive Responding," *Personality and Social Psychology Bulletin* 28, no. 6 (2002): 724–31; Keith G. Allred, "Anger and Retaliation in Conflict: The Role of Attribution," in *The Handbook of Conflict Resolution: Theory and Practice*, ed. Morton Deutsch and Peter T. Coleman (San Francisco: Jossey-Bass, 2000), 243–44; and Jennifer D. Parlamis, "Venting as Emotion Regulation: The Influence of Venting Responses and Respondent Identity on Anger and Emotional Tone," *International Journal of Conflict Management* 23, no. 1 (2012): 77–96. Another example of what I would consider to be a gap between research and what is being taught is in the area of apologies and forgiveness. See pp. 401–4.

62 See Maurice J. Elias and Steven E. Tobias, *Social Problem Solving: Interventions in Schools* (New York: Guilford Press, 1996), ix, xi, 3–5, 14–17.

action.[63] In researching conflict resolution curricula, numerous permutations of this model can be found.[64]

One example of an activity that is used to teach decision making and problem solving to children is when a teacher has his/her class listen to a story that is interrupted at a point in the narrative where the characters are faced with some type of dilemma or conflict. The class is then required to analyze the situation and to try to come up with various options for the characters by using their problem-solving model. In order to give students an opportunity to actually apply the theoretical knowledge they have acquired (which is one of the principal goals of conflict resolution education), some programs encourage students to use their decision-making and problem-solving model in some meaningful way; for example, they may use it in formulating class rules that they will agree to abide by.[65]

Principles of Conflict Resolution. This general theme covers an *exceptionally* wide range of topics. It deals with the basic concepts and theoretical underpinnings of conflict resolution, such as the definition of conflict, identifying the reasons for learning about conflict resolution, the potential negative and positive aspects of conflict, various conflict styles, typologies of conflict, how conflict escalates and deescalates (and all of the variables involved in these processes), the importance of not ignoring conflict, assessment of when it's appropriate to accommodate or to compromise, and issues of power and privilege. Within the broad range of topics that are covered, the dispute resolution techniques of negotiation and mediation stand out in that they receive special emphasis and attention, particularly the concepts and skills of cooperative negotiation (see p. 7).

---

63 See Sven Ove Hansson, *Decision Theory: A Brief Introduction* (Stockholm: Royal Institute of Technology, 1994), 5–10, http://home.abe.kth.se/~soh/decisiontheory.pdf. I am offering a slight variation of the sequential models that Hansson cites.

64 See, for example, Kreidler, *Creative Conflict Resolution,* 47; Elias et al., *Promoting Social and Emotional Learning,* 28–29; and Lantieri and Patti, *Waging Peace in Our Schools,* 42.

65 See Lantieri and Patti, *Waging Peace in Our Schools,* 41–42.

Cooperative/Collaborative Negotiation. In conflict resolution, the word "negotiation" is often used in very broad terms, in line with the dictionary definition of "communication or conference (with another) for the purpose of arranging some matter by mutual agreement; to discuss a matter with a view to some settlement or compromise."[66] Negotiation in this context is understood as one of the most fundamental and prevalent forms of human interaction. As mentioned earlier (p. 7), in negotiation that is "cooperative," the goals of the parties are seen as being potentially compatible and the parties are attempting to work together to find a mutually agreeable resolution. Cooperative negotiation, which is also often referred to as collaborative negotiation, has become the dominant paradigm for resolving conflicts in the field of conflict resolution, and it is a prominent component of conflict resolution education.

Cooperative negotiation encompasses manifold concepts, abilities, and skills. In addition to incorporating the elements that were discussed previously (i.e., cooperation, communication, perspective taking, anger management, and problem solving through the use of a multi-step heuristic), cooperative negotiation also typically entails that the parties set the stage for negotiation by considering the proper timing of negotiations (i.e., when the parties will be most amenable to engage in a constructive dialogue) and the proper location, and by creating a cooperative climate in place of a naturally occurring adversarial one. A cooperative climate is created by setting ground rules that promote mutual respect and commitment to resolving the conflict, and by using such strategies as reframing the issues as mutual problems, pointing out commonalities between the parties, minimizing differences (when appropriate), looking towards the future and not harping on the past, and proposing to work on easier issues first.

---

66 *The Oxford English Dictionary*, 2nd ed., s.v. "negotiate"; cf. Garner, *Black's Law Dictionary*, in which negotiation is described as a "bargaining process" (cited above, on p. 6)

The process of cooperative/collaborative negotiation requires that the problems at hand be clearly defined and analyzed. This necessitates that the parties "separate the people from the problem" and that they state their positions clearly and accurately. They must subsequently explore the underlying issues, focusing on deeper "interests and needs," and differentiate between them and their stated positions. The uncovering and addressing of the interests and needs that are at the root of the conflict are critical steps towards the attainment of win–win solutions.

Finding a win–win solution, whereby a conflict is resolved in a manner that is mutually beneficial to both parties, is one of the main goals of collaborative negotiation. This requires that the parties come up with viable options that satisfy their respective underlying interests and needs. In conflicts in which the parties are arguing over specific, limited resources (e.g., money, time, or land), which are often the most difficult to resolve, instead of assuming a "fixed pie," the parties attempt to "expand the pie," that is, they brainstorm and search for innovative ways of expanding the possible resources available and by bringing to the table new "bargaining chips" that could satisfy each other's needs. In situations where there is a clear, incontrovertible conflict of interests, and a win–win solution is simply not attainable, the parties need to establish certain objective and fair criteria that can serve as the basis for resolving their issues. Once a realistic agreement is reached, the parties formalize their agreement, either verbally or in writing.[67]

Despite the immense popularity of this type of collaborative problem-solving approach for resolving conflict, it is not the only one that exists. A notable alternative, which has emerged from the "mediation movement" and has received considerable attention from scholars and professionals in the field, is known as the "transformative approach." This approach, whose major proponents are Robert A. Baruch Bush and Joseph P. Folger, de-emphasizes "problem solving" and the satisfaction of personal "interests and needs" per se, where

---

67 See above, p. 28 footnote 10.

reaching an agreement is paramount, and instead emphasizes certain intra- and interpersonal aspects of conflict. Bush and Folger specifically focus on what they term as "empowerment" and "recognition." Empowerment refers to helping the parties develop a sense of personal strength—in other words, their self-respect, self-reliance, self-confidence, and self-efficacy. This is accomplished through allowing them to do such things as define "their problems and goals in their own terms" and exercising "self-determination in deciding how, or even whether, to settle their dispute."[68] Recognition refers to helping the parties be responsive to each other, and feeling and expressing mutual understanding and concern, which is shown through their interpersonal communication, perspective taking, decision making, and other interactions. The transformative approach does not emphasize underlying issues, common ground, or focusing on the future and not on the past, as does a collaborative problem-solving approach. Rather, it leaves it up to the parties involved in the conflict to determine what are the important issues that they should focus on.[69]

Bias Awareness. Many conflict resolution education programs have come to include some form of anti-bias education in their curricula.[70] These programs have students study and discuss the harm caused by prejudice, discrimination, racism, sexism, classism, and other similar discriminatory attitudes and behaviors that are prevalent in society. Students explore their own personal prejudices and biases, and teachers try to help them see that these prejudices and biases are unjustified and unfair. Besides combating prejudice and bias, these programs try to nurture respect for all people, regardless of the differences that may exist between them. By having

68 Robert A. Baruch Bush and Joseph P. Folger, *The Promise of Mediation: Responding to Conflict through Empowerment and Recognition* (San Francisco: Jossey-Bass, 1994), 20, 81–226.

69 Ibid.; and Robert A. Baruch Bush and Sally Ganong Pope, "Changing the Quality of Conflict Interaction: The Principles and Practice of Transformative Mediation," *Pepperdine Dispute Resolution Law Journal* 3, no. 1 (2002–2003): 67–96.

70 See Kreidler, *Creative Conflict Resolution*, 151–78; Kreidler, *Conflict Resolution in the Middle School*, 231–87; Lantieri and Patti, *Waging Peace in Our Schools*, 89; Sadalla et al., *Conflict Resolution*, p. i; and Prutzman, Johnson, and Fountain, *CCRC's Friendly Classrooms*, sec. Bias Awareness Concepts.

students who come from different religious, cultural, or socioeconomic backgrounds interact and work together on joint projects, and highlighting the positive aspects of diversity, an attempt is made to break down barriers that exist among the students, to help them develop respect and an appreciation for others, and to become comfortable with and embrace their differences.

An Analytic-Comparative Framework for Comparing and Contrasting Contemporary Conflict Resolution with Traditional Jewish Approaches

There are various conceptual frameworks that may come to mind when one wants to analyze and categorize the seven components of conflict resolution that have been outlined above. For example, the popular social-psychological framework that differentiates between cognitive, affective, and behavioral aspects of human functioning or an analytic framework that explores the theoretical bases and underlying assumptions of complex models for behavior could be frameworks that one may consider using. Even though these frameworks would certainly be more than satisfactory for analyzing the seven components I have outlined, for the sake of comprehensibility and to facilitate the comparison to traditional Jewish approaches that will be offered later in this work, I will use an alternative framework. The framework that I will employ incorporates elements of the ones mentioned above, but I believe that it is somewhat simpler than they are,[71] that it lends itself to a relatively nice, neat comparison to Jewish approaches, and, as I mentioned in the preface of this work, it embraces veritably all models of interpersonal conflict resolution.

The framework that I will employ takes the components of conflict resolution education programs and classifies them under the

71 The frameworks mentioned above would require breaking down every core component to its cognitive, affective, and behavioral elements or theoretical bases and underlying assumptions, as opposed to the one I will use, which, for the most part, will treat each component as a whole, allowing for a nice, neat categorization of the components.

following five categories: (1) *fundamental, underlying values,* which I will explain in terms of core goals and ultimate concerns;[72] (2) *fundamental, underlying theoretical concepts about conflict;* (3) *behavioral guidelines and rules of conduct* that the parties should follow in attempting to resolve their conflict; (4) internal *cognitive processes* the parties should engage in; and (5) an *affective component,* which deals with the constructive expression of emotions. The behavioral guidelines and rules of conduct, cognitive processes, and the affective component of the education programs are relatively easy to identify. The primary behavioral guidelines and rules of conduct are "communication," which encompasses many guidelines and rules, and the process of "collaborative negotiation," which takes up the greater part of the "principles of conflict resolution"[73] The cognitive processes are "perspective taking," with its cognitive and empathic understanding, and "problem solving," with its prescribed heuristic steps. And "anger management" is clearly the affective component.[74] However, the question of what constitutes the fundamental underlying values and fundamental underlying theoretical concepts of conflict resolution are open to considerable debate.

A compelling argument could be made that cooperation is the underlying value of conflict resolution education and of all contemporary conflict resolution. Cooperation is certainly a core goal and an ultimate concern, which, to some degree, can be seen as the basis for all of the other components of conflict resolution and informing all of their procedures. But, for that matter, when one considers each of the other components, every one of them

72 For a discussion of what is meant by "values," which offers various possible explanations of the term, see Luigi Tomasi, "Values," in *Encyclopedia of Religion and Society,* ed. William H. Swatos (Walnut Creek, CA: AltaMira Press, 1998), 537–39.

73 Of course, there are also normative aspects to cooperation and anger management. Assuming that cooperation is primarily expressed through the other six components (see further on in the text), I will treat it as an underlying value. Anger management I will treat as a category in and of itself due to its unique standing as the affective component of conflict resolution.

74 As I mentioned in the preface, there is going to be some overlap between these categories. This is certainly going to be the case when it comes to anger management, which encompasses behavioral, cognitive, and affective elements.

could also theoretically be viewed as a separate underlying value. For example, problem solving (not in the narrow sense of the use of a multi-step heuristic, but rather in its broader, literal sense of solving the problems that one is facing) is certainly a fundamental, pervasive concern of conflict resolution, and could therefore possibly be categorized as an underlying value. Or, to a lesser extent, showing respect to others (which is one of the essential features of bias awareness), effective communication, and the proper expression of emotions, are also major concerns of conflict resolution, which could also possibly be classified as underlying values.

I would posit that, just as showing respect to others, effective communication, the proper expression of emotions, and the like could rightfully be described as "subvalues" of problem solving or cooperation (in that problem solving and cooperation are the ultimate goals and concerns of these elements), so, too, could problem solving and cooperation be classified as subvalues. Assuming that the most basic and fundamental goal and concern of conflict resolution is simply the promotion of peaceful coexistence, which was cited earlier (see p. 5) as the intersect between the fields of peace studies and conflict resolution, one may justifiably propose that peaceful coexistence is *the* foundational value of all conflict resolution. All of the core components and all of the elements that they encompass in one way or another contribute to peaceful coexistence between people and may be seen as flowing from, and as an expression of, this most basic value.

Of course, there are also many implicit values that can be seen as part and parcel of conflict resolution. Conflict resolution incorporates values such as compassion, caring concern, self-respect, justice, appreciation of controversy, and so forth.[75] As an educational

75 See Bodine and Crawford, *Conflict Resolution Education*, 55–56. See also Raymond Shonholtz, "The Promise of Conflict Resolution as a Social Movement," *The Journal of Contemporary Legal Issues* 3 (1989–1990): 59–74; and Craig N. Shealy, "The Visions and Values of Conflict Resolution Education: Frontline Achievements and Real-World Aspirations," *Beliefs and Values* 2, no. 2 (2010): 104–10, doi: 10.1891/1942-0617.2.2.104.

endeavor, every aspect of conflict resolution training is meant to contribute to one's personal and social development and well-being, and it therefore follows that personal and social development and well-being (which I have chosen to group together and refer to as elements of character development)[76] can be viewed as fundamental values of conflict resolution. Therefore, to not overcomplicate our analysis, I would propose that, aside from the overarching values of peaceful coexistence and character development, there are essentially only two other fundamental pervasive values (or subvalues) that are accentuated by, and readily discerned from, the seven components that I have outlined: cooperation and problem solving. All other values are either limited in the scope of their effect on the processes and procedures of conflict resolution or are not explicitly addressed and emphasized.

The fundamental, underlying theoretical concepts that relate to conflict are even more difficult to definitively identify than the fundamental values. There are a multitude of theoretical concepts that underlie the processes and procedures of conflict resolution; once again, it would be highly debatable as to which should be designated as the fundamental underlying ones. Therefore, for simplicity's sake, I would propose that we restrict the category of fundamental, underlying theoretical concepts of contemporary conflict resolution to specifically refer to the "basic concepts and theoretical underpinnings of conflict resolution," which were touched on in the discussion of "principles of conflict resolution,"[77] and from among those basic concepts and theoretical underpinnings only to those that are not already covered by any of the other analytic categories (which would exclude the entire process of "collaborative negotiation," in that it is already covered under the behavioral guidelines and rules of conduct). This would mean that

76 The term "character development" can be understood in many different ways; see, for example, B. Edward McClellan, *Moral Education in America* (New York: Teachers College Press, 1999), 50–59, 89–93; Thomas Lickona, *Educating for Character* (New York: Bantam Books, 1992), 50–51; and Kevin Ryan and Karen E. Bohlin, *Building Character in Schools* (San Francisco: Jossey-Bass, 1999), 5–9.

77 P. 26.

when I reference the fundamental, underlying theoretical concepts of contemporary conflict resolution in this book, I will be limiting the parameters of this category only to such things as explanations of how conflict escalates and deescalates, of when it's appropriate to accommodate or to compromise, the various conflict styles, systems for classifying different types of conflicts, and so on.[78]

Summary

This introductory chapter has presented an overview of the field of contemporary conflict resolution, with a marked focus on conflict resolution education. Initially, it delineated and differentiated between the fields of peace studies, alternative dispute resolution, and conflict resolution, and pointed out the conceptual relationships that exist between these fields. It then discussed the field of conflict resolution at length, first focusing on the interdisciplinary nature of the field by highlighting major historical contributions of various disciplines, and then went on to explain the seven core components of conflict resolution's educational programs.

In the final section, I outlined the framework—of underlying values, theoretical concepts, behavioral guidelines, cognitive processes, and an affective component—that will be employed whenever I refer back to this chapter later in this work. At the end of each of the coming chapters, I will categorize the various elements of the traditional Jewish approaches using this framework, and compare and contrast the traditional Jewish elements with those of contemporary conflict resolution. In the concluding chapter, I will summarize the similarities and differences that have been highlighted, and offer a possible explanation for the differences. This will all hopefully help in attaining a better understanding of, and appreciation for, the two different systems of conflict resolution that will be discussed in this work.

---

78 Ibid.

PART II

Foundational Values and Concepts

CHAPTER 2

Pursuing Peace and Refraining from Destructive Conflict

God has created no more beautiful quality than peace.

Midrash, *Numbers Rabbah* 11:7

There is nothing in the world to which a person is drawn to more than conflict, and there is nothing in the world which in its end result will be as evil.

R. Judah Loew of Prague, *Derekh Ḥayim*, 5:17

This chapter will analyze the principal elements that form the underlying basis and framework of the Jewish perspective on peace and conflict. It will be divided into two major sections: (1) *Shalom* (Peace) in the Traditional Sources and (2) *Maḥaloket* (Conflict) in the Traditional Sources. Both of these sections will (*a*) define basic terminology (availing themselves of the conclusions of modern Hebraists and traditional rabbinic scholars); (*b*) present talmudic and midrashic perspectives; and (*c*) explicate the basic normative obligations that relate to their respective topics (i.e., pursuing peace and refraining from conflict). For this chapter, the elements that will be covered have extremely broad applications and not only serve as the underlying foundation of the paradigm for interpersonal conflict resolution that is being presented in this book (see p. xxii), but are also germane to all forms of interpersonal and intergroup conflict resolution, whether they involve a third-party intervention (i.e., mediation, arbitration, and judicial procedures) or not, and even to large-scale conflicts (e.g., conflicts between social and ethnic groups, or even international conflicts). In the conclusion of this chapter, after a summary of its main points, I will highlight certain basic similarities and differences that exist between traditional Jewish approaches and contemporary conflict resolution in respect to the focal topics that were covered.

Shalom (Peace) in the Traditional Sources

Defining the Biblical Term Shalom

Results of Research Done by Modern Hebraists. The word שלום (*shalom*), in its various grammatical forms, appears approximately 250 times in the Hebrew Bible.[1] Philologists and theologians who have done extensive studies of the range of semantic nuances and theological implications of the term have proposed that to define it simply as "peace" would be an egregious misrepresentation:

> *Šālôm* is a fundamental concept of ancient Israel's thought world and psychic life ... [it] indicates *everything* [emphasis mine] that constitutes healthy, harmonious life, the full development of the powers of the healthy psyche. This interpretation has been accepted almost without exception as an assured result of research.[2]

Unless otherwise noted, all citations from the Mishnah, Babylonian Talmud, Jerusalem Talmud, *Midrash Rabbah*, and *Mikra'ot Gedolot* are from the standard Vilna editions of these works.

1 According to Wald, it appears 249 times (Marcus Wald, *Shalom: Jewish Teaching on Peace* [New York: Bloch Publishing Company, 1944], 22); according to the Even-Shoshan concordance, it appears 237 times (Abraham Even-Shoshan, ed., *A New Concordance of the Bible: Thesaurus of the Language of the Bible: Hebrew and Aramaic Roots, Words, Proper Names, Phrases and Synonyms* [Jerusalem: Kiryat Sefer Publishing House, 1993], s.v. "*shalom*" and in Aramaic four times, s.v. "*shelam*" It should be understood that there are also derivatives of the root *sh-l-m* that are closely related to the biblical concept of peace (e.g., Gen. 33:18, and the eleven times Even-Shoshan explains the word "*shalem*" as referring to peace).

2 Gillis Gerleman, "*šlm*: to have enough," in *Theological Lexicon of the Old Testament*, ed. Ernst Jenni and Claus Westerman, trans. Mark E. Biddle (Peabody, MA: Hendrickson

The word *shalom* is so rich in meaning that it is difficult to provide any sort of accurate translation that encompasses all of its implied and associated ideas.[3] According to Gillis Gerleman (1912–1993), the Septuagint's translation of the word *shalom* as εἰρήνη (*eirēnē*, "peace") signifies "a marked limitation of the semantic range of the Hebrew term."[4] Modern biblical lexicons and commentaries often explain the word so that it encompasses a wide range of concepts, such as prosperity, security, good health, satisfaction, and friendship.[5]

Etymologically, the word *shalom* and its root שלם (*sh-l-m*) have cognates in Ugaritic, Akkadian, Aramaic, Syriac, Arabic, and Ethiopic.[6] The comparability of meaning is remarkably consistent across all the major languages of the ancient Near East.[7] The core concept that the *root* (*sh-l-m*) always seems to convey is the idea of being whole or complete.[8] Based on analyses of biblical usage and other Semitic languages, it would appear that the basic meaning of the word *shalom* is "well-being."[9] It should also be noted that modern scholars have suggested that the root שלם is a derivative of the roots שלה (*sh-l-h*) and שלו (*sh-l-v*), which denote being at ease and tranquil.[10]

Publishers, 1997), 1339, citing Johannes Pedersen, *Israel: Its Life and Culture*, vol. 2 (London: Oxford University Press, 1926), 311, 313, 330.

3 Adrianus van den Born, *Encyclopedic Dictionary of the Bible*, trans. Louis F. Hartman (New York: McGraw-Hill, 1963), s.v. "peace."

4 Gerleman, "*Šlm*," 1348.

5 See Ludwig Koehler and Walter Baumgartner, *The Hebrew and Aramaic Lexicon of the Old Testament*, trans. and ed. M. E. J. Richardson, Study Edition (Leiden, The Netherlands: Brill, 2001), s.v. "*šālôm*," 1506–10; and Gerleman, "*Šlm*," 1337–48. It should be noted that, based on biblical parallelism, there are places in Scripture in which *shalom* clearly denotes "negative peace" (i.e., the absence of violence or war), as in Eccles. 3:8 and 1 Kings 2:5.

6 Eliezer Ben-Yehuda, *A Complete Dictionary of Ancient and Modern Hebrew*, 8 vols. (New York: Yoseloff, 1960), vol. 8, 7132 n. 3; and Ernest Klein, *A Comprehensive Etymological Dictionary of the Hebrew Language for Readers of English* (New York: Collier Macmillan, 1987), s.v. "*shalom*."

7 Gerleman, "*Šlm*," 1339–40.

8 *The Anchor Bible Dictionary*, s.v. "peace," 206.

9 Ben-Yehuda, *Complete Dictionary of Ancient and Modern Hebrew*, vol. 8, 7132 n. 4.

10 See Harry Torczyner [Naphtali H. Tur-Sinai], *Die Entstehung des Semitischen Sprachtypus ein Beitrag zum Problem der Entstehung der Sprache* (Wein: R. Löwit, 1916),

Based on biblical parallelism, certain scholars associate *shalom* with the concepts of righteousness (see Ps. 85:11), justice (Zech. 8:17) and equity (Ps. 37:37).[11] Gerleman makes a cogent point when he asserts that the highly poetic nature of certain passages precludes the possibility of determining the meaning of the word solely based on biblical parallelism,[12] as was done by these scholars. Even though there is no doubt that there exists a relationship between these concepts in the Hebrew Bible, one should not lose sight of the fact that there also exist distinctions between them.

Definitions Offered by Traditional Rabbinic Scholars. In traditional rabbinic literature, a number of well-developed analyses and interpretations of the term *shalom* can be found. One of the most comprehensive analyses of the term is that of R. Isaac Arama (1420–1494), whose work *Akedat Yitsḥak* exerted a major influence in the field of Jewish homiletics.[13] Even though his analysis is often cited,[14] it has never been properly translated and elucidated in English.

In his classic philosophic-homiletic style, R. Arama attempts to identify and analyze the underlying concept and essential meaning of *shalom*. As an introduction to his analysis, he first dismisses the conventional wisdom that sees *shalom* merely as a resolution of conflict, a form of "negative peace":[15]

> The average person assumes that *shalom* is an agreement reached between parties that were initially quarreling … but,

243; Ben-Yehuda, *Complete Dictionary of Ancient and Modern Hebrew*, vol. 8, s.v. "*shalem,*" 7178 n. 1; and Klein, *Etymological Dictionary*, s.v. "*shalom.*"

11 Harold Louis Ginsberg, *Encyclopaedia Judaica*, 1st ed., s.v. "peace," columns 194–96; *The Anchor Bible Dictionary*, s.v. "peace"; cf. Wald, *Jewish Teaching on Peace*, 22–24.

12 Gerleman, "*Šlm,*" 1347–48.

13 See Ḥayyim Joseph David Azulai, *Shem ha-Gedolim* (New York: Grossman Publishing House, 1960), *Ma'arekhet Sefarim*, s.v. "*Akedat Yitsḥak.*"

14 Cited by Wald, *Jewish Teaching on Peace*, 6–12; Louis Jacobs, *Encyclopaedia Judaica*, 1st ed., s.v. "peace," col. 198; and Joseph David Epstein, *Mitzvot ha-Shalom: The Commandments on Peace; A Guide to the Jewish Understanding of Peace and Harmony in Interpersonal and Communal Life in Light of Torah* (in Hebrew) (Brooklyn: Torath HaAdam Institute Inc., 1987), 59–61.

15 For an explanation of this term, see p. 13 above.

> in truth, they have not recognized its beauty nor expressed its glory ... *Shalom,* in accordance with their terms, becomes something unsavory in that it implies the existence of a previous quarrel and conflict ... In actuality, *shalom* does not demand as a prerequisite the existence of prior strife or conflict; rather, it is that which prevents such things, for it is *shalom* that represents the indispensable common good that must prevail among humans who need interconnectedness and cohesion.

R. Arama goes on to develop this theme, proposing that we should conceive of *shalom* as something positive, a *ma'amid,* "something that gives support," or a "supportive agent," that maintains the unity and stability of a collective. He elucidates this concept with the following analogy:

> [*Shalom*] is comparable to a type of silver or golden thread that strings together many precious gems, thereby securing each individual unit as a part of the greater whole and giving to the chain its appropriate form and appearance ... This "thread," which holds together and gives strength to all the individual parts and promotes their well-being, in accordance with the greater good, as it stands and endures so does it vivify with life and prevent adverse occurrences, both on the individual and collective levels.

Using this simile, R. Arama explains the multivalent usages of the word. In addition to its applicability to groups of two or more human beings, it may also be used in reference to the well-being of a single living creature, whose body can be viewed as a complex biological system consisting of many parts:

> This concept is therefore applicable to individual human beings. How so? If a person lost the use of his teeth, the "thread" that binds together in that particular area has been "severed," or [similarly] if his eyesight fails ... , or if any of his limbs

> become weakened ... It is in this sense that the noun is also applied to the animal kingdom as well: "[Go now, and see] the *shalom* of your brothers and the *shalom of the flock*" (Gen. 37:14). Surely, animals are incapable of producing mutual agreements. Rather, their *shalom* is referring to the well-being and health of each individual [animal], in and of itself. Similarly, in reference to a single human being it states that "There is no *shalom* in my bones because of my sins" (Ps. 38:4).

R. Arama then goes on to explain that, as a consequence of being a "supportive agent," *shalom* can be applied to three distinct types of entities: individual living creatures, social groups, and even something that is not physically tangible, such as a state or a condition:

> "Furthermore, the term is even applicable to entities that are not made up of either singular or multiple physical objects: "And David inquired concerning the *shalom* of Joab, the *shalom* of the people, and the *shalom of the war*" (2 Sam.11:7); thus, we find in one passage that it is applied to all three categories [i.e., an individual human, a group, and an intangible entity]. The "*shalom* of Joab" refers to the well-being of the person in respect to his component elements; the "*shalom* of the people" is used in respect to the concordance among the individual people; and the "*shalom* of the war" refers to the idea that it [i.e., *shalom*] is that which upholds and supports all other types of things.

R. Arama finally offers the following concise definition of the term:

> We may therefore conclude that *shalom* is the element in nature that holds together and stabilizes the components of all things so that they maintain their essential quality [i.e., their integrity], and with its absence there is division and degeneration.[16]

16 Isaac Arama, *Akedat Yitsḥak* (Pressburg: Victor Kittseer, 1849), *sha'ar* 74, p. 19b–21b.

R. Isaac Abravanel (1437–1508), in his restatement of R. Arama's interpretation,[17] after employing the simile of the "thread that binds together," offers a much more simplified definition of the term. Similar to the conclusions of modern Hebraists,[18] he is of the opinion that *shalom*, which is related to the words *shelemut* (perfection) and *shalem* (whole), is a general term for a state of well-being:

> Generally speaking, *shalom* is used in the sense of the health, wholeness, well-being, and attractiveness of something … it is a synonym for that which is good or healthy … The primary application of the noun *shalom* is to *shelemut* (perfection) and to that which is full and *shalem* (whole) and lacks nothing … The prophet stated that "[I am He] Who forms light and creates darkness, Who makes *shalom* and creates evil [i.e., that which is 'bad']" (Isa. 45:7). Just as "light" is [used in the verse as] the opposite of "darkness," *shalom* is [used in the verse as] the opposite of "bad," and therefore means *that which is good.*[19]

R. Joseph Albo (c. 1380–1444) advances a definition of *shalom* that attributes to it certain additional characteristic properties that are noteworthy. He posits that *shalom* subsumes the existence of a naturally occurring tension between things that are antithetical or diametrically opposed and the achievement of a harmonious, *balanced* coexistence. He therefore, in explaining the underlying concept of *shalom*, only applies the term to a relationship between people that exhibits a marked degree of parity:

> The agreement between opposites is referred to as *shalom* … *Shalom* is thus a noun that describes concordance between

17 Abravanel's works were clearly influenced by those of R. Arama's; see Sarah Heller-Wilensky, "Isaac Arama on the Creation and Structure of the World," in *Essays in Medieval Jewish and Islamic Philosophy*, ed. Arthur Hyman (New York: Ktav Publishing House, 1977): 274–75, n. 94.

18 See p. 38 above.

19 Isaac Abravanel, *Naḥalat Avot* (New York: D. Silberman, 1953), chap. 1 mishnah 11, pp. 74–75.

individuals wherein *one does not dominate over another* [emphasis mine].[20]

In contradistinction to the conclusions of the modern Hebraists who understand the word *shalom* as an all-inclusive term that encompasses "everything that constitutes healthy, harmonious life,"[21] there are certain rabbinic works that significantly restrict it to specific domains. For those rabbinic scholars who, as a rule, have tried to consistently define and discriminate between Hebrew synonyms, *shalom* does not encompass every form of peace. For example, both R. Solomon Pappenheim (1740–1814) and R. Meir Loeb ben Jehiel Michael Weisser (*Malbim*, 1809–1879) maintain that, even though the word is used as an all-encompassing descriptor for human tranquility and equanimity, precise usage dictates that one use the adjective *shaket* to describe emotional calm or intrapsychic peace (e.g., Ezek. 16:42) and *sha'anan* for peaceful quietude (e.g., Job 3:18).[22]

Though it may be difficult to identify a singular foundational theme, one may conclude, as does Aviezer Ravitzky,[23] that it is the linguistic identification of *shalom* with wholeness (*shalem*) and perfection (*shelemut*) that has undergirded the conceptualization and development of the term in Jewish literature.

---

20 Joseph Albo, *Sefer ha-Ikarim ha-Shalem* (Jerusalem: Ḥorev, 1995), 4:51, pp. 632–33.

21 See p. 37 above.

22 See Meir Loeb ben Jehiel Michael Malbim, *Sefer Ya'ir Or; Sefer ha-Karmel* (Jerusalem: Mishor, 1982), *Ya'ir Or*, s.v. *"shalom, shalev, sha'anan, shaket"*; and Solomon Pappenheim, *Yeri'at Shelomoh*, vol. 1 (Dihrenfurt: Be-Defus Yeḥi'el Mikhal Mai, 1784), *ḥoveret* 3 *yeriah* 31, s.v. *"shalom, shalev, sha'anan, shaket"*; cf. Moses Sofer, *Ḥatam Sofer: Derashot*, vol. 1 (New York: The Rabbi Joseph Nehemiah Institute, 1961), 65b col. 2.

23 See Ravitsky's survey of the different usages of the term *shalom* in Jewish sources; Aviezer Ravitzky, *Al Da'at ha-Makom: Meḥkarim ba-Hagut ha-Yehudit uve-Toldoteha* (Jerusalem: Keter, 1991), 13, 33. Originally published in English; Aviezer Ravitzky, "Peace," in *Contemporary Jewish Religious Thought: Original Essays on Critical Concepts, Movements, and Beliefs*, ed. Arthur A. Cohen and Paul Mendes-Flohr (New York: The Free Press, 1987), 684, 701. Even though the focus of Ravitsky's essay is primarily on *medieval* Jewish literature, it appears to this author that his conclusion is equally true for the totality of traditional Jewish literature.

Talmudic and Midrashic Perspectives on the Meaning and Significance of Peace

According to R. Daniel Sperber, "There exists an inner organic continuity between the Bible's understanding of *shalom* and that of the later rabbinic sages."[24] In talmudic and midrashic literature, in conjunction with *all* of its biblical meanings, the import of *shalom* is considerably amplified. Its overall significance, connotations, and normative status are developed in such a way that it acquires a number of superlative qualities that are simply without equal.[25]

Encomiums in Praise of Shalom. Rabbinic literature is replete with pithy sayings that thoroughly glorify *shalom*.[26] In major midrashic works such as *Sifre*,[27] *Midrash Rabbah*,[28] and in the twenty *baraitot* (see Glossary) known as *Perek ha-Shalom* (The Chapter of Peace),[29] there are numerous aphorisms that extol peace as the ultimate good[30] and the pinnacle of ethical ideals, for example:

> Great is peace, for all blessings are encompassed within it.[31]

---

24 Daniel Sperber, introduction to *Perek ha-Shalom*, in *Masekhet Derekh Erets Zuta u-Ferek ha-Shalom* (Jerusalem: Tsur-Ot, 1994), 185.

25 Cf. Jacobs, *Encyclopaedia Judaica*, s.v. "peace," col. 196.

26 See George Foot Moore, *Judaism in the First Centuries of the Christian Era, the Age of the Tannaim*, vol. 2 (Peabody, MA: Hendrickson Publishers, 1997), 195–97; for a chronological list of rabbinic works that discuss *shalom*, see Sperber, introduction to *Perek ha-Shalom*, 188; for a compilation and translation of passages from the Talmud, Midrashim, and the *Zohar*, see Wald, *Shalom: Jewish Teaching on Peace*, 215–91; and for an anthological compilation of later sources, see Avraham Meshi Zahav, *Dover Shalom* (Jerusalem: Shmuel Dov Eisenblatt, 1980), 173–373.

27 Primarily in *Sifre de-Ve Rav: Maḥberet Rishonah ... al Sefer ba-Midbar*, ed. Saul Horovitz (Leipzig: n.p., 1917), *Naso, piska* 42. (Unless otherwise noted, all citations from the *Sifre* on Numbers are from the Horovitz edition.)

28 They are interspersed throughout the *Midrash Rabbah*. The majority of them are found in *Leviticus Rabbah* 9:9, and *Numbers Rabbah* 11:7.

29 *Perek ha-Shalom* is appended to the last chapter of the minor tractate *Derekh Erets Zuta*.

30 This should not be taken as a final or definitive statement on what Judaism views as the *summon bonum* (highest good). There are many other sources that indicate other possibilities. Also, the wording of the midrashim, *Great* is peace ... ," seems to indicate that peace is not the one and only ultimate good.

31 *Leviticus Rabbah* 9:9.

> Great is peace, for it is equal in weight to all things, as we say [in the daily liturgy]: "[Blessed are You, Lord our God, King of the universe . . .] who makes peace and creates all things."[32]

> Great is peace, for it is only peace that the prophets have implanted in the mouths of all humanity.[33]

> God created the world only on the condition that there will be peace among humans.[34]

Shalom's Earthly and Supernal Functions. The Rabbis viewed *shalom* as playing the most fundamental of roles in an organized social system. Together with justice and truth, it is designated by a *mishnah* in *Pirke Avot* (1:18) as one of the three pillars upon which the world endures. Tractate *Kallah Rabbati* cites three parallel teachings that express this idea:

> It has been taught: Great is peace, for the world stands upon it [35] as we have learnt in a mishnah: The world endures through three things: justice, truth, and peace; [and] it is written in the book of Ben Sira:[36] "Love peace, for the world stands upon it, [and] love all people."[37]

Shalom provides stability not only to the human social order, but also to the entire cosmological order as well. As Max Kadushin

32 *Numbers Rabbah* 11:7.

33 Ibid.

34 Ibid., 12:4.

35 It is noteworthy that this text equates the Hebrew expressions *omed alav* ("stands upon") and *kayam* ("endures"), which is a point of contention among the commentators on the mishnah in *Pirke Avot.*

36 This quotation is not found in extant versions of Ben Sira (Ecclesiasticus). See Michael Higger, introduction to *Masekhtot Kalah* (New York: De-Be Rabanan, 1936), 75.

37 My translation follows the punctuation of *Masekhtot Kalah*, ed. Michael Higger (New York: De-Be Rabanan, 1936), 223; cf. *Masekhet Kalah Rabati,* in the standard Vilna edition of the Babylonian Talmud, chap. 3 col. 2. As to my translating the last phrase of the quote as "love all people," see A. E. Cowley and Adolf Neubauer, eds., *The Original Hebrew of a Portion of Ecclesiasticus* (Oxford: Clarendon Press, 1897), xxviii; and Saul Lieberman, *Yevanit ve-Yavnut be-Erets Yisrael* (Jerusalem: Mosad Bialik, 1962), 55 n. 29.

(1895–1980) puts it, it becomes "a cosmic principle and is not only a value concept relating to man."[38] Moreover, its metaphysical properties transcend the physical realm into the supernal (i.e., heavenly) realm:

> If the heavens, in which there is no jealousy, hatred, rivalry, strife, antagonism, conflict, and ill-will, are in need of *shalom* [as it is written]: "He makes peace in His high places" (Job 25:2), the earthly abode, in which all these traits exist, how much more so![39]

Shalom's Numinous Qualities.[40] Beyond intimating that *shalom* transcends the physical world, the talmudic sages—basing themselves on a verse in Judges (6:24) that uses the expression *"Adonai shalom,"* "[The] Lord [is] peace"—also considered the word *shalom* as one of the names of God and as such accorded it a level of sanctity.[41] This is reflected in practical terms in the Talmud and *halakhic* (see Glossary) codes, which prohibit one from offering the greeting *shalom* in an "unclean" place, such as an outhouse;[42] thus, in essence, the word *shalom* takes on the status of a holy word. As a corollary of this, there were later halakhic authorities who prohibited spelling out the word *shalom* as a salutation in social correspondence, out of the concern that it may be thrown away in a degrading manner.[43]

---

38 See Max Kadushin, *A Conceptual Commentary on Midrash Leviticus Rabbah: Value Concepts in Jewish Thought* (Atlanta: Scholars Press, 1987), 69; cf. Ravitzky, *Al Da'at ha-Makom*, 16; and Ravitzky, "Peace," in *Contemporary Jewish Religious Thought*, 687–88. I believe that a close reading of Kadushin and Ravitzky reveals that neither of them touches on the rabbinic view that *shalom* transcends the physical realm.

39 *Leviticus Rabbah* 9:9. This translation is based on the critical edition of *Leviticus Rabbah* (*Midrash Wayyikra Rabbah,* annotated by Mordecai Margulies [New York: Jewish Theological Seminary of America, 1993], 189). For various midrashic interpretations of "He makes peace in His high places," see *Mishnat Rabi Eliezer-Midrash Sheloshim u-Shetayim Midot,* annotated by H. G. Enelow (New York, Bloch Publishing, 1933), 69–71.

40 I am using the word numinous in the sense of something that relates to the divine and embodies an aspect of holiness.

41 For a listing of sources, see Jedidiah Solomon Raphael Norzi, *Minḥat Shai,* in the standard *Mikra'ot Gedolot* (multi-commentary rabbinic Bible), Judges 6:24.

42 See *Shabbat* 10a–b; and *Shulḥan Arukh, Oraḥ Ḥayim* 84:1.

43 See Tosafot, *Sotah* 10a, s.v. *ela* (all citations from Tosafot are from the standard Vilna edition of the Babylonian Talmud); and *Shulḥan Arukh, Yoreh De'ah* 276:13.

Shalom's spiritual/holy attributes were even further developed by the talmudic sages. In one talmudic passage (which has been incorporated into Jewish liturgy),[44] *shalom*, together with it being designated as one of the names of God, comes to have even a closer identification with the Almighty: "*You are shalom* and your name is *shalom*" (*Berakhot* 55b).[45] In expressing such a close association between God and *shalom*, in that God is being portrayed as the very embodiment of, or is coming to represent, or signify, peace,[46] the Rabbis exalted *shalom* to the level of the highest good and the summit of holiness, and bestowed upon it the ultimate form of praise.

Shalom as a Torah Value. In addition to its numinous qualities, *shalom* is portrayed in a number of sources as not only a paramount—if not the supreme—Torah value, but also as the quintessence of the Torah:

> Great is peace, for even if a person has done numerous *mitsvot* [commandments, see Glossary under *mitzvah*], if he has not made peace, he has acquired nothing.[47]

> God said [at Sinai], "The whole Torah is peace and who shall I give it to? To a nation that loves peace."[48]

---

44 Recited after the "Blessing of the Priests." See Phillip Birnbaum, trans. and ed., *Daily Prayer Book, Ha-Siddur ha-Shalem* (New York: Hebrew Publishing Co., 1949), 632.

45 For textual variants, see Isaac Alfasi, *Hilkhot ha-Rif*, in the standard Vilna edition of the Babylonian Talmud, *Berakhot*, p. 43a in the pages of the *Rif*; and The Sol and Evelyn Henkind Talmud Text Databank, *Berakhot* 55b, http://www.lieberman-institute.com/.

46 It should be understood that this statement is not literally equating God with peace or defining what God is. See [Aharon Yehudah Leib Steinman], *Yemale Pi Tehilatekha: Iyunim ba-Tefilah* (Bnei Brak: n.p., 2012), 247. R. Steinman understands the statement of "You are peace" as referring to particularly strong manifestations of peace in God's governance of the world; ibid. Cf. Avie Gold, *Bircas Kohanim: The Priestly Blessings* (Brooklyn, NY: Mesorah Publications, 1981), 87, in which the phrase is understood as saying that God is the source of all peace.

47 *Mishnat Rabbi Eliezer*, Enelow edition, p. 75.

48 Quoted in *Yalkut Shimoni*, *Shemot* 18:273; cf. *Pesikta de-Rav Kahana*, vol. 1, ed. Bernard Mandelbaum (New York: Jewish Theological Seminary of America, 1962), 12:14, p. 215.

> The whole Torah is for the sake of *darkhe shalom* (literally: "paths of peace") as it is stated: "Its ways are ways of pleasantness and all of its paths are peace." (Prov. 3:17).[49]

This view of *shalom* as an overarching Torah value is rounded out with unequivocal rabbinic guarantees of finding favor in the eyes of God for those who live in peace and pursue peace:

> Great is peace, for even if Israel worships idols, yet there is peace among them, God says (as if it was possible) "I do not have power to rule over them [i.e., I cannot hurt them][50] because there is peace among them.[51]

> Whosoever pursues peace, his prayers will not go unanswered.[52]

Even when taking into account certain factors that may play down its significance, such as the tendency for rabbinic hyperbole[53] and other instances in which the Rabbis designate certain commandments

---

49 *Gittin* 59b. I have slightly altered the wording of this quote; to fully understand its meaning, one has to see it in its original context (see *Gittin* 59b). An earlier formulation of the notion that *shalom* is the ultimate focus and purpose of the Torah can be found in Philo's *De virtutibus* (On the Virtues): "That is primarily what Moses, the devout prophet wishes to achieve through his law: harmony, community, a common ethos, and harmonious nature; characteristics, through which families of the cities, nations and lands, the entire world in fact, can achieve the highest state of blessedness" (quotation and translation is from Walter Homolka and Albert H. Friedlander, *The Gate to Perfection: The Idea of Peace in Jewish Thought* [Providence: Berghohn Books Inc., 1994], 28 n. 26; cf. Philo, *The Works of Philo Judaeus*, vol. 3, trans. C. D. Yonge [London: Henry G. Bohn, 1855], 439).

50 See *Midrash Tanḥuma*, ed. Solomon Buber (Vilna: n.p., n.d.), *Tsav* 10.

51 *Genesis Rabbah* 38:6.

52 In the standard Vilna edition of the Babylonian Talmud, *Masekhet Kalah Rabati*, chap. 3 col. 2; in the Higger edition of *Masekhtot Kalah*, 219.

53 See Isaac ben Sheshet Perfet, *She'elot u-Teshuvot ha-Rivash* (Jerusalem: n.p., 1968), responsum 171, p. 39a col. 2; Isaiah ben Elijah di Trani, cited in Yehoshua Boaz le-vet Barukh, *Shilte ha-Giborim*, in the standard Vilna edition of the Babylonian Talmud, *Avodah Zarah*, p. 6a in the pages of the *Rif*; and Zevi Hirsch Chajes, *Mevo ha-Talmud*, in *Kol Sifre Maharits Ḥayot*, vol. 1 (Jerusalem: Divre Ḥakhamim, 1958), chap. 19, pp. 320–22.

as being "equal in weight to all the other *mitsvot*,"[54] the unique phraseology, unequivocal nature, and forcefulness of the maxims that are used in reference to *shalom* can still serve as a clear indication that it is one of the preeminent values of Judaism.

The Nature and the Extent of the Obligation of Promoting Interpersonal Peace

Menachem Elon (1923–2013), in his classic overview of Jewish law, *Jewish Law: History, Sources, Principles*, describes *shalom* as a "meta-principle" that pervades the world of *Halakhah* and Judaism.[55] In talmudic literature, *shalom* primarily appears as having a normative status, which translates into principles and precepts that are supposed to guide one's conduct.[56] There can be no doubt that it is inherent to innumerable biblical and rabbinic laws whose purpose is the avoidance of harmful conflict and the promotion of harmonious relations. As we proceed through the following chapters, we shall see numerous examples of this. At this stage, we will examine the general imperative that mandates the active promotion of peaceful relations.

The General Imperative to Pursue Peace. The verse in Psalms (34:15) that exhorts one to "seek peace and pursue it"[57] served as the basis of various rabbinic exhortations, maxims, and homiletic interpretations regarding the promotion of peace. One example of this would be the *gemara* (see Glossary) in tractate *Yevamot* (109a) that states that this verse was the source of the admonition that "a person should always cling to ... the promotion of peace."[58] Another example would be the

54 See Yehudah Levi, *Mul Etgere ha-Tekufah: Siḥot al ha-Yahadut* (Jerusalem: Olam ha-Sefer ha-Torani, 1993), 55. See also Walter S. Wurzburger, *Ethics of Responsibility: Pluralistic Approaches to Covenantal Ethics* (Philadelphia: The Jewish Publication Society, 1994), 41–42; cf. Walter S. Wurzburger, *"Darkhei Shalom,"* *Gesher* 6 (1977–1978): 81.

55 Menachem Elon, *Jewish Law: History, Sources, Principles* (Philadelphia: The Jewish Publication Society, 1994), 1840.

56 Ravitzky, *Al Da'at ha-Makom*, 14; cf. Ravitzky, "Peace," 686.

57 In Hebrew, בַּקֵּשׁ שָׁלוֹם וְרָדְפֵהוּ (*bakesh shalom ve-rodfehu*).

58 See Samuel Edels, *Ḥidushe Halakhot va-Agadot*, in the standard Vilna edition of the Babylonian Talmud, *Ḥidushe Agadot*, *Yevamot* 109a; and Jacob Ettlinger, *Arukh la-Ner* (Brooklyn: Mefitse Torah, 1959), *Yevamot* 109b; cf. Rashi, *Yevamot* 109b, s.v. *atya redifah*

mishnah in tractate *Pe'ah* that teaches that the reward for "promoting peace (*hava'at shalom,* literally: 'bringing of peace') between a person and their friend" is something which "one enjoys the fruits in this world and whose principal remains for the world to come." According to the Gemara in *Kiddushin* (40a), this teaching is derived from a *gezerah shavah* (a hermeneutic principle of biblical exegesis; see Glossary) that employed this verse from Psalms.

From the dual expression of *seeking* and *pursuing* that is used in the verse, the Rabbis deduced that one is obligated to try to attain peace even when it is elusive and may call for a degree of extra effort on the part of the individual (for examples, see footnote).[59] According

(all citations from Rashi's commentary to the Babylonian Talmud are from the standard Vilna edition).

59 This seems to be a reoccurring theme in Midrashim that discuss the concept of "pursuing peace": "There is no one who is as humble as he who *pursues peace* ... if a person curses him, he responds 'peace be upon you,' if a person quarrels with him, he will remain silent." (*Masekhet Kalah Rabati,* in the standard Vilna edition of the Babylonian Talmud, chap. 3 col. 2; *Masekhtot Kalah,* Higger edition, p. 216); similarly, *Deuteronomy Rabbah* relates how R. Meir personified the attribute of *seeking* and *pursuing peace* by convincing a woman to spit in his face in order to resolve a domestic dispute that had taken place between her and her husband (*Deuteronomy Rabbah* 5:15). R. Israel Meir ha-Kohen, the *Ḥafets Ḥayim,* cites a number of other interpretations in the name of the talmudic sages (*Ḥazal*) that focus on the dual expression of seeking and pursuing, from which it is derived that one is supposed to seek peace even when it is elusive and calls for a degree of extra effort:

> You should *seek* it among those you love and *pursue* it among your enemies.
> You should *seek* it in your place and *pursue* it in other places.
> You should *seek* it with your body and *pursue* it with your finances.
> You should *seek* it for yourself and *pursue* it for others.
> You should *seek* it today and *pursue* it tomorrow.

It is noteworthy that the *Ḥafets Ḥayim* explains the last line, of "seek it today and pursue it tomorrow," as teaching that one should not give up hope when it comes to the seeking peace—"[O]ne should seek peace today and tomorrow and the next day, until he attains it." Israel Meir ha-Kohen, *Shemirat ha-Lashon,* in *Kol Kitve Ḥafets Ḥayim ha-Shalem,* vol. 1 (New York: Avraham Yitsḥak Friedman, n.d.), *Sha'ar ha-Zekhirah* chap. 17 (this explanation of the last line is based on the interpretation of R. Jehiel Anav, see below). I have searched through all the major Midrashim and I have not been able to find a midrashic source for the interpretations cited by the *Ḥafets Ḥayim.* The earliest source that I could find was in Jehiel ben Jekuthiel Anav

to various *Midrashim* (see Glossary under *Midrash*), this translates into searching for opportunities to promote peace even when they do not readily present themselves, which is something that is, generally speaking, not required for other commandments:[60]

> The Torah is not so strict that one should have to run after *mitsvot;* rather, if they present themselves to you, you are commanded to fulfill them, [as it says:] "If by chance you come upon ..." (Deut. 22:6), "If you encounter ... If you see ..." (Exod. 23:4–5), "When you gather ..." (Deut. 24:21), but when it comes to peace, you should "seek peace" in your place and "pursue it" in other places.[61]

Both R. Levi ibn Ḥabib (c. 1480–c. 1545) and R. Shneur Zalman of Lyady (1745–1813), in their respective halakhic works, cite this midrash as proof that according to the Rabbis, the mandate to promote peace in effect imposes a greater obligation on an individual than do other commandments.[62]

Later rabbinic scholars cite sources from the Torah (i.e., the Pentateuch) for the general mandate to pursue peace, which supplement the hagiographical source from Psalms and allows it to be counted as one of the "613 commandments."[63] The earliest work

---

(13th century), *Ma'alot ha-Midot* (Jerusalem: Eshkol, 1967), *Ma'alat ha-Shalom*, p. 321. The wording does indicate that this was a midrash, and *Ma'alot ha-Midot* is known to cite Midrashim that are no longer extant. R. Isaiah Horowitz (c. 1565–1630) also cites these interpretations but does not attribute them to the sages; rather, he just quotes R. Anav verbatim; Isaiah Horowitz, *Shene Luḥot ha-Berit*, 5 vols. (Jerusalem: Oz ve-Hadar, 1993), vol. 1, *Sha'ar ha-Otiyot, ot bet* 13.

60 See Maimonides, *Mishneh Torah, Hilkhot Berakhot* 11:2; and David Feldman, *Lev David* (London: Defus Feiner, 2000), p. 24.

61 This is the version of this midrash as it is found in *Numbers Rabbah* 19:27. See also *Leviticus Rabbah* 9:9; *Masekhet Kalah*, chap. 3; and Jer. Tal. *Peah* 4a.

62 Levi ibn Ḥabib, *She'elot u-Teshuvot Maharalbaḥ* (Brooklyn: M. J. Finkelstein, 1962), near the end of *siman* 110; and Shneur Zalman of Lyady, *Shulḥan Arukh ha-Rav* (Brooklyn: Kehot, 1968), *Oraḥ Ḥayim* 156:2.

63 According to the Talmud (*Makkot* 23b), "613 commandments were told to Moses at Mount Sinai." This tradition gave birth to a genre of rabbinic literature that attempts to enumerate these commandments.

to count the promotion of peace as a biblical commandment was *Halakhot Gedolot* (eighth or ninth century).[64] Unfortunately, the author of this work does not cite a specific verse that could serve as the basis for this.[65] Later authorities, such as R. Isaac ben Joseph of Corbeil (thirteenth century) and R. Eleazar Azikri (1533–1600), cited various proof texts to support their opinion that promoting peace is mandated by the Torah. R. Isaac ben Joseph considered it a component of the biblical commandment "You shall love your neighbor as yourself" (Lev. 19:18).[66] R. Azikri was of the opinion that a general imperative to promote peace is implicit in the biblical command to offer peace prior to engaging in warfare: "When you come near to a city to wage war upon it, *you shall call out to it for peace*" (Deut. 20:10).[67]

Citing a kabbalistic source, R. Azikri also viewed promoting peace as encompassed by the biblical commandment of "And you shall walk in His ways" (Deut. 28:9). According to the Rabbis, "walking" in God's ways should be construed as an injunction to imitate to the best of one's ability any positive trait that is attributed to God in Scripture (i.e., *imitatio Dei*, emulating God's ways).[68] Hence, according to R. Azikri, if God is portrayed by the prophet Isaiah as being in a perpetual state of making peace—in the verse that states that God is "[He] Who forms light and creates darkness, Who *makes peace* and

64 Written either by R. Yehudai ben Naḥman (eighth century) or by R. Shimon Kayara (ninth century).

65 See Naftali Zevi Hildesheimer, ed., "*Hakdamat Sefer Halakhot Gedolot*," in *Sefer Halakhot Gedolot*, vol. 3 (Jerusalem: Ḥevrat Mekitse Nirdamim, 1988), positive commandment 37, p. 73 n. 333. It is worthy to note a slight discrepancy between the different versions of this work. The manuscript of *Halakhot Gedolot* that is found in the Vatican lists the precept as "*bringing about* peace" (הבאת שלום, "*hava'at* shalom"), whereas the Venice, 1548 edition lists it as "*loving* peace" (אהבת שלום, "*ahavat* shalom").

66 Isaac ben Joseph of Corbeil, *Sefer Amude Golah-Sefer Mitsvot Katan* (*Semak*) (Israel: Mefitse Or, 1959), *siman* 8, p. 6. This opinion is also found in Israel Meir ha-Kohen, *Sefer ha-Mitsvot ha-Katsar*, in *Kol Kitve Ḥafets Ḥayim*, vol. 1, positive commandment 60.

67 Eleazar Azikri, *Sefer Ḥaredim ha-Shalem* (Jerusalem: n.p., 1990), 12:57.

68 *Sifre al Sefer Devarim*, ed. Louis Finkelstein (Berlin: Ha-Agudah ha-Tarbutit ha-Yehudim be-Germanyah, 1940), *Ekev*, *piska* 49. (Unless otherwise noted, all citations from the *Sifre* on Deuteronomy are from the Finkelstein edition.) See Maimonides, *Sefer ha-Mitsvot* (Jerusalem: Hotsa'at Shabse Frankel, 2001), positive commandment 8; and id., *Mishneh Torah* (Bnei Brak, Israel: Hotsa'at Shabse Frankel, 2001), *De'ot* 1:5–6. See below, p. 130.

creates evil" (Isa. 45:7)[69]—it is therefore mandatory to follow His example and aspire to continuously promote peace.[70]

The Principle of "Positive Peace"

R. Joseph D. Epstein (d. 2002), in his seminal analysis of the Jewish perspective on peace, discusses a fundamental question regarding the nature of the general obligation of pursuing interpersonal peace. The fundamental question he addresses is: Does the obligation of pursuing peace require that one only attain a level of "negative peace," namely, the prevention of animosity, petulant bickering, strife, aggression, and so forth, or does it require that one must strive to achieve, if at all possible (with the understanding that often it is not possible), some type of "positive peace,"[71] such as a sense of interconnectedness between people or possibly even feelings of fraternity and love? R. Epstein contends that the traditional sources indicate that it is incumbent upon the individual to try to attain a level of positive peace. He proposes that when Hillel (first century BCE–first century CE) uses Aaron as the exemplar of promoting peace—"Hillel says, 'Be of the disciples of Aaron, loving peace and pursuing peace'" (*Pirke Avot* 1:12)[72]—Hillel is not just presenting some sort of pious ideal, but rather he is delineating the extent of the obligation to pursue peace. Accordingly, if the Rabbis write elsewhere that Aaron "would establish peace, *love*, and *friendship* between a man and his fellow [who were previously engaged in

69 See also Job 25:2. Citing the Zohar, R. Azikri explains that the verse uses the expression *oseh shalom*, a tense of the Hebrew verb that can be understood in the present progressive tense (He "*is making* peace," denoting continuous action), instead of the simple past tense *asah shalom* (*made* peace).

70 Azikri, *Sefer Ḥaredim*, 66:101.

71 Cf. above, Chapter 1, p. 13.

72 The basis for the rabbinic view that Aaron embodied these attributes is the verse in Mal. 2:6, "He walked with me in peace," which was interpreted by the Rabbis as referring to Aaron (*Sanhedrin* 6b). For a thoroughgoing analysis of this rabbinic concept, see Daniel Roth, "*Masoret Aharon Rodef Shalom ben Ish le-Ish ke-Model Rabani le-Fiyus*" [The Tradition of Aaron Pursuer of Peace between People as a Rabbinic Model of Reconciliation] (PhD dissertation, Bar-Ilan University, 2012), 15–33.

a quarrel],"[73] or that Aaron could bring about a reconciliation in which the disputants in the end result "would come together and hug and kiss each other,"[74] it may be reasonable to assume that this was the standard of peace which Hillel and the Rabbis intended that one should strive to attain.[75] (Support for this may also possibly be found in the rabbinic prescription that specifically instructs one to "pursue peace in *the manner that Aaron did.*")[76]

Further support for this thesis of positive peace may possibly be found in reference to the talmudic discussion of "altering [the truth] for the sake of peace" (*Yevamot* 65b). The question of "altering [the truth] for the sake of peace" revolves around cases in which there exists the probability that one would harm a relationship with someone if one would be truthful and brutally honest regarding some given topic. Situations such as these present one with a direct clash between the value of peace and the value of truth (i.e., the biblical injunction of "You shall distance yourself from falsehood" [Exod. 23:7]). Citing various proof texts, the Gemara in *Yevamot* (65b) teaches that there was a dispute among the *tannaim* as to the exact halakhah in such cases. It was the opinion of R. Eleazar ben R. Simeon (end of the second century CE) that in these circumstances it is *permissible* to alter the truth,[77] whereas according to R. Nathan (second century CE) it is *obligatory* to do

73 *Masekhet Derekh Erets Zuta-Perek ha-Shalom*, in the standard Vilna edition of the Babylonian Talmud, p. 59b col. 2. Also see Rashi's commentary to Num. 20:29, "Aaron pursued peace and *established love* among people who were involved in conflict ... ." (unless otherwise noted, all citations from Rashi's commentary to *Tanakh* are from the standard *Mikra'ot Gedolot*).

74 *Avot de-Rabbi Nathan* 12:3.

75 Epstein, *Mitzvot ha-Shalom*, 548–49, 577.

76 *Avot de-Rabbi Nathan*, Solomon Schechter Edition (New York: The Jewish Theological Seminary, 1997), *nusaḥ alef*, chap. 12, p. 53. Cf. the textual emendation of R. Elijah ben Solomon in the standard printing of *Avot de-Rabbi Nathan* in the Vilna edition of the Babylonian Talmud, *Avot de-Rabbi Nathan* 12:6, which deletes this section. There are other classic rabbinic sources that seem to indicate that shalom encompasses not only negative peace but positive peace as well; for example, the midrash that states, "If the heavens, in which there is no jealousy, hatred, rivalry, strife, antagonism, conflict, and ill-will, are in need of *shalom* ... (see above, p. 46); cited by Epstein, *Mitzvot ha-Shalom*, 574.

77 This is, apparently, the opinion accepted by Maimonides, *Mishneh Torah, Hilkhot Gezelah ve-Avedah* 14:13.

so.[78] This leads to the question as to whether this dispensation only applies to cases that involve the promotion of negative peace (the prevention of quarrelling and strife), or can it even apply to opportunities to promote positive peace (improving and enhancing an already satisfactory relationship).[79] This issue may have been a matter of dispute between the School of Shammai (first century CE) and the School of Hillel (first century CE). According to one possible interpretation, the School of Shammai would only permit one to alter the truth for the sake of negative peace, whereas the School of Hillel would even permit one to alter the truth for the sake of positive peace (see footnote).[80]

---

78 This is, apparently, the opinion accepted by Isaac Alfasi, *Hilkhot ha-Rif, Bava Metsia,* p. 13a in the pages of the *Rif;* and by Israel Meir ha-Kohen, *Sefer Ḥafets Ḥayim* in *Kol Kitve Ḥafets Ḥayim,* vol. 1, *Isure Rekhilut, Be'er Mayim Ḥayim* 1:14.

79 See Hillel D. Litwack, *Mi-Devar Sheker Tirḥak* (Brooklyn: Simcha Graphic, 1978), 54–55; and Ya'akov Ḥizkiyahu Fish, *Titen Emet le-Ya'akov* (Jerusalem: n.p., 2004), 224.

80 This dispute between the School of Shammai and the School of Hillel is in relation to the case in tractate *Ketubot* (16b–17a) that discusses the custom of singing the praises of a bride at her wedding. The gemara there deals with the question of whether it is permissible to deviate in any way from the absolute truth and to praise a woman as being beautiful who in reality is considered unattractive. The School of Shammai is of the opinion that the assemblage should find some beautiful quality that the bride possesses and praise her for it. The School of Hillel deems it proper to refer to her as "A beautiful and graceful bride," even though this may not seem objectively true. From the context of the talmudic discourse in *Ketubot,* it appears that the entire concern was regarding the *enhancement* of the groom's feelings and appreciation for his bride (to endear her to her husband, a type of positive peace). Therefore, we may posit that altering the truth for the sake of peace according to the School of Hillel is even permissible in an attempt to promote positive peace. And we may also posit that according to the opinion of the School of Shammai (for whom the Talmud does not indicate that they disagree with the fundamental concept of altering the truth for the sake of peace) it is only permissible to alter the truth for the sake of promoting negative peace (i.e., preventing an actual conflict). This is one possible explanation of the dispute between the School of Shammai and the School of Hillel in regard to singing the praises of a bride. This explanation is based on interpretations and observations that are found in Jacob Reischer, *Iyun Ya'akov,* in Jacob ibn Ḥabib, *En Ya'akov* (New York: Sifre Kodesh, 1971), *Ketubot* 17a; Epstein, *Mitzvot ha-Shalom,* 577; *Bet Yeḥiel: Ḥoshen Mishpat,* vol. 1 (Jerusalem: Kolel Bet Yeḥiel, 1999), 182; *Kallah Rabbati,* chap. 10, *Masekhtot Kalah,* Higger edition, pp. 324–25; Nissim ben Reuben Gerondi, *Shitah le-Ran, le-Rabenu Nisim, al Masekhet Ketubot* (Jerusalem: n.p., 1966), *Ketubot* 17a, p. 61; Yom-Tob ben Abraham Ishbili, *Ḥidushe ha-Ritba al ha-Shas,* 21 vols. (Jerusalem: Mossad Harav Kook, 2008), *Ketubot* 17a, p. 146. For

The normative halakhah in this case, as in most, follows the opinion of the School of Hillel.[81]

Maḥaloket (Conflict) in the Traditional Sources

Defining the Primary Hebrew Terms for Conflict

In traditional Jewish literature, there are various words that denote "conflict" (e.g., *madon,*[82] *matsah,*[83] *merivah,*[84] *ketatah,*[85] and *tigra*[86]). In biblical Hebrew, the most common term by far is ריב (*riv*, e.g., Gen. 13:7, Deut. 25:1, Prov. 26:21);[87] in post-biblical Hebrew, the most common term is מחלוקת (*maḥaloket*).[88] For the past two millennia, in both rabbinic and common parlance, the term *maḥaloket* has been *the* primary term used and, therefore, after briefly touching upon the biblical term, will be the main focus of this section.

---

further elaboration of this explanation, see Howard G. Kaminsky, "Traditional Jewish Perspectives on Peace and Interpersonal Conflict Resolution" (EdD diss. Teachers College, Columbia University, 2005), 75–77. For an alternative interpretation, see the commentary of R. Joseph Ḥayyim ben Elijah ("Ben Ish Ḥai," c. 1834–1909), who indicates that even according to the School of Hillel, one may only alter the truth to prevent an actual conflict. Joseph Ḥayyim ben Elijah al-Ḥakam, *Sefer Ben Yehoyada* (Jerusalem: Yitsḥak Bakal, 1965), *Ketubot* 16b, s.v. *u-vet Hilel omerim*.

81 See *Shulḥan Arukh, Even ha-Ezer* 65:1.

82 See Jer. 15:10, Hab. 1:3, Prov. 17:14.

83 See Isa. 58:4, Prov. 17:19, 13:10.

84 See Gen. 13:8, *Exodus Rabbah* 30:17.

85 See *Yevamot* 44a, *Genesis Rabbah* 8:5.

86 See *Ta'anit* 22a, *Bava Metsia* 59a, cf. Psa. 39:11

87 In its various grammatical forms, this term appears in the Hebrew Bible over 130 times. G. Liedke, "*Rîb*: to quarrel," in *Theological Lexicon of the Old Testament*, ed. Ernst Jenni and Claus Westerman, trans. Mark E. Biddle (Peabody, MA: Hendrickson Publishers, 1997), 1233; cf. Even-Shoshan, *A New Concordance of the Bible*, s.v. "*ryb*." For some of the alternative English translations of the word (e.g., "quarrel," "strife," "dispute," and so forth), see *The Layman's Parallel Bible* (Grand Rapids; Zondervan Bible Publishers, 1973), Gen. 13:7, Deut. 25:1, Prov. 26:21.

88 Depending on the context, the word *maḥaloket* has various alternative meanings or connotations, such as "argument," "dispute," "controversy," and "dissension" (see below, p. 57).

Defining the Biblical Term "Riv." The rabbinic commentator R. Jacob Meklenburg (1785–1865) cites R. Solomon Pappenheim[89] who theorized that the word *riv* is etymologically related to *hitravravut* (self-aggrandizement) and *rabanut* (mastery). It therefore expresses the idea that "each one of the disputants attempts to defeat his friend and to command mastery over the other or the topic that is being argued."[90] Modern Hebraists have done numerous studies on the term and its biblical denotation.[91] Even though linguistic connections to other Semitic languages have been established (e.g., *rāb* in Syriac means "to cry out" or "to make noise," and *rāyb* in Arabic means "disquiet"),[92] the root *r-y-b* as specifically denoting a quarrel is unique to Hebrew.[93]

Defining the Post-Biblical Term Maḥaloket. In the Bible, the word *maḥaloket* has nothing to do with conflict; rather, it denotes a "division" or "group" of people (e.g., 1 Chron. 27:1 ff.). It is derived from the root חלק (*ḥ-l-k*), which means, "[to] divide."[94] In its biblical sense, *maḥaloket* refers to "an independent segment of something";[95] in its rabbinic sense, it refers to a wide spectrum of disputes—from constructive controversy (i.e., a division between opinions) to pernicious, or destructive, conflict (i.e., a severe, far-reaching, negative division between people).[96] When used in the latter sense (of pernicious, or destructive,

89 Solomon Pappenheim, *Yeri'at Shelomoh*, vol. 2 (Rodelheim: Wolf Heidenheim, 1831), *ḥoveret* 4 *yeriah* 8, pp. 26b–27b.

90 Jacob Zevi Meklenburg, *Ha-Ketav veha-Kabalah* (Paris: Centre de Recherches des Escrits Sacres, n.d.), Exod. 23:2, Deut. 25:1.

91 See the list of sources quoted in G. Johannes Botterweck and Helmer Ringgren eds., *Theologisches Worterbuch zum Alten Testament*, vol. 7 (Stuttgart: W. Kohlhammer, 1993), s.v. "*rîb*," p. 496.

92 Koehler and Baumgartner, *The Hebrew and Aramaic Lexicon of the Old Testament*, s.v. "*ryb*," p. 1224; and Klein, *Etymological Dictionary*, s.v. "*ryb*," p. 616.

93 Ben-Yehuda, *Complete Dictionary of Ancient and Modern Hebrew*, vol. 7, s.v. "*ryb*," p. 6567, col. 1 n. 3; and G. Liedke, "*rîb*: to quarrel," 1232.

94 See Klein, *Etymological Dictionary*, s.v. "*maḥaloket*"; H. H. Schmid, "*ḥlq*: to divide," in *Theological Lexicon of the Old Testament*, ed. Ernst Jenni and Claus Westerman, trans. Mark E. Biddle (Peabody, MA: Hendrickson Publishers, 1997), 431; cf. Abraham ben Solomon ha-Levi Bukarat, *Sefer ha-Zikaron al Perush Rashi la-Ḥumash* (Petaḥ Tikvah: Mosheh Filip, 1985), *Vayikra* 2:3, s.v. *le-Aharon ule-vanav*.

95 Ben-Yehuda, *Complete Dictionary of Ancient and Modern Hebrew*, vol. 4, s.v. "*maḥaloket*," p. 2916.

96 See, for example, *Pirke Avot* 5:17. See also Shlomo Naeh's discussion of the term in "*Aseh Libkha Ḥadre Ḥaderim: Iyun Nosaf be-Divre Ḥazal al ha-Maḥaloket*," in *Renewing*

conflict), it appears as an antonym of *shalom*, for example, "You should love *shalom* and hate *maḥaloket* ..."[97] or "Great is *shalom* and hated is *maḥaloket* ..."[98]

Notwithstanding the talmudic dictum of "the terminology of the Bible is distinct from that of the Sages" (*Avodah Zarah* 58b, *Ḥullin* 137b), R. Judah Loew (the *Maharal* of Prague, 1525–1609) poses the question as to why in talmudic literature did the Rabbis, for the most part, cease to use the word *riv* and in its place began to use the word *maḥaloket* when referring to conflict.[99] One answer that suggests itself is that the word came to be employed because it says something about the nature of conflict, in the words of R. Baḥya ben Asher (c. mid-13th century-1340), "The very *cause* and *essence* of *maḥaloket* is separation" [100] or, according to R. Epstein, the word reflects the underlying issue with, or essential prohibition of, conflict as perceived by the Rabbis: "The Sages' term *maḥaloket* reflects any type of separation of minds and hearts, even if it cannot be categorized as contentious conflict ... this is so as to teach that the essence of the prohibition is

Jewish Commitment: The Work and Thought of David Hartman, ed. Avi Sagi and Zvi Zohar, vol. 2 (Tel Aviv: Shalom Hartman Institute, 2001), 853–56. It should be noted that even though in over four hundred places in mishnaic and talmudic literature the word *maḥaloket* denotes a "dispute" or "conflict," we do find that in approximately twenty places the word still retains its biblical sense, referring to a "group" or "division."See Chayim Yehoshua Kasovsky, *Otsar Leshon ha-Mishnah*, vol. 2 (Jerusalem: Massadah, 1957), 700; id., *Otsar Leshon ha-Tosefta*, vol. 3 (Jerusalem: n.p., 1942), 232–33; id., *Otsar Leshon ha-Talmud*, vol. 14 (Jerusalem: Misrad ha-Ḥinukh veha-Tarbut shel Memshelet Yisrael, 1965), 517–24; Biniamin Kosovsky, *Otsar Leshon ha-Tanaim: Sifra*, vol. 2 (Jerusalem: The Jewish Theological Seminary, 1967), 820; id., *Otsar Leshon ha-Tanaim: Sifre*, vol. 2 (Jerusalem: The Jewish Theological Seminary, 1972), 815; id. *Otsar Leshon ha-Tanaim: Mekhilta debe-Rabi Yishmael*, vol. 2 (Jerusalem: The Jewish Theological Seminary, 1965), 558.

97 *Derekh Erets Zuta*, in the standard Vilna edition of the Babylonian Talmud, chap. 9; *Masekhtot Derekh Erets*, ed. Michael Higger (New York: De-Be Rabanan, 1935), 147.

98 *Masekhtot Derekh Erets*, Higger edition, 149.

99 Judah Loew ben Bezalel, *Sifre Maharal mi-Prag* (Bnei Brak: Yahadut, 1999), *Netivot Olam, Netiv Shalom*, chap. 1, p. 217.

100 Baḥya ben Asher, *Kad ha-Kemaḥ*, in *Kitve Rabenu Baḥya* (Jerusalem: Mossad Harav Kook, 1970), s.v. *sinat ḥinam*, p. 282 (R. Baḥya's focus is on the concept of *maḥaloket*, not on the etymology of the word). See also Joseph ben Abraham Ḥayyun, *Mile de-Avot*, in *Perushe ha-Rishonim le-Maskehet Avot*, ed. Moshe Kasher and Ya'akov Blacherowicz (Jerusalem: Mekhon Torah Shelemah, 1973), 251 (in which, in passing, he briefly touches on the implication of the word itself).

separation and division ..."[101] (see below, p. 65, regarding R. Epstein's theory of "passive conflict").

General Talmudic and Midrashic Perspectives on Conflict

The Ruinous Effects of Conflict. In talmudic and midrashic literature, *shalom* and *maḥaloket* are often contrasted with and are antithetical to each other. Just as the Rabbis extolled the virtues of *shalom* and underscored its potential for good, they also denigrated destructive conflict and emphasized its potential for evil. Illustrative of this perspective is the following homiletic interpretation of the word *maḥaloket*, which (among other things) highlights conflict's perceived potential to debase and bring misfortune:

> *MaḤaLoKeT* [alludes to an acronym:][102] *M* [stands for] *makah* (a blow), *Ḥ* [for] *ḥaron* (anger), *L* [for] *likui* (impairment), *K* [for] *kelalah* [a curse], *T* [for] *to'evah* [an abomination], and there are those who say [that *T* stands for] *takhlit* [an end], because it brings destruction to the world.[103]

The likelihood that those who engage in destructive conflict will suffer the severest forms of divine judgment and calamitous misfortunes is even further accentuated by the following midrashic teachings:

---

101 Epstein, *Mitzvot ha-Shalom*, 97. Also pertinent to this is the rabbinic association of *maḥaloket* with a verse in Hosea: "You should love *shalom* and hate *maḥaloket* ... Regarding a matter of *maḥaloket* what does it say? 'Their *heart is divided*, now they shall bear their guilt' (Hos. 10:2)." *Derekh Erets Zuta*, chap. 9; *Masekhtot Derekh Erets*, Higger edition, 147–49; see also *Genesis Rabbah* 28:6; *Numbers Rabbah* 11:7. (This translation of Hos. 10:2 comes from *The Holy Scriptures: According to the Masoretic Text* [Philadelphia: Jewish Publication Society, 1964]; see Max L. Margolis, *Notes on the New Translation of the Holy Scriptures* [Philadelphia: Jewish Publication Society, 1921], Hos. 10:2.)

102 In Hebrew, words consist solely of consonants; vowels are represented by way of vowel signs. Thus, the word *maḥaloket* in actuality only consists of the letters *MḤLKT.* This midrash is employing an aggadic method of interpretation that was used by the Rabbis known as *"notarikon"*; for an explanation and examples of this method, see Zvi Chaim Zalb, *Gematria ve-Notarikon* (Jerusalem: n.p., 1955), 33–43.

103 *Numbers Rabbah* 18:12.

> Great is *shalom* and hated is *maḥaloket*! How so? A city in which there is *maḥaloket*, its end will be destruction ... ; a synagogue in which there is *maḥaloket*, its end will be destruction; a home in which there is *maḥaloket*, its end will be destruction.[104]

> How severe is *maḥaloket*! The heavenly tribunal does not condemn a person until they are twenty years old, an earthly tribunal not until they are thirteen years old, but in the *maḥaloket* of Korah even infants a day old were burned and consumed [see Num. 16:27–33].[105]

Working with the theological principle of *midah ke-neged midah* (that there exists a correspondence between the punishments meted out by God and the offense committed), which the Rabbis used in explaining acts of divine retribution,[106] these midrashic passages may also be interpreted as reflecting the rabbinic perspective on the individuals who engage in conflict and the suffering that they inflict. In depicting such dire consequences befalling those who contribute to *maḥaloket*, the Rabbis are correspondingly commenting upon the suffering and havoc these individuals initially caused in the lives of others.[107] Consequently, it comes as no surprise that we find the Rabbis censuring those who are prone to engaging in conflict by

---

104 *Derekh Erets Zuta*, chap. 9.

105 *Numbers Rabbah* 18:4

106 "According to the measure by which a person measures out, so is it measured out to him" (Mishnah *Sotah* 1:7; see also *Sanhedrin* 90a).

107 For sources that grapple with the theological question of why according to *Numbers Rabbah* even innocent children should suffer, see the textual variant of Rashi's commentary to Numbers 16:27, cited in Shmuel Yehoshua Gold, *Sefer Iyunim be-Rashi: api. 15 Kit. Y. ve-15 Defusim Rishonim* (Bnei Brak: Mekhon Mishnat Rabbi Akiva, 2009), 223; Baḥya ben Asher, *Rabenu Baḥya: Be'ur al ha-Torah* (Jerusalem: Mossad Harav Kook, 2006), Numbers 16:29; Judah Loew ben Bezalel, *Sefer Gur Aryeh: Be'ur al Pe. Rashi*, vol. 4 (Bnei Brak: n.p., 1972), Numbers 16:27, pp. 84–85; Ḥayim Leib Shmuelevitz, *Siḥot Musar* (Jerusalem: n.p., 1980), *ma'amar* 33, 5732, p. 122; and see also the related comments of Sa'adia Gaon, in Sa'adia ben Joseph, *Ha-Nivḥar ba-Emunot uva-De'ot* (New York: Sura, 1970), 5:3, p. 177–78, and 9:2, p. 266; and Aaron ben Meshullam of Lunel, *Teshuvat R. Aharon b.R. Meshulam mi-Lunil leha-Ramah*, in *Sanhedre Gedolah: al Masekhet Sanhedrin*, vol. 1 (Jerusalem: Machon Harry Fischel, 1968), 187.

applying to them the appellation of *"resha'im"* (wicked people): "Our Rabbis have taught: Four [types of people] are called *resha'im* ... and he who is prone to *maḥaloket.*"[108]

Two Elements of Destructive Conflict That Were of Particular Concern to the Rabbis. In conjunction with its destructive potential, there were other deleterious aspects of *maḥaloket* that were highlighted by the Rabbis. There is a talmudic passage in tractate *Sanhedrin* that seems to focus in on two particular elements of conflict: the manner in which it escalates and its intractable nature.

The Talmud in *Sanhedrin* (6b–7a) cites various interpretations of the verse "The beginning of strife [is like] the letting forth of water; therefore, abandon a quarrel before it breaks out" (Prov. 17:14). One of the interpretations that the Gemara cites is that of R. Huna (third century CE), who explained the verse by using the imagery of a river that overflows its banks: "Conflict is comparable to [a river that overflows and breaks off into] a channel of flowing water, which will continue to widen" (see the alternative translation cited in the footnote).[109] Based on the implications of the simile—of an unwieldy pouring forth of water that continuously spreads out and cannot be contained—we may justifiably assert that R. Huna came to highlight the escalatory manner in which a conflict tends to expand in the scope of its issues and to draw in new participants, thereby becoming increasingly more difficult to manage.[110]

---

108 *Numbers Rabbah* 18:12.

109 This translation is based on Rashi, *Sanhedrin* 7a, s.v. *le-tsinora de-videka*. Alternatively, based on Rashi's commentary to Prov. 17:14, R. Huna's saying can be translated differently and understood as using the imagery of someone who had bored a hole (or opening) into the wall of a water aqueduct, and consequently the hole in the wall becomes progressively wider: "Conflict is comparable to a channel of water from a hole [in the wall of an aqueduct], where it [the hole in the wall] will continue to widen." Cf. Michael Sokoloff, *A Dictionary of Jewish Babylonian Aramaic of the Talmudic and Geonic Periods* (Ramat Gan, Israel: Bar Ilan University Press, 2002), s.v. *bideka*.

110 Based on the alternative translation cited in the previous footnote, which focuses on the widening of the hole, which allows for an increase in the amount and intensity of the flow of water, R. Huna's simile may not only be highlighting the tendency of a conflict to expand in its scope and number of participants, but also to increase in its intensity. Even if R. Huna did not intend to highlight the increase in intensity, R. Elijah ben Solomon (the "Vilna Gaon," 1720–1797) in his commentary to Proverbs certainly does; see Elijah ben Solomon, *Be'ur ha-Gera: Mishle* (Jerusalem: Mossad

The Gemara then goes on to cite a saying of Abaye Kashisha (c. 300 CE) that underscores conflict's intractable nature, in the sense of its tendency to become entrenched and increasingly more difficult to resolve as it progresses. Abaye Kashisha accentuates this issue by comparing conflict to "a board on a bridge that [starts off loose but once tread upon] becomes imbedded in its place."

Citing the verse mentioned above ("The beginning of strife ... "), R. Isaiah Horowitz (c. 1565–1630) writes that it was specifically because of the conflagrative potential—"that from one spark of a flame [a small argument] the bonfire[111] will become great [a major destructive conflict may ensue]"—which, according to R. Horowitz, is embodied in R. Huna's teaching, that even "an infinitesimal amount of *maḥaloket* is prohibited."[112] This leads us to our next section, in which we will consider the nature and extent of the normative obligation to refrain from conflict.

The Halakhic Obligation of Refraining from Conflict

The Prohibition of "Holding on to a Quarrel." The Talmud states that there is a general prohibition against engaging in deleterious conflict, which is referred to as "holding on to a quarrel (*maḥaloket*)" (*Sanhedrin* 110a). This prohibition is derived from the biblical episode of Korah's

---

Harav Kook, 2005), 17:14. One can also find other interpretations of the verse in Proverbs that relate to conflict escalation interspersed throughout the spectrum of classic rabbinic texts, some of which appear in rather obscure places. One example would be the explanation of Samuel b. Kalonymus Ḥazan (twelfth to thirteenth centuries) appearing in his commentary to one of Solomon ha-Bavli's (tenth century) liturgical poems; see "*Perush Shemuel Ḥazan la-Piyut En Tsur Ḥelef*," *Yeshurun* 18 ([Kislev] 5767 [2006]): 125.

111 In traditional Jewish literature that discusses conflict, one often encounters the metaphor *esh ha-maḥaloket*, "the fire of conflict." In a search of the *Otzar HaHochma* online database of Jewish books, ver.14.0, accessed September 25, 2016, http://www.otzar.org, this expression appears in over 2,000 works. For some noteworthy explanations of the comparison of conflict to fire, see Naphtali Zevi Judah Berlin, *Hosafot le-Ferush Ha'amek Davar ve-Harḥev Davar* (Jerusalem: Bamberger et Vahrmann, 1928), Numbers 16:2; Naphtali Zevi Judah Berlin, *Meshiv Davar* (Jerusalem: Yeshivat Voloz'in be-Erets Yisrael, 1993), *ḥelek* 2 *siman* 3, and *siman* 8, p. 72 col. 2; Yosef Eliyahu Henkin, *Kitve ha-Ga'on Rabi Yosef Eliyahu Henkin*, vol. 1 (New York: Ezras Torah, 1980), 225b; and Yonason Binyomin Goldberger, *Avne Ḥefets*, vol. 4 (Brooklyn, NY: Imre Shafer, 2005), 271.

112 Horowitz, *Shene Luḥot ha-Berit, Sha'ar ha-Otiyot, ot bet* 10.

rebellion (Num. 16:1–17:15). According to R. Simeon ben Lakish (third century CE), when the Torah writes that "Moses rose up and went to Dathan and Abiram" (Num. 16:25) it is using Moses as an example of how someone who is embroiled in a conflict must take it upon himself to appease his antagonists: "From here we learn that one does not hold on to a quarrel." The Gemara then quotes Rav (third century CE), who cites the verse "And he shall not be as Korah and his assembly" (Num. 17:5) as teaching that "whoever holds on to a quarrel violates a negative commandment."

This talmudic passage establishes a paradigm from which later authorities derive certain principles and delineate the parameters of the prohibition. The earliest one to do so was R. Aḥa of Shabḥa (680–752) in *She'iltot de-Rav Aḥai Gaon*. Basing himself on this gemara in *Sanhedrin*, which uses Moses' behavior as a model of how one should behave in a conflict, R. Aḥa formulates the principle that "even he who is great is required to humble himself to one who is small so as to avoid a conflict."[113]

R. Jonathan ben David (c. 1135–c. 1211), one of the leading medieval Jewish scholars of Lunel, France, deduces from this talmudic passage that if Moses had not attempted to appease Dathan and Abiram and quell their dispute, this would have constituted a case of holding on to (i.e., perpetuating) a quarrel. Even though, according to the biblical narrative, Moses was in the right and it was Dathan, Abiram, and Korah who had unjustly instigated the conflict, if Moses had neglected an opportunity to end it (thereby *holding on to* it), on a certain level this would be comparable to the conduct of Korah. In other words, R. Jonathan is saying that, even if someone has been unjustly attacked and enmeshed in a conflict, that individual cannot use this fact as an excuse to perpetuate it, and if that individual should ignore an opportunity for reconciliation he or she will be held guilty for transgressing the prohibition.[114]

113 Aḥa of Shabḥa, *She'iltot de-Rav Aḥai Gaon*, 5 vols., annotated by Samuel K. Mirsky (Jerusalem: Institute for Research and Publication, Sura, 1960–1977), vol. 5, *Koraḥ, she'ilta* 148.

114 Jonathan ben David ha-Kohen of Lunel, *Perushe Rabenu Yehonatan mi-Lunil al 21 Masekhtot ha-Shas* (Jerusalem: n.p., 1975), *Sanhedrin*, p. 16 col. 1. In this commentary, chapter *Kol Yisrael* precedes *Elu Hen ha-Neḥenakin*.

The idea of using the talmudic paradigm of the Korah rebellion and Moses' response to it to define the prohibition of "holding on to a quarrel" is further developed by R. Nathan Zevi Finkel (1849–1927). In addition to making observations similar to those of R. Aḥa and R. Jonathan, R. Finkel also calls attention to another detail that they do not touch on. A close reading of the talmudic passage and the biblical verse it cites (i.e., Num. 16:25) reveals that it is referring to a point in the episode when Moses had already made an attempt to reconcile with the other parties (Num. 16:8–11), which they had summarily rejected with the utmost contempt (Num. 16:12–14). Consequently, it would follow that the obligation to take the initiative to resolve a conflict applies even when one is dealing with someone who has rejected, in no uncertain terms, a previous overture at reconciliation.[115] R. Josef Hirsch Dunner (1913–2007) goes even further than this and asserts that since Dathan and Abiram are depicted by the Rabbis as *"resha'im"* (wicked people)[116] and as Moses' prime antagonists who had assailed him on numerous occasions,[117] it would follow that the obligation to take the initiative to resolve a conflict applies even when the other party can be characterized as being wicked, and has an established reputation as being belligerent and attacking the person on previous occasions.[118]

As to the status of the prohibition of holding on to a quarrel, there is a dispute as to whether it is actually considered one of the 613 commandments or is only an *asmakhta* (see Glossary).[119] The manner in which it is referred to in various responsa and halakhic works seems

115 Nathan Zevi Finkel, *Or ha-Tsafun* (Jerusalem: Elḥanan Hoffman and Tsevi Weinreb, 1978), vol. 1, pp. 192–93 (cf. vol. 3, pp. 41–45).

116 See *Megillah* 11a, where they are described as "wicked from beginning to end."

117 *Nedarim* 64b; *Avodah Zarah* 5a; and *Exodus Rabbah* 1:31.

118 Yosef Tsevi ha-Levi Dunner, *Mikdash ha-Levi* (Bnei Brak: n.p., 2009), 460–61. Cf. Abraham Danzig, *Kitsur Sefer Ḥaredim* (Jerusalem: Mekhon Me'orot ha-Da'at, 1986), chap. 8: 28–29, pp. 69–70; Jonah ben Abraham Gerondi, *Sha'are Teshuvah* (Brooklyn: Zundel Berman, 1974), 3:58–59; and see Yehuda Shaviv, *Yodukha Aḥikha* (Alon Shvut: Yeshivat Har Etzion, 2004), 59 n. 2, 62 n. 6.

119 Maimonides was of the opinion that it is only an *asmakhta*; see Maimonides, *Sefer ha-Mitsvot*, *shoresh* 8, and negative commandment 45.

to indicate that it was considered by a considerable number of *poskim* (halakhic authorities; see Glossary) as biblical in nature.[120]

R. Epstein's Theory of "Passive Conflict." In the course of his analysis of *maḥaloket*, R. Epstein proposes that within the normative halakhic realm, there are two distinct types of *maḥaloket*:[121] (1) a conflict in which there exists antagonistic behaviors, such as verbal insults or provocative acts; and (2) a type of "passive conflict"[122] or "distancing" between individuals that is not accompanied by discordant behaviors but is still manifest in some way.[123] There is no question as to the validity of the first assertion that classifies actual conflictual behaviors under the rubric of *maḥaloket*. As to the validity of the second, which views "conflict" that is devoid of active clashing as falling within the halakhic category of *maḥaloket*, it is debatable whether this can actually be substantiated.

Apart from the philological implications of the term *maḥaloket* (see pp. 58–59 above), R. Epstein bases his opinion on the premise mentioned earlier[124] that in talmudic literature *shalom* and *maḥaloket* appear as having an obverse relationship with each other. Working with this premise, R. Epstein posits that if *shalom* on the interpersonal level is viewed as something positive, namely, a sense of unity among people, then *maḥaloket* should rightfully be viewed as the negation of *shalom*—in other words, the absence of that sense of unity, even though there is no manifest enmity or discord. This is in contrast to the commonly accepted approach that construes *shalom* as something negative (for

---

120 See Israel Meir ha-Kohen, *Sefer Ḥafets Ḥayim*, *petiḥah*, negative commandment 12, quoting Gerondi, *Sha'are Teshuvah*, 3:58, and Moses ben Jacob of Coucy, *Sefer Mitsvot Gadol* (*Semag*) (Israel: n.p.,1991), negative commandment 157; Isaac Jacob Weiss, *Minḥat Yitsḥak*, 10 vols. (Jerusalem: Hotsa'at Sefarim Minḥat Yitsḥak, 1989-), vol. 3, *siman* 13:16 (quoting Isaac ben Joseph of Corbeil, *Semak*, *siman* 132); and Berlin, *Meshiv Davar*, *ḥelek* 2 *siman* 8, 9, p.73 col. 1, p. 74 col. 2). Cf. Issachar Baer Eilenburg, *Sefer Be'er Sheva* (Jerusalem: n.p., 1969), *Sanhedrin* 110, p. 72b.

121 Epstein, *Mitzvot ha-Shalom*, 95–98.

122 The designation "passive conflict" is never actually used by R. Epstein. I have coined the phrase "passive conflict" because I believe that it expresses very clearly the idea he is trying to convey, albeit that at one point he does categorize this as something "positive" (see Epstein, *Mitzvot ha-Shalom*, 114).

123 Epstein, *Mitzvot ha-Shalom*, 95–98. It is difficult to know for sure if R. Epstein is referring to a distancing that is manifest in actions (as he seems to indicate on p. 97) or if he is even referring to an emotional distancing (as he seems to indicate on p. 96).

124 See pp. 57–58 above.

instance, the absence of fighting and strife)[125] and *maḥaloket* as something positive (such as overt hostility or active clashing).[126]

R. Epstein cites various halakhic sources in support of this theory. However, some of his interpretations of these sources may, possibly, be viewed as being a little tenuous. For example, in dealing with the halakhic prohibition of "You shall not create factions" (*lo ta'asu agudot agudot*) (*Yevomot* 13b), which forbids factionalism in religious observances, he quotes Maimonides' explanation[127] that the concern of this law (i.e., what it is ultimately concerned or worried about) is not divisiveness per se, but rather the potential of large-scale conflicts that can develop out of divisiveness. R. Epstein offers a highly cogent but what may, nevertheless, be regarded as a somewhat novel interpretation of this halakhah, which he cites as supporting his theory of passive conflict.[128]

Even R. Epstein, who repeatedly refers back to his theory of passive conflict, does not seem to accept it without some reservations. He himself at a certain point concedes that, at best, he has proven that passive conflict between individuals "contains within it a *connection*" to the prohibition of *maḥaloket* (*lata de-isur maḥaloket*) or is "at least an *offshoot* of *maḥaloket*" (*me'avizraihu de-maḥaloket*).[129]

Summary

This chapter has analyzed the general principles of *shalom* and *maḥaloket*, which form the foundation of Jewish conflict resolution. It has done this with a threefold approach: (1) to precisely define the terms *shalom* and *maḥaloket*; (2) to elucidate major

125 See the quote above on pp. 39–40 in the name of R. Arama.

126 Epstein, *Mitzvot ha-Shalom*, 114–15.

127 Maimonides, *Mishneh Torah, Hilkhot Avodah Zarah* 12:14. R. Epstein is quoting from the standard Warsaw-Vilna edition of the *Mishneh Torah;* cf. the Frankel edition, *Mishneh Torah, Hilkhot Avodah Zarah* 12:14.

128 See Epstein, *Mitzvot ha-Shalom*, 98–101. For other sources that R. Epstein cites in support of this theory, see ibid., pp 101–14.

129 Ibid., 110, and see also pp. 97, 99, 105, 114, 118–19, and 134.

talmudic and midrashic themes that pertain to the concepts of *shalom* and *maḥaloket*; and (3) to examine the nature and parameters of the basic *halakhot* that require one to pursue peace and to eschew conflict.

Each of the two principal subheadings of this chapter (i.e., "*Shalom* in the Traditional Sources" and "*Maḥaloket* in the Traditional Sources") began by initially presenting the conclusions of preeminent scholars regarding the proper denotation of some of the most basic, Hebrew "peace terminology." These sections brought together and contrasted (possibly for the first time) the results of modern, Hebrew linguistic research with those of traditional rabbinic scholarship that deal with the primary Hebrew terms for "peace" and "conflict."

The second section of each major division in this chapter brought together and explained a number of fundamental principles that have served as the bedrock of the rabbinic approach to conflict resolution for over fifteen hundred years. These include the following: that peace is the ultimate good, it is one of the "pillars" of society, it represents the quintessence of the Torah, and that it is ranked as one of the highest Torah values. Conversely, destructive conflict is permeated by an array of baneful qualities that require it to be regarded, basically, as anathema.

The final subsections explored the normative aspects of their respective focal topics by initially presenting the possible hagiographical and/or pentateuchal sources for pursuing peace and refraining from conflict. In doing so, it was shown how the general imperative of pursuing peace imposes (in a certain respect) a greater obligation on an individual than do other commandments and how the prohibition of holding on to a quarrel requires the rejection of the standard rationalizations for perpetuating a conflict. These subsections concluded with brief critical examinations of the theories of R. Joseph Epstein. Support was found for his theory of promoting positive peace, whereas his theory of passive conflict, even though theoretically sound, there was some question as to whether it could be fully substantiated by authoritative halakhic sources.

The results of the analysis done in this chapter may be viewed, for the sake of simplicity, as coalescing into two germinal principles: (1) there exists in Judaism a sacred obligation to do one's utmost to actively promote harmonious relations and (2) there also exists a corresponding obligation to do one's utmost to avoid potentially destructive conflict. These principles, which have served as the hallowed underpinnings of the traditional Jewish approach to conflict resolution, will provide us with the foundation and basic frame of reference for all of the coming chapters of this book.

Similarities and Differences between Contemporary Conflict Resolution and Traditional Jewish Approaches in Respect to the Fundamental Value of Promoting Peace[130]

Using the analytic-comparative framework that was detailed at the end of the first chapter (pp. 30–34), I would like to touch on what I consider to be a few significant similarities and a few significant differences that exist between contemporary conflict resolution and traditional Jewish approaches[131] in respect to the fundamental value of promoting peace.

130 In the following section, I will only offer what I perceive as being just some of the significant similarities and differences that exist between contemporary conflict resolution and traditional Jewish approaches in respect to the fundamental, underlying value of promoting peace. I have no doubt that one could readily come up with other significant similarities and differences that are very noteworthy; I myself am cognizant of some of these. What I will be highlighting are only a few select elements that have stood out in my mind, which I personally consider to be of significant import, and are discernible from the sources I have researched. This qualification of not giving an exhaustive account of all feasible similarities and differences will hold true for all the other instances in this work in which I will compare and contrast contemporary conflict resolution with traditional Jewish approaches.

131 I have decided that when I discuss the manner in which Judaism deals with conflict, I will use the plural "traditional Jewish approach*es*," so as not to give the impression that I subscribe to the notion of a single, monolithic, traditional Jewish approach. Not worrying that anyone would actually suggest that I believe that there is a single, monolithic, contemporary approach to conflict resolution, when I discuss commonalities or prevalent trends among contemporary

In Chapter 1, I proposed that the promotion of peaceful coexistence is the core goal and ultimate concern of all aspects of contemporary conflict resolution and, as such, should be designated as contemporary conflict resolution's most fundamental, underlying value. The attainment of peaceful coexistence is what lies behind all of the behavioral guidelines, rules of conduct, cognitive processes, and other components of contemporary conflict resolution and, as a value, peaceful coexistence encompasses all of contemporary conflict resolution's subvalues, and extends to the broader field of conflict resolution, serving as the foundational value of peace studies and alternative dispute resolution as well. As we proceed in our study of Judaism's approach to interpersonal conflict in the coming chapters, we shall see a multitude of behavioral guidelines, rules of conduct, subvalues, and other components of traditional Jewish approaches, all of whose core goals and ultimate concerns are the pursuit of peace and refraining from (or avoidance of) destructive conflict. It would therefore follow that pursuing peace and refraining from destructive conflict could, and should, be designated as the most fundamental, underlying values of traditional Jewish approaches (which can also find clear support from the rabbinic teaching that "the whole Torah is for the sake of *darkhe shalom*")[132] and that we may rightfully compare and contrast them with contemporary conflict resolution's value of promoting peaceful coexistence.

In discussing contemporary conflict resolution, I at one point defined "peaceful coexistence" as the fundamental concern for resolving conflicts using peaceful means, repudiating all types of violence, and the cultivation of positive human relationships.[133] In our study of traditional Jewish approaches, it will become quite evident that all of these aspects of peaceful coexistence are clearly part and

---

approaches, I will simply group the contemporary approaches together under the heading of "contemporary conflict resolution."

132 See pp. xxvii–xxviii and 48.

133 See p. 5.

parcel of traditional Jewish approaches as well. However, we shall also see a significant difference between contemporary conflict resolution's value of promoting peaceful coexistence and traditional Jewish approaches' value of promoting peaceful coexistence (or pursuing peace), as reflected in many *halakhot*. It should eventually become quite clear that traditional Jewish approaches seem to repeatedly focus on higher levels of peace and harmonious coexistence than those that are the focus of contemporary conflict resolution.

We have seen some indication of traditional Jewish approaches' stress on higher levels of peaceful coexistence already in this chapter in the context of the discussion of the principle of "positive peace." As R. Epstein had pointed out, there are traditional Jewish sources that indicate that one should not only be satisfied with a situation in which there exists a level of "negative peace" (the absence of active aggression, hatred, and so on), rather, if at all possible (with the understanding that often it is not), one should aim to attain a level of "positive peace," that is, a sense of interconnectedness, feelings of friendship, fraternity, and even love. This dual understanding of the concept of peace and the associated normative obligations that go with it stand in contrast to what we had seen in the first chapter's overview of the broader field of conflict resolution. As a general rule, the primary focus of the broader field—particularly in the areas of mediation, negotiation, and arbitration—is clearly on "negative peace" (the resolution of conflicts) and not on the development of "positive peace" (developing interconnectedness, friendship, and so on). The exceptions to this general rule were the "transformative" approaches that I had touched on, which do emphasize certain aspects of positive peace (e.g., Bush and Folger's "Transformative Mediation," which emphasizes the enhancement of the parties' relationship through mutual "recognition").[134]

In our discussion of the field of Peace Studies, we had seen that contemporary conflict resolution most certainly employs a concept of "positive peace," but for contemporary conflict resolution,

134 See pp. 28–29; see also p. 15, which briefly touches on John Paul Lederach's "Conflict Transformation."

"positive peace" has a different meaning than it does in traditional Jewish approaches. Johan Galtung explained contemporary conflict resolution's concept of "negative peace" as the "absence of personal [physical] violence" and "positive peace" as the "absence of structural [violence]." The term "structural violence" refers to social, political, and economic structures that lower the quality of life of particular groups or classes of people.[135] Thus, for contemporary conflict resolution, the term "positive peace" refers to the eradication of structural violence through initiatives that attempt to fulfill basic human needs, and eliminate poverty, hunger, disease, oppression, discrimination, and so forth, which clearly differs from R. Epstein's understanding of the "positive peace" of traditional Jewish approaches.[136]

However, it should be noted that contemporary conflict resolution's "positive peace" does parallel certain traditional Jewish conceptualizations of peace, one example of which would be that of R. Isaac Arama's. We had seen how R. Arama explained *shalom* as not only referring to "an agreement reached between parties that were initially quarreling" or necessarily implying "the existence of a previous quarrel and conflict," but rather as representing "the indispensable common [or shared] good that must prevail among humans" and the "supportive agent" that maintains the unity and stability of a collective, giving "strength to all the individual parts and [promoting] their well-being, in accordance with the greater good." All of these elements of peace are analogous to elements that were delineated by Galtung, for whom the concept of peace refers to positive initiatives that promote societal stability and encompass all members of society.

135 See pp. 5 and 13.

136 I am presently only focusing on the definition of "positive peace" in contemporary conflict resolution and traditional Jewish approaches. It goes without saying that initiatives that attempt to fulfill basic human needs, and eliminate poverty, hunger, disease, oppression, discrimination, and the like, are absolute imperatives in the Jewish tradition, which are mandated by numerous biblical and rabbinic sources. It also goes without saying that contemporary conflict resolution theorists, practitioners, and educational programs support and contribute to initiatives that attempt to promote interconnectedness, friendship, fraternity, and so forth.

In any case, when it comes to comparing contemporary conflict resolution's value of promoting peaceful coexistence with traditional Jewish approaches' value of promoting peaceful coexistence, there are indications even at this early stage of our study that traditional Jewish approaches place a greater stress on certain higher levels of positive peace than does contemporary conflict resolution. I would also venture to say that this is true not only in relation to contemporary conflict resolution's approach to mediation, negotiation, and arbitration, but even in regard to interpersonal conflict resolution that does not involve an intermediary, as reflected in contemporary conflict resolution's educational programs.

Contemporary conflict resolution's approach to interpersonal conflict resolution, as embodied in the core components of its educational programs, certainly attempts to advance positive peace (in the sense of promoting interconnectedness, friendship, and the like) by nurturing "positive interpersonal relationships."[137] Contemporary conflict resolution's core components of cooperation, effective communication, perspective taking, anger management, and decision making and problem solving are all integral elements of social and emotional intelligence[138] that not only help to avoid destructive conflict, but also contribute in the most important ways to all levels of interpersonal relationships, from courteous interactions with a stranger in the street to deep, loving relationships between a parent and child, between oneself and one's spouse, and so on. Nevertheless, even when it comes to contemporary conflict resolution's educational programs, there still seems to be an overall general stress on negative peace rather than positive peace. The difference between contemporary conflict resolution's stress and that of traditional Jewish approaches becomes discernable (to a certain degree) when one compares occurrences of explicit references to and the standard characterization of peace in the basic conflict resolution literature of

137 See p. 17.
138 See p. 17 n. 41.

traditional Jewish approaches[139] (or what may possibly be deemed as Judaism's conflict resolution education literature) with that of contemporary conflict resolution's educational literature.

The basic conflict resolution literature of traditional Jewish approaches is replete with references to concepts of peace, both negative and positive, that are repeatedly being emphasized and presented as being of paramount importance in all of one's interactions with all other human beings. This literature also commonly refers to and focuses on relational levels such as love (*ahavah*), friendship (*re'ut*), and fraternity (*aḥavah*), which have yet to be established in our study of Jewish approaches, but eventually will be. In contrast, contemporary conflict resolution's literature—I am referring even to its educational literature—generally focuses on negative peace, addressing how to resolve conflicts, and for the most part does not address higher relational levels and relational issues of the parties. When taken together, the above (in conjunction with the earlier observation of R. Epstein, that Jewish sources indicate that one should strive to attain a level of positive peace) may serve as an initial indication that, generally speaking, traditional Jewish approaches seem to put a consistently stronger emphasis on the attainment of certain higher levels of positive peace than those normally emphasized in contemporary conflict resolution's literature.[140] As we proceed, this contention in regard to a difference in standard emphasis between contemporary conflict resolution and traditional Jewish approaches will receive clear-cut substantiation from multiple sources (see, for example, pp. 173–74, 179, 183, 259–60, and 296). After we have examined some of these sources, in Chapter 4, I will elaborate further on the differences in emphasis that exist between contemporary conflict resolution and traditional Jewish approaches.

---

139 I refer to the "basic conflict resolution literature" of traditional Jewish approaches being fully aware of the difficulty in identifying a specific, discrete body of traditional Jewish conflict resolution literature. What I have in mind are the Jewish sources that I have delimited as being basic conflict resolution related and are presented in this work.

140 I believe that contemporary conflict resolution theorists have reasons for *not* emphasizing these levels of positive peace; see pp. 173–74, 186–87, 463 n. 24.

CHAPTER 3

Rabbinic Perspectives on Constructive Conflict: A "Dispute for the Sake of Heaven"

Introduction

As a complement to the Rabbis' denouncement of destructive conflict,[1] one finds that they also had an unequivocal reverence for constructive conflict. Anyone who is even vaguely familiar with rabbinic studies is well aware of the integral role that argumentation and controversy play in the talmudic dialectic and the halakhic process. In fact, it would be reasonable to propose that constructive conflict is one of the most prominent earmarks of rabbinic Judaism.

Having had ample firsthand experience with the widest spectrum of conflicts (i.e., from amicable disagreements and debates to inordinately contentious disputes and even violent conflicts[2]), it comes as no surprise that rabbinic scholars down through the ages have expressed their opinions as to the essential elements that constitute constructive conflict and destructive conflict. By the third century CE, we find that the *tannaim* (mishnaic Sages), in the fifth chapter of *Pirke Avot* (*Chapters of the Fathers*), had already established a basic, and somewhat cryptic, typology and standards by which one may identify and classify conflicts. The Mishnah states that

1 See pp. 59–61.

2 See, for example, Jer. Tal. *Shabbat* 1:4; and Saul Lieberman, *Ha-Yerushalmi ki-Feshuto* (New York: The Jewish Theological Seminary of America, 1995), 38; cf. Israel Eisenstein, *Amude Esh* (Lemberg: U.V.Z. Salat, 1880), *Kuntres Amude Yerushalayim*, 7b. See also R. Moshe Feinstein's interpretation of Jer. Tal. *Shabbat* 1:4, Moses Feinstein, *Igrot Mosheh*, 9 vols. (New York: Moriyah, 1959-), *Oraḥ Ḥayim*, vol. 5, *Yoreh Deah*, vol. 4, p. 55.

> Any dispute (*maḥaloket*)[3] that is for the sake of Heaven (*le-shem shamayim*) will in its end endure (*sofah le-hitkayem*),[4] but one that is not for the sake of Heaven will in its end not endure. What is a dispute that is for the sake of Heaven? This is a dispute of Hillel and Shammai. And one that is not for the sake of Heaven? This is the dispute of Korah and his group.[5]

---

3 E. Z. Melamed (*Iyunim be-Sifrut ha-Talmud* [Jerusalem: Magnes Press, 1986], 239–40, 244) and Shimon Sharvit (*Leshonah ve-Signonah shel Masekhet Avot le-Doroteha* [Be'er-Sheva: Ben-Gurion University of the Negev Press, 2006], 117–20) have both proposed that the word *maḥaloket* in this mishnah, which has traditionally been interpreted as a "dispute" or "conflict," should actually be understood in its biblical sense, namely, a "division" or "group" of people (see 1 Chron. 27:1 ff.). For various reasons, in this author's opinion, this interpretation is somewhat tenuous. Therefore, the assumption that will be followed throughout this work is that the word *maḥaloket* in the mishnah in *Avot* should be understood as a "conflict," as it was for the past millennium by almost all of the commentators, with (as far as I am aware of) the exception of four of them (three of whom are cited by Sharvit [ibid.], and Naphtali Herz Wessely, who is not cited by Sharvit).

4 It is difficult to express in English the richness of the phrase *sofah le-hitkayem* (literally, its end—to endure). I have provided a rather simple translation ("will in its end endure"), which conveys the rhetorical effect of conjoining contradictory terms (i.e., "ending" and "enduring"). Conceptually speaking, there is a glaring problem with this line—in the words of Sharvit (paraphrasing R. Yom Tov Ishbili and R. Menaḥem Meiri): "It is not proper to say regarding a *maḥaloket* that it will endure or will not endure, since in all cases only one opinion will endure—the one that is accepted or the one that becomes the established normative halakhah" (Sharvit, *Leshonah*, 118). In addressing the conceptual difficulty of this phrase, R. Judah Lerma (sixteenth century) offers a highly cogent and coherent explanation. He explains "will in its end endure" as simply saying that, even after the original proponents of the dispute are no longer around to debate the issue, future generations will continue to seriously discuss the matter and weigh the pros and cons of the two sides, as opposed to a dispute that is not for the sake of heaven, which, as it loses its original proponents, will also lose its vitality. Judah Lerma, *Leḥem Yehudah*, 2nd ed. (Brooklyn: Aḥim Goldenberg, 1994), 128a, quoted in Samuel Uceda, *Midrash Shemuel* (Jerusalem: Mekhon ha-Ketav, 1989), 422–23. From a purely contextual standpoint, *sofah le-hitkayem* should probably be rendered "it will have enduring (or perpetual) value."

5 The Hebrew version of this mishnah that appears in most of the contemporary printed editions of *Avot* reads as follows:

> כל מחלוקת שהיא לשם שמים סופה להתקיים; ושאינה לשם שמים אין סופה להתקיים. איזו היא מחלוקת שיהא לשם שמים? זו מחלוקת הלל ושמאי. ושאינה לשם שמים? זו מחלוקת קרח וכל עדתו.

For textual variants, see Shimon Sharvit, *Masekhet Avot le-Doroteha* (Jerusalem: Mosad Bialik, 2004), 202–3. The exact placement of this mishnah in the fifth chapter

This rudimentary *tannaic* system of conflict classification[6] and its defining criteria were later expounded on, and underwent considerable development, by literally hundreds of rabbinic commentators over a period of approximately nine hundred years (eleventh century to the present).[7]

To complete our study of foundational values and concepts,[8] we will examine the rabbinic conceptualization of constructive conflict, based on the mishnah in *Avot*. This chapter consists of three sections. The first section will present an analysis and interpretation of the mishnah, which will be in accordance with the literal-primary sense of the mishnah. The second section will highlight certain salient exegetical motifs pertaining to a "dispute for the sake of Heaven" and constructive conflict that are found in the works of the *rishonim* (the "early" rabbinic authorities, who lived between circa the

varies according to the edition of *Avot* that one uses. In the *"Yakhin u-Voaz"* edition of the *Mishnayot*, and in the standard Vilna edition of the Babylonian Talmud, it can be found in *Avot* 5:17.

6 It should be noted that this mishnah is dealing with two types of conflict: (1) halakhic arguments (conflicts of opinion), and (2) what would be categorized in contemporary terminology as "social" (or intrasocietal) conflicts. This is evident from the examples being offered—a dispute of Hillel and Shammai is representative of a halakhic argument and the dispute of Korah is representative of a social conflict. See Hanina Ben-Menahem, Neil Hecht, and Shai Wosner, eds., *Ha-Maḥaloket ba-Halakhah*, 3 vols. (Boston: The Institute of Jewish Law, Boston University, 1991-), vol. 3 (*Part Two—Sources and Commentary*), 69–70.

7 The earliest known commentators to discuss the mishnaic concept of "a dispute for the sake of Heaven" are R. Nathan ben Abraham II (d. before 1102); Maimonides (1135–1204), in his commentary to *Avot*; and the anonymous author of the commentary to *Avot* that is found in the *Maḥzor Vitry*, which has been ascribed to various possible authors, most often to R. Jacob ben Samson (early twelfth century).

8 Similar to Chapter 2, this chapter will examine concepts that have widespread applications. The concepts that will be discussed are not only germane to interpersonal conflict resolution that does not involve third-party intervention, they are also highly relevant to all forms of interpersonal and intergroup conflict resolution. For those who may be tempted to argue that the concept of a dispute for the sake of Heaven is not really germane to the sort of interpersonal conflict resolution that is the focus of this book, but rather to differences of opinion, controversies, and debates of an intellectual nature, I would recommend that they first read through the chapter before they decide that this is the case. After doing so, it should be quite clear that the material covered is pertinent to all forms of conflict.

mid-eleventh century and the late fifteenth century) and the *aḥaronim* (the "later" rabbinic authorities, who lived between circa the late fifteenth century and the present). These two sections, based on their respective methodological approaches, one being analytic in nature and the other "synthetic," will set forth hypotheses regarding what may be viewed as traditional rabbinic perspectives on constructive conflict. The third, and concluding, section will touch on some of the significant similarities and differences that exist between traditional Jewish perspectives and contemporary conflict resolution in respect to the fundamental, underlying concepts of conflict that will be discussed.

The Literal-Primary Sense of the Mishnah

A Conceptual Analysis of the Mishnah

Preliminary Points. From a conceptual standpoint, the mishnah in *Avot* can be viewed as primarily doing three things: (1) it establishes two distinct categories of conflict, one positive and one negative, and in the course of doing so, it assigns a descriptive designation to each ("a dispute that is for the sake of Heaven" and "a dispute that is not for the sake of Heaven," respectively); (2) it definitively guarantees the positive outcome/ultimate value of one and the negative outcome/lack of value of the other (one "will in its end endure" and the other "will in its end not endure"); and (3) it provides defining examples for each category (Hillel and Shammai, and Korah and his group). Our analysis will focus on the mishnah's categorization of disputes and its descriptive designations (1), and the exemplars it provides (3). Through an examination of the exemplars, we will attempt to understand the descriptive designations and ascertain the essential qualities of the two categories of "a dispute that is for the sake of Heaven" and "a dispute that is not for the sake of Heaven," and thereby uncover what the Rabbis viewed as being the primary attributes, or characteristic features, of constructive conflict (and, conversely, destructive conflict).

Even on a simple level, the mishnah's designation of constructive conflict as a "dispute that is for the sake of heaven" and destructive conflict as a "dispute that is not for the sake of Heaven" should not be taken at face value and understood in a purely literal sense. It would be a grievous mistake to construe these terms as simply implying that the determining factor as to whether a conflict will take a constructive or destructive course solely depends on one's religious motivation and that as long as an individual is bent on the glorification of Heaven, any conflict that individual may instigate will inevitably have positive results. Such an explanation may be summarily rejected because of the inherent implausibility of such a notion, in as much as such disputes, from antiquity, have always seemed to precipitate the most destructive and intractable of conflicts,[9] and from the fact that the mishnah itself immediately asks the question "What is a dispute that is for the sake of Heaven?" and finds it necessary to offer specific defining examples, which may indicate that the author of the mishnah feels that the concepts of "a dispute for the sake of Heaven" and "a dispute that is not for the sake of heaven" require clarification. In the course of the ensuing analysis, it will become quite apparent that such a superficial reading is not tenable, and that the appellations a "dispute for the sake of Heaven" and a "dispute that is not for the sake of heaven" carry with them a considerably deeper import than one would have initially imagined.

A Simple Rudimentary Explanation. In order to properly understand this mishnah, one of the first points that needs to be highlighted is that

9 The volatile nature of such disputes has been repeatedly bemoaned by rabbinic authorities; for example, "The majority of suffering and hardships are a result of disputes that are 'for the sake of Heaven' " (Shneur Zalman of Lyady [1757–1813], *Igrot Kodesh: Admur ha-Zaken, Admur ha-Emtsa'i, Admur ha-Tsemaḥ Tsedek* [Brooklyn: Kehot, 1980], 80); similarly, "If our intention in a conflict is 'for the sake of Heaven,' there can be nothing more hazardous than that" (Israel Salanter [1810–1883], quoted in Dov Katz, *Tenuat ha-Musar*, 6 vols. [Jerusalem: Feldheim, 1996], vol. 1, 285); and "To carry on a dispute 'for the sake of Heaven' that by no means [is acceptable]. That is the worst possible thing" (Abraham Isaiah Karelitz [1878–1953], quoted in Yisrael Shpigel, *She'al Avikha ve-Yagedkha*, vol. 1 [Jerusalem: Mekhon Da'at, 1990], 172).

the expressions "for the sake of heaven" (*le-shem shamayim*)[10] and "not for the sake of Heaven" (*she-lo le-shem shamayim*) are common terms in talmudic and midrashic literature.[11] Something "for the sake of heaven" invariably denotes an act that was performed with a pure, noble, or holy intention and, as a result, is imbued with a positive quality (or possibly multiple positive qualities);[12] and something that is "not for the sake of Heaven" invariably refers to an act that was performed with some type of ulterior motive that is, to some degree, impure, ignoble, or unholy and as a result of this is imbued with a negative quality (or possibly multiple negative qualities).[13]

Keeping this basic clarification in mind, on a simple level, when the mishnah proceeds to cite the cases of "a dispute of Hillel and Shammai" and "the dispute of Korah and his group," it may merely be providing concrete and eminent models of constructive conflict and destructive conflict. The disputes of Hillel and Shammai—who were two of the "fathers of the world" (see *Eduyyot* 1:4), the most revered progenitors of a new historical period in Judaism[14]—came to serve as the prototypical example of a pure, noble, and holy

10 One also often encounters the synonymous expression "*le-shum shamayim*" (e.g., Jer. Tal. *Berakhot* 2:9; Bab. Tal. *Ta'anit* 24a; [*Genesis Rabbah*] *Midrash Bereshit Rabba*, ed. J. Theodor and Chanoch Albeck [Jerusalem: Wahrmann Books, 1965], p. 1031).

11 See, for example, *Avot* 2:2, 12, 4:11; *Mekhilta debe-Rabi Yishmael*, ed. S. Horovitz and I. A. Rabin (Frankfurt am Main: n.p., 1931), *Pisḥa* 7, p. 23, *Amalek* 1, pp. 191, 193; *Sifre, Pinḥas, piska* 136, p. 182; *Tosefta*, 5 vols., ed. Saul Lieberman (New York: Bet ha-Midrash le-Rabanim sheba-Amerikah, 1993–2007), *Bikkurim* 2:15; Bab. Tal. *Avodah Zarah* 8a, *Betsah* 16a, *Bava Kamma* 81b, *Sanhedrin* 39b, *Sotah* 12a, *Zevaḥim* 116b.

12 For example, Jer. Tal. *Kiddushin* 4:1; Bab. Tal. *Ta'anit* 31a, *Bava Batra* 16a, *Tamid* 28a; *Genesis Rabbah*, Theodor-Albeck edition, p. 1293; see also *Derekh Erets Zuta* 10 and *Kallah Rabbati* 4.

13 For example, Jer. Tal. *Ḥagigah* 2:1; Jer. Tal. *Gittin* 1:4; Bab. Tal. *Rosh Hashanah* 17a; *Midrash Tanaim al Sefer Devarim*, ed. David Zevi Hoffmann (Berlin: Ts. H. Itskovski, 1908), Deut. 17:14; *Genesis Rabbah*, Vilna edition, 42:8.

14 Regarding the designation "fathers of the world," see Avraham Orenstein, *Entsiklopedyah le-To'are-Kavod be-Yisrael*, vol. 1 (Tel Aviv: Netsaḥ, 1958), 114–19; Efrayim Rokeaḥ, "*Hilel ve-Shamai*," *Shanah be-Shanah* (5756 [1996]): 459–60; Stephen G. Wald, "Hillel," in *Encyclopaedia Judaica*, 2nd ed., 108; David Fraenkel, *Korban ha-Edah*, in the standard printed edition of the Jerusalem Talmud, *Shekalim* 3:2, s.v. *she-ken neḥleku*, *Rosh ha-Shana* 1:1, s.v. *she-ken neḥleku*, *Ḥagigah* 2:2, s.v. *avot ha-olam*; cf. David Zevi Hoffmann, *Ha-Mishnah ha-Rishonah* (Jerusalem: n.p., 1968), 28, 40.

conflict. The dispute of Korah—who according to the biblical narrative was the infamous demagogue who instigated a seditious rebellion against Moses (see Num. 16:1–17:15)[15]—came to represent an impure, ignoble, and unholy conflict.

Veritably every single commentator who discusses this mishnah dismisses, either implicitly or explicitly, this, or a similar, explanation as being inadequate and ascribes a much deeper significance to the mishnah's choice of exemplars. We shall see that there is considerable evidence to support this approach of the commentators. There are indications—based on an examination of biblical, mishnaic, talmudic, and midrashic sources that relate to the disputes of Hillel and Shammai and the dispute of Korah—that the Rabbis choose these representative cases because of their associations with certain highly specific aspects of conflict. It should also become evident that in identifying the concept of "a dispute for the sake of Heaven" with the disputes of Hillel and Shammai, and "a dispute not for the sake of Heaven" with the dispute of Korah, the Rabbis were not merely attempting to define these concepts on a theoretical level, but rather they were intent on prescribing practical standards of comparison to be used in testing and evaluating the true nature of real-life conflicts that one either encounters or engages in.

The Evidence from the Mishnah and the Tosefta

The Attributes of Hillel and Shammai. When exploring the prima facie evidence from the mishnaic period (or shortly thereafter) that could possibly shed some light on the implications of the mishnah's focus on Hillel and Shammai, certain distinctive clues can be found that reveal a profound connection between their disputes and constructive conflict. The first fact that should be considered is that there are significantly few disputes between Hillel and Shammai that have been recorded in talmudic

15 For a close, analytic reading of Numbers 16:1–17:15, see Yeḥiel Zvi Moskowitz, *Sefer be-Midbar* (*Da'at Mikra*) (Jerusalem: Mossad Harav Kook, 1988), Numbers 16:1–17:15.

literature. The Babylonian Talmud (*Shabbat* 14b)[16] cites a statement in the name of R. Huna (third century CE) that the three disputes between Hillel and Shammai in the beginning of *Eduyyot* (1:1–3) are the only known instances of Hillel and Shammai disagreeing with each other.[17] The second fact that should be considered is that, even in regard to these disputes, the Mishnah in *Eduyyot* recounts how both Hillel and Shammai in one of the cases ultimately retracted their opinions in favor of a third opinion.[18] The Mishnah then goes on to state that it was important to record this in order "to teach future generations that a person should not [stubbornly] adhere to his words" (*Eduyyot* 1:4). It would not be all that presumptuous to suggest that it was specifically Hillel and Shammai's propensity to keep their conflicts to a minimum by being able to reconcile any possible differences, and their receptivity to alternative opinions that lead the Sages to their association of Hillel and Shammai's disputes with positive, or constructive, conflict (i.e., a "dispute for the sake of Heaven"). The propensity and ability to keep their conflicts to a minimum by reconciling differences could, possibly, have come to represent in the eyes of the Sages the effective resolution of conflicts, while the ability and willingness to admit that one is wrong and to accept an alternative opinion would certainly have been viewed as an indication of a commitment to principles of intellectual honesty and objectivity,

16 Cf. Jer. Tal. *Ḥagigah* 2:2.

17 The Talmud (*Shabbat* 15a) goes on to explain that there were other instances when Hillel and Shammai argued with each other. According to the Gemara, R. Huna did not include a case in which they argued about a topic that was already disputed by their predecessors, and he also excluded a case in which Hillel had (promptly) conceded to Shammai (see Tosafot, *Shabbat* 14b, s.v. *ve-ilu*).

18 *Eduyyot* 1:3. There are a number of possible interpretations of the mishnah in *Eduyyot*, some of which may negate certain premises I am working with (e.g., whether or not Hillel and Shammai actually retracted their opinions in favor of a third opinion); see Maimonides, *Mishnah im Perush Rabenu Mosheh ben Maimon*, trans. Joseph Kafih, vol. 4 (Jerusalem: Mossad Harav Kook, 1963), *Eduyyot* 1:4; Abraham ben David of Posquières, *Perush Rabad al Masekhet Eduyot*, in the Vilna edition of the Babylonian Talmud, *Eduyyot* 1:4; and Pinḥas Kehati, *Mishnayot Mevoarot*, vol. 8 (Jerusalem: Hekhal Shelomoh, 1966), *Eduyyot* 1:3–4.

or, from the perspective of the Rabbis, a pure and deep, theocentrically motivated, inner integrity.[19]

The Tosefta (see Glossary) sheds additional light on another significant aspect regarding Hillel and Shammai, which may require us to modify the above interpretation and help clarify the correlation between their disputes and a dispute for the sake of Heaven. In a highly terse statement, the Tosefta offers an explanation for the proliferation of halakhic disputes in the generations following Shammai and Hillel:

> When the students of Shammai and Hillel, who did not attend [to their teachers] as was necessary for them [i.e., they did not apply themselves sufficiently to their studies],[20] began to increase [in number], disputes increased in Israel.[21]

According to this excerpt from the Tosefta, for the Rabbis, Hillel and Shammai represented a critical turning point in rabbinic scholarship.[22] This passage is describing a historic scenario in which, in the words of Maimonides, "the disciples' studiousness in the pursuit of wisdom slackened and [the quality of] their logical argumentation weakened in comparison to the logical argumentation of Hillel and Shammai, their teachers; [consequently] in the course of

---

19 This explanation is based on certain insights that I have gleaned from the commentaries of R. Joseph Alashkar (fl. c. 1500), R. Shelomoh Zalman Hershman [Ragoler] (nineteenth century), and R. Naphtali Herz Wessely (1725–1805). See Joseph Alashkar, *Mirkevet ha-Mishneh* (Lod, Israel: Orot Yahadut ha-Megrab, 1993), 292–93; Shelomoh Zalman Hershman, *Bet Avot* (Berlin: Tsvi Itskowitz, 1889), 98a; and Naphtali Herz Wessely (1725–1805), *Yen Levanon* (Warsaw: Yitsḥak Goldman, 1884), 287.

20 See the quote from Maimonides below; cf. Rashi, *Sotah* 22a, s.v. *ve-lo shimesh talmide ḥakhamim*.

21 In the Tosefta found in the Vilna edition of the Babylonian Talmud, *Ḥagigah* 2:4, *Sotah* 14:1, and *Sanhedrin* 7:1; in *Tosefta*, ed. M. S. Zuckermandel (Jerusalem: Wahrmann, 1975), *Ḥagigah* 2:9, *Sotah* 14:9, and *Sanhedrin* 7:1; also quoted by the Gemara in *Sotah* 47b, *Sanhedrin* 88b, Jer. Tal. *Ḥagigah* 2:2, and Jer. Tal. *Sanhedrin* 1:4.

22 See Alon Goshen-Gottstein, "*Ha-Maḥaloket ba-Olamam shel Ḥakhamim*" (Jerusalem: Hebrew University, 1980), 12, 40.

their scholarly debates, disputes took place between them regarding many topics."[23] Thus, based on this passage from the Tosefta, the rarity of disputes between Hillel and Shammai was evidently not attributed to a simple propensity and ability to reconcile their differences as compared to future generations, as was suggested earlier (see p. 81).[24] Rather, Hillel and Shammai were deemed as being considerably more assiduous in their pursuit of wisdom than their students and successors. It may very well have been this fact that had led to the association between the disputes of Hillel and Shammai and constructive conflict. We may assert that, from the perspective of the Sages, such diligence in the pursuit of knowledge would be perceived—as would be the case with their receptivity to alternative opinions—as reflecting a pure and deep, theocentrically motivated, inner integrity and desire to ascertain objective truth in regard to the issues that were being dealt with at the time.[25]

Attention should be called to an additional factor, which is discussed by both R. David Zevi Hoffmann (1843–1921) and R. Saul Lieberman (1898–1983),[26] and is relevant to this analysis. Immediately preceding the passage from the Tosefta cited above, there is a statement that, depending on how it is interpreted, may further illuminate the rabbinic perspective on the proliferation of disputes subsequent to the period of Hillel and Shammai. The line before the above passage reads: "When there was an increase in the

23 This quote is taken from Maimonides' introduction to his commentary on the Mishnah. My explanation of the Tosefta does *not* actually reflect that of Maimonides. Maimonides attributes the rarity of halakhic disputes between Hillel and Shammai to their possessing similar methodologies and knowledge of "fundamental principles." Maimonides, *Hakdamah leha-Rambam mi-Seder Zeraim*, in the Vilna edition of the Babylonian Talmud, the third page of the introduction, s.v. *ha-ḥelek ha-shelishi*; cf. Maimonides, *Mishnah im Perush Rabenu Mosheh ben Maimon*, trans. Kafih, vol. 1, 20–21.

24 That does not mean to say that the earlier explanation has to be totally rejected. The explanation that is now being proposed may be understood as a modified version of the earlier explanation.

25 See Hershman, *Bet Avot*, 98a.

26 Hoffmann, *Ha-Mishnah ha-Rishonah*, 52, n. 54; Saul Lieberman, *Tosefta ki-Feshutah*, vol. 8 (New York: Jewish Theological Seminary of America, 1973), 755.

number of those who were arrogant (*zeḥuḥe ha-lev*),[27] there was an increase in the number of disputes."[28] R. Hoffmann and R. Lieberman cite a debate among the commentators as to whether this statement is coming to explain the underlying cause for the slackened performance and studiousness of the disciples of Shammai and Hillel (in other words, that there was some degree of arrogance prevalent among them, which had a detrimental effect on their scholarship), which is the interpretation offered by Rashi (R. Solomon ben Isaac, 1040–1105),[29] or whether this statement is referring to the proliferation of a different type of *maḥaloket* that was not characteristic of the disciples of Shammai and Hillel, but of a different group of people (e.g., the various sectarian groups that flourished during the Second Temple period), which is the interpretation of R. Samuel Eliezer Edels (*Maharasha*, 1555–1631).[30] Both R. Hoffman and R. Lieberman contend that the debate regarding how to interpret this line in the Tosefta revolves around textual variants that exist.[31] Consequently, the relevance of this line to Hillel and Shammai, and rabbinic perspectives on constructive conflict and the mishnah in *Avot*, is somewhat debatable.

Taking into consideration all of the above, we may propose that the diligent pursuit of wisdom and truth, which is alluded to in the Tosefta, and the receptivity to alternative opinions, which is mentioned in the mishnah in *Eduyyot*, can account for the Rabbis' equating the disputes of Hillel and Shammai with a noble, pure, and holy conflict. A conflict

27 This is the standard translation of this expression: see Lieberman, *Tosefta ki-Feshutah*, vol. 8, 755; David Kimḥi, *Sefer ha-Shorashim* (Jerusalem: n.p., 1967), s.v. *zaḥaḥ*; cf. Joseph Kimḥi, *Sefer ha-Galui* (Berlin: T. H. Itskovski, 1887), s.v. *yazaḥ*, 37.

28 Tosefta *Sotah*, Lieberman edition, 14:10, p. 238; Bab. Tal. *Sotah* 47b, *Ḥullin* 7a.

29 Rashi, *Sotah* 47b, s.v. *zeḥuḥe*; idem, *Ḥullin* 7a, s.v. *zeḥuḥe*. For a very clear articulation of this interpretation, see Menaḥem Meiri, *Ḥibur ha-Teshuvah* (New York: Talpiyot Yeshivah University, 1950), *ma'amar* 1, chap. 5, p. 119.

30 Samuel Eliezer Edels, *Ḥidushe Halakhot ve-Agadot*, in the Vilna edition of the Babylonian Talmud, *Sotah* 47b, s.v. *mishe-rabu*; see also Naphtali Zevi Judah Berlin, *Meshiv Davar* (Jerusalem: Yeshivat Voloz'in, 1993), vol. 1, *siman* 46, p. 29.

31 Hoffman, *Ha-Mishnah ha-Rishonah*, 52; Lieberman, *Tosefta ki-Feshutah*, 755; cf. Eliezer Paltiel, *"Ikvotav shel Menaḥem ha-Galili be-Agadat Ḥazal,"* in *Sefer Refa'el: Ma'amarim u-Meḥkarim ba-Torah uve-Mada'e ha-Yahadut le-Zikhro shel Dr. Yitsḥak Refael*, ed. Yosef Movshovitz (Jerusalem: Mossad Harav Kook, 2000), 466.

in which the parties show such intellectual integrity—that is to say, an intense dedication to the uncovering of objective and unmitigated truth in regard to the given topic at hand, and will readily admit that they are wrong—would be perceived by the Rabbis as being theocentrically motivated ("for the sake of Heaven") and free from ulterior motives that impair a person's ability to be objective and admit to the truth. Such a conflict would presumably possess concrete, positive qualities within the course of the disagreements and ultimately produce a positive outcome.

The Attributes of Korah and His Group. The setting of the dispute of Korah in diametric opposition to those of Hillel and Shammai could be explained in a simple and straightforward manner. When the Rabbis examined the arguments of Korah and his group, which are found in the biblical narrative in Numbers 16:3, 16:12–14, they simply understood them to be inherently unjustifiable or fallacious. Even though, according to Scripture, these selfsame arguments had enough outward appeal to have caused the whole community to rebel against Moses (Num. 16:19), from the Rabbis' perspective they were nothing more than specious arguments (which would account for the Midrashim that ascribe petty ulterior motives to Korah in instigating the rebellion [see footnote and pp. 93–94 below]).[32] In conjunction with this issue, there is another discernible flaw in the manner in which the Korah dispute was conducted, which may have been a focus of the Rabbis. A cursory examination of the biblical account of the dispute that took place between Korah and Moses reveals that it was conspicuously one-sided. We find that Moses responded to the accusations brought against him (Num. 16:8–11) and attempted to

32 See, for example, *Midrash Tanḥuma* [the "standard edition"], with the commentaries *Ets Yosef* and *Anaf Yosef*, by Enoch Zundel ben Joseph (Jerusalem: Levin-Epshtayn, n.d.), *Koraḥ* 1 (unless otherwise noted, all citations from the *Tanḥuma* are from the standard edition); Buber edition, *Koraḥ* 3, *Hosafah le-Farshat Koraḥ* 2; *Numbers Rabbah* 18:16; *Exodus Rabbah* 33:5 (these sources attribute Korah's actions to either arrogance, jealousy, or a bruised ego, all of which are reflected in the talmudic passage discussing Korah's wife, *Sanhedrin* 110a); and Menaḥem Kasher, *Torah Shelemah*, 45 vols. (Jerusalem: Hotsa'at Bet Torah Shelemah, 1992), *Koraḥ*, Numbers 16, nn. 1, 4*, 6, 8, 12, 104, 132, 136; see also Ben Sira 45:18 (cf. Psalms 106:16); and Josephus *Ant.* 4:14, 20.

convene with his accusers (Num. 16:12a). This is in stark contrast to those who opposed him, who throughout the story never respond to what Moses had to say and at one point adamantly refuse to meet with him (Num. 16:12b). This facet of the narrative is clearly picked up on by a number of Midrashim (see below, p. 95).[33]

The elements of unjustifiable, or flawed, arguments and the disregard for the other party's argument are almost perfectly antithetical to those attributed to Hillel and Shammai (i.e., an honest, conscientious, and discerning analysis of the issues at hand and the receptivity to alternative opinions) and may serve as an appropriate symmetrical explanation for the association of Korah and his group with conflict that is ignoble and counterproductive. A conflict in which the parties show such a fundamental lack of intellectual integrity, in the eyes of the Rabbis is seen as lacking a pure and holy motivation (it is considered "not for the sake of Heaven," i.e., some ulterior motive must be at play that is impairing their ability to be objective and admit to the truth). Such a conflict would presumably possess various negative qualities and lead to an unfavorable outcome.

Conclusions Based on the Primary Evidence. Based on the primary evidence from the Mishnah and Tosefta and the proposed correlation with the Korah narrative, which all seems to center around the concept of sound intellectual integrity, which is largely dependent on the quality of one's underlying motivations, we may propose that the Rabbis of the Mishnah were of the opinion that

➢ The basic prerequisite for constructive conflict is *the adherence to principles of intellectual integrity*. In accordance with the concomitant elements that are associated with Hillel, Shammai, and Korah, these principles would require *a diligent, objective, and honest analysis of the issues involved* in combination with *an open-mindedness to views that oppose one's own*, which should be *grounded in the most honorable and righteous motives*. When these conditions are in place and are functioning in conjunction with each other, they

33 See *Tanḥuma, Koraḥ* 6; Buber edition, 15, 17; see Kasher, *Torah Shelemah, Koraḥ*, Numbers 16, nn. 77, 91, 115, and p. 18, citation 51.

allow for constructive responses to the discordant opinions and situations that will be encountered in the course of a conflict and ultimately lead to a constructive outcome.

Interpretations of the *Rishonim* and *Aḥaronim*

A historical analysis of the interpretations of our mishnah readily reveals the existence of certain *exegetical motifs*, that is, certain reoccurring expository themes. As is the nature of rabbinic literature, later scholars often cite, expound on, and modify the interpretations that are found in the writings of earlier scholars. The result of this is the existence of certain highly salient themes that surround our mishnah that, for our purposes, can translate into principles of constructive conflict. As we move on to examine the commentaries of rabbinic scholars who have discussed our mishnah, one should take note of certain parallels between the interpretation offered in the first part of this chapter and a number of the interpretations they have offered, which may accord a degree of support for the conclusions we have and will reach.

Before proceeding with a synthesis of exegetical motifs, it is necessary to call attention to a fundamental question regarding the interpretation of the mishnah in *Avot*. There is a major debate among the commentators as to whether the proper nouns "Hillel" and "Shammai" in this mishnah are referring to the actual personages of Hillel and Shammai, or are they referring, idiomatically, to *Bet Hillel* (the "School of Hillel") and *Bet Shammai* (the "School of Shammai"), in the terminology of the Talmud (in reference to a different topic), "[When it speaks of 'Shammai,' it means] Shammai and his group [of students] and [when it speaks of 'Hillel,' it means] Hillel and his group [of students] (*Shabbat* 14b)." Both possibilities have been entertained by the commentators. As we shall see, this question plays a crucial role in the elucidation of this mishnah.

Motif A: The Positive Aspects of Conflict

The desirability of argumentation by the juxtaposition, contrast, and analysis of opposing views is an axiomatic principle in the

Jewish tradition. This is self-evident on almost every page of the Talmud, the halakhic codes, and the responsa literature. A number of commentators to our mishnah have mentioned this concept in passing.[34] One of the most eloquent to take up this theme and expound on it was R. Solomon (II) ben Isaac Levi (1532–1600) in his work *Lev Avot*:

> It is well known that debating opposing viewpoints in the course of in-depth study and acquiring knowledge is *the* factor that sheds light upon a matter and makes known that which is true . . . and it is also well known that uncertainties cannot be resolved without pitting group against group and questioning and responding, so as to bring forth a conclusive decision. This concept is unknown to those who mock[35] that which the talmudic sages have said that if every member of the *Sanhedrin* [the supreme rabbinic court in Jerusalem] decided that someone deserves to be sentenced to death, they would *not* execute him; even though, if there was a minority [of judges] who found in favor of the accused and a majority who found him guilty, he *would* be executed (*Sanhedrin* 17a) . . . The very sound reason for this, which I have heard quoted in the name of Maimonides of blessed memory, is exactly what I have written—that it is to make known and to proclaim that when there does not exist a dissenting group, which challenges with questions and arguments, in whatever inquiry that it may be, it is impossible

34 See Isaac Abravanel (1437–1508), *Naḥalat Avot* (New York: D. Silberman, 1953), 357; Obadiah Bertinoro (c. 1450-c. 1516), *Perush Rabenu Ovadyah mi-Bartenura*, in *Mishnayot Zekher Ḥanokh* (Jerusalem: Ḥ. Vagshal, 1999), *Avot* chap. 5 mishnah 17; Obadiah Sforno (c. 1470–c. 1550), *Bet Avot* (Tel Aviv: Nehdar, 1966), 225; Israel Lipschutz (1782–1860), *Tiferet Yisrael: Yakhin u-Voaz*, in *Mishnayot Zekher Ḥanokh* (Jerusalem: Ḥ. Vagshal, 1999), *Avot* chap. 5 mishnah 17, *Yakhin* 124. This concept is discussed at somewhat greater length by Samson Raphael Hirsch (1808–1888), *Pirkei Avot: Chapters of the Fathers* (Jerusalem: Feldheim, 1972), 90.

35 See Simeon ben Zemaḥ Duran, *Sefer Milḥemet Mitsvah*, in *Sefer Keshet u-Magen* (Jerusalem: Makor, 1970), 33a, quoted in Reuben Margulies, *Margaliyot ha-Yam* (Jerusalem: Mossad Harav Kook, 1958), *Sanhedrin* 17a, p. 72.

> for the matter to be properly resolved, and it is possible for all [involved] to be mistaken.[36]

This passage has been quoted (with slight variations) by later authors who want to emphasize the intrinsic value of "a dissenting group."[37] R. Ya'akov Sofer (1853–1920) cites R. Levi's explanation and suggests that the same basic idea can be found in the writings of another early authority.[38] This earlier authority—whose commentary appears in R. Abraham ben Solomon Akra's *Me-Harere Nemerim* (Venice, 1599)—expressed the opinion that in the majority of cases the level of understanding attainable by critically examining something in isolation cannot be compared to the deeper level of understanding attainable when one's perspective is being challenged by an opposing viewpoint:

> We cannot understand something by itself, in comparison to how we will understand [it] from that which is opposed to it. Therefore, the Holy One, blessed be He, desired to give us opposing logical arguments[39] so that when we arrive at the true opinion we will understand it with the utmost clarity.[40]

---

36 Shelomoh ben Yitsḥak ha-Levi ha-Sefaradi, *Lev Avot* (Salonika: n.p., 1565), 95b.

37 Uceda, *Midrash Shemuel*, 421; Abraham Azulai (c. 1570–1643), *Pirke Avot im Pe'[rush] me-Etsem Ketav Yad . . . Avraham b. k. h.-R. Mordekhai Azulai* (Jerusalem: Orot Ḥayim, 1987), 115; and Dov Berish Gottlieb (eighteenth century), *Yad ha-Ketanah* (Jerusalem: Or ha-Sefer, 1976), *De'ot* 10:51, p. 234. Cf. Baruch ha-Levi Epstein, *Torah Temimah* (New York: Hebrew Publishing Co., 1928), Exodus 23:2, n. 17.

38 Ya'akov Shalom Sofer, *Sefer Yeshovev Sofer* (Jerusalem: David Sofer, 1976), 20.

39 See *Ḥagigah* 3b.

40 [Meisterlin of Gornish?], quoted in Abraham ben Solomon Akra, *Me-Harere Nemerim* (Venice: Daniel Zaniti, 1599), in the section entitled "The First Chapter of *Ḥagigah*," s.v. *kulan ro'eh*, p. 19a. This quote can also be found in Solomon Nissim Algazi (1610–1677), *Yavin Shemuah*, in Jeshua ben Joseph ha-Levi, *Halikhot Olam* (Jerusalem: Mekhon Sha'ar ha-Mishpat, 1996), *kelal* 59, p. 85; Ḥayyim Joseph David Azulai (1724–1806), *Devash le-Fi* (Jerusalem: Ha-Ma'amin, 1962), *ot dalet*, p. 15; and Shemuel Binyamin Sofer (1873–1943), *Divre Sofrim: Kelalim be-Mevo ha-Talmud*, vol. 1 (Jerusalem: Hotsa'at Divre Sofrim, 1956), 79–80. R. Algazi and R. Sofer ascribe this quote to [Moses?] Ibn Musa ("Ramban Musa"); based on the title page of R. Akra's *Me-Harere Nemerim*, this ascription is questionable. See Aron Freimann, *Kuntres ha-Mefaresh ha-Shalem* (New York: American Academy for Jewish Research, 1946), 15;

Conclusions Based on Motif A. Taken in the context of our mishnah, we may summarize the central premise of this motif with the following simple proposition:

- Argumentation and conflict are not only potentially beneficial, but they can be invaluable in the attainment of objectivity and truth.[41]

Motif B: Ascription of Positive Attributes to Hillel and Shammai and Negative Attributes to Korah

In searching for reoccurring and prominent themes among the *rishonim* and *aḥaronim*, one discovers that there are certain specific distinguishing qualities that have been repeatedly assigned to the disputes of Hillel and Shammai, while the opposite qualities (more or less) have been assigned to the dispute of Korah and his group. The sincere desire "to establish the truth"[42] is unquestionably *the* signature characteristic that is associated with the disputes of Hillel and Shammai by the commentators, and thereby becomes, for these commentators, the defining characteristic of "a dispute for the sake of Heaven."[43] The dispute

---

and Haim Z. Dimitrovsky, "*Al Derekh ha-Pilpul,*" in *Sefer ha-Yovel le-Khvod Shalom Baron* (Jerusalem: American Academy for Jewish Research, 1974), 172.

41 For other sources that convey the same basic idea, and a number of related concepts, see Naftali Tsevi Yehudah Bar-Ilan, *Mishtar u-Medinah be-Yisrael al pi ha-Torah*, vol. 3 (Jerusalem: Ariel, 2007), 1065–68.

42 See R. Travers Herford, *Pirke Aboth* (New York: Jewish Institute of Religion, 1945), 139. The commentators employ various expressions to convey the same basic idea; for example, Maimonides uses the expression "seeking the truth" (Maimonides, *Masekhet Avot im Perush Rabenu Mosheh ben Maimon*, trans. Isaac Shailat [Jerusalem: Ma'aliyot, 1994], 115); R. Joseph ibn Aknin uses the expression "to attain the truth" (Joseph ibn Aknin, *Sefer Musar: Perush Mishnat Avot le-Rabi Yosef ben Yehudah* [Berlin: Tsvi Hersh Itskovski, 1910], 167); and the commentary in *Maḥzor Vitry* uses the expression *le-ha'amid davar al bureyo*, "to clearly establish the matter" (i.e., to ascertain the truth, see *Gittin* 89b with Rashi's commentary, s.v. *va-ha'amidu davar*) ([Jacob ben Samson?], *Maḥzor Vitry*, in *Mishnayot Zekher Ḥanokh* [Jerusalem: Ḥ. Vagshal, 1999], p. 529, chap. 5 Mishnah 17).

43 Included among the commentators who, within the course of interpreting the mishnah, at some point associate the disputes of Hillel and Shammai with seeking, clarifying, and/or establishing the truth are the following authors: [Jacob ben Samson?,

instigated by Korah has correspondingly been appraised as being the embodiment of speciousness (i.e., having the outward appearance of being sincere and credible but beneath the surface being disingenuous and of a dubious nature) and as being spurred on by various petty and ignoble ulterior motives.[44] Thus, dissimilation and corrupt ulterior motives become the defining characteristics of "a dispute that is not for the sake of Heaven."

Sources for Ascribing Positive Attributes to Hillel and Shammai. In addition to the primary sources that were cited earlier in this chapter from the Mishnah and the Tosefta,[45] the association of the disputes of Hillel and Shammai with an all-embracing concern for the establishment of truth has been routinely based on a number of talmudic sources. For many (possibly the majority) of commentators,

---

early twelfth century], *Maḥzor Vitry*, 529; Maimonides (1135–1204), *Masekhet Avot*, 115;. Ibn Aknin (c. 1150–1220), *Sefer Musar*, 167; Jonah ben Abraham Gerondi (c. 1200–1263), *Perushe Rabenu Yonah mi-Gerondi al Masekhet Avot* (Jerusalem: Mekhon Torah Shelemah, 1980), 91 (not found in the commentary of *Rabenu Yonah* that appears in the Vilna edition of the Babylonian Talmud); Menaḥem Meiri (1249–1306), *Bet ha-Beḥirah al Masekhet Avot* (Jerusalem-Cleveland: Mekhon Ofek, 1994), 262–63; Joseph Naḥmias (fourteenth century), *Perushe Rabi Yosef Naḥmi'as al Megilat Ester, Yirmiyahu, Pirke Avot, ve-Seder Avodat Yom ha-Kipurim* (Tel Aviv: n.p., n.d.), 59b; Bertinoro (c. 1450–c. 1516), *Perush Rabenu Ovadyah, Avot* chap. 5 mishnah 17; Abraham Farissol (c. 1451–1525), *Perushe Avraham Faritsol al Masekhet Avot* (Jerusalem: Mekhon Torah Shelemah, 1964), 85; Sforno (c. 1470–c. 1550), *Bet Avot*, 225; and Moses Almosnino (c. 1515–c. 1580), *Pirke Mosheh* (Jerusalem: Mekhon Torah Shelemah, 1970), 208.

44 For commentators who ascribe these attributes to Korah, see pp. 93–95 nn. 51–56 below.

45 The mishnah in *Eduyyot* and/or the gemara in *Shabbat* 14b (which mentions the mishnah in *Eduyyot*) are cited by the following commentators to the mishnah: Mattathias ha-Yitshari (fourteenth to fifteenth centuries), *Perush Masekhet Avot le-Rabi Matityah ha-Yitshari* (Jerusalem: Mekhon Ben-Tsevi, 2006), 260; Joseph Ḥayyun (d. 1497, quoting Mattathias [ha-Yitshari]), *Mile de-Avot* in *Perushe Rishonim le-Masekhet Avot* (Jerusalem: Mekhon Torah Shelemah, 1973), 250–51; Alashkar (fl. c. 1500), *Mirkevet ha-Mishneh*, 292–93; Wessely (1725–1805), *Yen Levanon*, 287; and Hershman (nineteenth century), *Bet Avot*, 98a. The Tosefta is referred to in the following commentaries: Abravanel (1437–1508), *Naḥalat Avot*, 358; Yom Tov Lipman Heller (1579–1654), *Tosafot Yom Tov*, in *Mishnayot Zekher Ḥanokh* (Jerusalem: Ḥ. Vagshal, 1999), *Avot* chap. 5 mishnah 17; Wessely, *Yen Levanon*, 287; Lipschutz (1782–1860), *Tiferet Yisrael, Avot* chap. 5 mishnah 17, *Yakhin* 123 (citing the gemara in *Sanhedrin* 88b); and Hershman, *Bet Avot*, 98a.

this was predicated on the assumption that the names "Hillel" and "Shammai" are actually referring to the "School of Hillel" and the "School of Shammai":

- A significant number of commentators[46] cite cases in which one of the schools retracts its opinion in favor of the opinion of the other school (e.g., *Eduyyot* 1:12–14 and Jer. Tal. *Terumot* 5:2). This is seen as a manifestation of the schools' adherence to principles of truth.

- Other commentators and rabbinic scholars[47] find the pure devotion to truth as being expressed through the positive relationships the two schools were able to maintain while in the throes of their most critical debates. Even when grappling over the weightiest of issues (e.g., laws regarding marriage and personal status, i.e., questions of *mamzerut*, "bastardism"), the Talmud says that "they treated each other with love and friendship, so as to fulfill that which is stated in Scripture: 'Love truth and peace' (Zech 8:19)"

46 Simeon ben Zemaḥ Duran (*Rashbats*, 1361–1444), *Magen Avot* (Jerusalem: Erez, 2000), 377; Judah ibn Shu'aib (fourteenth century), *Derashot R. Y. Ibn Shu'aib* (Jerusalem: Mekhon Lev Same'aḥ, 1992), 363–64; Alashkar, *Mirkevet ha-Mishneh*, 292; Wessely, *Yen Levanon*, 287; Meir ben Elijah Ragoler (d. 1842), *Derekh Avot*, in *Sifre ha-Gera ve-Talmidav al Masekhet Avot* (Jerusalem: Yerid ha-Sefarim, 2001), 33a; cf. Jacob Reischer (c. 1670–1733), *Masekhet Avot im Perush Iyun Ya'akov* (Brooklyn: Tiferet Baḥurim de-Bobov, 1994), 88; and Lipschutz, *Tiferet Yisrael, Avot* chap. 5 mishnah 17, *Yakhin* 123.

47 Ibn Aknin, *Sefer Musar*, 167; Wessely, *Yen Levanon*, 287; Ragoler, *Derekh Avot*, 33a; Ezekiel Sarna, *Daliyot Yeḥezkel*, vol. 1 (Jerusalem: Mosad Haskel, 1975), 308–10; Eliezer Ben-Zion Bruk, *Hegyone Musar* (New York: n.p., 1969), 182–83. See also Jonathan Eybeschuetz (d. 1764), *Sefer Ya'arot Devash*, vol. 2 (Jerusalem: Mekhon Even Yisrael, 2000), *ḥelek* 2, *derush* 8, p. 184; Reischer, *Iyun Ya'akov*, 88 n. 6; Gottlieb, *Yad ha-Ketanah, De'ot* 10:49–52, pp. 233b–34a; Lipschutz, *Tiferet Yisrael, Avot* 5:17, *Yakhin* 122–23; and Israel Bornstein (1882–1942), *Kerem Yisrael* (Piotrków: Ḥanokh H. Folman, 1929), 169–70, quoted in Asher Rossenbaum, *Binat Asher* (Tel Aviv: n.p., 1968), 38–39. (Rabbis Eybeschuetz, Gottlieb, Reischer, Lipschutz, and Bornstein cite the gemara in *Yevamot* that teaches that the schools treated each other with love and friendship, which they find as being indicative of a dispute for the sake of Heaven, but they do not at any point define a dispute for the sake of Heaven as being specifically for the purpose of establishing the truth.)

(*Yevamot* 14b).[48] R. Ezekiel Sarna (1889–1969) eloquently sums up this approach when he writes that the clearest indication that their arguments were motivated solely by the pursuit of truth was in the fact that these arguments never became personal; rather, they always simply remained differences of opinion.[49]

Sources for Ascribing Negative Attributes to Korah and His Group. The commentators consistently contrast the dispute of Korah with the disputes of Hillel and Shammai by ascribing to it a duplicitous veneer of sincerity and credibility that conceals some petty or ignoble ulterior motive. This is primarily based on a number of midrashic and/or biblical sources that indicate as much:

- The most common source to be cited is a passage in the *Midrash Tanḥuma,* which states that underlying Korah's complaints against Moses was his jealousy over the appointment of Elzaphon the son of Uziel as the leader of

48 The Tosefta (in the Zuckermandel edition, *Yevamot* 1:1; in the Vilna edition of the Babylonian Talmud, *Yevamot* 1:3) cites an alternative version: "They 'conducted' truth and peace between them." This was evidently the source for the Jerusalem Talmud's recension of this teaching, "They conducted [themselves] in truth and peace" (Jer. Tal. *Kiddushin* 1:1).

49 Sarna, *Daliyot Yeḥezkel,* 309–10. In connection with this, it is noteworthy that in reference to this mishnah a number of commentators, such as R. Joseph Gibianski (b. 1846), Prof. Ben Zion Dinur (1884–1973), and R. Ḥayim Shmuelevitz (1901–1979), cite the gemara in *Eruvin* (13b) that teaches that the School of Hillel would "study their opinion and the opinion of the School of Shammai, and in addition to this, they would put the words of the School of Shammai before their own words." According to Rashi (*Eruvin* 13b, s.v. *ve-shonin divrehen* and *she-makdimin divre Vet Shamai*), this gemara is teaching that the School of Hillel (1) made a point of addressing the opinion of the School of Shammai and (2) showed deference to the opinion of the School of Shammai by mentioning it first. See Joseph Gibianski, *Zekhut Avot* (Warsaw: Alexander Ginz, 1876), 82–83; Ben Zion Dinur, *Masekhet Avot* (Jerusalem: Mosad Bialik, 1973), 127–28; and Ḥayim Shmuelevitz, *Siḥot Musar* (Jerusalem: n.p., 1980), section 2, *ma'amar* 33, pp. 123–24. (The reason, evidently, that there are relatively few sources that cite this gemara in connection with a dispute for the sake of Heaven is because the gemara attributes these qualities only to Bet Hillel and not to Bet Shammai; therefore, the association between it and a dispute for the sake of Heaven, which applies to both Hillel and Shammai, is somewhat tenuous.)

the Levites.[50] Based on this midrash, Korah's arguments are characterized by many commentators as being fundamentally motivated by the "pursuit of honor" and the desire "to rule [over others]."[51]

- In the view of some commentators, it is the *perceptible display of acrimony* on the part of Korah that is the clearest indication of a corrupt motivation. According to R. Menaḥem Meiri (1249–1306), this occurs in the biblical narrative when Korah and his group come with a sweeping and total condemnation of Moses.[52] R. Joseph Ḥayyun (d. 1497) is of the opinion that this occurs when "they present themselves before Moses in an insolent manner and insult him."[53] And according to R. Jonathan Eybeschuetz (c. 1690–1764), this is reflected in "the animosity and hatred" that Korah and his group exhibited towards Moses

50 *Midrash Tanḥuma, Koraḥ* 1; Buber edition, *Koraḥ* 3.

51 Among the commentators who, within the course of interpreting the mishnah, at some point associate the dispute of Korah (i.e., a dispute that is not for the sake of Heaven) with the pursuit of honor and/or the desire to rule over others are the following: [Jacob ben Samson?], *Maḥzor Vitry*, 529; Eliezer ben Nathan (*Ra'avan*, twelfth century), *Masekhet Avot im Perush Rashi ve-im Perush Ra'avan* (Bnei Brak: Mishor, 1992), 107; Ibn Aknin, *Sefer Musar*, 167; Isaac ben Solomon ben Isaac (b. circa 1340), *Perushe Yitsḥak b. R. Shelomoh mi-Toledo al Masekhet Avot* (Jerusalem: Mekhon Torah Shelemah, 1965), 189, quoted in Uceda, *Midrash Shemuel*, 422; Naḥmias, *Perushe Rabi Yosef Naḥmi'as*, 59b; Joseph ibn Shoshan (fourteenth century), *Perushe Rabenu Yosef ben Shoshan* (Jerusalem: Mekhon Torah Shelemah, 1968), 153; Ibn Shu'aib, *Derashot R. Y. Ibn Shu'aib*, 363–65; Bertinoro, *Perush Rabenu Ovadyah, Avot* chap. 5 mishnah 17; Wessely, *Yen Levanon*, 288; Gottlieb, *Yad ha-Ketanah, De'ot* 10:47–48, p. 233a–b; Hershman, *Bet Avot*, 98a; and Meir Ragoler, *Derekh Avot*, 33a.

52 Meiri, *Bet ha-Beḥirah*, 263. This is in line with the midrashic interpretation that has Korah saying, "I argue against and nullify all things that were done through him" (*Midrash Tanḥuma, Koraḥ* 1; Buber edition, *Koraḥ* 3).

53 According to R. Ḥayyun, they insult Moses when they say, "Is it not enough that you have brought us out from a land flowing with milk and honey so as to kill us in the desert, yet you still rule over us?" (Num. 16:13). Ḥayyun, *Mile de-Avot*, 251. (See also Sarna, *Daliyot Yeḥezkel*, 304; Bruk, *Hegyone Musar*, 183; and *Targum Pseudo-Jonathan*, Num. 16:2, "They stood up with *ḥutspa* [insolence] ....")

and (based on a midrashic source) how they were "on the verge of stoning him."[54]

- Other rabbinic scholars[55] view Korah's *reluctance to engage in dialogue* as a sure sign of an impure motivation and dissimulation. In support of this explanation, some of these scholars[56] cite (aside from the intransigent stance of Korah and his group that is evident in the biblical narrative) a midrash that focuses on Korah's reticence and his rejection of Moses' conciliatory overtures:

> With all these words Moses attempted to appease Korah, and you do not find that he responded in any way; this is because he was prudent in his wickedness. He said, "If I respond to him, I know that he is exceptionally wise and he will hereupon overwhelm me with his words ... it is best that I do not engage him [in conversation]."[57]

Conclusions Based on Motif B. A common element in the overwhelming majority of commentaries to our mishnah is the idea that for a conflict to be carried on in a constructive manner and to produce constructive results, its underlying motivation should be the establishment of the objective truth in regard to the matter at hand.[58] Any type of ulterior motive outside of this that

54 See *Numbers Rabbah* 18:4, which states that "they desired to stone him." Eybeschuetz, *Sefer Ya'arot Devash, ḥelek* 2, *derush* 8, p. 184.

55 Wessely, *Yen Levanon*, 289; Shmuelevitz, *Siḥot Musar*, section 2, *ma'amar* 33, p. 123; Bruk, *Hegyone Musar*, 183–84, quoted in Moshe Levi, *Mi-shel ha-Avot*, vol. 3 (Bnei Brak: M. Levi, 1992), 143; see also Gottlieb, *Yad ha-Ketanah*, 233b–34a; and Aharon Walkin (1865–1942), *Metsaḥ Aharon* (Jerusalem: 1971), 150–51, quoted in Levi, *Mi-shel ha-Avot*, 140.

56 Cited by Gottlieb, *Yad ha-Ketanah*, 233b; Shmuelevitz, *Siḥot Musar*, section 2, *ma'amar* 33, p. 123; and Bruk, *Hegyone Musar*, 183.

57 *Midrash Tanḥuma, Koraḥ* 6; Buber edition, *Koraḥ* 15. In quoting this midrash, I have purposely included an elision in the text that alters its meaning in order to facilitate a better understanding of the explanation offered by these authors.

58 See pp. 90–93 nn. 42–49 above.

becomes operative in the course of a conflict will inevitably have some deleterious effect on the process and the outcome of the conflict. The commentators enumerate an array of such psychological motivations that often come into play in interpersonal confrontations. In surveying the classic commentaries, one finds that the most frequently cited negative motivations are the "pursuit of honor" (*bakashat ha-kavod*) and the desire "to rule [over others]" (*le-histarer*),[59] "the desire to feel triumphant" (*natsḥanut*),[60] and the general inclination "to be disagreeable [or provocative]" (*le-kanter*)."[61] The implication is that there is a consensus of sorts among the commentators that, until these personal ulterior motives are addressed, they will impede the successful resolution of a conflict. In the words of R. Israel Lipschutz (1782–1860), "As long as they [the disputants] will not attain that [personal] objective, they will not be at peace."[62] We may therefore derive the following central proposition:

➢ The fundamental element that determines the overall nature and outcome of a conflict is its underlying motivation.

Based on the aggregate of positive attributions to Hillel and Shammai and negative attributions to Korah and his group, we may assert that the commentators' interpretative ascriptions would

59 See p. 94 n. 51.

60 Among the commentators who, at some point, associate a dispute that is not for the sake of Heaven with the desire to feel triumphant are David ben Abraham Maimuni (1222–1300), *Midrash David al Pirke Avot* (Jerusalem: Siaḥ Yisrael, 1987), 117; Meiri, *Bet ha-Beḥirah*, 262–63; Duran, *Magen Avot*, 377; Ḥayyun, *Mile de-Avot*, 250; Moses Alashkar (1466–1542), quoted in Uceda, *Midrash Shemuel*, 420–21; Bertinoro, *Perush Rabenu Ovadyah, Avot* chap. 5 mishnah 17; and Sforno, *Bet Avot*, 225.

61 Among the commentators who mention the inclination to be disagreeable or provocative are Maimonides, *Perush ha-Mishnayot leha-Rambam*, which is found in the Vilna edition of the Babylonian Talmud (though this is not found in Maimonides, *Masekhet Avot im Perush Rabenu Mosheh ben Maimon*, trans. Shailat, 115); Meiri, *Bet ha-Beḥirah*, 262–63; Ḥayyun, *Mile de-Avot*, 250–51; Isaac ben Solomon, *Perushe Yitsḥak b. R. Shelomoh*, 189, quoted in Uceda, *Midrash Shemuel*, 422; Almosnino, *Pirke Mosheh*, 208; Reischer, *Iyun Ya'akov*, 88 n. *vav*; and Gottlieb, *Yad ha-Ketanah, De'ot* 10:49, p. 233b.

62 Lipschutz, *Tiferet Yisrael, Avot* chap. 5 mishnah 17, *Yakhin* 121.

generally be in consonance with the conclusions that appeared in the first part of this chapter, which were based on the Mishnah and Tosefta and the correlation with the Korah narrative (which emphasized principles of intellectual integrity and its concomitant elements; see pp. 80–87), but would also include certain additional elements, and they would attest to the following:

- An essential element of constructive conflict is the emphasis on sincerely seeking and establishing the truth. In practical terms, this requires engaging in dialogue, the careful consideration of opposing opinions, and a willingness to retract one's opinion. A conflict such as this would also entail that it not be conducted in a hostile manner[63] and that it should not in any way negatively affect the personal relationships of the parties involved.

Motif C: Recognition of Ulterior Motives

Since the eighteenth century, an issue that has been addressed by various rabbinic scholars,[64] primarily by proponents of the "*musar* ("ethics") movement,"[65] is the intrinsic difficulty in correctly assessing one's own true motivations when one is embroiled in a conflict. Having acknowledged that constructive conflict is dependent on the actuation of the purest of motivations and that with the introduction

---

63 This does not mean to suggest that in the course of a conflict the parties may not at certain points resort to intense and impassioned forms of argumentation. The Gemara in *Kiddushin* (30b) states that "even a father and son, Rabbi and student, when they are preoccupied in Torah [study] in the same gate [i.e., the same study hall; alternatively, the same topic] they become 'enemies' of each other; however, they will not move from that spot until they come to love each other."

64 See Gottlieb, *Yad ha-Ketanah, De'ot* 10:46–52, pp. 233a–34a; Simḥah Zissel Ziv [Broida] (1824–1898), *Ḥokhmah u-Musar*, vol. 1 (New York: n.p., 1957), 226–27; Yehudah Leyb Ḥasman (1869–1935), *Or Yahel*, vol. 1 (Jerusalem: Yitsḥak ha-Kohen Shvadron, 2001), 80; and Sarna, *Daliyot Yeḥezkel*, 303–11.

65 This movement was founded by R. Israel Lipkin (Salanter, 1810–1893) and promoted the study and implementation of traditional Jewish ethics. A major component of R. Lipkin's approach was the emphasis on introspection and self-analysis. See Katz, *Tenuat ha-Musar*, vol. 1, 265–69.

of ignoble motivations there is the presumption of detrimental effects, these scholars were concerned about the proclivity of the average person to *unwittingly* attribute the most impeccable of motives to one's own actions, even when in actuality one is being driven by the most dishonorable of motives. In psychoanalytic terms, they were addressing the problem of identifying and effectively dealing with the defense mechanism of rationalization,[66] which often becomes operative in the course of a conflict.

By no means were these rabbinic scholars the first to discuss the innate tendency to justify one's attitudes and actions to oneself. The talmudic dictum that "a person does not see guilt in himself" (*Ketubot* 105b and *Shabbat* 119a) was already formulated in Scripture—"All the ways of a man are pure in his eyes" (Prov. 16:2).[67] These scholars merely applied this principle to conflict. They proposed that Korah and his group had wholeheartedly believed that their cause was just and that, from their perspective, they had the purest of intentions. (Such a positive assessment was not without precedent. There are various talmudic and midrashic sources that, with the exclusion of this episode, cast Korah and his group in an otherwise favorable light.)[68]

---

66 Rationalization is defined as "[when the] individual deals with emotional conflict or internal or external stressors by concealing the true motivations for his or her own thoughts, actions, or feelings through the elaboration of reassuring or self-serving but incorrect explanations." American Psychiatric Association, *Diagnostic and Statistical Manual of Mental Disorders*, 4th ed., text rev. (Washington, DC: 2000), s.v. "rationalization," 812.

67 See also Prov. 21:2. R. Ḥasman (*Or Yahel*, 79) mentions a related halakhic principle, *de-aved inish le-aḥazuke dibure*, "a person holds on to [alternatively, strengthens] his words"; that is, once a person has expressed an opinion, that person does not readily let go of it (see Isaac ben Abba Mari [twelfth century], *Sefer ha-Itur*, vol. 1 [Jerusalem: n.p., 1970], letter *kuf*, 59b, p. 118, quoted in Shabbetai ben Meir ha-Kohen [*Shakh*], *Sifte Kohen*, in the standard printed edition of the *Shulḥan Arukh*, *Ḥoshen Mishpat*, 33:9).

68 The two hundred and fifty people who comprised Korah's group are described by the Talmud and Midrashim as being *meyuḥadim sheba-edah*, "the most distinguished of the congregation [of Israel]" (*Sanhedrin* 110a; *Tanḥuma*, *Koraḥ* 10; Buber edition, *Koraḥ* 25), *hayah lahem shem be-khol ha-olam*, "world renowned" (ibid.), *hayu yode'im le-aber shanim veli-kboah ḥodashim*, which Rashi (*Sanhedrin* 52b, s.v. *le-mah talmid*) explains as "talmudic scholars," and as *rashe sandhedra'ot*, "heads of rabbinic courts" (*Tanḥuma*, *Koraḥ* 2; Buber edition, *Koraḥ* 5). Korah himself is characterized as being highly intelligent (*pike'aḥ hayah*) and as possessing prophetic ability (*Tanḥuma*,

One of the first to discuss at some length the tendency to rationalize one's actions and attitudes to oneself in connection with our mishnah was R. Dov Berish Gottlieb (d. 1796) in his moralistic-halakhic work *Yad ha-Ketanah*. R. Gottlieb maintains that it would be illogical to assume that Korah was aware of the true stimulus that was spurring him on in his rebellion. A much more plausible approach (and one that reflects a common human inclination) would be to say "that his heart had fooled him into believing that his dispute was totally for the sake of heaven."[69] In a similar vein, R. Eybeschuetz, in discussing the Korah rebellion in one of his sermons, expresses the same idea in universal terms: "As a general principle, there does not exist a conflict in which the evil inclination does not seduce us and say that the intention is entirely for the sake of heaven."[70]

As a natural corollary to this thesis, our mishnah is seen as providing the means by which a person may come to recognize if he or she is unwittingly justifying his or her attitudes and actions when engaged in conflict.[71] The proponents of this approach assert that according to the mishnah the key to revealing one's true motivations lies in the ability to scrutinize one's feelings and behavior towards the opposing party. If one's attitudes and actions conform to the *Hillel and Shammai paradigm*—that is to say, he or she is doing such things as engaging in dialogue, being receptive to the other party's opinion, maintaining benevolent feelings and exhibiting goodwill towards the other—then one can be confident that one's motives are truly "for the sake of heaven" and that one is thereby contributing to constructive conflict. If, on the other hand, a person's attitudes and actions correspond to the *Korah paradigm*—namely,

---

Koraḥ 5; Buber edition, *Koraḥ* 12). For other sources that attribute positive qualities to Korah and his group, see Sarna, *Daliyot Yeḥezkel*, 303–5.

69 Gottlieb, *Yad ha-Ketanah, De'ot* 10:46, p. 233a.

70 Eybeschuetz, *Sefer Ya'arot Devash*, *ḥelek* 2, *derush* 8, p. 184; cf. ibid., *ḥelek* 1, *derush* 5, p. 159. In a related vein, R. Ezekiel Landau (1713–1793) wrote that "In our times, a dispute that is [truly] for the sake of Heaven is something that is uncommon" (Ezekiel Landau, *Noda bi-Yehudah ha-Shalem* [Jerusalem: Mekhon Yerushalayim, 2004], *Mahadurah Kama, Yoreh Deah, siman* 1, p. 2).

71 Gottlieb, *Yad ha-Ketanah, De'ot* 10:52, p. 234a; Sarna, *Daliyot Yeḥezkel*, 309–10; Bruk, *Hegyone Musar*, 181–84; Eybeschuetz, *Sefer Ya'arot Devash*, *ḥelek* 2, *derush* 8, p. 184; and Walkin, *Metsaḥ Aharon*, 150–51.

that the person is resistant to dialogue, unable to even consider opposing views, experiences feelings of malevolence, and exhibits ill will—that individual is assuredly involved in a dispute that is "not for the sake of heaven" and may very well be promoting destructive conflict.

Conclusions Based on Motif C. Based on the concepts and principles that the Rabbis were employing within this motif, we may conclude that they were of the opinion that

- One of the most important and difficult aspects in bringing about constructive conflict is the conscious perception of one's underlying motivations for engaging in a conflict. This would require a degree of introspection and self-scrutiny in which the individual examines his or her overall cognitive, affective, and behavioral orientations towards the opposing party. A critical comparison must then be made to determine if these correspond to the Hillel and Shammai paradigm or to the Korah paradigm, which will reveal the true nature of one's motivations.

Summary

This chapter has attempted to present a formulation of the classic rabbinic conceptualization of constructive conflict. Beginning with an analysis of the primary mishnaic source that deals with constructive conflict, a simple interpretation (in rabbinic parlance, the "*peshat ha-pashut*") of the mishnah in *Avot* was presented. Subsequently, the interrelationship between the mishnah's two categories of conflict and the exemplars it offers for them was explored. This was done through an examination of the implicit characteristic features of the disputes of Hillel and Shammai, as reflected in the mishnah in *Eduyyot* and the Tosefta, as well as certain characteristic features of the dispute of Korah, as depicted in the biblical narrative and in a number of Midrashim. Finding a correspondence between the traits of the exemplars, this section concluded by propounding the rabbinic view on the central role of principles of intellectual integrity, which were seen as being rooted in the underlying motivations of the conflict.

The second part of this chapter presented a synthesis of significant exegetical themes that relate to constructive conflict resolution and the mishnah in *Avot*. This section brought together comparable thematic elements from the writings of rabbinic scholars spanning a period of over eight hundred years. These elements were combined to form coherent and salient motifs. From out of these motifs, fundamental propositions were derived regarding the positive functions of conflict, the principal role of underlying motivations, the emphasis on "establishing the truth" (which is actualized in one's attitudes and actions), and the accurate assessment of one's motivations.

It should be stressed that, in tandem, all of the propositions put forth in this chapter, at best, only represent a very small part of a much larger rabbinic perspective on constructive conflict. There exists an enormous amount of material dispersed throughout the corpus of traditional Jewish writings that directly relates to the rabbinic concept of constructive conflict, for which a similar sort of analysis and synthesis as was offered in this chapter would be apropos. If that material would be properly researched, a much more comprehensive and nuanced explication of rabbinic perspectives on constructive conflict than the one I have presented could be developed.[72]

72 An extremely laudable work in this area is Ben-Menahem, Hecht, and Wosner's three volume set *Ha-Maḥaloket ba-Halakhah* (which has been cited earlier). These authors have put together a very impressive compilation of source material related to the topic of *maḥaloket*. Particularly germane to the topic of this chapter is the section of their work entitled "The Conduct of a Controversy: Etiquette and Rules of Debate," 67–144. I should point out that, for all intents and purposes, the paradigm that will be developed in the coming chapters could be viewed as further elaboration on Judaism's perspective on various features of constructive conflict.

Similarities and Differences between Contemporary Conflict Resolution and Traditional Jewish Approaches in Respect to Fundamental, Underlying Concepts about Constructive/ Destructive Conflict

In accordance with the analytic-comparative framework set forth in the first chapter,[73] when I talk about fundamental, underlying concepts of contemporary conflict resolution in this work, I will be referring to a wide spectrum of concepts that I have termed the "basic concepts and theoretical underpinnings of conflict resolution."[74] As I explained in the preface,[75] in my search for comparable underlying concepts within the traditional Jewish sources, I decided to focus on the concept of a dispute for the sake of Heaven and perspectives on constructive/destructive conflict that are associated with it. In this section, I would like to touch on what I consider to be some significant similarities and differences that exist between contemporary conflict resolution and traditional Jewish approaches in respect to these elements.

Constructive Conflict as Understood in Contemporary Conflict Resolution and a Dispute for the Sake of Heaven in Traditional Jewish Approaches

In comparing the concepts of constructive/destructive conflict that are associated with a dispute for the sake of Heaven with comparable concepts in contemporary conflict resolution, numerous similarities and numerous differences can be found. I would like to highlight what I consider to be some of the more notable ones that stand out from among these similarities and differences.

---

73 See p. 33.

74 These basic concepts and theoretical underpinnings of conflict resolution were touched on in the first chapter and are not covered under any of the other analytic categories that were set forth; see pp. 33–34.

75 See p. xxvi.

The Concept of Constructive Conflict in Contemporary Conflict Resolution. In contemporary conflict resolution, the concept of "constructive conflict" has been explained in many different ways. For example, Mary Parker Follet, whose views on constructive conflict have been enormously influential,[76] understood constructive conflict as an approach that employs an integrative problem-solving method, that is to say, a mutual-gains approach that seeks win–win solutions.[77] Another possible explanation is that of Louis Kriesberg's. Kriesberg, a world-renowned conflict resolution scholar, has explained constructive conflict as an approach that avoids violence and coercive tactics, preserves relationships, provides mutually satisfying outcomes, and requires that the parties recognize each other as legitimate entities.[78] Another way of understanding constructive conflict is that of John Crawley's. Crawley, who is a well-known trainer of mediators in the United Kingdom, associates constructive conflict with "clear perception and good judgment," "self-awareness and control," "ability to analyze and balance different views and positions" and "openness to others."[79]

Deutsch's Understanding of Constructive/Destructive Conflict. In 1973, Morton Deutsch published his now classic *Resolution of Conflict: Constructive and Destructive Processes. Resolution of Conflict* presents Deutsch's theories and summarizes research on the elements that engender the competitive interactions that normally take place during conflicts, which are generally counterproductive and lead to negative outcomes, and those that promote cooperative interactions,

---

76 See above, p. 10.

77 Ibid.; and Mary Parker Follett, *Dynamic Administration: The Collected Papers of Mary Parker Follett*, eds. Henry C. Metcalf and L. Urwick (New York: Harper and Brothers, n.d.), 16–17, 30–49.

78 Louis Kriesberg and Bruce W. Dayton, *Constructive Conflicts: From Escalation to Resolution*, 4th ed. (Lanham, MD: Rowman and Littlefield, 2012), 4, 21–22.

79 John Crawley, *Constructive Conflict Management: Managing to Make a Difference* (San Diego, CA: Pfeiffer and Company, 1994), 14–15. Crawley's approach is promoted in a United Nations training manual on conflict resolution; see Fred Fisher, *Building Bridges between Citizens and Local Governments to Work More Effectively Together through Managing Conflict and Differences: Part 1, Concepts and Strategies* (n.p.: United Nations Centre for Human Settlements [Habitat], 2001), 26, accessed November 7, 2016, http://www.gdrc.org/decision/BuildingBridges.pdf.

which are generally positive and productive. In the book's concluding essay, Deutsch sets forth his views on the characteristic features of constructive and destructive conflicts.

Deutsch discusses many variables that he believes contribute to constructive conflict. Without going into the intricate details and interplay of these variables, as Deutsch does, the following are some of what he sees as being characteristic features of constructive conflict: The parties have an appropriate level of motivation to solve the problems at hand; engage in open and honest communication; identify the underlying issues; recognize the legitimacy of and are responsive to the needs and interests of each other; avoid coercive and deceptive tactics; minimize the saliency of their differences (when appropriate); maintain trusting and friendly attitudes and behaviors; possess a requisite level of intelligence and apply their "cognitive resources" [80] to resolving the problem at hand; eschew simplistic, polarized thinking that views things as being black or white; and are open-minded and flexible.[81]

According to Deutsch, the characteristic features of destructive conflict are, more or less, the opposite of all of the above (i.e., the parties do not have an appropriate level of motivation to solve the problems at hand, do not engage in open and honest communication, and so on). In discussing destructive conflict, Deutsch also emphasizes certain motivational, perceptual, and psychological elements that affect the course of a conflict. He specifically focuses on the need to justify one's behaviors to others and to oneself, which he links to the theory of "cognitive dissonance" (that states that a person will attempt to decrease internal "dissonance," or uncomfortable inconsistencies, between one's beliefs, attitudes, and behaviors), and the tendency to at times have distorted, negative views of other people's conduct. These elements, as a general rule, come into play in conflicts and are

---

80 Morton Deutsch, *The Resolution of Conflict: Constructive and Destructive Processes* (New Haven: Yale University Press, 1973), 362.

81 For the sake of brevity and clarity, I have taken the liberty of rewording and rearranging the order of many of these variables from the way they appear in Deutsch's work. See Deutsch, *The Resolution of Conflict*, 351–76.

reflected in the typical biased, negative misperceptions of the other party's motives and actions, as opposed to the favorable judgments of one's own motives and actions.

Similarities and Differences between Contemporary Conflict Resolution and Traditional Jewish Approaches. There are a number of clear distinctions that stand out when comparing the concepts of traditional Jewish approaches associated with a dispute for the sake of Heaven with contemporary conflict resolution's elements of constructive conflict. There are two things that, for me, immediately come to mind. In my research of contemporary conflict resolution, I only infrequently encountered any sort of discussion of the importance of sincerely seeking and establishing "the truth" on the given topic or issue that is at the center of a dispute.[82] Also, I don't believe that I have ever seen, nor will I ever see, in contemporary conflict literature a discussion about the importance of having pure, noble, or holy motivations, as one finds in traditional Jewish approaches. For contemporary conflict resolution, these issues (particularly in regard to the second; in regard to the first, only generally speaking) are seen as being moot and not something that the parties should concern themselves with in order to constructively resolve their conflict. Even though clarifying the facts revolving around the issue at hand is certainly an important component of contemporary conflict resolution, there is (generally speaking) a preference not to emphasize the seeking or establishing of a singular, identifiable, objective truth (*see footnote*).[83] And even though

82 Some examples of discussions in contemporary conflict resolution that do emphasize (certain aspects of) the importance of seeking "the truth," would include David W. Johnson, Roger T. Johnson, and Dean Tjosvold, "Constructive Controversy: The Value of Intellectual Opposition," in *The Handbook of Conflict Resolution*. 2nd ed., ed. Morton Deutsch, Peter T. Coleman, and Eric C. Marcus (San Francisco: Jossey Bass, 2006), 69–70; Priscilla B. Hayner, "Past Truths, Present Dangers: The Role of Official Truth Seeking in Conflict Resolution and Prevention," in *International Conflict Resolution after the Cold War*, ed. Paul C. Stern and Daniel Druckman (Washington, DC: National Academy Press, 2000), 338–382; and John Paul Lederach, *Building Peace: Sustainable Reconciliation in Divided Societies* (Washington, DC: United States Institute of Peace Press, 1999), 28–30.

83 Contemporary conflict resolution's preference for not emphasizing the seeking or establishing of a singular, identifiable, objective truth, was pointed out to me by Professor Peter Coleman during my dissertation defense, May 2005. One should,

contemporary conflict resolution may readily admit that there are certain objectionable motivations that would have a detrimental effect on the course of a conflict (e.g., having a malevolent and vindictive desire for revenge), it does not emphasize in any way the need to have pure, noble, or holy motivations.

Despite these differences, many of the hallmark features of seeking and establishing the objective truth and having pure, noble, or holy motivations do correspond to concepts that appear in contemporary conflict resolution. From our study, we have seen that seeking and establishing the truth requires a diligent, objective, and honest analysis of the issues involved, engaging in dialogue, the careful consideration of opposing opinions, a willingness to retract one's opinion, that the conflict should not be conducted in a hostile manner, and it should not negatively affect the personal relationships of the parties involved. I believe that all of these features are similar, in varying degrees, to aspects of constructive conflict that appear in contemporary conflict resolution that I have touched on. A diligent, objective, and honest analysis of the issues are, to a certain extent, analogous to Deutsch's requirements that the parties properly apply their cognitive resources to resolving the conflict; identify underlying issues; and eschew simplistic, polarized thinking. Engaging in dialogue, taking into careful consideration opposing opinions, and

---

however, not mistakenly derive from what I have written here in the text, that Judaism necessarily subscribes to a belief in only one singular, identifiable, objective truth. Within Judaism, there is the talmudic concept of *elu va-elu divre Elohim ḥayim*, "[both] these and those are the words of the living God" (*Gittin* 6b and *Eruvin* 13b), which has been interpreted as teaching that it is possible for there to exist simultaneously more than one singular truth on a given topic. See, for example, Elijah Eliezer Dessler, *Mikhtav me-Eliyahu*, 5 vols. (Jerusalem: Yotse la-Or al Yede Ḥever Talmidav, 1997), vol. 3, 353; [Shlomo Wolbe], *Ale Shur*, vol. 2 (Jerusalem: Bet ha-Musar a"sh. R' H. M. Lehman, 1986), 560; Jacob Kamenetsky, *Emet le-Ya'akov: Sefer Iyunim ba-Mikra al ha-Torah*, 3rd ed. (New York: Makhon Emet le-Ya'akov, 2007), 28, 515; Avi Sagi, *Elu va-Elu: Mashmauto shel ha-Siaḥ ha-Hilkhati: Iyun Be-Sifrut Yisrael* (Tel Aviv: Kibbutz Hameuchad, 1996); Michael Avraham, "*Ha-Im ha-Halakhah hi Pluralistit*," *Ha-Mayan* 47, no. 2 [2006]: 41–56; and Michael Rosensweig, "*Elu va-Elu Divre Elokim Hayyim*: Halakhic Pluralism and Theories of Controversy," *Tradition* 26, no. 3 (1992): 4–23.

a willingness to retract an opinion correspond to Deutsch's elements of engaging in open and honest communication, and being open-minded and flexible. Not conducting the conflict in a hostile manner and that it not negatively affect personal relationships parallel Deutsch's elements of the parties maintaining trusting and friendly attitudes and behaviors.

In regard to the characteristic features of having pure, noble, or holy motivations, the commentators focused in on various psychological motivations that tend to have a deleterious effect on the conflict process and its outcome. The most frequently cited motivations that were discussed were the "pursuit of honor," the desire "to rule [over others]," "to feel triumphant," and the general inclination "to be disagreeable [or provocative]." In a similar vein, in discussing the problem of "issue rigidity" in his concluding essay, Deutsch specifically mentions the difficulty in resolving conflicts in which having "[g]reater power than the other," "victory over the other," or "having more status than the other" are at stake,[84] which correspond to a number of the elements that were highlighted by traditional Jewish commentators.

In connection with our discussion of motivations, we had also seen commentators who focused in on the proclivity of the average person to unwittingly rationalize his or her behavior by attributing the most impeccable of motives to one's own actions, even when in actuality he or she is being driven by dishonorable motives. There is a clear correspondence between this facet of a dispute not for the sake of Heaven and certain perceptual and psychological elements that Deutsch highlighted, such as the need to justify one's behaviors to oneself and to reduce cognitive dissonance between one's beliefs, attitudes, and behaviors. Also, implicit to contemporary conflict resolution's concern with perceptual and psychological elements is the need for the parties to recognize how these elements affect them on a personal level and to effectively address them, which is analogous to the emphasis of traditional Jewish approaches on the

84 Deutsch, *The Resolution of Conflict*, 370–71.

need for the parties to be aware of their cognitive, affective, and behavioral orientations through introspection and self-analysis and to subsequently take the appropriate steps to rectify the situation should they determine that there are destructive desires, interests, or drives that are adversely affecting them and the conflict.

There are many other aspects to constructive conflict that never came up in our study of a dispute for the sake of Heaven, for example, avoiding coercive and deceptive tactics and minimizing the saliency of the differences between the parties, which were elements that Deutsch discusses. And we have not discussed the similarities and differences between traditional Jewish approaches and the views of other scholars outside of those of Deutsch's, such as Kriesberg's or Crawley's. In respect to these lacuna, one should keep in mind that, as I pointed out in the summary (see p. 101), all of the material that was covered in this chapter represents only a small fraction of a much larger rabbinic perspective on constructive conflict that is interspersed throughout the vast corpus of traditional Jewish texts. What I have attempted to do in this last section is to merely offer a representative sample of some of the significant similarities and differences between contemporary conflict resolution and traditional Jewish approaches in respect to constructive conflict that are discernible from the sources I have researched and that stand out in my mind. Assuredly, there are many other clear-cut similarities and differences when it comes to contemporary conflict resolution's and traditional Jewish approaches' respective views on constructive conflict that have yet to be explored and elucidated, and, hopefully, one day will be.

PART III

Foundational Commandments And Laws

Chapter 4

Basic Interpersonal Obligations and Prohibitions

According to the Talmud (*Makkot* 23b), "613 commandments (*mitsvot*) were told to Moses at Mount Sinai." Elsewhere, the Talmud (*Gittin* 59b) asserts that all of these commandments, in one way or another, contribute to peaceful coexistence between people: "The entire Torah is for the sake of *darkhe shalom*" (literally: "paths of peace").[1] From out of the 613 commandments, R. Shmuel Eisenblatt lists thirty-eight commandments (twenty-one "negative commandments" and seventeen "positive commandments" [see Glossary under "*mone ha-mitsvot*"]) that one is liable to violate when one is involved in a conflict.[2] Though all of the commandments that R. Eisenblatt lists deserve to be properly elucidated, in that each one plays a unique role in a complete and comprehensive Jewish paradigm for harmonious coexistence, we will only touch on six fundamental commandments that play a pivotal role in the prevention of destructive conflict and serve major functions throughout the entire process of interpersonal conflict resolution. The six commandments that we will discuss encompass some of the most basic interpersonal obligations and prohibitions of Judaism—to love one's neighbor, the prohibition against hatred, the prohibition against physical violence, and the commandments that pertain to verbal abuse,

1 See pp. xxvii–xxviii and 48.

2 Shmuel D. Eisenblatt, *Ḥayim shel Shalom: Hilkhot Isure Maḥaloket* (Jerusalem: n.p., 1989), 17–56. R. Eisenblatt's list is based on R. Israel Meir ha-Kohen's list of commandments that one is liable to violate when one speaks *lashon ha-ra* ("evil speech"; see Glossary). Israel Meir ha-Kohen, *Sefer Ḥafets Ḥayim*, in *Kol Kitve Ḥafets Ḥayim ha-Shalem*, vol. 1 (New York: Avraham Yitsḥak Friedman, n.d.), *petiḥah*, pp. 9–36.

which enjoin an individual from cursing, embarrassing, or saying hurtful things to another person. For each of the commandments discussed, pertinent biblical, talmudic, and midrashic sources will be cited, and the basic normative obligations will be delineated. The final section of this chapter will compare and contrast the Jewish concepts that are discussed with analogous concepts from contemporary conflict resolution.

"You Shall Love Your Neighbor as Yourself"

The commandment of "You shall love your neighbor[3] as yourself"[4] (Leviticus 19:18) can be considered one of the great "meta-ethics" of Judaism.[5] The centrality of this commandment was sententiously expressed by two of the most prominent *tannaim* (sages of the Mishnah), R. Akiva (c. 50–135 CE) and Hillel (first century BCE–first century CE). According to R. Akiva, "This is a major principle in the Torah."[6] According to Hillel,

---

3 There are a number of alternative ways to translate the word *re'akha* (your neighbor), for example, "your friend," "your companion," "your fellow human being," and so on. See Ludwig Koehler and Walter Baumgartner, *The Hebrew and Aramaic Lexicon of the Old Testament*, Study Edition, trans. and ed. M. E. J. Richardson (Leiden, The Netherlands: Brill, 2001), s.v. "*rēaᶜ*," 1253–55.

4 In Hebrew, וְאָהַבְתָּ לְרֵעֲךָ כָּמוֹךָ (*ve-ahavta le-re'akha kamokha*). "You shall love your neighbor as yourself" is counted as one of the 613 commandments by all of the *mone ha-mitsvot*. See, for example, Shimon Kayara [alternatively, Yehudai ben Naḥman], *Sefer Halakhot Gedolot*, vol. 3 (Jerusalem: Ḥevrat Mekitse Nirdamim, 1988), positive commandment 69; Maimonides, *Sefer ha-Mitsvot*, positive commandment 206; Moses ben Jacob of Coucy, *Sefer Mitsvot Gadol* (*Semag*) (Israel: n.p.,1991), positive commandment 9; [Aaron?] ha-Levi of Barcelona, *Sefer ha-Ḥinukh*, (Netanya, Israel: Mifal Torat Ḥakhme Polin, 1988), commandment 243; Eliezer ben Samuel of Metz, *Sefer Yere'im ha-Shalem* (Israel: n.p., n.d.), 224 (38); and Isaac ben Joseph of Corbeil, *Sefer Amude Golah-Sefer Mitsvot Katan* (*Semak*) (Israel: Mefitse Or, 1959), *siman* 8, p. 6.

5 See Shalom Rosenberg, "*Ve-Halakhta bi-Drakhav,*" in *Filosofyah Yisre'elit*, ed. Asa Kasher and Moshe Halamish (Tel Aviv, Papyrus, 1983), 74. The term "meta-ethic" may have various possible connotations. In categorizing something as a meta-ethic of Judaism, I mean to say that it is a major principle that forms the basis and represents the essence of numerous laws and concepts within Judaism.

6 Jer. Tal. *Nedarim* 9:4 and *Sifra de-Ve Rav: Hu Sefer Torat ha-Kohanim*, ed. Isaac Hirsch Weiss (Vienna: Ya'akov ha-Kohen Shlosberg, 1862), *Kedoshim, perek* 4:12. (Unless otherwise noted, all citations from the *Sifra* are from the Weiss edition.)

it represents the very essence of the Torah: "This is all of the Torah in its entirety, the rest is commentary."[7] Love of one's neighbor may also rightfully be viewed as the fundamental concept that underlies and informs all aspects of Jewish interpersonal conflict resolution (see pp. 170–72). Because of the all-important foundational role of this concept in Judaism and Jewish conflict resolution, we will explore in depth in this section the primary rabbinic formulations of this commandment.

Rabbinic Formulations of "You Shall Love Your Neighbor as Yourself"

Reasons for Rejecting a Literal Interpretation. The basic questions of how does one define "love your neighbor as yourself" and what are the exact obligations that it imposes on the individual have been topics of ongoing debate in rabbinic literature since antiquity. In surveying the interpretations of rabbinic scholars, it appears that, generally speaking, they did not take the imperative of "love your neighbor as yourself" literally, and attempted to limit the form/degree of love that a strictly literal interpretation would require. It may be postulated that the reason for this is that from a traditional Jewish perspective the Torah establishes binding and practical (i.e., realistic) rules of conduct. Therefore, if the verse were taken literally, it would have been imposing an obligation that goes beyond the capacity of the average, or possibly any, person and would not meet these criteria. This idea is expressed by Naḥmanides (1194–1270) when he writes that "[this is a] hyperbole, for the heart of a human being will not accept that one [literally] loves his friend as he loves himself."[8] R. Naphtali Herz Wessely (1725–1805), in elaborating on the difficulties that exist with a literal reading of the verse, develops Naḥmanides' theme:

---

7 *Shabbat* 31a; see below, p. 115.

8 Naḥmanides, *Perush ha-Ramban al ha-Torah,* annotated by Charles B. Chavel (Jerusalem: Mossad Harav Kook, 1988), Lev. 19:17, p. 119.

> It would be quite astounding that He should command us regarding something that is not within the capacity of any human; it is impossible that a person should love another [literally] as himself, especially someone who is a [total] stranger. In addition to this, one cannot issue a command regarding love and hate, which a person cannot forcibly control[9] ... and furthermore, if this was so [i.e., that the verse should be understood literally], a person is thereby required to mourn for the suffering of all others as he would for himself and [as a result of this] his life would be unbearable, for an hour will not pass in which he will not see or hear of the suffering of another Jew.[10]

There are other alternatives that have been suggested to explain the rabbinic delimitation of the commandment.[11] R. Jacob ben

9 Clearly, there are commandments in the Torah regarding love and hate (e.g., "You shall love the Lord your God with all your heart" [Deut. 6:5] and "You shall not hate your brother in your heart [Lev. 19:17]). See the related discussion in She'ar Yashuv Kohen, *"Mitsvat Ahavat Yisrael: Be-Halakhah uve-Hagadah," Torah shebe-al Peh* 36 (1995): 49–50, quoted in Daniel Z. Feldman, *The Right and the Good: Halakhah and Human Relations,* expanded edition (Brooklyn: Yashar Books, 2005), 176–77; and Ha-Levi, *Sefer ha-Ḥinukh,* commandment 416.

10 [Naphtali Herz Wessely], *Netivot ha-Shalom*: *Va-Yikra* (Vienna: Adalbert Della Tore, 1861), Lev. 19:18, quoted in Nehama Leibowitz, *Studies in Vayikra* (*Leviticus*), translated by Aryeh Newman (Jerusalem: The World Zionist Organization, 1980), 195–96; and paraphrased in Meir Loeb ben Jehiel Michael Malbim, *Sefer ha-Torah veha-Mitsvah,* vol. 2 (Israel: Shiloh, n.d.), Leviticus, *ot* 45, p. 503. This train of thought may account for the widespread circumscription and negative formulation of the "Golden Rule" in antiquity. In such diverse sources as the Apocrypha (Tobit 4:15a), the Talmud (*Shabbat* 31a), the New Testament (the "Western Text" of Acts 15:29), the Apostolic Fathers (*Didache* 1:2), the writings of Confucius (*Analects,* bk. XII [Yen Yuan], chap. 2), Herodotus (*Hist.* III. 142), and Isocrates (*Nicocles* 61), the idea of loving your neighbor as yourself takes a considerably less arduous negative form. One example of this is "What you yourself hate, do not do to anyone" (Tobit 4:15a). See Carey A. Moore, *The Anchor Bible: Tobit: A New Translation with Introduction and Commentary* (New York: Doubleday, 1996), 178–79; and James L. Kugel, *The Bible As It Was* (Cambridge: The Belknap Press, 1997), 455–56.

11 Another alternative, offered by Naḥmanides himself, as to why the Rabbis rejected a literal reading of the verse is that they could not accept that one must actually love another as much as one loves oneself since this would contradict the halakhic

Asher (c. 1269–c. 1340), R. Judah Loeb Shapira (seventeenth to eighteenth centuries), R. Meir Loeb Weisser (*Malbim*, 1809–1879), R. David Zevi Hoffmann (1843–1921), and others have proposed that the unusual phraseology of the verse influenced the rabbinic interpretation of the commandment. The Torah's use of the Hebrew preposition *le* ("to")—*ve-ahavta* **le**-*re'akha* (literally, "You shall [show] love *to* your neighbor")—instead of the particle *et* (untranslatable, it serves as the direct object marker in Hebrew), *ve-ahavta* **et** *re'akha* ("You shall love your neighbor"), implies a limitation of the range of one's obligation (for further elaboration, see below, the section *The Centrist Position*).[12]

The Form and Degree of Love Required by the Commandment. Interspersed throughout rabbinic literature, there are a multitude of diverse and copious interpretations of "You shall love your neighbor as yourself."[13] In analyzing these interpretations, one can discern three basic approaches in regard to the form/degree of love encompassed by the biblical imperative. We may refer to these as the "minimalist," "centrist," and "maximalist" positions.[14]

---

dictum of *ḥayekha kodemim*, "Your life takes precedence" (*Bava Metsia* 62a), which teaches that one is not obligated to sacrifice one's own life in order to preserve the life of another. Naḥmanides, *Ramban al ha-Torah*, Lev. 19:17, p. 119.

12 Jacob ben Asher, *Perush ha-Tur ha-Arokh al ha-Torah* (Jerusalem: Hotsa'at be-Ferush uve-Remez, 1964), Lev. 19:18; Judah Loeb Shapira, *Rekhasim le-Vikah*, in *Moda le-Vinah* (Brooklyn: Moshe Stern, n.d.), Lev. 19:18, p. 8; Malbim, *Ha-Torah veha-Mitsvah*, vol. 2, Lev. *ot* 45, p. 503; David Zevi Hoffmann, *Sefer Va-Yikra Meforash* [*Das Buch Leviticus*], vol. 2, trans. Tsevi Har Shefer [Hebrew] (Jerusalem: Mossad Harav Kook, 1954), 36. Others who have offered this explanation include Moses Schick, *Maharam Shik al Taryag Mitsvot* (Brooklyn: Yisrael Brach, 1964), mitzvah 244; Wilhelm Bacher, *Agadot ha-Tana'im*, vol. 1 (Jerusalem: Devir, 1922), 3; and Jacob Kamenetsky, *Emet le-Ya'akov* (Baltimore: Kisvei Reb Yaakov Publications, 1986), Lev. 19:18, p. 209.

13 See Reinhard Neudecker, "'And You Shall Love Your Neighbor as Yourself—I am the Lord' in Jewish Interpretation," *Biblica* 73, no. 4 (1992): 496–517; and Emanuel B. Quint, "An Anthology of Rabbinic Views on the Commandment to Love Your Neighbor," *The Annual Volume of Torah Studies of the Council of Young Israel Rabbis in Israel* 3 (1991): 59–79. These articles offer just a miniscule sampling of Jewish interpretations of this commandment.

14 For an extensive treatment of this topic that offers many alternatives to my presentation, see Asi Halevi Even Yuli, *Shulḥan Arukh ha-Midot*, vol. 2 (Jerusalem: n.p., 2009), 3–39.

The Minimalist Position. One of the most well-known rabbinic explanations of the commandment to love your neighbor is that of the mishnaic sage Hillel. When asked by a would-be proselyte to be taught the whole Torah while standing on one foot, Hillel responded, "That which is hateful to you, do not do to your friend; this is all of the Torah in its entirety, the rest is commentary" (*Shabbat* 31a). Even though Rashi (R. Solomon ben Isaac, 1040–1105) offers an interpretation of Hillel's reply that understands it as being totally unrelated to the commandment in Leviticus (Rashi, *Shabbat* 31a, s.v. *da-alakh sene,* his first explanation), there are many other commentators who either equate it with or, at least, relate it to the concept of loving your neighbor.[15] Hillel's negative formulation of the commandment (aside from having sparked considerable polemical debate in later generations)[16] was a focus of considerable rabbinic commentary. One of the most halakhically significant interpretations is that of R. Samuel Edels (*Maharsha,* 1555–1631), who construes Hillel's negative formulation as establishing halakhic parameters for this mitzvah that makes it comparable to a prohibition or a "negative commandment." According to this view, the commandment to "love your neighbor" does *not* obligate one to do positive acts of good towards one's neighbor (*la-asot lo tovah*), but simply requires one to refrain from harming or hurting him (*she-lo ta'aseh lo ra'ah*).[17]

---

15 See, for example, *Targum Pseudo-Jonathan,* Lev. 19:18, which paraphrases Hillel in its explanation of the verse; R. Toviyahu ben Eliezer (eleventh century) in *Midrash Lekaḥ Tov,* vol. 2 (Jerusalem: n.p., 1960), Lev. 19:18, p. 54a, who writes that Hillel's statement is derived from Lev. 19:18; R. Nissim ben Reuben Gerondi (c. 1310–c. 1375) in *Derashot ha-Ran* (Jerusalem: Mekhon Shalem, 1974), *Ha-Derush ha-Ḥamishi,* p. 72, who renders Hillel's aphorism as "You shall love your neighbor as yourself"; and Moses ben Jacob, *Semag,* positive commandment 9.

16 See Neudecker, "And You Shall Love Your Neighbor," 496; Joseph H. Hertz, "Leviticus-Additional Notes: 'Thou Shalt Love Thy Neighbor as Thyself,' " in *The Pentateuch and Haftorahs* (London: Soncino Press, 1952), 563–64; Israel Abrahams, *Studies in Pharisaism and the Gospels: First and Second Series* (New York: Ktav Publishing House, 1967), 21–23; and George Foot Moore, *Judaism in the First Centuries of the Christian Era, the Age of the Tannaim,* vol. 2 (Peabody, MA: Hendrickson Publishers, 1997), 87–88.

17 Samuel Edels, *Ḥidushe Halakhot va-Agadot,* in the standard Vilna edition of the Babylonian Talmud, *Ḥidushe Agadot, Shabbat* 31a, s.v. *da-alakh sene,* quoted in Joseph Teomim, *Peri Megadim,* in the standard printed edition of the *Shulḥan Arukh, Oraḥ Ḥayim* 156, *Eshel Avraham* 2; and id., *Sefer Matan Sekharan shel Mitsvot,* in *Sifre Ba'al*

The Centrist Position. In opposition to the minimalist position, the centrist position requires one to not only refrain from doing harm, but to actively do good as well. According to this view, "love" must be expressed through *actions* that reflect loving concern for others, which is comparable, in some respect and limited degree, to the loving concern that one has for oneself.

It is quite clear that Maimonides accepts the centrist position and understands "love your neighbor" as a positive obligation.[18] This is evident from a number of places where he expresses the view that this precept encompasses all acts of *ḥesed,* "loving-kindness." One place where he mentions this is in his "Laws of Mourning":

> [One must] visit the sick, comfort mourners, be involved with burying the dead, assist a bride, escort [one's] guests ... these constitute acts of loving-kindness that one performs with his body ... these are [all] included in "You shall love your neighbor as yourself"—all the things that you want others to do unto you, you should do unto [he who is] your brother in Torah and commandments."[19]

Peri Megadim (n.p., n.d.), *ḥakirah* 4, p. 14. This explanation also appears in the earlier commentary of Yehudah ben Eliezer, *Rabotenu Ba'ale ha-Tosafot al Ḥamishah Ḥumshe Torah* (Bnei Brak: Ha-Makhon le-Hafatsat Perushe Ba'ale ha-Tosafot al ha-Torah, n.d.), *Perush Riva,* Lev. 19:18; quoted in Eliyahu Aryeh Friedman, *Kuntres ve-Ahavta le-Re'akha kamokha: Ha-Mitsvah ve-Gidreha ba-Halakhah, ba-Maḥshavah, ba-Musar uva-Ḥasidut* (Brooklyn: Moriah, 1994), 11. It appears that the majority of commentators understood Hillel's negative formulation differently than R. Edels. According to one approach, Hillel reformulated the commandment to the would-be proselyte (who was specifically asking for a reductionist explanation) in the negative, and did not explain the full extent of the commandment, so as not to overwhelm him with everything that the precept asks of the individual and thereby cause him to lose all interest in Judaism (see Jacob Reischer, *Iyun Ya'akov,* in Jacob ibn Ḥabib, *En Ya'akov* [New York: Sifre Kodesh, 1971], *Shabbat* 31a; and Ezekiel Sarna, commentary to *Mesilat Yesharim,* by Moshe Ḥayyim Luzzatto [Jerusalem: Mosad Haskel, 1979], chap. 10, p. 87, final explanation).

18 See also Naḥmanides, *Sefer ha-Mitsvot leha-Rambam im Hasagot ha-Ramban,* (Jerusalem: Mossad Harav Kook, 1981), *Ha-Shoresh ha-Rishon,* p. 25.

19 Maimonides, *Mishneh Torah, Evel* 14:1. See also Maimonides, *Sefer ha-Mitsvot, shoresh* 2 and 9. As to whether, according to Maimonides, there is an obligation of showing loving-kindness to a Gentile, see below, pp. 132–34.

R. Jacob Kamenetsky (1891–1986) explains that the source for this position is the grammatical construction of "you shall love" that is used in this verse—*ve-ahavta* ***le*** (see earlier discussion, p. 114)—which implies "that one must *do* for his friend that which he desires for himself," that is, express love through his actions; this is in contradistinction to "you shall love" that uses the grammatical construction of *ve-ahavta* ***et***, which, in R. Kamenetsky's opinion, refers to "*inner* love," in other words, that one inwardly *feel* the emotion of love.[20] R. David Zevi Hoffmann explains the verse similarly and writes:

> As opposed to "you shall love [with the Hebrew particle *et*], [our verse reads] "you shall love [with the Hebrew preposition *le*]," which without a doubt refers to love that is expressed through actions, that means to say, acts of loving-kindness ... In reference to God it says "You shall love the Lord"[with the particle *et*] since everyone is capable of loving God with their whole heart, for all that is necessary is the attainment of knowledge of Him, but a person is not capable of loving every human being, [which would include] even someone who does not find favor in his eyes. However, the *performance* of loving-kindness constitutes an obligation and is feasible in respect to every human being.[21] (emphasis mine)

The Maximalist Position. Even though the centrist position, by including positive actions, encompasses much more than the minimalist position, it still restricts the parameters of the commandment to the behavioral realm. This is as opposed to the maximalist position, which takes the verse much more literally. According to the maximalist position, when the Torah says "You shall love your neighbor," it means that one should not only *act* in a way that reflects love, but one must also strive to develop *feelings* of love as well.[22]

---

20 Kamenetsky, *Emet le-Ya'akov*, Lev. 19:18, p. 209.

21 Hoffmann, *Sefer Va-Yikra Meforash*, 36.

22 This may possibly be accomplished through a form of self-identification with the other person, through which an emotional bond is forged and emotional responses are

Notwithstanding the fact that it goes much further in the literal understanding of love for one's neighbor, the maximalist position still nevertheless clearly accepts the postulate that it is beyond the capacity of the average person to experience feelings for another that are exactly equivalent to what one would feel for oneself. Therefore, we find that proponents of this position propose that the commandment only entails that one should experience some type of feeling that would fall within the normal range of feelings of the average person, such as experiencing empathy.[23]

There are quite a number of authorities that subscribe to the maximalist position. One such authority is R. Eleazar Azikri (1533–1600), who categorizes this commandment among "Positive Commandments from the Torah *That Involve the Heart*,"[24] and explains it as follows:

> [The verse states] "You shall love your neighbor as yourself"; therefore, one is required to tell over his praise and be concerned about his money as he would be concerned about his own money, and he should be desirous of the honor of his

effectuated. This concept of self-identification is found in Jer. Tal. *Nedarim* 9:4, which, in turn, is quoted by R. Moses ben Jacob (*Semag*, positive commandment 9), and is reflected in the following comment of R. Joseph Albo [c. 1380–1444]: "'You shall love your neighbor [literally, your friend] as yourself,' that means to say, that just as [in] your love for yourself there is no [sense of] 'otherness,' so too [regarding] your love of your friend, you should not think of him as being separate from yourself" (Joseph Albo, *Sefer ha-Ikarim ha-Shalem*, vol. 2 [Jerusalem: Ḥorev, 1995], *ma'amar* 4 chap. 45, p. 613). See also Yeḥiel Neuman, *"Ve-Ahavta le-Re'akha kamokha: Berur ha-Shitot," Torat ha-Adam le-Adam: Kovets Torani ba-Mitsvot she-ben Adam la-Ḥavero* 4 (2001): 91.

23 I am using the word "empathy" in the sense that, among other things, it describes a "vicarious affective response" that mirrors the emotional experiences of another person. See Norma D. Feshbach and Kiki Roe, "Empathy in Six- and Seven-Year-Olds," *Child Development* 39, no. 1 (March 1968): 133; Arthur S. Reber, Rhianon Allen, and Emily S. Reber, *Penguin Dictionary of Psychology* (London: Penguin Books, 1985), s.v. "empathy"; *APA Dictionary of Psychology* (Washington, DC: American Psychological Association, 2007), s.v. "empathy"; cf., the sources cited below, 217 n. 77.

24 For each of the commandments he lists in this category, R. Azikri goes out of his way to highlight some aspect of the commandment that involves an emotion, belief, or cognitive process.

> friend as he is desirous of his own honor, and his love and compassion for his friend should be comparable to his love and compassion for himself; he should seek out that which is beneficial for him; *he should feel joy when good comes upon him and pain when he suffers*, and he should always speak to him gently in a loving and respectful manner ... [25]

R. Azikri's wording is a combination of the phraseology of Maimonides in the *Mishneh Torah* (*De'ot* 6:3) and *Sefer ha-Mitsvot* (positive commandment 206) with an interpolation from R. Azikri. In the passage above, everything is taken from Maimonides except for the final section starting from the italics, where R. Azikri begins to add his own original thoughts. The clearest indication in this passage that in addition to expressing "love" through deeds love should also be expressed through feelings is the clause "he should feel joy when good comes upon him and pain when he suffers." (As far as other possible indications are concerned, see below in the discussion of Maimonides' view.) Most significantly, in defining this commandment, R. Azikri specifically emphasizes vicarious emotional responses—in other words, empathy. This association between loving one's neighbor and empathy also appears in a number of other sources.[26]

---

25 Eleazar Azikri, *Sefer Ḥaredim ha-Shalem* (Jerusalem: n.p., 1990), chap. 9 mitzvah 28, p. 61.

26 For example, Moses ben Joseph Trani, *Igeret Derekh Hashem* (Venice, n.p., 1553), *Sha'ar 2 perek* 1, p. 7a; Alexander Susskind ben Moses, *Yesod ve-Shoresh ha-Avodah ha-Shalem* (Bnei Brak, Israel: Ḥasde Ḥayim, 1987), *sha'ar* 1 chaps. 7 and 8; Eliezer Papo, *Pele Yo'ets ha-Shalem* (Jerusalem: Mekhon Merav, 1994), s.v. *"ahavat re'im,"* p. 18 (R. Susskind and R. Papo are cited in Zelig Pliskin, *Love Your Neighbor* [Jerusalem: Aish ha-Torah Publications, 1977], 301, 306.); Dov Berish Gottlieb, *Yad ha-Ketanah* (Jerusalem: Or ha-Sefer, 1976), *De'ot* 5:5, *aseh* 9; Yosef Shalom Elyashiv, cited in [Yosef Yisraelzon] *Kuntres Kitsur Hilkhot ben Adam la-Ḥavero* (Reḥovot: Kolel Avrekhim Reḥovot, 1998), 8; see also Moses Feinstein, *Igrot Mosheh*, 9 vols. (New York: Moriyah, 1959–1996), *Yoreh De'ah* 4 *siman* 51:1, p. 277; Jonah ben Abraham Gerondi, *Sefer ha-Yirah im Beur Mekor ha-Yirah* (Jerusalem: Ha-Teḥiyah, 1959), 42–43, n. 165; and Shimon Vanunu, *Sefer ve-Ahavta le-Re'akha kamokha* (Jerusalem: Shimon Ḥen and Mordekhai Ḥen, n.d.), 12, 27–28, 33. It should be noted that R. Jeroham Lebovitch is of the opinion that even though empathy is a dimension of character development that serves as "the basis of [the] Torah and the

Even though a simple reading of Maimonides seems to indicate that he is a proponent of the maximalist position, it is difficult to say with any certainty that this is actually the case. In two different passages, he apparently frames the commandment as including an affective element. In the *Mishneh Torah* he writes, "It is incumbent upon every person to love every single individual of Israel[27] as himself, as it states: 'You shall love your neighbor as yourself'" (*De'ot* 6:3), and in the *Sefer ha-Mitsvot* he writes, "We are commanded to love one another as we love ourselves, and my compassion and love for my brother should be similar to my compassion and love for myself" (positive commandment 206)—which seems to indicate that Maimonides considered the higher level of experiencing, on some level, feelings of love as obligatory. However, in both instances he immediately seems to qualify this. In the passage from the *Mishneh Torah,* he immediately continues by specifying what appear to be behavioral aspects: "Therefore, one is required to tell over his [friend's] praise and be concerned about his money as he would be concerned about his own money, and as he is desirous of his own honor";[28] and in the passage from *Sefer ha-Mitsvot,* he also immediately continues by modifying what he had said by, seemingly, moving away from the affective realm and focusing on behavioral components: "This is in regards to his money, his body,

basis of [the] *mitsvot,*" it is not encompassed by the commandment of loving your neighbor. See Jeroham Lebovitch, *Da'at Ḥokhmah u-Musar,* 3 vols. (New York: Daas Chochmo U'Mussar Publications, 1966–1972), vol. 1, *ma'amar* 12, p. 29. An example of an alternative explanation that understands the commandment as related to feelings but does not focus on empathy is that of Naḥmanides. According to Naḥmanides, the commandment to love another as oneself relates to feelings of wanting to be superior to others and jealousy, and requires that one should desire that one's neighbor should attain all of the good things that one desires for oneself, and that one's neighbor should attain all of these things to the same degree that one would want for oneself (Naḥmanides, *Ramban al ha-Torah,* Lev. 19:17).

27 See below, p. 122.

28 Maimonides, *Mishneh Torah, De'ot* 6:3. For explanations of the wording of this halakhah, see Jacob ben Eliezer Kohen, annot., *Sefer ha-Mada* (Jerusalem: Mossad Harav Kook, 1964), *De'ot* 6:3, p. 168 n. 21; the paraphrase of this halakhah in Israel Meir ha-Kohen, *Sefer Ahavat Ḥesed,* in *Kol Kitve Ḥafets Ḥayim,* vol. 2, section 3, chapter 7, p. 53a; and Aryeh Pomeranchik, *Emek Berakhah* (Tel-Aviv: T. Pomeranchik, 1971), 63.

and everything he possesses ..."[29] This may, or may not, indicate that according to Maimonides, the normative range of the commandment only encompasses behavioral aspects.[30]

In reviewing the different approaches among rabbinic authorities, it appears that many of them did not view the three approaches to loving your neighbor (i.e., the minimalist approach of refraining from doing that which is hateful to you, the centrist approach of actively performing deeds of loving-kindness, and the maximalist approach of emotional responses) as being mutually exclusive from one another; rather, they viewed them as existing on a continuum and representing progressive levels or ways of fulfilling the commandment.[31]

Ahavat ha-Beriyot, Love for All Humanity

In the earlier discussion of the commandment of loving one's neighbor, Maimonides' opinion was cited, which, apparently, limits a Jew's obligation to perform acts of loving-kindness only to his "brother in Torah and commandments" (see p. 116), in other words, to a fellow Jew,[32] and limits the overall obligation of loving one's

29 Maimonides, *Sefer ha-Mitsvot*, positive commandment 206.

30 See Abraham Weinfeld, "*Mitsvat Ahavat ha-Ger le-Da'at ha-Rambam*" *Torat ha-Adam le-Adam: Kovets Torani ba-Mitsvot she-ben Adam la-Ḥavero* 5 (2004): 139–41. Cf. Halevi Even Yuli, *Shulḥan Arukh ha-Midot*, vol. 2, 4–10.

31 See Halevi Even Yuli, *Shulḥan Arukh ha-Midot*, vol. 2, 27–28; see also David Ari'av, "*Ve-Ahavta—le-Re'akha kamokha*," *Torat ha-Adam le-Adam: Kovets Torani ba-Mitsvot she-ben Adam la-Ḥavero* 4 (2001): 97. Even though all three approaches may fulfill the commandment of loving one's neighbor, that does not mean that they are all classified the same and are of equal status. R. Abraham Isaiah Karelitz (1878–1953), for example, is quoted as saying that not doing things that hurt or harm another (i.e., the minimalist approach) represents the primary requirement of the commandment, whereas performing positive actions to help another (the centrist approach) would only be considered a "*mitsvah kiyumit*" (a mitzvah that one fulfills if and when one decides to do so). See Tsevi Yavrov, *Ma'aseh Ish*, vol. 2 (Bnei Brak: n.p., 1999), 166; see also Moses Joshua Judah Leib Diskin, *She'elot u-Teshuvot Maharil Diskin* (Jerusalem: Defus Moriyah, 1911), 108. For many other sources and an in-depth discussion of views regarding the different possible levels of obligation of the three positions, see Halevi Even Yuli, *Shulḥan Arukh ha-Midot*, vol. 2, 118–33. See also below, p. 178.

32 As to whether this also excludes certain groups of Jews, see Maimonides, *Perush ha-Mishnayot leha-Rambam, Sanhedrin*, introduction to the tenth chapter, *Ha-Yesod*

"neighbor" by only requiring that one "love every single individual *of Israel* as himself" (see p. 120), which evidently excludes Gentiles.[33] This formulation, at face value, certainly seems to be an example of halakhic particularism, where the Halakhah is only promoting concern for fellow Jews, to the exclusion of the rest of humankind.

In reference to this (and other similar statements that one may encounter in halakhic/rabbinic literature),[34] it would be apropos to cite the words of R. Abraham Isaac Kook (1865–1935):

> [The concept of] love of humanity requires an extensive treatment ... This is in order to combat *the superficial understanding that emerges from an initial examination [of the traditional Jewish sources], due to a lack of proper training in Torah [texts], and the prevailing ethics,* which [give the impression] as if there exists [in Judaism] contradictions, or at least an indifference, concerning this type of love, which [in reality] needs to constantly fill all the chambers of one's soul.[35] (emphasis mine)

Sheloshah Asar; and Ha-Kohen, *Ahavat Ḥesed, Dine Hilkhot Halva'ah* 3:2, *Netiv ha-Ḥesed* 2–4. For other pertinent sources, see Elimelech Bar Shaul, *Mitsvah va-Lev*, vol. 1 (Jerusalem: Or Etsiyon, 1992), 172–74; Yehudah Zeraḥyah Segal, "*Yaḥas Torani le-Foshe Yisrael*," *Shanah be-Shanah* (5754 [1994]): 198–205; and She'ar-Yashuv Kohen, *Ḥikre Halakhah* (Jerusalem: Va'ad Talmidim, Yedidim ve-Shome Likḥo, 1992), 165–70. This topic is discussed in many other sources as well.

33 See also Maimonides, *Sefer ha-Mitsvot*, positive commandment 206.

34 Unfortunately, it is not feasible for me to adequately address every instance in which the sources cited in this work differentiate in some way between Jews and Gentiles. To do so would require a much, much lengthier and in-depth study than I could possibly provide within the constraints of the present work.

35 Abraham Isaac Kook, *Orot ha-Kodesh*, 4 vols. (Jerusalem: Mossad Harav Kook, 2006), vol. 4, p. 405; see also vol. 3, p. 318. R. Kook's mentioning that people have a false (and negative) impression about Judaism because of a lack of training in Jewish religious texts calls to mind what R. Joseph Albo (c. 1380–c. 1440) had written about people denigrating concepts they find in certain books because they have never attained an understanding of the methodology and literary style of the author, or because they do not have a comprehensive grasp of everything the author has written related to a given topic. See Joseph Albo, *Sefer ha-Ikarim*, vol. 1, *Ha-Ma'amar ha-Sheni, He'arah*, pp. 137–39. The predilection to understand halakhic concepts superficially by people who are inappropriately trained, and thereby erroneously attribute attitudes to Judaism that it in no way promotes, is discussed by R. Joseph Soloveitchik: Joseph

As we are about to see, what Maimonides has written about love of one's neighbor may serve as a perfect example of what R. Kook is referring to.

We may reasonably assume that Maimonides limits the commandment of loving one's neighbor to one's "brother in Torah and commandments" or to "every single individual of Israel" based on the premise that the word *re'akha* (your neighbor) in Leviticus 19:18 is only referring to a fellow Jew (see footnote).[36] This verse, according to Maimonides, would therefore be the source of the concept that is known in Jewish tradition as *ahavat Yisrael*, "love of Israel," that is, love for a fellow Jew. In Judaism, however, together going hand-in-hand with the concept of *ahavat Yisrael*, there is also the concept of *ahavat ha-beriyot*, literally, "love of humanity,"[37] that is, love for all humanity.[38]

B. Soloveitchik, "Korach Rebellion Part 2," accessed November 11, 2016, http://www.yutorah.org/lectures/lecture.cfm/767863/Rabbi_Joseph_B_Soloveitchik/_Korach_Rebellion_Part_2_#, at 22 to 34 minutes into the lecture.

36 The truth is that it is highly debatable if and how Maimonides derives that a Gentile is excluded from the word *re'akha*; see Baḥya ben Asher, *Rabenu Baḥya Be'ur al ha-Torah* (Jerusalem: Mossad Harav Kook, 2006), Exodus 11:2, cf. 20:13; Ḥayyim Ozer Grodzinski, *Aḥiezer*, vol. 3 (n.p., n.d.), responsum 37:5–6; Baruch ha-Levi Epstein, *Barukh she-Amar: Pirke Avot* (Tel Aviv: Am Olam, n.d.), *Avot* 3:14, pp. 122–23; Moses ben Jacob, *Semag*, positive commandment 9; Eliezer ben Samuel, *Sefer Yere'im*, 224 (38), where he focuses on the word *kamokha*, "like yourself"; and Epstein, *Mitzvot ha-Shalom*, 314–15.

37 Alternatively, "love of people" or "love of [God's] creatures."

38 Depending on the context, the term *ahavat ha-beriyot* could refer to love for all humanity, love for all of God's creatures (which may even include animals [see Simḥah Zissel Ziv, *Ḥokhmah u-Musar*, vol. 1 (New York: n.p., 1957), 31]), or love for one's fellow Jews. I will be using the term in the first sense, of love for all humanity. It should be noted that the universalistic concept of *ahavat ha-beriyot* and the particularistic concept of *ahavat Yisrael* are seen as going together naturally, augmenting and enhancing each other. See Abraham Isaac Kook, *Orot* (Jerusalem: Mossad Harav Kook, 2005), 149 par. 5; Benjamin Rabinowitz-Teomim, "*Ḥazon ha-Shalom*," *Sinai* 1 nos. 5–6 (Tishre–Ḥeshvan 5698 [1937]): 584–85; and Abraham Meir Habermann, *Mi-Peri ha-Et veha-Et* (Jerusalem: R. Mas, 1981), 10. I have discussed this topic with Morton Deutsch. Professor Deutsch fundamentally agreed to the thesis that, from the perspective of social psychology, love for all humankind and love for one's fellow Jew can certainly work together without any necessary contradictions. He suggested that a comparison can be drawn between their relationship and that of "multiple social identities" (see Paul Pederson, "Multicultural Conflict Resolution," in *Handbook of Conflict Resolution*, 2nd ed., ed. Morton Deutsch, Peter T. Coleman, and Eric C. Marcus [San Francisco, CA: Jossey Bass, 2006], 654–56). He pointed out how it is quite normal and natural for people to have a certain cultural

Primary Sources for the Concept of Ahavat ha-Beriyot. There are many sources in Judaism that are routinely cited as teaching love for all humanity. In this section, I will present five basic sources for this concept that are commonly cited.

(1) *Ben Azzai's Teaching regarding "This is the Book of the Descendants of Man."* One of the fundamental primary sources that is cited as teaching love for all humanity is a passage in the Jerusalem Talmud in tractate *Nedarim* (9:4). After quoting R. Akiva's teaching that love of one's neighbor is "a major principle in the Torah," the Talmud cites Simeon ben Azzai (early second century CE) as teaching that there is another principle in the Torah that is even greater (literally, "bigger") than (which evidently means to say that it goes beyond, and may even encompass) loving one's neighbor:

> Ben Azzai says, "This is the book of the descendants of man" (Genesis 5:1) is a greater principle.[39]

There is a debate among the commentators as to what exactly Ben Azzai means to say in this passage. There are two basic questions that they raise: (1) what principle, embodied in this verse, is he referring to, and, once we have identified that principle, (2) in what way is it greater (or "bigger") than the principle of loving one's neighbor?

What Principle Embodied in this Verse is Ben Azzai Referring To? There are two basic approaches[40] among the commentators in answering the first question, of what principle Ben Azzai is referring to:

Approach A: Many major commentators, such as R. Samuel ben Meir (*Rashbam*, c. 1080–c. 1174), R. Abraham ben David of

---

or ethnic group that they closely identify with and, at the same time, they can develop a global perspective and come to identify with the global community as a whole. Morton Deutsch, in discussion with the author, June 4, 2013.

39 Jer. Tal., *Nedarim* 9:4; also *Sifra, Kedoshim, perek* 4:12; and *Genesis Rabbah* 24:7. As to the correct text and interpretation of the passage in *Genesis Rabbah*, see J. Theodor and Chanoch Albeck, *Midrash Bereshit Raba u-Ferush Minḥat Yehudah*, vol. 1 (Jerusalem: Wahrmann Books, 1965), pp. 236–37; and Shraga Abramson, *Inyanut be-Sifrut ha-Ge'onim* (Jerusalem: Mossad Harav Kook, 1974), 127–30.

40 Of course, as is often the case with rabbinic texts, the commentators offer a wide range of possible alternative interpretations.

Posquières (*Rabad* III, c. 1125–1198), and R. Jacob of Orleans (d. 1189),[41] are of the opinion that when Ben Azzai cited the verse "This is the book of the descendants of man," he was actually referring to the words that appear in the second half of the verse, which are not cited in the talmudic text.[42] The second half of Genesis 5:1 reads, "On the day that God created man, He made him in the likeness of God." In other words, the principle Ben Azzai was referring to was that of *imago Dei*, the concept that every human is created in the *tselem Elohim*, "image of God."[43] This interpretation of Ben Azzai's statement appears for the first time already in the early Midrashic work *Genesis Rabbah*.[44]

Approach B: Other major commentators, such as R. David Fraenkel (1707–1762, the author of the commentary *Korban ha-Edah* on the Jerusalem Talmud), R. Samuel Strashun (*Rashash*, 1794–1872), and R. Shalom Mordecai Schwadron (*Maharsham*, 1835–1911),

---

41 Samuel ben Meir, quoted in *Moshav Zekenim al ha-Torah* (Jerusalem: Keren Hotsa'at Sifre Rabane Bavel, 1982), Leviticus 19:18; Abraham ben David of Posquières, *Perush ha-Ra'avad*, commentary on *Sifra de-Ve Rav hu Sefer Torat Kohanim* (Jerusalem: Sifra, 1959), *Kedoshim*, *perek* 4:12; Jacob of Orleans, quoted in Ḥayyim Paltiel ben Jacob, *Perush ha-Torah le-R'Ḥayim Paltiel* (Jerusalem: Y. S. Langeh, 1981), Leviticus 19:18.

42 One often encounters this type of elliptical style of writing in the Talmud.

43 See Gen. 1:27, 5:1, 9:6. There are many possible interpretations of what it means to be created in "the image of God." For a small sampling of traditional Jewish interpretations of the concept, see Shimon Kasher, *Peshuto shel Mikra* (Jerusalem: Mekhon Torah Shelemah, 1963), Genesis 1:26–27; and Chaim Navon, *Genesis and Jewish Thought* (New Jersey: Ktav, 2008), 43–57. It should be noted that some of the definitions of the "image of God" allow for the possibility that a person could theoretically debase himself to such an extent and become so corrupted that he loses this designation; see, for example, the view of Ezekiel Landau, *Derashot ha-Tselaḥ ha-Shalem* (Jerusalem: Mekhon ha-Tselaḥ, 2003), 369; Moses Joshua Judah Leib Diskin, *Ḥidushe Maharil Diskin al ha-Torah* (Jerusalem: n.p., 1985), Leviticus, p. 18; cf. Nathan Zevi Finkel, quoted in Dov Katz, *Tenu'at ha-Musar*, 6 vols. (Jerusalem: Feldheim, 1996), vol. 3, 125; A. Henach Leibowitz, *Ḥidushe ha-Lev*, vol. 1 (New York: Rabbinical Seminary of America, 2009), 22–23; and Yeḥezkel Levinshtain, *Or Yeḥezkel*, vol. 4 (*Midot*) (Bnei Brak: n.p., 1988), p. 145.

44 *Genesis Rabbah* 24:7. There are some ambiguities in the passage in *Genesis Rabbah*, and in the commentary of R. Abraham ben David of Posquières (see above, n. 41), that allow for alternative explanations; see Abramson, *Inyanut be-Sifrut ha-Ge'onim*, 129–30.

assert that Ben Azzai was indeed referring to the first part of the verse, "This is the book of the descendants of man." According to these commentators, the principle that is embodied in this half of the verse is the concept that all human beings descend from a single common ancestor, that is, the idea of the universal common ancestry of humankind, or, in other words, the brotherhood of humanity. It is noteworthy that all of the aforementioned commentators, when they offer this explanation, also paraphrase the verse in Malachi, "Have we not all one father? Has not one God created us all? Why do we betray, each person his brother ..." (Malachi 2:10).[45]

In What Way is This Principle Greater than the Principle of Loving One's Neighbor? Based on the premise that Ben Azzai was referring either to the principle that all humans are created in the image of God or to the principle of the universal common ancestry of humankind, the commentators go on to address the second question: in what way is the principle that is embodied in this verse greater than, or surpasses, the principle of loving one's neighbor? There is a wide range of possibilities. Two relatively simple and well-known approaches follow.

Approach A: Assuming that Ben Azzai was referring to the principle that every human is created in the image of God, R. Samuel ben Meir, R. Abraham ben David of Posquières, R. Jacob of Orleans, and others propose that this principle requires that one use a stricter, or higher, standard in determining how one should conduct oneself towards a fellow human being, who is created in God's image, than does the precept of loving one's neighbor. In respect to "You shall love your neighbor as yourself," the Torah instructs one to use the guideline of *"as yourself,"* that one is required to interact with a fellow human being in a manner that is comparable to what one would

45 David Fraenkel, *Korban ha-Edah*, in the standard printed edition of the Jerusalem Talmud, *Nedarim* 9:4, s.v. *zeh sefer*; Samuel Strashun, *Ḥidushe ha-Rashash*, in the standard Vilna edition of the *Midrash Rabbah*, *Bereshit*, 24:6; and Shalom Mordecai Schwadron, *Tekhelet Mordekhai*, vol. 1 (Brzezany: M. I. Feldmann, 1913), p. 5b, *ot* 52.

personally desire for oneself from others, which may allow for a considerable amount of leeway or leniency. (For example, if one would personally find acceptable and not be offended by certain statements that others may consider as being insulting, by using the standard of "as yourself" one may theoretically not be prohibited from saying such things to others; whereas the concept that every human is created in the image of God demands that even if one may not personally be offended by such statements, one must still avoid saying such disrespectful things to others who would be offended by them.) Thus, Ben Azzai is teaching that the principle of *imago Dei* imposes a higher standard of conduct on the person than the principle of loving one's neighbor. This explanation of Ben Azzai's opinion (similar to the first explanation that was discussed on p. 125) appears in the Midrash *Genesis Rabbah*.[46]

Approach B: Assuming that Ben Azzai was referring to the principle of the common ancestry of humankind, a number of commentators assert that Ben Azzai is saying that this principle is greater than the precept to love one's neighbor in that it encompasses not only Jews but all of humanity. This explanation is most often cited in the name of R. Fraenkel, who explains the passage with Ben Azzai by first quoting the verse "This is the book of the generations of man" and then tersely stating, "[That is to say] that all human beings come from the same father is a greater principle than 'You shall love your neighbor as yourself,' which only applies to 'your neighbor.'"[47] Presumably, R. Fraenkal understands the term "your neighbor" similar to the understanding of Maimonides, who applies the term only to a fellow Jew, and is saying that Ben Azzai is teaching that the principle of universal common ancestry, or the brotherhood of humanity, imposes a greater, or more extensive, obligation on the person than the principle of loving one's neighbor, in that it encompasses the entire human race, whereas loving one's neighbor only applies to a fellow Jew.

---

46 See above p. 125 n. 44.

47 Fraenkel, *Korban ha-Edah, Nedarim* 9:4, s.v. *zeh sefer*.

R. Schwadron offers a slightly clearer (and slightly different) formulation of this approach. R. Schwadron quotes the passage from the Jerusalem Talmud that mentions Ben Azzai and goes on to write that

> it appears to me that [the term] "your neighbor" [in "You shall love your neighbor as yourself"] is only applicable to one who is associated with you "in Torah and mitsvot," that means to say, a *Yisrael kasher* ("proper Jew").[48] When it comes to *ḥaside umot ha-olam* (the "righteous of the nations of the world," or "righteous Gentiles")[49] they are not encompassed by this principle ... That love [for a righteous Gentile] is derived from that which is written "This is the book of the generations of man," similar to that which is stated in Malachi chapter 2, "Have we not all one father?"[50]

Combining approaches A and B,[51] R. Joseph Hertz (1872–1946) basically, and quite eloquently, sums up these approaches, and explains Ben Azzai as saying that Genesis 5:1 teaches "reverence for

48 As to who is included in the category of a *Yisrael kasher*, see the sources cited above, p. 121 n. 32.

49 For a halakhic definition of "*ḥaside umot ha-olam*," see Maimonides, *Mishneh Torah, Melakhim* 8:11; Mordecai Gifter, "*Ha-Halakhah be-Midrash R. Eliezer Beno shel RYH"G*," *Talpiyot* 1, no. 2 (Tevet-Adar 5704 [1943–1944]): 334–35; Nahum Rakover, *Shilton ha-Ḥok be-Yisrael* (Jerusalem: Misrad ha-Mishpatim, 1989), 19–20; Ḥayyim David Halevi, *Aseh lekha Rav*, 9 vols. (Tel Aviv: Ha-Va'adah le-Hotsa'at Kitve ha-G. R. Ḥ. D. Halevi, 1976–1989), vol. 1, 157–60; Moshe Shternbukh, *Teshuvot ve-Hanhagot*, vol. 1 (Jerusalem: Netivot ha-Torah veha-Ḥesed, 1986), responsum 721; and Zevi Hirsch Chajes, *Kol Sifre Maharats Ḥayot*, vol. 1 (Jerusalem: Divre Ḥakhamim, 1958), 489; and other sources as well.

50 Schwadron, *Tekhelet Mordekhai*, p. 5b. The same basic idea also appears in Zevi Hirsch Kalischer, *Ḥamishah Ḥumshe Torah im ... u-Shene Perushim ... Sefer ha-Berit ...* (Warsaw: N. Shriftgisser, 1875), Leviticus 19, p. 175. It is noteworthy that R. Schwadron goes on to quote R. Samuel Shmelke Horowitz of Nikolsburg (1726–1778), who taught that one should "also love *resha'im* (wicked people), and that which the Sages have said that there is a mitzvah to hate a wicked person, that means to say, to hate the evil within him, but to love the good." Schwadron, *Tekhelet Mordekhai*, p. 5b.

51 To be exact, R. Hertz is combining the first set of approaches A and B (which were presented above on pp. 124–26) and approach B from the second set (see p. 127).

the divine image in man, and proclaims the vital truth of the unity of mankind, and the consequent doctrine of the brotherhood of man; and, therefore, all are our fellowmen and entitled to human love."[52]

(2) *"Beloved is a Human Being, Who is Created in the Image of God."* A primary source that is cited as teaching love for all humanity, and in all probability is much more well known than Ben Azzai's teaching, is the mishnah in *Pirke Avot* (3:14) that quotes R. Akiva as having taught:

> Beloved is a human being, who is created in the image [of God]) ... as it states, 'For in the *tselem Elohim* (image of God) He made the human being' (Genesis 9:6).[53]

Similar to the first approach mentioned earlier in explaining Ben Azzai, this teaching of R. Akiva has been interpreted as expressing the doctrine that every human is endowed with the image of God, and is therefore deserving of respect[54] and love.[55] In the words of the work

52 Hertz, "Leviticus—Additional Notes," p. 563.

53 From the fact that the verse in Genesis refers to all human beings, and that the next section in the mishnah goes on to discuss the special love for the Jewish people, the commentators point out that it is clear that this first section of the mishnah is referring to all human beings and not only Jews. See Yom Tov Lipman Heller, *Tosafot Yom Tov*, in *Mishnayot Zekher Ḥanokh* (Jerusalem: Ḥ. Vagshal, 1999), *Avot* 3:14; and Israel Lipschutz, *Tiferet Yisrael: Yakhin u-Voaz*, in *Mishnayot Zekher Ḥanokh* (Jerusalem: Ḥ. Vagshal, 1999), *Avot* 3:14, *Yakhin* 88. There are many others who mention in passing that the concept of "Beloved is a human being" is applicable to the entire human race. See, for example, Isaac Abravanel, *Naḥalat Avot* (New York: D. Silberman, 1953), p. 172; and Avraham Grodzinski, *Torat Avraham* (Bnei Brak: Yeshivat Kolel Avrekhim Torat Avraham, 1978), 1. See also Israel Schepansky, *Ha-Takanot be-Yisrael*, 4 vols. (Jerusalem: Mossad Harav Kook, 1991–1993), vol. 2, *Takanot ha-Talmud*, p. 325 n. 67, in which he addresses the view of R. Ḥayyim Vital.

54 The concept that a human being is created in the image of God is often cited in Jewish sources as the basis for *kevod ha-beriyot*, "respect for people" or "human dignity"; see Joseph Dov Soloveitchik, *Yeme Zikaron* (Jerusalem: Sifriyat Aliner, 1986), 9; Lebovitch, *Da'at Ḥokhmah u-Musar*, vol. 3, *ma'amar* 33, p. 63; Refael Reuven Grozovsky, *Siḥot Rabi Reuven* (n.p., 2007), 21–22; and Nahum Rakover, *Gadol Kevod ha-Beriyot: Kevod ha-Beriyot ke-Erekh Al* (Jerusalem: Moreshet ha-Mishpat be-Yisrael, 1998), 18–23.

55 This source is cited by Ahron Soloveichik, *Logic of the Heart, Logic of the Mind* ([Jerusalem]: Genesis Jerusalem Press, 1991), 70–71; and Yehudah Gershoni, *"Li-Dmuto shel ha-Rav Hertsog," Or ha-Mizraḥ* 9, nos. 3–4 (Shevat 5722 [1962]): 7.

Moshav Zekenim (a compilation of commentaries on the Torah from the medieval scholars known as the *Ba'alei ha-Tosafot*), "All human beings are created in the image of God ... therefore it is proper to respect and love all humans. And so have the Sages of blessed memory said, 'Beloved is a human being, who is created in the image [of God].'"[56]

(3) *"You Shall Love the Lord Your God."* The concept of *ahavat ha-beriyot* has also been understood as a component of the commandment of "You shall love the Lord your God" (Deut. 6:5). One of the most well-known rabbinic authorities who is cited as a proponent of this idea is R. Judah Loew (*Maharal* of Prague, 1525–1609), who describes *ahavat ha-beriyot* as a "branch," or offshoot, of *ahavat Hashem*, "love of God."[57] The *Maharal* explains the connection between the two concepts as stemming from the fact that "one who loves someone will also love all the things that he created with his hands. Therefore, when one loves God, it is impossible not to love his creations."[58]

(4) *"And You Shall Walk in His Ways."* Another source for the concept of love for all humanity that has been cited is the commandment of *ve-halakhta bi-drakhav*, "And you shall walk in His ways" (Deut. 28:9), which is understood by the Rabbis as an injunction that one should strive to emulate God's divine attributes (*imitatio Dei*).[59] Rabbinic

---

56 In Hebrew, this quote reads as follows:

"הואיל וכל בני אדם נבראים בצלם אלקים . . . על כן ראוי לכבד ולאהוב את כל האדם. וכן ארז"ל (אבות פ"ג) חביב אדם שנברא בצלם"

Moshav Zekenim al ha-Torah; Kovets Perushe Rabotenu Ba'ale ha-Tosafot (Jerusalem: Keren Hotsa'at Sifre Rabane Bavel, 1982), Leviticus 19:18, p. 350.

57 Judah Loew ben Bezalel, *Derekh Ḥayim: Ve-Hu Perush le-Masekhet Avot*, vol. 1 (Jerusalem: Mekhon Yerushalayim, 2007), chap. 1, mishnah 12–15, p. 342.

58 Judah Loew ben Bezalel, *Netivot Olam*, vol. 2 (Tel Aviv: Mekhon Yad Mordekhai, 1988), *Netiv Ahavat Re'a*, p. 129. Cited by R. Moshe Tsuriel, *"Ahavah Universalit—Yaḥas Ḥiyuvi le-Umot ha-Olam,"* accessed November 11, 2016, http://www.yeshiva.org.il/midrash/4453; cf. Zvi A. Yehuda, *"Leumiyut ve-Enoshiyut be-Diyune Ḥakhme Yisrael," Ha-Doar* 80, no. 11 (May 4, 2001): 8. This connection between love of God and love of humanity appears in a number of places in the works of R. Tzvi Yehuda Kook (1891–1982); see Tzvi Yehuda ha-Kohen Kook, *Siḥot ha-Rav Tsevi Yehudah*, ed. Shlomo Ḥayim Aviner (Jerusalem: n.p., 1993–2005), vol. 4, pp. 272–74, and vol. 5, pp. 125–27, n. 24.

59 *Sifre, Ekev, piska* 49, Deut. 11:22; *Sotah* 14a; *Shabbat* 133b. *Ve-halakhta bi-drakhav* is considered one of the 613 biblical commandments; see Kayara, *Sefer Halakhot Gedolot*, vol. 3, positive commandment 32; Maimonides, *Sefer ha-Mitsvot*, positive

authorities down through the ages have highlighted a wide array of *midot* (traits) that are associated with God and which one is therefore obligated to try to develop within oneself and express through one's actions.[60] R. Ahron Soloveichik (1917–2001) asserts that love for humanity is certainly one of God's traits and it therefore follows that love for humanity is encompassed within the commandment to emulate God.[61] In connection with this, it is worth noting that R. Simḥah Zissel Ziv (Broida, 1824–1898), one of the great nineteenth-century proponents of *musar*, writes that God's trait of *ahavat ha-beriyot*—"that He loves all"—stands out from among all of His other traits, since "we do not find that any of the *midot* of the Holy One, blessed be He, is as evident to the extent that *ahavat ha-beriyot* is."[62]

(5) *The View that "You Shall Love Your Neighbor" Applies to All Humankind.* One source for *ahavat ha-beriyot* that is often cited is the view that takes issue with Maimonides and interprets the word *re'akha* (your neighbor) in Leviticus 19:18 as also referring to Gentiles. Though this view appears in a few different sources,[63] it is generally attributed to R. Phinehas Elijah Hurwitz (1765–1821) in his work *Sefer ha-Berit*.[64]

---

commandment 8; Moses ben Jacob, *Semag*, positive commandment 7; Ha-Levi, *Sefer ha-Ḥinukh*, commandment 611; Eliezer ben Samuel, *Sefer Yere'im*, 408 [4]; Isaac ben Joseph, *Semak, simanim* 46–47; and many other sources as well.

60 See, for example, *Sifre, Ekev, piska* 49, Deut. 11:22; *Sotah* 14a; Maimonides, *Mishneh Torah, De'ot* 1:5–6, *Avadim* 9:8; Moses Cordovero, *Tomer Devorah* (London, n.p., 2003); and Joseph Dov Soloveitchik, quoted in Hershel Schachter, *Nefesh ha-Rav* (Jerusalem: Reshit Yerushalayim, 1995), 59–71.

61 Ahron Soloveichik, "*Sovlanut ba-Halakhah*," *Torah shebe-al Peh* 40 (1999): 61.

62 R. Ziv, however, does not categorize *ahavat ha-beriyot* as a component of the commandment of *ve-halakhta be-derakhav*, as does R. Soloveichik; rather, he views it as a means by which one becomes close to God. Ziv, *Ḥokhmah u-Musar*, vol. 1, p. 31.

63 See, for example, Ḥayyim Hezekiah Medini, *Sede Ḥemed*, 10 vols. (Brooklyn: Kehot, 1959), vol. 3, *ma'arekhet ha-resh, kelal* 60:6, vol. 8, *Pe'at ha-Sadeh, kelalim ma'arekhet ha-gimel, siman* 6:9 (citing the work *Taharat ha-Mayim*, by R. Abraham ben Naḥman ha-Kohen); Epstein, *Barukh she-Amar, Avot* 3:14, p. 122; Jonathan Steif, *Mitsvot Hashem*, vol. 2 (n.p., n.d.), pp. 32–33 (citing R. Ḥayyim Vital); and Eliezer Shulevits, *Or Eliezer*, vol. 2 (Petaḥ Tikvah: Yeshivat Lomza, n.d.), 229.

64 Phinehas Elijah Hurwitz, *Sefer ha-Berit ha-Shalem* (Jerusalem: Yerid ha-Sefarim, 1990), 530.

It should be noted that even though R. Hurwitz broadens the concept of loving one's neighbor to encompass all humankind, he nevertheless adds two highly significant qualifications to this. First, he emphatically states that one is not obligated to love a person whom he terms a *"vilder man"* (savage) nor an individual who is "involved with the destruction of society, such as murderers, thieves, bandits, and the like."[65] A second extremely important qualification that R. Hurwitz adds is that love of one's neighbor should be exhibited in accordance with the closeness of the relationship that exists between oneself and the other person. A person has an obligation of exhibiting a proportionally greater degree of love and caring concern for one's immediate family than for all others. After one's immediate family, the next highest level of love and caring concern one should show is for one's extended family. After one's extended family, the next level of love would be for one's neighbors and members of one's own community. Then, after one's neighbors and members of one's own community, comes the love for the other members of society.[66]

Maimonides' View. Even though, as we had seen earlier (p. 120), Maimonides limits the commandment of loving one's neighbor to a fellow Jew, nevertheless, there are unquestionably other halakhic

65 Hurwitz, *Sefer ha-Berit*, 526–27. R. Hurwitz defines "savages" as those who "live like animals of the land," who do not exhibit any form of friendship; do not live in houses; do not cultivate their land; who walk around naked; and whose women are all promiscuous. Ibid.

66 Hurwitz, *Sefer ha-Berit*, 551, 558. In support of this concept, R. Hurwitz cites the talmudic passage that instructs one who is faced with the question of how to distribute charitable funds to be guided by the principle of "Your poor and the poor of another city—the poor of your city take precedence" (*Bava Metsia* 71a); ibid. Interestingly, Professor Resianne Fontaine has pointed out that R. Hurwitz's formulation closely parallels that of Cicero's. Cicero, whose writings R. Hurwitz was familiar with (see *Sefer ha-Berit*, 565), views such an approach as being socially responsible and beneficial for society as a whole: "The interests of society, however, and its common bonds will be best conserved, if kindness be shown to each individual in proportion to the closeness of his relationship" (Cicero, De Officiis [*On Obligations*] 1.16.50–52). Resianne Fontaine, "Love of One's Neighbour in Pinhas Hurwitz's *Sefer ha-Berit*," in *Studies in Hebrew Literature and Jewish Culture*, ed., Martin F. J. Baasten and Reinier Munk (Dordrecht: Springer, 2007), 291–92.

sources according to Maimonides that obligate a Jew to perform acts of loving-kindness for and behave in a compassionate manner towards all other human beings. Maimonides is patently clear about this when he writes:

> We conduct ourselves with *derekh erets* [good manners and respect] and *gemilut ḥasadim* [loving-kindness][67] towards resident aliens [i.e., Gentiles who accept to observe the basic universal "Noahide" laws, see footnote][68] similar to a Jew, for we are commanded to sustain them ... Even when it comes to idolaters, our sages have commanded us to visit their sick, to bury their dead along with our dead, and to support their poor together with the Jewish poor, *mi-pene darkhe shalom* (for the sake of promoting peace). Surely it states "God is good to all and His compassion is upon all of his creations" [Psalms 145:9], and it also states, "Its [i.e., the Torah's] ways are ways of pleasantness and all of its paths are peace" [Proverbs 3:17] (Maimonides, *Mishneh Torah, Melakhim* 10:12).

Whether in regard to Gentiles classified as "resident aliens," for which there is a special obligation to help provide for them, or in regard to "idolaters," for which there are the universalistic obligations of *mi-pene darkhe shalom*, of promoting harmonious

67 Literally, "the performance of [acts of] loving-kindness."

68 The seven basic Noahide commandments are the prohibitions against (1) idolatry, (2) blasphemy, (3) homicide, (4) sexual sins, (5) theft, (6) and eating meat from a living animal; and the positive obligation of (7) establishing a legal system. For a basic overview of these laws, see *Sanhedrin* 56a; and [Yoel Schwartz], *Or la-Amim* (Jerusalem: Devar Yerushalayim, 1983), 109–18. For a much more extensive treatment, see Eliyahu Berakhah, *Toldot Noaḥ* (Jerusalem: n.p., 2012); and Nahum Rakover, *Law and the Noahides: Law as a Universal Value* (Jerusalem: Ministry of Justice, 1998). As to other possible prerequisites that a Gentile must fulfill in order to receive the designation of a resident alien, and whether this status is applicable to modern-day Gentiles, see *Entsiklopedyah Talmudit*, s.v. "*ger toshav*"; Abraham Elijah Kaplan, *Divre Talmud*, vol. 1 (Jerusalem: Mossad Harav Kook, 1958), 280–87; and the sources cited in Ariel Finkelstain, *Derekh ha-Melekh* (Netivot: Yeshivat ha-Hesder Ahavat Yisrael, 2010), 53–60.

coexistence between people,[69] and *ve-halakhta bi-drakhav*, of emulating God's ways (which Maimonides is evidently alluding to when he quotes the verse "God is good to all and His compassion is upon all of his creations"), evidently according to Maimonides a Jew's obligation to perform acts of loving-kindness and show compassion towards others encompasses the entire human race.

"You Shall Not Hate Your Brother in Your Heart"

Hatred can be viewed as having far-reaching negative effects and implications that parallel the positive effects and implications of love for one's neighbor; in the words of R. Azikri, "Just as 'You shall love your neighbor as yourself' embodies the fulfillment of the entire Torah, so too the opposite is true in relation to hatred, [that it embodies] the violation of the entire Torah."[70] The Rabbis, however, understood the relationship between the precepts regarding love and hate as not only being one of opposites,[71] but as one of antecedence—"If one transgresses 'You shall love your neighbor as yourself,' he will eventually transgress [other commandments, including] ... 'You shall not hate your brother in your heart' (Lev. 19:17) ... "; where, in the emerging sequence of events, the degenerative potential of hatred is viewed as being seemingly limitless—"and he will eventually come to bloodshed." (Midrash, *Sifre*, *Shoftim*, 187).[72] This rabbinic portrayal, which situates hatred on a moral slippery slope and emphasizes its degenerative potential, sheds light on another talmudic dictum that equates hatred with the three "cardinal sins":[73] "*sinat ḥinam* (literally, baseless

---

69 See above, p. 110.

70 Azikri, *Sefer Ḥaredim*, 66:85, p. 244.

71 The oppositional relationship between hatred and love is reflected in Proverbs 10:12, "Hatred stirs up quarrels, but love covers over all wrongs"; and see Abraham ibn Ezra, *Perush Rabenu Avraham ibn Ezra*, in the standard *Mikra'ot Gedolot*, Lev. 19:17.

72 This midrash is addressing a verse in Deuteronomy that suggests the existence of a direct connection between hatred and murder: "When there will be one who hates his neighbor, and lies in wait for him, and rises up against him, and strikes him mortally, and he dies . . ." (Deut. 19:11).

73 The three "cardinal sins" of idolatry, illicit sexual relations, and bloodshed have a unique status in Jewish law: "For all prohibitions in the Torah, if they say to a

hatred)[74] is on par with three sins: idolatry, illicit sexual relations, and bloodshed" (*Yoma* 9b). In classic *aggadic* (see Glossary) style, by correlating ostensibly remote sins (one generally regarded as being much less serious than the others), this statement conveys what the Rabbis perceived as the incredible destructive power of hatred.[75]

In light of the fundamental role that hatred plays in interpersonal relations and particularly in conflict, in this section we will explore the biblical commandment of "You shall not hate your brother in your heart" (Leviticus 19:17).[76] I will present two classic rabbinic formulations of the commandment and two of the primary approaches to dealing with hatred that appear in the traditional literature.

Rabbinic Formulations of "You Shall Not Hate Your Brother in Your Heart"

The Form of Hatred That is Prohibited. Just as the form of love required by "love your neighbor" is a topic of debate among rabbinic scholars, similarly, the form of hatred prohibited by "You shall not hate your

---

person 'Transgress and you will not be killed,' he should transgress and not [allow himself to] be killed, except for idolatry, illicit sexual relations, and bloodshed" (*Sanhedrin* 74a).

74 The term "baseless hatred" should not be understood as hatred without any basis whatsoever, but rather as hatred without a valid basis, or rationalized hatred. See Nathan Zevi Finkel, quoted in Jehiel Jacob Weinberg, *Seride Esh*, vol. 4 (Jerusalem: Mossad Harav Kook, 1977), 312–13 (based on *Yoma* 9b).

75 Other examples of this aggadic method would include: "Whoever tells over *lashon ha-ra* [i.e., something derogatory about someone without a constructive, halakhically sanctioned purpose; see Glossary], he 'increases sins' that are equivalent to three sins: idolatry, illicit sexual relations, and bloodshed" (*Arakhin* 15b); and "One who tears his garments in his anger, or one who breaks his utensils in his anger, or one who scatters his money in his anger, he should be viewed by you as one who worships idols. For this is the way the evil inclination works: today he tells him 'do such and such,' and the next day he tells him 'do such and such,' until he tells him 'worship idols,' and he goes and worships" (*Shabbat* 105b).

76 In Hebrew, לֹא־תִשְׂנָא אֶת־אָחִיךָ בִּלְבָבֶךָ (*lo tisna et aḥikha bi-lvavekha*). "You shall not hate your brother in your heart" is counted as a biblical commandment by all of the *mone ha-mitsvot*: see, for example, Kayara, *Sefer Halakhot Gedolot*, vol. 3, negative commandment 98; Moses ben Jacob, *Semag*, negative commandment 5; Ha-Levi, *Sefer ha-Ḥinukh*, commandment 238; Eliezer ben Samuel, *Sefer Yere'im*, 195 (39); Isaac ben Joseph, *Semak*, *siman* 17; and Gerondi, *Sha'are Teshuvah*, 3:39.

brother in your heart" is also debated. The Talmud in tractate *Arakhin* (16b) cites a *baraita* (see Glossary) that establishes the basic parameters of the prohibition:

> One might have thought that ["You shall not hate your brother" teaches that] he should not hit him, slap him, or curse him; therefore, the verse states: "in your heart"; Scripture is talking about hatred in the heart.

The ambiguity of this passage, particularly the phrase "Scripture is talking about hatred in the heart," led to a fundamental halakhic dispute regarding the purview of this commandment. R. Aḥa of Shabḥa (680–752 CE) puts forth what can be considered the "simple" approach. After quoting the *baraita*, he adds on the following short addendum:

> This is saying that God prohibited hatred by itself, *even though* he has *not done anything* [i.e., he has in no way acted upon it].[77] (emphasis mine)

Evidently, R. Aḥa interprets the phrase in the *baraita*, "Scripture is talking about hatred in the heart" as saying that Scripture is *even* talking about hatred in the heart. One is forbidden from even harboring *concealed* hatred, which does not express itself outwardly in any way. The implication is that *revealed* hatred, which expresses itself through actions, is certainly prohibited by this commandment.[78]

---

77 Aḥa of Shabḥa, *She'iltot de-Rav Aḥai Gaon*, 5 vols. (Jerusalem: Institute for Research and Publication, Sura, 1960–1977), vol. 2, *parashat Va-yeshev, she'ilta* 29, p. 196.

78 This explanation of R. Aḥa's opinion is found in Naphtali Zevi Judah Berlin, *Ha'amek She'elah*, commentary to *She'iltot de-Rav Aḥai Gaon*, by Aḥa of Shabḥa, vol. 1 (Jerusalem: Mossad Harav Kook, 1958), *parashat Va-yeshev, she'ilta* 27, p. 182 n. 3. For other *rishonim* whose views correspond to that of R. Aḥa's, see ibid.; Yosef Ḥazan, *Sefer She'elot u-Teshuvot Ḥikre Lev*, vol. 6 (Jerusalem: Mekhon ha-Me'or, 1998), *Yoreh De'ah*, responsum 80, p. 101; and Ya'akov Yisrael Kanevski, *Kehilot Ya'akov al Masekhtot Shevuot, Makot* (Bnei Brak: n.p., 1967), *Makkot, siman* 16. According to R. Abraham Isaac Kook (*Mitsvot Re'iyah* [Jerusalem: Mossad Harav Kook, 1970], *He'arot le-Sefer Ḥafets Ḥayim*, p. 97), R. Jeroham Fishel Perla (commentary to *Sefer ha-Mitsvot le-Rabenu Sa'adyah: Im Be'ur Meva'er Devarav vi-Yesodotav ve-Shitato*, by Sa'adia ben Joseph, 3 vols. [New York: E. Grossman, 1962], vol. 1, pp. 267, 274), and R. Abraham A. Price

Maimonides' explanation, which is diametrically opposed to that of R. Aḥa's, may be considered the "novel" approach. Maimonides discusses this commandment in two places. In *Sefer ha-Mitsvot* he explains it as follows:

> He has said "You shall not hate your brother in your heart" ... when one shows another his hatred and makes known to him that he hates him, he has *not* transgressed this negative commandment, but he has transgressed "You shall not take revenge" and "You shall not bear a grudge," and he has also transgressed a positive commandment, that which He has said, "You shall love your neighbor as yourself"; but hatred of the heart, that is a more powerful sin than all others.[79]

And in the *Mishneh Torah*, Maimonides writes:

> This is a negative commandment that does not entail a physical act. The Torah only proscribed hatred in the heart, but one who hits his friend or insults him, even though he is not allowed to, he has not transgressed "You shall not hate."[80]

It is evident that Maimonides interpreted the phrase in the *baraita*, "Scripture is talking about hatred in the heart" to mean that Scripture is *only* talking about hatred in the heart. The implication is that "You shall not hate your brother" does not encompass every form of hatred, *only* a concealed and pernicious "hatred of the heart," but other types of clearly visible displays of hatred, though prohibited based on other sources, do not fall under the purview of this commandment.[81]

(*Mishnat Avraham al ha-Semag*, 3 vols. [Toronto: Yeshiva Torath Chaim, 1972–1985], vol. 1, p. 33) this *may* actually have been Maimonides' view as well. See also Joseph Karo, *Kesef Mishneh*, in the standard printed edition of the *Mishneh Torah*, *De'ot* 6:5.

79 Maimonides, *Sefer ha-Mitsvot*, negative commandment 302.

80 Maimonides, *Mishneh Torah*, *De'ot* 6:5.

81 Maimonides' view is cited by later authorities, such as Abraham Abele Gombiner, *Magen Avraham*, in the standard printed edition of the *Shulḥan Arukh*, *Oraḥ Ḥayim* 156:2; and Israel Meir ha-Kohen, *Mishnah Berurah*, 6 vols. (Zikhron Ya'akov: Merkaz le-Ḥinukh Torani, 1975), *Oraḥ Ḥayim* 156:4.

As R. Zvi Weinberger and R. Baruch Heifetz point out, the logic that underlies R. Aḥa's opinion seems relatively simple to grasp, whereas Maimonides' logic regarding this topic is somewhat elusive. R. Aḥa is evidently of the opinion that hatred that is not expressed is simply considered less intense and less destructive than open, or expressed, hatred. Therefore, when the Torah prohibits hatred of the heart, one must conclude, *a fortiori*, how much more so, that revealed hatred is certainly forbidden.[82] The logic underlying R. Aḥa's opinion is therefore quite sound and simple to grasp.

As to explaining Maimonides' opinion—that concealed hatred is "a more powerful sin than all others," even more so than open hatred, which seems counterintuitive—there are various possible approaches. All of these approaches regard pent up and suppressed hatred as one of the most dangerous and volatile of emotions. One such explanation, offered by R. Dov Berish Gottlieb (d. 1796) and others,[83] proposes that if hatred is not vented in some way it will never dissipate; rather, it will continue to ferment within one's heart and build up until it reaches critical proportions and eventually "burst forth" with an intensity that may lead one to do serious harm to someone else. R. Eliezer Papo (c. 1784–1827) offers two alternative explanations. In paraphrasing Jeremiah 9:7, "Their tongue is a deadly arrow, it speaks deceit; through his mouth he speaks peace with his friend, but inwardly he lays an ambush for him,"[84] R. Papo suggests that the destructive potential of concealed hatred lies in the fact that the other party will not be aware of it and will therefore not be able to be on guard and protect himself from the other individual.[85]

82 See Zvi H. Weinberger and Baruch A. Heifetz, *Sefer Limud le-Hilkhot ben Adam la-Ḥavero: Lo Tisna et Aḥikha be-Lvavekha* (Safed, Israel: Makhon Torat ha-Adam le-Adam, 1995), 134–36.

83 Gottlieb, *Yad ha-Ketanah, De'ot* 7:4, quoted in Weinberger and Heifetz, *Lo Tisna et Aḥikha,* 135; see also Mordechai Lichtstein, *Mitsvot ha-Levavot* (Brisk, Lithuania: Avraham Hendler, 1924), *Hilkhot Ahavat Yisrael, Derekh Mitsvotekha,* 17, p. 22; and Isaac Simḥah Hurwitz, *Yad ha-Levi,* commentary to Maimonides' *Sefer ha-Mitsvot* (Jerusalem: S. Zuckerman, 1926), negative commandment 302, p. 264, quoted in Weinberger and Heifetz, *Lo Tisna et Aḥikha,* 135 n. 17.

84 See also Proverbs 3:29, 10:18.

85 A similar explanation is also found in Ha-Kohen, *Sefer Ḥafets Ḥayim, petiḥah, lavin* 7, *Be'er Mayim Ḥayim* 7.

In addition to this concern, R. Papo also suggests that concealed hatred precludes the possibility that "mediators of peace" will ever come along and bring about a reconciliation between the parties.[86]

The Degree of Hatred That is Prohibited. In halakhic literature, the Hebrew noun *sinah*, "hatred," and other derivatives of its consonantal root שנא (*s-n-'*, "[to] hate," e.g., *sone*, "enemy" or "foe") find a range of applications. Depending on the context, they may have various meanings and refer to different *intensities* of hatred. For example, in one instance, one finds that they are applied to what is described as "minimal hatred" (*sinah mu'etet*, literally, a "little hatred") in which "one's mind is distant [from another]";[87] in another instance, they refer to a much more severe hatred in which "one takes pleasure in the misfortune of another";[88] and in another instance, they are used in relation to an intense hatred in which "one torments another ... and tries to make him suffer any way he can."[89]

According to R. Israel Meir ha-Kohen (Kagan, 1838–1933, commonly referred to as the "*Ḥafets Ḥayim*"; see Glossary), from the perspective of practical Halakhah, the degree of animosity that constitutes "hate" and is considered a violation of the prohibition is described in a mishnah in tractate *Sanhedrin*. In listing various things that disqualify someone from serving as a judge or testifying in a rabbinic court, the mishnah states that

> one who hates [is disqualified from serving as a judge or testifying in a court case that involves the person that he hates] ... [The definition of] "one who hates" is anyone

86 Papo, *Pele Yo'ets*, s.v. "*sinah.*"

87 See Asher ben Jehiel, *Sefer Rabenu Asher* [*Piske ha-Rosh*], in the standard Vilna edition of the Babylonian Talmud, *Sanhedrin*, chap. *Zeh Borer* 23 (in conjunction with *Sanhedrin* 29a), quoted in Joseph Karo, *Bet Yosef*, in the standard printed edition of Jacob ben Asher's *Arba'ah Turim*, *Ḥoshen Mishpat* 7, s.v. *en ha-dayan*.

88 See Shabbetai ben Meir ha-Kohen, *Sifte Kohen*, in the standard printed edition of the *Shulḥan Arukh*, *Yoreh De'ah* 335:2; in conjunction with Moses Isserles, *Shulḥan Arukh*, *Hagahot ha-Rama*, *Yoreh De'ah* 335:2; and *Sanhedrin* 19a.

89 Sherira ben Ḥanina Gaon, quoted in [Joseph Bonfils?], *Teshuvot Ge'onim Kadmonim* (Tel Aviv: n.p., 1964), responsum 100; quoted in Weinberger and Heifetz, *Lo Tisna et Aḥikha*, 28.

> who does not speak to him [to the person that he hates] for three days out of animosity.[90]

Based upon this mishnah, the *Ḥafets Ḥayim* makes the following observation:

> One very often finds that because of disputes over relatively minor matters people form grievances against each other. Notwithstanding the fact that there does not exist outright hatred between them, they still do not want to have any contact with each other. This is what is referred to in the vernacular as *eno shaveh be-shaveh imo* ("he isn't on good terms with him"). But, in truth, we see from the talmudic passage mentioned above that by maintaining this type of relationship with the other person one receives the designation of "one who hates," and thereby transgresses the prohibition of "You shall not hate your brother in your heart."[91]

It is evident that the *Ḥafets Ḥayim* is of the opinion that, from a halakhic standpoint, the appropriate standard in gauging whether one transgresses the prohibition against hatred is if one's dislike for another person has reached an intensity resulting in one not speaking to that person for three days out of animosity. It therefore follows that since it is relatively commonplace for even minor differences to produce a level of disaffection in which individuals are simply "not on good terms" and do not want to talk to each other, people may possibly come to violate the prohibition much more often than one would normally have imagined. (For exceptions to the general prohibition, see footnote.[92])

90 *Sanhedrin* 27b.

91 Israel Meir ha-Kohen, *Kuntres Ahavat Yisrael*, in *Kol Kitve Ḥafets Ḥayim*, vol. 1, 48–49.

92 If one does not speak to someone whom he or she does not like for three days *not* out of animosity, but because of some other valid reason, for example, the opportunity does not present itself or because the person wants to avoid conflict, it would appear that one does not violate the commandment. Also, there may be many

While the standard of not speaking to a person for three days is also used by R. Azikri, R. Mordecai Lichtstein (b. 1865), and others,[93] R. Joseph D. Epstein cites the opinion of R. Ḥayyim ben Attar (1696–1743), who offers an alternative standard to be used in determining what constitutes "hate":

> A person should not assume that something does not fall under the category of "hate" unless it is total, unadulterated hatred, in which one seeks the detriment and ruin of the other individual, but that [a mere] distancing of the heart could not be categorized as "hate" ... [rather] the standard for determining what is considered hate, which God has established a precept regarding, is whatever can be perceived [as a relative diminishment in feelings] by using the standard of a "brother" [which is implied by the verse in Leviticus]. On the basis of this standard measure, even *a minute distancing of another from the heart,* perforce lowers one from the level of a "brother" and thereby contravenes "You shall not hate."[94]

Rabbis Weinberger and Heifetz, who have done extensive research on the topic, write that they have not found any other major halakhic authority who expresses a view similar to that of R. Attar. Even R. Epstein himself, who often refers to R. Attar's opinion, questions its practical halakhic import in light of the fact that it sets a standard that goes beyond the normal, natural capacity of a human being.[95]

---

possible exceptions to the general rule that one should not hate someone; see Weinberger and Heifetz, *Lo Tisna et Aḥikha,* 145 n. 11; 152–54, 206–53.

93 Azikri, *Sefer Ḥaredim,* 21:19, p. 103; Lichtstein, *Sefer Mitsvot ha-Levavot, Ahavat Yisrael* 12, p. 22. For other authorities who are also of this opinion, and for further elaboration, see Weinberger and Heifetz, *Lo Tisna et Aḥikha,* 140–49.

94 Ḥayyim ben Moses Attar, *Or ha-Ḥayim,* in the standard *Mikra'ot Gedolot,* Lev. 19:17. Epstein, *Mitzvot ha-Shalom,* 74, 78, 97, 118, 332, 530, and 553.

95 See Weinberger and Heifetz, *Lo Tisna et Aḥikha,* 148 n. 17; and Joseph D. Epstein, *Mitsvat ha-Etsah* (New York: Torat ha-Adam, 1983), 277 n. 8.

Two Approaches to Dealing with Hatred

The Primary Method. Leviticus 19:17, in its entirety, reads as follows: "You shall not hate your brother in your heart; you shall surely reprove your friend, and you shall not bear sin because of him." The juxtaposition of the commandment of "You shall not hate your brother in your heart" with the imperative of "you shall surely reprove your friend" led biblical exegetes and halakhic authorities to read this verse as follows: "You shall not hate your brother in your heart; *but instead* you shall surely reprove your friend." In other words, after initially establishing a prohibition against harboring feelings of hatred towards another, the verse goes on to instruct one who is experiencing such feelings to confront the other person and discuss the issue with him. In this verse, the Torah is presenting what may be viewed as its primary method for dealing with hatred. By discussing one's grievances with the person one is feeling malice towards, one can potentially produce a purgative effect, and do away with feelings of ill will, and resolve the issues between them. This approach will be discussed in detail in Chapter 6.

Subduing the Inclination to Hate. In classic rabbinic sources, we find that another method for dealing with hatred was discerned from the following verses:

> If you encounter your enemy's ox or donkey wandering about, you shall surely return it to him. If you see the donkey of one who hates you [alternatively, someone whom you hate][96] lying under its burden, you shall not leave him, you must surely help him (Exodus 23:4–5).

According to the Midrash, in these verses "the Torah is speaking in response to [97] the [evil] inclination."[98] In other words, as numerous

96 See *Targum Pseudo-Jonathan*, Exod. 23:4–5 (and *Pesaḥim* 113b).

97 Alternatively, "against the [evil] inclination" (see *Kiddushin* 21b).

98 *Sifre, Tetse, piska* 222, 225. See also Menaḥem M. Kasher, *Torah Shelemah*, 45 vols. (Jerusalem: Hotsa'at Bet Torah Shelemah, 1992), Exod. 23:4–5, pp. 165–66 nn. 47–50, 168–69 nn. 65–68.

commentators explain,[99] the Torah is demanding that one go against his or her natural inclination to hate and be helpful to the person that he or she has negative feelings towards, if the opportunity presents itself. By behaving in a manner that runs contrary to one's natural inclination towards the person, one may develop a positive attitude and goodwill towards that person.[100] This process is known in the Talmud and halakhic literature as *la-khof et yitsro,* "subduing one's inclination [to hate]."[101]

The concept of "subduing one's inclination [to hate]" appears in all of the major halakhic codes.[102] The *Shulḥan Arukh*'s version reads as follows:

> When one encounters two [animals], one crouching down under its burden [unable to move] and one whose load had fallen off, and there is no one to assist him [i.e., the owner of each animal], [in normal circumstances] there is a mitzvah to first unload because of the suffering of a living creature [i.e., the animal under its burden] ... but if one of these people is someone he hates and the other is someone

99 See, for example, Hillel ben Eliakim, in *Sifre leha-Tana ha-Elohi Rabi Shimon ben Yoḥai,* vol. 2 (Jerusalem: n.p., 1983), *Tetse* 222, p. 93; Ḥakham Kadmon Sefaradi, in *Sifre leha-Tana ha-Elohi Rabi Shimon ben Yoḥai,* vol. 2 (Jerusalem: n.p., 1983), *Tetse* 222, p. 93; Joseph Bekhor Shor, *Perushe Rabi Yosef Bekhor Shor al ha-Torah* (Jerusalem: Mossad Harav Kook, 1994), Exod. 23:4, p. 151; Moses ben Joseph Trani, *Kiryat Sefer,* 2 vols. (Jerusalem: Hotsa'at Yerid ha-Sefarim, 2002), vol. 2, p. 338; and Malbim, *Sefer ha-Torah veha-Mitsvah, Mishpatim* 201.

100 See Avraham Ya'akov ha-Kohen Pam, *Atarah la-Melekh* (Brooklyn, NY: Yo.l. a.Y. Talmidav, 1993), 22; Eliyahu Bakshi-Doron, *Sefer Binyan Av: Teshuvot u-Meḥkarim,* vol. 3 (Jerusalem: Mekhon Binyan Av, 2002), *siman* 78, pp. 357–58; and Elijah Eliezer Dessler, *Mikhtav me-Eliyahu,* 5 vols. (Jerusalem: Yotse la-Or al Yede Ḥever Talmidav, 1997), vol. 1, p. 37. This may possibly be understood as a means of creating "cognitive dissonance" (see above, p. 104), which helps facilitate attitude change. For other possible mechanisms that may also come into play, see below, p. 444 nn. 130–31 and p. 446 n. 141.

101 See *Bava Metsia* 32b. Literally, *la-khof et yitsro* should probably be translated as "to subdue one's [evil] inclination."

102 See Isaac Alfasi, *Hilkhot ha-Rif,* in the standard Vilna edition of the Talmud, *Bava Metsia,* p. 17b in the pages of the Rif; Maimonides, *Mishneh Torah, Hilkhot Rotse'aḥ* 13:13; Asher ben Jehiel, *Rabenu Asher, Bava Metsia, perek Elu Metsiot* 30; Jacob ben Asher, *Arba'ah Turim, Ḥoshen Mishpat, siman* 272; and Joseph Karo, *Shulḥan Arukh, Ḥoshen Mishpat* 272:10.

> he loves, there is a mitzvah to first help someone he hates in order to subdue his inclination [to hate].[103]

In other words, in a normal situation in which one encounters two people on a road, one whose animal has collapsed underneath a heavy load and is suffering, and another whose animal's load fell off and the load is now lying on the ground, the Halakhah dictates that one should first assist the person whose animal is suffering, out of a concern for *tsa'ar ba'ale ḥayim* (the suffering of a living creature). However, if the animal that is suffering belongs to someone he has a good relationship with and personally likes, and the other animal whose load fell off belongs to someone he dislikes, he must first assist the person he dislikes in order to suppress (and eliminate) his natural inclination to hate.

In addition to evoking positive feelings in the person who performs the gesture of kindness, the Rabbis also noted the positive psychological effect on the other party as well:

> "If you see the donkey of one who hates you ..." this is [an example of] that which is stated in the biblical verse "Its [the Torah's] ways are ways of pleasantness and all of its paths are peace" (Prov. 3:17). When an enemy sees that you come to his aid, he will say in his heart, "I assumed this [person] was my enemy. Heaven forfend! If he was my enemy, he would not help me. He must be my friend, and I have been his enemy without cause. I will go and appease him." He then goes to him and makes peace.[104]

Aside from the two methods for addressing hatred that we have touched on here, there are a variety of other approaches for dealing with hatred that can be found in traditional Jewish works. Some of

---

103 Karo, *Shulḥan Arukh, Ḥoshen Mishpat* 272:10.

104 *Midrash Agadah, Mishpatim* 23:5, quoted in Kasher, *Torah Shelemah*, vol. 18, p. 169 n. 68. See also *Tanḥuma, Mishpatim* 1; *Midrash Tehilim*, 99:3; Rashi, Psalms, 99:4 (citing *Tanḥuma*); Isaiah Horowitz, *Shene Luḥot ha-Berit*, vol. 1 (Jerusalem: Oz ve-Hadar, 1993), *Sha'ar ha-Otiyot, ot bet* 13, p. 278; and Ḥayyim Vital, *Sefer Sha'are Kedushah* (Jozefow, Poland: S. Y. Vaks, 1842), *ḥelek* 1, *sha'ar* 6, p. 9a.

these will be discussed in Chapter 9, in the context of traditional approaches to anger management.

The Commandment Prohibiting Physical Violence

In connection with the biblical sanction for court-administered corporal punishment (see footnote),[105] the Torah spells out a prohibition against exceeding a designated limit—"Forty [lashes] he may strike him, he shall not add [on to this]; lest he strike him an additional blow beyond these, an excessive flogging, and your

105 Court-administered corporal punishment is biblically sanctioned for the willful transgression of negative commandments (*Sifre, Ki Tetse, piska* 286, 243; *Makkot* 16a; Maimonides, *Mishneh Torah, Sanhedrin* 18:1 and chapter 19, *Yesode ha-Torah* 5:4; for which types of negative commandments are excluded, see Maimonides, *Mishneh Torah, Sanhedrin* 18:1–3, 6). This type of punishment is only sanctioned when certain conditions are met: The person is given a "warning" (*Sanhedrin* 40b–41a; Maimonides, *Mishneh Torah, Sanhedrin* 16:4), in which he must be told that he should not perform this act because it is a sin that carries with it the punishment of flogging (Maimonides, *Mishneh Torah, Sanhedrin* 12:2; according to other opinions, the one giving the warning must also spell out the exact prohibition the person will transgress, see Rashi, *Shevuot* 20b, s.v. *ve-azharateh*, s.v. *akhalti*; Tosafot, *Moed Katan* 2b, s.v. *mishum*; and Isaiah ben Mali di Trani, *Tosafot Rid* [Jerusalem: Machon Harry Fischel, 1962], *Shabbat* 138a). The person must then verbally accept the warning by saying "I am doing it on this condition," that is, I am aware of this and I accept it (*Sanhedrin*, 72b, 81b; Tosefta, *Sanhedrin*, chapter 11; Maimonides, *Mishneh Torah, Sanhedrin* 12:2, 18:5; Abraham de Boton, *Leḥem Mishneh*, in the standard printed edition of the *Mishneh Torah, Sanhedrin* 12:2; cf. the opinions cited in Medini, *Sede Ḥemed*, vol. 2, *ma'arekhet mem, kelal* 31). He then must immediately (within approximately three seconds) perform the forbidden act (*Sanhedrin*, 40b; Maimonides, *Mishneh Torah, Sanhedrin* 12:2); the act must be clearly witnessed by two "kosher" witnesses (*Sifre, Shoftim, piska* 188; Maimonides, *Mishneh Torah, Sanhedrin* 16:4, 20:1; Joseph Babad, *Minḥat Ḥinukh* [Jerusalem: Mekhon Yerushalayim, 1997], 82:1); and the witnesses must undergo a cross-examination process (*Sanhedrin*, 32a, 40a; Maimonides, *Mishneh Torah, Sanhedrin* 16:4, *Edut* 3:2). (Even if all of the above conditions are met, a contemporary rabbinic court would not be halakhically permitted to administer this punishment [see Medini, *Sede Ḥemed*, vol. 2, *ma'arekhet mem, kelal* 32].) In reference to imposing extralegal lashes and "lashes for rebelliousness" (*makot mardut*), see Maimonides, *Mishneh Torah, Sanhedrin* 18:5 and 24:4. According to the Talmud, thirty-nine lashes is the maximum number of lashes that may be administered (see *Makkot* 22a–b; Maimonides, *Mishneh Torah, Sanhedrin* 17:1; and Kalman Kahane, *"Arba'im Ḥaser Aḥat," Ha-Mayan* 10, no. 1 [1970]: 18–25). The court assesses the person's physical condition and makes a determination of how many lashes he is actually capable of receiving, up to thirty-nine (Tosefta, *Makkot*, 3:10; *Makkot* 22a–23a; Maimonides, *Mishneh Torah, Sanhedrin* 17:1–6).

brother will be degraded before your eyes"[106] (Deuteronomy 25:3). The Rabbis state that this prohibition of striking another individual is not only applicable to the court-appointed representative who implements the flogging, but is also applicable to anyone who would strike another person.[107] Veritably, all of the *mone ha-mitsvot* (the "enumerators of commandments"; see Glossary) view this prohibition against striking another person as constituting one of the 613 biblical commandments.[108]

In condemning physical violence, the Talmud in tractate *Sanhedrin* (58b) cites R. Simeon ben Lakish (third century CE) as teaching that "one who raises his hand against his friend, even if he does not hit him, receives the designation of a *rasha* ('wicked person')" (for his source, see footnote).[109] (In later generations, this saying of R. Simeon ben Lakish becomes quite well known[110] and is cited often by rabbinic authorities when they discuss or censure

106 In Hebrew, the verse reads, אַרְבָּעִים יַכֶּנּוּ, לֹא יֹסִיף; פֶּן־יֹסִיף לְהַכֹּתוֹ עַל־אֵלֶּה, מַכָּה רַבָּה, וְנִקְלָה אָחִיךָ לְעֵינֶיךָ.

107 *Mekhilta* (Horovitz and Rabin edition), *Mishpatim* 5, p. 266. See also *Sanhedrin* 85a; *Ketubot* 33a; *Sifre, Ki Tetse* 286, p. 304. How exactly this is derived from the verse is a matter of debate among the commentators; see Ḥayyim Benveniste, *Keneset ha-Gedolah*, vol. 9, *Ḥoshen Mishpat* (Jerusalem: Haktav Institute, 2005), *siman* 620, pp. 224–28.

108 See, for example, Kayara, *Sefer Halakhot Gedolot*, negative commandment 244; Maimonides, *Sefer ha-Mitsvot*, negative commandment 300; Moses ben Jacob, *Semag*, negative commandment 199; Ha-Levi, *Sefer ha-Ḥinukh*, commandment 595; Eliezer ben Samuel, *Sefer Yere'im*, 217 (247); and Isaac ben Joseph, *Semak*, *siman* 84. There is a minority opinion that views the two phrases "he shall not add [on to this]" (*lo yosif*) and "lest he strike him an additional blow" (*pen yosif*...) as constituting *two* separate commandments prohibiting physical violence; see Jonah ben Abraham Gerondi, *Sha'are Teshuvah* (Brooklyn: Zundel Berman, 1974), 3:77; Samuel de Medina, *She'elot u-Teshuvot Maharashdam* (Lemberg: P. M. Balaban, 1862), *Yoreh De'ah*, responsa 98, 190, *Even ha-Ezer*, responsum 122; and Judah Aszod, *Teshuvot Mahari'a: Yehudah Ya'aleh* (New York: Hotsa'at Ḥayim u-Verakhah, 1965), part 2, *Yoreh De'ah*, responsum 164, p. 52a.

109 R. Simeon ben Lakish derives this from the passage in Exodus that describes Moses' encounter with two Hebrew men who were fighting. The verse states, "He [Moses] went out on the next day and behold there were two Hebrew men fighting; and he said to the *rasha* ("wicked person"), 'Why are you hitting your friend?'" (Exodus 2:13). The Hebrew word for "hitting" in this verse, *takeh*, is written in the future tense and could be translated literally as "going to hit." Based on this reading of the verse, R. Simeon ben Lakish goes on to say that "[the verse] does not state 'Why did you hit?' [in the past tense], but rather 'Why are you going to hit?' [This implies that] even though he has not hit him [yet] he still receives the designation of a *rasha*" (*Sanhedrin* 58b).

110 This can be partially attributed to Rashi paraphrasing this teaching in his commentary on the Torah; see Rashi, Exodus 2:13.

physical violence.[111]) The Talmud then goes on to quote R. Ḥanina [bar Ḥama] (early third century CE) as assigning the alternative designation of "a sinner"[112] to one who raises his hand against his friend. R. Ḥanina's source for this is the biblical episode that discusses the children of Eli (1 Samuel 2:12–17). The Bible goes into some detail as to how the servants of Eli's children would inappropriately demand certain priestly gifts, and that if someone would not accede to their demands, a servant would threaten him by saying, "you will give [it], and if not, I will take it by force" (1 Samuel 2:16). Taking it "by force" is understood by R. Ḥanina as implying that the servants were threatening to use violent means if the person would continue to refuse.[113] The very next verse goes on to describe their behavior by saying that "The *sin* of the servants was very great before the Lord" (1 Samuel 2:17), thus indicating that one who threatens another with violence, or by "raising his hand," is considered a sinner.

111 See, for example, Maimonides, *Mishneh Torah, Ḥovel u-Mazik* 5:2; Jacob ben Asher, *Arba'ah Turim, Ḥoshen Mishpat* 420, at the beginning of the *siman*; and Karo, *Shulḥan Arukh, Ḥoshen Mishpat* 420:1.

112 There is some ambiguity as to the connotation of being considered a "sinner" in this context. The commentators are troubled by the fact that the Talmud quotes R. Ḥanina's opinion, that such a person is designated a "sinner," after citing the opinion of R. Simeon ben Lakish, who had already designated him as being a *rasha*. The appellation *rasha* seems to be a *much* stronger form of censure than "sinner." It would therefore seem incongruous with the normal aggadic style of the Talmud—of proceeding progressively, by first teaching what is less novel (i.e., most obvious), and then teaching what is more novel (less obvious)—for the Gemara to first condemn the threat of physical violence with the stronger reproach, of being a *rasha*, and then cite the weaker reproach, of being a sinner, which should be self-evident in that the person was already categorized as a *rasha*. To resolve this issue, some commentators suggest that in certain contexts, such as this gemara, the term "sinner" may actually refer to a worse type of person than the term *rasha*. See Judah Loew ben Bezalel, *Ḥidushe Agadot Maharal mi-Prag*, vol. 3 (Jerusalem: n.p., 1972), *Sanhedrin* 58b; Jacob Joseph of Polonoye, *Toldot Ya'akov Yosef* (Jerusalem: Ha-Mesorah, 2010), *parashat Emor*, p. 521; and Epstein, *Barukh She-amar, Pirke Avot* 1:8, p. 36. Cf. Joseph Ḥayyim ben Elijah al Ḥakam, *Sefer Ben Yehoyada* (Jerusalem: Yitsḥak Bakal, 1965), *Sanhedrin* 58b; and *Yalkut Shemoni*, 1 Samuel, *remez* 85 (where R. Ḥanina's opinion is quoted before that of R. Simeon ben Lakish's).

113 Rashi, *Sanhedrin* 58b, s.v. *im lo lakaḥti ve-ḥazekah*. See also Shemaryahu Yosef Berman, *Sefer Birkat Shai al Masekhet Sanhedrin* (Bnei Brak: Berman, 2002), 242; and Ya'akov Yeshayahu Bloi, *Pitḥe Ḥoshen*, 8 vols. (Jerusalem: Yeshivat Ohel Moshe Diskin, 1982–), vol. 5, p. 35 n. 4.

The Talmud then cites R. Huna (third century CE) as stating that "His hand [i.e., of the one who raises his hand against another] should be 'cut off.'" There are some commentators who point out that a similar expression, that one's hand should be "cut off," appears elsewhere in the Talmud (*Niddah* 13a–b) as a curse that is invoked against someone.[114] Alternatively, a number of commentators propose that in this context having a hand "cut off" should be understood as a talmudic idiom for the imposition of a monetary fine, as the term is used elsewhere (see *Sifre, Ki Tetse, piska* 293 and *Bava Kamma* 28a, in explanation of Deut. 25:12).[115] (As to the possibility that R. Huna meant that the person's hand should literally be cut off, see footnote.)[116]

In later generations, a *ḥerem* (ban of excommunication) was also imposed, in all probability by R. Gershom ben Judah Me'or ha-Golah

---

114 See Berman, *Sefer Birkat Shai*, 242; Yitsḥak Arieli, *Enayim la-Mishpat* (Jerusalem: Ha-Ivri, 1971), *Sanhedrin* 58b (the third explanation); and see Samuel Schotten, *Kos ha-Yeshuot* [Podgórze, Poland: M. Traube, 1903], *Sanhedrin* 58b (whose explanation of the gemara may lend support to such an interpretation).

115 Ḥananel ben Ḥushiel, *Otsar ha-Geonim le-Masekhet Sanhedrin* (Jerusalem: Mossad Harav Kook, 1966), *Likute Perush Rabenu Ḥananel, Sanhedrin* 58b, p. 552; Menaḥem Meiri, *Bet ha-Beḥirah al Masekhet Sanhedrin* (Jerusalem: Kedem, 1965), *Sanhedrin* 58b (second explanation); and Meir Abulafia, *Ḥidushe ha-Ramah al Masekhet Sanhedrin* (Jerusalem: n.p., 1999), *Sanhedrin* 58b (second explanation, which he questions). See also Schotten, *Kos ha-Yeshuot, Sanhedrin* 58b (which may also lend support to this explanation, as well as the first; see previous footnote).

116 Even though the Gemara subsequently states that there was a case in which R. Huna "cut" someone's hand off, which is understood literally as referring to actually amputating a hand, by a number of major commentators (see below, cf. the commentators cited in the previous footnote), it does not appear that when R. Huna had said that one who raises his hand against another "his hand should be cut off," he meant that this should be taken literally and carried out in practice. This is evident from a talmudic passage in *Bava Kamma* (37a, which relates how R. Huna fined a person a sum of money when that person had hit someone) and from the commentators who point out that R. Huna only implemented his ruling in practice due to the unique circumstances of the case he was dealing with. See, for example, Rashi *Sanhedrin* 58b, s.v. *kats yada* (who explains R. Huna's implementing his ruling as an extralegal measure for dealing with a perpetrator who had become accustomed to committing violent acts); Tosafot, *Sanhedrin* 58b, s.v. *kats yada* (who, similar to Rashi, write that R. Huna was dealing with a recidivist, violent offender); Yom Tov ben Abraham Ishbili, cited in Ḥayyim Benveniste, *Ḥamra ve-Ḥaye* [Jerusalem: S. L. A., 1988], *Sanhedrin* 58b (who states that such a punishment could only be imposed in a case in which a "prestigious court," made up of "great sages," after "extensive deliberation," determines that it is necessary); and Solomon ben Adret, *She'elot u-Teshuvot ha-Rashba*, 8 vols. (Jerusalem: Mekhon Or ha-Mizraḥ, Mekhon Yerushalayim, 1997–2001), vol. 5, responsum 238.

(c. 960–1028),[117] as a method of enforcing the prohibition against physical violence.[118] Based on the talmudic passage that was cited above, rabbinic authorities ruled that a person who strikes another should be subject to monetary fines,[119] could be reported to the gentile authorities,[120] and subjected to other forms of coercion until he abstains from any further violence.[121] They also ruled that if one merely raises his hand to another, he should be categorized as a *rasha* and be disqualified from serving as a witness and from being able to swear in a court case.[122] In addition to all of the above, one who assaulted another also had a halakhic obligation to compensate the person for (1) permanent physical damage, (2) pain suffered,

---

117 Israel Schepansky, "*Takanot Rabenu Gershom Me'or ha-Golah,*" *Ha-Dorom* 22 (1966): 111, 114. Idem, *Ha-Takanot be-Yisrael,* vol. 4, *Takanot ha-Kehilot,* 96–97.

118 Schepansky, "*Takanot Rabenu Gershom,*" 109. In reference to this ban, R. Moses Isserles quotes R. Menaḥem of Merseburg (first half of the fourteenth century) as writing that "There was a ban from the early sages placed upon one who hits his friend. The community must first release him from this 'ban of sinfulness' before he can be counted in a *minyan* of ten people (the requisite quorum for public worship) … [He is released from the ban] only on the condition that he will accept upon himself everything that the court will want [to impose upon him]." Moses Isserles, *Darkhe Mosheh ha-Shalem al Tur Ḥoshen ha-Mishpat,* vol. 2 (Jerusalem: Mekhon Yerushalayim, 1983), *siman* 620, p. 248; idem, *Shulḥan Arukh, Ḥoshen Mishpat,* 420:1; and Menaḥem of Merseburg, *Nimuke Menaḥem Mirzburk,* in *She'elot u-Teshuvot ve-Hilkhot Sheḥitah u-Vedikah ve-Ḥidushe Dinim,* by Jacob Weil (Jerusalem: Yisrael Wolf, 1959), 172–73.

119 See, for example, Jacob ben Meir (*Rabenu Tam*), cited in Meir ben Baruch of Rothenburg, *Sifre She'elot u-Teshuvot Piske Dinim u-Minhagim Maharam mi-Rotenburg,* vol. 4, Prague edition (Bnei Brak: Ha-Sifriyah ha-Ḥaredit ha-Olomit, 1999), p. 159b; Jacob Weil, *She'elot u-Teshuvot Rabenu Ya'akov Vail,* vol. 1, annotated by Yonatan Shraga Domb (Jerusalem: Mekhon Yerushalayim, 2001), responsum 28, p. 39; and Solomon ben Adret, *She'elot u-Teshuvot ha-Rashba,* vol. 3, responsum 393.

120 Menaḥem of Merseburg, *Nimuke Menaḥem Mirzburk,* p. 174; Meir ben Baruch of Rothenburg, *She'elot u-Teshuvot,* vol. 4, Prague edition (Bnei Brak: Ha-Sifriyah ha-Ḥaredit ha-Olomit, 1999), p. 160a; Isserles, *Shulḥan Arukh, Ḥoshen Mishpat* 388:7; Shabbetai ben Meir ha-Kohen, *Sifte Kohen, Ḥoshen Mishpat,* 388:45; Elijah ben Solomon, [*Be'ure*] *Ha-Gra al Shulḥan Arukh,* in the standard printed edition of the *Shulḥan Arukh, Ḥoshen Mishpat* 388:7; and Bloi, *Sefer Pitḥe Ḥoshen,* vol. 5, 141–43.

121 Weil, *She'elot u-Teshuvot Rabenu Ya'akov Vail,* p. 38; Solomon Luria, *Yam shel Shelomoh* (Jerusalem: Mishnat David, 1995), *Bava Kamma* chap. 8:63; and Isserles, *Shulḥan Arukh, Even ha-Ezer* 154:3 (in reference to domestic violence).

122 Mordecai ben Hillel ha-Kohen, *Sefer Mordekhai,* in the standard Vilna edition of the Babylonian Talmud, *Bava Kamma, siman* 102–3; Joseph Karo, *She'elot u-Teshuvot Bet Yosef* (Jerusalem: Tiferet ha-Torah, 1960), *Dine Kidushin,* responsum 2, pp. 10–11; and Isserles, *Shulḥan Arukh, Ḥoshen Mishpat* 34:4.

(3) medical expenses, (4) loss of income, and (5) humiliation suffered (see *Bava Kamma* 83b and *Shulḥan Arukh, Ḥoshen Mishpat* 420:3).[123]

Even in cases when one is being physically attacked, and it is therefore halakhically permitted to respond with physical force in self-defense, according to the *Shulḥan Arukh* one is still required to maintain enough self-control so as not to inflict greater harm than is necessary to protect oneself.[124] R. David ben Samuel ha-Levi (*Taz*, 1586–c. 1667) and other authorities were of the opinion that the *Shulḥan Arukh's* requirement to exhibit self-control also obligates one who finds oneself in a fistfight to desist *immediately* from using physical force once the threat of physical violence ceases.[125]

Commandments Prohibiting Verbal Abuse—The Prohibitions against Saying Things That Are Hurtful/Embarrassing and Cursing Someone

There are two biblical commandments that focus on what may be designated as "verbal abuse"[126]: "You shall not hurt one another"

123 As to the details of these (and other) forms of compensation for assaulting someone, see *Shulḥan Arukh, Ḥoshen Mishpat, siman* 420, with commentaries. As to whether a rabbinic court is empowered to collect these types of compensation in modern times, see *Bava Kamma* 84b; *Shulḥan Arukh, Ḥoshen Mishpat* 1:2; and Jehiel Michal Epstein, *Arukh ha-Shulḥan* (n.p., n.d.), *Ḥoshen Mishpat* 1:3.

124 Karo, *Shulḥan Arukh, Ḥoshen Mishpat* 421:13. R. Jacob ben Asher (c. 1269–c. 1340) cites the opinion of his father, R. Asher ben Jehiel (1250–1327), that this is comparable to the law set down in *Sanhedrin* (74a) regarding someone who is pursuing another with the intent to kill him. Even though it is permissible to kill the pursuer in order to save the victim, one is obligated to try to only physically disable him and avoid the use of excessive force. Jacob ben Asher, *Arba'ah Turim, Ḥoshen Mishpat* 421.

125 David ben Samuel ha-Levi, *Ture Zahav*, in the standard edition of the *Shulḥan Arukh, Ḥoshen Mishpat* 421:13. See also Moses ben Joseph Trani, *She'elot u-Teshuvot Rabenu Moshe bar Yosef mi-Trani* (Jerusalem: Yad ha-Rav Nissim, 1990), responsum 311; Joseph ben Moses Trani, *She'elot u-Teshuvot Maharit*, vol. 2 (Tel Aviv: Sifriyati, 1959), responsum 29, p. 57; Joel Sirkes, *Bayit Ḥadash*, in the standard printed edition of the *Arba'ah Turim, siman* 421, s.v. *shenayim*; and Shneur Zalman of Lyady, *Shulḥan Arukh ha-Rav* (Brooklyn: Kehot, 1968), *Ḥoshen Mishpat, Hilkhot Nizke ha-Guf* 2. Other authorities have a considerably more lenient opinion regarding this issue; see Joshua ben Alexander Falk, *Sefer Me'irat Enayim* (*Sma*), in the standard edition of the *Shulḥan Arukh, Ḥoshen Mishpat* 421:24; and Elijah ben Solomon, [*Be'ure*] *Ha-Gra, Ḥoshen Mishpat* 421:17.

126 As to how to exactly define the term "verbal abuse," and the ambiguity that surrounds it, see Grace H. Ketterman, *Verbal Abuse: Healing the Hidden Wound*

(literally, "A man shall not hurt his friend"; Leviticus 25:17)[127] and "You shall not bear sin because of him" (Leviticus 19:17).[128] According to the Talmud, the first verse prohibits one from saying anything that is hurtful to another individual (*Bava Metsia* 58b) and the second verse prohibits one from embarrassing another person (*Arakhin* 16b). The commandment that enjoins one from saying hurtful things, which is known in rabbinic literature as *ona'at devarim,* "distress of words," prohibits one from "saying things to someone that will hurt him and anger him" (Maimonides, *Sefer ha-Mitsvot,* negative commandment 251).[129] The commandment against embarrassing someone dictates "that we are prohibited from shaming one another" (Maimonides, *Sefer ha-Mitsvot,* negative commandment 303).[130] After a few short introductory comments on the overall rabbinic stance toward verbal abuse, we will examine the

---

(Ann Arbor, MI: Servant Publications, 1992), 12–13, 149. According to Ketterman, it is very difficult to establish a formal definition of verbal abuse. She describes how she herself "has sat in committees for hours trying to formulate statements that could be useful in such an effort." Ibid., 12.

127 In Hebrew, וְלֹא תוֹנוּ אִישׁ אֶת־עֲמִיתוֹ (*ve-lo tonu ish et amito*). There are various alternative translations for the Hebrew root of the word *tonu,* which I have translated as "hurt," for example, "annoy," "afflict," "wrong," "oppress," and so on. See G. Johannes Botterweck and Helmer Ringgren, eds., *The Theological Dictionary of the Old Testament,* 14 vols. (Grand Rapids: William B. Eerdsmans, 1974–), vol. 6, s.v. *"yānâ,"* p. 104.

128 In Hebrew, וְלֹא־תִשָּׂא עָלָיו חֵטְא (*ve-lo tisa alav ḥet*).

129 The entire phrase in the *Sefer ha-Mitsvot* reads as follows: "saying things to someone that will hurt him, and anger him, and he will not be able to stand [up against] because he will be embarrassed." For other versions of this text, see the footnotes in the Frankel edition of Maimonides' *Sefer ha-Mitsvot* (Jerusalem: Hotsa'at Shabse Frankel, 2001), p. 369. (Cf. the translation in Moses Maimonides, *Sefer ha-Mitsvot,* trans. Joseph Kafih [Jerusalem: Mossad Harav Kook, 1971], 300; and Ha-Levi, *Sefer ha-Ḥinukh,* commandment 338.) See also Kayara, *Sefer Halakhot Gedolot,* negative commandment 136, p. 48 n. 167; Moses ben Jacob, *Semag,* negative commandment 171; Eliezer ben Samuel, *Sefer Yere'im,* 180 (51); Isaac ben Joseph, *Semak,* 122; Ha-Levi, *Sefer ha-Ḥinukh,* commandment 338; Gerondi, *Sha'are Teshuvah* 3:24, 49, 214; and Maimonides, *Mishneh Torah, Mekhirah* 14:12–14, 18.

130 Alternatively, "that we are prohibited from embarrassing one another" (see below, p. 160). My translation is based on Maimonides, *Sefer ha-Mitsvot,* trans. Joseph Kafih, p. 322. For the word I have translated as "shaming," Maimonides uses the Judeo-Arabic word אכ‘ג‘אל, which, according to R. Kafih, is derived from the Arabic term خجل and apparently indicates intense embarrassment. Maimonides, *Sefer ha-Mitsvot,* trans. Joseph Kafih, p. 322 n. 75; and Maimonides, *Mishnah im Perush ha-Rambam,* trans. Joseph Kafih, 7 vols. (Jerusalem: Mossad Harav Kook, 1963), vol. 3, p. 424 n. 16, 380 n. 12, 433 n. 23.

parameters of these prohibitions, and then subsequently compare and contrast them, thereby highlighting the unique function of each one. This section will conclude with a brief discussion of the prohibition against cursing someone.

The Rabbinic Stance toward Verbal Abuse

The all too often routine acceptance and callous indifference with which people insult and say hurtful things to each other, especially when they are involved in a conflict, stands in stark contrast to how the Rabbis viewed this type of behavior. Indicative of their extremely negative view of these forms of verbal abuse are such rabbinic pronouncements as

> All [sins] are punished through an intermediary [of God] except for distress [of words].
>
> All the [heavenly] gates are locked[131] except for the gates [through which pass the cries] of [one who suffers from] distress [of words].[132]

Correspondingly, we find that the *Shulḥan Arukh* denounces someone who insults and embarrasses people by declaring that he is "nothing more than an idiot, a wicked person, and arrogant."[133]

---

131 R. Abraham Ḥayyim Schor (d. 1632) explains that this does not mean that the petitions of others are not answered; rather, they are not answered as readily as those of one who has suffered from *ona'at devarim*. Abraham Ḥayyim Schor, *Torat Ḥayim* (Jerusalem: n.p., 1969), *Bava Metsia* 59a, p. 65, quoted in Adin Steinsaltz, *Talmud Bavli im Kol ha-Mefarshim al ha-Daf im Hosafot Ḥadashot* (Jerusalem: Ha-Mekhon ha-Yisraeli le-Firsumim Talmudiyim, 1998), *Bava Metsia* 59a; see also Maimonides, *Mishneh Torah, Mekhirah* 14:18.

132 See *Bava Metsia* 59a (where the order of these two sayings is reversed); in conjunction with Rashi, *Bava Metsia* 59a, s.v. *ḥuts me-sha'are ona'ah*; Eliezer ben Samuel, *Sefer Yere'im*, 180 (51); Moses ben Jacob, *Semag*, negative commandment 171; and Maimonides, *Mishneh Torah, Mekhirah* 14:18.

133 Karo, *Shulḥan Arukh, Ḥoshen Mishpat* 420:39; based on Jacob ben Asher, *Arba'ah Turim, Ḥoshen Mishpat* 420, towards the end of the *siman*; and Maimonides, *Mishneh Torah, Ḥovel u-Mazik* 3:7.

The Rabbis found public embarrassment particularly abominable and execrated such behavior in no uncertain terms:

> It is better for a person to throw himself into a fiery furnace than to embarrass his friend in public.[134]

> Anyone who embarrasses his friend in public has no share in the world to come (see footnote).[135]

> All those who descend into Gehenna [Hell] will [right away][136] ascend except for three who descend and will not ascend [right away] ... [and one of these three is] someone who embarrasses his friend in public.[137]

We also find sanctions and fines imposed by rabbinic authorities in an attempt to discourage people from insulting and embarrassing others.[138] For example, R. Asher ben Jehiel (*Rosh*, 1250–1327) cites R. Sherira ben Ḥanina Gaon (c. 906–c. 1006) who writes that a ban of excommunication is imposed on one who embarrasses another, until such time that the person appeases him (the offended party) in

---

134 *Berakhot* 43b; *Ketubot* 67b; *Sotah* 10b. We also find the statement, "Anyone who embarrasses his friend in public, it is as if he has shed blood" (*Bava Metsia* 58b). See also Tosafot, *Sotah* 10b, s.v. *no'aḥ lo*; and Gerondi, *Sha'are Teshuvah*, 3:139.

135 *Pirke Avot* 3:11; *Sanhedrin* 99a. According to Maimonides, this is only the case if someone does this on a regular basis (Maimonides, *Mishneh Torah, Teshuvah* 3:14). Maimonides in his commentary to tractate *Sanhedrin* writes that one who embarrasses another in public has no share in the world to come because he has "a soul of inferior quality that does not have integrity and is not worthy for the world to come" (Maimonides, introduction to the tenth chapter of *Sanhedrin*, in the standard Vilna edition of the Babylonian Talmud, *Sanhedrin* 124a, first col., three lines before *Ha-Yesod ha-Rishon*); cited in Feldman, *The Right and the Good*, 15–16. Regarding this teaching, see the noteworthy comment of Abraham Danzig, *Bet Avraham* (Vilna: Yosef Reuven Rom, 1847), section 20, p. 11a.

136 See *Tosafot, Bava Metsia* 58b, s.v. *ḥuts me-g'*; cf. Menaḥem Azariah da Fano, *Sefer Asarah Ma'amarot* (Jerusalem: Mekhon Yismaḥ Lev, 2000), *Ḥikur Din* 3:16, p. 224.

137 *Bava Metsia* 58b.

138 See Isserles, *Darkhe Mosheh*, vol. 2, 249–51; and the commentators to *Shulḥan Arukh, Ḥoshen Mishpat* 420:38.

an appropriate fashion (*le-fi kevodo,* in accordance with the dignity of the person he had insulted).[139]

The severity with which the Rabbis dealt with verbal abuse can be understood both in terms of its adverse social/communal effects and out of concern for the emotional suffering of the individual victim— "because this is very difficult for the human heart [to bear]" (*Sefer ha-Ḥinukh, "The Book of Education,"* traditionally ascribed to R. Aaron ha-Levi of Barcelona, c. 1235–c. 1300),[140] this "rip[s] apart his heart" (R. Eleazar ben Judah of Worms, c. 1165–c. 1230),[141] or, in the words of the Bible, "There is one who speaks [and it is] like the piercing of a sword" (Proverbs 12:18).[142] In all likelihood, the rabbinic stance toward verbal abuse also stems from the perspective that every insult hurled against another human being is, in essence, an affront to God himself. This perspective would be based on the concept that every human being is created in the image of God (and, as we saw on p. 129, is therefore beloved by God). In the words of the Midrash: "If you have done this [to belittle another human being], be cognizant of whom you are disgracing—'He made him [man] in the likeness of God' (Gen. 5:1)."[143]

---

139 Asher ben Jehiel, *Rabenu Asher, Bava Kamma, perek Ha-Ḥovel* 15. Another example would be the opinion that is cited by R. Mordecai ben Hillel (c. 1240–1298) that even if one testifies that someone had said something (extremely) hurtful to him and there are witnesses that support his claim, the person who said the hurtful thing should be flogged. Mordecai ben Hillel ha-Kohen, *Sefer ha-Mordekhai, Bava Metsia, perek Ha-Zahav* 306 (cf. Maimonides, *Mishnah im Perush ha-Rambam,* trans. Kafih, *Makkot,* chap. 3, p. 236; Meir ben Baruch of Rothenburg, *She'elot u-Teshuvot Maharam BR' Barukh,* "Prague-Budapest edition" [Budapest: Y. Shternberg, 1895], responsum 785; Ha-Kohen, *Sefer Ḥafets Ḥayim, petiḥah, lavin, Be'er Mayim Ḥayim* 17).

140 Ha-Levi, *Sefer ha-Ḥinukh,* commandment 338.

141 Eleazar ben Judah of Worms, *Sefer Moreh Ḥata'im,* in *Kol Bo,* vol. 4, (Jerusalem: D. Avraham, 1993), *siman* 66, p. 214, quoted in Epstein, *Mitzvot ha-Shalom,* 184.

142 Quoted by R. Joshua Falk (*Sma, Ḥoshen Mishpat* 420:48), in explaining the opinion cited by R. Mordecai ben Hillel ha-Kohen (see above, n. 139).

143 *Genesis Rabbah* 24:7. See Epstein, *Mitzvot ha-Shalom,* 29–30, n. 23; Feldman, *The Right and the Good,* 17 (citing Heller, *Tosafot Yom Tov, Pirke Avot* 3:11); Lebovitch, *Da'at Ḥokhmah u-Musar,* vol. 3, *ma'amar* 33, p. 63; and Soloveitchik, *Yeme Zikaron,* 9.

Ona'at Devarim—The Prohibition against Saying Things That Are Hurtful

Rashi, in a number of places, defines *ona'at devarim* as "provoking," or "vexing," someone (see his commentary to Exodus 22:20, Leviticus 25:17, and Isaiah 49:26).[144] An alternative, and slightly lengthier, definition of *ona'at devarim*, which one periodically encounters in contemporary halakhic works, is that of the *Sefer ha-Ḥinukh*. Basing himself on the wording of Maimonides in his *Sefer ha-Mitsvot* (cited above, p. 151), the author of the *Sefer ha-Ḥinukh*, explains *ona'at devarim* as encompassing

> words that will hurt him and cause him pain, for which he will be unable to defend himself ...[145] [the laws of which require that one] not cause pain to human beings in any way and not to embarrass them."[146]

Two alternative, noteworthy definitions are offered by R. Moses Zacuto (1625–1697) and R. Judah Loew of Prague, the *Maharal* of Prague (1525–1609). R. Zacuto defines the Hebrew noun *ona'ah* as an act of "forcibly stealing" something; therefore, he interprets *ona'at devarim* (literally, "*ona'ah* of words")[147] as encompassing *genevat ha-kavod ve-ḥamisat ha-ratson*, "stealing away [the other person's] dignity and robbing [his] will [with one's words]."[148] The *Maharal*

---

144 Rashi in his commentary to Exodus (22:20) translates *ona'ah* in French as *contrarier* (alternatively, *contralier*; see Moshe Catane, "*Ha-Le'azim be-Rashi*," in *Da'at Mikra: Shemot*, vol. 1 [Jerusalem: Mossad Harav Kook, 1991], p. 51 n. 25). For the exact meaning of this word, see Raphael Levy, *Contribution à la Lexicographie Française selon d'Anciens Textes d'Origine Juive* (Syracuse, NY: Syracuse University Press, 1960), s.v. "*contraliement*," p. 214.

145 For an explanation of the significance of the phrase "for which he will be unable to defend himself," see Shemuel Vozner, *Shevet ha-Levi*, 3rd ed., 10 vols. (n.p., 2002), vol. 8, responsum 309:5, p. 276, vol. 5, *Kuntres ha-Mitsvot*, *siman* 51, p. 283.

146 Ha-Levi, *Sefer ha-Ḥinukh*, commandment 338. See also Jonah ben Abraham Gerondi, *Sha'are Teshuvah* 3:24.

147 As a feminine Hebrew noun in the construct state, the word *ona'ah* becomes *ona'at*.

148 Moses Zacuto, *Sefer Kol ha-Remez* (Moshav Bitḥah, Israel: Mekhon Kol Bitḥah, 1999), *Bava Metsia* 4:10, p. 51; quoted in David Ari'av, *Le-Re'akha kamokha*, 9 vols. (Jerusalem: Mekhon Le-Re'akha kamokha, 2000–), vol. 3, 19–20 n. 2.

explains it as "[when] another person is considered insignificant and anything relating to him is viewed as lowly, inferior, and is looked down upon, and he says to him things that lead him to realize that he is considered insignificant."[149]

The talmudic discourse on *ona'at devarim* and the major halakhic codes offer a number of examples of *ona'at devarim* from which there are indications that an *exact* halakhic definition of *ona'at devarim* may be considerably more complex than any of the aforementioned explanations (for the examples that the Talmud cites, see footnote).[150] The one common denominator that all of the examples of *ona'at devarim* that appear in the Talmud and major halakhic codes seem to share is that they all deal with situations in which someone says

---

149 Judah Loew ben Bezalel, *Sifre Maharal mi-Prag* (Bnei Brak: Yahadut, 1999), *Bava Metsia* 58b, pp. 21–22. Two other alternative noteworthy definitions are those of R. Aaron ibn Ḥayim (1545–1632) and R. Moshe Ḥayyim Luzzatto (1707–1747). R. Aaron ibn Ḥayim understands *ona'at devarim* as a duplicitous show of good intentions (Aaron ibn Ḥayyim, *Sefer Korban Aharon: Ve-Hu Perush le-Sefer Sifra*, vol. 2 [Jerusalem: n.p., 1969], *Behar, perek* 4, p. 273a); and R. Moshe Ḥayyim Luzzatto equates it with embarrassing someone (Moshe Ḥayyim Luzzatto, *Sefer Mesilat Yesharim* [Jerusalem: Mosad Haskel, 1979], chap. 11, p. 82 n). See also Epstein, *Mitzvot ha-Shalom*, 179–253. Cf. Shaul Gabai, "*Be-Geder Ona'at Devarim,*" *Torat ha-Adam le-Adam: Kovets Torani ba-Mitsvot she-ben Adam la-Ḥavero* 4 (2002): 203–5; and Barukh Moshe Kubin, "*Be-Inyan Ona'at Devarim,*" *Torat ha-Adam le-Adam: Kovets Torani ba-Mitsvot she-ben Adam la-Ḥavero* 4 (2002): 206–10.

150 The Mishnah gives the following three examples: "One should not say [to a merchant] 'How much does this item cost,' if he is not interested in purchasing it"; "If someone has [sinned and] repented, one should not say to him 'Remember your former deeds'"; and "If someone is a child of converts, one should not say to him 'Remember the deeds of your forefathers.'" The Gemara then cites a *baraita* that adds the following examples: "If someone is a convert and has come to study Torah, one should not say to him 'A mouth that has partaken of carrion, animals possessing mortal defects, abominations, and creeping things [i.e., non-kosher food] is coming to study the Torah, which was said over by the mouth of the Almighty?'"; "If one is suffering, sick, or if he has had children who have died, one should not say to him something similar to that which the friends of Job said to him: 'Your fear [of God] should give you confidence, and the integrity of your ways should give you hope. Please consider, does there exist such a thing that a truly innocent person is ever [totally] lost.'"; "If donkey-drivers ask him about acquiring grain, one should not say to them 'go to so-and-so who sells grain,' when he knows that that person has never sold [grain]"; and "Rabbi Judah said: 'One should not even 'attach his eyes to' [examine] merchandise when he has no money'" (*Bava Metsia* 58b). An explanation of the significance and novelty of each of these examples goes beyond the scope of the present work. For an analysis of these examples as they appear in the halakhic codes, see Kaminsky, "Traditional Jewish Perspectives," 356–66.

something to another person that would normally upset the average person to some (unspecified) degree.

The Intensity and Duration of the Distress. Rabbi J. David Bleich contends that *ona'at devarim* is totally independent of the subjective level of emotional pain that the individual who it is directed towards (i.e., the person on the receiving end) experiences; instead, it is solely dependent on whether the speaker exhibits disrespect towards the other person. By merely saying something that bespeaks one's perception of another as being insignificant, one may violate the prohibition. In conjunction with various arguments in support of this view, R. Bleich cites the definition of the *Maharal* of Prague, mentioned above, that *ona'at devarim* occurs when one person views another as "insignificant" and subsequently says something to that person that allows him to realize this.[151] Even though he does not mention R. Zacuto, whose definition focuses on "stealing away [the other person's] dignity," at one point R. Bleich explains *ona'at devarim* in an almost identical fashion to that of R. Zacuto.

The *Ḥafets Ḥayim*, however, was apparently of the opinion that one must induce *some* degree of emotional distress or discomposure in the other person for it to be considered a violation of this prohibition. This can be inferred from the fact that the *Ḥafets Ḥayim* combines the definitions of Maimonides[152] and the *Sefer ha-Ḥinukh* cited earlier, and defines *ona'at devarim* as "words that anger and confound him, and for which he will not be able to defend himself."[153]

Assuming that there must be some degree of discomposure present for a statement to be considered a violation of the commandment (in accordance with what appears to be the *Ḥafets Ḥayim*'s opinion, and not like R. Bleich), the question of the *duration* of the discomposure becomes relevant. Is there some minimum duration of time for how long the verbally induced pain must last, or does one violate the

151 J. David Bleich, "*Ona'at Devarim*," *Ha-Dorom* 35 (1972): 140–43.

152 From the wording that the *Ḥafets Ḥayim* employs, it is evident that he was using one of the popular printed editions of Maimonides' *Sefer ha-Mitsvot*. When I quoted Maimonides earlier, I used the Frankel edition (see above, p. 151 n. 129), which has a slightly different wording for negative commandment 251.

153 Ha-Kohen, *Sefer Ḥafets Ḥayim*, *petiḥah*, *lavin* 13.

halakhic prohibition even if there is only some fleeting emotional pain that is suffered? R. Abraham Isaiah Karelitz (1878–1953) certainly seems to be of the latter opinion. In one of his letters, in the midst of exhorting someone to be careful with his interpersonal relationships, he comments that "one must be careful not to cause pain to his friend [even] with a simple little utterance, *even for a moment* [emphasis mine], for there is a biblical prohibition regarding this, as they [the Sages] have stated at the end of chapter *Ha-Zahav* [the fourth chapter in tractate *Bava Metsia,* in which the topic of *ona'at devarim* is discussed].[154]
(As to the question of saying hurtful things for a constructive purpose, such as when one is attempting to resolve an interpersonal conflict, see p. 163.)

The Prohibition against Embarrassing Someone

The Rabbis in tractate *Arakhin* (16b) derive the prohibition against embarrassing someone from the second half of Leviticus 19:17, which reads: "You shall surely reprove your friend, *and you shall not bear sin because of him*":

> "You shall surely reprove [your friend]" ... One might have assumed that [you may reprove the person] even if [it is to

154 Abraham Isaiah Karelitz, *Kovets Igrot me-et Maran Ba'al Ḥazon Ish,* vol. 1 (Bnei Brak: S. Grainiman, 1990), letter 211, p. 192, quoted in Avraham Dov Levin, ed., *Piske Din mi-Bet ha-Din le-Dine Mamonot ule-Virur Yahadut shel ha-Rabanut ha-Rashit le-Yerushalayim,* vol. 5 (Jerusalem: Ha-Mo'atsah ha-Datit Yerushalayim, 1998), 175(b); Mordekhai Potash, "*Kuntres Ona'at Devarim,*" in *Sefer Darkhe Shalom: Ve-Kuntres Ona'at Devarim* (Jerusalem: n.p., 1993), 3; and Ari'av, *Le-Re'akha kamokha,* vol. 3, 53 n. 81, 317. It is interesting to note that R. Judah ben Samuel (c. 1150–1217), in his pietistic work *Sefer Ḥasidim,* writes in reference to a talmudic passage in *Ḥagigah* (5a)—which warns against doing anything in front of another person that he might find disgusting, such as killing a bug or spitting on the floor—that "one may be exempt from guilt by human legal standards, but he will be guilty by the standards of Heaven, even if this is an *infinitesimal* amount of distress. For every single instance of causing distress to one's friend, one will be punished by Heaven." Judah ben Samuel, *Sefer Ḥasidim* (Jerusalem: Mossad Harav Kook, 2002), *siman* 44, p. 103, quoted in Hillel D. Litwack, *Kuntres Sha'are Ona'ah* (Brooklyn: Oraḥ Mesharim, 1979), 7; and Ari'av, *Le-Re'akha kamokha,* vol. 3, 53 n. 81. For further discussion of the degree of suffering necessary to violate the prohibition, see Ari'av, *Le-Re'akha kamokha,* vol. 3, pp. 314–17; and Epstein, *Mitzvot ha-Shalom,* 232–34.

> the extent that] his face changes [color] [i.e., he will be embarrassed], therefore the verse states "and you shall not bear sin because of him."[155]

This talmudic passage is interpreting the verse in Leviticus as follows: "You shall surely reprove your friend," that one is required to reprove his friend for a misdeed, but, in the course of doing so, one still must be careful not to embarrass him and thereby "bear sin because of him."

R. Moses ben Jacob of Coucy (thirteenth century) explains the broader implication of this passage:

> If the Torah is concerned about not embarrassing someone in the course of reproof [for a wrongdoing], how much more so not in the course of reproof [when he has not done anything wrong]. [156]

That means to say that if a person is prohibited from embarrassing someone even when the other person has committed some misdeed, for which he deserves to be reprimanded, yet even in such a case the Torah prohibits one from embarrassing him, it follows ("how much more so") that one is certainly prohibited from embarrassing an innocent person who has not committed any type of misdeed.

There is a basic aspect of this prohibition that deserves some clarification. The Talmud in the passage cited above uses the terminology "his face changes [color]" (*panav mishtanim*)[157] when it refers to embarrassing someone. Even though this may possibly be understood as saying that the face of the one who is embarrassed must literally

155 *Arakhin* 16b; and *Sifra, Kedoshim, perek* 4:8.

156 Moses ben Jacob, *Semag*, negative commandment 6. See also Kayara, *Sefer Halakhot Gedolot*, negative commandment 99, p. 43; Maimonides, *Sefer ha-Mitsvot*, negative commandment 303; Eliezer ben Samuel, *Sefer Yere'im ha-Shalem*, 195 (39); Isaac ben Joseph, *Semak*, 126; Ha-Levi, *Sefer ha-Ḥinukh*, commandment 240; Gerondi, *Sha'are Teshuvah*, 3:24, 49, 214; and Maimonides, *Mishneh Torah, De'ot* 6:8.

157 This is the wording of the Gemara according to the emendation of Bezalel Ashkenazi, *Shitah Mekubetset*, in the standard Vilna edition of the Babylonian Talmud, *Arakhin* 16b n. 6. The order of the wording is switched in the text of the Vilna edition [*mishtanim panav*]; however, the meaning is the same.

change color (which may require a relatively strong level of embarrassment) for one to have transgressed the commandment,[158] this does not seem to be the view of Maimonides. When Maimonides (whose opinion regarding this halakhah is cited by the *Ḥafets Ḥayim*)[159] discusses this prohibition, in a number places, he does not at any point specify that one's face must actually change color to transgress the commandment.[160] The prohibition simply entails that one not "shame" (*le-hakhlim*) or "embarrass" (*le-vayesh*) the other person.[161] The implication is that Maimonides understands the phrase "his face changes [color]" simply as a talmudic idiom for a state of embarrassment or humiliation, and not as an additional necessary condition in order for one to have violated the prohibition. This is the basic conclusion that is reached by R. Jeroham Fishel Perla (1846–1934), R. Yehudah Henkin, and R. David Ariav.[162] It appears that this is also the view of the *Ḥafets Ḥayim*, who after quoting the words of the Gemara, which seem to require that one's face literally change color, immediately qualifies this and writes, "This means to say that he becomes embarrassed. I have [herein] employed the terminology of the Talmud in *Arakhin.*" The *Ḥafets Ḥayim*, apparently, means to dispel the possibility of taking the expression "his face changes" literally, and is saying that all one needs to do to violate the commandment is to simply embarrass the person, even without any external facial indication that he has done so.[163]

Another basic point that deserves consideration in reference to this commandment is the fact that in most instances when the Talmud

158 See Moshe Rosmarin, *Sefer Devar Mosheh: Al Masekhet Horiyot, Masekhet Pirke Avot, Sugya de-Kiyum Shetarot* (Jerusalem: n.p., 1978), 213–14, quoted in Feldman, *The Right and the Good*, 6 n. 27.

159 Ha-Kohen, *Sefer Ḥafets Ḥayim, petiḥah, lavin, Be'er Mayim Ḥayim* 14.

160 See Maimonides, *Perush ha-Mishnayot, Avot* 3:11; Maimonides, *Sefer ha-Mitsvot*, negative commandment 303; and Maimonides, *Mishneh Torah, De'ot* 6:8, *Ḥovel u-Mazik* 3:7. In *De'ot* 6:8, Maimonides quotes the talmudic passage from *Arakhin* that mentions one's face changing color and then immediately goes on to explain that we learn from this the prohibition against "shaming" a fellow Jew.

161 In *De'ot*, he uses the word *le-hakhlim*; in the *Sefer ha-Mitsvot*, the word that is used is *le-vayesh*.

162 Perla, commentary to *Sefer ha-Mitsvot*, vol. 1, 341; Yehudah H. Henkin, *Sefer She'elot u-Teshuvot Bene Vanim*, vol. 1 (Jerusalem: n.p., 1981), responsum 41, pp. 139–40, quoted in Feldman, *The Right and the Good*, 6 n. 27; and Ari'av, *Le-Re'akha kamokha*, vol. 3, pp. 330–31.

163 Ha-Kohen, *Sefer Ḥafets Ḥayim, petiḥah, lavin, Be'er Mayim Ḥayim* 14.

discusses the prohibition of embarrassing someone, it specifically mentions embarrassing the person *in public*,[164] which may signify that the prohibition applies only in public. Rashi certainly seems to indicate that this is the case.[165] However, the talmudic discourse in *Arakhin* does not mention this as a necessary condition, which supports the opinion of Maimonides, who states clearly that the prohibition applies even in private.[166] In accordance with Maimonides' view, which is accepted by later *poskim* (halakhic authorities) as authoritative,[167] the repeated rabbinic emphasis on *public* embarrassment may just be seen as reflecting the Rabbis' recognition of and concern over the heightened sense of humiliation or mortification that a person experiences when embarrassed in public and, consequently, the greater deplorability of the sin,[168] which is accentuated by repeatedly mentioning public embarrassment.

---

164 For example, *Pirke Avot* 3:11; *Berakhot* 43b; *Ketubot* 67b; *Bava Metsia* 58b-59a; and *Sanhedrin* 99a.

165 Rashi comments: "'His face changes': That he reproves him in *public* ..." Rashi, *Arakhin* 16b, s.v. *u-fanav mishtanin*. R. Ḥayyim Benveniste and R. Shneur Zalman of Lyady take Rashi at face value and understand him as being of the opinion that the embarrassment must take place in public for it to be considered a violation of the commandment (Ḥayyim Benveniste, *Dina de-Ḥaye: Be'ur al Sefer ha-Semag*, [Jerusalem: Haktav Institute, 1997], vol. 1, negative commandment 6, pp. 26–27; and Shneur Zalman of Lyady, *Shulḥan Arukh ha-Rav, Oraḥ Ḥayim* 156:8). The *Ḥafets Ḥayim* suggests that Rashi is of the opinion that embarrassing someone in private is also prohibited and the only reason Rashi mentions embarrassing the person in public is because he wanted to discuss a clear-cut case (*milta di-fesika leh*) in which a person in normal circumstances would inevitably be embarrassed (Ha-Kohen, *Sefer Ḥafets Ḥayim, petiḥah, lavin, Be'er Mayim Ḥayim* 14). A close reading of R. Eliezer ben Samuel of Metz (*Sefer Yere'im ha-Shalem*, 195 [39]) lends support to the *Ḥafets Ḥayim*'s interpretation of Rashi. See also Isaac ben Joseph, *Semak*, 126; Perla, commentary to *Sefer ha-Mitsvot*, vol. 1, pp. 341–42; and Ḥayim Daniel Penso, *Sefer Shem Ḥadash*, vol. 1 (Jerusalem: n.p., 1848), commandment 39, p. 25b.

166 Maimonides, *Mishneh Torah*, De'ot 6:8; see also Moses ben Jacob, *Semag*, negative commandment 6.

167 See Joseph Teomim, *Peri Megadim, Eshel Avraham* 156; Shneur Zalman of Lyady, *Shulḥan Arukh ha-Rav, Oraḥ Ḥayim* 156:8; Ha-Kohen, *Sefer Ḥafets Ḥayim, petiḥah, lavin* 14, *Be'er Mayim Ḥayim* 14; Epstein, *Arukh ha-Shulḥan, Oraḥ Ḥayim* 156:10; and Feinstein, *Igrot Mosheh, Ḥoshen Mishpat* 2, responsum 66, p. 291.

168 This is reflected in the severity of the punishment. As pointed out above (p. 153), according to the Rabbis, as a result of public embarrassment one "has no share in the world to come." (See Teomim, *Peri Megadim, Eshel Avraham* 156; Perla, commentary to *Sefer ha-Mitsvot*, vol. 1, 342; and Feinstein, *Igrot Mosheh, Ḥoshen Mishpat* 2, responsum 66, p. 291.)

Comparing and Contrasting the Two Commandments

In comparing and contrasting the commandment that prohibits saying hurtful things with the commandment that prohibits embarrassing someone, one must address the question of the unique function of each and the fundamental differences that may exist between them. It is quite clear that it is possible for someone to say something hurtful to another person, yet at the same time not to embarrass him.[169] In such a case, one would transgress the prohibition of *ona'at devarim* but not the prohibition against embarrassing a person. However, it is not feasible for someone to embarrass another person without hurting him. Therefore, evidently, embarrassing someone would be proscribed by the prohibition against *ona'at devarim*, and for every instance when someone has embarrassed another person, he or she has transgressed two commandments—the prohibition against embarrassing a person and the prohibition against saying something hurtful. Therefore, the question must be raised as to whether there is actually any practical purpose the prohibition against embarrassing a person serves that is not already served by the prohibition against *ona'at devarim*.[170]

Both the *Ḥafets Ḥayim*[171] and R. Perla[172] propose that there is a very common case for which the prohibition against embarrassing a person would apply, but the prohibition against saying something hurtful would not. This would be when one is engaged in "*tokhaḥah*"—reproving a person for something the person has done.[173]

169 Embarrassment in this context should be understood as a painful emotion that is associated with a sense of shame and disgrace. For general source material on the topic of embarrassment, see William Sharkey, "Bibliography of Embarrassment Research," accessed November 11, 2016, www2.hawaii.edu/~sharkey/embarrassment/embarrassment_references.html.

170 This question is discussed in Ḥazan (1741–1820), *She'elot u-Teshuvot Ḥikre Lev*, vol. 6, *Yoreh De'ah*, responsum 80, p. 105.

171 Ha-Kohen, *Sefer Ḥafets Ḥayim, petiḥah, lavin, Be'er Mayim Ḥayim* 14.

172 Perla, commentary to *Sefer ha-Mitsvot*, vol. 1, 342.

173 The *Ḥafets Ḥayim* does not clearly spell out what I am attributing to him in this section. He writes as follows: "One who embarrasses [another] without a doubt also transgresses the prohibition of '[a man] shall not hurt [his friend, i.e., *ona'at devarim*],' since one who is embarrassed also feels pain; and this that the Torah writes [i.e., *finds it necessary to write*] 'You shall not bear sin because of him' [the prohibition against embarrassing another person] is because it wanted to juxtapose

In the course of reproving a person, which is something that we shall see (in Chapter 6) is mandated by the Torah, and is a central feature of Jewish interpersonal conflict resolution, there may be times when it will be simply impossible to avoid and one, by necessity, will have to say something disconcerting, causing some distress for the person on the receiving end of the reproof. In such instances, the prohibition of *ona'at devarim*, apparently, is not applicable (at least to some degree) according to the Torah while one is engaged in the "*tokhaḥic* dialogue" (*see footnote*).[174] On the other hand, when it comes to the prohibition against embarrassing a person, it is clear from the talmudic discourse in tractate *Arakhin*, which was cited earlier (see pp. 158–59), that even in the course of reproving someone, it is forbidden to embarrass him.[175] As we shall see in Chapter 6 (pp. 236–37 and 240–42), this conclusion may have a major impact on the halakhic procedure for negotiating interpersonal conflicts.

---

it to the law of reproof, so as to teach us that even in the course of reproof it is prohibited to embarrass [someone]." Ha-Kohen, *Sefer Ḥafets Ḥayim, petiḥah, lavin, Be'er Mayim Ḥayim* 14. The implication of this is that the prohibition against embarrassing someone is still operative even when one is engaged in *tokhaḥah*, whereas *ona'at devarim* (for some reason) is not (at least to some degree).

174 See Elḥanan Bunim Wasserman, *Sefer Kovets He'arot le-Masekhet Yevamot* (n.p., n.d.), *siman* 70 (where R. Wasserman discusses a number of interpersonal prohibitions that are not applicable in certain situations when one's actions serve a constructive purpose). R. Asher Weiss is of the opinion that this concept should be explained differently from the way I have explained it. According to R. Weiss, one cannot say that the prohibition of *ona'at devarim* is not applicable in the course of *tokhaḥah*. In his view, it most certainly is. However, the prohibition of *ona'at devarim* is dependent on the intent of the person who is saying the potentially hurtful thing. If one intends to insult or hurt the other party, then *ona'at devarim* is applicable. Therefore, in regard to *tokhaḥah*, when the person does not intend to insult or hurt the other party, there would be no prohibition of *ona'at devarim*. This is in contrast to the prohibition against embarrassing a person, which would nevertheless still be applicable. Asher Weiss, in a (brief) conversation with the author, November 19, 2016. Cf. Perla, commentary to *Sefer ha-Mitsvot*, vol. 1, 342 (where R. Perla offers an alternative explanation for why *ona'at devarim* is not applicable to *tokhaḥah*, which may not be relevant to most cases of interpersonal offenses). See also Hillel D. Litwack, *Kuntres Sha'are Ona'ah* (Brooklyn, NY: Oraḥ Mesharim, 1979), 17; and, below, Chapter 6, pp. 235–39.

175 Maimonides points out (*Mishneh Torah, De'ot* 6:8), this may only be true if one is dealing with an offense that is categorized as "between a man and his fellow man."

The Prohibition against Cursing Someone

Even though the halakhic prohibition against cursing someone may not necessarily be categorized as a prohibition against "verbal abuse" (see the discussion below), it is closely related to the concept, and it is highly pertinent to an understanding of the Jewish approach to interpersonal relations and conflict resolution. Therefore, in this section, we will discuss the source and basic parameters of the prohibition, and touch upon the underlying rationale that has been offered for it.

The first thing that needs to be stated clearly about the halakhic prohibition against cursing someone is that it has nothing to do with swearing, uttering profanities, or name-calling. The type of cursing that we are talking about in this context is the kind in which one verbally expresses a wish that some sort of misfortune or harm befalls someone.[176]

There is considerable debate as to the exact source for the prohibition (which all of the *mone ha-mitsvot* categorize as one of the 613 commandments).[177] Two talmudic passages seem to indicate that Leviticus 19:14, "You shall not curse a deaf person,"[178] is the source for the prohibition of cursing someone, even though that someone is not deaf.[179] Another talmudic passage indicates that Leviticus 19:14 taken in conjunction with other verses in the Torah that discuss cursing different types of individuals (i.e., a leader of the people [Exod. 22:27], a judge [ibid.], or one's father or mother

176 Price, *Mishnat Avraham al ha-Semag,* vol. 3, *mitzvah* 209–12, *ot* 3, pp. 144–45; Shemaryahu Yosef Ḥayim Kanevski, quoted in Ari'av, *Le-Re'akha kamokha,* vol. 1, 348; Aharon Bu'aron, *"Be-Geder Kelalah," Torat ha-Adam le-Adam: Kovets Torani ba-Mitsvot she-ben Adam la-Ḥavero* 4 (2001): 197–200; and Ari'av, *Le-Re'akha kamokha,* vol. 1, 210.

177 See, for example, Kayara, *Sefer Halakhot Gedolot,* vol. 3, negative commandment 111; Maimonides, *Sefer ha-Mitsvot,* negative commandment 317; Moses ben Jacob, *Semag,* negative commandment 211; Ha-Levi, *Sefer ha-Ḥinukh,* commandment 231; Eliezer ben Samuel, *Yere'im,* 189 (42); Isaac ben Joseph, *Semak,* 123; and Gerondi, *Sha'are Teshuvah,* 3:46.

178 In Hebrew, לֹא־תְקַלֵּל חֵרֵשׁ (*lo tekalel ḥeresh*).

179 *Shevuot* 36a, *Temurah* 4a. See Toviyahu ben Eliezer, *Midrash Lekaḥ Tov,* Lev. 19:14; with the commentary of Karo, *Kesef Mishneh, Hilkhot Sanhedrin* 26:1, and *Mamrim* 5:4. Cf., Naḥmanides, *Hasagot ha-Ramban,* mitzvah 317, p. 377; Tosafot, *Shevuot* 36a, s.v. *mekalel;* id., *Sanhedrin* 66b, s.v. *mai lo tekalel.*

[Lev. 20:9]) collectively serve as the source.[180] And there is a midrashic passage that indicates that the phrase in Exodus 22:27 that reads "among your people you shall not curse" is the source.[181]

Citing "You shall not curse a deaf person" as the source for the prohibition, R. Jacob ben Asher (c. 1269–c. 1340) paraphrases Maimonides and explains the derivation of the law as follows:

> The verse specifies a deaf person to teach us that *even* one who does not hear and does not suffer [from what is being said, it is prohibited to curse]; it follows that one who does hear and suffers by being cursed it would certainly [be prohibited to curse] ...[182]

Hence, the prohibition against cursing someone applies to any person, even though that person is not present at the time he or she is being cursed, and therefore is totally unaware of what is being said and, apparently, suffers in no way because of the curse. This is implied in the wording of the verse in Leviticus,[183] and is the ruling of all of the major codes.[184] Consequently, as mentioned earlier,

180 *Sanhedrin* 66a–b; with the commentaries of Tosafot, *Shevuot* 36a, s.v. *mekalel*; id., *Sanhedrin* 66b, s.v. *mai lo tekalel*; Yom-Tob ben Abraham Ishbili, *Ḥidushe ha-Ritba al ha-Shas*, 21 vols. (Jerusalem: Mossad Harav Kook, 2008), *Shevuot* 36a, p. 315; and Nissim ben Reuben Gerondi, *Ḥidushe ha-Ran: Masekhet Sanhedrin* (Jerusalem: Mossad Harav Kook, 2008), *Sanhedrin* 66a, p. 467.

181 *Sifra, Kedoshim, parashah* 2, *perek* 3:13; Rashi, *Kedoshim* 19:14; and Naḥmanides, *Ramban al ha-Torah*, Lev. 19:14.

182 Jacob ben Asher, *Arba'ah Turim, Ḥoshen Mishpat, siman* 27; Maimonides, *Mishneh Torah, Hilkhot Sanhedrin* 26:1. The clause "it follows that one who does hear ..." does not appear in the *Mishneh Torah* nor in most of the manuscripts of the *Tur*; see Jacob ben Asher, *Arba'ah Turim ha-Shalem*, 21 vols. (Israel: Mekhon Yerushalayim, 1993–1994), vol. 14, *Ḥoshen Mishpat* 27, p. 190, *Hagahot ve-He'arot* 6.

183 See Naḥmanides, *Ramban al ha-Torah*, Lev. 19:14; and Sa'adia ben Joseph, *Mishle im Targum u-Ferush ha-Ga'on Se'adyah ben Yosef Fayumi* (Jerusalem: Ha-Va'ad le-Hotsa'at Sifre Rasag, 1976), p. 267 (where he writes that the biblical term *ḥeresh*, "a deaf person," in this context is merely a metaphor for a person who is not present at the time); cited in Nachum L. Rabinovitch, *Mishneh Torah: Hu ha-Yad ha-Ḥazakah le-Rabenu Mosheh b. R. Maimon im Perush Yad Peshutah*, 20 vols. (Jerusalem: Ma'aliyot, 1997–2011), *Sefer Shoftim*, vol. 1, *Hilkhot Sanhedrin* 26:1–3, p. 670.

184 See above, n. 182, and Karo, *Shulḥan Arukh, Ḥoshen Mishpat, siman* 27 (in which, even though it is not clearly spelled out, it is implied). See Karo, *Kesef Mishneh, Sanhedrin* 26:1 (where he quotes Toviyahu ben Eliezer, *Midrash Lekaḥ Tov*, Lev. 19:14).

the prohibition against cursing someone may not necessarily be categorized as a prohibition against "verbal abuse," which (understood simply) entails that one is aware of what is said and suffers because of it.

The halakhic codes discuss a number of different forms of curses that are prohibited. The severest form[185] is when one invokes one of the names of God, with which one expresses a wish that some type of misfortune or harm befall a person (e.g., "God should punish him"), or uses one of the alternative descriptive names of God (e.g., "The merciful one should punish him"). A somewhat less severe form, which is still prohibited, is when one expresses a wish that some type of misfortune or harm befall the person but does not mention the name of God (e.g., "So-and-so should suffer")[186] or when the imprecation is indirectly implied ("God should not bless so-and-so").[187] Notably, R. David Ariav cites the opinion of R. Ḥayim Kanievsky that there is no such thing as a minimum degree of suffering or misfortune that one has to wish that the other person suffer for one to transgress this commandment. Rather, any type of bad occurrence that one (verbally) wishes upon another would be categorized as a form of cursing.[188]

185 That is to say that it is biblically prohibited and one is *ḥayav malkot* ("deserves [court administered] flogging," see above, p. 145 n. 105).

186 As to the status of this prohibition, R. Perla cites three sources that indicate that without mentioning God's name or a descriptive name of God there is no prohibition whatsoever; he then cites a number of *rishonim* and *aḥaronim* who are of the opinion that not only is this prohibited, but it is biblically prohibited. See Perla, commentary to *Sefer ha-Mitsvot*, vol. 1, *mitsvat aseh* 1, p. 34b, and vol. 2, *lo ta'aseh* 47, p. 43a. See also Abraham Isaiah Karelitz, *Ḥazon Ish: Ḥoshen Mishpat* (Bnei Brak: n.p., 1991), *Sanhedrin* 20:7; and Babad, *Minḥat Ḥinukh*, mitzvah 69:4.

187 See Maimonides, *Mishneh Torah, Hilkhot Sanhedrin* 26:3–4; Jacob ben Asher, *Arba'ah Turim, Ḥoshen Mishpat, siman* 27; Karo, *Shulḥan Arukh, Ḥoshen Mishpat, siman* 27:1–2; Harry Fischel Institute, *Halakhah Pesukah*, vol. 2 (Jerusalem: Machon Harry Fischel, 1987), *siman* 27, pp. 338–40; Karelitz, *Ḥazon Ish: Ḥoshen Mishpat, Sanhedrin* 20:10; Ari'av, *Le-Re'akha kamokha*, vol. 1, 210–16, 229–45; and Jacob ben Jacob Moses, of Lissa, *Netivot ha-Mishpat: Ve-Hu Ḥidushim u-Ve'urim al Ḥoshen Mishpat (Jerusalem: Me'ore Or, 2004), 27:2*. As to the exact meaning of "God should not bless so-and-so," see Falk, *Sma, Ḥoshen Mishpat* 27:7; Elijah ben Solomon, [*Be'ure*] *Ha-Gra, Ḥoshen Mishpat* 27:9; and Barukh Rakover, *Birkat Eliyahu al Be'ure ha-Gera, Ḥoshen Mishpat*, vol. 1 (Jerusalem: Machon Harry Fischel, 1991), 27:9, pp. 287–88.

188 Ari'av, *Le-Re'akha kamokha*, vol. 1, 219–20, 345.

There are various traditional explanations that have been offered for this prohibition, almost all of which have taken into account that the prohibition applies even if the person who is cursed is totally unaware of it. Maimonides (*Sefer ha-Mitsvot*, prohibition 317) proposes the following explanation, which focuses on the detrimental effect to one's own character when one curses another:

> When one's soul is driven to retaliate against someone who has inflicted harm, in accordance with the damage it believes it has suffered, it will not be at rest until it reciprocates in kind ... Once he has reciprocated, the drive will be at rest and subside. At times, [he may be satisfied] by reciprocating through cursing and insulting ... [and, at times, he may be satisfied] even if the person is not present and does not hear him ... [One may believe that] there is nothing wrong with doing so [i.e., cursing people if they are unaware of it]; however, He surely has apprised us that this is something that is forbidden and has warned us against doing so. *The Torah is not only concerned about the one who is being cursed, it is also concerned with the one doing the cursing, in that he should not allow his soul to be driven to take revenge, nor should he become accustomed to losing his temper.* (emphasis mine)

Apparently, Maimonides is saying that the reason behind the prohibition is that when one gives into or attempts to purge vindictive angry emotions through verbally expressing the wish that a human being should suffer, even when done privately to oneself, there will be some type of negative effect to one's own soul, or character, as a result of doing so.

An alternative explanation for the prohibition against cursing someone is that it is connected to, or an outgrowth of, the fundamental concept that a human being is created in the image of God. One commentator who makes such a connection is R. Naphtali Zevi Judah Berlin (1817–1893). R. Berlin cites the earlier commentary of R. Abraham ben David of Posquières (*Rabad* III) who paraphrases a midrashic text (cited above on p. 154) and writes that "[When you curse someone,] who are you cursing? The image of the Omnipresent."[189] In a similar vein, R. Meir Poppers (d. 1662) exhorts against cursing others by stating that when someone curses another human being, who possesses a "portion of God" within him, he in essence is cursing God himself.[190] And R. Moses Ḥagiz (1672–c. 1751) likewise warns that when one curses another, he himself will be deserving of a curse because "he is cursing a human being who is created in the image of God."[191]

Summary

In light of the Jewish tradition's stress on *mitsvot* and Halakhah, this chapter has examined some of Judaism's basic commandments and laws for the promotion of peaceful coexistence—the obligation to love your neighbor, the prohibition against hatred, the prohibition against physical violence, and the prohibitions against saying things that are hurtful or embarrassing, and cursing someone. For each of these, the primary sources and basic parameters and obligations were discussed in some detail.

In analyzing the six commandments that were discussed in this chapter, one can readily perceive a number of possible common denominators that they all share. One such common denominator, which straightaway comes to mind in the context of exploring Jewish approaches to interpersonal conflict resolution, is that all of these commandments, in one way or another, help to preclude the development of destructive conflict. The insensitive remarks,

---

189 Naphtali Zevi Judah Berlin, *Ha'amek Davar* (Jerusalem: Y. Kuperman, 2009), Lev. 19:14 (according to R. Berlin, this concern for the image of God in turn promotes peace amongst people); Abraham ben David, *Perush ha-Ra'avad, Kedoshim parashata* 2, *perek* 4:12; *Genesis Rabbah*, Theodor-Albeck edition, *Bereshit* 24:7.

190 Meir Poppers, *Or ha-Yashar* (Jerusalem: H. Y. Valdman, 1981), *Amud ha-Avodah, siman* 13:53, p. 285; cited in Ya'akov Ḥayim Sofer, *Menuḥat Shalom*, vol. 9 (Jerusalem: n.p., 2002), p. 87.

191 Moses Ḥagiz, *Eleh ha-Mitsvot* (Jerusalem: Ḥorev, 1964), mitzvah 71, p. 94. For other possible explanations for the prohibition, see Maimonides, *Guide for the Perplexed*, section 3:41; Ha-Levi, *Sefer ha-Ḥinukh*, commandment 231; and Solomon ben Adret, *She'elot u-Teshuvot ha-Rashba*, vol. 1, *siman* 408.

accusations, scurrilous insults, maledictions, and torrents of invective that generally accompany interpersonal conflict contravene the commandments that deal with verbal abuse and cursing someone. The alienation, ill will, bitter disdain, inveterate rancor, and deep-seated malice that are produced through conflict run contrary to, and potentially violate, the precept regarding hatred. The intolerance, rigidity, negative assessments, double standards, and, for that matter, all of the elements that constitute destructive conflict are the very antithesis of even the most basic prescriptive level of loving one's neighbor as oneself. And, when an interpersonal conflict goes beyond the negative emotions and verbal abuse and escalates into physical violence, the fundamental commandment that forbids such behavior is often violated in the ugliest of ways.

In addition to the prevention of destructive conflict, it should be understood that the commandments covered in this chapter represent what Judaism would regard as (some of) the most fundamental rules of interpersonal relations, and play an ongoing and intrinsic role throughout the entire process of interpersonal conflict resolution. They therefore add another important basic layer to the framework and understanding of Jewish conflict resolution, and consequently they will be referred to in the coming chapters. That being the case, we have now basically set the stage for Part IV of this book, Basic Commandments and Laws of Interpersonal Conflict Resolution, which we will proceed to after a discussion of some of the similarities and differences between contemporary conflict resolution and traditional Jewish approaches in regard to concepts that were discussed in this chapter.

Similarities and Differences between Contemporary Conflict Resolution and Traditional Jewish Approaches in Respect to Underlying Values and Behavioral Guidelines of the Basic Interpersonal Obligations and Prohibitions

In Chapter 2, I proposed that promoting peaceful coexistence (what I referred to there as "pursuing peace and refraining from destructive conflict") should be designated as traditional Jewish approaches' most fundamental underlying value for interpersonal conflict resolution. This was based on the assertion that in the course of our study we will see that promoting peaceful coexistence is the core goal and ultimate concern of all of the behavioral guidelines, rules of conduct, subvalues, and other components of traditional Jewish approaches. It is quite apparent that the basic interpersonal obligations and prohibitions that were covered in this chapter—which attempt to prevent and address hatred, physical violence, and verbal abuse, and to promote love—lend firm support to that thesis.

Aside from the evidence from the material that we have seen, and which we will see later in this work, I also mentioned parenthetically in Chapter 2 that the proposition that the promotion of peaceful coexistence is the fundamental underlying value of traditional Jewish approaches can also obviously be substantiated by the well-known rabbinic saying that "the whole Torah is for the sake of *darkhe shalom* (the promotion of peaceful coexistence)" (*Gittin* 59b; see above, p. 110).

However, alongside the promotion of peaceful coexistence, one also finds other rabbinic statements from the talmudic period regarding the ultimate purpose of the Torah that highlight other basic values. Probably the most famous of these statements is Hillel's, that love of one's neighbor represents the essence of the Torah (see p. 115). Another rabbinic statement that offers an alternative fundamental underlying value is "The commandments were only given in order to purify [alternatively: refine][192] people" (*Genesis Rabbah* 44:1). The implication of this statement being that the ultimate goal of the Torah is character development.

The rabbinic designations of love for one's neighbor and character development as the values that underlie the entire Torah

192 See Naḥmanides, *Ramban al ha-Torah*, Deut. 22:6; cf. Maimonides, *Guide for the Perplexed*, 3:26 (in conjunction with *Mekhilta de-Rabi Shimon ben Yoḥai*, ed. J. N. Epstein and Ezra Zion Melamed [Jerusalem: Mekitse Nirdamim, 1955], p. 144); and Solomon ben Adret, *She'elot u-Teshuvot ha-Rashba*, vol. 8, *siman* 366, p. 237.

are readily applicable to Jewish interpersonal conflict resolution. All of the behavioral guidelines and rules of conduct of traditional Jewish approaches that we have seen and will see can be simply understood as aimed at promoting love for one's neighbor (see below). Any other possible fundamental underlying Torah value, such as, for example, *kevod ha-beriyot* ("respect for people," or "human dignity"), may be viewed as being subsumed by the broader overarching value of expressing love for one's neighbor (or fellow human being).[193] One's personal social and emotional growth and well-being (which in Chapter 1, I explained would be referred to as "elements of character development")[194] is also certainly part and parcel to all of the behavioral elements of Jewish conflict resolution, and we may therefore also rightfully assign "character development" as one of the fundamental underlying values of traditional Jewish approaches.

Working with the classic rabbinic statements cited above regarding underlying values, and their simple, straightforward application to interpersonal conflict resolution, I will now offer what I believe are some of the major similarities and differences between contemporary conflict resolution and traditional Jewish approaches in respect to the fundamental underlying values and the basic interpersonal behavioral guidelines and rules of conduct that were covered in this chapter. I will first focus on the value of love for one's neighbor, then go on to compare and contrast some of traditional Jewish approaches' and

193 *Kevod ha-beriyot* can be seen as the fundamental underlying value for all of Judaism's interpersonal laws; see Lebovitch, *Da'at Ḥokhmah u-Musar*, vol. 3, p. 63, vol. 2, pp. 34–35; and Soloveitchik, *Yeme Zikaron*, 9. R. Aryeh Pomeranchik (1908–1942) calls attention to the fact that Maimonides views showing respect to people as being subsumed by the injunction to love one's neighbor (see *Mishneh Torah, De'ot* 6:3), whereas R. Jonah Gerondi does not (see Jonah ben Abraham Gerondi, *Perushe Rabenu Yonah mi-Gerondi al Masekhet Avot* [Jerusalem: Mekhon Torah Shelemah, 1980], *Avot* 2:10) (Pomeranchik, *Emek Berakhah*, 63; see also Epstein, *Barukh she-Amar: Pirke Avot*, 77). R. David Kronglas points out that when one understands "love" as performing acts of loving-kindness (see above, pp. 116–17, the "centrist position"), *kevod ha-beriyot* would have to be considered a broader, more expansive concept than *ahavat ha-beriyot* (David Kronglas, *Siḥot Ḥokhmah u-Musar: Ḥoveret* 3 [Jerusalem: Yotse le-Or be-Siyu'a Kevutsat Talmidav, 1982], 29–30). See also Tsevi Krizer, *Be'er Tsevi* (Bnei Brak: Ts. Krizer, 2011), 316.

194 See p. 33 n. 76.

contemporary conflict resolution's behavioral guidelines and rules of conduct, and conclude with a discussion of the value of character development.

The Value of Loving One's Neighbor as Opposed to Cooperation

In Chapter 1, I proposed that there are four primary underlying values of contemporary conflict resolution: (1) peaceful coexistence, (2) cooperation, (3) problem solving, and (4) character development.[195] I dealt with similarities and differences between contemporary conflict resolution and traditional Jewish approaches in respect to peaceful coexistence at the end of Chapter 2; the similarities and differences in respect to problem solving will be dealt with in Chapter 6; and similarities and differences relating to character development will be discussed later in this chapter (pp. 184–88). At this point, I would like to address traditional Jewish approaches' and contemporary conflict resolution's respective values of love for one's neighbor and cooperation.

As we have seen in this chapter, love of one's neighbor is a clearly articulated core goal and ultimate concern of the Jewish approach to interpersonal relations. "You shall love your neighbor as yourself" is a familiar concept that one repeatedly encounters throughout traditional Jewish literature, and it would probably be safe to say that anyone who has had any type of decent Jewish education is aware of the concept. Even though when one examines traditional Jewish conflict resolution literature and its approaches, one may not necessarily find that love for one's neighbor is being overtly addressed, it does not take all that much to see beneath the surface and to perceive that, beyond just preventing destructive conflict and promoting peaceful coexistence, love for one's neighbor can very well be the impetus behind all of traditional Jewish approaches' discussions and behavioral guidelines. This is in contrast to contemporary conflict resolution, in which one would generally be

195 See pp. 31–33, where I point out that cooperation and problem solving could also be viewed as subvalues of promoting peaceful coexistence.

hard-pressed to find any type of reference to or real indication in its mainstream literature and approaches that *love* for one's neighbor, or fellow human being, is a core goal or ultimate concern.

Outside of works on conflict resolution that have a clear religious orientation, as a general rule, as far as I have been able to determine based on my research, one does not find contemporary conflict resolution discussing the concept of love for one's neighbor, or fellow human being. Contemporary conflict resolution has established what may be seen as considerably more modest, and, what it would view as, more realistic goals. As was highlighted in the introductory essay of this work, a major component of contemporary conflict resolution's approach to preventing destructive conflict and promoting peace is to emphasize that people should interact in a cooperative, or collaborative, fashion. In its theory, practice, and educational programs, contemporary conflict resolution consistently accentuates the importance of people working together and relating to each other in a constructive, respectful, and responsive manner that is mutually beneficial to both parties, which are the essential elements that constitute cooperation.

Of course, it goes without saying that traditional Jewish approaches' emphasis on love does not take away from the importance of the value of cooperation. Love for one's neighbor, or fellow human being, by necessity encompasses cooperation, just as it encompasses showing respect for people (see p. 171). As a broad, overarching value, love for one's neighbor would entail that people should always try to interact and work with each other in a manner that is both respectful and responsive to their mutual needs. Traditional Jewish approaches would unquestionably encourage cooperation; however, they are not satisfied only with cooperation. Judaism wants people to set their sights higher, and strive for greater levels of unity and interconnectedness, such as love of one's neighbor, with the understanding that very often due to the challenges of the real world, in many cases this may not be attainable.

Contemporary conflict resolution focuses on what can be viewed as the basics—cooperation and its subvalues, such as civility, showing respect to others, proper expression of emotions, and so on. These may all fall under the category of what traditional Jewish sources have termed *"derekh erets,"* or proper social behavior, which is viewed as a basic prerequisite of proper Torah observance (see footnote).[196] Taking into consideration that mainstream Jewish approaches generally do not understand "love your neighbor" literally, but instead offer various more realistic interpretations of the injunction (see pp. 112–121), it could be argued that the gap between traditional Jewish approaches and contemporary conflict resolution in respect to the fundamental underlying values of cooperation and love of one's neighbor may not be as great as one might have imagined. Nevertheless, even when one understands love in its weakest sense, there is still an undeniable and very significant difference between having cooperation, even with all of its associated concepts, as a core goal and ultimate concern as compared to love of one's neighbor. This difference should become quite evident as we go on to consider the differences between contemporary conflict resolution and traditional Jewish approaches in respect to their behavioral guidelines and rules of conduct.

Basic Interpersonal Behavioral Guidelines and Rules of Conduct

In this chapter, we have touched on some of Judaism's basic interpersonal behavioral guidelines and rules of conduct. Each of the six commandments that we discussed encompasses certain normative standards of conduct: In relation to the commandment of "You shall love your neighbor as yourself," we saw a number of approaches to its

196 The term *"derekh erets"* literally means "way of the land." The term has multiple connotations in rabbinic literature (see *Encyclopaedia Judaica*, 2nd ed., s.v. *"derekh erez"*). My reference to the concept that *derekh erets*, understood as proper social behavior, is seen as a prerequisite of proper Torah observance is based on the often cited expression *"derekh erets* precedes the Torah" (see *Leviticus Rabbah* 9:3; Moshe Tsuriel, *Otsrot ha-Musar*, vol. 1 [Jerusalem: Yerid ha-Sefarim, 2002], 479–81 [citing the interpretations of R. Judah Loew ben Bezalel and R. Nathan Zevi Finkel]; and *Wikipedia*, s.v. "proper behavior precedes the Torah," http://en.wikipedia.org/wiki/Proper_behavior_precedes_the_Torah).

practical application (e.g., that one refrain from harming or hurting others or that one express love through actions). The commandment of "You shall not hate your brother in your heart" in practical halakhic terms, according to the *Ḥafets Ḥayim* and others, is an injunction against going three days without talking to someone "out of animosity." The commandment of "he shall not add; lest he strike him an additional blow" prohibits physical violence. The commandments of "You shall not hurt one another," "You shall not bear sin because of him," and "You shall not curse a deaf person," respectively, proscribe saying hurtful things to, embarrassing, and cursing people.

Contemporary conflict resolution's approach to dealing with conflict also encompasses behavioral guidelines and rules of conduct. As proposed in Chapter 1, the most prominent normative behavioral aspects of contemporary conflict resolution are the series of steps and procedures that are associated with the process of collaborative negotiation and constructive communication.[197] The closest thing that may possibly correspond to contemporary conflict resolution's collaborative negotiation (in respect to interpersonal conflict resolution that does not involve an intermediary) in traditional Jewish approaches is *tokhaḥah*, "reproof," for interpersonal offenses, which may be viewed as Judaism's basic approach to resolving interpersonal conflict through dialogue. *Tokhaḥah* for interpersonal offenses will be discussed in Chapter 6. At the end of that chapter is where I will offer what I believe to be some of the major similarities and differences between contemporary conflict resolution and traditional Jewish approaches in regard to collaborative negotiation.

As far as behavioral guidelines for constructive communication are concerned, even though we have discussed in this chapter traditional Jewish approaches' prohibitions of saying hurtful things and embarrassing people, which certainly relate to constructive communication, I will push off the discussion of similarities and differences in respect to this topic until the end of Chapter 6 as well. It will not be until Chapter 6, when we have gone through the *halakhot*

197 See p. 31.

of reproof and get a much better picture of traditional Jewish approaches' guidelines for constructive communication, will we be able to accurately and intelligently compare and contrast the two systems' respective approaches to communication.

We will therefore at this point only focus on traditional Jewish approaches' normative obligations that relate to love, hatred, and the prohibition against physical violence, and compare and contrast them with contemporary conflict resolution's approach to these elements.

The Normative Obligations of Love. As alluded to earlier (on pp. 168–69), when one is involved in a conflict one is liable to violate all of the commandments that were discussed in this chapter.[198] In regard to love for one's neighbor, when one considers the three approaches to the form/degree of love that have been discussed, it is quite evident how true this assertion is. The first approach we had seen (that of the minimalist position) proposed that "you shall love your neighbor" is a commandment that one should refrain from hurting or harming others; the second approach (the centrist position) proposed that it is a commandment to perform positive acts, among which, based on Maimonides and the examples that he offers, includes that one actively shows concern for another's honor;[199] and the third approach (the maximalist position) proposed that it is a commandment that one strive to have feelings for others that can be seen as expressing a certain degree of love, such as empathy. Needless to say, all of these normative aspects of loving one's neighbor, whether in regard to refraining from hurting or harming others, being concerned about another's honor, or showing empathy, routinely come into play and are often[200] violated in interpersonal conflicts.

198 See p. 110, where I mention R. Eisenblatt's list of commandments that one is liable to violate when involved in a conflict. As previously noted, R. Eisenblatt's list is based on what the *Ḥafets Ḥayim* had written in respect to the commandments that one may violate when speaking *lashon ha-ra*.

199 See p. 120.

200 One does not necessarily always violate the commandment to love your neighbor in every interpersonal conflict. See p. 178.

Contemporary conflict resolution, of course, firmly advocates that one should in no way hurt or harm others, that one should be concerned about another's honor, and show empathy. These are all basic aspects of contemporary conflict resolution's fundamental values (or what I have referred to as its "subvalues") that underlie, or are inherent to, the behavioral guidelines and rules of conduct of contemporary conflict resolution.[201] The difference between traditional Jewish approaches and contemporary conflict resolution in respect to these elements, when they are translated into normative standards of behavior, are, first, in regard to how they are formulated and their binding nature and imperativeness. Being grounded in Western secular social-ethics, contemporary conflict resolution does not talk in terms of "commandments" (i.e., "*mitsvot*") and "laws" (the English equivalent of "*halakhot*") that dictate one's interpersonal behaviors for the resolution of conflicts. This is in contrast to Judaism, in which binding interpersonal obligations, in the form of *mitsvot* and *halakhot*, with the inherent imperativeness of these types of obligations, are essential concepts.[202] As we have seen, this clearly holds true for the normative elements of love for one's neighbor that we have focused on in this chapter, which appear in the form of an explicit biblical commandment and practical *halakhot* that are applicable to the process of interpersonal conflict resolution.

---

201 See pp. 31–33. Not hurting or harming others and being concerned about another's honor are all subvalues of contemporary conflict resolution's four primary underlying values of peaceful coexistence, cooperation, problem solving, and character development, and they are inherent to all of the seven components of conflict resolution that were outlined in Chapter 1. Showing empathy, aside from being a subvalue of contemporary conflict resolution's primary underlying values, is also an integral part of contemporary conflict resolution's core component of perspective taking.

202 Regarding differences in formulation, there are many unique aspects to Halakhah and the halakhic process that do not have parallels in contemporary conflict resolution literature. A discussion of these differences would require a familiarity with Halakhah that goes way beyond the scope of the present work. For a very good introductory text on Halakhah and the halakhic process, see Menachem Elon, *Jewish Law: History, Sources, Principles* (Philadelphia: The Jewish Publication Society, 1994).

Admittedly, even in traditional Jewish approaches, the normative elements of loving one's neighbor are not rigid, ironclad rules that are set in stone. Rather, they are only broad principles or guidelines of conduct that take into consideration the wide array of complex, real-world variables that come into play in interpersonal relations, and therefore they show considerable flexibility. In practice, there are many possible scenarios in which the Halakhah would maintain that it is permissible, and even advisable, that in a certain practical respect one not be overly concerned about showing love for one's neighbor. One common example of such a case would be where an individual is in a bad or abusive relationship and decides to end it. Even though by doing so the individual may cause a degree of emotional pain for the other person in the relationship, it goes without saying that the injunction to love your neighbor would not prevent the individual from doing so.[203] However, that does not mean to say that even in these types of cases the injunction to love one's neighbor is totally inoperative. Even when one would have to unavoidably cause some degree of pain to another person through one's actions, the commandment would apparently still dictate that one should do his or her utmost to keep any suffering to the absolute bare minimum, show empathy for the other person, and, if the opportunity should present itself, to even perform acts of loving-kindness for the other person. This being the case, even though one may possibly be tempted because of the inherent ambiguity in the practical application of "you shall love your neighbor" to make some type of comparison between contemporary conflict resolution and

203 This would also theoretically hold true for innumerable other cases in which one's sole intent is to prevent some type of suffering for oneself or for some other justifiable constructive purpose, so long as the degree of pain that one's actions may cause another is ethically sanctionable, and is unavoidable and unintended. See the related discussion in Diskin, *She'elot u-Teshuvot Maharil Diskin*, 108; and Abraham Isaac ha-Kohen Kook, *Oraḥ Mishpat* (Jerusalem: Mossad Harav Kook, 1985), *Ḥoshen Mishpat, siman* 26, pp. 238–39. Both of these sources appear in Makhon Torat ha-Adam le-Adam, *"Likutim ba-Mitsvat 'Ve-Ahavta le-Re'akha kamokha,'" Torat ha-Adam le-Adam: Kovets Torani ba-Mitsvot she-ben Adam la-Ḥavero* 4 (2001): 136–40. For other possible instances when the obligation to love one's neighbor may not apply (in regard to the performance of acts of loving-kindness), see Shemaryahu Yosef Ḥayim Kanevski, *Sefer Sha'are Emunah ... al Mas. Pe'ah* (Bnei Brak: Ḥ. Kanevski, 2000), 22–23.

traditional Jewish approaches in regard to these elements, this would probably not be a valid comparison. Even in conflict situations in which the precept may not bar certain behaviors that could be viewed as being of a self-concerned nature and hurtful to the other person, it may still nevertheless be operative and could affect interactions between the parties involved in a very profound way.

Another difference between contemporary conflict resolution and traditional Jewish approaches in respect to the behavioral guidelines and rules of conduct associated with love your neighbor—aside from differences in formulation, binding nature, and imperativeness—is in regard to the range, or scope, of what they ask of the individual. Contemporary conflict resolution may advocate that one should in no way hurt or harm others, that one should be concerned about another's honor, and show empathy, but it does not ask that one show love to another person by doing such things, as Maimonides had mentioned, as "[telling] over his praise" and being "concerned about his money as he would be concerned about his own money,"[204] or to, as a general principle, do those things that you want him to do for you. These normative elements of traditional Jewish approaches' imperative to love one's neighbor could potentially have a major transformative impact on interpersonal relations and conflicts (if they are put into practice), whereby, in the context of a conflict, the typical confrontational dynamics could be greatly diminished, and the likelihood for a quick, amicable resolution greatly increased. We may reasonably assert that this difference between contemporary conflict resolution and traditional Jewish approaches in respect to the range of their elements all goes back to and reflects what was discussed earlier in relation to differences in underlying values. Contemporary conflict resolution emphasizes basic cooperation, civility, showing respect to others, and so forth, whereas traditional Jewish approaches encompass these basic values but also try to go beyond them by emphasizing love for one's neighbor.

---

204 Maimonides, *Mishneh Torah, De'ot* 6:3; see above, p. 120.

Taking all of the above into consideration—that some of the basic normative aspects of love your neighbor can be seen as underlying and inherent to the behavioral guidelines of contemporary conflict resolution, that there are differences between traditional Jewish approaches and contemporary conflict resolution in respect to the formulation, binding nature, and imperativeness of their normative standards, that despite the flexibility in the practical application of love your neighbor the injunction would still remain operative, and the difference in the range of their normative elements—we may therefore conclude that there is some basic similarity between contemporary conflict resolution and traditional Jewish approaches but there are also very significant differences between them in respect to the normative obligations associated with love your neighbor. Contemporary conflict resolution and traditional Jewish approaches apparently share a number of the same basic underlying standards, but they differ in that in contemporary conflict resolution these standards are not expressed as clearly articulated imperatives that obligate the parties to act in a certain fashion. This is as opposed to traditional Jewish approaches, in which they take the form of elements of an explicit, abiding commandment. Additionally, apart from the basic normative standards that they do share, there are highly significant normative elements of love, which may be of major practical import, that traditional Jewish approaches ask the parties to engage in, whereas contemporary conflict resolution does not.

The Normative Obligations of the Prohibition against Hatred. Unquestionably, both contemporary conflict resolution and traditional Jewish approaches view hatred as contributing to destructive conflict; they both are concerned about preventing its development and, if it has already developed, its elimination, and when that is impossible, the amelioration of its destructive effects. Similar to what was said earlier in relation to the normative obligations of love, the prevention, elimination, and amelioration of hatred can be viewed as subvalues of contemporary conflict resolution's primary underlying values (of peaceful coexistence, cooperation, problem solving, and character development) and as being implicit to the behavioral guidelines and rules of conduct of contemporary conflict resolution. However, when one considers the connection between contemporary conflict resolution's behavioral guidelines and rules of conduct and hatred, particularly when it comes to forms of internalized "hatred of the heart" that does not openly express itself, one may possibly view this connection as being a little more tenuous than the connection between contemporary conflict resolution and the normative elements of love that we focused on earlier (i.e., that one should not hurt or harm others, should be concerned about another's honor, and show empathy).[205] Granting that there does exist such a connection in contemporary conflict resolution in regard to hatred, the differences between contemporary conflict resolution and traditional Jewish approaches emerge, as they did with regard to the normative obligations of love, in respect to the formulation, binding nature, and imperativeness of their normative standards, and in respect to the range of what they ask of the individual.

The guidelines and rules of conduct of contemporary conflict resolution that could possibly be seen as related to preventing, eliminating, and ameliorating hatred would include many of the rules and procedures of collaborative negotiation, such as setting ground rules that promote mutual respect and commitment to resolving the conflict, pointing out commonalities between the parties, minimizing differences when appropriate, and addressing underlying issues.[206] In addition to the behavioral elements of collaborative negotiation, there are also behavioral rules that the other core components of contemporary conflict resolution incorporate that could also be seen as related to the prevention, elimination, and amelioration of hatred, such as the use of techniques to regulate anger and the use of communication techniques that

---

205 I am well aware that this is counterintuitive, and debatable (cf. pp. 293–98, what I have written in regard to contemporary conflict resolution's approach to dealing with resentment.)

206 See pp. 27–28.

promote nonconfrontational communication.[207] Admittedly, the acknowledged primary purposes of these elements are the effective negotiation of differences between the parties, anger management, and constructive communication, but at the same time they also help, on a secondary level, to address to some degree issues related to hatred. For all of these behavioral elements of contemporary conflict resolution, even if we should grant the connection between them and hatred, we would also probably have to concede that dealing with hatred, and certainly hatred that is not manifest in some open way, is not their primary concern.

The existence of a clear-cut and emphatic precept that addresses hatred, even when it is not manifest in some open way, in traditional Jewish approaches is quite evident. We have seen that the Bible, Talmud, Midrash, and major medieval and later rabbinic authorities discuss it, that it received the serious attention of halakhic authorities, and that it has practical, prescriptive guidelines that relate to it. Two examples of the behavioral guidelines and rules of conduct that relate to hatred that were examined in this chapter were the *halakhot* regarding what constitutes a violation of "you shall not hate your brother in your heart" and the principle of *la-khof et yitsro* (that one should "subdue" the inclination to hate). We had seen how halakhic authorities rule that one transgresses the prohibition against hatred if one's dislike for another person has reached an intensity that as a result of which he or she does not speak to that person for three days out of animosity. And we had seen how the halakhah of *la-khof et yitsro* teaches that one should attempt to suppress (and eliminate) his or her natural inclination to hate someone by being helpful to the person that one has ill will towards, if the opportunity presents itself.[208] These *halakhot* (and as we shall see in Chapter 6 other *halakhot* as well) basically preclude, under normal circumstances,[209] the possibility for one to just nonchalantly

---

207 See pp. pp. 20–21 and 24–25.

208 See pp. 139–44.

209 As I have previously pointed out, if one does not speak to someone not out of animosity but for some other valid reason, it appears that one does not violate the commandment, and I have also pointed out that there may be other possible exceptions to the general prohibition that one should not hate someone (see p. 140 n. 92).

decide to have nothing to do with someone else because one hates that person. From a halakhic standpoint, this would be an unacceptable course to take, generally speaking. Rather, when someone has feelings of animosity or hatred in one's heart for another, the person should engage in certain positive behaviors, such as initiating a dialogue and discussing one's grievances with the other person,[210] and try to do away with these feelings.

Contemporary conflict resolution incorporates many behavioral guidelines that may be seen as helping to prevent, eliminate, and ameliorate hatred, but it does not encompass a clear-cut injunction that tells a person that he cannot go walking around with hatred in his heart. Nor does it have any type of rule that says that a person cannot without due consideration simply break off ties with someone that he or she hates, and it does not require in any way that a person should be helpful to someone that he or she feels ill will towards. These rules of conduct, which traditional Jewish approaches incorporate, go beyond the range of what contemporary conflict resolution would probably consider as being reasonable to ask of people. Thus, similar to what was stated in reference to the normative obligations of love, contemporary conflict resolution and traditional Jewish approaches may share a number of basic underlying standards in regard to hatred (i.e., they both view hatred as contributing to destructive conflict and are concerned about its prevention, elimination, and amelioration), but they differ in relation to the formulation, binding nature, and imperativeness of their standards, in that in traditional Jewish approaches there is an explicit commandment (and associated rules) that addresses hatred, whereas in contemporary conflict resolution there is not, and there are some highly significant normative elements related to hatred that traditional Jewish approaches incorporate, which do not appear in contemporary conflict resolution.

The Prohibition against Physical Violence. One of the most basic normative elements that contemporary conflict resolution and traditional Jewish approaches clearly share is that they both repudiate physical violence in no uncertain terms. In both contemporary conflict

210 See above, p. 142.

resolution and traditional Jewish approaches, any and all types of physical violence are unequivocally denounced, proscribed, and potentially punishable by law. Nevertheless, in examining even just the very small amount of material that relates to physical violence in traditional Jewish approaches that we have seen in this chapter, one may pick up on a degree of intensity in traditional Jewish approaches' exhortations and attempts to stem the development of physical violence that, possibly, go beyond what appears in contemporary conflict resolution.[211] For example, we find the often cited saying of R. Simeon ben Lakish that "one who raises his hand against his friend even if he does not hit him receives the designation of a *rasha* ('wicked person')" and R. Huna saying that, theoretically, one's hand deserves to be "cut off" (understood as possibly a talmudic idiom for the imposition of a monetary fine or a curse invoked against someone), which may serve as illustrations of the type of very strong rabbinic language and means used in censuring and trying to prevent physical violence.[212] However, one could no doubt also put up a valid argument that, on a practical level, both contemporary conflict resolution and traditional Jewish approaches try to outlaw physical violence to basically the same extent. One may therefore justifiably simply state that when it comes to comparing and contrasting contemporary conflict resolution and traditional Jewish approaches in relation to physical violence, they exhibit a much greater similarity than when it comes to the normative elements of love and hatred that we have previously examined, and that contemporary conflict resolution's guidelines are very much akin to those of traditional Jewish approaches.

The Value of Character Development

In Chapter 1, I had pointed out that one of the primary goals of contemporary conflict resolution education is the personal and

211 I write this with the understanding that contemporary conflict resolution works in conjunction with educational and legal systems that are categorically dedicated to stemming violence, and incorporate a *massive* amount of material and legislation that do so quite forcefully.

212 See the discussion, and other examples, on pp. 146–50.

social development and well-being of its students, which I have chosen to refer to as elements of character development.[213] The core components of conflict resolution education (i.e., cooperation, constructive communication, perspective taking, anger management, decision making, collaborative negotiation, and so on) represent contemporary conflict resolution's essential approach to interpersonal conflict resolution and encompass some of the most important interpersonal skills that one needs in order to grow and flourish in life. The interpersonal skills of contemporary conflict resolution contribute to the development of strong, healthy, and happy relationships; they play an important role in whether or not one will succeed in his/her career; and they have also all been found to promote one's overall emotional and physical well-being.[214]

At this stage in our study, the emphasis of traditional Jewish approaches on elements of character development should already be self-evident. Just from what we have seen in this chapter alone, in relation to the six commandments and their associated concepts that were examined, Judaism's concern for an individual's personal and social development and well-being should be quite apparent. The basic interpersonal obligations of showing love for one's neighbor, not walking around with hatred in one's heart, and not physically or verbally hurting one another can all potentially contribute in various and very profound ways to an individual's personal and social growth, health, happiness, and prosperity, and they can serve as clear indications of traditional Jewish approaches' marked focus on character development.

---

213 See p. 33.

214 There is empirical research that has shown that the skills that the conflict resolution education programs focus on, which constitute a considerable part of the larger field of social and emotional learning, help to prevent aggressive behaviors, violence, the abuse of alcohol and drugs, and help to promote a wide range of positive prosocial behaviors. See Wendy M. Garrard and Mark W. Lipsey, "Conflict Resolution Education and Antisocial Behavior in U.S. Schools: A Meta-Analysis," *Conflict Resolution Quarterly* 25, n. 1 (Fall 2007): 9–38; Tricia S. Jones, "Conflict Resolution Education: The Field, the Findings, and the Future," *Conflict Resolution Quarterly* 22, no. 1/2 (Fall/Winter 2004): 233–67; and Joseph A. Durlak et al., "The Impact of Enhancing Students' Social and Emotional Learning: A Meta-Analysis of School-Based Universal Interventions," *Child Development* 82, no. 1 (2011): 405–32.

I believe that when one compares traditional Jewish approaches' concern for character development with that of contemporary conflict resolution's, specifically in the realm of school-based conflict resolution education, one could theoretically argue that, on a basic level, there is not much appreciable difference between the two systems. Contemporary conflict resolution and traditional Jewish approaches are both clearly dedicated to the individual's personal and social development and well-being. These elements of character development are core goals and ultimate concerns of both systems; therefore, they rightly deserve to be designated as fundamental underlying values that the two share.

The difference between contemporary conflict resolution and traditional Jewish approaches, however, does emerge quite clearly in regard to how they would define this shared value. Contemporary conflict resolution's understanding of personal and social development and well-being basically reflects current trends in the field of social and emotional learning. As was explained in Chapter 1, the field of social and emotional learning essentially tries to help people develop the fundamental life skills they need to effectively handle themselves and their relationships.[215] Traditional Jewish approaches' understanding of personal and social development and well-being is based on the classic biblical and rabbinic conceptualizations of these constructs. Considering what we have seen in this chapter, it should already be clear, at least to some extent, that the classic biblical and rabbinic approaches to personal and social development and well-being often set goals and standards that are somewhat, and at times significantly (and possibly even quite significantly),[216] higher than those of contemporary conflict resolution. The goals and standards of traditional Jewish approaches go beyond the

215 This is a paraphrase of the definition of social and emotional learning that appears on The Collaborative for Academic, Social, and Emotional Learning's website, at http://casel.org/why-it-matters. For further elaboration, see above, p. 17 n. 41.

216 See below, p. 456, where I quote Gopin, who in discussing religious approaches to dealing with conflict (including Judaism's) at one point describes them as "quite rigorous, almost monastic, demands of piety that, if they are followed, ... most conflicts are nipped in the bud, or never even arise."

fundamental life skills, and reflect what appears to be an alternative perspective on what should be considered a reasonable level of interpersonal functioning to ask the average person to strive for.

By merely reviewing and weighing the evidence from what was highlighted in the sections above that compare and contrast the two systems, the divergence between what traditional Jewish approaches ask and expect from the average person and what contemporary conflict resolution asks and expects should start to become apparent. In the previous sections, we have highlighted how in relation to basic values contemporary conflict resolution emphasizes that people should interact in a cooperative fashion, whereas traditional Jewish approaches stress that people should go beyond cooperation and strive for love of one's neighbor. In the realm of normative obligations, contemporary conflict resolution advocates that one should in no way hurt or harm others, that one should be concerned about another's honor, and show empathy; in contrast, traditional Jewish approaches expect that one should not only do all of these things, but also ask that one engage in positive actions that reflect a certain degree of love for the other person by doing those things that you want the other person to do for you. Contemporary conflict resolution incorporates behavioral guidelines that may be seen as helping to prevent, eliminate, and ameliorate hatred; however, contemporary conflict resolution does not encompass a clear-cut injunction that tells a person that he cannot go walking around with hatred in his heart, nor does it have a rule that says that a person should attempt to suppress and eliminate hatred by being helpful to the one he or she has ill will towards, as in traditional Jewish approaches.

All of the abovementioned elements reflect established goals and standards of character development that traditional Jewish approaches incorporate which to a certain extent go further than those of contemporary conflict resolution. But, perhaps, even a clearer indication than all of these elements that accentuates this difference between traditional Jewish approaches and contemporary conflict resolution, which we have seen in this chapter, is the halakhic prohibition against cursing someone. From the verse "You shall not curse a deaf person," halakhic authorities derive that one is prohibited from verbally expressing a wish that some type of misfortune or harm befall another person, even though the other person is not present at the time, is totally unaware of what is being said, and apparently suffers in no way because of it. The simplest explanation, as Maimonides suggests, for this prohibition is that when one curses another person, even if the other person is totally unaffected by what is being said, the one who is doing the cursing is. By losing his temper and verbally expressing the wish that a human being should suffer in some way, the one doing the cursing engenders some type of negative effect to his own soul, or character. It appears that contemporary conflict resolution has no definitive guideline or rule in its system that is (really) comparable to this (see footnote).[217]

The divergence between what contemporary conflict resolution asks of the average person and what traditional Jewish approaches ask will be discussed further in the conclusion of this work. At this point, we may conclude that on a basic level contemporary conflict resolution and traditional Jewish approaches are both dedicated to and actively promote personal and social development and well-being. These elements of character development are clearly fundamental underlying values that the two share. However, traditional Jewish approaches do seem to set specific goals and standards of character development that are, to some degree, higher than contemporary conflict resolution's, and consequently ask and expect more from the average person than does contemporary conflict resolution. As we proceed through our study, this assertion will find strong and repeated support from numerous sources that will be examined in the following chapters.

---

217 One may possibly suggest that contemporary conflict resolution's guidelines that relate to venting anger could conceivably be viewed as comparable. However, we had seen in Chapter 1 that contemporary conflict resolution's stance on the question of venting anger is somewhat ambiguous. Despite the fact that there is empirical research that discourages its use, some of the popular programs nevertheless recommend venting as a viable technique for dealing with anger (see p. 25).

PART IV

Basic Commandments and Laws of Interpersonal Conflict Resolution

Chapter 5

Judging People Favorably: Countering Negative Judgmental Biases

This that we have said that everyone is obligated to judge their friend favorably ... will promote peace and friendship among people.

Sefer ha-Ḥinukh, Mitzvah 235

The Talmud (*Shevuot* 30a) cites the verse "In righteousness you shall judge your friend"[1] (Leviticus 19:15) as teaching that "You should judge your friend towards the scale of merit." The simple explanation of what it means to judge someone "towards the scale of merit" is that it is referring to situations in which a person performed an action that can be interpreted either positively or negatively—the person may have committed some sort of misdeed, or may not have committed a misdeed—and, using the analogy of a balance scale that can lean to either side, the Rabbis are teaching that one should judge the person "*le-khaf zekhut*," "towards the weighing pan [which in English is also referred to as a "scale"] of merit," that is, give the person the benefit of the doubt and judge him or her favorably.[2]

1 In Hebrew, בְּצֶדֶק תִּשְׁפֹּט עֲמִיתֶךָ (*be-tsedek tishpot amitekha*). For sources that support the translation of the word *amitekha* as "your friend," see p. 224 n. 4.

2 See Rashi, *Shevuot* 30a, s.v. *have dan*; and Obadiah Bertinoro, *Perush Rabenu Ovadyah mi-Bartenura*, *Avot* 1:6.

The Talmud (*Shabbat* 127a–b) also states that judging one's friend *le-khaf zekhut*, towards the scale of merit, is something that falls under the category of *hava'at shalom ben adam la-ḥavero*, "bringing peace between a person and his friend."[3] Rashi explains this to mean that when one commits some type of interpersonal offense against another, and the aggrieved party judges the other person favorably by saying such things as "'He didn't [really] commit a misdeed against me by doing such and such,' 'He couldn't help himself,' or 'He meant well,' there will then be peace between them."[4] Based on this rabbinic (and the common sense) connection between judging a person favorably and the promotion of peace,[5] in this chapter we will examine the basic halakhic parameters of this mitzvah and a number of related perspective-taking concepts that appear in the traditional sources.

The mitzvah of judging someone favorably could rightfully be categorized as one of Judaism's basic interpersonal obligations that plays a key role in preventing destructive conflict and promoting peace. As such, it may very well have been appropriate to have included it in Chapter 4, together with the other basic interpersonal obligations. However, because of the unique cognitive nature of the precept and the vital function, of countering judgmental biases, that it serves throughout the process of interpersonal conflict resolution (see p. 220), I have decided to dedicate an entire chapter to it and to group it together with "commandments and laws of interpersonal conflict resolution" in Part IV of this work.

The primary focus of our analysis will be on what the Halakhah requires one to think about and consider when an interpersonal offense has ostensibly taken place. We will only discuss tangentially the much more complex associated question of how one should interact and behave towards the person based on one's judgment of the person's actions. Considering the complexity of the *halakhot* that will be discussed, taken together with the multiplicity of real-life variables that

3 This is based on the text and explanation of Rashi, *Shabbat* 127b, s.v. *h'g hane name*.

4 Ibid.

5 As far as the role of judging people favorably in contemporary conflict resolution is concerned, see pp. 218–21.

affect them, and the potential for suffering and harm that one might expose oneself and others to (which also includes the person who is being judged) if one mistakenly misjudges someone, one has to approach this topic with a requisite degree of caution and concern. As with all such weighty halakhic issues, in many cases to ascertain the correct practical application of this mitzvah, one would have to consult with a halakhic authority who is intimately familiar not only with all of the pertinent *halakhot* but also with all of the relevant facts and variables that could come into play in the question at hand. With that said, and hopefully clearly understood, we will proceed to examine the commandment and its basic halakhic parameters.

The Commandment of "In Righteousness You Shall Judge Your Friend"

Leviticus 19:15 reads as follows: "You shall do no unrighteousness in judgment; you shall not show favor to the poor, nor show honor to the great; in righteousness you shall judge your friend." This passage has been interpreted, according to the simple explanation of the verse (the "*peshuto shel mikra*"), as addressing and exhorting a judge who is serving in a court case that he should not be swayed by the litigants' backgrounds in rendering his decision, but rather should decide the case objectively based on the merits of the evidence presented.[6] The final clause of the verse, "in righteousness you shall judge your friend," in Hebrew, *be-tsedek tishpot amitekha,* would accordingly be just a positive restatement of the introductory prohibition of "You shall do no unrighteousness in judgment," which was mentioned at the beginning of the verse.[7]

The Talmud, however, offers a number of other possible interpretations of "in righteousness you shall judge your friend."[8] One of

6 See Samson Raphael Hirsch, *The Hirsch Chumash*, 6 vols., trans. Daniel Haberman (Jerusalem: Feldheim, 2000), Lev. 19:15; Chaim Dov Rabinowitz, *Da'at Sofrim* (Tel Aviv: Sifriyati, 1958), Lev. 19:15; and Menachem Bolle, *Sefer Va-Yikra* (*Da'at Mikra*) (Jerusalem: Mossad Harav Kook, 1992), Lev. 19:15.

7 See Rashi's commentary to Lev. 19:15, first explanation, with the commentary of David Pardo, *Maskil le-David* (Jerusalem: Mekhon Even Yisrael, 1986), Lev. 19:15, s.v. *be-tsedek*.

8 See *Shevuot* 30a, *Sanhedrin* 32b, and *Sanhedrin* 3a.

these interpretations, which was cited above, is that this part of the verse is not dealing with a court proceeding, but rather it is a general precept that instructs one to judge other people's questionable behaviors favorably—"You should judge your friend towards the scale of merit" (see p. 190).[9] Consequently, we find that Maimonides and other authorities in their works that enumerate and explain the 613 commandments include "judging one's friend towards the scale of merit" as a biblical commandment.[10]

In their analyses of this commandment, later rabbinic scholars have focused on the fact that the talmudic sages derive the injunction to judge others favorably specifically from the statement "*in righteousness* (*be-tsedek*) you shall judge your friend."[11] A number of contemporary scholars assert that by emphasizing that one judge another's questionable behavior favorably in accordance with "*tsedek*," "righteousness" (which basically means, in accordance

9 *Shevuot* 30a and *Sifra, Kedoshim, perek* 4:4. There are various possibilities as to what served as the basis for this interpretation of the verse. The Rabbis may have viewed the entire final clause as being superfluous if it was still referring to judging a court case (see Abraham ben Solomon ha-Levi Bukarat, *Sefer ha-Zikaron al Perush Rashi la-Ḥumash* [Petaḥ Tikvah: Mosheh Filip, 1985], Lev. 19:15, s.v. *be-tsedek*); or some aspect of the verse's use of the word *amitekha*, "your friend," was viewed as being anomalous in the context of judging a court case (see Aaron ibn Ḥayyim, *Sefer Korban Aharon, Kedoshim, perek* 4:4, p. 205b).

10 A number of *rishonim* describe the requirement of judging others favorably as being "included within," or a component of, the mitzvah of "in righteousness you shall judge your friend." See Maimonides, *Sefer ha-Mitsvot*, positive commandment 177; Moses ben Jacob, *Semag*, positive commandment, 106; Ha-Levi, *Sefer ha-Ḥinukh*, commandment 235; Isaac ben Joseph, *Semak, siman* 224; cf. Gerondi, *Sha'are Teshuvah, sha'ar* 3:218. In two places, the *Ḥafets Ḥayim* writes that judging someone towards the scale of merit is a positive biblical commandment "according to a *number* of *poskim*" (*Sefer Ḥafets Ḥayim*, in *Kol Kitve Ḥafets Ḥayim ha-Shalem*, vol. 1 [New York: Avraham Yitsḥak Friedman, n.d.], *Hilkhot Isure Lashon ha-Ra, kelal* 4 *sa'if* 3 and *kelal* 6 *sa'if* 7). As to what exactly the *Ḥafets Ḥayim* means by attributing this view to only a number of *poskim*, see *Sefer Ḥafets Ḥayim, Hilkhot Isure Lashon ha-Ra, kelal* 3 *Be'er Mayim Ḥayim* 9; together with Hillel Zaks, "*Lashon ha-Ra u-Rekhilut ve-Lav shebe-Khlalot*," *Kol ha-Torah* 54 (Tishre 5764 [2003]): 58–59; and Moshe Kaufman, *Sefer Ḥafets Ḥayim ... ve-Nilvah alav Ḥibur Netivot Ḥayim* (Bnei Brak: n.p., 2011), *Hilkhot Lashon ha-Ra, kelal* 4, *Netiv Ḥayim* 5, and *kelal* 6, *Netiv Ḥayim* 11.

11 See, for example, Meir Loeb ben Jehiel Michael Malbim, *Sefer ha-Torah veha-Mitsvah* (Israel: Shiloh, n.d.), *Sifra* 39, Lev. 19:15; Hirsch, *The Hirsch Chumash*, Lev. 19:15; and David Kronglas, *Siḥot Ḥokhmah u-Musar*, vol. 1 (Jerusalem: n.p., 1998), 82–83.

with "what is correct and proper"),[12] the Torah is teaching that when one makes a determined effort to take into account all of the extenuating circumstances and factors that might possibly shed a favorable light on another person's somewhat questionable behavior, one is thereby counterbalancing a natural human tendency to often judge others in a harsh and negative fashion. In doing so, one may reduce an array of prejudices, cognitive distortions, and emotional biases that produce inaccurate perceptions and evaluations of others' behaviors,[13] which would then allow for an objective and accurate assessment of the person's conduct. Consequently, as a result of the attempt to lean towards a positive explanation for the questionable behavior, one may then properly judge the person in accordance with "*tsedek*."[14] To support this interpretation of the verse, some authors cite Targum Onkelos's translation (Lev. 19:15) of "in righteousness you shall judge your friend," which reads "*in truth*[15] you shall judge your friend." The implication of this paraphrase is that when one takes into consideration all of the factors that may allow for a positive judgment, one may thereby overcome prejudices,

12 See *Ha-Entsiklopedyah shel Tanakh* (Jerusalem: The Jerusalem Publishing Company, 1987), vol. 4., s.v. "*tsedek, tsedakah*"; B. Johnson, "*ṣāḏaq*," in *The Theological Dictionary of the Old Testament*, vol. 12 (Grand Rapids: William B. Eerdsmans, 2003) p. 248; for additional possible translations, see Zvi Raday and Chaim Rabin, *Ha-Milon he-Ḥadash la-Tanakh* (Jerusalem: Keter Publishing House, 1989), s.v. "*tsedek.*" Cf., Naḥmanides, *Perush ha-Ramban al ha-Torah*, annotated by Charles B. Chavel (Jerusalem: Mossad Harav Kook, 1988), Gen. 6:9 (who explains it as referring to "guiltlessness"); and Jonah ibn Janaḥ, *Sefer ha-Shorashim* (Jerusalem: n.p., 1966), s.v. "*tsadi dalet kuf.*"

13 See the related discussion of factors that may distort one's perceptions and negatively affect one's judgment, in Daniel Z. Feldman, *False Facts and True Rumors: Lashon Hara in Contemporary Culture* (New Milford, CT: Maggid Books, 2015), 44–82.

14 Avraham Ehrman, *Sefer Halikhot Olam: Kitsur Dinim ben Adam la-Ḥavero; Ve-Sefer Kodesh Yisrael* (Bnei Brak: n.p., 1996), *Kodesh Yisrael*, 118–19; Betsalel Shelomoh Gantserski, *Darkhe Tsedek: Al ha-Mitsvah la-Dun be-Tsedek* (Tifraḥ: n.p., 2002), 17; [Tzvi Meir Zilberberg], *Siḥot Hitḥazkut: She-Ne'emru be-Vet ha-Midrash Naḥalat Ya'akov: Be-Inyene Diyun le-Khaf Zekhut* (Jerusalem: Ḥaverim Makshivim, 2006), 24–25; and Avraham Ya'akov ha-Kohen Pam, *Atarah la-Melekh* (Brooklyn, NY: Yo.l. a.Y. Talmidav, 1993), 82–83.

15 Onkelos translates the Hebrew *be-tsedek* in Lev. 19:15 as *be-kushta (Targum Onkelos*, in the standard *Mikra'ot Gedolot*, Lev. 19:15). Included among the possible English translations would be "in truth," "in honesty," or "faithfully" (see ibid., Lev. 19:36, Deut. 1:16, 16:18, 20, 25:15).

distorted perceptions, and biases, and then be able to judge others in accordance with what is factually true.[16]

Alternatively, other rabbinic scholars propose that judging favorably in "righteousness" implies that when one judges another, one should take into consideration the pertinent facts, *both* positive and negative, that could help shed light on what took place. This would explain the halakhic parameters, which we are about to examine in the next section, that require one to take into consideration and differentiate between categories of actions (analyzing the nature of the questionable action, that is, does it or does it not appear that a wrong was committed) and categories of people (i.e., considering the character of the person who performed the action as it relates to the present action) when one judges others favorably.[17]

The Basic Halakhic Parameters of Judging Someone Favorably

There are *many* questions and issues that come into play that affect the practical halakhic application of the commandment to judge someone favorably. Two of the most basic questions that the sources indicate must be raised in its application are

> (1) What type of action did the person engage in? That is, objectively speaking, just viewing the action by itself, separate from the person who performed it, does it or does it not appear that a wrong was committed.
>
> (2) Who performed the action? That means to say, we have to consider the overall character of the person who performed the action as it relates to the present action.

16 See [Zilberberg], *Siḥot Hitḥazkut*, 25; and Gantserski, *Darkhe Tsedek*, 17.

17 Hillel Zaks, *"Ba-Mitsvat be-Tsedek Tishpot ba-Isur Lashon ha-Ra," Marpe Lashon* 3 (1984): 8–9; Kaufman, *Netivot Ḥayim*, 286–7; Yeḥiel Neuman, *"Ha-Mitsvah la-Dun le-Khaf Zekhut," Torat ha-Adam le-Adam: Kovets Torani ba-Mitsvot she-ben Adam la-Ḥavero* 5 (2004): 201 (in explaining Maimonides' opinion); Shimon Finkelman and Yitzchak Berkowitz, *Chofetz Chaim: A Lesson a Day* (Brooklyn: Mesorah Publications, 1998), endnote 91.

Taking the answers to these two questions together in conjunction with each other, the Halakhah will begin to direct us as to whether one should or should not judge the person favorably. However, there are also a number of other basic issues that come into play in the practical application of the *halakhot* of judging someone favorably:

(3) The question of the level of one's obligation in judging someone favorably. In other words, when the Halakhah states that one should judge a person favorably, sometimes one is halakhically obligated to do so (*"mi-tsad ha-din,"* literally, "from the perspective of the law [i.e., Halakhah]") and at other times, one is not halakhically obligated to judge the person favorably, but the Halakhah would recommend it as something that is proper to do (as a *"midah tovah,"* "a good character trait").[18]

(4) How should one judge someone favorably? Assuming that the Halakhah dictates that in a given case one should view what a person did as something positive, or favorably, practically speaking, if it appears that the person did something negative (i.e., wrong), how does one go about viewing it as something positive? Does one just employ the explanations that were cited earlier (p. 191) in the name Rashi (i.e., the person did not really commit a misdeed, he could not help himself, or he meant well),[19] or are there other possible positive interpretations that may be employed?

And, as so often is the case in halakhic discussions such as this:

(5) There are differences of opinion among halakhic authorities about the practical application of these *halakhot*, and

(6) There are different possible interpretations of the opinions expressed by these authorities.

---

18 There is also the related question of when one may judge someone unfavorably, whether this is something that is permissible, proper, or even obligatory to do.

19 See p. 191.

To help simplify the following discussion, we will primarily focus on questions 1 through 4 and the views expressed by R. Israel Meir ha-Kohen, the *Ḥafets Ḥayim*. We will only touch on issues related to questions 5 and 6 in the footnotes.

The Ḥafets Ḥayim on Judging "Towards the Scale of Merit"

Interspersed throughout the *Sefer Ḥafets Ḥayim* (his work on the laws of *lashon ha-ra*), in a number of different places the *Ḥafets Ḥayim* discusses the *halakhot* of judging people favorably.[20] Primarily basing himself on the opinions of Maimonides[21] and R. Jonah ben Abraham Gerondi (*Rabenu Yonah*, 1200–1263),[22] the *Ḥafets Ḥayim* addresses the first two questions cited above that relate to judging someone favorably—(1) What type of action did the person engage in, and (2) Who performed the action? The *Ḥafets Ḥayim* basically delineates three broad categories of questionable actions and four broad categories of people (see footnote):[23]

Categories of Actions

(1) "The matter is leaning towards the scale of merit."[24] The person engaged in an action that leans towards the positive.

20 The primary places where he focuses on this topic are Ha-Kohen, *Sefer Ḥafets Ḥayim, petiḥah, Asin* 3, *Be'er Mayim Ḥayim* 3; *Hilkhot Isure Lashon ha-Ra, kelal* 3 *se'ifim* 7–8, *Be'er Mayim Ḥayim* 8–12; *kelal* 4 *se'ifim* 3–4 (see also 6–7), *Be'er Mayim Ḥayim* 10, 18, 29; *kelal* 6 *se'ifim* 7–8 (and the *hagahah* on *sa'if* 8), *Be'er Mayim Ḥayim* 20, 28 (with the *hagahah*); (*kelal* 8 *sa'if* 7;) *kelal* 10 *Be'er Mayim Ḥayim* 3, 7 (at the end); *Hilkhot Rekhilut, kelal* 5 *sa'if* 6, *Be'er Mayim Ḥayim* 8; and *kelal* 6 *sa'if* 3.

21 See Maimonides, *Sefer ha-Mitsvot*, positive commandment 177; Maimonides, *Mishneh Torah, De'ot* 5:7; and Maimonides, *Perush ha-Mishnayot, Avot* 1:6.

22 Jonah ben Abraham Gerondi, *Sha'are Teshuvah, sha'ar* 3:218.

23 It goes without saying that, in the real world, there are many more than just three types of actions and four types of people. In his discussions of this topic, the *Ḥafets Ḥayim* gets involved in extremely intricate discussions of how the Halakhah categorizes different types of actions and people. The categories that I am presenting here should just be understood as very broad general classifications and guidelines to help explain the basic *halakhot*.

24 See Ha-Kohen, *Sefer Ḥafets Ḥayim, Hilkhot Isure Lashon ha-Ra, kelal* 3 *sa'if* 7; *kelal* 6 the *hagahah* on *sa'if* 8; *Hilkhot Rekhilut, kelal* 5 *Be'er Mayim Ḥayim* 8.

In other words, even though there is some doubt about the nature of what the person did, most probably the person did something good or proper.

(2) "An even doubt."[25] There is a 50/50 doubt as to the nature of the action. That means that there is an equal probability that the person did something good or that he did something bad.[26]

(3) "The matter is leaning towards the scale of guilt." [27] The person engaged in an action that leans towards the negative. Even though there is some doubt about the nature of what the person did, most probably he did something bad or improper.

Categories of People

(1) A "righteous person" ("*tsadik*"), or a "God fearing individual."[28]

---

25 Ha-Kohen, *Sefer Ḥafets Ḥayim, Hilkhot Isure Lashon ha-Ra, kelal* 3 *sa'if* 7.

26 At one point, the *Ḥafets Ḥayim* mentions the difficulty in definitively knowing when something actually constitutes an "even doubt"; see *Hilkhot Rekhilut, kelal* 5 *Be'er Mayim Ḥayim* 8.

27 (Alternatively, this may also be translated as "the scale of culpability.") Ha-Kohen, *Sefer Ḥafets Ḥayim, petiḥah, Asin* 3; *Hilkhot Isure Lashon ha-Ra, kelal* 3 *se'ifim* 7, 8; *kelal* 6 the *hagahah* on *sa'if* 8.

28 Maimonides uses the term "righteous" (specifically, "a righteous person, who is well-known for good deeds"; Maimonides, *Perush ha-Mishnayot, Avot* 1:6 [Kafih and Sheilat editions; cf., the standard printed edition in the Vilna *Shas*]) and *Rabenu Yonah* uses the term "God fearing" (Gerondi, *Sha'are Teshuvah, sha'ar* 3:218). The *Ḥafets Ḥayim* equates Maimonides' view regarding this category with that of *Rabenu Yonah*'s (*Sefer Ḥafets Ḥayim, petiḥah, Asin, Be'er Mayim Ḥayim* 3; and *Hilkhot Isure Lashon ha-Ra, kelal* 6 *sa'if* 8). The *Ḥafets Ḥayim* generally uses the term "God fearing" when discussing this category (see *Sefer Ḥafets Ḥayim, petiḥah, Asin* 3; *Hilkhot Isure Lashon ha-Ra, kelal* 3 *sa'if* 7; *kelal* 6 *sa'if* 8), and at times applies it to a "*talmid ḥakham*" (Torah scholar) (see *kelal* 4 *sa'if* 4, in which he is discussing "a person who is a Torah scholar and is fearful of committing a sin"; and *kelal* 6 the *hagahah* on *sa'if* 8, in which he is discussing "someone who has an established reputation in the city as being a Torah scholar").

(2) An "average person" ("*benoni*").[29] This refers to people who "are [generally] careful to abstain from sins but occasionally stumble."[30]

(3) A "wicked person" ("*rasha*").[31]

(4) A "person you are not familiar with."[32]

(It should be noted that according to a number of contemporary halakhic authorities, one individual can simultaneously fall into multiple categories; see footnote.[33])

---

29 Ha-Kohen, *Sefer Ḥafets Ḥayim, petiḥah, Asin* 3, *Be'er Mayim Ḥayim* 3; *Hilkhot Isure Lashon ha-Ra, kelal* 3 *sa'if* 7; *kelal* 6 *sa'if* 8.

30 Ha-Kohen, *Sefer Ḥafets Ḥayim, Hilkhot Isure Lashon ha-Ra, kelal* 3 *sa'if* 7; quoting Gerondi, *Sha'are Teshuvah, sha'ar* 3:218. The *Ḥafets Ḥayim* at one point describes this type of person as "an average Jew, whose path is that he guards himself from sin and stumbles only periodically" (*Hilkhot Isure Lashon ha-Ra, kelal* 4 *sa'if* 3; see also *kelal* 6 the *hagahah* on *sa'if* 8).

31 Maimonides uses the term "wicked" (specifically, "a wicked person, whose [bad] deeds are well-known"; Maimonides, *Perush ha-Mishnayot, Avot* 1:6); *Rabenu Yonah* describes this category of person as one who "the majority of his deeds are wicked or you have examined the person [and determined] that there is no fear of God in his heart" (Gerondi, *Sha'are Teshuvah, sha'ar* 3:218). Once again, the *Ḥafets Ḥayim* equates Maimonides' view regarding this category with that of *Rabenu Yonah*'s (*Sefer Ḥafets Ḥayim, petiḥah, Asin, Be'er Mayim Ḥayim* 3; and *kelal* 4 *Be'er Mayim Ḥayim* 29). See also *kelal* 6 the *hagahah* on *Be'er Mayim Ḥayim* 28.

32 Ha-Kohen, *Sefer Ḥafets Ḥayim, petiḥah, Asin, Be'er Mayim Ḥayim* 3. Maimonides describes this category of person as "a person who is not known to you, who you do not know if he is a righteous or wicked person" (Maimonides, *Perush ha-Mishnayot, Avot* 1:6 [Kafih and Sheilat editions, cf., the standard printed edition in the Vilna *Shas*]). See also *Kallah Rabbati*, chap. 9 (cited in David Ari'av, *Le-Re'akha kamokha*, vol. 8, *Halakhot u-Ve'urim ba-Mitsvah la-Dun le-Khaf Zekhut ve-Isur Sheker* [Jerusalem: Mekhon Le-Re'akha Kamokha, 2012], 439 n. 3).

33 For example, a person may be considered a "*tsadik*" in regard to one certain area (e.g., the person is always extremely honest and would never tell a lie), a "*benoni*" in another area (e.g., periodically, the person is insensitive to other people's feelings and transgresses the prohibition of *ona'at devarim*), and a "*rasha*" in another (e.g., the person is always speaking derogatorily about others, and constantly transgresses the prohibition of *lashon ha-ra*). See Shlomo Zalman Auerbach, quoted in *Mareh Mekomot al ha-Halakhot she-ben Adam la-Ḥavero*, vol. 1 (Jerusalem: Reshet ha-Kolelim Linat ha-Tsedek, 2006), 62; Shemaryahu Yosef Ḥayim Kanevski, quoted in Gantserski, *Darkhe Tsedek*, 60 (in which he expressed some doubt about this) and in Ari'av, *Le-Re'akha kamokha*, 486 (in which R. Kanievsky responded that this is "correct"); and Zaks, "*Ba-Mitsvat be-Tsedek Tishpot*, 8–9; cf. Hillel D. Litwack, "*Ba-Inyan Geder Benoni*," *Marpe Lashon* 7 (1994): 145–48.

Working with these three categories of actions and four categories of people, and the two basic levels of obligation in judging someone favorably that were mentioned earlier (i.e., that the Halakhah requires one to do so or that the Halakhah would just recommend it as something proper to do; see p. 196, question number 3), and assuming that there are three basic options to choose from when it comes to judging a person's questionable act—to either judge it positively, negatively, or deciding that one does not know one way or another if it was positive or negative—the *Ḥafets Ḥayim* sets forth the following basic guidelines:

Categories of People	*Categories of Actions:* An Action That Leans towards the Positive	An "Even Doubt"	An Action That Leans towards the Negative
Tsadik ("Righteous Person")	Favorably	Favorably	Favorably
Benoni ("Average Person")	Favorably	Favorably	It is proper that it should remain as a doubt[34]
Rasha ("Wicked Person")	Unfavorably	Unfavorably	Unfavorably
A Person You Are Not Familiar With	It is proper to judge the person favorably		

Figure 5.1. A basic (and oversimplified) summary of the rulings of the *Ḥafets Ḥayim* regarding judging others favorably. Adapted from Silver, *Mishpete ha-Shalom*, p. 12.[35] For an explanation of these rulings, see below, pp. 201–3, footnotes 36–40.

34 In his chart, R. Silver also adds that it is a righteous character trait to judge the person favorably in this case; see below, p. 201 n. 38.

35 Yitsḥak Isaac Silver, *Mishpete ha-Shalom: Hilkhot ben Adam la-Ḥavero* (Jerusalem: n.p., 2005), 12. For an English version of *Mishpete ha-Shalom*, see id., *The Code of Jewish Conduct: The Laws of Interpersonal Relationships* (Jerusalem: Center for Jewish Values, 2008).

In regard to a

- *Tsadik* – As a general rule, one is required to judge a "righteous person" favorably, even when the action leans towards the negative.[36]

- *Benoni* – One is required to judge an "average person" favorably when the action leans towards the positive. If there is an "even doubt" about the nature of the action, one is also required to judge the person favorably.[37] If the action leans towards the negative, the basic Halakhah would permit one to judge the person unfavorably; however, it is still proper for one not to do so, but rather for it to remain a doubt in one's mind and view the action as something that one does not know one way or another if it was positive or negative.[38]

---

36 The *Ḥafets Ḥayim* cites both *Rabenu Yonah* (Gerondi, *Sha'are Teshuvah, sha'ar* 3:218) and Maimonides (*Perush ha-Mishnayot, Avot* 1:6) as stating so (Ha-Kohen, *Sefer Ḥafets Ḥayim, petiḥah, Asin, Be'er Mayim Ḥayim* 3). According to the *Ḥafets Ḥayim,* their source for this ruling is the gemara in *Berakhot* 19a, which teaches, "If you see that a talmudic scholar has committed a sin at night, do not think [negatively] about him during the [next] day ... for he has certainly repented" (Ha-Kohen, Sefer Ḥafets Ḥayim, *Hilkhot Isure Lashon ha-Ra, kelal* 3 *Be'er Mayim Ḥayim* 8). I have written that this is only a *general* rule because, as many authors have pointed out, the gemara in *Berakhot* immediately qualifies what it says about the talmudic scholar and states that this rule does not apply in every case—"When it comes to monetary matters, not until he returns it to its owner." See Silver, *Mishpete ha-Shalom,* 10, n. 11; Ari'av, *Le-Re'akha kamokha,* 43; Gantserski, *Darkhe Tsedek,* 21 n. 15 (and 20 n. 14); Binyamin Cohen, *Sefer Ḥafets Ḥayim im Perush Ḥelkat Binyamin* (Brooklyn: n.p., 1993), *Hilkhot Isure Lashon ha-Ra, kelal* 3 *Ḥelkat Binyamin* 11, *kelal* 10 *Be'urim* 2; and Kaufman, *Netivot Ḥayim, Hilkhot Isure Lashon ha-Ra, kelal* 4, *Shevile Ḥayim* 20. All of these authors (excluding, possibly, R. Silver) are of the opinion that the talmudic exception regarding monetary matters can also apply to various other interpersonal transgressions as well.

37 Ha-Kohen, *Sefer Ḥafets Ḥayim, petiḥah, Asin* 3, *Be'er Mayim Ḥayim* 3 (where the *Ḥafets Ḥayim* cites Gerondi, *Sha'are Teshuvah, sha'ar* 3:218, and Maimonides, *Sefer ha-Mitsvot,* positive commandment 177, in conjunction with Maimonides, *Perush ha-Mishnayot, Avot* 1:6, as his sources); *Hilkhot Isure Lashon ha-Ra, kelal* 3 *sa'if* 7; *kelal* 6 *se'ifim* 7–8.

38 Ha-Kohen, *Sefer Ḥafets Ḥayim, Hilkhot Isure Lashon ha-Ra, kelal* 3 *se'ifim* 7–8, and *Be'er Mayim Ḥayim* 10. When the *Ḥafets Ḥayim* refers to this halakhah, he uses a

- *Rasha* – As a general rule, one should judge a "wicked person" unfavorably, even if the action is leaning towards the positive.[39]

---

number of different expressions that convey, more or less, the same basic idea: In *sa'if* 7, the *Ḥafets Ḥayim* writes that, in regard to a *benoni*, when it appears that the action the person engaged in was something negative "it is *very proper* that the matter should remain as a doubt for him and that one does not judge him negatively." In *Be'er Mayim Ḥayim* 10, he refers to this as a "*midah tovah be-alema*" (merely a good character trait), and cites Gerondi, *Sha'are Teshuvah, sha'ar* 3:218, taken in conjunction with talmudic passages in *Bava Metsia* 75b and *Sanhedrin* 26a, as his source. When he refers to this in *sa'if* 8, he writes that "from the perspective of the Halakhah, there is *not that much of a prohibition* to judge him negatively." At the end of *Be'er Mayim Ḥayim* 10, he adds that there is an additional level of "*midah tovah*" that dictates that even when there is a great likelihood that the action was something negative, the matter should not just remain as a doubt, but one should rather judge the person favorably. The source he cites for this is the talmudic passage in *Shabbat* 127b (see Mosheh Samsonovits, "*Kuntres Min ha-Ḥayim Meshisihu*," *Marpe Lashon* 3 [1984]: 52–53). For an alternative interpretation of what *Rabenu Yonah* had written in *Sha'are Teshuvah, sha'ar* 3:218, see [Binyamin Yehoshua Zilber], *Sha'are Teshuvah im Beur Zeh ha-Sha'ar* (Bnei Brak: Hotsa'at Ḥokhmah u-Musar, 1977), 290, s.v. *ve-im ha-davar*. According to R. Zilber, the wording of *Sha'are Teshuvah* indicates that even though the action leans towards the negative, it is not only "proper" but there is an obligation for it to remain as a doubt.

39 According to the *Ḥafets Ḥayim*, as a general rule, one is required to judge the questionable action of a *rasha* unfavorably; see Ha-Kohen, *Sefer Ḥafets Ḥayim, petiḥah, Asin, Be'er Mayim Ḥayim* 3 (in which the *Ḥafets Ḥayim* cites Gerondi, *Sha'are Teshuvah, sha'ar* 3:218 and Maimonides, *Perush ha-Mishnayot, Avot* 1:6); *kelal* 4 *sa'if* 7 (in which he briefly touches on judging someone whom it has "been established that he is a completely wicked person in respect to other areas"); and *kelal* 6 the *hagahah* on *Be'er Mayim Ḥayim* 28. R. Samuel Kolin (*Maḥasit ha-Shekel*, in the standard printed edition of the *Shulḥan Arukh, Oraḥ Ḥayim* 156, near the end of the *siman*, s.v. *heve dan*) quotes R. Obadiah Bertinoro (*Perush Rabenu Ovadiyah mi-Bartenura, Avot* 1:6) as stating that, in respect to a *rasha*, "it is *permissible* to judge him unfavorably" (as opposed to being required). A number of authors have pointed out that apparently there are those who disagree with the *Ḥafets Ḥayim*'s view and write that one should judge even a *rasha* favorably. Those who are of this opinion base their view on the wording of *Pirke Avot* 1:6—"Judge *all people* towards the scale of merit," which seems to imply that one should even judge a wicked person favorably (see the next footnote for an alternative interpretation of what the phrase "all people" may imply). For a number of *rishonim* who were possibly of this opinion, see Neuman, "*Ha-Mitsvah la-Dun le-Khaf Zekhut*," 211–14 (R. Neuman argues that one can interpret Maimonides as also being of this opinion); Daniel Biton, *Shisha Sidre Mishnah im Perush ha-Mishnah leha-Rambam* (Jerusalem: Mekhon ha-Ma'or, 2009), *Avot* 1:6, *he'arot u-ve'urim* 44; and

- *A Person You Are Not Familiar With* – Even though one may not be required to do so, it is still proper for one to judge a person one is not familiar with favorably.[40]

Encyclopedia Talmudit, vol. 17, s.v. *ḥashad*, column 564, n. 76. It should be noted that the *Ḥafets Ḥayim* himself points out that it could very well be that one is *not* allowed to judge someone who is a *rasha* negatively by assuming that he has committed a worse offense than those he has committed up until now (*Sefer Ḥafets Ḥayim, kelal* 6 the *hagahah* on *Be'er Mayim Ḥayim* 28).

40 Ha-Kohen, *Sefer Ḥafets Ḥayim, petiḥah, Asin, Be'er Mayim Ḥayim* 3. The *Ḥafets Ḥayim* cites Maimonides (*Perush ha-Mishnayot, Avot* 1:6, and *Mishneh Torah, De'ot* 5:7) as his source. In his commentary to the mishnah in *Avot*, Maimonides writes that it is "the path of righteousness" ("*ba-derekh ha-ḥasidut*," this is according to the translation of Samuel ibn Tibbon in the standard Vilna edition of the Babylonian Talmud, and Yosef Kafih, trans. and annot., *Mishnah im Perush Rabenu Mosheh ben Maimon: Makor ve-Targum, Seder Nezikin* [Jerusalem: Mossad Harav Kook, 1965], *Avot* 1:6; cf. Isaac Shailat, trans., *Masekhet Avot im Perush Rabenu Mosheh ben Maimon* [Jerusalem: Ma'aliyot, 1994], 10 n. 37), which the *Ḥafets Ḥayim* refers to as a "*midah tovah*," a "good character trait," that one should judge a person that one is not familiar with favorably. (Thus, according to Maimonides, the phrase "all people" in "Judge all people towards the scale of merit," comes to include even people that one is not familiar with.) There is, however, a fundamental debate among contemporary scholars as to what exactly Maimonides (and the *Ḥafets Ḥayim*) means by this. Some argue that Maimonides means that it is only recommended that one judge favorably a person one is not familiar with when there is an "even doubt" about the nature of the action, but if the matter is "leaning towards the scale of guilt," one may judge the person unfavorably. This interpretation of Maimonides appears in the commentaries of R. Menaḥem Meiri (*Bet ha-Beḥirah al Masekhet Shabat* [Jerusalem: n.p., 1976], *Shabbat* 127b; and *Ḥibur ha-Teshuvah* [New York: Talpiyot Yeshiva University, 1950], 85) and R. Simeon ben Zemaḥ Duran (in his commentary to *Avot*, in *Mishnat Re'uven: Masekhet Avot im Perushe ha-Rishonim* [Jerusalem: Mossad Harav Kook, 2005], *Avot* 1:6) (see Neuman, "*Ha-Mitsvah la-Dun le-Khaf Zekhut*," 201; Ari'av, *Le-Re'akha kamokha*, 48 n. 52; and Gantserski, *Darkhe Tsedek*, 29–30). However, others understand Maimonides as saying that it is recommended that one always judge favorably a person one is not familiar with even if it appears that the person did something improper (see Silver, *Mishpete ha-Shalom*, 11–12, and above, p. 200, in the chart). This view appears in the commentary of *Rabenu Yonah* on *Pirke Avot* (Jonah ben Abraham Gerondi, *Perushe Rabenu Yonah mi-Gerondi al Masekhet Avot* [Jerusalem: Mekhon Torah Shelemah, 1980], *Avot* 1:6). R. Yitsḥak Sheilat points out that this question of how to interpret Maimonides revolves around how one translates the original Judeo-Arabic wording of Maimonides. According to R. Sheilat, R. Samuel ibn Tibbon's and R. Kafih's translations support the first interpretation, whereas an exact rendering of the original Judeo-Arabic wording lends support to the second interpretation (Shailat, *Masekhet Avot*, p. 10 n. 36). For an alternative perspective on these *halakhot*, see Asher Weiss, *Minḥat Asher: Leket*

How Should One Judge Someone Favorably? The next practical question we should address is, in those cases that the Halakhah requires or recommends that one judge another favorably, how does one do so if it really seems that the person did something improper? The *Ḥafets Ḥayim* offers a number of plausible interpretations that one may give for what appears to be improper conduct on the part of another, so as to judge the person favorably (see above, p. 191, for the three interpretations that Rashi offers in such a case). These include: (1) The person did something wrong but it was unintentional, and possibly afterwards he himself regretted what he did;[41] (2) he acted or said something improper as a result of anger and/or pain he was experiencing at the time because of something unrelated to the present situation;[42] (3) the person simply did not understand that what he did was "prohibited," or wrong;[43] (4) the person realized that what he did was wrong, but did not realize how wrong it was;[44] and (5) that one has totally misunderstood what took place and in reality the other person's actions were totally justified and he did nothing wrong.[45]

Based on the above, it appears that the *Ḥafets Ḥayim* was of the opinion that as a general rule there is almost always some possible justification for what the person had done or at least some mitigating factor that could, to a certain degree, lessen a person's guilt or culpability. This view is clearly expressed when at one point the *Ḥafets Ḥayim* writes that

---

Shiurim ve-Siḥot al Sefer Va-Yikra (Jerusalem: Mekhon Minḥat Asher, 2003), 263, where he argues, based on *Rabenu Yonah* and the *Vilna Gaon*, that we should treat a person we are not familiar with the same as a *benoni*.

41 Ha-Kohen, *Sefer Ḥafets Ḥayim, petiḥah, Asin, Be'er Mayim Ḥayim* 3; *Hilkhot Isure Lashon ha-Ra, kelal* 4 *sa'if* 3; and *Hilkhot Rekhilut, kelal* 5 *sa'if* 6.

42 Ha-Kohen, *Sefer Ḥafets Ḥayim, petiḥah, Asin, Be'er Mayim Ḥayim* 3.

43 Ha-Kohen, *Sefer Ḥafets Ḥayim, Hilkhot Isure Lashon ha-Ra, kelal* 4 *sa'if* 3.

44 Ibid.; and Ha-Kohen, *Shemirat ha-Lashon, Sha'ar ha-Tevunah*, chap. 4.

45 Ha-Kohen, *Shemirat ha-Lashon, Sha'ar ha-Tevunah*, chap. 4 (what he refers to as "*sheha-din imo*"); see also Ha-Kohen, *Sefer Ḥafets Ḥayim, Hilkhot Isure Lashon ha-Ra, kelal* 6 the *hagahah* on *sa'if* 8; and *kelal* 10 *Be'er Mayim Ḥayim* 7 (at the end).

> One who desires to judge [someone] favorably, the paths for [finding] a favorable judgment are never closed off before him.[46]

Related Concepts

"Respect Him and Suspect Him"

There are a number of perspective-taking concepts that are related to the commandment of judging someone favorably that we should also touch on. By far, one of the most pertinent concepts is what is popularly referred to in traditional sources as *"kabdehu ve-ḥoshdehu,"* "respect him and suspect him,"[47] which seems to suggest that one show respect to people and at the very same time also suspect them of potential wrongdoing.

There are many possible explanations of what exactly *kabdehu ve-ḥoshdehu* means, and how one may possibly reconcile it with the requirement of judging a person favorably and the related concept known as *"ḥoshed bi-khsherim"* (literally, "suspecting 'kosher' people"), which teaches that one should not suspect an innocent person of wrongdoing.[48] One simple approach is that of R. Eleazar Azikri (1533–1600). According to R. Azikri, "respect him and

---

46 Ha-Kohen, *Sefer Ḥafets Ḥayim, petiḥah, Asin, Be'er Mayim Ḥayim* 3. (Personally speaking, this calls to mind what the social psychologist Bernard Weiner once wrote in relation to "attribution theory" [see below, pp. 213–14]—that "[a] virtually infinite number of causal ascriptions are available in memory" [Bernard Weiner, "An Attributional Theory of Achievement Motivation and Emotion," *Psychological Review* 92, no. 4 (1985): 549].)

47 The source for this concept appears in *Kallah Rabbati*, chap. 9; *Derekh Erets Rabbah*, Chap. 5; and is cited by Rashi, *Ta'anit* 23b, s.v. *de-lo bedikitu li*. The wording of *Kallah Rabbati* and *Derekh Erets Rabbah* is "All people should be in your eyes as bandits, and you should honor them as you would Rabban Gamliel." See the illustrative story that these sources also offer, with the comments of R. Shlomo Zalman Auerbach, *Minḥat Shelomoh: Tinyana* (Jerusalem: n.p., 2000), *siman* 133, p. 472.

48 See *Shabbat* 97a and *Yoma* 19b. For a discussion of the relationship between judging people favorably and the prohibition of being *ḥoshed bi-khsherim*, see Yitsḥak Ḥayim Fus, *"Ha-Mitsvah la-Dun le-Khaf Zekhut veha-Isur la-Ḥshod bi-Khsherim," Torat ha-Adam le-Adam: Kovets Torani ba-Mitsvot she-ben Adam la-Ḥavero* 3 (1999): 126–29; and Ari'av, *Le-Re'akha kamokha*, 449–53.

suspect him" simply means that one should show the utmost respect to a person whom one is unfamiliar with, but at the same time be prudently cautious, in order to protect oneself (or others), and suspect that the person has the potential to do something improper or harmful—"One should view a person as being completely righteous and wholeheartedly honor him (not merely as a pretentious show), but one must still guard oneself from him . . . ."[49] R. Azikri compares this to one of the fundamental rules of *lashon hara* ("evil speech," i.e., saying derogatory things about someone without a constructive, halakhically sanctioned purpose), which teaches that "one may not accept it [i.e., believe *lashon hara*] to be true, but one should suspect that it is possibly so [in order to protect oneself or others]."[50]

"Vindicating the Wicked"

The sources that elaborate on the concept of judging others favorably inevitably at some point in their discussions touch on the potentially negative and harmful flip slide of the concept, of when one erroneously judges favorably someone who really does not deserve a favorable judgment, such as someone who is guilty of a crime or serious wrongdoing. In addressing this concern, rabbinic scholars cite an array of sources that caution against being naïve and gullible, and inadvertently justifying morally reprehensible behavior. Often, these scholars cite biblical verses that underscore this concern in one way or another. The most common verses that are cited include: "He who vindicates the wicked

49 Eleazar Azikri, *Sefer Ḥaredim ha-Shalem* (Jerusalem: n.p., 1990), 66:33. For alternative explanations and further elaboration, see *Kallah Rabbati*, chap. 9 (the "Gemara"); Judah ben Samuel, *Sefer Ḥasidim* (Jerusalem: Mossad Harav Kook, 2002), *siman* 1088; Joseph ben Ḥayyim Jabez, *Masekhet Avot im Perush . . . Yosef Yabe'ts* (Jerusalem: Mekhon Ma'oz ha-Torah, 1990), *Avot* 1:6; Moses Sofer, *Ha-Ḥatam Sofer al Masekhet Avot* (n.p., n.d.), *Avot* 1:1, s.v. *hevu metunim ba-din*; Fus, "*Ha-Mitsvah la-Dun le-Khaf Zekhut*," 135–37; and Neuman, "*Ha-Mitsvah la-Dun le-Khaf Zekhut*," 210–11.

50 *Niddah* 61a; and Ha-Kohen, *Sefer Ḥafets Ḥayim, Hilkhot Isure Lashon ha-Ra, kelal* 6 *se'ifim* 10–11. See also Shemaryahu Yosef Ḥayim Kanevski, quoted in Ari'av, *Le-Re'akha kamokha*, 490 (question 22). For more on how one should interact and behave towards a person based on one's judgment of the person's actions, see the sources cited in Gantserski, *Darkhe Tsedek*, 40–43.

and he who condemns the righteous—both of them are an abomination to God" (Proverbs 17:15),[51] "He who is righteous is wise regarding the abode of the wicked, interpreting [the deeds of] the wicked as evil" (Proverbs 21:12),[52] "Woe unto them that say about bad that it is good, and about good that it is bad" (Isaiah 5:20),[53] "A fool will believe anything, but a prudent person's steps will be with understanding" (Proverbs 14:15),[54] and "When his voice tries to find favor, do not believe him" (Proverbs 26:25).[55]

"Do Not Judge Your Friend until You Are in His Place"

Another perspective-taking concept that most certainly deserves to be touched on is the teaching of Hillel in *Pirke Avot,* "Do not judge your friend until you are in his place" (*Avot* 2:4). According to R. Joseph Jabez (the "*Ḥasid Yavets,*" d. 1507), this concept should be viewed as being "a major principle in maintaining peace and love between people."[56]

There is a plethora of rabbinic commentaries that discuss the concept of "do not judge your friend until you are in his place." From among the many different commentaries, there are a number of reoccurring interpretive themes that appear in the traditional sources. For example, there is one line of interpretation that understands this mishnah as saying that in order to accurately judge another person, one has to try to put oneself in the other person's place and take into consideration all of the variables that

51 Cited by Moses Almosnino, *Pirke Mosheh* (Jerusalem: Haktav Institute, 1995), *Avot* 1:6; Ben-Zion Meir Ḥai Ouziel, *Derashot Uziel al Masekhet Avot* (Jerusalem: Ha-Va'ad le-Hotsa'at Kitve ha-Rav, zatsal, 1991), 47–49; and Yehoshua Falk Ze'ev [Wolfsohn], *Sefer ha-Midot* (Munkacs: Kahn and Fried, 1906), 23a.

52 See, for example, Gerondi, *Sha'are Teshuvah, sha'ar* 3:218; Gerondi, *Rabenu Yonah al Masekhet Avot, Avot* 1:6; and Isaac Hutner, *Paḥad Yitsḥak: Sha'ar Yeraḥ ha-Etanim* (Brooklyn: Ha-Mosad Gur Aryeh, 1974), 104.

53 Cited in Jacob Emden, *Sefer Migdal Oz* (Jerusalem: Hotsa'at Fisher, 1993), 276.

54 Cited in Silver, *Mishpete ha-Shalom,* 9.

55 See, for example, Maimonides, *Perush ha-Mishnayot, Avot* 1:6; Gerondi, *Rabenu Yonah al Masekhet Avot, Avot* 1:6; and Meiri, *Ḥibur ha-Teshuvah,* 85.

56 Jabez, *Masekhet Avot im Perush Yosef Yabe'ts, Avot* 2:5.

may have influenced the other person's behavior; this would include such things as "his nature, his intellectual level, his environment, his friends, and things that he is dealing with."[57] Another line of interpretation understands it as saying that even when it is clear that someone has done something wrong, one should not judge the person too harshly since one never knows whether or not if he was in the other person's place and had to deal with that person's challenges if he would act any better.[58] And a third line of interpretation understands it as saying that since it is impossible to ever really totally put oneself in another person's place, no one, outside of God, really has the right to pass judgment on another human being.[59]

The *Ḥafets Ḥayim* discusses "do not judge your friend until you are in his place" (as far as I have been able to determine) only three times in his written works.[60] Each of these times, he seems to equate it with the act of going over to the person, questioning him, and discussing with him his ostensibly improper behavior, and

---

57 Abram. Jelen, *Orekh Apayim* (Brooklyn: Yofi, n.d.), 37b, *Va-Yosef Avraham* n. 14. For similar interpretations, see Elijah Meyer Bloch, *"Ha-Roeh,"* in *Shi'ure Da'at*, vol. 3, by Joseph Leib Bloch (Tel Aviv: Netsaḥ, 1956), 157; Moshe ibn Makhir, *Seder ha-Yom* (Warsaw: Levenzohn, 1873), 28–29; and Ari'av, *Le-Re'akha kamokha*, 24.

58 Dov Berish Gottlieb, *Yad ha-Ketanah* (Jerusalem: Or ha-Sefer, 1976), *sha'ar* 7, *perek* 4. For similar interpretations, see Jacob ben Samson, commentary to *Avot*, in *Mishnat Re'uven: Masekhet Avot im Perushe ha-Rishonim* [Jerusalem: Mossad Harav Kook, 2005], *Avot* 2:4; Menaḥem Meiri, *Bet ha-Beḥirah al Masekhet Avot* (Jerusalem: Mekhon ha-Talmud ha-Yisraeli ha-Shalem, 1968), *Avot* 2:4; and Israel Lipschutz, *Tiferet Yisrael: Yakhin u-Voaz*, in *Mishnayot Zekher Ḥanokh* (Jerusalem: Ḥ. Vagshal, 1999), *Avot* 2:4, *Yakhin* 34.

59 Naḥman of Bratslav, *Likute Moharan* (Jerusalem: Keren Hadpasah shel Ḥaside Breslav, 1976), *Tinyana*, 2b; Judah Aryeh Leib Alter, *Masekhet Avot im Perush Sefat Emet* (Jerusalem: Y.Y.A. Alter, 2002), *Avot* 2:4; Azriel Meir Eger, cited in *Eleh Ezkerah: Osef Toldot Kedoshe 5700–5705*, vol. 5 (New York: Ha-Makhon le-Ḥeker Be'ayot ha-Yahadut ha-Ḥaredit, 1963), 128; and Elijah Eliezer Dessler, *Mikhtav me-Eliyahu: Divre Ḥokhmah u-Musar ba-Avodat Ḥodesh Elul ve-Yeraḥ ha-Etanim*, 2 vols. (Bnei Brak: Sifsei Chachamim, 2008), vol. 1, 95.

60 Ha-Kohen, *Sefer Ḥafets Ḥayim, Hilkhot Isure Lashon ha-Ra, kelal* 6 the *hagahah* on *sa'if* 8; *kelal* 10 *Be'er Mayim Ḥayim* 7 (at the very end); and Israel Meir Ha-Kohen, *Kuntres Ahavat Yisrael*, in *Kol Kitve Ḥafets Ḥayim ha-Shalem*, vol. 1, chap. 5, p. 53. He does mention it a fourth time in passing, in Ha-Kohen, *Shemirat ha-Lashon, Sha'ar ha-Tevunah*, chap. 4.

determining his reason for this behavior.[61] In one of these sources, the *Ḥafets Ḥayim* emphasizes that after clarifying the motivation behind the person's actions, one should try to mentally put oneself in the other person's place and reflect on how he would have dealt with that person's situation, and if possibly he would have acted in a similar manner.[62] Notably, in one of the other places that the *Ḥafets Ḥayim* discusses it,[63] he compares this concept to the mitzvah of *tokhaḥah* for interpersonal offenses, which requires that one respond to an interpersonal provocation by going over to the person who committed the offense, discussing what had occurred, and trying to thereby resolve the matter (see Chapter 6).

Summary

In this chapter, we have examined the mitzvah of judging people favorably. After initially introducing the basic concept, terminology, and sources that relate to this commandment, the basic halakhic parameters of the mitzvah, as set forth by the *Ḥafets Ḥayim*, were presented. We then concluded by briefly touching on a number of pertinent related concepts.

In going through the sources that were presented in this chapter, we have seen how rabbinic authorities stressed the vital role that judging people favorably and its associated concepts play in positive interpersonal relations. The ability to go against one's natural tendency to often judge people unfavorably, and to strike the proper balance between viewing questionable behavior favorably and at the same time not inappropriately justifying bad behavior, in other words, being able to judge the other person fairly, were viewed by the Rabbis as essential life skills that serve a major function in promoting peace between people.

---

61 The same explanation also appears in Simḥah Zissel Ziv [Broida], *Bet Kelm*, vol. 2 (Bnei Brak: Sifte Ḥakhamim, 2010), 578–79; and Avraham Mader, cited in Shalom Schnitzler, *Kitsur Shulḥan Arukh ve-Nilvu alav Shene Sefarim: Sha'are Shalom, Mevaser Shalom*, vol. 2 (Jerusalem: College for Higher Rabbinical Studies, 1978), *siman* 29, p. 101 n. 27.

62 Ha-Kohen, *Kuntres Ahavat Yisrael*, p. 53.

63 Ha-Kohen, *Sefer Ḥafets Ḥayim*, *Hilkhot Isure Lashon ha-Ra*, *kelal* 6 the *hagahah* on *sa'if* 8.

There are a number of things that should be highlighted from out of our discussion. First, it should be self-evident that the *halakhot* of judging people favorably are based on the fundamental premise that things are often not as they appear to be. We have seen how the Halakhah teaches that there are certain cases in which a person has engaged in an action that leans towards the negative, yet one should nevertheless assume a positive explanation, and that there are other certain cases in which a person has engaged in an action that leans towards the positive, but one should still nevertheless assume a negative explanation. In all cases, the Halakhah requires that one rise above the superficial impressions, emotional biases, and distorted perceptions that so often adversely affect interpersonal relations and contribute to conflict, and instead render a careful and fair assessment of other people's behaviors.

Another point that I feel has to be underscored, as I tried to do earlier in this chapter, is that the practical application of the *halakhot* and concepts that were discussed may be far from a simple matter. Aside from the challenge of overcoming the natural tendency, and possibly the nurturing that one received, which may run contrary to a lot of what we have learned, the entire process requires a nuanced perspective on different types of people and different types of actions, and a solid grasp of the pertinent *halakhot*. However, I believe that the basic *halakhot* that were presented in this chapter are quite logical and for most people would be quite easily and intuitively grasped (I found this to be the case when I taught this topic to over two hundred fifty ninth graders between 2007 and 2012). The one concern that I have is that in going through the summary of the *halakhot* that I have presented (pp. 197–203) one may mistakenly not realize that what I have offered is only an oversimplified presentation of these *halakhot*. I therefore, once again, would like to emphasize that the appropriate real-world application of what we have learned may be much more complicated than one may realize, and may require that one consult a qualified halakhic authority.

I would like to conclude with an insight that was offered by R. David Kronglas (1910–1973). Aside from the simple explanation that the purpose of the mitzvah of judging others favorably is to help promote peace (see the citation from *Shabbat* 127a–b, on p. 191, and the epigraph at the beginning of this chapter), R. Kronglas proposed that this mitzvah is meant to help develop within the individual a compassionate way of thinking and looking at people and the world. Highlighting the unique cognitive nature of the commandment, he wrote as follows:

> God, may He be blessed, has given us many interpersonal commandments, the purpose of which is to implant and enroot within our hearts good character traits, such as loving-kindness, compassion, pity, mercy, love of humanity, and the like. All of these are encompassed in the term *"lev tov,"* [a "good heart"]. And God has also given to us one commandment, singular and unique in its character ... whose purpose is to implant and enroot within our minds loving-kindness, compassion, pity, and mercy. All of these are encompassed in the term *"sekhel tov"* [a "good intellect"], that means to say, an intellect of loving-kindness and compassion ... This is the commandment of "In righteousness you shall judge your friend"—"You should judge all people towards the scale of merit."[64]

Similarities and Differences between Contemporary Conflict Resolution and Traditional Jewish Approaches in Respect to Judging People Favorably

Though the exact terminology may hardly ever appear in contemporary conflict resolution literature, nevertheless the concept of "judging people favorably" plays a major role in contemporary conflict resolution. There exists a large body of social-psychological research on how people perceive the behavior of others and its effect on conflict. From

64 Kronglas, *Siḥot Ḥokhmah u-Musar*, vol. 1, 79.

out of this research, many concepts have emerged that have influenced contemporary conflict resolution theory and practice. Particularly germane to the focal topic of this chapter is the research on negative perceptions of other people's behaviors and the impact of these perceptions on interpersonal conflict.[65] After briefly presenting some of the findings of this research, we will examine contemporary approaches to countering common judgmental biases and what contemporary conflict resolution has adopted from out of these approaches. We will then go on to compare and contrast these elements with the traditional Jewish approaches that were presented in this chapter.

Research on Negative Judgmental Biases

Contemporary social psychology postulates the existence of a fundamental, innate human "motivation" (i.e., a need or drive) to comprehend the behaviors of people that one encounters.[66] The processes by which one categorizes, judges, and evaluates other people are often referred to in social-psychological literature as "person perception."[67] Some of the most significant aspects of these

---

65 See Chapter 3, pp. 104–5, where I briefly touched on this topic.

66 One finds many different formulations of this concept in the social-psychological literature. Some describe this simply as a "motivation"; see, for example, Susan T. Fiske, *Social Beings: A Core Motives Approach to Social Psychology* (Hoboken, NJ: Wiley, 2004), 14–15, 17–19, 123–25. Citing earlier researchers and theorists, Michael Andreychik describes this as a "proclivity" and a "fundamental human activity"; see Michael R. Andreychik, "Social Explanatory Style as a Foundation of Social Orientation" (master's thesis, Lehigh University, 2006), 3–4, accessed November, 7, 2016, http://preserve.lehigh.edu/cgi/viewcontent.cgi?article=1016&context=cas-campbell-prize. Gordon Moskowitz and Michael Gill refer to it as a "drive," "need," and "desire"; see Gordon B. Moskowitz and Michael J. Gill, "Person Perception," in *The Oxford Handbook of Cognitive Psychology*, ed. Daniel Reisberg (Oxford: Oxford University Press, 2013), 919 ("the drive to understand behavior"), 920 (part of the "causal drive"), 930 and 920 (perceivers have "epistemic needs—to impose meaning on stimuli" and behavior observed), and 925 (perceivers are motivated by "their desire for prediction and control").

67 For basic definitions of "person perception," see the *APA Dictionary of Psychology* (Washington, DC: American Psychological Association, 2007), s.v. "person perception"; and Andrew M. Colman, *Oxford Dictionary of Psychology*, 3rd ed., s.v. "person perception." For a much more extensive treatment of the concept, see

processes in respect to interpersonal conflict are the biased ways in which people negatively interpret and draw negative inferences about the conduct of others. Two categories of biases that especially stand out in this regard are what are known as "negativity biases" and "attributional biases."

"Negativity biases" refers to a group of phenomena wherein negative (or, alternatively, "bad") acts, information, and stimuli have been found to have in many ways a much greater impact on people than positive (or "good") acts, information, and stimuli. The pervasive tendency of people to systematically focus on and overemphasize what is negative, and even what is just *possibly* negative, in others is well documented.[68] This acute sensitivity to and overemphasis on the negative, and possibly negative, conduct of another person, as well as the propensity to formulate unfounded and irrational negative inferences about others, all together contribute in the most profound ways to conflict (see explanation below).

Closely related to negativity biases are "attributional biases," which are periodically discussed in contemporary conflict resolution literature. In the context of the social-psychological discussions of how people interpret the conduct of others, the term "attribution" refers to the "inferring [of] underlying

---

Moskowitz and Gill, "Person Perception," 918–42. Person perception overlaps with (or, to be precise, is a subcategory of) the social-psychological construct "social cognition" (i.e., the cognitive processes by which people interpret, categorize, and judge social behavior [see *APA Dictionary of Psychology*, s.v. "social cognition"; Colman, *Oxford Dictionary of Psychology*, s.v. "social cognition"; Gordon B. Moskowitz, *Social Cognition: Understanding Self and Others* (New York: Guilford Press, 2005), 2–3; and Gordon B. Moskowitz, e-mail message to the author, March 24, 2015]).

68 See, for example, David E. Kanouse, "Explaining Negativity Biases in Evaluation and Choice Behavior: Theory and Research," in *Advances in Consumer Research*, vol. 11, ed. Thomas C. Kinnear (Provo, Utah: Assoc. for Consumer Research, 1984), 703–8; Andrew Galperin and Martie G. Haselton, "Error Management and the Evolution of Cognitive Bias," in *Social Thinking and Interpersonal Behavior*, ed. Joseph P. Forgas, Klaus Fiedler, and Constantine Sedikides (New York: Taylor & Francis, 2012), 45–47, 50–53, 56; and the landmark review of research by Roy F. Baumeister et al., "Bad is Stronger Than Good," *Review of General Psychology* 5 no. 4 (2001): 323–70.

conditions or causes regarding behavior of others or self,"[69] in other words, the explanations that one gives for someone's behavior by which one ascribes to the person certain characteristics, intentions, feelings, and traits.[70] "Attributional biases" therefore refer to certain prevalent tendencies that people have to make flawed inferences and errors in judgment regarding the *causes* of behavior (most often, positive ones when it comes to judging oneself and negative ones when it comes to judging others).[71] Negative attributional biases towards others have a very significant bearing on conflict, one classic example of which would be what has been dubbed the "fundamental attribution error," with which people tend to attribute others' bad behavior to internal, dispositional factors—which encompasses such things as negative personality traits (e.g., "he's arrogant," "she's a very nasty person," "he's irresponsible and lazy," and so on), motives (e.g., "he was intentionally trying to insult and hurt me"), and attitudes (e.g., "she must hate me")—as opposed to external, situational factors (e.g., others' behavior is attributed to some type of external pressure or as being accidental).[72]

Among the potential adverse effects that negativity and attributional biases have been found to have, which directly relate to conflict, are reduced empathy for the other, the assignment of blame, the fostering of poor communication, the development of anger

69 See Raymond J. Corsini, *The Dictionary of Psychology* (Philadelphia, PA: Brunner/Mazel, 1999), s.v. "attribution."

70 See David Kanouse and L. Reid Hanson, Jr., "Negativity in Evaluations," in *Attribution: Perceiving the Causes of Behavior*, ed. Edward E. Jones et al. (Morristown, NJ: General Learning Press, 1972), 47; Colman, *Oxford Dictionary of Psychology*, s.v. "attribution"; *APA Dictionary of Psychology*, s.v. "attribution"; and Gifford Weary, John A. Edwards, and Shannon Riley, "Attribution," in *Encyclopedia of Human Behavior* (San Diego: Academic Press, 1994), 291.

71 See David Matsumoto, ed., *The Cambridge Dictionary of Psychology* (Cambridge: Cambridge University Press, 2009), s.v. "attributional bias"; Colman, *Oxford Dictionary of Psychology*, s.v. "attributional bias"; and *APA Dictionary of Psychology*, s.v. "attribution error."

72 See Lee Ross, "The Intuitive Psychologist and His Shortcomings: Distortions in the Attribution Process," *Advances in Experimental Social Psychology* 10 (1977): 175–76, 183–86.

and hostility, and the adoption of harsh and dysfunctional tactics. All of these effects are known to significantly contribute to conflict and serve as strong barriers to its resolution.[73]

Countering Negative Judgmental Biases

Research on methods for countering judgmental biases has explored various different approaches to negating or minimizing the effects of common biases that contribute to conflict. Some of the "debiasing" techniques that this research has promoted have been, to varying degrees, adopted by contemporary conflict resolution, with one in particular (in respect to interpersonal conflict resolution) standing out from the rest. In this section, we will touch on select highlights of this research.

Debiasing Techniques. A considerable amount of research on judgmental biases has concerned itself with the process of "debiasing," that is, eliminating or diminishing the intensity and frequency of common errors and fallacies in judgment.[74] There are a

73 See Morton Deutsch, "Educating for a Peaceful World," *American Psychologist* 48, no. 5 (1993): 514; Jeffrey Z. Rubin, Dean G. Pruitt, and Sung Hee Kim, *Social Conflict: Escalation, Stalemate, and Settlement,* 2nd ed. (New York: McGraw Hill, 1994), 84–88, 102–7; Alan L. Sillars, "Attributions and Interpersonal Conflict Resolution," in *New Directions in Attribution Research,* vol. 3, ed. John H. Harvey, William Ickes, and Robert F. Kidd (Hillsdale, NJ: Lawrence Erlbaum Associates, 1981), 279–305; Keith G. Allred, "Anger and Retaliation in Conflict: The Role of Attribution," in *The Handbook of Conflict Resolution: Theory and Practice,* ed. Morton Deutsch and Peter T. Coleman (San Francisco: Jossey-Bass, 2000), 243–44; Emily Pronin, Carolyn Puccio, and Lee Ross, "Understanding Misunderstanding: Social Psychological Perspectives," in *Heuristics and Biases: The Psychology of Intuitive Judgment,* ed. Thomas Gilovich, Dale W. Griffin, and Daniel Kahneman (New York: Cambridge University Press, 2002), 636–42; Susan S. Raines, *Conflict Management for Managers: Resolving Workplace, Client, and Policy Disputes* (San Francisco: Jossey-Bass, 2013), 42–44; and Deutsch, *The Resolution of Conflict,* 352–56.

74 See Roy F. Baumeister and Brad J. Bushman, *Social Psychology and Human Nature,* 2nd ed. (Belmont, CA: Cengage Learning, 2011), 154–55; Max H. Bazerman and Don A. Moore, *Judgment in Managerial Decision Making,* 7th ed. (Hoboken, NJ: Wiley, 2009), 189; Scott O. Lilienfeld, Rachel Ammirati, and Kristin Landfield, "Giving Debiasing Away: Can Psychological Research on Correcting Cognitive Errors Promote Human Welfare?" *Perspectives on Psychological Science* 4, no. 4 (2009): 391. For general research on debiasing that encompasses a very broad spectrum of areas, see Richard

number of popular approaches that have been promoted by this research. Based on the postulate that biased evaluative judgments primarily occur spontaneously, one proposed approach to countering biases has been to try to slow down and improve the judgmental process by shifting from an "automatic" mode of thinking to an "analytic," or "rational," one that is "controlled and rule-governed." By employing such a controlled, rule-governed mode of thinking, one may potentially override the perfunctory processing of information and, to a certain extent, counter judgmental biases.[75]

Working in conjunction with the above, there is a related approach that has been promoted which builds on various theories of how people ascribe blame to others. Studies have shown that, generally speaking, in order to ascribe blame to others for conduct that they have engaged in, one needs to disregard acceptable excuses or justifications for the conduct in question. Therefore, it follows that one may counter the process of erroneously ascribing blame by considering possible extenuating circumstances and mitigating factors (e.g., the other person did not act with malicious intent or failed to appreciate what his actions signify). Comparable to how legal decision makers are asked to withhold judgment until the relevant evidence and plausible explanations have been taken into consideration and weighed, in a similar fashion, so as to avoid common pitfalls in judgment (e.g., emotional reactions, cognitive shortcomings, selective perception, and the like), one is advised to try to engage in an analogous process before ascribing blame.[76]

P. Larrick, "Debiasing," in *Blackwell Handbook of Judgment and Decision Making*, ed. Derek J. Koehler and Nigel Harvey (Oxford, UK: Blackwell Publishing, 2004), 316–37.

75 See Lilienfeld, Ammirati, and Landfield, "Giving Debiasing Away," 393; and Baumeister and Bushman, *Social Psychology*, 155. For research dealing with the two modes of thinking and their impact on judgmental biases, see Keith E. Stanovich and Richard F. West, "Individual Differences in Reasoning: Implications for the Rationality Debate," *Behavioral and Brain Sciences* 23, no. 5 (2000): 658–59.

76 See Mark D. Alicke, "Culpable Control and the Psychology of Blame," *Psychological Bulletin* 12, no. 4 (2000): 556–74; Allred, "Anger and Retaliation in Conflict," 250;

Another approach that has garnered overwhelming support in countering biases that are operative in conflict is the use of perspective taking (and empathy).[77] There is a substantial body of research that advocates perspective taking, which is basically understood as seeing things from another person's perspective (i.e., that one comprehends how another is cognitively and emotionally reacting to a situation), as one of the best possible ways to overcome biases and their associated adverse effects on conflict. By taking the perspective of the other party, one may potentially decrease attributional biases, the assignment of blame, prejudice, stereotyping, aggressive responses, and retaliatory actions, and increase objectivity, positive attitudes and feelings, and the use of constructive communication and problem-solving strategies.[78]

Kenneth W. Thomas and Louis R. Pondy, "Toward an 'Intent' Model of Conflict Management Among Principal Parties," *Human Relations* 30, no. 12 (1977): 1089–102; and the related discussion in Dolf Zillman, "Mental Control of Angry Aggression," in *The Handbook of Mental Control*, ed. Daniel M. Wegner and James W. Pennebaker (Englewood Cliffs, NJ: Prentice Hall, 1993), 375–78, 382–83.

77 For a general overview on perspective taking, see Sara D. Hodges, Brian A.M. Clark, and Michael W. Myers, "Better Living through Perspective Taking," in *Positive Psychology as Social Change*, ed. Robert Biswas-Diener (Dordrecht: Springer, 2011), 193–218; for an explanation of the relationship between "perspective taking" and "empathy," see Mark H. Davis, "Measuring Individual Differences in Empathy: Evidence for a Multidimensional Approach," *Journal of Personality and Social Psychology* 44, no. 1 (1983): 114; and Adam D. Galinsky, William W. Maddux, Debra Gilin, and Judith B. White, "Why It Pays to Get Inside the Head of Your Opponent: The Differential Effects of Perspective Taking and Empathy in Negotiations," in *Psychological Science* 19, no. 4 (2008): 378–79; for a historical overview of what exactly is meant by "empathy," see Lauren Wispé, "History of the Concept of Empathy," in *Empathy and Its Development*, ed. Nancy Eisenberg and Janet Strayer (Cambridge: Cambridge University Press, 1990), 17–37.

78 See Allred, "Anger and Retaliation in Conflict," 250; Hodges, Clark, and Myers, "Better Living through Perspective Taking," 204–9; Ximena B. Arriaga and Caryl E. Rusbult, "Standing in My Partner's Shoes: Partner Perspective Taking and Reactions to Accommodative Dilemmas," *Personality and Social Psychology Bulletin* 24, no. 9 (1998): 927–48; Deborah R. Richardson et al., "Empathy as a Cognitive Inhibitor of Interpersonal Aggression," *Aggressive Behavior* 20, no. 4 (1994): 275–89; Adam D. Galinsky, Debra Gilin, and William W. Maddux, "Using Both Your Head and Your Heart: The Role of Perspective Taking and Empathy in Resolving Social Conflict," in *The Psychology of Social Conflict and Aggression*, ed. Joseph P. Forgas, Arie W. Kruglanski, and Kipling D. Williams (New York: Psychology Press, 2011), 103–18; and David W. Johnson, "Cooperativeness and Social Perspective Taking," *Journal of Personality and*

Contemporary Conflict Resolution's Approach to Addressing Negative Judgmental Biases. From among the aforementioned approaches to addressing negative judgmental biases, it appears that perspective taking is *the* prevailing approach that is being used in contemporary conflict resolution. Perspective taking is very frequently referenced in contemporary conflict resolution literature,[79] and, as was highlighted in the introductory essay of this work, perspective taking is also a major component of programs of conflict resolution education, which reflect contemporary conflict resolution's mainstream approaches to interpersonal conflict resolution (that do not involve third-party interventions).[80] This is as opposed to the use of debiasing techniques that use controlled, rule-governed modes of thinking or require that one consider possible extenuating circumstances and mitigating factors to combat negativity and attributional biases, which, as far as I have been able to determine, are generally not being employed in contemporary conflict resolution.[81]

Comparing Contemporary Conflict Resolution's and Traditional Jewish Approaches' Respective Methods

In this chapter, we have seen how traditional Jewish approaches embrace an approach to judging people that attempts to be rational,

---

Social Psychology 31, no. 2 (1975): 241–44. For some notable exceptions to the general positive effects of perspective taking in conflict situations, see Nicholas Epley, Eugene M. Caruso, and Max H. Bazerman, "When Perspective Taking Increases Taking: Reactive Egoism in Social Interaction," *Journal of Personality and Social Psychology* 91, no. 5 (2006): 872–89; and Adam D. Galinsky, Cynthia S. Wang, and Gillian Ku, "Perspective-Takers Behave More Stereotypically," *Journal of Personality and Social Psychology* 95, no. 2 (2008): 404–19.

79 For example, the term "perspective taking" appears over forty times, in various contexts, in Morton Deutsch, Peter T. Coleman, and Eric C. Marcus, eds., *The Handbook of Conflict Resolution: Theory and Practice* (San Francisco: Jossey-Bass, 2006).

80 See pp. 21–24, 31, where I had designated perspective taking as one of the primary cognitive processes of contemporary conflict resolution.

81 Controlled, rule-governed modes of thinking are certainly being employed by contemporary conflict resolution in the context of collaborative negotiation (see p. 28), but not for countering the negative judgmental biases that I have been discussing.

analytic, and rule-governed, and focuses on possible extenuating circumstances and mitigating factors. This approach is embodied in the *halakhot* of judging a person *"le-khaf zekhut,"* "towards the scale of merit." By requiring one to judge a person's ambiguous and ostensibly negative behaviors based on a critical evaluation of what took place, the person involved, and possible mitigating factors, and then, when determined appropriate, to give the person the benefit of the doubt, traditional Jewish approaches are setting forth a prescriptive model that incorporates the first two methods of debiasing that were discussed above (see pp. 216–17). As was pointed out in our discussion of the commandment of "in righteousness you shall judge your friend," contemporary rabbinic scholars have proposed that the halakhic guidelines for judging others are specifically meant to counter what may be categorized as negative judgmental biases.[82] In addition to this halakhic model, towards the end of the chapter we had seen that traditional Jewish approaches also incorporate an approach that emphasizes perspective taking, as embodied in the concept of "do not judge your friend until you are in his place" and its associated rabbinic interpretations. Using the analytic-comparative framework that was set forth in the introductory essay,[83] all of the above would fall under the category of what was designated as "internal cognitive processes the parties should engage in."

As explained in the previous section, the prevailing approach that is employed in contemporary conflict resolution for debiasing is perspective taking, as opposed to the use of controlled, rule-governed modes of thinking or an approach that requires one to consider possible extenuating circumstances and mitigating factors. One may speculate on the possible reasons for this.[84] However, whatever the reasons may be, by emphasizing perspective taking in its contemporary present form (as outlined in Chapter 1) contemporary conflict

82 See pp. 193–95.

83 See pp. 30–34.

84 The preference for perspective taking may just be because it has been found to be extremely effective and it is the simplest and most direct approach. Also, there may be certain inherent limitations and issues with the use of the alternative approaches; see Lilienfeld, Ammirati, and Landfield, "Giving Debiasing Away," 394–95.

resolution is promoting an approach to countering negative judgmental biases that essentially requires that one first discuss the issues with the other party and hear (i.e., understand and absorb) what he or she has to say, and then put oneself in the other person's place (and to try to show empathy).[85] This is in contrast to the *halakhot* of judging someone "towards the scale of merit" and giving the person the benefit of the doubt, which pertain to doubts, suspicions, and mistrust that may possibly crop up in interpersonal relations and conflicts either prior, during, or after conversations with the other party. By being concerned with ambiguities and unknowns, and the biases that they engender, and working with a rational system for when it is appropriate to give the other person the benefit of the doubt based on reasonable explanations for the other person's conduct, traditional Jewish approaches have set forth an approach to dealing with biases that can be used at any stage of the conflict process, in that it does not require that one first discuss the issues with the other party and focus on the overt information that is acquired through doing so. Discussing the issues, hearing what the other party has to say, and focusing on overt information, however, is certainly required by traditional Jewish approaches in the context of *tokhaḥah* for interpersonal offenses, which will be discussed in the next chapter.[86]

It should be understood that there are compelling reasons to be concerned about ambiguities and unknown factors and their associated judgmental biases at all stages of conflict, and to try to find some way to address them in a manner that does not focus

---

85 Even without discussing the issues and hearing what the other party has to say, the mere realization that one needs to see things from the other person's perspective or guessing what the other person is thinking and feeling may produce a positive effect on conflict dynamics. However, the robust effect of perspective taking that is described in social-psychological research and in contemporary conflict resolution calls for a degree of comprehension of the other's perspective that, in most cases, is only attained through meeting with the other party, discussing the issues, and hearing what the other party has to say.

86 We have also seen in this chapter (pp. 208–9) that according to the *Ḥafets Ḥayim* discussing one's issues with the other party, hearing what he or she has to say, and focusing on overt information is also necessary in the context of "do not judge your friend until you are in his place."

solely on the overt information that one acquires through discussions with the other party. In their analysis of judgmental biases in conflict resolution and ways to overcome them, Leigh Thompson, Janice Nadler, and Robert Lount point out that "much of the information we need to know about people is not directly accessible; rather, we must infer it on the basis of their behavior and spoken words"

> … Given the complexity of the task, it is not surprising that misunderstanding, error, and bias in judgment occur naturally even under favorable circumstances. In conflict, bias is apt to occur because conflict often leads to inadequate communication between the negotiating parties; arousal of emotional tensions that constrict thinking to stereotypes and to black-and-white viewpoints; primary focus on opposed interests; and anxiety …"[87]

The issues that Thompson, Nadler, and Lount raise highlight the need for an approach to countering judgmental biases that is not based solely on the overt information that is acquired through dialogue. In a similar vein, other conflict resolution scholars have also proposed that when faced with unknowns and biases in the context of conflicts, what the parties really need to be able to do is to give each other "the benefit of the doubt."[88]

Taking the above into consideration, and that there has also been a call for the crafting of alternative interventions for debiasing, in that many current techniques do not seem to be sufficiently

---

87 Leigh Thompson, Janice Nadler, and Robert B. Lount, Jr., "Judgmental Biases in Conflict Resolution and How to Overcome Them," in *The Handbook of Conflict Resolution: Theory and Practice*, 2nd ed., ed. Morton Deutsch, Peter T. Coleman, and Eric C. Marcus (San Francisco, CA: John Wiley and Sons, 2006), 244.

88 See, for example, James A. Schellenberg, *Conflict Resolution: Theory, Research, and Practice* (Albany, NY: State University of New York Press, 1996), 71 (in explaining Deutsch's approach to constructive conflict); Rubin, Pruitt, and Kim, *Social Conflict*, 85–86; and Raines, *Conflict Management*, 42–43. See also Baumeister and Bushman, *Social Psychology*, 299.

robust to generate enduring attitudinal or behavioral changes,[89] traditional Jewish approaches may very well offer an alternative model contemporary conflict resolution could possibly learn from. An approach that focuses on both overt information and unknowns, and integrates a prescriptive rule-governed mode of thinking that considers possible extenuating circumstances and mitigating factors, as well as incorporating perspective taking, which, as cited earlier, is all supported by contemporary research and theory, and is analogous to traditional Jewish approaches' method, may possibly be a viable alternative that is worth exploring.

89 See, for example, Lilienfeld, Ammirati, and Landfield, "Giving Debiasing Away," 391, 395; and Larrick, "Debiasing," 334.

Chapter 6

Tokhaḥah: Judaism's Basic Approach to Resolving Interpersonal Conflict through Dialogue

Rabbi Yose bar Ḥanina said, "Tokhaḥah brings to love ... any love without tokhaḥah is not [true] love." Resh Lakish said, "Tokhaḥah brings to peace ... any peace without tokhaḥah is not [true] peace."

Midrash, *Genesis Rabbah* 54:3

One of the most fundamental principles of conflict resolution is that when two parties find themselves embroiled in a conflict, the most desirable and efficacious way of resolving their issues is through some form of dialogue.[1] This being the case, dialogue has become the central characteristic feature of contemporary conflict resolution. According to

1 This is only a general rule for which there may be many possible exceptions; see Kenneth Thomas, "Conflict and Conflict Management," in *Handbook of Industrial and Organizational Psychology*, ed. Marvin D. Dennette (New York: John Wiley & Sons, 1983), 900–902, 913–16, 929; Kenneth W. Thomas and Ralph H. Kilmann, *Thomas-Kilmann Conflict Mode Instrument* (Mountain View, CA: CPP, 2007), 11–16 (where they offer various scenarios in which avoidance, assertiveness, or accommodation would be called for); and Roger Fisher, William Ury, and Bruce Patton, *Getting to Yes: Negotiating Agreement Without Giving In*, 2nd ed. (New York: Penguin Books, 1991), 164–65 (where they discuss cases in which it would make more sense not to negotiate but to rather choose one's BATNA [Best Alternative to a Negotiated Agreement]).

rabbinic authorities, the resolution of an interpersonal issue through dialogue, without the involvement of an intermediary, is mandated by an explicit biblical commandment, known as *tokhaḥah*, "reproof." *Tokhaḥah* may rightfully be designated as the centerpiece of the paradigm of interpersonal conflict resolution that is being presented in this work, and will be elaborated on in this chapter.

The Hebrew word תּוֹכָחָה (*tokhaḥah*)[2] is often translated either as "reproof," "rebuke," or "admonition."[3] In rabbinic literature, the word is often used in reference to the biblical injunction of Leviticus 19:17, הוֹכֵחַ תּוֹכִיחַ אֶת־עֲמִיתֶךָ (*hokheaḥ tokhiaḥ et amitekha*), "You shall surely reprove your friend."[4] This injunction, which is considered one of the 613 biblical commandments,[5] is understood by halakhic

2 The word *tokhaḥah* is an alternative or "secondary" form of the word *tokheḥah*. See Abraham Even-Shoshan, ed., *Ha-Milon he-Ḥadash*, 8th ed. (Jerusalem: Kiryat Sefer, 1977), s.v. "*tokhaḥah*"; and David Kimḥi, *Sefer Mikhlol* (Jerusalem: n.p., 1967), s.v. "*to'alah*," 168b.

3 See Jacob Milgram, *The Anchor Bible: Leviticus 17–22, A New Translation with Introduction and Commentary* (New York: Doubleday, 2000), 1647–48; Ernst Jenni and Claus Westerman, eds., *Theological Lexicon of the Old Testament*, trans. Mark E. Biddle, 3 vols. (Peabody, MA: Hendrickson Publishers, 1997), s.v. "*ykḫ*, to determine what is right"; G. Johannes Botterweck and Helmer Ringgren, eds., *The Theological Dictionary of the Old Testament*, 14 vols. (Grand Rapids: William B. Eerdsmans, 1974–), vol. 6, s.v. "*ykḫ*"; and Ya'akov Levy, ed., *The Oxford English-Hebrew/Hebrew-English Dictionary* (n.p.: Kenerman Publishing, 1995), s.v. "*tokhaḥah*." I have decided, as a general rule, to translate the word *tokhaḥah* as "reproof," as opposed to other common translations, because the noun "reproof," and the verb "reprove," often carry the connotation of "gentle criticism" (*The American Heritage College Thesaurus*, s.v. "chastise") or criticism "without harshness" (*Merriam Webster's Dictionary of Synonyms*, s.v. "reprove"), which, as we shall see, are essential halakhic features of *tokhaḥah*.

4 For the various possible translations of the word *amitekha*, which I have translated as "your friend," see Ludwig Koehler and Walter Baumgartner, *The Hebrew and Aramaic Lexicon of the Old Testament*, trans. and ed. M. E. J. Richardson, study ed. (Leiden, The Netherlands: Brill, 2001), s.v. "*amit*"; and Botterweck and Ringgren, *The Theological Dictionary of the Old Testament*, vol. 11, s.v. "*amîṯ*." In translating the word *amit* as "friend," I am following the Aramaic of *Targum Onkelos* (*Targum Onkelos*, in the standard *Mikra'ot Gedolot*, Lev. 19:17), and Ernest Klein, *A Comprehensive Etymological Dictionary of the Hebrew Language for Readers of English* (New York: Collier Macmillan, 1987), s.v. "*amit*."

5 See Shimon Kayara (alternatively, Yehudai ben Naḥman), *Sefer Halakhot Gedolot*, 3 vols. (Jerusalem: Ḥevrat Mekitse Nirdamim, 1988), vol. 3, positive commandment 65; Maimonides, *Sefer ha-Mitsvot*, (Jerusalem: Hotsa'at Shabse Frankel, 2001), positive commandment 205; Moses ben Jacob of Coucy, *Sefer Mitsvot Gadol* (*Semag*) (Israel: n.p.,1991), positive commandment 11; [Aaron?] ha-Levi of Barcelona, *Sefer*

authorities as incorporating two distinct facets: (1) it establishes a requirement to admonish someone who has committed a sin (even if the sin does not directly affect the individual on a personal level), and (2) it encompasses a paradigmatic process for dealing with interpersonal issues through respectful and sensitive communication.

This chapter will attempt to elucidate those aspects of *tokhaḥah* that relate to interpersonal issues. After a basic explanation of the biblical source for the commandment, a detailed analysis of Maimonides' halakhic rulings regarding *tokhaḥah* for interpersonal issues will be presented. This analysis will attempt to define terminology, uncover sources, explain the logic behind the rulings, and offer interpretations of later authorities. Subsequent to this, there will be a brief discussion of the dialogic component of *tokhaḥah*. The chapter will conclude by comparing and contrasting a number of aspects of *tokhaḥah* with analogous components of contemporary conflict resolution.

The Biblical Source

The verse in Leviticus (19:17) states, "You shall not hate your brother in your heart; you shall surely reprove your friend, and you shall not bear sin because of him." From antiquity, there have existed various exegetical approaches to explaining this verse.[6] One approach found in rabbinic literature understands the verse as establishing an obligation to rebuke someone when he or she has engaged in any

ha-Ḥinukh (Netanya, Israel: Mifal Torat Ḥakhme Polin, 1988), commandment 239; Eliezer ben Samuel of Metz, *Sefer Yere'im ha-Shalem* (Israel: n.p., n.d.), *siman* 223 (37); and in numerous other sources as well.

6 See James L. Kugel, "On Hidden Hatred and Open Reproach: Early Exegesis of Leviticus 19:17," *Harvard Theological Review* 80, no. 1 (1987): 43–61; Lawrence H. Schiffman, "Reproof as a Requisite for Punishment in the Law of the Dead Sea Scrolls," in *Jewish Law Association Studies II: The Jerusalem Conference Volume*, ed. B. S. Jackson (Atlanta, GA: Scholars Press, 1986), 59–74; and Dennis C. Duling, "Matthew 18:15–17: Conflict, Confrontation, and Conflict Resolution in a 'Fictive Kin' Association," *Society of Biblical Literature: Seminar Papers* 37, no. 1 (1998): 253–95.

type of improper behavior,[7] or, in the words of the Talmud (*Arakhin* 16b), when one perceives any sort of "unseemly thing in one's friend."

Another approach to interpreting this verse, which seems to be less well known, understands it as offering a method for dealing with contentious interpersonal issues through dialogue. One of the earliest sources for this interpretation in classic rabbinic literature appears in the Midrash *Tanna de-Ve Eliyahu*.[8] The Midrash cites the following explanation of the verse in the name of R. Eleazar ben Matya (second century CE):

> If there is some issue between you and him, speak to him [about it], and do not be one who has sinned through that person.[9]

7 See, *Arakhin* 16b, *Bava Metsia* 31a; see also *Berakhot* 31a–b, *Yevamot* 65b, *Betsah* 30a, *Shevuot* 39a, and *Shabbat* 55a.

8 The Talmud refers to a two-part work known as *Seder Eliyahu Rabbah* and *Seder Eliyahu Zuta* (*Ketubot* 106a), which traditionally has been identified with the Midrash *Tanna de-Ve Eliyahu;* see Ḥayyim Joseph David Azulai, *Shem ha-Gedolim* (New York: Grossman Publishing House, 1960), *ma'arekhet sefarim*, s.v. "*Seder Eliyahu Rabba*." Modern scholars have questioned this assertion. For a summary of the different views, see William G. Braude and Israel J. Kaplan's introduction to *Tanna debe Eliyahu: The Lore of the School of Elijah* (Philadelphia: The Jewish Publication Society of America, 1981), 3–12.

9 R. Eleazar ben Matya's statement consists of three parts, each of which apparently corresponds to one of the three parts of the verse: (1) "If there is some issue between you and him" corresponds to "You shall not hate your brother in your heart"; (2) "speak to him [about it]" corresponds to "you shall surely reprove your friend"; (3) "and do not be one who has sinned through that person" corresponds to "and you shall not bear sin because of him." *Tanna de-Ve Eliyahu* (*Seder Eliyahu Rabah ve-Seder Eliyahu Zuta*, ed. Meir Ish Shalom [Friedmann] [Vienna: Aḥiasaf, 1902]), chap. 18, p. 109; also cited in *Yalkut Shemoni, Kedoshim, remez* 613. It should be noted that many of the popular editions of *Tanna de-Ve Eliyahu* have a significantly different text than the one I have based my translation on (see, for example, *Tana de-Ve Eliyahu: Seder Eliyahu Raba ve-Seder Eliyahu Zuta* [Jerusalem: Eshkol, 1991], chap. 18, sec. 99; and the edition with a commentary by Ya'akov Meir Shechter, *Tana de-Ve Eliyahu Raba ve-Zuta: Im Perush ... Mishpat u-Tsedakah* [Jerusalem: n.p., 1959], 320). I have used Meir Ish Shalom's edition of *Tanna de-Ve Eliyahu*, which is based on the oldest existing manuscript of *Tanna de-Ve Eliyahu*, and is considered to be one of the more reliable ones. It should also be noted that R. Zvi H. Weinberger and R. Baruch A. Heifetz (*Sefer Limud le-Hilkhot ben Adam la-Ḥavero: Lo Tisna et Aḥikha be-Lvavekha* [Safed, Israel: Makhon Torat ha-Adam le-Adam, 1995], 168) cite R. Benjamin Ze'ev Boskowitz (*Sefer Seder Mishneh*, vol. 1 [Jerusalem: Mosdot Ziv ha-Torah, 1991], 190), R. Menaḥem Krakovski (*Avodat ha-Melekh* [Jerusalem: Mossad

It appears that the Midrash is focusing on the verse's tripartite structure and is interpreting it as follows: "You shall not hate your brother in your heart, *but instead* you shall surely reprove your friend, and *thereby* you shall not bear sin because of him."[10] In other words, the verse is instructing one who feels that he has been mistreated by another—and is therefore experiencing feelings of hatred towards that person—to deal with the issue at hand by confronting the person and presenting his grievances, and thereby avoid sin.[11] This verse is evidently understood in a similar fashion in *The Wisdom of Ben Sira* (c. early second century BCE) and in the *Testaments of the Twelve Patriarchs* (composed between c. third century BCE.–c. second century CE).[12] James Kugel has pointed out that virtually all modern critical commentaries have elucidated Leviticus 19:17 in a similar fashion.[13]

As far as traditional Jewish commentators are concerned, there is a litany of biblical exegetes who offer similar explanations; this would include R. Samuel ben Meir (*Rashbam*, c. 1085–1174),

---

Harav Kook, 1971], 57), and R. Elijah David Rabinowitz-Te'omim (*Bene Binyamin*, in the back of the standard printed editions of the *Mishneh Torah, De'ot* 6:6) who all clearly understood the quote from *Tanna de-Ve Eliyahu* as I have translated it. However, R. Abraham Abele Gombiner, in his commentary on *Yalkut Shemoni* (*Zayit Ra'anan* [Jerusalem: Mekhon le-Hotsa'at Sefarim ve-Ḥeker Kitve Yad, 1971], 48a), interprets R. Eleazar ben Matya's statement in a manner so that it is in accord with the alternative versions of *Tanna de-Ve Eliyahu*.

10 See Kugel, "Hidden Hatred," 45.

11 There is a dispute among the commentators as to how to interpret the final clause, "you shall not bear sin because of him." For some examples of different interpretations of this clause, see Naḥmanides, *Perush ha-Ramban al ha-Torah*, annotated by Charles B. Chavel (Jerusalem: Mossad Harav Kook, 1988), Lev. 19:17; Joseph Bekhor Shor, *Perushe Rabi Yosef Bekhor Shor al ha-Torah* (Jerusalem: Mossad Harav Kook, 1994), 213; and Hezekiah ben Manoah, *Perush ha-Ḥazekuni al ha-Torah*, annotated by Charles B. Chavel (Jerusalem: Mossad Harav Kook, 1989), 389 n. 48. Maimonides, in *Sefer ha-Mitsvot*, positive commandment 205 (together with negative commandment 303), interprets it to mean that one should not "entertain a sinful thought of him [the person who committed the offense]"; in the *Mishneh Torah, De'ot* 6:8, he quotes the interpretation of the Talmud in *Arakhin* 16b, which understands it as referring to a prohibition against embarrassing someone (see pp. 158–59 above).

12 Sir 19:13–17; *T. Gad* 6:1–7. See Kugel's explanation of the passages in *Ben Sira* and the *Testaments of the Twelve Patriarchs*; Kugel, "Hidden Hatred," 47–52.

13 Kugel, "Hidden Hatred," 45. See also Milgram, *The Anchor Bible: Leviticus*, 1646–49; and Baruch J. Schwartz, "Selected Chapters of the Holiness Code: A Literary Study of Leviticus 17–19," (Ph.D. thesis, Hebrew University, 1987), 145–46.

R. Joseph Bekhor Shor (twelfth century), Naḥmanides (*Ramban*, 1194–1270), R. Jacob ben Asher (c. 1269–1340), R. Hezekiah ben Manoah (thirteenth century), R. Levi ben Gershom (*Ralbag*, 1288–1344), R. Isaac Abravanel (1437–1508), R. Ḥayyim ben Attar (1696–1743), R. Samson Raphael Hirsch (1808–1888), R. Naphtali Zevi Judah Berlin (1817–1893), R. David Zevi Hoffmann (1843–1921), and others.[14] In addition to these biblical exegetes, preeminent halakhic authorities, such as R. Eliezer ben Samuel of Metz (c. 1115–c. 1198), R. Moses ben Jacob of Coucy (thirteenth century), the *Sefer ha-Ḥinukh* (*The Book of Education*, written c. 1258, traditionally ascribed to R. Aaron ha-Levi of Barcelona, c. 1235–c. 1300),[15] and Maimonides (see next section), have also understood this passage to be the source for a biblical commandment that enjoins one to resolve interpersonal issues through verbal communication.

Maimonides on *Tokhaḥah*

Maimonides' presentation of the laws of *tokhaḥah* for interpersonal issues serves as *the* primary normative halakhic source on this topic in rabbinic literature. In the first volume of the *Mishneh Torah*, in the sixth chapter of *Sefer ha-Mada: Hilkhot De'ot* (*Book of Knowledge: Laws of Dispositions*) subsections six through nine, Maimonides delineates the core halakhic components of *tokhaḥah*.

14 Samuel ben Meir, *Perush ha-Rashbam ha-Shalem* (Breslau: Shlomo Shattlander, 1882), 161; Joseph Bekhor Shor, *Perushe Bekhor Shor*, 213; Naḥmanides, *Perush ha-Ramban*, Lev. 19:17; Jacob ben Asher, *Perush ha-Tur ha-Arokh al ha-Torah* (Jerusalem: Hotsa'at be-Ferush uve-Remez, 1964), 232; Hezekiah ben Manoah, *Perush ha-Ḥazekuni*, 389; Levi ben Gershom, *Perushe ha-Torah le-Rabenu Levi ben Gershom*, 5 vols., ed. Ya'akov Levi (Jerusalem: Mossad Harav Kook, 1996–2000), vol. 3, 298; Isaac Abravanel, *Perush al ha-Torah: Ḥibro Don Yitsḥak Abravanel*, vol. 3 (Jerusalem: Bene Arabel, 1964), Lev. 19:17, p. 111; Ḥayyim ben Moses Attar, *Or ha-Ḥayim*, in the standard *Mikra'ot Gedolot*, Lev. 19:17; Samson Raphael Hirsch, *The Hirsch Chumash*, 6 vols., trans. Daniel Haberman (Jerusalem: Feldheim, 2000–2009), *Sefer Vayikra*, vol. 2, 619–20; Naphtali Zevi Judah Berlin, *Ha'amek Davar*, vol. 3 (Jerusalem: Y. Kuperman, 2009), Lev. 19:17; and David Zevi Hoffmann, *Sefer Va-Yikra Meforash* [*Das Buch Leviticus*], vol. 2, trans. Tsevi Har Shefer (Jerusalem: Mossad Harav Kook, 1954), 35–36.

15 Eliezer ben Samuel, *Yere'im*, *siman* 195 (39); Moses ben Jacob, *Semag*, negative commandment 5; and Ha-Levi, *Sefer ha-Ḥinukh*, commandment 239.

Hilkhot De'ot (Laws of Dispositions), Subsection 6:6

In *De'ot* 6:6, Maimonides begins[16] his discussion of the laws of *tokhaḥah* by introducing the basic idea of reproof for interpersonal issues—when A commits a perceived offense against B, B should meet with A, ask for an explanation, and attempt to resolve the issue:

> **כשיחטא איש לאיש לא ישטמנו וישתוק** כמו שנאמר ברשעים: "ולא דבר אבשלום את אמנון מאומה למרע ועד טוב כי שנא אבשלום את אמנון", **אלא מצוה עליו להודיעו ולומר לו "למה עשית לי כך וכך? ולמה חטאת לי בדבר פלוני?" שנאמר: "הוכח תוכיח את עמיתך"**. ואם חזר ובקש ממנו למחול לו צריך למחול, ולא יהא המוחל אכזרי שנאמר: "ויתפלל אברהם אל האלקים וגו'".

When a man commits a transgression against a [fellow] man,[17] he [the fellow man] should not hate[18] him [the

---

16 R. Meir ha-Kohen Kaplan (*Mitsvat ha-Tokhaḥah* [Jerusalem: Mossad Harav Kook, 1951], 6–7), R. Joseph D. Epstein (*Mitsvat ha-Etsah* [New York: Torat ha-Adam, 1983], 225 n. 1), and R. Mordekhai Shelomoh Movshovits (*Shalme Mordekhai* [Tel Aviv: Lipa Friedman, 1983], 72) have called attention to the fact that in the *Mishneh Torah*, Maimonides discusses *tokhaḥah* for interpersonal issues before discussing *tokhaḥah* for general sins, whereas in Maimonides' *Sefer ha-Mitsvot*, the order is reversed. (See also Eleazar Azikri, *Sefer Ḥaredim ha-Shalem* [Jerusalem: n.p., 1990], 12:29.)

17 The phrase "a man commits a transgression against a man" comes from 1 Samuel 2:25. As to the question of what specific types of transgressions Maimonides meant to encompass with this phrase, see *Orḥot Tsadikim ha-Shalem* (Jerusalem: Feldheim, 1988), *Sha'ar ha-Sinah*, p. 45, which, when paraphrasing Maimonides' formulation of this halakhah, applies it to monetary losses, physical violence, embarrassing someone, spreading a slanderous report, and similar offenses that would breed hatred between people. It is noteworthy that *Orḥot Tsadikim* understands this halakhah as being relevant even to offenses for which a person may choose to initiate a judicial proceeding in a rabbinic court. This is certainly indicated by the wording of Maimonides. The implication would be that before one resorts to taking another person to court, one should first try to resolve the issue on one's own through interpersonal *tokhaḥah*. The wordings of other *rishonim* who discuss this halakhah imply that this mitzvah encompasses an extremely broad spectrum of interpersonal issues. See, for example, Joseph Bekhor Shor, *Perushe Bekhor Shor*, 213, where he applies it to cases in which someone does something "*she-kasheh be-enekha*" (which can be translated as, "that upsets you"); and Naḥmanides, *Perush ha-Ramban*, Lev. 19:17, where he applies it to cases of "*ba-asoto lekha she-lo ki-rtsonekha*" (in which someone "does something to you contrary to your will"). Cf. the view of R. Dov Berish Gottlieb cited in Chapter 7, pp. 291–92 n. 85.

18 Alternatively, "bear a grudge against."

> **offender] and keep silent,** which would be similar to that which is stated regarding iniquitous[19] individuals: "And Absalom did not speak with Amnon, neither good nor bad, because Absalom hated Amnon" (2 Sam 13:22);[20] **rather, there is a mitzvah incumbent upon him to inform him [the one who committed the transgression] and say to him, "Why did you do such and such to me?"[21] and, "For what reason did you commit a transgression against me in regard to the specified matter?" as it is stated: "You shall surely reprove your friend."[22]** If he responds and asks that he should be forgiven, it is necessary to forgive [him]; and the forgiver should not be cruel, as it is stated: "And Abraham prayed unto God [i.e., for Abimelech, who had wronged him] . . ." (Gen 20:17).

In this subsection, Maimonides presents *tokhaḥah* as the Torah's basic method for dealing with hatred. *Tokhaḥah* apparently serves as a means of bringing to the fore the negative feelings and thoughts that one has towards an interpersonal offender, which in turn prevents those feelings and thoughts from festering, and forestalls the development of open aggression. This understanding of *tokhaḥah* parallels Maimonides' portrayal of this mitzvah in his *Sefer ha-Mitsvot*:

19 Alternatively, "wicked" or "evil."

20 R. Kaplan discusses the significance of mentioning the incident of Absalom and Amnon; see Kaplan, *Mitsvat ha-Tokhaḥah,* 7. Cf. Ephraim Ardit, *Mateh Efrayim* (Thessaloniki: Mordekhai Naḥman u-Mishnehu David Yisraelig'ah, 1771), 5b–6a; and Krakovski, *Avodat ha-Melekh, De'ot* 6:6.

21 In his restatement of this halakhah, R. Eleazar Azikri applies it not only to the individual against whom the offense was personally committed, but also *"li-krovo,"* which is literally translated as "to someone who is close to him," and is often used idiomatically to refer to a relative. See Azikri, *Ḥaredim,* 12:29.

22 It is worth noting that this halakhah is cited by many later halakhic authorities: for example, Abraham Abele Gombiner, *Magen Avraham,* in the standard printed edition of the *Shulḥan Arukh, Oraḥ Ḥayim* 156: 4; Shneur Zalman of Lyady, *Shulḥan Arukh: Oraḥ Ḥayim,* vol. 1 (Brooklyn: Kehot, 1968), 156:6; Solomon Ganzfried, *Kitsur Shulḥan Arukh ha-Shalem* (Vilna: Rozenkrants and Shriftzetser, n.d.), *siman* 29:13; Jehiel Michal Epstein, *Arukh ha-Shulḥan* (n.p., n.d.), *Oraḥ Ḥayim* 156:8; Israel Meir ha-Kohen, *Mishnah Berurah* (Zikhron Ya'akov: Merkaz le-Ḥinukh Torani, 1975), 156:4 (who cites the wording of Maimonides in the *Sefer ha-Mitsvot*); as well as in many other sources.

> Included in this commandment is that we should reprove one another[23] when one of us commits a wrong against another, and not bear a grudge against nor entertain a sinful thought of the person. Instead, we are commanded to verbally reprove him until[24] there is no remnant [of ill will] left in the soul.[25]

As it will become clear in our analysis of the laws of *tokhaḥah* in the *Mishneh Torah*, Maimonides is not suggesting that one engage in an emotional tirade, through which one will release pent up anger. Rather, he is advocating that a productive conversation ensue, in which the parties will work through points of contention and resolve their issues in a respectful and sensitive manner.

Sources for This Subsection. Working with the accepted presupposition that Maimonides' halakhic rulings in the *Mishneh Torah* are based on earlier rabbinic dicta that appear in talmudic and midrashic sources,[26] the commentators have offered various possible sources for this subsection. Aside from the aforementioned quote in the name of R. Eleazar ben Matya[27] (see p. 226), there is another notable

---

23 This English translation is based on the standard edition's Hebrew translation of the Arabic by R. Moses ibn Tibbon. According to R. Joseph Kafih's translation of the Arabic and R. Ḥayyim Heller's edition of the *Sefer ha-Mitsvot*, this should be translated slightly differently, possibly as "*reproach* one another." See Moses Maimonides, *Sefer ha-Mitsvot*, trans. Joseph Kafih (Jerusalem: Mossad Harav Kook, 1971), positive commandment 205; and Moses Maimonides, *Sefer ha-Mitsvot*, ed. Ḥayyim Heller (Jerusalem: Mossad Harav Kook, 1995), positive commandment 205.

24 Once again, this translation is based on R. Moses ibn Tibbon's translation of the Arabic. R. Kafih's translation differs slightly from this, and reads, "*in order that* there remains no remnant [of ill will] in the heart." See Maimonides, *Sefer ha-Mitsvot*, Kafih edition, positive commandment 205.

25 Maimonides, *Sefer ha-Mitsvot*, positive commandment 205.

26 See Isadore Twersky, *Introduction to the Code of Maimonides* (*Mishneh Torah*) (New Haven: Yale University Press, 1980), 49–53.

27 This apparently is the primary rabbinic source according to Boskowitz, *Seder Mishneh*, *De'ot* 6:6; Krakovski, *Avodat ha-Melekh*, *De'ot* 6:6; and Rabinowitz-Teomim, *Bene Binyamin*, *De'ot* 6:6. Maimonides' reference to Abraham reproving Abimelech corresponds to *Genesis Rabbah* 54:3.

midrashic source that has been suggested.[28] R. Ḥayim Kanievsky[29] and R. Nachum Rabinovitch[30] cite the Midrash *Sifre* that discusses the episode described in Numbers 12:1–16, in which "Miriam and Aaron spoke against Moses because of the Cushite woman … ." After the biblical narrative recounts how God had confronted Miriam and Aaron and admonished them for casting aspersions on Moses' conduct, it goes on to state that "the anger of the Lord was kindled against them …" (Num. 12:9). In reference to this passage, the *Sifre* teaches:

> Only after He had made known to them their misdeed did He decree banishment upon them. Surely [one can derive from this] the [following] matter [which] is an *a fortiori*: If He who created the world did not become upset with those who are flesh and blood until He made known to them their misdeed, how much more so should he who is flesh and blood not become upset with his friend until he makes known to him his misdeed."[31]

According to R. Naphtali Zevi Judah Berlin, the import of the midrash's *a fortiori* is as follows: If God who is omniscient, and must have known that there was no valid excuse for what Miriam and Aaron had done, and nevertheless He gave them the opportunity to explain themselves before He became "upset" (and punished them), how much more so a human being, who cannot know if his friend

28 It is worth noting that R. Shem Tov ibn Gaon (1283–c. 1340) is of the opinion that the talmudic passage in *Arakhin* 16b served as Maimonides' source for this halakhah. Shem Tov ben Abraham ibn Gaon, *Migdal Oz*, in the standard printed edition of the *Mishneh Torah, De'ot* 6:6. For an explanation of how one may derive this halakhah from the gemara in *Arakhin*, see Boskowitz, *Seder Mishneh, De'ot* 6:6.

29 Shemaryahu Yosef Ḥayim Kanevski, *Kiryat Melekh*, 3rd ed. (Bnei Brak: n.p., 1983), *De'ot* 6:6.

30 Nachum L. Rabinovitch, *Yad Peshutah*, 20 vols. (Jerusalem: Maaliyot Press, 1997–2011), *Sefer ha-Mada*, vol. 1, 314.

31 *Sifre* (Horovitz edition), *Be-Ha'alotekha*, *piska* 104, quoted in Rashi's commentary to Num. 12:9.

has some hidden justification for his actions, should be obligated to give the person a chance to defend himself before becoming upset.[32]

Though one may possibly question whether this midrash actually served as the basis for Maimonides' ruling in this subsection,[33] it clearly does offer an alternative source for the requirement that people broach and discuss the interpersonal issues that come up between them.

The Implications of the Interrogative Statements. The straightforwardness of the two interrogative statements in this subsection—"Why did you do such and such to me?" and "For what reason did you commit a transgression against me ... "—is somewhat striking. This is particularly true when they are contrasted with the nonconfrontational approaches to *tokhaḥah* that were formulated by other authorities, which take into account the likelihood that a direct approach is not necessarily the best way of reproving someone.[34]

32 Naphtali Zevi Judah Berlin, *Emek ha-Netsiv*, vol. 1 (Jerusalem: n.p., 1977), 318.

33 Maimonides' focus in this subsection is on the expunging of hatred through *tokhaḥah*. This seems to be the exact same idea that is conveyed in the source cited from *Tanna de-Ve Eliyahu*. This is in contrast to the source cited from the *Sifre*, which just seems to be emphasizing that before becoming upset with someone one is obligated to explain to, or discuss with, the person why he is becoming upset.

34 See, for example, Solomon Astruc (fourteenth century), *Midreshe ha-Torah* (Berlin: Tsevi Hirsch Itskovski, 1899), *Kedoshim*, p. 147; Moses Alshekh (1508–c. 1593), *Torat Mosheh*, vol. 3 (Jerusalem: Mekhon Lev Same'aḥ, 1990), 137–38; Ḥayyim Capusi (c. 1555–1639), *Sefer Be'or ha-Ḥayim* (Jerusalem: Ahavat Shalom, 1989), 212; Isaiah Horowitz (c. 1565–1630), *Shene Luḥot ha-Berit*, 5 vols. (Jerusalem: Oz ve-Hadar, 1993), vol. 5, *Torah she-Bikhtav, parashat Devarim*, p. 95, and vol. 1, *Sha'ar ha-Otiyot, ot lamed*, p. 310; Azariah Figo (1579–1647), *Sefer Binah le-Itim*, vol. 1 (Jerusalem: Hotsa'at Ḥ. Vagshal, 1989), 129–30; Zevi Hirsch Kaidanover (d. 1712), *Sefer Kav ha-Yashar*, 2 vols. (Jerusalem: n.p., 1993), vol. 1, chap. 48, pp. 227–28, and vol. 2, chap. 62, pp. 299–300; Jacob Joseph of Polonoye (d. c. 1782), *Toldot Ya'akov Yosef* (Jerusalem: n.p., 1966), 94a; Ḥayyim Joseph David Azulai (1724–1806), *Naḥal Kedumim* (Israel: n.p., 1968), 40b; id., *Devarim Aḥadim* (Jerusalem: Yahadut, 1986), 199–200; Jacob Kranz (1740–1804), *Ohel Ya'akov* (Vienna: Josef Schlesinger, 1863), 48a; Moses Sofer (1762–1839), *Ḥatam Sofer he-Ḥadash al ha-Torah* (Jerusalem: Mekhon Da'at Sofer, 2000), 89; Eliezer Papo (1784–1827), *Pele Yo'ets ha-Shalem* (Jerusalem: Mekhon Merav, 1994), 664; Jacob Zevi Meklenburg (1785–1865), *Ha-Ketav veha-Kabalah* (Paris: Recherches des Ecrit Sacres, n.d.), Lev. 19:17; Jacob Ettlinger (1798–1871), *Minḥat Ani*, vol. 1 (Jerusalem: Oz ve-Hadar, 1997), 230–33; Elijah Eliezer Dessler (1891–1954), *Mikhtav me-Eliyahu*, 5 vols. (Jerusalem: Yotse la-Or al Yede Ḥever Talmidav, 1997), vol. 3, 139. The majority of these sources are quoted in the

Maimonides, on the other hand, seems to endorse a frank and forthright approach, in which the person clearly spells out the issues involved and asks for some type of explanation or justification—"*Lamah asita li kakh ve-khakh*" ("Why did you do such and such to me?"); and also allows, or even possibly calls for, the sharing of one's subjective perception of the events—"*Lamah **ḥatata** li bi-dvar peloni*" ("For what reason did *you commit a transgression* against me in regard to the specified matter?").[35] It should be noted, however, that major halakhic authorities who quote this halakhah very often leave out the question of "For what reason did you commit a transgression against me?" (see footnote).[36] As far as practical Halakhah is concerned, R. Weinberger, R. Heifetz, and R. David Ariav assert that despite the fact that Maimonides and other *rishonim* present *tokhaḥah*

anthologies of Moshe Kharif, ed., *Sefer Yalkut Ahavat Yisrael* (Jerusalem: Gamaḥ Ḥamishai, 1999), 88–126; and Hillel D. Litwack, *Ḥovat ha-Tokhaḥah* (Brooklyn: n.p., 1991). These authorities, who were primarily discussing *tokhaḥah* for general sins, recommend various possible strategies for reproving a person in a manner that would hopefully make him receptive to what is said and avoid the virulent verbal exchanges that reproof typically engenders. The main principles that they underscore are that the reprover shows sensitivity for the other person's feelings, demonstrates unconditional regard for the person, considers the other person's perspective, and does not assail the person as a whole, or even sharply impugn the person's improper behavior. See Kaminsky, "Traditional Jewish Perspectives," 215–18.

35 The subjective nature of this question is highlighted in David Kenigsberg, "*Rekhishat Samkhuyot le-lo Hafalat Koaḥ be-Ḥinukh*," in *Ha-Madrikh ha-Ishi shelkha: Yeme Iyun le-Horim u-Meḥankhim* (Jerusalem: Darkhe Noam ve-Tiferet Baḥurim-Hatsalat ha-Noar, 2009), 247.

36 See Moses ben Jacob, *Semag*, negative commandment 5; Gombiner, *Magen Avraham*, 156: 4 (who not only left out the entire question of "For what reason did you commit a transgression against me?" but also left out the words "*to me*" in the question "Why did you do such and such to me?"); Shneur Zalman of Lyady, *Shulḥan Arukh: Oraḥ Ḥayim*, 156:6; Epstein, *Arukh ha-Shulḥan, Oraḥ Ḥayim* 156:8; and Israel Meir ha-Kohen, *Sefer ha-Mitsvot ha-Katsar*, in *Kol Kitve Ḥafets Ḥayim ha-Shalem*, vol. 1 (New York: Avraham Yitsḥak Friedman, n.d.), negative commandment 78. The implication of leaving out the question of "For what reason did you commit a transgression against me?" by these authorities is that they felt that it was preferable not to reveal, at least not totally, one's negative (subjective) perspective on the other person's actions to that person. (In response to a letter that I had sent him in which I had offered this explanation for why the question was left out by these authorities, R. Ḥayim Kanievsky wrote that "[this is] correct." Shemaryahu Yosef Ḥayim Kanievsky, letter to the author, May 2016.)

as starting off with a clarifying question that focuses on the actions of the one being reproved (which may come across as somewhat accusatory), it does not appear that one is halakhically obligated to incorporate such a question if it will in any way be counterproductive or impede the process. Rather, one should express oneself in a manner that will be the most helpful in facilitating dialogue and is conducive to a peaceful resolution.[37]

Hilkhot De'ot, Subsection 6:7

In *De'ot* 6:7, Maimonides begins to spell out the guidelines, or rules, to be followed when reproving another person. After starting the subsection by discussing reproof for general sins (i.e., sins that have nothing to do with the reprover on a personal level; see above, pp. 225–26), Maimonides states as follows:

> **המוכיח את חבירו** בין בדברים שבינו לבינו, בין בדברים שבינו לבין המקום **צריך להוכיחו בינו לבין עצמו, וידבר לו בנחת ובלשון רכה**... אם קיבל ממנו מוטב ואם לאו יוכיחנו פעם שניה ושלישית...

> **He who reproves his friend**—whether in regard to things that relate to the other person and himself or in regard to things that relate to the other person and God—**is required to reprove him in private** [literally, between the other person and himself], **and to speak to him gently and in a soft manner**... If he accepts [it] from him, it is good; if not, he should reprove him a second and third time ...[38]

---

37 R. Weinberger, R. Heifetz, and R. Ariav recommend as a good alternative that one use I-messages (see Chapter 1, p. 21) in *tokhaḥah;* see [Zvi H. Weinberger and Baruch A. Heifetz], *"Yom Yom," Torat ha-Adam le-Adam: Kovets Torani ba-Mitsvot she-ben Adam la-Ḥavero* 2 (1998): 139–40; also David Ari'av, *Le-Re'akha kamokha,* 9 vols. (Jerusalem: Mekhon Le-Re'akha kamokha, 2000–), vol. 5, 112–13.

38 As to the question of whether one is required to make repeated attempts at reproof for interpersonal issues, see Litwack, *Ḥovat ha-Tokhaḥah,* 151–52 n; Epstein, *Mitsvat ha-Etsah,* 225; and Weinberger and Heifetz, *Lo Tisna et Aḥikha,* 178. From the wording of Jacob ben Judah Ḥazzan of London, *Ets Ḥayim* (Jerusalem: Mossad Harav Kook,

In this subsection, Maimonides sets forth two basic requirements for the "tokhaḥic dialogue": (1) privacy and (2) stating one's position in a gentle manner.[39] According to R. Moses ben Jacob of Coucy, the functional purpose of these requirements is to make the other party more receptive to one's remarks;[40] according to the *Sefer ha-Ḥinukh*, these requirements are in place to prevent the reprover from embarrassing the other party.[41]

Privacy. R. Joseph D. Epstein addresses the question as to what exactly constitutes privacy in respect to *tokhaḥah*. He notes that Maimonides requires that the reproof takes place *beno le-ven atsmo*, "between the other person and himself"; whereas the *Sefer ha-Ḥinukh* [42] and R. Judah ben Samuel (c. 1150–1217)[43] describe the requirement of privacy as being that the parties' discussion takes place *ba-seter*, "in seclusion."[44] Even though there is no apparent practical difference between the two expressions,[45] R. Epstein does raise the possibility that the term *ba-seter* may indicate a greater degree of privacy than *beno le-ven atsmo*. According to R. Epstein, "in seclusion" may connote that the discussion must take place in total and absolute seclusion, hidden from the view of other people and using the utmost discretion.[46] Whatever the requirement of privacy may exactly entail, the obligation to confer with the other person in

---

1962), 13, it appears that he understood the requirement to make a second and third attempt at *tokhaḥah* as being applicable to *tokhaḥah* for interpersonal issues.

39 Maimonides also mentions what seems to be a third requirement, of expressing concern for the other party's spiritual welfare—that one has "to make known to him that he is speaking to him only for his benefit, to bring him to the world to come." However, as R. Weinberger and R. Heifetz point out, this requirement would, apparently, only be applicable to reproof for general sins, not to reproof for interpersonal issues. See Weinberger and Heifetz, *Lo Tisna et Aḥikha*, 176; and Kaminsky, "Traditional Jewish Perspectives," 203–4.

40 Moses ben Jacob, *Semag*, positive commandment 11. See also below, p. 239, the quote from *Orḥot Tsadikim*.

41 Ha-Levi, *Sefer ha-Ḥinukh*, commandment 239.

42 Ibid.

43 Judah ben Samuel, *Sefer Ḥasidim* (Jerusalem: Mossad Harav Kook, 2002), *siman* 5, p. 56

44 Alternatively, "secretly" or "in a hidden manner."

45 See Epstein, *Mitsvat ha-Etsah*, 234.

46 R. Epstein suggests that this requirement for total seclusion is either out of the concern that others will become aware of what is taking place or that the recipient

private apparently stems from the second half of Leviticus 19:17, "you shall not bear sin because of him," which, based on its talmudic interpretation (*Arakhin* 16b), teaches that one is not allowed to embarrass someone in public (see Chapter 4, pp. 158–61)."[47]

Stating One's Position in a Gentle Manner. The phrase *be-naḥat uve-lashon rakah*, "gently and in a soft manner" (literally, "with gentleness and a soft tongue"), which Maimonides uses in explaining the requirement of speaking in a gentle manner, is a combination of the wording of two verses from Scripture. In contrasting a subdued and gentle communication style with a loud and cantankerous one, Ecclesiastes 9:17 teaches, "The words of the wise are heard when spoken with gentleness (*be-naḥat*), more so than the shouting of a ruler in [the manner of] the fools";[48] and in espousing the efficacy of a soft verbal approach in confronting one who is obdurate and resistant to persuasion, Proverbs 25:15 teaches, "With a soft tongue (*lashon rakah*) one can break through [something that is as hard as] a bone." Though one may deduce, based on the phraseology and context, that it was these specific verses that had served as the basis for what

---

of the reproof may be sensitive to bystanders observing them. Epstein, *Mitsvat ha-Etsah*, 234.

47 See Ha-Levi, *Sefer ha-Ḥinukh*, negative prohibition 239 and 240; Eliezer ben Samuel, *Yere'im*, *siman* 195 (39), and Krakovski, *Avodat ha-Melekh*, *De'ot* 6:7. This explanation of why one must reprove another person in private is based on the understanding that when one reproves a person in a public setting, there is a much greater likelihood that one will embarrass the person, and that a "public setting" is defined as a time and place where even one other (i.e., a third) person is present. For other halakhic sources regarding the question of what constitutes a public setting in respect to the prohibition against embarrassing someone, see Daniel Z. Feldman, *The Right and the Good: Halakhah and Human Relations*, expanded edition (Brooklyn: Yashar Books, 2005), 17–18. In addition to the verse from Leviticus, R. Krakovski also suggests that the midrashic quote in the name of R. Eleazar ben Matya (see p. 226 above) may have served as the source for this requirement (this would follow the reading of R. Gombiner; see p. 227 n. 9 above); see also Kanevski, *Kiryat Melekh*, 30.

48 Cf. the translation of this verse in Harold Louis Ginsberg, trans., *The Five Megilloth and Jonah: A New Translation* (Philadelphia: The Jewish Publication Society of America, 1969), 73 footnote n; and Jehiel Hillel Altschuler, *Metsudat David; Metsudat Tsiyon*, in the standard *Mikra'ot Gedolot*, Eccles. 9:17.

Maimonides has written, R. Eliezer of Metz does offer a talmudic source for the concept. Citing the Gemara in *Shabbat* (34a), he writes that "it is [incumbent] upon the one who reproves to do so in a pleasant[49] and gentle manner in order that his words should be accepted, as it is stated in [tractate] *Shabbat*, 'Three things one must say on the eve of the Sabbath [to his family] ... [and] *one must say them in a gentle manner so that they accept them from him* [emphasis mine].'"[50]

As to how one should define speaking "gently and in a soft manner," common sense would dictate that this entails that one carefully regulate the volume, tone, physical gestures, choice of words, and verbal content of what is being said when expressing disapproval of the other person.[51] The presentation of this halakhah in *Orḥot Tsadikim* (a classic anonymous work on Jewish ethics, probably written

---

49 Attention should be drawn to the fact that in his discussion of the mitzvah of *tokhaḥah*, R. Eliezer of Metz not only states that one speak in a gentle manner, but also writes that one speak with *ne'imut*, "pleasantness," as well; see Ḥayim Penso, *Shem Ḥadash: ... al Sefer Yere'im*, vol. 1 (Jerusalem: n.p., 1848), 25a. See also Rashi, *Arakhin* 16b, s.v. *she-yode'a le-hokhiaḥ*, where he implies that *tokhaḥah* needs be offered [*be-*]*derekh kavod*, "[in] a respectful manner."

50 Eliezer ben Samuel, *Yere'im*, *siman* 223 (37). This talmudic source is also cited in Moses ben Jacob, *Semag*, positive commandment 11. According to R. Moshe Shmuel Shapira (1917–2006), the halakhah that reproof should be given in a gentle manner is derived from the gemara in *Arakhin* 16b. See Moshe Shmuel Shapira, "*Ba-Inyan Tokhaḥah*," *Yeshurun* 18 ([Kislev] 5767 [2006]): 403.

51 Halakhic sources do not elaborate on what exactly constitutes speaking "gently and in a soft manner." In proposing that speaking gently and in a soft manner would entail that one regulate the volume, tone, physical gestures, choice of words, and verbal content of what is being said, I have in mind the conventional division of communication into three primary components: (1) the verbal component—the actual words that we use, and the message that they convey; (2) the "paralinguistic" component—the vocal features of speech, such as volume (how loud one speaks), tone (i.e., the vocal "quality" of one's voice, e.g., a voice that sounds harsh and angry vs. a voice that sounds warm and friendly), tempo (how fast one talks), and the like; and (3) the nonverbal component—all the other ways we communicate thoughts, attitudes, and emotions, aside from the words we use and their vocal features, for example, the messages we communicate with facial expressions, hand gestures, or other parts of our bodies. (See Robert M. Krauss et al., "Verbal, Vocal, and Visible Factors in Judgments of Another's Affect," *Journal of Personality and Social Psychology* 40, no. 2 [1981]: 312.)

c. fifteenth century) focuses on the volume and tone of one's voice, and their psychological effect:

> Initially you reprove him gently and in seclusion, and you speak to him in a soft manner ... but if you should reprove your friend with *a loud voice and with anger* ... [he] will not accept the reproof from you, since it is the nature of human beings that when one comes upon his friend with force, his friend hardens himself in opposition and will not humble himself beneath him. Regarding this, the wise one [Solomon] has said: 'The words of the wise are heard when spoken with gentleness' (Eccles. 9:17)."[52] (emphasis mine)

In other words, according to *Orḥot Tsadikim*, by speaking in a subdued manner and calmly, one may reduce the intensity of the confrontation and avoid (at least to some extent) the other party's natural resentment to adverse criticism.

Before proceeding, it would be worthwhile to once again refer back to what Maimonides has written in *Sefer ha-Mitsvot*: "[In regard to *tokhaḥah* for interpersonal issues] we are commanded to verbally reprove him until there is no remnant [of ill will] left in the soul."[53] From this, it appears that, according to Maimonides, by verbally expressing to the other party what is being ruminated within, one can induce a cathartic effect, which helps to release and purge potentially destructive emotions and thoughts. Taken by itself, this excerpt from the *Sefer ha-Mitsvot* could have been interpreted as sanctioning a vituperative tirade of complaints against the other person, which allows one to vent one's emotions. However, when it is taken together with what Maimonides has written in *De'ot* 6:7, which makes it compulsory to speak to the other person in a gentle

---

52 See *Orḥot Tsadikim, Sha'ar ha-Ka'as*, pp. 79–80 (for the complete quote), quoted in Elijah ben Moses de Vidas, *Reshit Ḥokhmah ha-Shalem*, vol. 2 (Jerusalem: Or ha-Musar, 1990), *Sha'ar ha-Anavah*, p. 678. (It should be noted that this excerpt, and many other sections of *Orḥot Tsadikim*, are clearly derived from Maimonides' rulings in the *Mishneh Torah*.)

53 Maimonides, *Sefer ha-Mitsvot*, positive commandment 205.

manner, it becomes clear that Maimonides is of the opinion that it is not permitted, nor is it necessary, to express one's feelings with vehemence and anger to induce such a cathartic effect.[54]

Hilkhot De'ot, Subsection 6:8

In *De'ot* 6:8, Maimonides continues to spell out the guidelines to be followed when reproving another person. As we had seen in Chapter 4, as a general rule, Halakhah is *extremely* concerned about not embarrassing, or shaming, another human being. Maimonides now addresses the concern of not embarrassing the other person in the course of *tokhaḥah*:

המוכיח את חבירו תחלה לא ידבר לו קשות עד שיכלימנו, שנאמר: "ולא תשא עליו חטא..."

He who reproves his friend, initially must not speak to him harshly up to the point that he puts him to shame, as it states: "You shall not bear sin because of him ..."[55]

Based on the subsection that precedes this one (*De'ot* 6:7), it would appear that the requirement to speak in a gentle manner is an absolute one and does not terminate at any point. However, *De'ot* 6:8 seems to indicate that, in some respect, this is not necessarily true.[56] If Maimonides writes that "he who reproves his friend, *initially*

54 See also Maimonides, *Sefer ha-Mitsvot*, negative commandment 317, cited above on p. 167, in which he explains that the Torah prohibited one from cursing someone who is deaf because it is concerned about the negative effect losing one's temper will have on the person doing the cursing.

55 For the explanation of how the prohibition against shaming someone is derived from this verse, see p. 159.

56 We may possibly differentiate between the requirement of speaking "to him gently and in a soft manner" in *De'ot* 6:7 and the requirement of initially not speaking "to him harshly up to the point that he puts him to shame" in *De'ot* 6:8. *De'ot* 6:7 establishes a broad general requirement to speak gently, which encompasses a wide range of elements (e.g., that one avoid using an angry tone, not raise his voice [see above, p. 238], not demonize, or severely censure, the other person's improper behavior, not assail the other person's character as a whole [see above p. 234 n. 34], etc.);

must not speak to him harshly up to the point that he puts him to shame," the implication is that at some later stage one *is* permitted to say something that may shame the other person. Among the commentators, one finds various possible interpretations of this ruling. These interpretations are highly diverse and range from one possible extreme to the other.

Three Interpretations of De'ot 6:8. At one end of the spectrum of interpretations of this subsection is (1) the (lenient) view of R. Ephraim ha-Kohen (1616–1678), who maintains that Maimonides is of the opinion that after one starts off the conversation by being careful and avoiding embarrassing the other person, it would be permissible, if the other person is unreceptive to what is being said, to say something that may embarrass him as long as this is done in private.[57] On the other end of the spectrum is (2) the (strict) view of R. Ovadiah Hadayah (1890–1969), who proposes that when Maimonides makes a distinction between the initial and later stages in regard to shaming the person, he is *not* referring to reproof for interpersonal issues; rather, he is only discussing reproof for sins that are between the other person and God. R. Hadayah therefore maintains that the obligation set forth in *De'ot* 6:7, which requires a person to speak in a gentle manner when he is reproving someone for an interpersonal issue, is an ongoing one and never ceases in any way throughout the entire tokhaḥic dialogue.[58]

---

whereas *De'ot* 6:8 is only focusing on what one says in relation to embarrassing the other person, for which there exists a limited exemption from the general rule (see further on in the text for what that exemption may be). Nevertheless, there are commentators who certainly do equate the requirements of these two subsections; see Ḥayim Yosef Elyakim, *Shem Yosef* (Saloniki: Yuda Kelai and Mordekhai Naḥman, 1769), 4b; Ovadiah Hadayah, *Eved ha-Melekh* (Jerusalem: Y. A. Itaḥ, 1941), 10b; and Shapira, "*Ba-Inyan Tokhaḥah,*" *Yeshurun*, 403.

57 Ephraim ben Jacob ha-Kohen, *Sha'ar Efrayim* (Jerusalem: n.p., 1981), responsum no. 65, p. 25b. It should be noted that R. Abraham de Boton cites an interpretation that parallels the explanation of R. Ha-Kohen's and apparently rejects it. Abraham de Boton, *Leḥem Mishneh*, in the standard printed edition of the *Mishneh Torah*, *De'ot* 6:8.

58 Hadayah, *Eved ha-Melekh*, *De'ot* 6:8. R. Joseph Babad (c. 1800–1875) has a view that is diametrically opposed to that of R. Hadayah. He maintains that *De'ot* 6:8 is *specifically* referring to reproof for interpersonal issues; see Joseph Babad, *Minḥat Ḥinukh* (Jerusalem: Mekhon Yerushalayim, 1997), commandment 240.

Midway between these two interpretations is (3) the view of R. Mas'ud Raccah (1690–1768). R. Raccah explains that when Maimonides writes that initially one must not speak to the other person in a harsh manner up to the point that he puts him to shame, he never meant to imply that at some later stage in the tokhaḥic process one would be permitted to come straight out and shame the other person. The only thing that is being condoned is that within the due course of the dialogue, one may "make a harsh comment as is necessary to the topic [of conversation] ... although, invariably it is never permissible for him to, God forbid, openly embarrass him."[59] R. Raccah evidently means to say that after one has set the tone by initially speaking to the other person in a gentle manner, if the conversation calls for it (e.g., in order to get across a point and explain what one is thinking) one would be permitted to say something a little harsh, but one would never be permitted to blatantly and insensitively insult and embarrass the other person.

Hilkhot De'ot, Subsection 6:9

In *De'ot* 6:9, Maimonides discusses cases in which one feels that it would be extremely difficult to engage in *tokhaḥah* with the other party, and would prefer not doing so. In such cases, according to Maimonides, the option of not doing so is totally acceptable if one can find it in his or her heart to forgive the person:

> **מי שחטא עליו חבירו ולא רצה להוכיחו ולא לדבר לו כלום מפני שהיה החוטא הדיוט ביותר, או שהיתה דעתו משובשת, ומחל לו בלבו ולא שטמו ולא הוכיחו הרי זו מדת חסידות ; לא הקפידה תורה אלא על המשטמה.**

59 Masud Raccah, *Ma'aseh Rokeaḥ* (Jerusalem: n.p., 1976), *De'ot* 6:8. The logic behind this ruling, according to R. Raccah, is that we assume that the other person will not be all that embarrassed, since the appropriate tone was set at the beginning of the conversation. For an alternative interpretation of this subsection, see R. Boskowitz's commentary (*Seder Mishneh, De'ot* 6:8, pp. 197–98), in which he attempts to resolve all difficulties by differentiating between various degrees of embarrassment.

One whose friend has committed a transgression against him, yet he does not desire to reprove him or to say anything to him because the offender is an exceptionally common person [*hedyot be-yoter*] or there is something wrong with the way his mind functions [or perceives things] [*dato meshubeshet*],[60] **and he [the offended party] has forgiven him in his heart, bears him no ill will, and does not reprove him, this is a pious character trait [since] the Torah is only concerned with the bearing of ill will.**

In this subsection, Maimonides rules that the obligation to reprove someone for an interpersonal issue is not an absolute one. Unfortunately, the wording of this halakhah opens itself up to two vastly different and opposing interpretations. One may interpret this subsection either as saying that (*a*) the *only* exemption from offering *tokhaḥah* is when one is dealing with a difficult individual who falls under the category of, or is comparable to, what Maimonides describes as being exceptionally "common" or as having "something wrong with the way his mind functions"; or (*b*) *anyone* who wishes to abstain from *tokhaḥah* is given the option of doing so, as long as he has the strength of character not to bear ill will towards the other person. Before proceeding to analyze these two interpretations, we will first discuss some of the possible explanations for the terms *hedyot be-yoter*, "an exceptionally common person," and *dato meshubeshet*, "something wrong with the way his mind functions."

Defining the Terms Hedyot be-Yoter (an Exceptionally Common Person) and Dato Meshubeshet (Something Wrong with the Way His Mind Functions [or Perceives Things]). R. Asher Feuchtwanger

60 There are various possible translations for the term *dato meshubeshet*. The term appears four times in the *Mishneh Torah*: once in *Hilkhot De'ot* (the halakhah that we are discussing), once in *Hilkhot Tefilah* (4:15), and twice in *Hilkhot Edut* (9:9). In *Hilkhot Tefilah, dato meshubeshet* refers to someone whose "mind is unsettled," in the sense of being discomposed and unable to concentrate; in *Hilkhot Edut*, it refers to someone whose "mind is not well," in the sense of being sick or mentally disturbed. See also *Hilkhot Megilah* 2:7, in which the word *meshubeshet* appears by itself and refers to something that is "faulty," or filled with mistakes.

(1911–1977) seems to understand the term "exceptionally common person" as indicative of a boorish obstinacy, with which a person is *unwilling* to listen to adverse criticism. Someone who has "something wrong with the way his mind functions [or perceives things]" he explains as referring to one who is *incapable* of comprehending what he is being told.[61] R. Epstein offers an alternative explanation of the term "exceptionally common person." He identifies it with the "common person" that the Talmud describes in *Megillah* 12b—"[T]he common person jumps ahead [out of his place,] to the front." This type of individual, apparently, is characterized by his crudity and as being devoid of a sense of propriety and good manners, which makes it difficult to deal with him.[62] The term "something wrong with the way his mind functions [or perceives things]" is interpreted by R. Epstein in a similar fashion to that of R. Feuchtwanger; however, R. Epstein goes on to offer a specific misperception, or deficiency, which inhibits a person's ability to reason and accept reproof. He proposes that the person who has something wrong with the way his mind functions has a convoluted and bloated perception of himself that leads him to denigrate other people's opinions.[63] R. Shlomo Lorincz (1918–2009) suggests that "an exceptionally common person" may refer to someone who is not aware that there is an obligation to engage in *tokhaḥah,* and someone who has "something wrong with the way his mind functions" may be applicable to an individual who lacks the common sense to realize that he should not be offended when the other person is trying to fulfill the mitzvah of *tokhaḥah,* which is something that the other person is required to do.[64]

Whether or not we accept the exact interpretations of R. Feuchtwanger, R. Epstein, or R. Lorincz, we may propose with a

61 Asher Feuchtwanger, *Asher la-Melekh,* vol. 1 (Jerusalem: F. Feuchtwanger, 1988), *De'ot* 6:9, p. 10.

62 See Epstein, *Mitsvat ha-Etsah,* 224. Cf. Raccah, *Ma'aseh Rokeaḥ, De'ot* 6:9, the first explanation.

63 Epstein, *Mitsvat ha-Etsah,* 223–24.

64 Shelomoh Zalman Lorints, *Milu'e Shelomoh: Berure Sugyot ve-Shu't im Maranan Gedole Torah* (Jerusalem: Feldheim, 2004), 81.

considerable amount of certainty that Maimonides is referring to individuals who suffer from the types of temperamental and intellectual shortcomings that inevitably lead to an inordinate amount of difficulty when one is forced to engage in dialogue with them in trying to resolve an interpersonal issue.

The Two Approaches to Interpreting De'ot 6:9. There are two basic approaches to interpreting this subsection:

> *Interpretation A: The only time there exists an exemption from reproving someone is when one is dealing with a person who would fall under the category of, or is comparable to, what Maimonides describes as being "exceptionally common" or as having "something wrong with the way his mind functions."*

R. Jedidiah Tarika (1713–1769),[65] R. Feuchtwanger,[66] and others[67] are of the opinion that the exemption from reproving someone is a limited one, which stems from the inability of the person being reproved to accept what is being said. This leniency would be based on the talmudic dictum of "Just as there is a mitzvah upon a person to say something that will be accepted, so too there is mitzvah upon a person *not* to say something that will *not* be accepted … as it states: 'Do not reprove a scorner, lest he hates you' (Prov. 9:8)" (*Yevamot* 65b). The commentators who cite this gemara as the source for *De'ot* 6:9 understood Maimonides as having derived from it that if one knows that the other party will obstinately reject whatever one has to say and that discussing the matter will be counterproductive, the option of finding it in one's heart to forgive the other party is preferable to reproving him.[68]

---

65 Jedidiah Samuel Tarika, *Sefer Ben Yedid* (Solonika: Sa'adi Ishkenazi [*sic*], 1806), 10b, *De'ot* 6:9.

66 Feuchtwanger, *Asher la-Melekh*, *De'ot* 6:9.

67 R. Weinberger and R. Heifetz also cite R. Azikri (*Ḥaredim* 47:2) and R. Raccah (*Ma'aseh Rokeaḥ*, *De'ot* 6:9) as accepting this first interpretation. Weinberger and Heifetz, *Lo Tisna et Aḥikha*, 179–82.

68 Closely related to this is an opinion that is cited in the name of R. Yosef Shalom Elyashiv (1910–2012), who is quoted as saying that it is preferable not to engage in

Interpretation B: The option of not offering tokhaḥah is applicable to all people.

When R. Shneur Zalman of Lyady (1745–1813) and R. Jacob Ḥazzan (thirteenth century) paraphrase this ruling of Maimonides in their halakhic compendia,[69] they make no reference to the exceptionally common person or to one who has something wrong with the way his mind functions. They simply state that in regard to an interpersonal offense, it is a pious character trait to forgive the other person in one's heart and not to reprove him. R. Weinberger and R. Heifetz point out that this implies that both R. Shneur Zalman and R. Ḥazzan understood *De'ot* 6:9 as giving blanket approval to not offering *tokhaḥah* for interpersonal offenses committed by anyone if one can find it in one's heart to overlook the offense and forgive the person. In addition to R. Shneur Zalman and R. Ḥazzan, R. Weinberger and R. Heifetz also cite a number of other commentators who seem to understand Maimonides in a similar vein.[70] R. Weinberger and R. Heifetz go on to explain that even though Maimonides states the law only in reference to an exceptionally common person or someone who has something wrong with the way his mind functions, he did not mean to thereby exclude other people; Maimonides simply wanted to offer two common examples

tokhaḥah for interpersonal issues if, in doing so, it will lead to *maḥaloket*; see Yosef Shalom Elyashiv, cited in [Yosef Yisraelzon] *Kuntres Kitsur Hilkhot ben Adam la-Ḥavero* (Reḥovot: Kolel Avrekhim Reḥovot, 1998), 9.

69 Shneur Zalman of Lyady, *Shulḥan Arukh ha-Rav, Oraḥ Ḥayim* 156:6; Ḥazzan, *Ets Ḥayim*, 13.

70 R. Weinberger and R. Heifetz cite the following authorities: R. Shem Tov ibn Gaon (*Migdal Oz, De'ot* 6:9), R. Yosef ben Ya'akov Yitsḥak Hochgelehrter (*Mishnat Ḥakhamim* [Jerusalem: Hotsa'at Rashbats, 1996], 39), R. Ovadiah Hadayah (*Eved ha-Melekh, De'ot* 6:9), R. Samson Raphael Hirsch (*The Hirsch Chumash, Vayikra*, vol. 2, 619–20), and R. Menaḥem Treves (*Oraḥ Mesharim: Shulḥan Arukh le-Midot* [Jerusalem: Meir Kleiman, 1969], chap. 31, *be'ur* 12, p. 160). Weinberger and Heifetz, *Lo Tisna et Aḥikha*, 180–81. R. Avraham Shlozover (*Be'er Yehudah* [Brooklyn: Aḥim Goldenberg, 1991], *De'ot* 6:8) cites R. de Boton (*Leḥem Mishneh, De'ot* 6:8) as also being of this opinion. It is also clear that R. Isaac Jacob Weiss (*Minḥat Yitsḥak*, 10 vols. [Jerusalem: Hotsa'at Sefarim Minḥat Yitsḥak, 1989–], vol. 4, *siman* 79:11, p. 183, the bottom of col. 1–2) and R. Babad (*Minḥat Ḥinukh*, commandment 240) were also of the same view.

of when a person may elect to forgo reproving someone. The source for this interpretation, according to a number of authorities,[71] is the talmudic passage in *Arakhin* 16b that discusses the concept of not giving *tokhaḥah* out of "humility not for its own sake" (see footnote).[72]

The Dialogic Component of Tokhaḥah

Up until this point, we have been focusing only on the reprover (i.e., the person who was hurt and initiates the *tokhaḥah*) and his obligation to communicate to the other person that the other person has committed an offense against him. We will now briefly discuss the verbal exchange that should take place between the two parties during *tokhaḥah*.

---

71 See Weinberger and Heifetz, *Lo Tisna et Aḥikha*, 180–81. Cf. Treves, *Oraḥ Mesharim*, chap. 31, *be'ur* 12, p. 160. According to R. Treves, the option of not offering reproof and forgiving the person is implicit in the biblical verse "You shall not hate your brother in your heart; you shall surely reprove your friend." Evidently, in R. Treves's opinion, the import of this verse is that one should not hate another and that *tokhaḥah* is the means by which the average person should deal with feelings of hatred. In a situation when one does not harbor feelings of hatred, there would be no need to resort to reproof. According to R. Weinberger and R. Heifetz, this explanation is also alluded to in the words of R. Hirsch (*The Hirsch Chumash, Vayikra*, vol. 2, 620, quoted in *Lo Tisna et Aḥikha*, 181 n. 34).

72 In discussing various aspects of the commandment of *tokhaḥah*, the Talmud in tractate *Arakhin* (16b) raises a question as to whether it is better to give reproof to someone "for its own sake" or is it better not to give reproof, out of "humility not for its own sake." Giving "reproof for its own sake," apparently refers to the offering of *tokhaḥah* that is impelled by a pure motivation, such as the desire to fulfill the Torah's commandment of *tokhaḥah*. Not giving *tokhaḥah* out of "humility not for its own sake," at least according to Maimonides, would refer to someone who *acts* as a humble person (who would generally abstain from reproving others) and does not reprove someone who commits a transgression against him, not out of humility, but for some other reason, such as not wanting to engage in a discussion with a difficult person who is "exceptionally common" or has "something wrong with the way his mind functions" (see Jacob Ḥayyim Ben-Nayim, *Yeshuot Ya'akov* [Levorno: Avraham Yitsḥak Kastilo, 1784], 36a; and Yitzchok Mitnik, ed., *Avodah Berurah al Masekhet Arakhin*, vol. 1 [Lakewood, NJ: Mekhon Be'er ha-Torah, 2003], 427). The Talmud concludes that it is better *not* to reprove someone out of "humility not for its own sake." For further discussion of this gemara, see Kaminsky, "Traditional Jewish Perspectives," pp. 211–12, 214–15.

R. Weinberger and R. Heifetz point out that the *rishonim* who discuss *tokhaḥah* for interpersonal offenses indicate that in order to fulfill this mitzvah, one is required to not only talk and convey to the other person what he or she has done, but must also engage in a dialogue, which entails that one listens to and potentially accepts what the other person has to say:

> In analyzing the wording of the *rishonim*, we may ascertain that more than just *talking* to his friend, [the reprover] is supposed to *question* him[73] . . . It therefore follows that this mitzvah is fulfilled not only through the reprover talking but also through listening [i.e., he must both talk and listen]. The reprover must be prepared to listen to the response of his friend, for as long as he is only coming to *talk* and berate his friend, and he's not prepared to listen and *accept* what his friend has to say back and the explanation[74] that he may offer—he does not fulfill the mitzvah.[75] (italics in the original)

R. Weinberger and R. Heifetz subsequently go on to cite the wording of eight different authorities who discuss *tokhaḥah* for interpersonal issues (Naḥmanides, R. Hezekiah ben Manoah, R. Eleazar Azikri, Maimonides, R. Moses of Coucy, R. Joseph Bekhor Shor, the *Sefer ha-Ḥinukh*, and R. Eliezer of Metz), who all indicate that some form of verbal exchange should take place between the parties in the course of *tokhaḥah*.[76]

Maimonides in *De'ot* 6:6 indicates that a verbal exchange should take place when he writes that one should ask the other party "Why did you do such and such to me? . . ." and then offers a scenario in which the other party responds to what was said, "If he responds

73 See above, p. 229.

74 Regarding the meaning of the Hebrew word *hitnatslut* (which is a term that is used by the *rishonim* when they discuss the mitzvah of *tokhaḥah*), which I have translated as "explanation," see Weinberger and Heifetz, *Lo Tisna et Aḥikha*, 169 n. 7, 170.

75 Ibid., 169; and Ari'av, *Le-Re'akha kamokha*, 115.

76 Weinberger and Heifetz, *Lo Tisna et Aḥikha*, 169.

and asks that he should be forgiven ... ," to which the reprover is then required to respond back by forgiving the person, "it is necessary to forgive [him] .... "

One of the other authorities who indicates that *tokhaḥah* requires that the parties engage in dialogue, and is cited by R. Weinberger and R. Heifetz, is R. Joseph Bekhor Shor. Bekhor Shor describes *tokhaḥah* for interpersonal issues as follows:

> If your brother does something that upsets you, do not hate him in your heart. Rather, you should reprove him and say to him "Why did you do this to me?" Since it is possible that he never intended what you had thought, or he couldn't help himself, or he will give you some [other] explanation. And through this [mitzvah of *tokhaḥah*], you will come to realize that he never did something improper to you.[77]

Here we find the reprover asking the same type of question that Maimonides had him asking: "Why did you do this to me?"; subsequently, however, we encounter different scenarios from the one Maimonides used in respect to the dialogue that ensues. Maimonides presented a very simple, best-case scenario in which the person being reproved admits that he did something wrong and apologizes.[78] R. Bekhor Shor presents cases in which the person being reproved responds by clarifying that "he never intended what you had thought, or he couldn't help himself, or he will give you some [other] explanation." The reprover then comes to the realization that in actuality "he never did something improper."

77 Joseph Bekhor Shor, *Perushe Bekhor Shor*, 213.

78 There may be much greater significance to the scenario that Maimonides presented. When Maimonides' formulation in *De'ot* 6:6 is taken in conjunction with what he had written in the *Sefer ha-Mitsvot* (positive commandment 205), and it is contrasted with the formulations of other authorities (e.g., those of Naḥmanides, the *Sefer ha-Ḥinukh*, R. Bekhor Shor, and R. Moses of Coucy), there is a strong indication that Maimonides' formulation may very well reflect a fundamental disagreement between him and the other authorities as to the form and purpose of *tokhaḥah* for interpersonal issues. See the discussion in Weinberger and Heifetz, *Lo Tisna et Aḥikha*, 169–71.

From this depiction of *tokhaḥah*, and those of all of the other authorities that are cited by R. Weinberger and R. Heifetz, it appears that some form of discussion should take place in the course of *tokhaḥah*, in which the reprover will listen to and potentially accept what the other person has to say (regarding the exact nature of this dialogue, see below, pp. 253–55, and footnote 82).[79]

Summary

This chapter has examined the mitzvah of *tokhaḥah*, specifically, the facet of the commandment that directly relates to the resolution of interpersonal conflicts. After initially presenting the biblical source for reproof for interpersonal issues, a detailed analysis of Maimonides' treatment of the topic in the *Mishneh Torah* was offered. The four subsections that we examined dealt with the following:

> Subsection 6:6 introduced the basic idea of *tokhaḥah*—when one feels that a person has committed an improper act against him, and he is therefore experiencing

79 As far as the one who is being reproved is concerned, it is worth noting that R. Isaac of Corbeil (d. 1280) writes as follows:

> [There is a mitzvah] to "cut away the barrier of one's heart," as it states (Deut. 10:16), "You shall cut away the barrier of your heart." The explanation [of "cutting away the barrier of your heart"] is that one should love [receiving] reproof and love the person who is giving him reproof. Also Solomon, peace be upon him, has written in his work (Prov. 9:8) "Reprove a wise man and he will love you." And when it comes to this mitzvah, there is a [corresponding] negative commandment, as it states, (Deut. 10:16) "and you shall no longer stiffen your neck" [that one should not reject reproof] (Isaac ben Joseph of Corbeil, *Sefer Amude Golah-Sefer Mitsvot Katan* [Israel: Mefitse Or, 1959], *siman* 9).

In other words, as opposed to the common response of becoming defensive and feeling resentment towards one who offers *tokhaḥah*, and instinctively rejecting what he has to say, the person being reproved should instead be receptive to and appreciate the constructive criticism he is being offered. (See also Aaron Kotler, *Mishnat Rabi Aharon al ha-Torah* [Lakewood: Machon Mishnas Rabbi Aaron, 2001], Lev. 19:17, pp. 196–97.)

resentment, he should go to that person, broach the topic, and discuss the issue with the person.

Subsection 6:7 began to delineate the guidelines for *tokhaḥah*—"He who reproves his friend … is required to reprove him in private, and to speak to him gently and in a soft manner … ."

Subsection 6:8 continued to spell out the guidelines—"He who reproves his friend, initially must not speak to him harshly up to the point that he puts him to shame … ."

Subsection 6:9 discussed the question of when it may be preferable to simply overlook what had taken place—"One whose friend has committed a transgression against him, yet he does not desire to reprove him or to say anything to him … ."

Throughout the analysis of these *halakhot*, an attempt was made to examine methodically and in some detail the various elements of each subsection and to explore their import and implications, with an underlying focus on practical halakhic applications. Subsequent to the analysis of the *halakhot* in the *Mishneh Torah*, we concluded with a brief discussion of the dialogic component of *tokhaḥah*.

Tokhaḥah is clearly a fundamental component of the Jewish approach to interpersonal conflict resolution, in that it encompasses the basic halakhic guidelines for addressing interpersonal issues through dialogue (without resorting to a third-party intervention). The midrash that was quoted in the epigraph of this chapter—"Rabbi Yose bar Ḥanina said, '*Tokhaḥah* brings to love … any love without *tokhaḥah* is not [true] love.' Resh Lakish said, '*Tokhaḥah* brings to peace … any peace without *tokhaḥah* is not [true] peace'"—was evidently, as pointed out by a number of commentators, referring to *tokhaḥah* for interpersonal issues.[80] This midrash thus gives us some inkling of the

80 See *Genesis Rabbah* 54:3; and *Sifre, Parashat Devarim, piska* 2; De Vidas, *Reshit Ḥokhmah*, vol. 2, *Sha'ar ha-Anavah*, pp. 663–64; Horowitz, *Shene Luḥot ha-Berit*,

importance that the sages attached to this mitzvah when it comes to interpersonal relations and the promotion of peace.

The fundamental challenges of *tokhaḥah*—that the person on the receiving end of the *tokhaḥah* must contend with feelings that very often lead to the rejection of *tokhaḥah*, and that the reprover must know how to properly express him- or herself, and choose the proper time and place in which to engage in dialogue—were in essence summed up by two of the Jewish sages in the talmudic passage that reads:

> Rabbi Tarfon (first–second century CE) said: I wonder if there is anyone in this generation who accepts reproof—if one says to someone, "Remove the 'splinter from between your eyes,'" he would say [back], "Remove the 'beam from between your eyes.'"
>
> Rabbi Eleazar ben Azariah (first–second century CE) said: I wonder if there is anyone in this generation who knows how to reprove [in a proper manner].[81]

Rabbi Tarfon is concerned with the fact that when faced with criticism of any sort, even if it be in regard to just some small flaw ("Remove the 'splinter from between your eyes'"), there is an instinctive reaction to become defensive, reject what one hears, feel resentment, and respond back by verbally attacking the reprover ("Remove the 'beam from between your eyes'," i.e., by focusing on some major flaw that the reprover may have). Rabbi Eleazar ben Azariah is concerned with the inherent difficulty in knowing how to

vol. 4, *parashat Va-Yera* (right before the end), p. 90; and Eliezer Papo, *Orot Elim* (Ashdod: Mekhon Hadrat Ḥen, 2005), *Sha'ar ha-Midrashim: Midrash Rabah*, p. 202. The application of this midrash specifically to *tokhaḥah* for interpersonal issues was evidently based on its context (i.e., Abraham reproving Abimelech [Gen. 21:25–27] and Isaac reproving Abimelech [Gen. 26:27–31]) and that it allows for the simplest explanation of how *tokhaḥah* may lead to love and peace.

81 *Arakhin* 16b.

offer *tokhaḥah,* which encompasses the skills and insights that are required to know how to properly express oneself, and the ability to discern the appropriate time and place in which to offer *tokhaḥah.*

Unfortunately, outside of the basic requirements of maintaining privacy, speaking "with gentleness and a soft tongue," and avoiding embarrassing the other person, the halakhic sources do not detail the exact nature of the tokhaḥic dialogue (see footnote).[82] This may very

---

82 However, there are later sources, of a non-halakhic nature, that indicate that *tokhaḥah* should take the form of a process of "clarification," in which the parties discuss and clarify what had taken place. (It should be noted, however, that some of these sources were focusing on *tokhaḥah* for general sins.) See, for example, Solomon Pappenheim, *Yeri'at Shelomoh,* vol. 1 (Dihrenfurt: Be-Defus Yeḥi'el Mikhal Mai, 1784), *ḥoveret 2 yeriah* 11, s.v. *"neged, umat, mul, likrat, nokhaḥ,"* pp. 65b-66a (cited in Meklenburg, *Ha-Ketav veha-Kabalah,* Lev. 19:17) (R. Pappenheim emphasizes that the reprover should proceed in a slow and methodical fashion and that a *"vikuaḥ sikhli"* [a thoughtful and rational discussion, or debate] take place between him and the other party, whereby the other party comes to the realization of any wrongdoing); Ettlinger, *Minhat Ani,* vol. 1, 232 (R. Ettlinger emphasizes that the reprover should bring "proof and [employ] logic" in reproving the other party); Hirsch, *The Hirsch Chumash, Vayikra,* vol. 2, 619–20 (according to R. Hirsch, in the course of *tokhaḥah* the reprover should attempt to bring the other party to "self-awareness" in relation to what had occurred); Isaac ben Ḥayyim Volozhiner, *Peh Kadosh ha-Shalem* (Jerusalem: Mekhon Moreshet ha-Yeshivot, 1995), Lev. 19:17 (R. Isaac asserts that the Torah's wording of *hokheaḥ tokhiaḥ* implies that there should be a "clarification of the matters [at hand]"); Jeroham Lebovitch, *Da'at Torah,* vol. 2 (Exodus) (Jerusalem: Daas Torah Publications, 2001), 51 (R. Lebovitch writes that *"tokhaḥah* is a [process of] clarification of the matters [at hand] by way of contemplation and an in-depth, comprehensive analysis of all aspects [of the issues]"); [Shlomo Wolbe], *Ale Shur,* vol. 2 (Jerusalem: Bet ha-Musar a"sh. R' Ḥ. M. Lehman, 1986), 240. R. Wolbe and others cite Rashi's commentary to Genesis 20:16—that "the expression *'hokhaḥah'* [alternatively, according to the wording of other editions of Rashi, *'tokhaḥah'*] in every place is 'clarification of things'"—in support of the view that *tokhaḥah* is supposed to be a process of clarification. As to the correct wording of Rashi to Genesis 20:16 [i.e., should it read *"hokhaḥah"* or *"tokhaḥah"*], all of the early manuscripts of Rashi's commentary that appear on the Al HaTorah website ("Online Rashi Manuscripts - Torah," accessed September 13, 2016, http://alhatorah.org/Commentators:Online_Rashi_Manuscripts; that is, those manuscripts without broken links) have the word *"hokhaḥah,"* not *"tokhaḥah."* For the earliest printed edition of Rashi in which the word *"tokhaḥah"* appears, see *Ḥamishah Ḥumshe Torah, Ariel: Rashi ha-Shalem,* vol. 1 (Jerusalem: Ariel, Mif'ale Torah, Yahadut ve-Ḥevrah be-Yisrael, 1986), 364. For a related discussion, see Yoel Florsheim, *Rashi la-Mikra be-Ferusho la-Talmud,* vol. 2 (Jerusalem: Rubin Mass, 1984), 133–36. It should be

well be a case in which the Rabbis apply the concept of "everything is in accordance with the time, issue, place, and individual."[83] The underlying idea of this concept is that there are certain areas in life that are best left up to the discretion and good judgment of the individual, who will hopefully do what is called for based on the unique circumstances of the situation, the correct application of Torah values, and good common sense. In the case of the dialogic component of *tokhaḥah,* the Rabbis may have felt that this would qualify as such an area, and therefore, outside of the fundamental requirements of privacy and speaking with sensitivity, the parties are free to conduct their dialogue as they see fit.

Even if there are no detailed halakhic guidelines for the tokhaḥic dialogue, there are nevertheless many possible rabbinic maxims and sources that may help serve as guides to the dialogue that should take place during *tokhaḥah.* Personally, two sources come to mind that seem to be particularly apropos to the dialogue and the give and take that should occur during *tokhaḥah.* There is a passage in *Derekh Eretz Zuta* (chap. 2) that reads: "Listen attentively to the words of your friend,[84] do not be quick to respond, properly contem-

---

noted, in support of this idea that *tokhaḥah* should take the form of a process of clarification, that many of the halakhic authorities and commentators who discuss *tokhaḥah* for interpersonal issues, in explaining what this mitzvah entails, offer scenarios in which the reprover starts off by asking some type of clarifying question regarding the actions of the other party (i.e., the one being reproved), and then the other party responds back in some way, either by explaining his actions and what had taken place, or by coming to the realization that he had committed a wrong against the reprover, from whom he proceeds to ask forgiveness. See, for example, the sources cited above on p. 228.

83 One of the famous formulations of this concept appears in Vidal Yom Tov of Tolosa (fourteenth century), *Magid Mishneh,* in *Mishneh Torah* (Jerusalem: Shabse Frankel, 2002), *Hilkhot Shekhenim* 14:5. See also Israel Meir ha-Kohen, *Sefer Ḥafetz Ḥayim, Hilkhot Isure Lashon ha-Ra, kelal* 4, *Be'er Mayim Ḥayim* 38. The source for the wording that I am using is from Israel Bruna (c. 1400–c. 1480), *She'elot u-Teshuvot Yisrael mi-Bruna* (Jerusalem: n.p., 1973), *siman* 102, p. 77. See also the related concepts discussed in Naḥmanides, *Perush ha-Ramban,* Deut. 6:18, Lev. 19:2; and Meir Simḥah ha-Kohen of Dvinsk, *Or Same'aḥ* (Jerusalem: n.p., 1973), *Hilkhot Talmud Torah,* 1:2, s.v. *be-Yoma.*

84 This is the wording that appears in the standard Vilna edition of the Babylonian Talmud and is cited in Jehiel ben Jekuthiel Anav, *Ma'alot ha-Midot* (Jerusalem: Eshkol, 1978), *Ma'alat Derekh Erets,* p. 296; cf. *Masekhtot Derekh Erets,* ed. Michael Higger (New York: De-Be Rabanan, 1935), 71.

plate the matter, talk about first things first and last things last, and admit to the truth."[85] This passage teaches the importance of paying close attention to what is being said by the other person, considering and honestly evaluating different positions, responding in an orderly and methodical manner, and admitting when one has made a mistake. Also, the rule of "You shall do that which is right and good in the eyes of the Lord" (Deut. 6:18), which is interpreted by the Rabbis as an injunction to resolve disputes through compromise and the dictates of equity,[86] seems to be particularly apropos for settling many of the types of disputes that may come up in the course of *tokhaḥah*.

Similarities and Differences between Contemporary Conflict Resolution and Traditional Jewish Approaches in Respect to Their Methods for Resolving Interpersonal Conflict through Dialogue

As explained in the introductory essay, cooperative, or collaborative, negotiation is the primary approach that is used in contemporary conflict resolution for resolving interpersonal conflicts. Cooperative negotiation is a process that encompasses a series of steps that help the parties to a conflict effectively resolve their issues through dialogue. This process typically requires that the parties clearly define the problems at hand (by focusing on underlying issues as opposed to the stated positions and by "separating the person from the problem"), employ some form of multi-step heuristic for problem solving, and search for win–win solutions, and that all of this be done through the use of constructive communication. The

85 The traits listed in this passage correspond to those that are mentioned in the mishnah in *Avot* 5:7, which discusses the traits of a "wise [alternatively, learned] person." See also tractate *Kallah Rabbati*, chapter 4; *Masekhtot Kalah*, Higger edition, pp. 251–55.

86 See Rashi's commentary to Deut. 6:18. Naḥmanides and R. Baḥya ben Asher cite this interpretation in the name of a midrash. Naḥmanides, *Ramban al ha-Torah*, Exod. 15:26, Lev. 19:2, Deut. 6:18; and Baḥya ben Asher, *Rabenu Baḥya: Be'ur al ha-Torah* (Jerusalem: Mossad Harav Kook, 2006), Deut. 6:17.

process also typically asks that the parties engage in various other elements, which were discussed in Chapter 1.[87]

In the analytic-comparative framework that was put forth at the end of the introductory essay, I had proposed that collaborative negotiation represents one of the most prominent normative behavioral aspects of contemporary conflict resolution. I had also proposed that from out of the seven core components of contemporary conflict resolution, constructive communication, with its various guidelines and rules, stands out as another major behavioral aspect of contemporary conflict resolution. In this chapter, we have seen that *tokhaḥah* for interpersonal offenses is traditional Jewish approaches' basic method for resolving interpersonal issues through dialogue. *Tokhaḥah* also certainly represents one of the most prominent normative behavioral aspects of traditional Jewish approaches. It follows that *tokhaḥah* for interpersonal issues is probably the closest possible thing that would correspond to collaborative negotiation (in respect to interpersonal conflict resolution that does not involve a third-party intervention) in traditional Jewish approaches. *Tokhaḥah* also encompasses a number of rules for constructive communication that are analogous to those of contemporary conflict resolution. Consequently, I shall now attempt to compare and contrast elements of *tokhaḥah* for interpersonal offenses with contemporary conflict resolution's approach to cooperative negotiation and constructive communication.

Comparing and Contrasting Tokhaḥah with Cooperative Negotiation

There are certain basic elements of *tokhaḥah* that it obviously shares with cooperative negotiation, and there are others of which it does not. The most basic element of *tokhaḥah*—that when dealing with an interpersonal issue[88] that may serve as a source of conflict between two people, the parties involved should come together and engage in

87 See pp. 7, and 27–28.

88 The range of interpersonal issues that *tokhaḥah* addresses was discussed on p. 229 n. 17.

a dialogue in an attempt to resolve the issue at hand—certainly parallels the basic concept of cooperative negotiation, which requires the same. *Tokhaḥah* also asks the parties to openly discuss the issues at hand, yet at the same time, that they do so using respectful and sensitive communication. This would certainly be equivalent to the constructive communication that cooperative negotiation requires (see the next section). *Tokhaḥah*'s rule that there are certain cases that are not amenable to constructive dialogue and may call for some other best alternative to dialogue also finds parallels in cooperative negotiation.[89] However, outside of these basic elements, the similarities between *tokhaḥah* and cooperative negotiation basically end there.

As it is generally formulated, cooperative negotiation, in comparison to *tokhaḥah*, is a relatively involved process of problem solving. Cooperative negotiation's focus on underlying issues as opposed to the stated positions requires that the parties be reflective and uncover the interests and needs that are at the root of the conflict. After clearly defining the underlying issues, the parties then employ some type of multi-step heuristic for problem solving that typically has them generate a number of possible options, identify the possible consequences of these options, assess the likelihood of the different consequences and evaluate their desirability, and then go on to decide on the most prudent course of action. Cooperative negotiation's emphasis on trying to attain win–win solutions requires that the parties come up with viable options that can satisfy their mutual interests and needs, which usually calls for a good degree of creativity, and is not always feasible. In stark contrast to all of this, *tokhaḥah* for interpersonal issues incorporates a minimal amount of guidelines, all of which center around constructive communication.

We can, at best, only speculate on what may lie behind the absence of detailed guidelines for *tokhaḥah*. One distinct possibility, as mentioned above (p. 254), is that this absence of guidelines may simply be due to the fact that traditional Jewish approaches wanted to leave this area of conflict resolution open-ended, without establishing

89 See p. 223 n. 1.

definitive rules, because of the rabbinic concept of "everything is in accordance with the time, issue, place, and individual."[90]

Contemporary Conflict Resolution's and Traditional Jewish Approaches' Behavioral Guidelines for Communication

Positive, constructive communication is without a doubt something that contemporary conflict resolution puts a great emphasis on when it comes to interpersonal conflict resolution. Abstaining from insulting, blaming, patronizing, and threatening the other party,

90 Aside from this, for me, another possibility comes to mind. In the introductory essay, we had seen that "problem solving," that is, the goal of resolving the (immediate) problems one faces in a conflict, is a clearly articulated, pervasive concern of contemporary conflict resolution, which I proposed should be designated as one of contemporary conflict resolution's fundamental values. Contemporary conflict resolution's emphasis on problem solving has precipitated processes that can get quite involved and seem to favor "expert problem-solvers" (see Robert A. Baruch Bush and Sally Ganong Pope, "Changing the Quality of Conflict Interaction: The Principles and Practice of Transformative Mediation," *Pepperdine Dispute Resolution Journal* 3, no. 1 [2002–2003]: 72, n. 7). This emphasis on problem solving, as Lederach and Bush and Folger have pointed out, also seems to exhibit a preoccupation with resolving the specific, immediate issues at hand. (It is totally understandable that this should be the case, being that it is generally the specific, immediate issues that spark the conflict and are therefore in the foreground and would naturally capture the attention of the parties.) But, as a result of this, to a certain extent, contemporary conflict resolution may at times neglect to focus on other relevant, and bigger, conflict-related issues (e.g., addressing deep-seated relational issues that exist between the parties, promoting the parties' moral development, and potentially improving the overall character of one's community, or society as a whole) and get caught up with what may be relatively trivial details, which has become an area of concern and criticism of contemporary conflict resolution (see John Paul Lederach, *Little Book of Conflict Transformation* [Intercourse, PA: Good Books, 2003], 4–5, 8, 28; and Robert A. Baruch Bush and Joseph P. Folger, *The Promise of Mediation: Responding to Conflict through Empowerment and Recognition* [San Francisco: Jossey-Bass, 1994], xv, 20, 27–30, 81–103). To avoid these pitfalls, traditional Jewish approaches may have just wanted to keep things simple (so that the basic process of resolving interpersonal conflicts through dialogue is accessible and useful to the widest possible range of people) and did not want to become overly focused on the immediate issues at hand, and thereby lose sight of the bigger issues of creating strong and healthy relationships and nurturing social/personal development, which, we may reasonably assert, are the elements that underlie *tokhaḥah*'s stated biblical purpose (see above, pp. 142, 225–28) of "you shall not hate your brother in your heart."

regulating the volume and tone of one's voice, and even being careful with the choice of one's words are only some of the communication skills that were mentioned in Chapter 1 in connection with contemporary conflict resolution's educational programs' approaches to communication. In Chapter 4 and in this chapter, we have examined some of traditional Jewish approaches' halakhic guidelines for communication. In Chapter 4, we had seen how traditional Jewish approaches incorporate a basic interpersonal prohibition against *ona'at devarim*, which prohibits intentionally saying anything hurtful to another person, and that they also incorporate a basic interpersonal prohibition against saying things that will embarrass another person. In the discussion of these *halakhot*, authorities were cited who propose that in the course of *tokhaḥah*, the prohibition of *ona'at devarim* is possibly, at least to some degree, not applicable, whereas the prohibition against embarrassing someone remains in effect. In this chapter, we have seen that there is a halakhic requirement to "speak gently and in a soft manner" during *tokhaḥah* and that in regard to embarrassing someone there is a halakhic debate as to the exact extent that the prohibition remains in effect.

By imposing definitive restrictions that would prohibit one from ever intentionally saying anything hurtful to another person (even if it causes pain "for a moment"; see p. 158, the quote from R. Abraham Isaiah Karelitz) or embarrassing someone, traditional Jewish approaches have apparently laid down as their starting point a standard that goes beyond what can normally be found in contemporary conflict resolution. However, within the context of *tokhaḥah*, when traditional Jewish approaches may to a certain degree relax their restrictions on what one may say, traditional Jewish approaches' basic guidelines of speaking gently and in a soft manner and not embarrassing the other person may not be all that different from contemporary conflict resolution's, at least in respect to the ideal standards that are taught in its educational programs. As outlined in Chapter 1, the communication component of contemporary conflict resolution's educational programs tries to teach students how to maintain the optimal balance between openly expressing one's ideas, needs, and emotions and at the same time showing sensitivity towards the other person throughout the process of interpersonal conflict resolution, which appears to be basically akin to traditional Jewish approaches' guidelines for communication that we have examined in this chapter.[91] Nevertheless, I would contend that by emphasizing that one has to speak "gently and in a soft manner"[92] and that one make a conscious effort to avoid embarrassing the other person when engaged in dialogue, the Halakahah is requiring that a person maintain a heightened level of awareness of and sensitivity to the other person's feelings that goes beyond the guidelines that one normally encounters in contemporary conflict resolution.

---

91 There are of course significant differences between contemporary conflict resolution and traditional Jewish approaches in respect to the formulation, imperativeness, and binding nature of traditional Jewish approaches' *halakhot*, as opposed to the guidelines and recommendations of contemporary conflict resolution. For a discussion related to these types of differences, see what I have written in relation to the similarities and differences between contemporary conflict resolution and traditional Jewish approaches at the end of Chapter 4 regarding the normative obligations of love and the prohibition against hatred, pp. 177, 183.

92 This, of course, was only Maimonides' formulation of this requirement; for other formulations, see p. 238 n. 49.

CHAPTER 7

Retaliation and Resentment: Not Taking Revenge (*Nekamah*) and Not Bearing a Grudge (*Netirah*)

When one experiences an interpersonal provocation, there is a wide spectrum of possible responses; for example, one could simply ignore what had happened, one may confront the person who is the source of the provocation and discuss what had happened in a constructive manner, one may ruminate and brood over what had happened, or one may resort to physical violence, and so on. Two of the most common responses to an interpersonal provocation, which are generally categorized in Judaism as being counterproductive, would be that one either becomes seized by a feeling of ill-will that leads one to actively retaliate and "get even," in other words, that one takes some form of revenge,[1] or that one feels and nurses a significant degree of resentment because of what had taken place, that is to say, that one bears a grudge.[2] Considering the frequency

1 The English word "revenge" can be defined as "the act of retaliating for wrongs or injury received" (*Collins English Dictionary*, 10th edition) or "to avenge (as oneself) usually by retaliating in kind or degree" (*Merriam-Webster Collegiate Dictionary*, 10th edition). In scholarly literature, one finds various definitions of "revenge" (Susan Boon, "Revenge," in *Encyclopedia of Human Relationships*, ed. Harry T. Reis and Susan Sprecher [Thousand Oaks, CA: Sage Publications, 2009]).

2 The English word "grudge" can be defined as "a feeling of ill will or resentment because of some real or fancied wrong" (*Random House Webster College Dictionary*, 2000 edition). The word also "applies to cherished ill will against an individual which seeks satisfaction; it usually suggests deep resentment for some real or fancied slight or affront and, often, a determination to get even" (*Merriam Webster's Dictionary of Synonyms*, s.v. "malice"). We shall see in this chapter that the latter definition does

with which people respond to interpersonal provocations by taking revenge or bearing a grudge, and their profound effect on the course of a conflict,[3] the standards of conduct that are established by the traditional Jewish sources that address these two types of responses are reckoned as essential components of the paradigm of interpersonal conflict resolution that is being presented in this work (see p. xxx) and will be the focal topic of this chapter.

The verse in Leviticus (19:18)—"You shall not take revenge[4] and you shall not bear a grudge[5] against the children of your people"—is the source of two biblical prohibitions: (1) it prohibits taking revenge for offenses that one has committed and (2) it prohibits harboring feelings of resentment for such offenses. This chapter will examine rabbinic interpretations of these two *mitsvot*.[6] After initially presenting

---

not reflect the traditional Jewish usage of the term *netirah*. The former definition, which simply focuses on the experiencing of resentment for a wrong (without the qualifiers of "which seeks satisfaction," "suggests deep resentment," and "a determination to get even"), is however in line with the basic halakhic conceptualization of the term (as formulated by a number of major authorities; see below, p. 278 n. 41). I therefore will be translating *netirah* as "bearing a grudge," as it is commonly translated.

3 See p. 293.

4 In Hebrew, לֹא-תִקֹּם (*lo tikom*). The word *tikom* is derived from the root נקם (*nkm*), which expresses the notion of taking revenge (see G. Johannes Botterweck, and Helmer Ringgren, eds., *The Theological Dictionary of the Old Testament*, 14 vols. [Grand Rapids: William B. Eerdsmans, 1974–], vol. 10, s.v. "*nāqam*," p. 1). In rabbinic literature, the prohibition is referred to by the biblical noun *nekamah* or by its post-biblical form *nekimah*.

5 In Hebrew, וְלֹא-תִטֹּר (*ve-lo titor*). The word *titor* is derived from the root נטר (*ntr*), which expresses the act or state of watching, guarding, or preserving something. The verse is therefore commonly understood by traditional Jewish commentators as teaching that one "should not *guard over enmity in his heart*" even if he does not plan on taking revenge (see Rashi, Lev. 19:18; cf. Jacob Milgram, *The Anchor Bible: Leviticus 17–22, A New Translation with Introduction and Commentary* [New York: Doubleday, 2000], 1650–52). In rabbinic literature, the prohibition is referred to by the post-biblical noun *netirah*.

6 The prohibitions of not taking revenge and not bearing a grudge are included among the 613 biblical commandments by Shimon Kayara [alternatively, Yehudai ben Naḥman], *Sefer Halakhot Gedolot* (Jerusalem: Ḥevrat Mekitse Nirdamim, 1988), vol. 3, negative commandments 100–101; Maimonides, *Sefer ha-Mitsvot*, Frankel ed. (New York: Hotsa'at Shabse Frankel, 2001), negative commandments 304–5; Eliezer ben Samuel of Metz, *Sefer Yere'im ha-Shalem* (Israel: n.p., n.d.), *siman* 197–98 [40];

various reasons that have been offered to explain the rational basis for these commandments, a number of components of the practical halakhic discourse on the two prohibitions will be elucidated. The specific focus of this discussion will be on what the Talmud terms as *tsa'ara de-gufa,* "personal suffering." We will then briefly touch on how the prohibition against bearing a grudge is in consonance with the commandment of *tokhaḥah,* "reproof." The chapter will conclude with a discussion of similarities and differences between traditional Jewish approaches and contemporary conflict resolution in respect to retaliation and resentment.

Underlying Reasons for the Commandments

There have been various attempts to explain the rational basis for the prohibitions against taking revenge and bearing a grudge. We will examine a number of these. In going through these explanations, one should keep in mind that in addition to providing explanations of the purpose and significance of these commandments, it appears that the authors who have offered reasons for these commandments seem to have also had another goal in doing so. Apparently, these authors also intended to provide rationales, all of which employ some type of religio-social concept, that one may use to shape, or cognitively restructure, one's attitude so as to be able to deal with interpersonal provocations in a way so that the provocations will not come to serve as catalysts for bearing grudges or taking revenge.

Sa'adia Gaon's Explanation

R. Sa'adia ben Joseph (Sa'adia Gaon, 882–942) discusses the concept of taking revenge in the tenth treatise of his *Sefer ha-Emunot*

Moses ben Jacob of Coucy, *Sefer Mitsvot Gadol* (*Semag*) (Israel: n.p.,1991), negative commandments 11–12; [Aaron?] ha-Levi of Barcelona, *Sefer ha-Ḥinukh* (Netanya, Israel: Mifal Torat Ḥakhme Polin, 1988), commandments 241–42; Isaac ben Joseph of Corbeil, *Sefer Amude Golah-Sefer Mitsvot Katan* (*Semak*) (Israel: Mefitse Or, 1959), *siman* 130–31; as well as in many other sources.

veha-De'ot (*The Book of Beliefs and Opinions*). At one point in his discussion of the topic, R. Sa'adia lists the pros and cons of taking revenge. He enumerates two basic arguments that people use for taking revenge and ten arguments that he has against taking revenge.[7] The arguments for taking revenge are as follows:

> (1) It provides one with a multiplicity of psychological and emotional benefits—"Revenge removes anxiety from the soul, expels sadness from it, gives it pleasure in seeing what happens to its enemy, abates its anger, and does away with excessive brooding."
>
> (2) It serves as a deterrent to others who would duplicate the objectionable act that was done—"it will prevent another enemy from provoking him in a fashion that is similar to that of the first one."

After asserting that the positive psychological and emotional effects of taking revenge actually occur independent of the act of revenge, R. Sa'adia lists the following arguments against taking revenge:

> (1) Once a person begins to reflect on how he can take revenge, he becomes totally preoccupied and consumed by such thoughts—"[If one's soul] brings itself to conceive plans against an enemy, it will fall into 'the black ocean,'[8] for it will constantly be coming up with one plan after another."

---

7 R. Sa'adia is presenting these arguments in the midst of discussing the common idolization of certain behaviors and traits, and is not presenting them as formal explanations for the biblical commandment. He also does not group or number these arguments. I have grouped the arguments and assigned them numbers based on features that they share.

8 According to R. Kafih, this is a common expression in Arabic that is used in reference to someone who becomes absorbed in plotting against an enemy. Joseph Kafih, trans. and annot., *Ha-Nivḥar ba-Emunot uva-De'ot*, by Sa'adia ben Joseph (New York: Sura, 1970), 312 n. 45.

(2) He is led to hard-heartedness and implacability—"He will not accept appeasement; he will show no compassion; he will show no graciousness; and he will not listen to any plea."

(3) He imprudently dissipates his resources—"[He] will come to expend all of his money and resources for that revenge."

(4) He shows reckless disregard for the welfare of his friends and his own personal welfare—"even if he would not be able to kill his enemy unless he also kills a thousand friends or himself, he will not be deterred from doing so."

(5) He behaves in a manner that contravenes his belief in God and ignores his religious obligations—"and even though he will only attain this [his revenge] through denying God and [forsaking] His service [he will not be deterred from doing so]."

(6) There always exists the possibility that his actions will be totally futile—"and as he accepts upon himself all of these [negative aspects of revenge], it is still possible that he will not attain that which he seeks."

(7) His actions may very well backfire and have a detrimental, opposite effect—"and it is also possible that the matter might turn around and he will perish, as it states: 'He who digs a pit will fall into it; and he who rolls a stone, it will come back upon him' (Prov. 26:27)."

(8) He incurs divine punishment, which can only be avoided through the forgiveness of the person he has taken revenge against[9]—"He brings upon himself a weighty

9 See Chapter 8, pp. 301–2 below.

punishment from God, which he can only be saved from through the forgiveness of the person he has wronged."

(9) He is attempting to go against the will of God and tacitly expresses that he is not subject to God's providence[10]—"and what about the hopeless desire to go against the creator of the heavens and earth ... and they (*sic*) imagine that they are beyond His control."

(10) He will breed ill will towards himself—"and what about the hatred and animosity of people, and the jealousy of his good fortune and joy in his misfortune that he will instill in their hearts ... there will not be found anyone who feels troubled because of their trouble or pained when something disastrous happens to them; instead, they [other people] will eat and drink and be happy and rejoice in their downfall."[11]

Maimonides' Explanation

The rationale/religio-social concept for the prohibitions against taking revenge and bearing a grudge that is offered by Maimonides (1135–1204) is based on the premise that those things that commonly serve as catalysts for revenge and bearing a grudge are mundane matters that are inherently insignificant. According to Maimonides' explanation in the *Mishneh Torah,* one who possesses insight into the true nature of things will put such matters into their proper perspective and dismiss them as being inconsequential:

10 Conceptually, this argument is comparable to the explanation that appears in the *Sefer ha-Ḥinukh*; see pp. 269–70 below.

11 Sa'adia ben Joseph, *Sefer ha-Emunot veha-De'ot* (Tel Aviv: Sifriyati, 1959), *ma'amar* 10 *Sha'ar Ha-Nekamah*, pp. 245–56. My translation is primarily based on R. Kafih's Hebrew translation of the original Arabic; see Kafih, *Ha-Nivḥar ba-Emunot uva-De'ot*, chap. 10 [13], pp. 312–33.

> One who takes revenge against his companion transgresses a negative commandment, as it is stated: "You shall not take revenge" (Lev. 19:18); and even though he is not flogged because of it, it is an exceedingly bad trait. Rather, it is proper for a person to show forbearance regarding all worldly matters,[12] inasmuch as for those who have understanding all [worldly matters] are vanity and nonsense[13] and are not worth taking revenge on account of them ... [14]

In the subsection of the *Mishneh Torah* that immediately follows this one, Maimonides goes on to discuss the prohibition against bearing a grudge. After delineating the laws of the commandment, he asserts that the Torah prohibits bearing a grudge because it may lead to the taking of revenge:

> So too anyone who bears a grudge against one from among Israel[15] transgresses a negative commandment, as it is stated:

---

12 Alternatively, "it is proper for a person to overlook all worldly matters" (see "*Yalkut Shinuye Nusḥa'ot*," in Maimonides, *Mishneh Torah*, Frankel edition, *De'ot* 7:7, p. 525).

13 R. Ephraim of Luntshits (1550–1619) further develops Maimonides' theme: "God does not want people to take revenge concerning any secular matter. Using an analogy, to what can this be compared? To an infant who is playing, and is performing a childlike act of building, or something similar. Someone [then] comes along and destroys everything the child has built and sown. The child [subsequently] cries in front of his father with a loud and bitter cry because of this. If his father were to pay attention to the child and fulfill his desire, he would [have to] kill the person. Surely his father will totally disregard what he is saying, for even if the small child because of his limited intelligence will consider that which this person has done to him as being a terrible thing, nevertheless, the father will perceive with his [matured] intellect that it is not so and that everything that the son was doing is insignificant and illusionary and it is not worth becoming this person's enemy and to take revenge [on account of what happened] ... ." Ephraim Solomon ben Aaron of Luntshits, *Sefer Keli Yakar ha-Shalem* (Jerusalem: Orot Ḥayim, 2001), Lev. 19:18.

14 Maimonides, *Mishneh Torah, De'ot* 7:7. In his *Shemoneh Perakim*, after stating that the majority of the commandments serve to train, or discipline, one's character traits, Maimonides mentions in passing that the prohibition against taking revenge also helps to "weaken the traits of anger and rage" (Maimonides, *Shemoneh Perakim*, chap. 4).

15 The *Sefer ha-Mafte'aḥ* (in Maimonides, *Mishneh Torah* [Jerusalem: Hotsa'at Shabse Frankel, 2001], *De'ot* 7:8, p. 396) points out that based on the rationale Maimonides offers at the end of this subsection (i.e., that not bearing a grudge

> "you shall not bear a grudge against the children of your people" (Lev. 19:18) ... Rather, he should eliminate the matter from his heart and not "guard over" it, for as long as he guards over the matter and remembers it he might come to take revenge.[16] Therefore, the Torah objected to bearing a grudge, to the extent that one must eliminate from his heart the offense [committed against him] and not remember it at all [see footnote for explanation].[17]

Maimonides concludes his discussion of taking revenge and bearing a grudge by briefly putting forth what he believes are the far-reaching social ramifications of abiding by these commandments:

"is the proper moral disposition whereby the development of society and social interaction between people are maintained"), the prohibition against bearing a grudge should be equally applicable to dealings with a Gentile as well. This is cited in the name of Mordekhai Lurya, *Eleh ha-Mitsvot*, in *Mishneh la-Melekh Aḥaron* (Jerusalem: Shmuel ha-Levi Tsukerman, 1905), *siman* 21. For discussions of these prohibitions in relation to Gentiles, see Zvi H. Weinberger and Baruch A. Heifetz, *Sefer Limud le-Hilkhot ben Adam la-Ḥavero: Lo Tikom ve-Lo Titor* (Safed, Israel: Makhon Torat ha-Adam le-Adam, 2003), 80–85; Yehudah Levi, "*Am Yisrael ve-Umot ha-Olam*," *Ha-Mayan* 24, no. 4 (1984): 15–17; Ben Zion Rivkin, "*Ba-Inyan li-Fne Iver Etsel Goy* (*Hemshekh*)," *Ha-Darom* 58 (Elul 5749 [1988]): 85–87; Ahron Soloveichik, *Logic of the Heart, Logic of the Mind* ([Jerusalem]: Genesis Jerusalem Press, 1991), 75–77; Eleazar Simḥah Wasserman, *Be'ure Rabi Elḥanan al ha-Torah: Kovets Parshiyot* (Jerusalem: Yeshivat Or Elḥanan, 2012), Lev. 19:18, Gen. 18:19, Deut. 23:20–21; as well as in other sources.

16 Cf. Dov Berish Gottlieb, *Yad ha-Ketanah* (Jerusalem: Or ha-Sefer, 1976), *De'ot* 7:15, p. 208b.

17 Maimonides, *Mishneh Torah, De'ot* 7:8. My translation of the last sentence of this paragraph is based on the standard printed edition of the *Mishneh Torah*. Most manuscripts differ from the printed edition somewhat and read, "one must eliminate from his heart the offense [committed against him] in [its] totality and not remember it" (see "*Yalkut Shinuye Nusḥa'ot*," in Maimonides, *Mishneh Torah*, Frankel edition, *De'ot* 7:8, p. 525). According to R. Hillel D. Litwack (*Kuntres Yisrael ha-Kedoshim* [New York: n.p., 1978], 44 n. 8) and R. Shmuel D. Eisenblatt (*Ḥayim Shel Shalom: Hilkhot Isure Mahaloket* [Jerusalem: n.p., 1989], 70–71), when Maimonides writes that one is forbidden from remembering the offense, he did not mean for this to be taken literally; rather, Maimonides only means to prohibit one from "remembering" the occurrence in the sense that when one thinks about it, he should not allow it to stir ill will in his heart. This explanation is quoted in Weinberger and Heifetz, *Lo Tikom*, 70. See also R. Ḥayyim David Halevi's explanation, cited below, on pp. 357–58.

> For this is the proper moral disposition whereby the development of society and social interaction between people are maintained.[18]

The Sefer ha-Ḥinukh's Explanation

The Ḥinukh's First Explanation. An alternative rationale/religio-social concept that is based on the belief in divine providence is offered by the *Sefer ha-Ḥinukh* (*Book of Education,* traditionally ascribed to R. Aaron ha-Levi of Barcelona, c. 1235–c. 1300):

> [When] a Jew has mistreated or caused pain to his companion in any particular matter, it is customary for most people in the world to persist in going after the person who mistreated them until they have compensated him in accordance with his misdeed or have caused him pain as he has caused them pain. It is from this sort of thing that God, blessed be He, restrains us when He says, "You shall not take revenge"... Among the underlying root reasons for the commandment is that a person should be cognizant and take to heart that everything that occurs to him [in life], whether good or bad, is caused by God; and that which transpires between a man and his brother through a human [act], none of it occurs independent of the will of God. Therefore, when a person inflicts him with suffering or pain, he should know in his soul that his [own] sins have caused it [see explanation below] and that God decreed it upon him. One should [consequently] not set his thoughts to taking revenge against the other person, for he was not the cause of the mishap; rather, it was the sin [committed by oneself] which has brought it about. This is similar to that which David, peace be upon him, had said

18 Alternatively, "whereby the cultivation of the land and business dealings between people are maintained." Maimonides, *Mishneh Torah, De'ot* 7:8.

> [regarding Shimei the son of Gera], "leave him alone and let him curse [me], because the Lord told him [to do so]" (2 Samuel 16:11). [We see that] he attributed the matter to his [own] sin and not to Shimei the son of Gera.[19]

In this passage, the *Sefer ha-Ḥinukh* offers an explanation that is based on the belief that everything in life is brought about through the will of God, and there is a correlation, of some form, between what happens to a person and one's own deeds, even the provocative actions of another human being who possesses free will.[20] Consequently, the author is suggesting that when someone does something that may motivate one to take revenge, instead of simply blaming the other person, one should look inward and attribute what had happened to one's own sins. By doing so, there would thus be no motivation or desire to take revenge.

Some Clarifications of the Sefer ha-Ḥinukh's Perspective. I believe that there are a number of things that could easily be read into the above passage that the author never intended to say and require clarification. First and foremost, it should be understood that the author is by no means promoting what may be some type of perverse, psychologically harmful process of self-blame. Elsewhere in his work, when the author of the *Sefer ha-Ḥinukh* writes that one should attribute bad things that one experiences to his own sins, he presents this as a process of being introspective and examining one's deeds, and then engaging in *teshuvah* (repentance) and trying to improve oneself to the best of one's ability (see *Sefer ha-Ḥinukh,*

---

19 Ha-Levi, *Sefer ha-Ḥinukh,* commandment 241. In my translations of the *Sefer ha-Ḥinukh,* I have made use of Charles Wengrov's translation; [Aaron?] ha-Levi of Barcelona, *Sefer haHinnuch: The Book of (Mitzvah) Education,* trans. Charles Wengrov (Jerusalem: Feldheim, 1992).

20 For sources that apparently support and sources that apparently disagree with this view, see Yehudah Berakhah, *Ketsad Mitmodedim,* vol. 1 (Jerusalem: Y. Berakhah, 2006), 161–82; Elijah Eliezer Dessler, *Sefer ha-Zikaron le-Va'al Mikhtav me-Eliyahu* (Bnei Brak: Sifte Ḥakhamim, 2004), 16–17; Re'uven Chmiel, *Sha'ar Re'uven* (Jerusalem: R. Chmiel, 2008), 308–9; as well as in other sources.

commandments 169 and 264).[21] This process has been elucidated by R. Joseph B. Soloveitchik (1903–1993), in a related discussion. R. Soloveitchik describes it as an edifying and sound approach to turning severe hardships into positive experiences in which one is cleansed of "the refuse of superficiality, the dross of crudity; his soul becomes sensitive, and his horizons are expanded ... he achieves self-actualization ... [and] from out of the negative sprouts forth the positive."[22]

Another point that requires clarification is that, despite what seems to be an apparent contradiction, the belief in such an all-encompassing divine providence that even includes the actions of another human being does not contravene the basic principles that a human being is endowed with free will, and is therefore held unequivocally responsible for his actions, and that other people who suffer from those actions have every right to, and most definitely should, protest and try to do everything in their power to stop those actions. There have been various classic philosophical approaches that have attempted to resolve this seeming contradiction.[23] Without

---

21 This is evidently based on the talmudic concept of "If a person sees suffering befalling him, he should examine his deeds" (*Berakhot* 5a).

22 Joseph Dov Soloveitchik, "*Kol Dodi Dofek*," in *Divre Hagut ve-Ha'arakhah* (Jerusalem: Ha-Histadrut ha-Tsiyonit ha-Olamit, 1983), 13–16; for an English translation see Joseph B. Soloveitchik, "*Kol Dodi Dofek: Listen-My Beloved Knocks*," trans. David Z. Gordon, ed. Jeffrey R. Woolf ([New York]: Yeshiva University, 2006), 7–11. There may be a very significant difference between the process that the *Sefer ha-Ḥinukh* is discussing and the process that R. Soloveitchik is describing. R. Soloveitchik states clearly that the process he is describing is not dealing with any aspect of causality (i.e., attributing one's suffering to specific causes), whereas the wording of the *Sefer ha-Ḥinukh* ("that his [own] sins have caused it ... it was the sin [committed by oneself] which has brought it about ...") seems to indicate that it is dealing with causality. I would contend, based on the ambiguity of the *Sefer ha-Ḥinukh* in commandment 241, how this process is explained in commandments 169 and 264, and R. Soloveitchik's comments in footnote 3 of *Kol Dodi Dofek* (pp. 14–15 of *Divre Hagut ve-Ha'arakhah*), that they are both discussing the selfsame process of being introspective and examining one's deeds.

23 See, for example, Sa'adia ben Joseph, *Ha-Nivḥar ba-Emunot uva-De'ot* (New York: Sura, 1970), 4:5, pp. 160–62; Maimonides, *Mishneh Torah, Hilkhot Teshuvah* 6:5; Maimonides, *Shemonah Perakim*, chap. 8; Naḥmanides, *Perush ha-Ramban al ha-Torah*, annotated by Charles B. Chavel (Jerusalem: Mossad Harav Kook, 1988), Gen. 15:14; Baḥya ibn Pakuda, *Ḥovot ha-Levavot*, trans. Judah ibn Tibbon (Brooklyn: n.p., 1984),

referencing these philosophical approaches, R. Isaac Hutner (1907–1980) simply explains this as a representative case in which one finds a sharp division between religious domains, where each domain works with its own unique set of rules. When it comes to dealing with the realm of personal feelings that may prompt him to take revenge, a person should maintain one type of perspective regarding someone who has committed an offense against him, which would promote forbearance and forgiveness. However, in the legal realm, or "realm of justice," he should view the selfsame individual from a totally different perspective, which could mandate that the offender is held fully and personally responsible for his actions. According to R. Hutner, this approach is exemplified in the two seemingly contradictory attitudes that David exhibits towards Shimei the son of Gera in the Bible (see 2 Samuel 16:10–12 and compare it with 1 Kings 2:8–9).[24]

One final point that needs to be clarified is that one should not mistakenly read into this passage that the author is presenting any type of comprehensive explanation of how to view suffering. Even those Jewish philosophers who subscribe to the talmudic view that "there is no suffering without sin" (see *Shabbat* 55a, regarding which there are major debates among the commentators as to what exactly this concept means, how to reconcile it with other sources that indicate otherwise, and as to whether the Talmud actually accepts this view in its final conclusion), such as Maimonides and Naḥmanides, are also clearly of the opinion that this is not always the case.[25]

Sha'ar ha-Bitaḥon, chap. 4, pp. 112b–113b, 117b–118a; and Yom Tov Lipman Heller, *Tosafot Yom Tov*, in *Mishnayot Zekher Ḥanokh* (Jerusalem: Ḥ. Vagshal, 1999), *Avot* 2:6, s.v. *yetufun*.

24 Isaac Hutner, letter to Joseph D. Epstein, in *Mitzvot ha-Shalom: The Commandments on Peace* (Brooklyn: Torath HaAdam Institute Inc., 1987), 271–72. When R. Hutner addresses this issue, he does not mention the *Sefer ha-Ḥinukh*; however, R. Ḥayim Friedlander, who takes an approach that is similar to that of R. Hutner, does mention the *Sefer ha-Ḥinukh*. See Ḥayim Fridlander, *Sifte Ḥayim: Pirke Emunah ve-Hashgaḥah*, vol. 1 (Bnei Brak: Ha-Rabanit Fridlander, 1999), 380–81.

25 See Maimonides, *Guide for the Perplexed*, 3:17, 23–24; together with Hannah Kasher, "*Yisurin le-Lo Avon: Le-Mashma'ut shel ha-Nisayon ba-Moreh Nevukhim*," *Da'at* 26 (*Ḥoref* 5751 [1990–1991]): 40–41; and Jonathan Blass, *Minofet Tsuf*, vol. 2 (Neveh Tsuf: Kolel Retson Yehudah, 2006), 828–29; and Naḥmanides, *Sha'ar ha-Gemul*, in

Despite all of these clarifications, in later works the relationship between divine providence and these commandments is often presented quite differently from that of the *Sefer ha-Ḥinukh*'s presentation. One still finds that the provocative actions of another are attributed to divine providence, but there is no mention of connecting this to one's own sins. The emphasis is on the belief that God loves the individual and only wants what is best for the individual, and even though the provocative actions of the other person may appear to be detrimental, ultimately God in His wisdom felt that this was for the person's benefit. This being the case, one logically should approach the matter with equanimity and not feel motivated to take revenge or bear a grudge.[26]

The Ḥinukh's Second Explanation. The *Sefer ha-Ḥinukh* then goes on to offer a second root reason that focuses on the interpersonal/societal benefits of the commandment:

> Additionally, within this commandment there is great practical value in that it will quell conflict and remove harbored hatreds from the hearts of people; and when there is peace among men [in regard to things that are within their control], God will grant them peace [in regard to things that are beyond their control][27] ... [I]f a person violates this [prohibition] and infixes it in his heart that he will hate his companion because he has been mistreated by him, to the point that he will compensate him in accordance with his

---

Kitve Rabenu Mosheh ben Naḥman, vol. 2 (Jerusalem: Mossad Harav Kook, 1964), 269–74.

26 See, for example, Ezekiel Zevi Michaelson, *Bet Yeḥezkel* (Piotrków: H. Falman, 1924), 20b–21b; Yitsḥak Yeruḥem Brodianski, *"Be-Ve'ur Torat ha-Bitaḥon," Bet Va'ad: Siḥot u-Ma'amre Musar* 1 (Sivan 5757–Iyar 5758 [1997–1998]): 21–23; and Dan Segal, *"Emunah u-Vitaḥon: Ha-Derekh la-Avor et ha-Ḥayim," Bet Va'ad: Siḥot u-Ma'amre Musar* 3 (Sivan 5759–Iyar 5760 [1999–2000]): 97–100.

27 Alternatively, this may possibly mean that "when there is peace among men [on an individual level], God will grant them peace [on a societal and national level]." Whatever the exact meaning may be, the basic idea is that God grants peace to those who live in peace. (In connection with this, see *Genesis Rabbah* 38:6, which is quoted in Chapter 2, p. 48.)

> misdeed, he has transgressed this negative commandment and his evil is great for this can lead to an exceedingly bad situation [literally, stumbling-block].[28]

This second explanation proposes that the underlying reason for the commandment is the promotion of goodwill and social harmony. By abstaining from taking revenge, one avoids conflicts and contributes to peace among people. Conversely, the taking of revenge will inevitably lead to discord and may have potentially calamitous repercussions. As far as the bearing of a grudge is concerned, in the commandment that immediately follows this one (commandment 242), the *Sefer ha-Ḥinukh* goes on to state that "the entire concept of this commandment [i.e., the underlying 'root reason' for not bearing a grudge] is similar to that of the previous commandment about revenge."

An Essential Cognitive Component

There is evidence already in the Bible that there was a concern about the inherent challenges in fulfilling the commandments of not taking revenge and not bearing a grudge, that is, as to how to deal with the natural human inclination to feel resentment and to retaliate when provoked. Aside from the additional exhortation of Proverbs, "Do not say, 'As he has done unto me, so I will do unto him; I will render to the person according to his deed'" (Proverbs 24:29), which, at least on a simple level, seems to just be reinforcing the Torah's prohibition against taking revenge, we also find another verse in *Tanakh* that appears to be offering encouragement and inspiration to people so that they will not come to take revenge when they are tempted to do so. Proverbs 20:22 states, "Do not say, 'I will pay back evil'; put your hope in God, and He will save you." Apparently, this verse is advising a person who is tempted to transgress the Torah's commandment and to take revenge to instead

28 Ha-Levi, *Sefer ha-Ḥinukh,* commandment 241.

have faith and place his/her hope in God, who will assuredly come to the aid of that person in some way.[29]

That the explanations that were offered for the commandments against taking revenge and bearing a grudge were also providing concepts that could possibly help a person in shaping, or cognitively restructuring, his or her attitude when faced with interpersonal provocations, so as not to bear grudges or take revenge, was recognized by later authorities. Commenting on Maimonides' explanation for the prohibition against taking revenge, R. Eleazar Landau (1778–1831) states,

> [Maimonides] wrote with wisdom, finding a proper path in giving suggestions to the person as to how to lighten from upon himself the "yoke" of the desire to take revenge, which is implanted within the individual. [This is by] taking it to heart that all worldly matters are altogether [less] than vanity, to such an extent that they should not prompt a person to take revenge because of them. For without such curatives and things to make it easier for the person such as these, our teacher [Maimonides] knew that it would be impossible for a person to overcome himself and to totally eliminate the offense that his friend committed against him from his heart.[30]

In a similar vein, the first explanation of the *Sefer ha-Ḥinukh* (that everything in life is ultimately brought about through the will of God) was adopted by R. Eliezer Papo (1786–1827) and put forth as the proper mindset that one should embrace so as not to bear grudges and be driven to take revenge. R. Papo (who reformulates the *Sefer ha-Ḥinukh*'s explanation to a certain extent, and does not

29 See Menaḥem Meiri, *Perush ha-Meiri al Sefer Mishle* (Jerusalem: Otsar ha-Poskim, 1969), Proverbs 20:22; Yehudah Kil, *Sefer Mishle* [*Da'at Mikra*] (Jerusalem: Mossad Harav Kook, 1983), Proverbs 20:22; and Shmuel Huminer, *Mitsvat ha-Bitaḥon* (Jerusalem: n.p., 1999), pp. 62–63.

30 Eleazar Landau, *Yad ha-Melekh* (Jerusalem: Mekhon Yerushalayim, 2000), *De'ot* 7:7, p. 50.

cite the *Sefer ha-Ḥinukh* as his source) prefaces this concept by writing that when it comes to the prohibition of bearing a grudge, one may mistakenly assume that

> this commandment could only be appropriate for the ministering angels, for whom there is no jealousy, hatred, and rivalry. However, since our creator has commanded us regarding it, we can certainly fulfill it, for "the Holy One, blessed be He, does not deal in a tyrannical manner with His creations [i.e., He does not require that they do things that go beyond their abilities]" (*Avodah Zarah* 3a) and "the Torah was not given to the ministering angels [but rather to human beings, with all their inherent limitations]" (*Berakhot* 25b).[31]

R. Papo then goes on to offer his formulation of the *Sefer ha-Ḥinukh*'s explanation.[32] After this explanation, he concludes by emphasizing the vital role of one's thoughts (i.e., utilizing a cognitive approach) in facing the inherent challenges of interpersonal commandments:

> [O]ne should strengthen himself like a lion with pure thoughts such as these ... he should do likewise for all commandments that relate to the heart ... With strength, through pure thoughts, a person will prevail over his inclination ...[33]

---

31 Eliezer Papo, *Pele Yo'ets ha-Shalem* (Jerusalem: Mekhon Merav, 1994), s.v. *"nekimah u-netirah."* That does not mean to say that not bearing a grudge is an easy mitzvah to fulfill. In contemporary religious works that deal with revenge and bearing a grudge, R. Moses Ḥayyim Luzzatto (*Ramḥal*, 1707–1736) is often quoted as saying that "revenge is sweeter than honey ... [and not taking revenge and not bearing a grudge] is only easy for the ministering angels." Moses Ḥayyim Luzzatto, *Sefer Mesilat Yesharim* (Jerusalem: Mosad Haskel, 1979), chap. 11, p. 85.

32 Papo, *Pele Yo'ets*, s.v. *"nekimah u-netirah."*

33 Ibid.

Similarly, in discussions of not taking revenge and bearing a grudge in contemporary Jewish religious works, one periodically encounters the reasons that were offered by earlier authorities for these commandments and finds that they are being presented as concepts that may aid a person in cognitively dealing with the emotional and psychological challenges of not taking revenge and bearing a grudge.[34] Aside from the reasons offered by earlier authorities that we have seen, one also finds various other cognitive approaches that are suggested in these works, based on earlier sources, for dealing with resentment and the desire for retaliation.[35]

The Practical Halakhic Discourse

There are *many* different opinions as to the practical application of the commandments of "you shall not take revenge" and "you shall not bear a grudge." These opinions encompass an extremely wide range of views as to what is and what is not prohibited by these commandments. It would not be feasible to adequately present this material in this work.[36] I will therefore only be touching on the main halakhic opinions regarding one common category of situations that arise in interpersonal conflicts, known in rabbinic terminology as "*tsa'ara de-gufa*," "personal suffering."

To be able to appreciate and understand the halakhic discourse surrounding the prohibitions against taking revenge and bearing a

34 See, for example, Weinberger and Heifetz, *Lo Tikom*, 322–24; Ḥayyim David Halevi, *Mayim Ḥayim*, vol. 2 (Tel Aviv: Ha-Va'adah le-Hotsa'at Kitve ha-G.R.Ḥ.D. Halevi, 1995), 294; Ze'ev Grinvald, *Iture Halakhah: Midot Tovot* (Jerusalem: n.p., 1997), 100 (which is children's literature); and Yosef Ben-Amram, *Or ha-Torah*, vol. 3 (Jerusalem: Mekhon Naḥalat Yosef, 2013), 132–35.

35 See, for example, Israel Meir ha-Kohen, *Shemirat ha-Lashon*, in *Kol Kitve Ḥafets Ḥayim ha-Shalem*, vol. 1 (New York: Avraham Yitsḥak Friedman, n.d.), *Sha'ar ha-Tevunah* chap. 6; id., *Shem Olam*, in *Kol Kitve Ḥafets Ḥayim*, vol. 2, *Sha'ar Shemirat ha-Shabat*, chap. 3, p. 5b; [Moshe Seḥayek], *Mi-Zekenim Etbonen*, vol. 1, 2nd ed. (Bnei Brak: Mishpaḥat Seḥayek, 2012), 49–51; and Ḥanan Levi, *Shevile ha-Midot veha-Arakhim*, vol. 6 (Rekhasim: n.p., 2009), 337.

36 This material is covered quite thoroughly in Weinberger and Heifetz, *Lo Tikom*. I will reference some, but far from all, alternative opinions in the footnotes.

grudge, one must first be familiar with the classic rabbinic formulations of these prohibitions and certain basic concepts.

The examples of taking revenge and bearing a grudge that have become *the* defining rabbinic models for these prohibitions appear in the Midrash *Sifra* (*Kedoshim, perek* 4:11–12). The Midrash offers two illustrative cases, which convey the magnitude, or extent, of the prohibitions as they were understood by the Rabbis:

> "You shall not take revenge." How far does the prohibition of revenge extend?[37] [If] he says to someone, "Lend me your sickle," and that someone refuses to lend it; [then] the next day, that [same] someone says to him, "Lend me your axe,"[38] [and] he responds [see footnote],[39] "I will not lend to you, just as you did not lend to me your sickle." In reference to such [a case] as this, it is stated: "You shall not take revenge."

> "You shall not bear a grudge." How far does the prohibition of bearing a grudge extend?[40] [If] he says to someone, "Lend me your axe," and that someone refuses to lend it; [then] the next day, that someone says to him, "Lend me your sickle," [and] he responds,[41] "Here it is for you [to take]; I am not like you,

37 Literally, "To what extent is the power of revenge?"

38 Alternatively, "your spade." See the discussion in Alexander Kohut, *Arukh ha-Shalem*, vol. 7 (Vienna: Menorah, 1926), s.v. "*kardom*."

39 The consensus of *poskim* (halakhic decisors) is that the prohibition against taking revenge is applicable even if one does not verbally express to the other person that he is taking revenge. See Abraham ben David of Posquières, *Perush ha-Ra'avad*, commentary on *Sifra de-Ve Rav hu Sefer Torat Kohanim* (Jerusalem: Sifra, 1959), *Kedoshim, parashata* 2 *perek* 4:10; Israel Meir ha-Kohen, *Sefer Ahavat Ḥesed*, in *Kol Kitve Ḥafets Ḥayim*, vol. 2, *Dine Mitsvat Halva'ah*, 4:5. Cf. Mordechai Lichtstein, *Sefer Mitsvot ha-Levavot* (Brisk, Lithuania: Avraham Hendler, 1924), *Hilkhot Nekimah ve-Netirah, Derekh Mitsvotekha* 3, p. 30.

40 Literally, "To what extent is the power of bearing a grudge?"

41 R. Isaac Attia (1755–1830) and R. Israel Meir ha-Kohen cite the view of a number of *rishonim* that the prohibition against bearing a grudge is applicable even if one's feelings are kept to oneself and never verbally expressed. Isaac Attia, *Pene ha-Mayim* (Jerusalem: Ha-Sifriyah ha-Sefaradit, 2003), 15b; Israel Meir ha-Kohen, *Sefer Ḥafets Ḥayim*, in *Kol Kitve Ḥafets Ḥayim*, vol. 1, *petiḥah*, *lavin* 8, 9, *Be'er Mayim Ḥayim* 8, 9. For alternative opinions and a thoroughgoing discussion of the topic, see Weinberger and Heifetz, *Lo Tikom*, 50–63.

> who did not lend to me his axe." In reference to such [a case] as this, it is stated: "you shall not bear a grudge."

Based on these examples, the Talmud derives certain fundamental principles regarding the prohibitions against taking revenge and bearing a grudge. These principles, in turn, are used by later halakhic authorities in establishing guidelines for the everyday applications of the prohibitions (to be discussed below).

In addition to a familiarity with the classic rabbinic formulations, there are also certain basic concepts that should be clearly understood before the halakhic discourse on this topic can be elucidated. First, it is a given that the prohibition against taking revenge is *not* applicable to certain realms. For example, cases that involve legitimate monetary compensation, which even though they may resemble, in a certain respect, a form of "taking revenge," undoubtedly remain outside the realm of the prohibition. In all cases of theft, damage to one's person or property, payment of debts, and, for that matter, all cases of halakhically actionable lawsuits, an injured party is entitled to seek justifiable restitution for something that is rightfully his.[42] Similarly, those cases in which the Talmud specifically permits one to harbor "*taromet,*" "a [personal] grievance,"[43] against another person do not constitute halakhically forbidden forms of bearing a grudge.[44] In each of the cases of *taromet,* all of which relate in some way to a type of financial issue,[45] one has

42 Naḥmanides, *Ramban al ha-Torah,* Lev. 19:17; Joseph Bekhor Shor, *Perushe Rabi Yosef Bekhor Shor al ha-Torah* (Jerusalem: Mossad Harav Kook, 1994), Lev. 19:18; and in other sources as well. Naḥmanides and Bekhor Shor are cited in Elyakim Krumbein, *"Nekimah u-Netirah bi-M'kom Tsa'ar ha-Guf," Teḥumin* 6 (1985): 294.

43 R. Isaac Blaser defines *taromet* as "displeasure and ill will." Isaac Blaser, *"Netivot Or,"* in *Sefer Or Yisrael,* [n.p., n.d.], s.v. *hine be-shas,* pp. 58a–b. Cf. Rashi, *Bava Metsia,* 52b, s.v. *im le-ḥasid.*

44 Simon Grünfeld, *Sefer She'elot u-Teshuvot Maharshag,* vol. 2 (Jerusalem: Mordekhai Greenfeld, 1983), responsum 53, p. 68; Isaac Hutner, *Paḥad Yitsḥak: Sha'ar Yeraḥ ha-Etanim* (Brooklyn: Ha-Mosad Gur Aryeh, 1974), 181–83; Joseph D. Epstein, *Mitsvot ha-Musar,* vol. 2 (New York: Va'ad le-Hotsa'at Sifre Mitsvot ha-Musar, 1948), 48. R. Grünfeld, R. Hutner, and R. Epstein are cited in Weinberger and Heifetz, *Lo Tikom,* 239.

45 R. Blaser writes that one is also allowed to harbor *taromet* when someone has committed an interpersonal transgression and has not asked for forgiveness. Blaser, *"Netivot Or,"* 58a.

been wronged by another person in a manner and to a degree that entitles him to feel what the Talmud considers as being justifiable resentment, even though he would not have a halakhically viable legal claim against the person (for cases covered under this category, see *Bava Metsia* 49a, 52a–b, 75b–76b, 77b, 79a–b; *Bava Batra*, 145b; and Jerusalem Talmud *Bava Metsia* 5:3).[46]

Tsa'ara de-Gufa, "Personal Suffering"

One of the most fundamental practical halakhic questions regarding the prohibitions against revenge and bearing a grudge has to do with what the Talmud refers to as *tsa'ara de-gufa*, "personal suffering."[47] From the context of the talmudic discourse that deals with the concept,[48] it is apparent that the term *tsa'ara de-gufa* is referring to the sort of personal suffering that people experience when they have been insulted or ridiculed.[49] There is a long-standing debate among halakhic authorities (which can be traced back to at least the twelfth century)[50] as to whether one is allowed

46 See Weinberger and Heifetz, *Lo Tikom*, 236–41.

47 This is how the term *tsa'ara de-gufa* is translated in Artscroll's Schottenstein edition of the Talmud (*Yoma* 23a). For an explanation that supports this translation, see Weinberger and Heifetz, *Lo Tikom*, 120.

48 *Yoma* 23a. See below, p. 281 n. 53.

49 See Ḥananel ben Ḥushiel, *Perushe Rabenu Ḥananel bar Ḥushiel la-Talmud* (Jerusalem: Mekhon Lev Same'aḥ, 1993), *Yoma* 23a; Eliakim ben Meshullam, *Perush Rabi Elyakim le-Masekhet Yoma* (Jerusalem: Mekitse Nirdamim, 1964), *Yoma* 23a; Isaac ben Sheshet Perfet, *She'elot u-Teshuvot Rabenu Yitsḥak bar Sheshet*, vol. 1 (Jerusalem: Mekhon Or ha-Mizraḥ, 1993), *siman* 220 (quoted in Weinberger and Heifetz, *Lo Tikom*, 120 n. 74); and Menaḥem Meiri, *Ḥibur ha-Teshuvah* (New York: Talpiyot Yeshivah University, 1950), *ma'amar* 1 *perek* 5, p. 126. For alternative explanations of the term *tsa'ara de-gufa*, see Menaḥem Meiri, *Bet ha-Beḥirah al Masekhet Yoma* (Jerusalem: Mekhon ha-Talmud ha-Yisraeli ha-Shalem, 1970), *Yoma* 23a (in which he writes that *tsa'ara de-gufa* includes hitting, cursing, and degrading another person); and Grünfeld, *She'elot u-Teshuvot Maharshag*, vol. 2, p. 68. It is worth noting that the *Ḥafets Ḥayim* writes that insulting someone not in his or her presence could probably not be categorized as *tsa'ara de-gufa*. See Ha-Kohen, *Sefer Ḥafets Ḥayim, Hilkhot Isure Rekhilut, kelal* 5, *Be'er Mayim Ḥayim* 7, quoted in Weinberger and Heifetz, *Lo Tikom*, 123.

50 This is based on the assumption (see p. 284) that Maimonides (1135–1204) was the earliest authority to express the view that the prohibitions apply to personal

to bear a grudge and take revenge, that means to say, to *reciprocate in kind by saying something harsh back to the person,*[51] when he or she has been subjected to such personal suffering. Some authorities permit it and some prohibit it.[52]

The question of whether one is prohibited from or permitted to take revenge and bear a grudge in cases that involve *tsa'ara de-gufa* revolves around the interpretation of a rather cryptic talmudic passage in tractate *Yoma* (22b–23a, see footnote).[53] At one stage in

---

suffering. The earliest known authority to express the view that the prohibitions do not apply to personal suffering was R. Isaac ibn Ghiyyat (1038–1089), *Hilkhot ha-Rits Gi'at: Sefer Sha'are Simḥah,* vol. 1 (Brooklyn: Mekhon le-Hotsa'at Sefarim ve-Ḥeker Kitve Yad, 1998), *Hilkhot Teshuvah,* 65–66.

51 To reciprocate in a harsher manner would go against basic dictates of justice; see Avraham Ehrman, *Sefer Halikhot Olam: Kitsur Dinim ben Adam la-Ḥavero; Ve-Sefer Kodesh Yisrael* (Bnei Brak: n.p., 1996), *Hilkhot De'ot, siman* 24:9, n. 30, p. 89; and Weinberger and Heifetz, *Lo Tikom,* 128, 131. As to whether those who permit one to take revenge for personal suffering would allow one to do so by reciprocating in a "milder" manner, that is, by not doing an act of kindness for the person that involves an object of monetary value, see Ha-Kohen, *Sefer Ḥafets Ḥayim, petiḥah, lavin* 8, 9, *Be'er Mayim Ḥayim* 8, 9.

52 For specific authorities, see pp. 283–84. The reasons for prohibiting taking revenge and bearing a grudge even when subjected to personal suffering are rather clear-cut. All of the reasons that are offered for these prohibitions by the commentators (see pp. 264–74 above) can readably be applied to cases of personal suffering as well. To explain the view that exempts personal suffering from the prohibitions, various explanations have been offered. R. Abraham Isaac Kook suggested that the exemption is possibly due to the inherent difficulty of not bearing a grudge and reciprocating in such cases, and because of the frequency in which these cases occur. Abraham Isaac Kook, *Mitsvot Re'iyah* (Jerusalem: Mossad Harav Kook, 1970), *He'arot le-Sefer Ḥafets Ḥayim,* p. 98. For alternative explanations, see Weinberger and Heifetz, *Lo Tikom,* 110–14.

53 After faulting King Saul for not responding to being ridiculed by certain wicked individuals (see 1 Samuel 10:27–11:12–13), the passage in *Yoma* reads as follows:

> ואמר רבי יוחנן משום רבי שמעון בן יהוצדק: כל תלמיד חכם שאינו נוקם ונוטר כנחש אינו תלמיד חכם. והכתיב "לא תקם ולא תטר"! ההוא בממון הוא דכתיב – דתניא: איזו היא נקימה ואיזו היא נטירה? נקימה: אמר לו: "השאילני מגלך", אמר לו: "לאו". למחר אמר לו הוא: "השאילני קרדומך", אמר לו: "איני משאילך, כדרך שלא השאלתני" – זו היא נקימה. ואיזו היא נטירה? א"ל: "השאילני קרדומך", אמר ליה: "לא". למחר א"ל: "השאילני חלוקך", אמר לו: "הילך, איני כמותך, שלא השאלתני" – זו היא נטירה. וצערא דגופא לא? והא תניא: הנעלבין ואינן עולבין, שומעין חרפתן ואינן משיבין, עושין מאהבה ושמחין ביסורין – עליהן הכתוב אומר: "ואהביו כצאת השמש בגברתו" (שופטים ה:לא). לעולם דנקיט ליה בליביה. והאמר רבא: כל המעביר על מדותיו, מעבירין לו על כל כל פשעיו! דמפייסו ליה ומפייס.

the passage, the Talmud asserts that these two prohibitions are only applicable to cases that involve an object of "monetary value" (in which someone has refused to do an act of kindness for another

---

R. Johanan said in the name of R. Simeon ben Jehozadak, "Any Torah scholar who does not take revenge and bear a grudge like a snake is not a Torah scholar."

[How can this be?] Surely, it is written, "You shall not take revenge and you shall not bear a grudge"!

That is [only] stated regarding things of monetary value [and not in regard to cases involving "personal suffering"], as [can been seen from that which] was taught in a *baraita*:

What is considered taking revenge and what is considered bearing a grudge? Taking revenge [is when] he says to someone, "Lend me your sickle," and that someone says, "No"; [then] the next day, that someone says to him, "Lend me your axe," [and] he responds, "I will not lend to you in the same way that you did not lend to me." This is [a case of] taking revenge. What is considered bearing a grudge? [If] he says to someone, "Lend me your axe," and that someone says, "No"; [then] the next day, that someone says to him, "Lend me your shirt," [and] he responds, "Here it is for you [to take]; I am not like you, who did not lend to me." This is [a case of] bearing a grudge.

[But is it really true that these prohibitions would only apply to things of monetary value] and not to "personal suffering"? Surely, the following was taught in a *baraita*:

Those who are humiliated [by others] but do not humiliate [back], they listen to that which disgraces them, yet do not respond, they perform [the will of God] out of love and are joyous in [the midst] of suffering, concerning them the verse states, "But those that love Him are like the sun that goes forth in its might" (Judges 5:31).

[We can answer by saying that] he may keep the matter in his heart.

[But is this a satisfactory answer?] Surely, Rava has stated that "Anyone who shows forbearance, they [the heavenly tribunal] will overlook all of his sins"!

[We may answer] that [the teaching of Rava] is [only applicable to a case] when he has been appeased by the person.

There are *many* questions regarding this talmudic passage, and there are many different possible ways to explain it; see Weinberger and Heifetz, *Lo Tikom*.

person, e.g., lending him a sickle or an axe),[54] and not to cases involving personal suffering.[55] By the conclusion of the passage, it is not clear whether the Talmud has ultimately rejected or accepted this assertion. Those halakhic authorities who permit one to take "revenge" (i.e., they allow one who has been insulted to say something harsh back) and to bear a grudge for personal suffering are of the opinion that the Talmud ultimately accepted the assertion, while those authorities who prohibit revenge and bearing a grudge for personal suffering are of the opinion that the Talmud ultimately rejected it. R. Israel Meir ha-Kohen (Kagan, "the *Ḥafets Ḥayim,*" 1838–1933) cites R. Eliezer ben Samuel of Metz (c. 1115–c. 1198),[56] R. Moses ben Jacob of Coucy (thirteenth century),[57] and R. Jonah ben Abraham Gerondi (*Rabenu Yonah,* c. 1200–1263)[58] as permitting revenge and bearing a grudge for personal suffering,[59] and the

54 This definition is based on Eliezer ben Samuel, *Yere'im, siman* 197–98 [40], quoted in Ha-Kohen, *Sefer Ḥafets Ḥayim, petiḥah, lavin* 8, 9, *Be'er Mayim Ḥayim* 8, 9.

55 According to R. Eliezer of Metz, the Sages derived this from the biblical passage in Leviticus by way of the hermeneutic principle of *davar ha-lamed me-inyano,* "something derived from its context" (*Yere'im, siman* 197–98 [40]). For an explanation of exactly how this principle is applied to the passage in Leviticus, see Ḥayim Daniel Penso, *Sefer Shem Ḥadash: ... al Sefer Yere'im,* vol. 1 (Jerusalem: n.p., 1848), commandment 40, pp. 25b–26a.

56 Eliezer ben Samuel, *Yere'im, siman* 197–98 [40].

57 Moses ben Jacob, *Semag,* negative commandment 12.

58 Jonah ben Abraham Gerondi, *Sha'are Teshuvah* (Brooklyn: Zundel Berman, 1974), 3:38. R. Mordechai Lichtstein and R. Binyamin Zilber point out that a close reading of *Sha'are Teshuvah* (3:38) seems to indicate that in cases of personal suffering, *Rabenu Yonah* only permits bearing a grudge but that he does not permit taking revenge. Lichtstein, *Sefer Mitsvot ha-Levavot, Hilkhot Nekimah ve-Netirah, sa'if* 3, *Derekh Mitsvotekha sa'if* 4; [Binyamin Yehoshua Zilber], *Sha'are Teshuvah im Beur Zeh ha-Sha'ar* (Bnei Brak: Hotsa'at Ḥokhmah u-Musar, 1977), 3:38.

59 The *Ḥafets Ḥayim* writes that there are "many *poskim*" who are of this opinion (Ha-Kohen, *Sefer Ḥafets Ḥayim, petiḥah, lavin* 8, 9, *Be'er Mayim Ḥayim* 8, 9). Among the *rishonim* (aside from R. Eliezer of Metz, R. Moses of Coucy, and *Rabenu Yonah*), there is R. Isaac ibn Ghiyyat (*Hilkhot ha-Rits Gi'at, Hilkhot Teshuvah,* 65–66); R. Menaḥem Meiri (*Bet ha-Beḥirah al Masekhet Yoma, Yoma* 23a); and R. Menaḥem Recanati (*Sefer Rekanati* [n.p., n.d.], *siman* 557); among the *aḥaronim,* there is R. Yosef Hochgelehrter (*Mishnat Ḥakhamim* [Jerusalem: Hotsa'at Rashbats, 1996], *siman* 9–10 *Tsofnat Paneaḥ* 3); and R. Jacob Castro (*Maharikash*) (*Hagahot ha-Gaon Morenu ha-Rav Ya'akov Kastro,* in the back of the standard printed edition of the *Shulḥan Arukh, Yoreh De'ah* 243:9).

Sefer ha-Ḥinukh[60] and Maimonides[61] as prohibiting taking revenge and bearing a grudge for personal suffering. According to the *Ḥafets Ḥayim*, since this is a matter that involves a biblical prohibition, we must apply the halakhic rule of *safek de-oraita le-ḥumra*, that one must follow the stricter opinion when a doubt arises regarding a law that is from the Torah;[62] therefore, in practice, one would be prohibited from taking revenge and bearing a grudge in all cases, even those that involve personal suffering.[63]

Notwithstanding the fact that there is considerable evidence that can be brought in support of the *Ḥafets Ḥayim*'s conclusions,[64] there are certain questions that have been raised regarding them,[65] and some contemporary rabbinic scholars have reached conclusions

---

60 Ha-Levi, *Sefer ha-Ḥinukh*, commandments 241–42.

61 Maimonides, *Mishneh Torah, De'ot* 7:7–8. There are a number of authorities who interpret Maimonides as agreeing with those *rishonim* who permit one to take revenge and bear a grudge for personal suffering; see Weinberger and Heifetz, *Lo Tikom*, 102–4. One such authority is Joseph Zevi Duschinsky, *Sefer She'elot u-Teshuvot Maharits*, vol. 2 (Jerusalem: J. M. Duschinsky, 1975), responsum 140, s.v. *aval* (cited by Baruch A. Heifetz, in a conversation with the author, September 8, 2004).

62 See *Betsah* 3b, *Shabbat* 34a, and *Avodah Zarah* 7a.

63 Ha-Kohen, *Sefer Ḥafets Ḥayim, petiḥah, lavin* 8, 9, *Be'er Mayim Ḥayim* 8, 9. There are a number of later authorities who attempt to deduce from the writings of other *rishonim* that they were of the same opinion as Maimonides and the *Sefer ha-Ḥinukh*. For example, R. Jeroham Perla attempts to bring proof from the writings of R. Simeon ben Zemaḥ Duran (*Magen Avot* [Jerusalem: Erez, 2000], 5:14, p. 370) and Naḥmanides (*Ramban al ha-Torah*, Lev. 19:17) that they were of the same opinion. (Jeroham Fishel Perla, commentary to *Sefer ha-Mitsvot le-Rabenu Sa'adyah: Im Be'ur Meva'er Devarav vi-Yesodotav ve-Shitato*, by Sa'adia ben Joseph, 3 vols. [New York: E. Grossman, 1962], vol. 1, positive commandment 19, p. 268; vol. 2, negative commandments 53–55, p. 104.) R. Menaḥem Krakovski similarly deduces that R. Yom-Tob ben Abraham Ishbili (*Ḥidushe ha-Ritba al ha-Shas*, 21 vols. [Jerusalem: Mossad Harav Kook, 2008], *Rosh ha-Shanah* 17a) was also of the same opinion (Menaḥem Krakovski, *Avodat ha-Melekh* [Jerusalem: Mossad Harav Kook, 1971], *De'ot* 7:7). For other authorities and an analysis of this view, see Weinberger and Heifetz, *Lo Tikom*, 100–105.

64 See Weinberger and Heifetz, *Lo Tikom*, 100–105.

65 See, for example, Perla, *Sefer ha-Mitsvot*, vol. 1, positive commandment 19, p. 268 (i.e., the question he raises regarding R. Ḥazan's interpretation of the Gemara's question *"Ve-hatanya: Ha-ne'elavin,"* which is identical to the *Ḥafets Ḥayim*'s interpretation). See also Krumbein, *"Nekimah u-Netirah,"* 296 (i.e., R. Krumbein's question on the *Ḥafets Ḥayim*'s interpretation of the phrase in the talmudic discourse that reads "he may keep the matter in his heart").

that are very different than his.[66] One of the most notable authorities to take issue with the *Ḥafets Ḥayim*'s approach is R. Abraham Isaac Kook (1865–1935), who offers a highly novel alternative approach to the whole matter. After asserting that the clear implication of the talmudic discourse, even in its conclusion, is that the prohibitions against revenge and bearing a grudge do *not* apply to personal suffering, R. Kook goes on to propose that even though the *Sefer ha-Ḥinukh* and Maimonides indicate that they are of the opinion that the prohibitions *do* apply to personal suffering, this may in fact not have been their true opinion regarding the halakhah. The *Sefer ha-Ḥinukh* and Maimonides, according to R. Kook, may have been reluctant to publicize their true permissive view regarding this matter since, from the standpoint of Jewish ethics, taking revenge and bearing a grudge even for personal suffering is viewed as something improper and may lead to disastrous consequences. R. Kook concludes by stating that this halakhah requires further study and that even if it should be determined that the Torah prohibition of taking revenge does not apply to personal suffering, there still exists the prohibition of Proverbs 24:29, "Do not say, 'As he has done unto me, I will do unto him; I will render to the person according to his deed,'" which would be applicable.[67]

A third and exceptionally noteworthy approach to the question of *tsa'ara de-gufa* is that of R. Jeroham Fishel Perla (1846–1934). R. Perla writes that the clear implication of the talmudic discourse, even in its conclusion, is that the prohibitions of revenge and bearing a grudge do not apply to personal suffering (which is similar to R. Kook's opinion) and that this is clearly not the view of the *Sefer ha-Ḥinukh* and Maimonides (which is similar to the *Ḥafets Ḥayim*'s opinion). R. Perla proposes that even though it would appear that the *Sefer ha-Ḥinukh* and Maimonides are contradicting the ruling of the

66 See, for example, Abram. Jelen, *Orekh Apayim* (Brooklyn: Yofi, n.d.), *siman* 1, *Ve-Yosef Avraham* 22, p. 16a–b; Eisenblatt, *Ḥayim Shel Shalom*, 72–76; Moshe Kaufman, *Sefer Ḥafets Ḥayim . . . ve-Nilvah alav Ḥibur Netivot Ḥayim* (Bnei Brak: n.p., 2011), 11–12 (in *Shevile Ḥayim* 33); and Weinberger and Heifetz, *Lo Tikom*, 138.

67 Kook, *Mitsvot Re'iyah, He'arot le-Sefer Ḥafets Ḥayim*, p. 98.

Talmud (which is something highly improbable), there may be a very simple way of reconciling their view with that of the Talmud's. Citing a responsum that was written by Maimonides' son, R. Abraham ben Moses ben Maimon (1186–1237),[68] in which R. Abraham quotes the talmudic passage in *Yoma* that discusses revenge and bearing a grudge, R. Perla points out that R. Abraham's version of the passage differs considerably from the standard printed version that we have today.[69] In R. Abraham's version, the Talmud *never* asserts that the prohibitions of revenge and bearing a grudge are only applicable to cases that involve an object of monetary value and not to personal suffering. We may therefore assume that this was the version of the Talmud that was used by Maimonides and, possibly, the *Sefer ha-Ḥinukh,* which served as the basis for their rulings that the prohibitions would apply even to personal suffering.[70]

Responding to Insults and Ridicule during the Initial Verbal Exchange

One might assume, based on the view that prohibits taking revenge and bearing a grudge even for personal suffering, that these prohibitions are unconditional and never allow one to respond in kind to an insult or to ridicule;[71] however, this does not seem to be the case. According to the *Ḥafets Ḥayim,* at the time of the initial verbal exchange in which a person is insulted, it is permissible—even though it is most certainly not advisable (see footnote)[72]—for one to respond in kind

68 Abraham ben Moses ben Maimon, *Ma'aseh Nisim* (Paris: L. Guérin, 1866), responsum 13, p. 105; id., *Ha-Maspik le-Ovde ha-Shem* (Jerusalem: Salimon Śaśon, 1965), 47–48.

69 It should be noted that R. Abraham's version does not appear in any of the manuscripts found in the *Sol and Evelyn Henkind Talmud Text Databank,* accessed March 3, 2014, http://www.lieberman-institute.com/.

70 Perla, *Sefer ha-Mitsvot,* vol. 2, negative commandments 53–55, pp. 103–4.

71 According to the view that permits *nekamah* and *netirah* in cases of personal suffering (see p. 283 above), one would apparently be permitted to say something harsh back to the person at any point in time, even after the initial verbal exchange.

72 In the *sifrut ha-musar* (Jewish ethical literature), biblical and talmudic passages are often cited that emphasize that it is preferable not to respond or take it to heart when one is insulted. One of the most common sources cited is the gemara in *Ḥullin*

and insult the person back.[73] It is only after some period of time has passed,[74] in which one is able to regain one's composure (and put things into their proper perspective), do these prohibitions become operative and require that one overlook what has happened. The *Ḥafets Ḥayim* bases this ruling on the opinion of the *Sefer ha-Ḥinukh* in its discussion of *ona'at devarim* (saying something hurtful to someone; see Chapter 4, pp. 150–51, 155–58 above). The *Sefer ha-Ḥinukh* writes:

> It does not appear that this [prohibition against *ona'at devarim*] requires that if a Jew comes along and begins to act in a wicked manner and inflict pain on his friend with evil words that the listener should not respond, since it is impossible for a person to be like "a stone that cannot be moved" [i.e., an inanimate object, without feelings];[75] moreover, his silence would be construed as if he is agreeing to the disparaging remarks. Surely, the Torah would not command one to be as silent as a stone to those who insult him as [one would be] to those who bless him ...[76]

(89a): "The world exists only on account of one who shuts himself up during a conflict." See, for example, Elijah ben Moses de Vidas, *Reshit Ḥokhmah ha-Shalem*, vol. 2 (Jerusalem: Or ha-Musar, 1990), *Sha'ar ha-Anavah* 3:9, 4:43; Luzzatto, *Mesilat Yesharim*, chap. 11, p. 100; and Jacob Kranz, *Sefer ha-Midot* (Jerusalem: Mekhon Sha'are Yosher, 1993), *Sha'ar ha-Sinah* chaps. 5–11.

73 See Ha-Kohen, *Sefer Ḥafets Ḥayim, Hilkhot Isure Lashon ha-Ra, kelal* 2, *Be'er Mayim Ḥayim* 1. I am assuming that what the *Ḥafets Ḥayim* wrote in *kelal 2, Be'er Mayim Ḥayim* 1 should be taken in conjunction with what he had written in the *petiḥah, lavin, Be'er Mayim Ḥayim* 8, 9.

74 In relation to the amount of time that should pass, it is noteworthy that R. Jair Bacharach (1638–1702) in discussing the concept of "when his heart is in the heat of anger" (see p. 289 n. 83, below) writes that a night's sleep generally has the ability to dissipate anger. Jair Ḥayyim Bacharach, *Sefer She'elot u-Teshuvot Ḥavat Ya'ir* (Ramat Gan: Mekhon Eked Sefarim, 1997), *siman* 65, p. 192. Cited in Weinberger and Heifetz, *Lo Tikom*, 76. Cf. Abraham Isaac Kook, *Orot ha-Rambam*, in Ya'akov Filber, *Le-Oro* (Jerusalem: Mekhon le-Ḥeker Mishnat ha-Re'iyah, 1995), 191; and Levi ben Gershom, *Perushe ha-Torah le-Rabenu Levi ben Gershom*, 5 vols., ed. Ya'akov Levi (Jerusalem: Mossad Harav Kook, 1996–2000), vol. 4, Numbers 30, *Ha-to'elet ha-sheni*, p. 171.

75 This expression appears in *Sanhedrin* 14a.

76 Ha-Levi, *Sefer ha-Ḥinukh*, commandment 338, cited in Ha-Kohen, *Sefer Ḥafets Ḥayim, petiḥah, lavin, Be'er Mayim Ḥayim* 8, 9. Even though the *Ḥafets Ḥayim* does

It should be noted that the *Sefer ha-Ḥinukh* does, however, suggest that

> [When a person] is forced by one who insults him to respond to his words, it is proper for one who is wise to respond in a refined and nice manner, without getting very angry, "for anger rests in the bosom of fools" (Eccl. 7:9). Instead, he should defend himself before those who have heard the insults leveled against him, and place the burden on the one who has insulted him.[77]

Even though there are those (i.e., R. Solomon ibn Gabirol and R. Eleazar Azikri)[78] who evidently disagree with the view of the *Sefer ha-Ḥinukh* and prohibit one from responding to an insult by insulting the person back, the *Ḥafets Ḥayim* never cites their opinions;[79] rather, he characterizes such conduct as merely a righteous character trait.[80] Once again, he bases this on the *Sefer ha-Ḥinukh*, which states:

---

not mention it, the *Sefer ha-Ḥinukh* does offer another argument for allowing a person to respond to an insult:

> We can apparently derive this that it is permissible to respond to the fool [who insults him], from that which the Torah has permitted one to kill someone in advance [in self-defense] who stealthily breaks into one's home. There is no doubt that one is not obligated to suffer the injuries inflicted by his friend, for he is allowed to save himself from the other person [i.e., a physical attack]. Similarly, he should be allowed to save himself with every means [at his disposal, i.e., a verbal response] from the words of his [the insulter's] mouth that are filled with deceit and oppression. (Ha-Levi, *Sefer ha-Ḥinukh*, commandment 338.)

77 Ha-Levi, *Sefer ha-Ḥinukh*, commandment 338.

78 Ibn Gabirol prohibits responding to an insult based on his interpretation of Exodus 23:2. See Solomon ibn Gabirol, *Azharot le-Rabenu Shelomoh ben Gavirol* (Jerusalem: n.p., 1987), negative commandments 21–24, p. 108. R. Azikri prohibits responding to an insult based on the opinion of Ibn Gabirol (and R. Simeon ben Zemaḥ Duran). See Eleazar Azikri, *Sefer Ḥaredim ha-Shalem* (Jerusalem: n.p., 1990), 24:29. See also Ehrman, *Sefer Halikhot Olam*, p. 91 *sa'if* 18 and n. 4, *Kodesh Yisrael*, p. 98.

79 This assertion is based on a search of the works of the *Ḥafets Ḥayim* that are found in *Ha-Otsar: Otsar ha-Sefarim ha-Yehudi Torah Treasures*, version 10 (Jerusalem: Digital Book Systems, 2003), CD-ROM.

80 According to the *Ḥafets Ḥayim*, the *Shulḥan Arukh* (*Ḥoshen Mishpat* 228:1) itself rules that the commandment of *ona'at devarim* does not prohibit one who has had

> There is a class of people whose piety reaches to such a high level to the extent that they do not desire to avail themselves of this ruling, and will not respond in any way to those who insult them, lest [their] anger overpower them and they get unduly carried away with the matter. Regarding them [people of such piety], the talmudic sages of blessed memory have said,[81] "Those who are humiliated [by others] but do not humiliate [back], they listen to that which disgraces them, yet do not respond, regarding them Scripture states: 'But those that love Him are like the sun that goes forth in its might' (Judges 5:31)."[82]

In support of the distinction that he makes between responding to an insult during the initial verbal exchange and responding after a period of time has passed, the *Ḥafets Ḥayim* cites certain rulings of R. Moses Isserles (c. 1525–1572) and R. Joshua Falk (c. 1555–1614) that seem to employ a similar distinction.[83]

---

something hurtful said to him by someone from saying something hurtful back to that person. Ha-Kohen, *Sefer Ḥafets Ḥayim, Hilkhot Isure Lashon ha-Ra, kelal* 10, *Be'er Mayim Ḥayim* 31. See also Moses Rivkes, *Be'er ha-Golah*, in the standard printed edition of the *Shulḥan Arukh, Ḥoshen Mishpat*, 228:5. For an alternative interpretation of the *Shulḥan Arukh*'s ruling, see Joshua ben Alexander Falk, *Sefer Me'irat Enayim* (*Sma*), in the standard printed edition of the *Shulḥan Arukh, Ḥoshen Mishpat* 228:4.

81 *Shabbat* 88b; *Yoma* 23a; *Gittin* 36b.

82 Ha-Levi, *Sefer ha-Ḥinukh*, commandment 338.

83 Ha-Kohen, *Sefer Ḥafets Ḥayim, petiḥah, lavin, Be'er Mayim Ḥayim* 8, 9. In discussing the laws of monetary fines for insulting someone (see Chapter 4, p. 153 above), R. Isserles and R. Falk refer to a halakhic exemption for someone who insults another person in direct response to an insult that was leveled against him by that person. This exemption, in certain instances, exempts the second person from compensating the first person because this took place "when his heart is in the heat of anger" (*ki yeḥam levavo*, see Deuteronomy 19:6). R. Falk, in interpreting what R. Isserles had written, differentiates between when the response took place immediately after the insult (in which case the second party would be exempt) and when it took place sometime afterwards (in which case he would be liable), which seems to be perfectly analogous to the distinction that the *Ḥafets Ḥayim* makes in regard to responding to an insult. Moses Isserles, *Shulḥan Arukh, Ḥoshen Mishpat* 421:13; see also id., *Darkhe Mosheh ha-Shalem al Tur Ḥoshen ha-Mishpat*, vol. 2 (Jerusalem: Mekhon Yerushalayim, 1983), *siman* 421, p. 252; and Falk, *Sma*, *Ḥoshen Mishpat*

The Relationship between Tokhaḥah and the Commandment against Bearing a Grudge

One of the most basic components of the traditional Jewish approach to interpersonal conflict resolution is the mitzvah of *tokhaḥah*, "reproof." As we had seen in Chapter 6, *tokhaḥah* encompasses the basic halakhic guidelines for dealing with interpersonal provocations. When one feels that a person has committed an offense against him, the mitzvah of *tokhaḥah* obligates the individual to confront that person and discuss the issue with him. To once again quote the words of Maimonides in the *Mishneh Torah* (*De'ot* 6:6):

> When a man commits a transgression against a [fellow] man, he [the fellow man] should not hate the offender and keep silent ... rather, there is a mitzvah incumbent upon him to inform him and say to him, "Why did you do such and such to me?" and, "For what reason did you commit a transgression against me in regard to the specified matter?" as it is stated: "You shall surely reprove your friend" (Lev. 19:17).

There is what would seem to be, on the face of things, an apparent contradiction between the mitzvah of *tokhaḥah* and the mitzvah that prohibits one from bearing a grudge. The prohibition against bearing a grudge requires that "[we] do not bear a grudge, even if we do not [actively] reciprocate, which means to say, that we [merely] remember the misdeed the sinner committed against us and we remind him about it" (Maimonides, *Sefer ha-Mitsvot*, negative commandment 305); rather, one should "eliminate the matter from his heart and not 'guard over' it" (Maimonides, *Mishneh Torah*, *De'ot* 7:8; see above, p. 268 and footnote 17). It would seem to follow that if the prohibition against bearing a grudge requires that one ignore and, so to speak, "forget about" the whole matter, one should not be

---

421:24. For further elaboration and a discussion of the concept of "when his heart is in the heat of anger," see Kaminsky, "Traditional Jewish Perspectives," 178–84.

allowed to broach and discuss an interpersonal provocation in the course of *tokhaḥah.*

There are a number of possible explanations that have been offered to resolve this seeming contradiction between the two *mitsvot.*[84] R. Weinberger and R. Heifetz offer what is one of the simpler explanations. According to R. Weinberger and R. Heifetz, the mitzvah of *tokhaḥah* and the mitzvah of not bearing a grudge work in conjunction with each other. When one fulfills the commandment of *tokhaḥah* by confronting a person who has committed a perceived offense against him and discusses the matter with that person, one thereby purges hatred and resentment from his heart in a constructive manner (see Chapter 6, pp. 230–31, 239). In doing so, one is thereby in effect fulfilling the commandment of not bearing a grudge, which requires that one "erase the matter from his heart."[85]

84 See Weinberger and Heifetz, *Lo Tikom*, 208–9, and the next footnote.

85 Ibid., 209. Support for this approach can possibly be found in the wording of Maimonides when he discusses *tokhaḥah* and writes that "we should reprove one another when one of us commits a wrong against another, and not bear a grudge against nor entertain a sinful thought of the person. Instead, we are commanded to verbally reprove him until there is no remnant [of ill will] left in the soul" (Maimonides, *Sefer ha-Mitsvot*, positive commandment 205). See Yeḥiel Neuman, *"Kuntres 'Lo Titor,'" Torat ha-Adam le-Adam: Kovets Torani ba-Mitsvot she-ben Adam la-Ḥavero* 3 (1999): 80–81.

One other noteworthy approach to resolving the apparent contradiction between the mitzvah of *tokhaḥah* and the mitzvah of not bearing a grudge is that of R. Dov Berish Gottlieb's (d. 1796). R. Gottlieb has a completely different approach to that of R. Weinberger and R. Heifetz's and, for that matter, the commandments of *tokhaḥah* and of not bearing a grudge, as a whole. To understand how he resolves the contradiction between the two commandments, one first must be aware of R. Gottlieb's interpretation of the halakhic conclusion of the talmudic discourse in *Yoma* that deals with bearing a grudge. According to R. Gottlieb, the Talmud in *Yoma* only prohibits one from bearing a grudge for an act that does not constitute an infraction of Jewish law (e.g., not lending someone a sickle or an axe), but permits one to bear a grudge for an act that does constitute an infraction of Jewish law (e.g., ridiculing someone). Therefore, in the view of R. Gottlieb, the problem would resolve itself by the fact that the commandments of bearing a grudge and *tokhaḥah* are dealing with two totally different categories of offenses. The commandment against bearing a grudge only applies to offenses that do not constitute an infraction of Jewish law, whereas the commandment of *tokhaḥah*, in R. Gottlieb's opinion, would only apply to personal offenses that do constitute infractions of Jewish law, such as when one is subjected to insults or ridicule (i.e., *tsa'ara de-gufa*). It thus

Summary

This chapter has examined the prohibitions against bearing a grudge and taking revenge. It began by first citing the explanations that have been offered for these biblical commandments by Sa'adia Ga'on, Maimonides, and the *Sefer ha-Ḥinukh*. These explanations were understood not only as attempts to shed light on the rational basis for the two commandments, but also as attempts to offer religio-social concepts that could serve as the cognitive basis for effectively coping with the emotional and psychological challenges of not bearing a grudge and taking revenge. This understanding of these explanations, the concern about emotional and psychological challenges, and the need to address these challenges through a cognitive approach were underscored in the works of later authorities and are periodically encountered in contemporary religious works.

The second section of this chapter expounded on laws of revenge and bearing a grudge. The discussion centered on *halakhot* that relate to *tsa'ara de-gufa*, "personal suffering." A number of opinions were cited regarding when, and how, one should and should not respond to insults or ridicule. One point that deserves to be highlighted is that throughout this discussion we had seen that the Halakhah is taking into consideration, weighing, and trying to strike the proper balance between what can and cannot be expected from the average person. The diversity of opinions that emerges from out of this discussion, aside from its practical relevance for an observant Jew, reflects alternative—and, in certain cases, diametrically opposed—views as to the degree of fortitude and self-restraint an average person is capable of exhibiting in the face of personal insults and provocations.

---

emerges that, according to R. Gottlieb, one is supposed to overlook and not bear a grudge for what the Torah would perceive as petty issues, whereas more serious issues, that is, offenses that the Torah would categorize as infractions of laws, one could bear a grudge for. However, even in such a case in which one is permitted to bear a grudge, one is nevertheless obligated to discuss the matter with the other party and try to resolve the issue and do away with his resentment through *tokhaḥah*. Gottlieb, *Yad ha-Ketanah, De'ot* 7:7–35, pp. 207a–214a.

The final section took us back to, and highlighted once again, the all-important process of *tokhaḥah*. This section very briefly dealt with the relationship between the prohibition against bearing a grudge, which requires that one basically ignore a personal offense, and the mitzvah of *tokhaḥah*, which requires that one confront a person who commits a personal offense and discuss the matter with that person. The approach that was presented in reconciling these two precepts proposed that the process of *tokhaḥah* should be understood as a way of overcoming resentment and fulfilling the commandment against bearing a grudge. The two precepts thus work together and are in complete harmony with each other.

Similarities and Differences between Contemporary Conflict Resolution and Traditional Jewish Approaches in Respect to Retaliation and Resentment

In previous chapters, we have seen that on a basic level one finds many similarities between contemporary conflict resolution and traditional Jewish approaches. This is also certainly true in respect to retaliation and resentment, or the taking of revenge and the bearing of grudges. Both contemporary conflict resolution and traditional Jewish approaches are extremely concerned about the problems associated with retaliation and resentment. Revengeful or retaliatory behaviors in which one reciprocates in kind, insult for insult, wrong for wrong, injury for injury, and the harboring of ill will, bitterness, and anger (i.e., the bearing of a grudge, or resentment) can serve as major factors in the development and perpetuation of conflicts. Conflict resolution literature, and general literature, recount innumerable cases in which parties to a conflict fall into vicious and destructive cycles of resentment and retaliation.[86] Consequently, a significant percentage of contemporary

86 See, for example, Sung Kim and Richard H. Smith, "Revenge and Conflict Escalation," *Negotiation Journal* 9, no. 1 (1993): 37–43; Noreen Stuckless and Richard Goranson, "A Selected Bibliography of Literature on Revenge," *Psychological*

conflict resolution's and traditional Jewish approaches' systems of conflict resolution attempt to address issues of resentment and retaliation. For contemporary conflict resolution, its core components of anger management, perspective taking, constructive communication, and cooperative negotiation all relate, in varying degrees, to the prevention or elimination of resentments and retaliatory behaviors. The same may also be said about core components of traditional Jewish approaches. This was highlighted in this chapter in respect to the commandments that deal with taking revenge, bearing a grudge, and *tokhaḥah.* It will be evident that this is also the case in respect to traditional Jewish approaches' components of forgiveness and anger management, which will be discussed in the next two chapters.

Differences between contemporary conflict resolution and traditional Jewish approaches in respect to retaliation and resentment do emerge in regard to a number of areas, however. Probably the most basic difference is in regard to traditional Jewish approaches' direct focus on and approach to the taking of revenge and the bearing of grudges. Though both contemporary conflict resolution and traditional Jewish approaches attempt to address issues of retaliation and resentment through similar indirect means, such as the use of dialogue, constructive communication, and anger management techniques, which in various ways try to prevent retaliatory behaviors and the harboring of resentment, traditional Jewish approaches take the additional step in dealing with these issues head on, by directly focusing on and addressing retaliatory behaviors and issues of resentment with explicit prohibitions.

Reports 75, no. 2 (1994): 803–11; Jeffrey Z. Rubin, Dean G. Pruitt, and Sung Hee Kim, *Social Conflict: Escalation, Stalemate, and Settlement,* 2nd ed. (New York: McGraw Hill, 1994), 118–19, 124; Morton Deutsch, "Cooperation, Competition, and Conflict," in *The Handbook of Conflict Resolution: Theory and Practice,* 3rd ed., ed. Peter T. Coleman, Morton Deutsch, and Eric C. Marcus (San Francisco, CA: Jossey-Bass, 2014), 9, 17 (see also the introduction, p. xviii); and Richard H. Smith and David Ryan Schurtz, "Resentment," in *Encyclopedia of the Mind,* vol. 17, ed. Harold Pashler (Thousand Oaks, CA: Sage Publications, 2013), 658–60.

That traditional Jewish approaches employ explicit prohibitions to proscribe the taking of revenge and the bearing of grudges also subsumes other basic differences between contemporary conflict resolution and traditional Jewish approaches. As we have seen repeatedly throughout this study, contemporary conflict resolution and traditional Jewish approaches differ significantly in regard to the formulation, binding nature, and imperativeness of their behavioral guidelines and rules of conduct. Contemporary conflict resolution does not employ the terminology of "commandments" (i.e., "*mitsvot*") and "laws" (the English equivalent of "*halakhot*") and their associated concepts.[87] In stark contrast, for traditional Jewish approaches, the concepts of *mitsvot* and *halakhot*, with their interpersonal imperatives that obligate the parties to interact in a certain fashion, are essential elements of traditional Jewish approaches' method of conflict resolution. Thus, we find that contemporary conflict resolution may denounce and work to prevent retaliatory behaviors and the harboring of resentment, but it does not impose the same sort of firm requirements that traditional Jewish approaches do, which prohibit the parties from taking revenge and bearing grudges.

We have also seen repeatedly throughout this study that contemporary conflict resolution and traditional Jewish approaches differ significantly in regard to the range, or scope, of what they ask of the parties. As far as differences in this area in relation to retaliation and resentment are concerned, I am somewhat hesitant to take any type of definitive stand. The reason for this, as I had mentioned earlier (p. 277), is that my focus has been on only one major aspect of the *halakhot* of *nekamah* and *netirah* (i.e., *tsa'ara de-gufa*, "personal suffering"); therefore, I have not adequately presented the extremely wide range of halakhic opinions regarding the practical applications of the commandments against taking revenge and bearing a grudge. This being the case,

87 Aside from their simple formulation, binding nature, and imperativeness, there are other associated concepts that I have not discussed in this work; see p. 177 n. 202.

the following comments by necessity are qualified and should not be taken as a definitive statement on the matter.

In focusing on the standards of conduct established by traditional Jewish approaches that were covered in this chapter, we had seen that even though there are exceptions to the general precepts, there does exist fundamental prohibitions that bar one who experienced an interpersonal provocation from reciprocating in kind or harboring a grudge. Just to use the classic rabbinic formulations of these prohibitions, which prohibit a person from not lending an object to someone who had refused to lend a similar type of object to him, or to even bear a grudge because of this, and the halakhah promulgated by the *Ḥafets Ḥayim*, which prohibits reciprocating insult for insult, and from even bearing a grudge for an insult,[88] as representative examples of traditional Jewish approaches' behavioral guidelines and rules of conduct, I would contend that contemporary conflict resolution may find these standards of conduct in relation to retaliation and resentment to be ideals and as extremely commendable, but not something that it incorporates, and that it would more than likely view them as standards that could not realistically be maintained.

Aside from the similarities and differences discussed above,[89] which all relate to halakhic aspects of taking revenge and bearing grudges, and as such would fall under the heading of behavioral guidelines and rules of conduct, there is one other area that I feel should also be discussed, and that is, the emphasis on a cognitive approach in dealing with the challenges of not retaliating and not

88 As was pointed out earlier (see pp. 263, 268 n. 17, 287, and 291), that does not mean to say that one has to simply ignore and forget about what had happened. What is required is that one should attempt to put what had happened into its proper perspective or engage in *tokhaḥah* and thereby deal with feelings of ill will towards the other person.

89 All of the similarities and differences that I have highlighted up until this point in this section parallel ones that were discussed in Chapter 4 (pp. 180–83) in relation to traditional Jewish approaches' normative obligations of the prohibition against hatred.

harboring resentment, which were elaborated on in the first half of this chapter.

Contemporary conflict resolution fully recognizes that parties to a conflict need the requisite impetus and mindset to effectively engage in conflict resolution processes. This entails that the parties have an awareness and understanding of the negative aspects of the alternatives to conflict resolution, which includes the harm that may ensue from engaging in retaliatory behaviors and harboring grudges. Consequently, contemporary conflict resolution's literature abounds with material that describes the harmful effects of resentment and retaliation, and, as I had mentioned in the introductory essay, one finds that participants in contemporary conflict resolution's educational programs typically discuss the potential negative aspects of conflict, which invariably focus on the undesirable outcomes of resentment and retaliation.[90] We will also see, at the end of Chapter 9, that contemporary conflict resolution stresses various other cognitive elements related to resentment and retaliation in the context of anger management. This emphasis on a cognitive approach in dealing with the challenges of not retaliating and not harboring resentment in contemporary conflict resolution parallels the emphasis we had seen in traditional Jewish approaches in this chapter, which we will come back to discuss further when we elaborate on Jewish approaches to anger management.

Taking all of the above similarities and differences into consideration, we may conclude that contemporary conflict resolution and traditional Jewish approaches possess many basic similarities but also differ in certain respects when it comes to issues of retaliation and resentment. Both contemporary conflict resolution and traditional Jewish approaches recognize the dangers of, remonstrate against, and actively address retaliatory behaviors and the harboring of grudges. Differences between them emerge in regard to how they address retaliation and resentment. Contemporary conflict

90 See pp. 26 and 293.

resolution employs indirect approaches, whereas traditional Jewish approaches use both indirect and direct approaches. Traditional Jewish approaches' direct approaches take the form of explicit prohibitions against seeking revenge and bearing a grudge. Prohibitions such as these, with their binding nature, imperativeness, and distinctive formulation, do not find their equivalents in contemporary conflict resolution. As to possible differences in relation to what contemporary conflict resolution and traditional Jewish approaches ask of the parties, limiting myself only to the halakhic material that was focused on in this chapter (and pointing out that there are other halakhic opinions that were not discussed, and what I have written should not be taken as a definitive statement on the matter), I proposed that contemporary conflict resolution and traditional Jewish approaches differ in regard to their respective standards of conduct in relation to retaliation and resentment, with traditional Jewish approaches setting higher expectations and asking more of the individual than contemporary conflict resolution. I had also proposed that contemporary conflict resolution and traditional Jewish approaches are fundamentally similar in respect to their emphases on the need for cognitively addressing the emotional and psychological challenges of retaliation and resentment.

I had mentioned at the beginning of this section that traditional Jewish approaches have other core components that address issues related to resentment and retaliation, namely, the components of forgiveness and anger management. As we shall see in the next two chapters, traditional Jewish approaches incorporate an array of behavioral guidelines and rules of conduct relating to forgiveness and an array of strategies for controlling anger. Elements to be discussed pertain to such things as the pardoning of interpersonal offenses, the giving up of harbored resentments, and the constructive expression of emotions, all of which are relevant to the topics we have covered in this chapter. We are therefore not totally leaving behind the issues of resentment and retaliation; rather, we will be building on and augmenting concepts that were previously presented in this chapter.

CHAPTER 8

Apologies: The Asking and Granting of Forgiveness

When one explores the topic of interpersonal conflict in traditional Jewish sources, one becomes aware of an unmistakable emphasis on *meḥilah*,[1] "forgiveness." It is quite evident from the traditional sources, particularly the halakhic ones, that the asking and granting of *meḥilah* are considered essential elements of the process of interpersonal conflict resolution. Accordingly, forgiveness is reckoned as one of the core components of the paradigm being presented in this work.

This chapter will present an analysis of the halakhic obligations applicable to one who has committed an interpersonal offense, and is therefore required to ask for forgiveness,[2] and the obligations that are applicable to the one whom the offense

---

1 The noun מְחִילָה (*meḥilah*) comes from the verb מָחַל (*maḥal*), to forgive, pardon, or forgo. The word is post-biblical (Elijah Levita, *Sefer ha-Tishbi* [New York: Naḥliel, 1951], s.v. "*maḥal*"); it corresponds to the biblical סְלִיחָה (*seliḥah*) (see the discussion in Isaiah ben Judah Loeb Berlin, *Hagahot ha-GRY'P*, in *Shulḥan Arukh ha-Shalem, Oraḥ Ḥayim*, vol. 9 [Jerusalem: Mifal Shulḥan Arukh ha-Shalem, 2002], *Yalkut Mefarshim, siman* 607, p. 573). Etymologically, *maḥal* is probably related to the word מָחָה (*maḥah*), to erase, cleanse, or do away with (see Abraham Even-Shoshan, *Ha-Milon he-Ḥadash*, 8th ed. [Jerusalem: Kiryat Sefer, 1977], s.v. "*maḥal*"). For alternative explanations, see Joseph Teomim, *Peri Megadim*, in the standard printed edition of the *Shulḥan Arukh, Oraḥ Ḥayim, Ashel Avraham* 607:3; L. Gordon, *Avodat ha-Lev*, in *Otsar ha-Tefilot*, vol. 2 (New York: Avraham Yitsḥak Friedman, n.d.), *Iyun Tefilah*, at the conclusion of the *Amidah* prayer for Yom Kippur [p. 1119]; and Zevi Har-Zahab, "*Ha-Shorashim ha-Mesorasim*," *Ḥorev* 4, nos. 7–8 (Nisan 5697-Tishre 5698 [1937]): 159–60. See also Mitchell First, "What is the Origin of the Word *Meḥilah*?" *Ḥakirah* 18 (Winter 2014): 147–58.

2 As to the relationship between an apology and asking for forgiveness, see below, pp. 364–83.

was committed against and is being asked to grant forgiveness. The focus will be on those laws that have practical applications and those that embody foundational concepts of *meḥilah*. Reasons and fundamental principles that underlie the *halakhot* will be highlighted throughout the analysis.

The Obligations of the One Who Asks for Forgiveness

This first section will discuss the obligations of the one who asks for forgiveness. It will encompass six subtopics: (1) the primary talmudic sources for the obligation of asking for forgiveness; (2) the obligation of asking for forgiveness on the day before Yom Kippur; (3) if one must personally go to ask for forgiveness oneself; (4) the halakhic requirement of specifying the offense committed; (5) how many attempts one must make at asking for forgiveness; and (6) the appeasement of the person who has suffered. Within this array of subtopics, I will attempt to elucidate essential components and prominent themes of the halakhic discourse on the asking of forgiveness for interpersonal offenses.

The Talmudic Sources

There are two primary talmudic sources for the obligation of asking for forgiveness. There is a short talmudic passage in tractate *Bava Kamma* (92a), which deals with one's obligation to ask for forgiveness when one has physically harmed another person, and there is a considerably lengthier talmudic passage in tractate *Yoma* (85b, 86b, 87a–b), which deals with one's obligation to ask for forgiveness in order to attain atonement on the holiday of Yom Kippur (the "Day of Atonement"). These two passages serve as the basis for the majority of later halakhic rulings regarding the asking of forgiveness for an interpersonal offense.

The Talmudic Passage in Bava Kamma. In discussing the halakhic obligations of one who has caused another person physical harm, the Mishnah in *Bava Kamma* states:

> Even though he gives to him [financial compensation], he is not absolved[3] until he seeks [forgiveness] from him, as it is stated [in the biblical episode of Abraham and Abimelech]: "Now return the wife of..." (Gen. 20:7).[4]

The Gemara cites a *baraita* that parallels this mishnah and includes a number of additional points:

> The Rabbis taught that all of these [designated amounts of financial compensation cited in previous *mishnayot*] are [considered] financial remuneration for his embarrassment, but for his suffering,[5] even if he brings all of the 'rams of Nebaioth'[6] in the world [as a sacrifice], he will not be absolved until he seeks [forgiveness] from him, as it is stated: "Now return the wife of the man for he is a prophet, and he will pray for you" (Gen. 20:7).[7]

The Talmudic Passage in Yoma. In discussing the atonement that takes place on Yom Kippur, the Mishnah in tractate *Yoma* teaches that

3 Literally, "forgiven."

4 Mishnah, *Bava Kamma* 8:7, and in the Gemara, *Bava Kamma* 92a. For alternative versions of this mishnah, see *Shinuye Nusḥa'ot* in the standard *"Yakhin u-Voaz"* [the Vilna edition] *Mishnayot, Bava Kamma* 8:7. For explanations of how the mishnah derives this teaching from the verse in Genesis, see Menaḥem Meiri, *Bet ha-Beḥirah al Masekhet Bava Kama* (Jerusalem: K. Schlesinger, 1963), chap. 8 mishnah 4, p. 268, quoted in Bezalel Ashkenazi, *Shitah Mekubetset* (Jerusalem: Mekhon Tiferet ha-Torah, 1997), *Bava Kamma* 92a; Yom Tov Lipman Heller, *Tosafot Yom Tov*, in *Mishnayot Zekher Ḥanokh* (Jerusalem: Ḥ. Vagshal, 1999), *Bava Kamma* 8:7; Samson Raphael Hirsch, *The Pentateuch: Translated and Explained by Samson Raphael Hirsch*, trans. Isaac Levy (Gateshead, England: Judaica Press, 1989), Gen. 20:7; and Yehudah Ḥatab, *Sefer Mevin Shemu'ah Be'urim al Masekhet Bava Kama* (Jerusalem: Y. Ḥatab, 1998), *Bava Kamma* 92a.

5 For various possible explanations of what type of suffering is being referred to, see the sources cited in Shamma Friedman, annot., *Perush Yehonatan ha-Kohen mi-Lunel al ha-Mishnah veha-Rif Masekhet Bava Kama* (Jerusalem: Feldheim, 1969), 270 n. 838.

6 See Isa. 60:7.

7 *Bava Kamma* 92a.

> Transgressions that are between a man and God Yom Kippur atones for; transgressions that are between a man and his fellow man Yom Kippur does not atone for, until he appeases his friend. R. Eleazar ben Azariah [first–second centuries CE] interpreted the verse "From all of your sins before God you shall be cleansed" (Lev. 16:30) [as teaching that] transgressions that are between man and God Yom Kippur atones for; transgressions that are between man and his fellow man Yom Kippur does not atone for, until he appeases his friend.[8]

Basing itself on the interpretation of various verses, the Gemara on this mishnah (*Yoma* 87a) sets forth a number of teachings related to the asking of forgiveness. These include

- "If a man sins against another man and appeases him, God will forgive him";[9]

- "Whoever provokes his friend, even verbally, is obligated to appease him";

- "[If one has verbally provoked another] one should bring many friends to him [in order to appease him]";

- "[The friends that one brings to appease another should consist of] three rows of three people [i.e., a group of three for each one of the three attempts that one should make; see next quote]";[10]

---

8 Mishnah, *Yoma* 8:9, and in the Gemara, *Yoma* 85b.

9 The Gemara is citing the wording and interpreting 1 Samuel 2:25 as teaching this; see Rashi, *Yoma* 87a, s.v. *ve-hakhi ka'amar*; together with David Shperber, *Metsudat David: Al Shishah Sidre Mishnah* (Jerusalem: n.p., 2004), 556; and Ze'ev Wolf Einhorn, *Midrash Tanaim* (Lakewood, NJ: Machon Mishnas Rabbi Aaron, 2003), 44.

10 The explanation that is in brackets is based on Rashi's interpretation. See Rashi, *Yoma* 87a, s.v. *be-shalosh shurot*.

- "Whoever beseeches [forgiveness] from his friend should not beseech him more than three times."[11]

After discussing what someone should do if the person he had committed an offense against has died before he had an opportunity to ask for forgiveness, the talmudic discourse in *Yoma* concludes by offering a number of illustrative cases of different sages who attempted to appease and reconcile with people they had offended (see *Yoma* 87a–b).

Corresponding to the two talmudic passages cited above, the major halakhic codes (i.e., Maimonides' *Mishneh Torah*, R. Jacob ben Asher's *Arba'ah Turim*, and R. Joseph Karo's *Shulḥan Arukh*)[12] cite an obligation to ask for forgiveness in the sections that deal with the "Laws of One Who Causes Physical Harm to His Friend" and the "Laws of Yom Kippur."[13]

Asking for Forgiveness on the Day before Yom Kippur

Sources for the Obligation.[14] In his "Laws of Yom Kippur," R. Jacob ben Asher (c. 1269-c. 1340) states that "every person should take it to

---

11 *Yoma* 87a.

12 Maimonides, *Mishneh Torah, Hilkhot Ḥovel u-Mazik* 5:9, *Hilkhot Teshuvah* 2:9; Jacob ben Asher, *Arba'ah Turim, Ḥoshen Mishpat* 422, *Oraḥ Ḥayim* 606; and Joseph Karo, *Shulḥan Arukh, Ḥoshen Mishpat* 422:1, *Oraḥ Ḥayim* 606:1.

13 These are section titles that appear in R. Jacob ben Asher's *Arba'ah Turim* and R. Joseph Karo's *Shulḥan Arukh*. Maimonides discusses the obligation of asking for forgiveness that corresponds to the talmudic passage in *Bava Kamma*, in the fifth chapter of *Hilkhot Ḥovel u-Mazik*, the "Laws of One Who Inflicts Physical Harm and Damages"; and he discusses the obligation of asking for forgiveness that corresponds to the passage in *Yoma*, in the second chapter of *Hilkhot Teshuvah*, "Laws of Repentance" (2:9), in which he discusses the laws of repentance for Yom Kippur. In the section in *Hilkhot Teshuvah*, Maimonides also incorporates a certain element from *Bava Kamma* together with those of *Yoma*; see Joseph Karo, *Kesef Mishneh*, in the standard printed edition of the *Mishneh Torah, Hilkhot Teshuvah* 2:9.

14 Even though, technically speaking, asking for forgiveness on the day before Yom Kippur should probably be categorized as a *minhag*, "custom" (see the wording of Moses Isserles, *Shulḥan Arukh, Oraḥ Ḥayim* 606:2; Mordecai ben Hillel ha-Kohen, *Sefer Mordekhai le-Masekhet Yoma*, in the standard Vilna edition of the Babylonian Talmud,

heart that on the day before Yom Kippur they [*sic*] should appease anyone whom they had committed an offense against." He offers the following explanation for this requirement:

> We do this in order that the heart of all of Israel should be completely unified [lit., whole], each individual with his friend, and that Satan will be unable to speak against them [when they are being judged on Yom Kippur]. This [concept] is found in [the Midrash] *Pirke de-Rabbi Eliezer* (chap. 46):[15] "[The angel] Samael [i.e., Satan] sees that there does not exist [any] sin in [the people of] Israel on the day of atonement, and he says [to God], "Master of the world, you have one nation in the world that is comparable to the ministering angels ... just as the ministering angels are untainted by any sin, so too Israel is untainted by any sin; just as there is peace between the ministering angels, so too [the people of] Israel on the day of atonement; and [then] The Holy One blessed be He listens to the testimony of those who prosecute [and speak against Israel], and brings about their [the people of Israel's] atonement.[16]

Yoma, siman 723 [cited in the text below, p. 305]; and Aaron ben Jacob ha-Kohen of Lunel, *Orḥot Ḥayim* [Jerusalem: Y. D. Shtitsberg, 1956], *Din Erev Yom ha-Kipurim* 9, p. 230), nevertheless, I will refer to it throughout this chapter as an "obligation." This is based on many authorities who do refer to it as something required, or obligatory; see, for example, Jacob ben Asher, *Kitsur Piske ha-Rosh mi-Masekhet Yoma*, in the standard Vilna edition of the Babylonian Talmud, *Yoma*, chap. 8:24; Joseph Molkho, *Sefer Shulḥan Gevoah* (Jerusalem: Or va-Derekh, 1992), *Oraḥ Ḥayim* 606:11; Ephraim Zalman Margolioth, *Mateh Efrayim ha-Shalem* (Jerusalem: G. M. Eisenbach, 1989), *siman* 606:1; Jehiel Michal Epstein, *Arukh ha-Shulḥan* (n.p., n.d.), *Oraḥ Ḥayim* 606:2; and Zalman Nehemiah Goldberg, *"Ba-Inyan Ḥiyuv Piyus la-Ḥavero be-Erev YoH'K," Torat ha-Adam le-Adam: Kovets Torani ba-Mitsvot she-ben Adam la-Ḥavero* 3 (1999): 12–13. See also R. Jacob of Lissa's paraphrase of R. Isserles's ruling, Jacob ben Jacob Moses of Lissa, *Sidur Derekh ha-Ḥayim* (Tel Aviv: Sinai, 1954), *She-Yefayes Adam et Ḥavero be-Erev Yom ha-Kipurim* 3, p. 431.

15 There are a number of significant differences between the version of *Pirke de-Rabbi Eliezer* that R. Jacob ben Asher cites and the printed version that we have today. See *Pirke de-Rabbi Eliezer* 46.

16 Jacob ben Asher, *Arba'ah Turim, Oraḥ Ḥayim* 606.

In his commentary to R. Jacob ben Asher's code, R. Joseph Karo (1488–1575) points out that (1) R. Jacob ben Asher had based this ruling on the writings of his father, R. Asher ben Jehiel (1250–1327);[17] (2) R. Asher ben Jehiel not only cites the midrash from *Pirke de-Rabbi Eliezer* as the source for this ruling, but also cites two of the illustrative cases mentioned in the talmudic discourse in tractate *Yoma* (see above, p. 303), which emphasize that on the day before Yom Kippur, the talmudic sages attempted to appease and reconcile with people they had offended;[18] and (3) that R. Mordecai ben Hillel ha-Kohen (c. 1240–1298) cites an alternative midrashic source, *Midrash Shuvah Yisrael* (found in *Pesikta Rabbati*),[19] for the custom[20] of asking for forgiveness on the day before Yom Kippur.[21]

Two Different Obligations of Asking for Forgiveness. Rabbinic authorities address the question as to whether there exists a difference between the obligation of asking for forgiveness before Yom Kippur and the obligation of asking for forgiveness that is incumbent on the person year-round. Some of these authorities are of the opinion that the two obligations are not substantively different from each other, whereas others view the two as being essentially different.

R. Isaac Hutner (1906–1980) and R. Joseph Dov Soloveitchik (1903–1993) are of the opinion that there exists a difference

---

17 See Asher ben Jehiel, *Sefer Rabenu Asher* [*Piske ha-Rosh*], in the standard Vilna edition of the Babylonian Talmud, *Yoma*, chap. 8, *siman* 24.

18 Ibid.

19 This midrash reads as follows: "God who loves [the people of] Israel has established ten days of repentance [the ten days that start at the beginning of Rosh Hashanah and conclude at the end of Yom Kippur] in which the repentance of even a single individual will be as acceptable as a communal repentance; therefore, all of Israel is required to engage in repentance and to make peace between a man and his fellow man, and to forgive each other on the day before Yom Kippur in order that their repentance and their prayer be accepted before God in peace and abundant love; for we find that great is the power of peace ... for even if Israel worships idols, as long as they make peace between themselves and stand [together] as one group the attribute of justice cannot touch them" (*Pesikta Rabati*, ed. Meir Ish Shalom [Friedmann] [Vienna: Yosef Kaizer, 1880], p. 199b).

20 R. Mordecai ben Hillel ha-Kohen specifically refers to this as a "custom."

21 Mordecai ben Hillel ha-Kohen, *Sefer Mordekhai le-Masekhet Yoma*, *siman* 723. Joseph Karo, *Bet Yosef*, in the standard printed edition of the *Arba'ah Turim*, *Oraḥ Ḥayim* 606, s.v. *ve-yiten* and s.v. *ve-katav ha-Mordekhai*.

between the two obligations of asking for forgiveness. They both deduce this from the difference in wording between the mishnah in *Bava Kamma* and the mishnah in *Yoma* when these *mishnayot* describe the act of asking for forgiveness. The mishnah in *Bava Kamma* (92a) uses the expression of *ad she-yevakesh mimenu,* "until he *seeks* (or *asks for*) [forgiveness] from him," whereas the mishnah in *Yoma* (85b) uses the expression *ad she-yeratseh et ḥavero,* "until he *appeases* his friend."

According to R. Soloveitchik, this difference in wording reflects a fundamental difference between the obligation of asking for forgiveness that is incumbent on the person year-round and the obligation of asking for forgiveness on the day before Yom Kippur. Year-round, one merely has to seek *meḥilah,* "forgiveness," in other words, that the person he has committed an offense against should simply pardon his offense, whereas the obligation before Yom Kippur requires *ritsui,* "appeasement," which is understood by R. Soloveitchik as restoring the positive feelings of friendship that existed before the offense.[22] This obligation of *ritsui* would entail that one

> beg the aggrieved party to restore their old relationship ... [so that] the parties will be as friendly now as they were before the incident occurred ... [O]n *Erev Yom Kippur* [the day before Yom Kippur] it is not sufficient for one to ask for *meḥilah.* He must ask for his friendship ... he must ask that the relationship be restored and that it regain its old crystal clear qualities.[23]

22 Joseph Dov Soloveitchik, *Mi-Pi ha-Shemu'ah mi-Maran ha-GRY"D Solovets'ik, Mesorah* 2 (Tishre 5750 [1989]): 23; Joseph Dov Soloveitchik, *Sefer Harare Kedem,* lectures that were summarized by Michal Zalman Shurkin (Jerusalem: n.p., 2000), *siman* 39, p. 82; and Joseph Dov Soloveitchik, *Shiure ha-Rav ha-Ga'on Rabi Yosef Dov Solovets'ik, zatsal: Al Pesaḥim, R.H., Yo. ha-Kip., u-Megilah: Mi-Pi ha-Shemu'ah,* lectures summarized by Hershel Schachter (Jerusalem: n.p., 2002), 121.

23 Joseph Dov Soloveitchik, *Nora'ot ha-Rav,* vol. 13, lectures that were transcribed by B. David Schreiber (New York: n.p., 2000), 142–44.

R. Hutner understands the different terminologies that are used in the two *mishnayot* in a similar fashion to that of R. Soloveitchik, but with one very significant distinction. R. Hutner is of the opinion that the difference between the two obligations exists only in relation to what they are supposed to ultimately accomplish, but not in regard to what they require of the individual on a practical level. R. Hutner is certain that there is no practical difference between what is halakhically required in the process of asking for forgiveness before Yom Kippur and what is required in the process of asking for forgiveness year-round. Both obligations require one to articulate a request for forgiveness and attempt to appease the other person.[24] The difference between the two obligations is in regard to their respective ultimate goals. According to R. Hutner, the ultimate goal of asking for forgiveness year-round is simply the removal of the anger, or resentment, that the party who was hurt is feeling towards the one who committed the offense.[25] This is as opposed to the ultimate goal of asking for forgiveness before Yom Kippur, which is, in R. Hutner's words, the "restoration of the light of his friend's countenance towards him," that means to say, the restoration of positive, warm feelings between the parties.[26]

In contrast to these approaches, one finds authorities who apparently do not differentiate, fundamentally, between the obligation to ask for forgiveness before Yom Kippur and the obligation to ask for forgiveness year-round. One such authority is R. Joel Sirkes (1561–1640). R. Sirkes is apparently of the opinion that there does not exist any substantive difference between the two obligations. This can be seen from the fact that when he discusses

24 Isaac Hutner, *Paḥad Yitsḥak: Sha'ar Yeraḥ ha-Etanim* (Brooklyn: Ha-Mosad Gur Aryeh, 1974), 46–52. R. Hutner does propose, however, based on the view of R. Jonah Gerondi, that there is a practical difference between the two obligations in respect to the component of the sin that is *ben adam la-Makom* (between man and God), when it comes to the obligation of *vidui* (confession); see ibid. for the explanation of this difference.

25 R. Hutner writes that an additional objective in asking for forgiveness is that it should take away the right for maintaining a grievance against the offender. See ibid., 50–52.

26 Ibid., 49–52, 60.

the two obligations, the only difference between them that he points out is in relation to whether one is allowed to postpone the asking of forgiveness. Regarding the year-round obligation, he writes that even though "it is proper for every person to immediately appease someone whom he has committed an offense against, one is however allowed to postpone it to another day." This is as opposed to the obligation of asking for forgiveness before Yom Kippur, for which one cannot say, "I will appease him either today or tomorrow."[27] The implication seems to be that this is the only distinction that exists between the two obligations. (For others who may maintain that the obligation to ask for forgiveness before Yom Kippur and the obligation to ask for forgiveness year-round are fundamentally one and the same, see footnote.)[28]

(For the remainder of this chapter, it will be assumed that there does not exist any substantive difference between the two obligations; therefore, I will refer to "the obligation" [in the singular] of asking for forgiveness.)

---

27 Joel Sirkes, *Bayit Ḥadash,* in the standard printed edition of Jacob ben Asher's *Arba'ah Turim, Oraḥ Ḥayim* 606, s.v. *ve-yiten*. This view is cited in Margolioth, *Mateh Efrayim, siman* 606:1; Israel Meir ha-Kohen, *Mishnah Berurah* (Zikhron Ya'akov: Merkaz le-Ḥinukh Torani, 1975), *siman* 606:1. See also Jair Ḥayyim Bacharach, *Mekor Ḥayim* (Jerusalem: Mifal Torat Ḥakhme Ashkenaz, 1984), *siman* 606, s.v. *yaḥazor*; and Epstein, *Arukh ha-Shulḥan, Oraḥ Ḥayim* 606:2; cf. Binyamin Yehoshua Zilber, *Derekh Teshuvah* (Jerusalem: n.p., 2009), 141; and Makhon Torat ha-Adam le-Adam, *"Ve-Tsarikh Iyun," Torat ha-Adam le-Adam: Kovets Torani ba-Mitsvot she-ben Adam la-Ḥavero* 3 (1999): 217–18.

28 See Ze'ev Hoberman, *Ze'ev Yitrof: Be-Inyana di-Teshuvah ve-Yom ha-Kipurim* (Lakewood, NJ: Z. Hoberman, 1996), 213–19, 230–36, 244–48, where he argues that according to Maimonides, the two obligations are fundamentally the same, whereas according to R. Jonah of Gerondi, they are fundamentally different; Moshe Shternbukh, *Mo'adim u-Zemanim ha-Shalem,* 9 vols. (Jerusalem: n.p., n.d.), vol. 6, *siman* 20, the first paragraph; Baruch Leizerowski, *Sefer She'elot u-Teshuvot Ta'am Barukh* (Philadelphia: n.p., n.d.), *siman* 21, quoted in Daniel Z. Feldman, *The Right and the Good: Halakhah and Human Relations,* expanded edition (Brooklyn: Yashar Books, 2005), 151; and Ya'akov David Luban, *"Ad she-Yeratseh et Ḥavero," Ha-Darom* 64 (Elul 5755 [1995]): 40–53.

The Range of Interpersonal Offenses for Which One Must Seek Forgiveness—Appeasing Someone Even for Imagined Offenses. From the *poskim* (halakhic decisors; see Glossary), it appears that there is a requirement to ask for forgiveness for any type of interpersonal offense one has committed against another.[29] Maimonides indicates that this is the case when he writes that one must ask for forgiveness for "transgressions that are between a man and his fellow man, for example, physically harming his friend, or one who curses his friend, or steals, and things that are of a similar nature" (*Hilkhot Teshuvah* 2:9; according to Maimonides, there may be an exception to this general rule, see footnote).[30] There are situations, however, in which it is debatable as to whether one is halakhically required to ask for forgiveness from the other party. In this section, we will examine one such category of cases.[31]

Asking for Forgiveness for Imagined Offenses. R. Tsevi Katz (born c. 1590), R. Jair Ḥayyim Bacharach (1638–1702), and other authorities are of the opinion that before Yom Kippur, one is obligated to ask for forgiveness even for perceived, or imagined, offenses. That means to say that even if one is certain he has done nothing to offend or hurt the other person that would require him to ask for forgiveness, but that other person believes that he has committed such an act, before Yom Kippur one is supposed to appease and reconcile with that person.[32]

29 See, for example, Karo, *Oraḥ Ḥayim*, 606:1 and *Ḥoshen Mishpat* 422:1, where this may possibly be inferred from the fact that when he discusses asking for forgiveness, it is presented as a blanket obligation without differentiating between categories of interpersonal transgressions; cf. Maimonides, *Mishneh Torah*, *Hilkhot Ḥovel u-Mazik* 5:9, and the next footnote.

30 It should be noted that Maimonides in *Hilkhot Ḥovel u-Mazik* (5:9) seems to indicate that if one damages another person's property and then compensates the person for the damage incurred, he does not have to ask for forgiveness. For possible explanations of Maimonides' ruling in *Ḥovel u-Mazik* and how to reconcile it with what he had written in *Hilkhot Teshuvah*, see Kaminsky, "Traditional Jewish Perspectives," 251–55.

31 For examples of other possible categories, see Israel Meir ha-Kohen, *Sefer Ḥafets Ḥayim*, in *Kol Kitve Ḥafets Ḥayim ha-Shalem*, vol. 1 (New York: Avraham Yitsḥak Friedman, n.d.), *Hilkhot Isure Lashon ha-Ra*, *kelal* 4, *Be'er Mayim Ḥayim* 48; Epstein, *Arukh ha-Shulḥan*, *Ḥoshen Mishpat* 422:4; and Moses Feinstein, *Igrot Mosheh*, 9 vols. (New York: Moriyah, 1959–), *Ḥoshen Mishpat*, vol. 1, *siman* 88, p. 154.

32 See Tsevi ben Joseph Katz, *Naḥalat Tsevi*, *Ateret Tsevi*, vol. 2 (Jerusalem: Zikhron Aharon, 2003), *Ateret Tsevi* 606:1; Bacharach, *Mekor Ḥayim*, *siman* 606, s.v. *le-tovat*;

R. Katz explains that since the obligation to ask for forgiveness (before Yom Kippur) is based on the concept of "the heart of Israel should be completely unified, each individual with his friend" (see p. 304 above) it follows that one is required to ask for forgiveness from another person even if one is certain that he did not actually commit any type of offense against him. The mere fact that that other person is feeling animosity towards him is reason enough to appease him for the imagined offense.[33]

It should be noted that this view certainly seems to have a solid basis in the Talmud. In one of the illustrative cases in tractate *Yoma* of a talmudic sage attempting to appease someone on the day before Yom Kippur, the Gemara cites a story about Rav (third century CE), who went to appease someone who was unjustifiably bearing a grudge against him:

> There was an incident between Rav and a certain butcher [in which the butcher had committed an offense against Rav].[34] He [the butcher] did not come to [appease] him [Rav]. On

---

Judah Aryeh Leib Alter, *Sefer Sefat Emet* (Jerusalem: Mekhon Hotsa'at Sefarim Mir, 1996), *Yoma* 87b, s.v. *ba-gm' ikpid* (the second answer); and Ḥayyim Soloveichik, quoted in Ahron Soloveichik, *Paraḥ Mateh Aharon* (Jerusalem: Hotsa'at Targum, 1997), *Hilkhot Teshuvah* 2:9, p. 189. It should be noted that neither R. Katz nor R. Bacharach actually state that this halakhah is only applicable to Yom Kippur and not year-round. However, one may deduce that this was R. Katz's opinion based on the explanation that he offers (which I cite in the text). As far as R. Bacharach's opinion is concerned, even though he does not indicate that this is only applicable to asking for forgiveness before Yom Kippur, I believe that this may be implied by the fact that he bases his opinion on the gemara in *Yoma* with Rav and the butcher (or Rav and R. Ḥanina, *Yoma* 87a–b; see n. 35 below), which occurred on the day before Yom Kippur.

33 Katz, *Naḥalat Tsevi, Ateret Tsevi* 606:1. The reason for asking for forgiveness that R. Katz offers seems to be applicable only to a case that involves two Jews. R. Moshe Litsch-Rosenbaum (d. 1877) states that a Jew is certainly obligated to appease a Gentile against whom he has committed an offense. See Moshe Leib Litsch-Rosenbaum, *Mata di-Yerushalayim* (n.p., 1978), *Yoma* 8:7, s.v. *ve-da*, p. 63a, quoted in Ḥayim Tsevi Ehrenraikh, *Ketseh ha-Mateh*, commentary to *Sefer Mateh Efrayim*, by Ephraim Zalman Margolioth (Brooklyn: Ḥevrah Mefitse Torah mi-Mishpaḥat Kol Aryeh, 2001), *siman* 606:4; *Ketseh ha-Mateh* is quoted in Gavriel Zinner, *Sefer Nit'e Gavriel: Hilkhot Yom ha-Kipurim* (Jerusalem: n.p., 2001), 127.

34 See Rashi, *Yoma* 87a, s.v. *bahade tabaḥa*.

> the day before Yom Kippur, he [Rav] said, I will go to appease him [the butcher].[35]

Citing the case with Rav and the butcher,[36] R. Asher ben Jehiel writes that "every person should take it to heart that on the day before Yom Kippur he should appease *anyone who bears animosity towards him.*"[37] The implication of this is that one has to appease someone who bears animosity towards him even if the animosity is unwarranted.[38] It should be noted, however, that when R. Jacob ben Asher paraphrases this line from his father's writings, he significantly changes the wording and writes that "every person should take it to heart that on the day before Yom Kippur he should appease anyone whom *he has committed an offense against.*"[39] The inference that may be drawn from this change of wording is that one is only required to appease someone whom he has committed an actual offense against.[40]

Even though, as stated above, there are authorities who are of the opinion that a person should ask for forgiveness on the day before Yom Kippur even for an imagined offense, Rashi (R. Solomon ben Isaac, 1040–1105) and R. Abraham ben Isaac of Narbonne (c. 1110–1179) quote a *geonic* responsum that categorizes the act of going and appeasing a person whom one has not actually committed an offense against (i.e., the episode with Rav and the butcher) as

---

35 *Yoma* 87a. Apparently, R. Bacharach is referring to this story (or possibly to the story that immediately follows it in *Yoma*, with Rav and R. Ḥanina) when he writes that based on the Gemara even when "his friend is upset about something that was said or done for which it is not proper to be upset about, one is nevertheless obligated to ask for forgiveness." Bacharach, *Mekor Ḥayim, siman* 606, s.v. *le-tovat.*

36 R. Asher also cites the story with Rav and R. Ḥanina (*Yoma* 87a–b), which illustrates the same idea.

37 Asher ben Jehiel, *Piske ha-Rosh, Yoma* chap. 8 *siman* 24.

38 See Binyamin Yehoshua Zilber, *Az Nidberu*, 14 vols. (Bnei Brak: n.p., 1969–1987), vol. 8, *siman* 68, p. 153; and Shlomo Moshe Wallach, "*Me-Va'er de-Yesh Shene Dinim ba-Ḥiyuv le-Fayes et Ḥavero ba-Erev Yom ha-Kipurim,*" *Reshimot meha-Va'ad* 12 (Shevat 5766 [2006]): 93.

39 Jacob ben Asher, *Arba'ah Turim, Oraḥ Ḥayim* 606; see also Jacob ben Asher, *Kitsur Piske ha-Rosh, Yoma* 8:24.

40 See Wallach, "*Shene Dinim ba-Ḥiyuv le-Fayes,*" 92–93.

merely a "pious trait," which indicates that it is not a halakhically binding requirement.[41]

The Obligation of Personally Going to Ask for Forgiveness

When the obligation of asking for forgiveness is discussed in the talmudic passage in *Yoma* and in R. Jacob ben Asher's code, it is presented in the form of one person "going to" another to ask for forgiveness.[42] There is a dispute among halakhic authorities as to how literally this should be taken. In other words, is the one who committed an interpersonal offense obligated to personally go to ask for forgiveness him/herself, or is one allowed to have an intermediary do it for him/her, or, at least, have an intermediary speak to the other party first so as to make the other party more receptive to one's subsequent personal attempt at appeasement.

R. Jacob ibn Ḥabib (c. 1445–1515), R. Moses Mat (c. 1551–1606), and R. Joel Sirkes are of the opinion that one must personally go and ask for forgiveness without initially resorting to any type of intermediary.[43] R. Samuel Jaffe Ashkenazi (1525–1595), R. Hezekiah

41 Rashi, *Sefer ha-Orah* (Jerusalem: n.p., 1967), *ḥelek rishon*, pp. 3–4; Abraham ben Isaac of Narbonne, *Sefer ha-Eshkol*, (Jerusalem: Ḥ. Vagshal, 1980), 2–3; also quoted in Abraham Zacuto, *Sefer Yuḥasin ha-Shalem* (Jerusalem: n.p., 1963), *ma'amar sheni: Seder ha-Amoraim, ot resh*, p. 180. This is listed among the "Ten pious traits that Rav kept, and after him all those who served him [i.e., his students] were unable to maintain [as a whole] and [instead] each one [of his students only] kept one of them." *Sha'are Teshuvah: 353 Teshuvot ha-Ge'onim* (Leipzig: Leopold Shenois, 1858), *siman* 178. This is also cited in Ḥayyim Joseph David Azulai, *Sefer Petaḥ Enayim*, vol. 2 (Jerusalem: n.p., 1959), *Menaḥot* 110a, pp. 116a–b; as well as in other sources. For a discussion of the original source of this view, see Shalom Albeck, annot., *Sefer ha-Eshkol*, by Abraham ben Isaac of Narbonne (Jerusalem: Ḥ. Vagshal, 1980), 2 n. 1.

42 See *Yoma* 87a–b; Jacob ben Asher, *Arba'ah Turim, Oraḥ Ḥayim* 606. For an exact citation of sources in the talmudic discourse in *Yoma* and in the *Arba'ah Turim*, see Sirkes, *Bayit Ḥadash, Oraḥ Ḥayim* 606, s.v. *u-mah she-katav ve-tsarikh lelekh*.

43 Jacob ibn Ḥabib, *Sefer En Ya'akov* (New York: Sifre Kodesh, 1971), vol. 2, *Perush ha-Kotev*, Jer. Tal. *Yoma* chap. 8; Moses Mat, *Sefer Mateh Mosheh* (Jerusalem: n.p., 1984), section 5 *siman* 848; Sirkes, *Bayit Ḥadash, Oraḥ Ḥayim* 606, s.v. *matsati*. Both R. Mat and R. Sirkes quote the earlier opinion of R. Ibn Ḥabib, who bases himself on the opinion of the amoraic sage Samuel, cited in the Jerusalem Talmud, *Yoma* 8:7.

da Silva (1659–1698), and R. Ḥayyim Palache (1788–1869) permit one to not only initially resort to an intermediary (to make the other party more receptive to one's subsequent personal attempt at appeasement) but to have the entire process of asking for forgiveness conducted through the intermediary.[44] (As we shall shortly see, according to R. Ashkenazi, it would actually be acceptable if one simply forgives the person who committed the offense without having the person ask for forgiveness at all, even through an intermediary.) Later halakhic authorities, such as R. Ephraim Zalman Margolioth (1760–1828), R. Solomon Ganzfried (1804–1886), and R. Israel Meir ha-Kohen (Kagan, the *Ḥafets Ḥayim*, 1838–1933),[45] propose a compromise between these two views: "It is proper that he should personally go to him and not initially send an intermediary to placate him so that he [the person who is being asked to grant forgiveness] will [subsequently] accept [his attempts at] appeasement, but if it would be difficult for him to initially go himself, or if he knows that there is a greater likelihood that the person will be appeased through an intermediary, who will serve as a mediator between them, he may use an intermediary."[46]

In examining the opinions of R. Ibn Ḥabib and R. Ashkenazi, who were the earliest authorities to address this topic and are cited by later proponents of the two views, it becomes clear that this dispute is based on a fundamental difference that exists between these authorities concerning what asking for forgiveness is supposed

44 Samuel Jaffe Ashkenazi, *Yefeh Mareh*, in *Sefer En Ya'akov*, by Jacob ibn Ḥabib, vol. 2 (New York: Sifre Kodesh, 1971), Jer. Tal. *Yoma*, chap. 8; Hezekiah da Silva, *Peri Ḥadash*, in the standard printed edition of the *Shulḥan Arukh*, *Oraḥ Ḥayim* 606:1, s.v. *tsarikh;* Ḥayyim Palache, *Sefer le-Ḥayim bi-Yerushalayim* (Jerusalem: Mekhon Shuvi Nafshi, 2000), *Yoma* chap. 8 *halakhah* 7, p. 87, quoted in Ovadia Yosef, *Sefer She'elot u-Teshuvot Yeḥaveh Da'at*, vol. 5 (Jerusalem: n.p., 1977), *siman* 44, p. 198.

45 Margolioth, *Mateh Efrayim*, 606:1; Solomon Ganzfried, *Kitsur Shulḥan Arukh ha-Shalem* (Vilna: Rozenkrants and Shriftzetser, n.d.), 131:4; Ha-Kohen, *Mishnah Berurah*, 606: 2.

46 This is a translation of the *Ḥafets Ḥayim*'s version of this ruling (Ha-Kohen, *Mishnah Berurah*, 606: 2). R. Margolioth and R. Ganzfried present the same basic rule with some slight variations in their wordings; for example, instead of writing "It is *proper* that he should personally go to him . . . ," R. Margolioth and R. Ganzfried write that one is *"obligated"* to personally go.

to accomplish. The rationale that R. Ibn Ḥabib offers for one to personally go and ask for forgiveness is that the "shame and disgrace serve as an atonement for the misdeed he committed against his friend."[47] This ruling of R. Ibn Ḥabib and his explanation for it elicited the following criticism by R. Ashkenazi:

> I have not found any compelling reason to support this that he [R. Jacob ibn Ḥabib] has written that one who embarrasses another[48] must personally go [to ask for forgiveness without resorting in any way to an intermediary]. Eventually, he will go to appease him, [so] why should this matter one way or another ... and even if the one whom he had embarrassed is appeased without him going to see him at all, it would still be acceptable. What need is there for "shame and disgrace [to] serve as an atonement" if the one whom he has embarrassed will forgive him without this. The matter is [totally] dependent upon him [the one who grants the forgiveness].[49]

It seems that according to the view of R. Ashkenazi, and those who accept his opinion, the purpose of asking for forgiveness is simply the appeasement of the party who was hurt and his forgiving the offender. This is opposed to the view of R. Ibn Ḥabib, and those who accept his opinion, who seem to view asking for forgiveness as not only a means of appeasing the party who was hurt and having him grant forgiveness but as also a means of engendering some degree of shame, or embarrassment, on the part of the offender for what he had done, which serves, in some respect, as an atonement (see footnote).[50]

---

47 Ibn Ḥabib, *Sefer En Ya'akov*, vol. 2, *Perush ha-Kotev*, Jer. Tal. *Yoma*, chap. 8.

48 R. Ibn Ḥabib discusses a case in which someone embarrasses another person. However, he evidently was not only referring to such a case. This can be seen from the fact that he bases his view on the view of Samuel (Jer. Tal. *Yoma* 8:7), who is discussing all types of interpersonal offenses.

49 Ashkenazi, *Yefeh Mareh*, Jer. Tal. *Yoma* chap. 8.

50 To understand this view, one should be aware of the fact that many of the classic Jewish ethicists consider the experiencing of some degree of shame, or

Contemporary halakhic authorities continue to debate this issue. However, many of them do so in regard to the related question of whether it would be halakhically acceptable if the other person simply forgave the individual who committed the offense without the individual asking for forgiveness at all. Some authorities maintain that as long as the party who suffered has granted forgiveness, it is no longer necessary for the offender to go and ask for forgiveness, while other authorities are of the opinion that it would still be necessary to do so.[51] It is noteworthy that in discussing

---

embarrassment, as an important element of repentance. See, for example, Jonah ben Abraham Gerondi, *Sha'are Teshuvah* (Brooklyn: Zundel Berman, 1974), 1:21–22; Baḥya ben Asher, *Sefer Kad ha-Kemaḥ*, in *Kitve Rabenu Baḥya* (Jerusalem: Mossad Harav Kook, 1970), s.v. *rosh ha-shanah*, p. 373; and Isaac Aboab, *Sefer Menorat ha-Maor*, vol. 4 (Jerusalem: Mekhon Midrash ha-Mevoar, 1988), *ner* 5 *kelal* 1 *ḥelek* 2 *siman* 281, p. 43. Many of the authorities who discuss the connection between shame and repentance cite the talmudic teaching that "anyone who commits a sin and is ashamed because of it, is forgiven for all of his sins" (*Berakhot* 12b). According to R. Judah Loew of Prague, the relationship between shame and repentance is that "when a person is ashamed because of a sin it reflects that he is totally removing and distancing himself from the sin" (Judah Loew ben Bezalel, *Sefer Netivot Olam*, vol. 2 [Tel Aviv: Mekhon Yad Mordekhai, 1988], *Netiv ha-Teshuvah*, chap. 5, p. 393). There are some contemporary authors who suggest that engendering shame for an interpersonal offense is required in order to atone for the aspect of the offense that is a sin against God (*ben adam la-Makom*). See Ḥayim Shmerler, *Moade Ḥayim* (Jerusalem: Mekhon Arba, 2002), 208; and Yosef Lieberman, *Sefer She'elot u-Teshuvot Mishnat Yosef*, vol. 4 (Jerusalem: n.p., 2000), *siman* 44, p. 218–19.

51 Those authorities who do not require one to go and ask for forgiveness would include Yehoshua Menaḥem Mendel Ehrenberg, *Sefer Devar Yehoshua*, vol. 5 (Bnei Brak: Be-Hotsa'at Ḥotne ha-Meḥaber, 1998), *siman* 20, p. 11; Zilber, *Az Nidberu*, vol. 2:65, vol. 7:65; and Jekutiel Jehuda Halberstam, *Sefer She'elot u-Teshuvot Divre Yatsiv*, vol. 2 (Netanya: Mekhon Shefa Ḥayim, 1996), *Oraḥ Ḥayim*, *siman* 258, pp. 519–21. Those who do require one to go and ask for forgiveness include Shternbukh, *Mo'adim u-Zemanim ha-Shalem*, vol. 1, *siman* 54, p. 109; and Solomon Braun, *She'arim Metsuyanim ba-Halakhah*, commentary to *Kitsur Shulḥan Arukh*, by Solomon Ganzfried (Jerusalem: Feldheim, 1978), *siman* 131 *sa'if* 8, p. 179. See also Eliezer Papo, *Pele Yo'ets ha-Shalem* (Jerusalem: Mekhon Merav, 1994), s.v. *teshuvah*, pp. 652–53, who states that one is required to ask for forgiveness (when he caused someone pain), but if one would be embarrassed to do so, he may send an intermediary or write a letter to the person requesting forgiveness; and Shemaryahu Yosef Nissim Karelitz, *Sefer Ḥut Shani: Be'urim u-Verure Inyanim ve-Ḥidushe Dinim be-Hilkhot Rosh ha-Shanah, Yom ha-Kipurim, Sukot va-Ḥanukah* (Bnei Brak: n.p., 2010), 100, who cites a view in the name of R. Abraham Isaiah Karelitz that seems to indicate that one must go and ask for forgiveness; however, R. Nissim

the requirement to personally go and ask for forgiveness, some contemporary authors have offered explanations that significantly expand on, or are alternatives to, R. Ibn Ḥabib's understanding of the obligation (which focused on the experiencing of shame). Among the possible explanations that they have offered are that by personally going and asking for forgiveness one thereby humbles oneself,[52] which may make the party who was hurt more psychologically receptive to forgiving the person;[53] that this is called for because the person offended another human being and thereby exhibited disrespect to the image of God that resides within the individual;[54] and that this may help correct the bad character traits that led one to commit the offense.[55]

Specifying the Offense Committed

The Requirement of Specifying the Exact Offense. R. Joel Sirkes cites the opinion of R. Shalom of Neustadt (fourteenth century) that "he who asks for forgiveness from his friend for an offense he has committed against him is required in the [course of asking for] forgiveness to specify the offense."[56] This ruling was subsequently accepted by later authorities, such as R. Abraham Abele Gombiner

---

Karelitz concludes that when the party who was hurt has completely forgiven the offender this would not be necessary.

52 Cited in the name of Abraham Isaiah Karelitz, in Karelitz, *Sefer Ḥut Shani, Hilkhot Rosh ha-Shanah, Yom ha-Kipurim,* 100; Shternbukh, *Mo'adim u-Zemanim,* vol. 1, *siman* 54, p. 109; Yosef Kohen, *Sefer ha-Teshuvah,* vol. 1 (Jerusalem: Machon Harry Fischel, 1989), 148–49; and Baruch Razovsky, *Sefer Birkat Avot* (Jerusalem: n.p., 1990), *siman* 62, p. 502, quoted in Feldman, *The Right and the Good,* 148.

53 Kohen, *Sefer ha-Teshuvah,* vol. 1, 148–49 (see 150, where he writes that this may also atone for the sin that was committed).

54 Makhon Torat ha-Adam le-Adam, *"Kelal Gadol mi-Zeh," Torat ha-Adam le-Adam: Kovets Torani ba-Mitsvot she-ben Adam la-Ḥavero* 4 (Tishre 5762 [2001]): 302–4.

55 Lieberman, *Mishnat Yosef,* vol. 4, *siman* 44, p. 219. For other possible explanations, see Jeroham Lebovitch, *Sefer Ḥever Ma'amarim: Da'at Ḥokhmah u-Musar,* vol. 1 (Brooklyn: Daas Chochmo Umussar Publications, 1966), 368–69; and She'ar-Yashuv Kohen, *Shai Kohen,* vol. 1 (Jerusalem: Ariel, 1997), 211–12.

56 Shalom of Neustadt, *Hilkhot u-Minhage Rabenu Shalom mi-Noishtat* (Jerusalem: Mekhon Yerushalayim, 1997), *siman* 332, p. 102, quoted in Sirkes, *Bayit Ḥadash, Oraḥ Ḥayim* 606, s.v. *matsati.* For the talmudic source, see Elijah ben Solomon,

(c. 1637–1683), R. Shneur Zalman of Lyady (1745–1812), and the *Ḥafets Ḥayim*.[57] R. Sirkes explains this requirement by asserting that "[just as] one is required to specify the sin [he has committed] when he makes his verbal confession to God, so too when he makes his verbal confession to his friend, for in this regard one should not differentiate between sins that are [categorized as] 'between man and God' and those that are 'between man and his fellow man.'"[58]

In order to understand R. Sirkes's explanation, one must first be aware of the fact that in Judaism, the offering of some form of verbal confession to God[59] is reckoned as one of the essential elements of repentance.[60] The recognition and verbal acknowledgment of one's

---

[Be'ure] Ha-Gra al Shulḥan Arukh, in the standard printed edition of the *Shulḥan Arukh, Oraḥ Ḥayim* 606:1, s.v. *averot*.

57 Abraham Abele Gombiner, *Magen Avraham*, in the standard printed edition of the *Shulḥan Arukh, Oraḥ Ḥayim*, introduction to *siman* 606; Shneur Zalman of Lyady, *Shulḥan Arukh* (Brooklyn: Kehot, 1968), *Hilkhot Yom ha-Kipurim* 606:1; Ha-Kohen, *Mishnah Berurah*, 606:3.

58 Sirkes, *Bayit Ḥadash, Oraḥ Ḥayim* 606, s.v. *matsati*.

59 It should be understood that Judaism does not require any type of auricular confession to a Priest; rather, one's verbal confession for a sin takes place directly between the person and God. See Feinstein, *Igrot Mosheh, Oraḥ Ḥayim*, vol. 4, *siman* 118, p. 209, and *Even ha-Ezer*, vol. 4, *siman* 47:2–3, p. 100 (where he addresses the concept of public confession, which appears in Maimonides, *Mishneh Torah, Hilkhot Teshuvah* 2:5); and Meir Eisenstadt, *Panim Me'irot*, vol. 1 (New York: Kelilat Yofi Publishing, 1962), *she'elah* 178.

60 There are numerous biblical verses that emphasize the confession of sins, for example, "I acknowledged my sin to You, and my iniquity I have not hidden. I have said, 'I will confess my transgressions to the Lord,' and You have forgiven the iniquity of my sin" (Psalms 32:5). Maimonides cites two verses from the fifth chapter of Numbers as the source for the requirement: "When one repents from his sin, he is obligated to confess before God, blessed be He, as it is stated: 'When a man or woman shall commit any of the sins of men, committing a trespass against God, and that person becomes guilty, they shall confess the sin that they have committed (Num. 5:6–7) ...'" (Maimonides, *Mishneh Torah, Hilkhot Teshuvah* 1:1). As to why one should have to *verbalize* one's confession, as opposed to confessing one's sins in one's heart, there are various possible explanations. Baḥya ibn Pakuda understands it as a manifestation of one humbling oneself before God. Baḥya ibn Pakuda, *Sefer Torat Ḥovot ha-Levavot*, trans. Joseph Kafih (Jerusalem: Ha-Va'ad ha-Kelali li-Yehude Teman, n.d.), *Sha'ar ha-Teshuvah*, chap. 4, p. 311. For other explanations, see Kohen, *Sefer ha-Teshuvah*, vol. 1, 62; and Joseph B. Soloveitchik, *Soloveitchik on Repentance: The Thought and Oral Discourses of Rabbi Joseph B. Soloveitchik*, trans. Pinchas H. Peli (New York: Paulist Press, 1984), 91–96.

misdeed is considered something that is indispensable to the process of repentance. There is a general consensus among traditional authorities regarding this point.[61] However, in regard to specifying the exact sins one has committed, when one makes a verbal confession before God, there is considerable debate as to whether this is required or not. The Talmud in *Yoma* (86b) cites the opinion of R. Judah ben Bava (second century CE), who requires one to specify one's exact sins, and the opinion of R. Akiva (c. 50–c. 135 CE), who does not require one to do so. According to R. Sirkes, since R. Isaac Alfasi (1013–1103), Maimonides, and R. Asher ben Jehiel accept the opinion of R. Judah ben Bava, the halakhah follows R. Judah ben Bava's opinion, and therefore a person is required to specify his exact sins when he makes a verbal confession before God.[62] This being the case, R. Sirkes is of the view that the obligation of asking for forgiveness from a fellow human being is comparable to the asking of forgiveness from God, and therefore just as one must verbally acknowledge the specific sins he committed when he asks for forgiveness from God, so too one must also verbally acknowledge the specific interpersonal offenses he committed when asking for forgiveness from his friend.[63]

---

61 See, for example, Maimonides, *Mishneh Torah, Hilkhot Teshuvah* 1:1, 2:2–3; Gerondi, *Sha'are Teshuvah,* 1:19; Joseph Albo, *Sefer ha-Ikarim ha-Shalem,* 2 vols. (Jerusalem: Ḥorev, 1995), vol. 2, 4:26, p. 536; Baḥya ibn Pakuda, *Torat Ḥovot ha-Levavot, Sha'ar ha-Teshuvah,* chap. 4, p. 311; Baḥya ben Asher, *Kad ha-Kemaḥ,* vol. 2, p. 441–42; and Elijah ben Solomon, *Be'ur ha-Gera: Mishle* (Jerusalem: Mossad Harav Kook, 2005), Proverbs 28:13. For further elaboration, and authorities who differ, see Aaron Greenbaum, *"Gidre ha-Teshuvah al Pi ha-Gaon Rav Shemuel ben Ḥofni," Sinai* 77 (Nisan-Elul 5735 [1975]): 97–108.

62 See *Bayit Ḥadash, Oraḥ Ḥayim* 607, s.v. *u-mah she-katav ve-khen nireh.* Cf. Karo, *Bet Yosef, Oraḥ Ḥayim* 607, s.v. *u-mah she-katav ve-khen nireh* and s.v. *u-mah she-katav rabenu;* and Karo, *Shulḥan Arukh, Oraḥ Ḥayim* 607:2 (see next footnote).

63 Sirkes, *Bayit Ḥadash, Oraḥ Ḥayim* 606, s.v. *matsati.* R. Joseph Teomim (c. 1727–1792) and R. Samuel Kolin (1720–1806) raise a question that needs to be addressed by those later authorities who have accepted this ruling. The entire requirement of specifying interpersonal offenses when one asks for forgiveness from another person, according to R. Sirkes, is based on the premise that one is obligated to specify one's sins when confessing before God. The problem with this is that R. Joseph Karo, the author of the *Shulḥan Arukh,* rules that one is *not* obligated to specify his sins when confessing before God. According to R. Karo, R. Isaac Alfasi and R. Asher ben Jehiel do not follow the opinion of R. Judah ben Bava, as postulated by R. Sirkes; rather, they follow the opinion of R. Akiva, that one does not have to

An alternative explanation to the one that is offered by R. Sirkes for the requirement of specifying interpersonal offenses can be found in the writings of R. Joseph Trani (1568–1639). R. Trani compares the *meḥilah*, "forgiveness," for an interpersonal offense to the relinquishing of a monetary debt (which is also referred to by the Talmud and *poskim* as *meḥilah*, that is, the forgiving, or forgoing, of a monetary sum that is rightfully one's due), specifically, to the relinquishing of one's right to be compensated when one is being overcharged.[64] According to R. Trani, just as there is a halakhah that states that one does not waive one's right to collect such a monetary sum unless one is aware of the exact amount to be given up,[65] so, too, when asked to forgive an interpersonal offense, one does not forgive such an offense unless one knows exactly what is being forgiven.[66]

An Exception to the Requirement of Specifying the Offense. After citing R. Sirkes's earlier ruling, that one is obligated to specify the offense when asking for forgiveness from one's friend, R. Abraham Abele Gombiner writes, "It appears to me that if his friend [the person whom he is asking forgiveness from] will be embarrassed by this, he should not specify it [the offense]."[67] This exemption for cases in which one will embarrass the other person is cited by later

---

specify his sins, and therefore R. Karo rules in accordance with R. Akiva's view. The question therefore presents itself as to why later authorities (such as R. Abraham Abele Gombiner; see p. 316 above) who accept the ruling of R Karo, require one to specify interpersonal offenses when asking for forgiveness from a fellow human being. See Teomim, *Peri Megadim, Oraḥ Ḥayim* 606, *Ashel Avraham* s.v. *bi-she'at;* and Samuel Kolin, *Maḥatsit ha-Shekel,* in the standard printed edition of the *Shulḥan Arukh, Oraḥ Ḥayim* 606:1, s.v. *katav Magen Avraham.*

64 In rabbinic literature, overcharging is referred to as *"ona'at mamon,"* "financial harm [or oppression]." See *Entsiklopedyah Talmudit,* vol. 1, s.v. *"ona'ah"*; and Shmuel Shilo and Menachem Elon, *"ona'ah,"* in *Encyclopaedia Judaica,* 2nd ed., 423–26.

65 See *Bava Metsia* 51b; *Shulḥan Arukh, Ḥoshen Mishpat* 227:21; and Ya'akov Yeshayahu Bloi, *Sefer Pitḥe Ḥoshen,* 8 vols. (Jerusalem: Yeshivat Ohel Moshe Diskin, 1982–), vol. 4, 318, s.v. *uve-Imre Binah.*

66 Joseph ben Moses Trani, *She'elot u-Teshuvot Maharit,* vol. 2 (Tel Aviv: Sifriyati, 1959), *Oraḥ Ḥayim, siman* 8, p. 7. There is some slight ambiguity in R. Trani's wording. I am offering what I believe to be the simplest explanation of what he means to say.

67 Gombiner, *Magen Avraham, Oraḥ Ḥayim,* introduction to *siman* 606.

authorities,[68] including the *Ḥafets Ḥayim* in his *Mishnah Berurah* (his commentary to *Shulḥan Arukh, Oraḥ Ḥayim*).[69] There is, however, some question as to what exactly was the *Ḥafets Ḥayim*'s opinion regarding specifying the offense one committed if, in doing so, it will cause the other person emotional distress. The question revolves around a ruling of the *Ḥafets Ḥayim* that appears in his work *Sefer Ḥafets Ḥayim* and the following story that is told about it.

R. Abraham Kosowsky (died during World War II in Auschwitz) relates that the *Ḥafets Ḥayim* had told him that at the time he had written his *Sefer Ḥafets Ḥayim*, he had brought a copy of the work to R. Israel Lipkin (Salanter, 1810–1883) for R. Lipkin to review. After going through the work, R. Lipkin had told the *Ḥafets Ḥayim* that he had a major problem with one halakhah he had come across. In discussing the obligation of asking for forgiveness from a person whom one had spoken *lashon ha-ra* (see Glossary) against, the *Ḥafets Ḥayim* had written that "even if his friend is totally unaware of this, he is required to reveal to him what he had done against him."[70] In R. Lipkin's view, this would be unacceptable because "when he would tell him [what he had done] he would cause him pain." The *Ḥafets Ḥayim*'s response to this was that he had based his ruling on a ruling of R. Jonah Gerondi (c. 1200–1263).[71] This story and the view the *Ḥafets Ḥayim* had expressed, which at first blush seems to contradict his view in the *Mishnah Berurah* that was cited above, have sparked considerable discussion and debate among contemporary scholars. One finds an array of approaches to the topic in contemporary works (for a summary of some of these approaches, see footnote).[72]

---

68 For example, Shneur Zalman of Lyady, *Shulḥan Arukh, Hilkhot Yom ha-Kipurim* 606:1; Margolioth, *Mateh Efrayim*, 606:2; and Epstein, *Arukh ha-Shulḥan, Oraḥ Ḥayim* 606:1.

69 Ha-Kohen, *Mishnah Berurah*, 606:3.

70 Ha-Kohen, *Sefer Ḥafets Ḥayim, Hilkhot Isure Lashon ha-Ra, kelal* 4:12.

71 Abraham Abba Kosowsky, letter to Aryeh Leib Poupko, 21 Kislev 5698 (1937), in *Siḥot he-Ḥafets Ḥayim*, in *Kol Kitve Ḥafets Ḥayim*, vol. 3, p. 9. Gerondi, *Sha'are Teshuvah, Sha'ar* 3:207.

72 Some scholars simply question the *Ḥafets Ḥayim*'s interpretation of R. Gerondi's ruling. See, for example, Ḥayim Yitsḥak Lipkin, *Derekh Teshuvah*, commentary to *Sha'are Teshuvah*, by Jonah ben Abraham Gerondi (Bnei Brak: Hotsa'at Ḥokhmah u-Musar, 1977), *sha'ar* 3:207, p. 44 (at the end of the book), in which he offers a

In discussing this story, some sources[73] cite a letter from R. Naftali Amsterdam (1832–1916), one of R. Lipkin's foremost students, that directly relates to the topic. Based on what can be inferred from R. Amsterdam's letter, it seems that R. Isaac Blaser (1837–1907), another leading student of R. Lipkin, had asked R. Amsterdam for a halakhic ruling regarding a case in which he,

possible alternative interpretation to that of the *Ḥafets Ḥayim*'s. R. Binyamin Zilber contends that what R. Gerondi had written does not contradict R. Lipkin's view, and that it would appear that even the *Ḥafets Ḥayim* himself would agree to what R. Lipkin had said. See Zilber, *Az Nidberu*, vol. 7, *siman* 66. See Karelitz, *Sefer Ḥut Shani, Hilkhot Rosh ha-Shanah, Yom ha-Kipurim*, 106, where R. Karelitz states, similar to R. Zilber, that one cannot derive anything from what R. Gerondi had written that would contradict R. Lipkin's view, and that he is certain that the *Ḥafets Ḥayim* would never have entertained the possibility that one could transgress the prohibition against *ona'at devarim* (saying something hurtful to another person) in order to attain forgiveness for a previous sin. R. Karelitz goes on to offer two possible interpretations of the *Ḥafets Ḥayim*'s ruling so that it does not contradict R. Lipkin's view. R. Zilber's and R. Karelitz's approaches implicitly raise some questions about the veracity of the story itself, which indicated that the *Ḥafets Ḥayim* did disagree with R. Lipkin. See also Avigdor Nebenzahl, quoted in Moshe Harari, *Mikra'e Kodesh: Hilkhot Yom ha-Kipurim* (Jerusalem: Yeshivat Merkaz ha-Rav, n.d.), 34–35 n. 4, in which R. Nebenzahl alludes to the difficulty he has with the story. R. Aaron Soloveichik cites a slightly different version of the story, which he had heard from R. Isaac Hutner. In R. Hutner's version, R. Lipkin goes on to debate the issue with the *Ḥafets Ḥayim*. R. Lipkin presents an alternative reading of R. Gerondi to that of the *Ḥafets Ḥayim*'s, and the *Ḥafets Ḥayim* responds by disagreeing with R. Lipkin's reading. See Soloveichik, *Paraḥ Mateh Aharon, Hilkhot De'ot* 7:5, *Hilkhot Teshuvah* 2:9, pp. 88, 187. In discussing this topic, there are some who focus on resolving the contradiction between the *Ḥafets Ḥayim*'s ruling in the *Mishnah Berurah* and his ruling in *Sefer Ḥafets Ḥayim*. See, for example, Yitsḥak Trager and Aharon Auerbach, *Orḥot Halakhah*, in *Halikhot Shelomoh*, by Shlomo Zalman Auerbach, vol. 2 (Tel Aviv: Yeshivat Halikhot Shelomoh, 2003), p. 45 n. 24, who differentiate between embarrassing one's friend, which is the focus of the discussion in the *Mishnah Berurah*, and causing someone *tsa'ar*, "pain," which may be the focus of the discussion in *Sefer Ḥafets Ḥayim*. Cf. Shmuel Huminer, *Sefer Ikre Dinim* (Jerusalem: n.p., 1975), *kelal* 4 n. 6, p. 9b; and Abraham Shapira to Moshe Harari, letter, 25 Av 5754 (1994), in *Mikra'e Kodesh: Hilkhot Yom ha-Kipurim*, by Moshe Harari (Jerusalem: Yeshivat Merkaz ha-Rav, n.d.), 331. R. Huminer and R. Shapiro (and others) do not differentiate between embarrassment and *tsa'ar*. For additional sources, see Daniel Z. Feldman, *False Facts and True Rumors: Lashon Hara in Contemporary Culture* (New Milford, CT: Maggid Books, 2015), 234–41.

73 For example, Dov Katz, *Tenu'at ha-Musar*, vol. 1 (Jerusalem: Feldheim, 1996), 334 n. 58; Moshe Harari, *Mikra'e Kodesh: Hilkhot Yom ha-Kipurim* (Jerusalem: Yeshivat Merkaz ha-Rav, n.d.), 35 n. 4; and Yisrael Vinman, *Mishnat Yisrael: Be-Mitsvot she-ben Adam la-Ḥavero u-Shemirat ha-Lashon* (Jerusalem: n.p., 2009), 237–40.

R. Blaser, had spoken what he considered to be *lashon ha-ra* about a group of people, and he was not sure if he was required to reveal to them exactly what he had said, when he would ask forgiveness from them prior to his leaving the community in which they lived. R. Amsterdam's response to this was that even though it appears, based on what R. Trani had stated (see above, p. 319), that if one does not specify the offense, the forgiveness one would receive would be halakhically ineffective, R. Gombiner clearly states otherwise (see p. 319). Based on an approach he has for reconciling R. Trani's and R. Gombiner's opinions, R. Amsterdam concludes that it would be acceptable for one to ask for forgiveness without specifying exactly what he had done, as long as one does admit to committing an offense. R. Amsterdam therefore suggests that before leaving the community, R. Blaser should approach the group of people he had spoken *lashon ha-ra* against and

> ask them for forgiveness as is customary at that time, and say to them something along the lines of "Let us forgive each other, et cetera [i.e., for any misdeeds we may have committed against each other]" and to also say [to them] that "this includes that which I had said about you a long time ago"; or something similar, in accordance with what you will deem as being appropriate.[74]

As far as contemporary halakhic authorities are concerned, R. Shlomo Zalman Auerbach (1910–1995), R. Yosef Shalom Elyashiv (1910–2012), R. Ovadia Yosef (1920–2013), R. Binyamin Zilber (1906–2008), and R. Ḥayim Kanievsky (1928–) all support what R. Lipkin had said and rule that if it would cause pain to the person one is asking forgiveness from, one does not specify the offense.[75]

---

74 Naftali Amsterdam, "*Me-Igrotav shel Maran ha-Gaon he-Ḥasid R. Naftali Amsterdam*," *Tevunah: Inyane Torah u-Musar* 3, ed. Israel Zisel Dvoretz, *ḥoveret* 7 (Jerusalem, Adar 2, 5703 [1943]): 69.

75 Shlomo Zalman Auerbach, *Halikhot Shelomoh*, vol. 2 (Tel Aviv: Yeshivat Halikhot Shelomoh, 2003), pp. 44–45; Yosef Shalom Elyashiv, quoted in Moshe Frid, *Va-Yishma Mosheh*, vol. 1 (Jerusalem, n.p., 2010), 196 (cf. Yosef Shalom Elyashiv,

It should be noted, however, that R. Moshe Sternbuch (1926–) quotes in the name of R. Elijah E. Dessler (1892–1953) that R. Lipkin's opinion was that in such a situation as this, one should say to the person that "if he had offended him [at some point in the past], he is asking for forgiveness for everything [he had done]."[76]

The Obligation to Ask for Forgiveness Three Times

The Source of the Obligation. The talmudic passage in *Yoma* (above, pp. 302–3) indicates that one should make three attempts at asking for forgiveness. According to Rashi, this is first expressed in the passage by the teaching of R. Ḥisda (c. 217–309 C.E.) that "it is necessary to appease him with three rows of three people [i.e., that one is supposed to bring a group of three people for each one of the three attempts that one should make],[77] as it is stated in Scripture: 'He makes a row of men[78] and says "I have sinned, and I have perverted that which was straight, and it was not worth it for me"' (Job 33:27)" (*Yoma* 87a). Rashi explains that the three clauses in the person's confession in the verse in Job ("I have sinned," "I have perverted that which was straight," and "it was not worth it for me") midrashically allude to the three attempts one must make at asking for forgiveness.[79] Immediately following R. Ḥisda's teaching, the

---

quoted in Yitsḥak Zilberstein, *Kav ve-Naki*, vol. 2 [n.p., 2013], 240, in which R. Elyashiv offers an explanation for the *Ḥafets Ḥayim*'s opinion); Ovadia Yosef, *Ḥazon Ovadyah: Yamim Noraim* (Jerusalem: n.p., 2005), p. 244 n. 20; Zilber, *Az Nidberu*, vol. 7, *siman* 66; Shemaryahu Yosef Ḥayim Kanevski, Eliyahu Man, and Tsevi Yavrov, *Derekh Siḥah* (Bnei Brak: Sifre Or ha-Ḥayim, 2004), 623–24.

76 Shternbukh, *Mo'adim u-Zemanim*, vol. 1, *siman* 54; see also Elijah Eliezer Dessler, *Mikhtav me-Eliyahu: Divre Ḥokhmah u-Musar ba-Avodat Ḥodesh Elul ve-Yeraḥ ha-Etanim*, 2 vols. (Bnei Brak: Sifsei Chachamim, 2008), vol. 2, 483; and Zilber, *Az Nidberu*, vol. 7, *siman* 66.

77 Rashi, *Yoma* 87a, s.v. *be-shalosh shurot*.

78 In Hebrew, *yashor al anashim*. The literal sense of this expression is either "he goes unto men" or "he looks upon men," both of which express the idea that this confession takes place publicly in front of people. I have used Abraham J. Rosenberg's translation of this phrase, which is based on the midrashic interpretation cited in Rashi's commentary to Job. See *Job: A New English Translation*, trans. Abraham J. Rosenberg (New York: The Judaica Press, 1995), Job 33:27.

79 Rashi, *Yoma* 87a, s.v. *be-shelosh shurot* and s.v. *ḥatati*.

Gemara goes on to cite the teaching of R. Jose bar Ḥanina (third century CE), who mentions three attempts at asking for forgiveness when he sets down the maximum number of attempts that one should make: "R. Jose bar Ḥanina said, 'Whoever beseeches [forgiveness] from his friend should not beseech him more than three times, as it states [in reference to the brothers of Joseph, three expressions of pleading for forgiveness], "O please, please forgive ... and now please forgive ..." (Genesis 50:17).'"[80]

In order to comprehend the halakhic requirement of making three attempts at asking for forgiveness, it should first be understood that in Jewish law once something occurs three times a *ḥazakah* is established. A *ḥazakah* is a legal presumption that just as something has occurred three times in the past, it can be assumed that it will continue to do so in the future.[81] Therefore, according to an explanation offered by R. Judah Aryeh Leib Alter (1847–1905) and R. Yosef Shalom Elyashiv (1910–2012), once one has made three sincere attempts at asking for forgiveness and is rebuffed each time, from the standpoint of Halakhah one can assume that the person from whom one is asking for forgiveness will continue to reject future propitiatory gestures.[82]

As far as the requirement, which R. Ḥisda had referred to, of having other people accompany the one who asks for forgiveness, the gemara in *Yoma* immediately preceding the statement of R. Ḥisda had taught that "Whoever provokes his friend, even verbally, is obligated to appease him ... [and one should bring] many friends to him [the person being appeased]."[83] According to Maimonides,

80 *Yoma* 87a.

81 See *Entsiklopedyah Talmudit*, vol. 13, s.v. *ḥazakah*.

82 Alter, *Sefat Emet*, *Yoma* 87a-b, s.v. *ve-im met* and s.v. *Rav shane*; Yosef Shalom Elyashiv, *He'arot be-Masekhet Yoma* (Jerusalem: n.p., 2002), *Yoma* 87a-b, s.v. *ve-im met* and s.v. *Rav shane*. Alternatively, according to R. Ḥayim Zaichyk (1906–1989), the purpose of making three attempts is to test the sincerity of the person asking for forgiveness—that he exhibits an understanding of the harm he caused the other person, and that he sincerely wants to reconcile with him. Ḥayim Ephraim Zaichyk, *Va-Ani Tefilah*, vol. 4 (Bnei Brak: Lipa Friedman, 1974), 287–89.

83 *Yoma* 87a. The Gemara bases this teaching on the midrashic interpretation of the verses "[If] you have been ensnared by the words of your mouth, then do this, my son, and be saved ... go and humble yourself and increase your friends" (Proverbs 6:2–3). Rashi explains the Gemara's interpretation of these verses as follows: "If 'you

bringing along other people is only necessary in a case when the party who was hurt refuses to forgive. In such a case, these other people are there to assist the one who is asking for forgiveness by "entreating and requesting" from the other party that he grant forgiveness (for further elaboration and alternative explanations, see footnote).[84] In regard to the practical halakhic application of having other people present, see the next section (pp. 327–28).

---

have been ensnared by the words of your mouth,' by verbally provoking your friend, do this and 'you will be saved' ... 'increase your friends'—bring many friends to ask forgiveness from him." Rashi, *Yoma* 87a, s.v. *beni*, and s.v. *lekh*. I have translated the Hebrew *u-rhav re'ekha* in the verse from Proverbs, as "increase your friends." This phrase can alternatively be translated as "importune your friend." My translation is based on R. David Kimḥi's explanation (*Sefer ha-Shorashim le-Radak* [Jerusalem: n.p., 1967], s.v. "*rhv*," second explanation) and the commentary of Mordechai Zer-Kavod (*Sefer Mishle* [Jerusalem: Mossad Harav Kook, 1992], Prov. 6:3, p. 29 n. 7).

84 Maimonides, *Mishneh Torah, Hilkhot Teshuvah* 2:9. Rashi offers a similar explanation to that of Maimonides (however, Rashi does not specify that one only brings along other people after the other party refuses to forgive, as does Maimonides). Rashi, *Yoma* 87a, s.v. *lekh*, and s.v. *be-shalosh shurot*. Maimonides and Rashi's explanations should not be misconstrued as suggesting that the other people are in any way coercing the person into granting a forgiveness that is forced and insincere. R. Moses Feinstein (in discussing Rashi's view) explains that the other people help to facilitate that the forgiveness be completely sincere and wholehearted. See Feinstein, *Igrot Mosheh, Even ha-Ezer*, vol. 4, *siman* 47:2–3. A number of authors have pointed out that when the Jerusalem Talmud discusses having other people present when asking for forgiveness, it states that "he brings people and *appeases him in front of them*" (Jer. Tal. *Yoma* 8:7). This wording of the Jerusalem Talmud indicates that the other people do not take an active role in the process of appeasing the person, which differs from the view expressed by Maimonides and Rashi. See Shalom Tsevi Shapira, *Meshiv Nefesh: Al ha-Rambam, Hilkhot Teshuvah* (Bnei Brak: n.p., n.d.), *Hilkhot Teshuvah* 2:9; p. 117. The approach of the Jerusalem Talmud, that the other people do not take an active role, was apparently accepted by a number of authorities; see, for example, Shneur Zalman of Lyady, *Shulḥan Arukh, Hilkhot Yom ha-Kipurim* 606:2. A totally different approach is taken by R. Jonah of Gerondi to that of Maimonides, Rashi, and other halakhic authorities in regard to having other people present when asking for forgiveness. According to R. Gerondi, other people have to be present only if one had disgraced the other person in front of others; only then one has to compensate for what he had done by humbling himself and confessing to that person "publicly" (i.e., in front of three people). See Gerondi, *Sha'are Teshuvah*, 4:19; with [Binyamin Yehoshua Zilber], *Sha'are Teshuvah im Beur Zeh ha-Sha'ar* (Bnei Brak: Hotsa'at Ḥokhmah u-Musar, 1977), *sha'ar* 4:19, p. 329 (where R. Zilber points out that this view is clearly not accepted by other *poskim*). See also Lieberman, *Mishnat Yosef*, vol. 4, *siman* 44, p. 221.

Must One Make Three or Four Attempts? There are numerous questions that have been raised by *poskim* concerning the requirement of asking for forgiveness three times. One of the most basic questions is whether one is required according to Halakhah to make three attempts at appeasing one's friend or is one actually required to make four attempts.

This question regarding the number of attempts arises because, based on the reading of major halakhic authorities, there are two possible ways of understanding what the Talmud means when it says that a person has to ask for forgiveness "three times." One possibility is that a person is required to make three, and only three, attempts at asking for forgiveness, and for each of these three attempts he should be accompanied by three people, as is indicated by what may be viewed as the simple explanation of the gemara in *Yoma* (cited above). The other possibility is that one is supposed to initially go and ask the other person for forgiveness without anyone else present, and only if that person refuses to forgive him is he then required to resort to the bringing of three people to help appease the person, which he then must attempt to do three times (thus, making it a total of *four* attempts at asking for forgiveness). The latter possibility is what is indicated by the Jerusalem Talmud:

> Samuel (second–third century CE) said: "One who commits a sin against his friend is required to say to him 'I have committed an offense against you.' If he accepts [his apology and forgives him], it is good; if not, he [*then*] brings people and appeases him in front of them. For this is what is stated in the verse [Job 33:27] 'He makes a row of men' …" (Jer. Tal. *Yoma* 8:7).

> Rav said: "A person who commits an offense against his friend and seeks [forgiveness] from him, if his friend does not accept it [his request for forgiveness], he should [*then*] make a row of people and appease him, as it is written 'He makes a row of men …'" (Jer. Tal. *Bava Kamma* 8:7).

Both Samuel's statement and Rav's statement clearly indicate that one first attempts to appease the person by oneself, and only if this fails does one resort to bringing along other people.[85] The *Ḥafets Ḥayim* calls attention to the fact that R. Jacob ben Asher and R. Joseph Karo require one to initially start off with three people (as implied by a simple reading of the Babylonian Talmud), whereas Maimonides is of the opinion that initially one is not required to bring along other people, as is indicated by the Jerusalem Talmud.[86] According to R. Ḥayyim David Halevi (1924–1998) and R. Avigdor Nebenzahl (1935–), the approach of Maimonides reflects the accepted present-day custom. R. Nebenzahl also asserts that, in accordance with this approach, not only is one not required to initially bring along others when asking for forgiveness, but it is actually preferable not to do so.[87]

R. Shmuel Kamenetsky (1924–) maintains that it would appear that even according to the *Shulḥan Arukh* (i.e., R. Karo's opinion, cited above) being accompanied by three people is not something that one must be overly concerned about and that it would be acceptable to ask for forgiveness without being accompanied by anyone else, if one believes that his friend will forgive him without others being present.[88] R. Mordechai Eliyahu (1929–2010) also

---

85 The sources in the Jerusalem Talmud do not indicate how many attempts one must make with these groups of people, nor do they specify how many people one must bring along. See Aryeh Loeb Yellin, *Yefeh Enayim*, in the standard Vilna edition of the Babylonian Talmud, *Yoma* 87a, s.v. *shalosh shurot*. There are textual variants of Jer. Tal. *Bava Kamma* 8:7 according to which one should first make two or three attempts without being accompanied by others. See *Sha'are Teshuvah: 353 Teshuvot ha-Ge'onim* (Leipzig: Leopold Shenois, 1858), responsum 69 (according to R. Dov Baer Ratner, there are three [key] words missing in the original responsum; see Dov Baer Ratner, *Ahavat Tsiyon vi-Yerushalayim: Masekhet Yoma*, [Jerusalem: n.p., 1967], *Yoma* 8:9, p. 102); Isaac ben Moses of Vienna, *Or Zaru'a*, vol. 3 (Jerusalem: Mekhon Yerushalayim, 2010), *siman* 377; and Judah ben Samuel, *Sefer Ḥasidim* (Jerusalem: Mossad Harav Kook, 2002), *siman* 44, p. 103; and cf. Judah ben Samuel, *Sefer Ḥasidim, Mekitse Nirdamim* ed. (Frankfurt am Main: M. A. Wahrmann, 1924), *siman* 90, p. 55.

86 Ha-Kohen, *Mishnah Berurah, Be'ur Halakhah*, s.v. *yaḥazor*.

87 See Ḥayyim David Halevi, *Aseh lekha Rav*, 9 vols. (Tel Aviv: Ha-Va'adah le-Hotsa'at Kitve ha-G.R.Ḥ.D. ha-Levi, 1976–89), vol. 4, responsum 36, pp. 207–8; Nebenzahl, *Mikra'e Kodesh*, 38 n. 19.

88 Shmuel Kamenetsky, *Kovets Halakhot: Yamim Nora'im*, ed. Daniel Kleinman (Lakewood, NJ: n.p., 2011), 304 n. 1. See ibid., where R. Kamenetsky also offers an

expressed a similar view. He stated that if one believes that it would be more effective to ask for forgiveness without others present, that is what should done.[89] R. Shlomo Koraḥ (1935–) points out that the prevalent contemporary practice is that people ask for forgiveness without ever resorting to bringing three people, even after the other person refuses to grant forgiveness.[90]

(Even though there may actually be a requirement to make four attempts at asking for forgiveness, for the remainder of this section, I will refer to the *three* attempts that one should make, which is the number of attempts that is commonly referred to in halakhic sources.)

Asking for Forgiveness More than Three Times. The *poskim* debate the meaning of R. Jose bar Ḥanina's statement that "whoever beseeches [forgiveness] from his friend should not beseech him more than three times." A simple reading of the talmudic passage (see *Yoma* 87a–b) indicates that R. Jose bar Ḥanina was understood as saying that one is not *allowed* to ask for forgiveness more than three times.[91] According to R. Sirkes, this is the interpretation

---

explanation for why "we never see that anyone in practice is accompanied by three people when appeasing his friend."

89 Mordechai Eliyahu, *Hilkhot Ḥagim*, 2nd ed. (Jerusalem: Darkhe Hora'ah, 2003), 308. See also Ḥayim Pinḥas Scheinberg, quoted in G. Alon and Elḥanan Perets, *Orḥot ha-Rav ve-Rosh ha-Yeshivah* (Jerusalem: Mekhon Ḥukat Mishpat, 2012), 93–94.

90 Shlomo Koraḥ, *Sefat Melekh*, commentary to *Mishneh Torah, Sefer Mada*, vol. 2 (Bnei Brak: n.p., 1998), *Hilkhot Teshuvah* 2:9, p. 453. See ibid. for the justification that R. Koraḥ offers for the present-day practice. Cf. Kamenetsky, *Kovets Halakhot*, 304 n. 1. It should be noted that the *Ḥafets Ḥayim* writes that the halakhah that one is only required to make three (or four) attempts at asking for forgiveness only holds true if one follows the halakhic guideline of being accompanied by others (Ha-Kohen, *Mishnah Berurah*, 606:4). This would evidently mean that according to the *Ḥafets Ḥayim*, if one asks for forgiveness and the other person refuses to forgive, and one subsequently chooses not to be accompanied by others, he would have to continue to ask for forgiveness even beyond three or four attempts.

91 According to R. Joseph Escapa (1570–1662), R. Joseph Molkho (c. 1688–c. 1760), and R. Judah Aryeh Leib Alter (1847–1905), the logic behind prohibiting one from asking for forgiveness more than three times is that once a person has refused to

of R. Isaac Alfasi, R. Asher ben Jehiel, Maimonides, and R. Moses ben Jacob of Coucy (thirteenth century),[92] whereas Rashi and R. Jacob ben Asher (and R. Joseph Karo)[93] interpret R. Jose bar Ḥanina as saying that one is not *obligated* to ask for forgiveness more than three times.[94] The implication of the latter interpretation is that if the person wishes to ask for forgiveness more than three times, he may certainly do so[95] (and this may even be considered something praiseworthy[96]). From among the *aḥaronim* ("later" rabbinic authorities, see Glossary), R. Sirkes, R. Abraham Abele Gombiner, R. Elijah ben Solomon (1720–1797), and the *Ḥafets Ḥayim* permit one to ask for forgiveness more than three times,[97] whereas R. Hezekiah da Silva prohibits it.[98]

---

forgive someone three times (and it is clear that he will continue to do so), one would subsequently be considered responsible for leading the person to commit a sin (see pp. 335–41 below) by giving him the opportunity to repeatedly refuse to grant forgiveness. Joseph Escapa, *Sefer Rosh Yosef* (Monroe, NY: Yitsḥak Brakh, 1989), *Oraḥ Ḥayim* 606, p. 104b; Molkho, *Sefer Shulḥan Gevoah, Oraḥ Ḥayim* 606:4; and Alter, *Sefat Emet, Yoma* 87b, s.v. *Rav shane.*

92 For an alternative interpretation of R. Alfasi's view, see Elijah ben Solomon, *[Be'ure] Ha-Gra, Oraḥ Ḥayim* 606:1, s.v. *mihu*; and for an alternative explanation of Maimonides' view, see David ben Samuel ha-Levi, *Ture Zahav*, in the standard printed edition of the *Shulḥan Arukh, Oraḥ Ḥayim* 606:1.

93 R. Karo's view is not cited by R. Sirkes, but it seems quite clear from R. Karo's wording of this halakhah that he follows the opinion of R. Jacob ben Asher. See Karo, *Shulḥan Arukh, Oraḥ Ḥayim* 606:1.

94 Sirkes, *Bayit Ḥadash, Oraḥ Ḥayim* 606, s.v. *u-mah she-katav ve-hane mile.*

95 Ibid. According to R. Sirkes, an exception to the rule that allows one to ask for forgiveness more than three times would be when this would entail that one would thereby "demean the Torah," that means to say, diminish one's standing as a Torah scholar (see ibid. and Epstein, *Arukh ha-Shulḥan, Oraḥ Ḥayim* 606:3).

96 See Escapa, *Rosh Yosef, Oraḥ Ḥayim* 606, p. 104b, s.v. *ve-katav ha-Tur* (in explaining the opinion of R. Jacob ben Asher); with *Yoma* 87b, where the Gemara recounts how Rav attempted to appease R. Ḥanina bar Ḥama every *Erev Yom Kippur* [the day before Yom Kippur] for a period of thirteen years.

97 Sirkes, *Bayit Ḥadash, Oraḥ Ḥayim* 606, s.v. *u-mah she-katav ve-hane mile*; Gombiner, *Magen Avraham, Oraḥ Ḥayim* 606:2; Elijah ben Solomon, *[Be'ure] Ha-Gra, Oraḥ Ḥayim* 606:1, s.v. *mihu*; Ha-Kohen, *Mishnah Berurah*, 606:5.

98 Da Silva, *Peri Ḥadash, Oraḥ Ḥayim* 606:1, s.v. *u-mah she-katav eno zakuk.*

The Requirement of Appeasement

What Does It Mean to "Appease" Someone?[99] In setting forth the obligation of asking for forgiveness for an interpersonal offense, Maimonides writes as follows:

> [For] transgressions that are between a man and his fellow man, for example, physically harming his friend, or one who curses his friend, or steals, and things that are of a similar nature, a person is never absolved until he gives to his friend that which he is [financially] obligated to give him and appeases[100] him.
>
> Even if he has returned to him the money that he is obligated to give him, he is [still] required to appease him and ask for forgiveness. And even if one had only provoked his friend verbally, he is required to appease[100] and entreat him until he forgives him.[101]

In this halakhah, Maimonides is describing a process that encompasses three basic components:

> (1) (*financial*) *restitution* (when called for) — "a person is never absolved until he gives to his friend that which he is [financially] obligated to give him ..."

99 In English, the word *appease* is defined as "to bring to peace, calm, or quiet (persons at strife or in disorder)" or "to pacify, assuage, or allay (anger or displeasure)" (*Oxford English Dictionary*, s.v. "appease," 1b, 2a). Possible synonyms include "pacify," "placate," mollify," and "propitiate" (*Merriam Webster's Dictionary of Synonyms*, s.v. "pacify").

100 I am translating both Hebrew verbs פִּיֵּס (*piyes*) and רִצָּה (*ritsah*) as "appease," as they are commonly translated. See Teomim, *Peri Megadim, Oraḥ Ḥayim* 606, *Ashel Avraham*, s.v. *bi-she'at*, in which he indicates that these words are synonymous. Cf. Mordechai Gifter, *Hirhure Teshuvah: He'arot, He'arot u-Ve'urim ba-Rambam Hilkhot Teshuvah* (Brooklyn: Artscroll/Mesorah, 2007), 125.

101 Maimonides, *Mishneh Torah, Hilkhot Teshuvah* 2:9.

(2) *appeasement* — "... he is [still] required to appease him"

(3) *a request to be forgiven* — "and ask for forgiveness."[102]

It should be noted that the element of appeasement is emphasized three times by Maimonides in this halakhah, and it is something that is mentioned in innumerable other classic halakhic sources that discuss forgiveness.

Classic halakhic sources, however, do not spell out the exact nature of the appeasement that one should engage in. Evidently, it was felt that this should be left up to the discretion and good judgment of the party who asks for forgiveness, who will hopefully say the proper things and express the appropriate sentiment based on the unique circumstances of the situation and the needs of the individual that one is asking forgiveness from so that the individual will be able to find in his or her heart to forgive the person.[103]

In relation to the question of what exactly constitutes "appeasement," R. Yosef Shalom Elyashiv is quoted as stating that for one to just say to someone "I'm asking for forgiveness" or "Do you forgive me?" would not be considered "appeasement." According to R. Elyashiv, appeasement would entail that the one who seeks forgiveness sees to it that the person being asked to forgive understands that he (the one asking for forgiveness) recognizes the significance of what he has done, that is to say that he has committed a wrong against the other person, and is therefore seeking forgiveness from him.[104]

As we shall shortly see in the second half of this chapter, there are two or three[105] essential elements that will be discussed that may be highly relevant to the nature of the appeasement. In

102 See Yisrael Yisakhar Dov Klein, *Sefer Ve-Ezer mi-Tsarav: Al Hilkhot Teshuvah leha-Rambam* (Brooklyn: n.p., 2004), 298.

103 This would be in conformity with the principle of "everything is in accordance with the time, issue, place, and individual" (see p. 254).

104 Yosef Shalom Elyashiv, quoted in Avraham Tsevi Yisraelzon, "*Be-Inyane Yamim Noraim ve-Sukot*," *Kovets Sha'are Hora'ah* 8 (5767 [2007]): 108.

105 See the following footnote.

discussing when one is and is not obligated to forgive, we will see that the person asking for forgiveness is supposed to exhibit regret for what he has done, stop engaging in the wrongful behavior, and resolve to never engage in the behavior again.[106] R. Mordechai Gifter (1915–2001) specifically mentions these elements when he refers to the concept of appeasement. In the midst of an analysis of the requirement of asking for forgiveness for interpersonal offenses, R. Gifter writes that "included in appeasement is that one feels regret for what he had done, that he stops [the wrongful behavior] and takes it upon himself to not engage in it again."[107]

The elements of feeling remorse, stopping the wrongful behavior at present and resolving to never engage in it again in the future, and verbally acknowledging the transgression that was committed are viewed by classic Jewish halakhists and ethicists as constituting the essential components of *teshuvah*, "repentance," for sins when one seeks forgiveness from God.[108] The comparison between the asking of forgiveness from God and the asking of forgiveness from a fellow human being is a prominent theme in the halakhic sources that are examined in this chapter. As we have already seen, and will see again later,[109] there are

106 The concept of not engaging in the wrongful behavior may be viewed as encompassing two distinct aspects—to stop committing the offense at the present time and to firmly resolve to not commit the offense again in the future. When these two elements are discussed in the traditional literature, they are sometimes combined under one heading of *azivat ha-ḥet*, "abandoning of the sin" (see, for example, Gerondi, *Sha'are Teshuvah*, 1:11), and are sometimes divided into two distinct categories: (*a*) abandoning of the sin (i.e., to stop committing the sin at the present time) and (*b*) resolving to not engage in the sin in the future (see, for example, Elijah ben Solomon, *Be'ur ha-Gera: Mishle*, Proverbs 28:13). When I discuss this topic in the second half of this chapter, I only focus on (*a*), the abandoning of the sin. See below, p. 343 n. 143.

107 R. Gifter is presenting an in-depth theoretical analysis of the requirement of asking for forgiveness for interpersonal offenses. He mentions this tangentially in relation to an explanation that views the asking of forgiveness from a human being as a form of *teshuvah*, "repentance," offered to the person against whom one committed an offense. As such, appeasement would also include verbal confession of one's sins (see above, pp. 317–18, and below, p. 333). Gifter, *Hirhure Teshuvah*, 120.

108 For sources, see above, p. 318 n. 61.

109 See pp. 314 n. 50, 317–18, 344–45.

halakhic authorities who derive rules of asking forgiveness from one's friend from the rules of asking forgiveness from God.

Pertaining to our understanding of what it means to appease someone, it is noteworthy (though it is not of a prescriptive halakhic nature) that in explaining the significance of feeling remorse, stopping the wrongful behavior at present and resolving to never engage in it again, and verbally acknowledging the transgression in respect to asking forgiveness from God, R. Baḥya ibn Pakuda (eleventh century) describes a typical pattern of people asking and granting forgiveness to each other that highlights the role these elements play in appeasement:

> [W]hen the one who committed the offense shows his friend that he [sincerely] regrets committing the wrong against him, that is [one] of the strongest incentives for forgiving him ...
>
> When, together with the regret, the one who committed the offense against his friend stops engaging in the harmful act, he will then be deserving in his eyes for forgiveness and for his transgression to be pardoned ...
>
> When he humbles himself and [verbally] admits that he committed a transgression against him and that he wronged him ... he will then not delay in forgiving him, pardoning his transgression, and doing away with the resentment that he is feeling towards him in his heart ...
>
> [And] when the one who committed the offense accepts upon himself that he will not again hurt his friend, shows regret [for what he has done] and that he has stopped doing it, and admits to [the wrongdoing], these will be all of the [necessary] reasons for him to forgive [the offender], for the removal of his anger [towards him], and that he [the offender] not to be subjected to punitive measures.[110]

110 Baḥya ibn Pakuda, *Torat Ḥovot ha-Levavot, Sha'ar ha-Teshuvah*, chap. 4, pp. 311–12. In translating this passage, I have made use of Judah ibn Tibbon's and Shmuel Yerushalmi's translations. (Baḥya ibn Pakuda, *Ḥovot ha-Levavot*, trans. Judah ibn

Using Different Forms of Appeasement. In regard to the manner in which one appeases the person that one is asking forgiveness from, R. Gombiner, without going into specifics, writes that "he should appease him each time with a different type of appeasement."[111] R. Gombiner cites R. Sirkes as his source for this ruling. When one looks at what R. Sirkes wrote, one finds that R. Sirkes had cited the earlier halakhic authority R. Jacob Moellin (c. 1360–1427) as stating that when one asks for forgiveness and the other party refuses to grant forgiveness, one should try different approaches in each of his subsequent attempts—"with three types of appeasement he should appease him."[112] According to R. Sirkes, this requirement is implied in the gemara in *Yoma* (87a) when it cites the three different expressions of pleading for forgiveness used by Joseph's brothers in Genesis 50:17 (*ana* [O please], *sa na* [please forgive], and *ve-atah sa na* [now please forgive]) (see above, p. 324, the quote in the name of R. Jose bar Ḥanina).[113] According to R. da Silva, this is also implied by the three different expressions in Job 33:27 (which is cited by R. Ḥisda in the same gemara, see above, p. 323).[114] However, R. Sirkes points out that nowhere in the works of R. Isaac Alfasi, Maimonides, R. Moses ben Jacob of Coucy, or R. Asher ben Jehiel does one find any reference to such a requirement.[115] As far as the practical halakhah is concerned,

---

Tibbon [Brooklyn: n.p., 1984], *Sha'ar ha-Teshuvah*, chap. 4, p. 33a; and Baḥya ibn Pakuda, *Sefer Torat Ḥovot ha-Levavot*, trans. Shmuel Yerushalmi [Jerusalem: Me'ore Yisrael, 1972], 183–84.) For further discussion of what appeasement entails, see Hillel Cooperman, *Shuvi Nafshi*, commentary to Maimonides' *Hilkhot Teshuvah* (Jerusalem: n.p., 2010), *Hilkhot Teshuvah* 2:9, p. 46; Shimon Moshe Waldman, *Sefer Naḥalat Shimon: Al Dine Ḥodesh Elul ve-Rosh ha-Shanah, Aseret Yeme Teshuvah ve-Yom Kipur* (Monroe, NY: n.p., 2009), 284; and Daniel Palvani, *Ma'adane Daniyel*, commentary to *Shulḥan Arukh: Hilkhot Rosh ha-Shanah ve-Yom ha-Kipurim* (Jerusalem: Mosdot Hifkadeti Shomrim, 2013), *siman* 606:4.

111 Gombiner, *Magen Avraham*, 606:1.

112 See Jacob Moellin, *Sefer Maharil: Minhagim* (Jerusalem: Mekhon Yerushalayim, 1989), *Hilkhot Lel Yom Kipur*, p. 325.

113 Sirkes, *Bayit Ḥadash, Oraḥ Ḥayim* 606, s.v. *u-mah she-katav ve-tsarikh*.

114 Da Silva, *Peri Ḥadash, Oraḥ Ḥayim* 606:1, s.v. *u-mah she-katav pa'am*. R. Elijah ben Solomon cites both the verse from Genesis and the verse from Job as sources; Elijah ben Solomon, *[Be'ure] Ha-Gra, Oraḥ Ḥayim* 606:2.

115 Sirkes, *Bayit Ḥadash, Oraḥ Ḥayim* 606, s.v. *u-mah she-katav ve-tsarikh*.

numerous *aḥaronim* require one to use a different approach each time one asks for forgiveness.[116]

The Obligations of the One Who Forgives

This section will explore four subtopics: (1) the primary talmudic and midrashic sources for the obligation to forgive someone, (2) how readily must one grant forgiveness, (3) when one is and is not obligated to forgive, and (4) how sincere must one's forgiveness be. Within these subtopics, I will attempt to elucidate what I believe are some of the most fundamental concepts and practical aspects of the halakhic discourse on the granting of forgiveness.

The Primary Sources for the Obligation to Forgive Someone

There are various talmudic and midrashic passages that are cited by later authorities as sources for the obligation[117] to forgive someone

116 For example, Shneur Zalman of Lyady, *Shulḥan Arukh, Hilkhot Yom ha-Kipurim* 606:2; Abraham Danzig, *Ḥaye Adam* (Jerusalem: Mekhon Me'orot Da'at, 1988), 144:5; Margolioth, *Mateh Efrayim*, 606:1; Epstein, *Arukh ha-Shulḥan, Oraḥ Ḥayim* 606:3; and Ha-Kohen, *Mishnah Berurah*, 606:3.

117 A simple reading of the *poskim* indicates that one is *obligated* to grant forgiveness. Maimonides and R. Karo write that a "person is *forbidden* to be cruel and to withhold forgiveness" (Maimonides, *Mishneh Torah, Hilkhot Ḥovel u-Mazik* 5:10; Karo, *Shulḥan Arukh, Ḥoshen Mishpat* 422:1). Maimonides also writes that "If he responds and asks that he should be forgiven, it is *necessary* to forgive [him]; and the forgiver should not be cruel ... (*Hilkhot De'ot* 6:6). See Kohen, *Sefer ha-Teshuvah*, vol. 1, 217–18 nn. 107, 110 (in which he also addresses the view of R. Menaḥem Meiri, who seems to indicate that forgiveness is not an obligation); Eliezer Ginsburg, *Sefer ve-Atah be-Raḥamekha ha-Rabim: Al Hilkhot Teshuvah leha-Rambam* (Brooklyn: n.p., 1992), 73–74 (where he proposes that forgiveness is not considered an obligation according to the Jer. Tal. *Bava Kamma* 8:7); and Joseph Engel, *Gilyone ha-Shas* (New York: n.p., 1949), *Yoma* 87b, s.v. *tsarikh le-fayeso*. See also Jacob Joshua Falk, *Pene Yehoshua* (Jerusalem: Or ha-Ḥokhmah, 1998), *Bava Kamma* 92a, s.v. *Mishnah*; and Israel Lipschutz, *Tiferet Yisrael*, in *Mishnayot Zekher Ḥanokh* (Jerusalem: Ḥ. Vagshal, 1999), *Bava Kamma*, chap. 8, *Yakhin* 46; cf. Shlomo Aviner, "*Ha-Zekhut li-Teguvah Alimah ve-Ḥovat Hitpayesut,*" *Noam* 25 (5743–5744 [1983–1984]): 207–8, 214; and Zvi H. Weinberger and Baruch A. Heifetz, *Sefer Limud le-Hilkhot ben Adam la-Ḥavero: Lo Tikom ve-Lo Titor* (Safed, Israel: Makhon Torat ha-Adam le-Adam, 2003), 212. According to R. Solomon Kluger (1785–1869), since the Talmud in *Bava Kamma* (92a) derives the obligation to grant forgiveness from the verse in Genesis (20:17),

who asks for forgiveness. The following are some of the most commonly cited passages:

> From where do we know that if he [someone who was harmed by another] does not forgive him [the person who caused the harm and is now coming to ask for forgiveness] that he is [considered] cruel?[118] [We know this] as it states [in the biblical episode of Abraham and Abimelech (Gen. 20:17)]: "And Abraham prayed to God, and God healed Abimelech" (Mishnah, *Bava Kamma* 92a).[119]
>
> From where do we know that if a person commits an offense against his friend and that person [apologizes to him and] says, "I have sinned," that one is called a sinner if he does not forgive him? From that which it states [in Samuel's farewell address to the nation] (1 Samuel 12:23): "As for me, God forbid that I should sin against the Lord by ceasing to pray for you" (Midrash, *Tanḥuma, Hukat* 19).[120]
>
> [The people came to Moses and said, "We have sinned, for we have spoken against the Lord and against you. Pray to the Lord

this obligation should be viewed as being *min ha-Torah* (biblical). Solomon Kluger, *Sefer ha-Ḥayim* (New York: Avraham Yitsḥak Friedman, 1968), *siman* 606, p. 69a.

118 For alternative versions of this mishnah, see *Sefer ha-Mafteaḥ le-Masekhet Bava Kama, Sefer Shinuye Nusḥa'ot* (Bnei Brak: Yeshivat Ohel Yosef, 1996), 92a, p. 641; and *Shinuye Nusḥa'ot*, in the standard *"Yakhin u-Voaz" Mishnayot, Bava Kamma* 8:7.

119 Cited by Karo, *Kesef Mishneh, Hilkhot Teshuvah* 2:9, as one source for Maimonides' ruling that it is forbidden to be cruel and not be appeased. It is also cited by R. Elijah ben Solomon as one of the sources for R. Moses Isserles's ruling about the granting of forgiveness. Elijah ben Solomon, *[Be'ure] Ha-Gra, Oraḥ Ḥayim* 606:1. For explanations of why the Rabbis characterize someone who does not grant forgiveness as being cruel, see Meiri, *Bet ha-Beḥirah, Bava Kamma* chap. 8 mishnah 4, p. 268; and Jacob Reischer, *Iyun Ya'akov*, in Jacob ibn Ḥabib, *En Ya'akov* (New York: Sifre Kodesh, 1971), *Bava Kamma* 92a.

120 This midrash is cited by R. Menaḥem Krakowski (1869–1929) as the source for Maimonides' ruling that one is considered a sinner if he does not grant forgiveness. Menaḥem Krakovski, *Avodat ha-Melekh* (Jerusalem: Mossad Harav Kook, 1971), *Hilkhot Teshuvah* 2:9. For an explanation of how the verse in 1 Samuel is relevant to forgiving someone for an interpersonal offense, see the commentary of Jehiel Hillel Altschuler, *Metsudat David, Metsudat Tsiyon*, in the standard *Mikra'ot Gedolot*, 1 Samuel 12:23.

that He may remove the snakes from us." And Moses prayed on behalf of the people" (Numbers 21:7).] Upon them having said "we have sinned," he [Moses] was immediately appeased [and forgave them]. This comes to teach you that one who forgives is not considered [literally, does not become] cruel (Midrash, *Tanḥuma* [Buber], *Hukat* 46).[121]

How could R. Ḥanina [bar Ḥama] (third century CE) have done this [i.e., not to forgive the *amora* Rav, who had offended him and subsequently asked him for forgiveness]? Surely, Rava (d. 352 CE) has stated that "Anyone who shows forbearance, they [the heavenly tribunal] will overlook all of his sins" ... (*Yoma* 87b).[122]

The obligation to forgive someone is mentioned in R. Jacob ben Asher's *Arba'ah Turim* and in R. Karo's *Shulḥan Arukh*.[123] Both of these codes basically paraphrase the earlier ruling of Maimonides (see below, p. 339). Maimonides discusses the obligation to forgive someone in three places in the *Mishneh Torah*.[124] His lengthiest presentation of the topic is in *Hilkhot Teshuvah* (Laws of Repentance):

It is forbidden for a person to be cruel and not to be appeased. Rather, one should be readily pacified and come

---

121 This source is the basis for Rashi's commentary to Numbers 21:7, in which he writes "From here [the episode with Moses] we learn that he who is asked to forgive should not be cruel and refuse to forgive." There are slight variations between the version of this midrash as it appears in the Buber edition of the *Tanḥuma* and those of other sources that cite it. See Solomon Buber, annot., *Midrash Tanḥuma* (n.p., n.d.), *Hukat* 46 n. 339.

122 Cited by Karo, *Kesef Mishneh*, *Hilkhot Teshuvah* 2:9, as another source for Maimonides' ruling in *Hilkhot Teshuvah* regarding granting forgiveness; and by R. Elijah ben Solomon as another source for R. Isserles's ruling; Elijah ben Solomon, *[Be'ure] Ha-Gra*, *Oraḥ Ḥayim* 606:1.

123 Jacob ben Asher, *Arba'ah Turim*, *Ḥoshen Mishpat* 422; Karo, *Shulḥan Arukh*, *Ḥoshen Mishpat* 422:1. The obligation to forgive someone is also mentioned in R. Isserles's glosses to the *Shulḥan Arukh*; Isserles, *Shulḥan Arukh*, *Oraḥ Ḥayim* 606:1.

124 Maimonides, *Mishneh Torah*, *Hilkhot De'ot* 6:6, *Hilkhot Teshuvah* 2:10, *Hilkhot Ḥovel u-Mazik* 5:10.

> to anger with difficulty. At the time when one who had committed a sin [against him] asks him for forgiveness, one should forgive him with a whole heart and with a desirous soul. And even if he caused him pain and sinned against him to a great extent, he should not take revenge nor bear a grudge. This is the [characteristic] path of the offspring of Israel and their proper heart, but the Gentiles [who are] uncircumcised of heart[125] are not so, rather their "fury is maintained forever."[126] And so it states in reference to the Gibeonites, since they were unforgiving and would not be appeased: "The Gibeonites were not of the children of Israel" (2 Samuel 21:2).[127]

In this presentation of the obligation to forgive, Maimonides alludes to the mishnah in *Bava Kamma*, which was cited earlier (see p. 336), and also paraphrases two other early rabbinic sources. When he writes that "one should be readily pacified and come to anger with difficulty," he is paraphrasing the mishnah in *Pirke Avot* (5:11), "He who comes to anger with difficulty and is readily pacified is a pious person." When he writes that "this is the [characteristic] path of the offspring of Israel . . . ," Maimonides is basically summarizing a gemara in *Yevamot* (79a), which discusses the biblical episode of the Gibeonites (see 2 Samuel 21) and contrasts their being obdurate and unforgiving to what it identifies as being three

125 See Ezekiel 44:7, 9; Jeremiah 9:25; and Leviticus 26:41.

126 See Amos 1:11.

127 Maimonides, *Mishneh Torah, Hilkhot Teshuvah* 2:10. It is noteworthy that there is a clear correlation between this subsection in the *Mishneh Torah* and the *Midrash ha-Gadol* (a midrashic anthology ascribed to the thirteenth-century scholar R. David ben Amram Adani), Gen. 20:17. In addition to mentioning the concepts of being readily pacified, coming to anger with difficulty, forgiving someone with a whole heart and with a desirous soul, and not taking revenge nor bearing a grudge, which are all mentioned by Maimonides in this subsection, the *Midrash ha-Gadol* also quotes the talmudic saying "A person should always be as flexible as a reed and not as hard as a cedar" (*Ta'anit* 20a–b), and states that all of these concepts were derived from the biblical episode with Abraham and Abimelech. *Midrash ha-Gadol* (Jerusalem: Mossad Harav Kook, 1947), Gen. 20:17, p. 332.

characteristic traits of the Jewish people (which if the Gibeonites would have possessed, they would have felt compelled to grant forgiveness).[128] The three traits that the gemara mentions are the propensity to be compassionate,[129] shamefaced,[130] and perform acts of loving-kindness.[131]

How Readily Must One Grant Forgiveness?

The alacrity with which one is supposed to grant forgiveness is discussed in the halakhic codes in the sections that deal with someone who physically harms another person. As mentioned above (p. 337), R. Jacob ben Asher and R. Joseph Karo[132] basically paraphrase Maimonides' formulation of this law, specifically, what he had written in *Hilkhot*

---

128 This last point, which I put in parenthesis, is only implied in the talmudic passage. However, it is explicitly articulated by the version of this teaching that appears in *Numbers Rabbah, Be-Midbar* 8:4.

129 According to R. Joshua Falk, it is specifically the Gibeonites' cruelty (i.e., their unwillingness to forgive) that is being contrasted with the Israelites' compassion. Joshua ben Alexander Falk, *Sefer Me'irat Enayim* (*Sma*), in the standard editions of the *Shulḥan Arukh, Ḥoshen Mishpat* 422:4. This also seems to be Rashi's interpretation of the talmudic passage. Rashi, *Yevamot* 79a, s.v. *ha-raḥamanim*.

130 That means to say, they have a propensity to feel shame. In Hebrew, *"baishanim."* R. Samuel Jaffe Ashkenazi writes that the Gibeonites exhibited a complete lack of this trait in their refusing to be appeased. Samuel Jaffe Ashkenazi, *Yefeh To'ar*, commentary to the *Midrash Rabbah*, in the standard Vilna edition of the *Midrash Rabbah, Numbers Rabbah, Be-Midbar* 8:4, s.v. *ve-elu en*.

131 A connection between the propensity to perform acts of loving-kindness and the willingness to grant forgiveness may be found in a midrashic passage that is cited by R. Ḥayim Kanievsky. R. Kanievsky points out the correlation between the subsection in Maimonides' *Hilkhot Teshuvah* that discusses the obligation to grant forgiveness and the seventh chapter in the *Midrash le-Olam*, which reads as follows: *"A person should always perform an act of loving kindness even with someone who has done him wrong*; and he should not take revenge nor bear a grudge, as it states, 'You shall not take revenge and you shall not bear a grudge' (Lev. 19:18). And this is the way of the holy children of Israel, but the cruel Cuthites, the uncircumcised of heart, take revenge and bear a grudge. And so it is stated regarding the Gibeonites ..." (*Midrash le-Olam*, in Adolph Jellinek, ed., *Bet ha-Midrash*, vol. 3 [Jerusalem: Wahrmann Books, 1967], chap. 7, p. 113). Shemaryahu Yosef Ḥayim Kanevski, *Sefer Kiryat Melekh*, 3rd ed. (Bnei Brak: n.p., 1983), *Hilkhot Teshuvah* 2:10.

132 Jacob ben Asher, *Arba'ah Turim, Ḥoshen Mishpat* 422; Karo, *Shulḥan Arukh, Ḥoshen Mishpat* 422.

Ḥovel u-Mazik (Laws of One Who Inflicts Physical Harm and Damages). In *Ḥovel u-Mazik*, Maimonides states as follows:

> It is forbidden for the injured person to be cruel and withhold forgiveness. This is not the path of the offspring of Israel. Rather, once the person who caused the injury asks of him and entreats him a first and second time [alternatively, a first *or* second time] and he knows that he [the person who committed the offense] has repented from his sin and regrets his iniquity, he should forgive him. And whoever forgives quickly is surely praiseworthy, and the spirit of the Sages is pleased with him.[133]

In his commentary to the *Shulḥan Arukh*, R. Joshua Falk (c. 1555–1614) indicates that when it states in this passage[134] that one should forgive someone who asks to be forgiven "a first *and* second time," in Hebrew, *"pa'am rishonah u-sheniyah,"* the conjunction *u* ("ו"), which generally is translated as "and," should in this context be translated as "or";[135] that means to say that one should grant forgiveness when asked the first time or, at the very least, by the second time. R. Falk points out that, even though when it comes to the obligation of the one who asks for forgiveness the earlier *poskim* require that three attempts be made at appeasing the person, in reference to the obligation of the one who grants forgiveness they teach that one should be compassionate and not wait until the third attempt, but rather should grant forgiveness by the second attempt.[136]

R. Sirkes has a totally different interpretation of this halakhah. He is of the opinion that normally one should grant forgiveness the first time that one is asked. According to R. Sirkes, when the earlier *poskim* mention that one may delay the granting of forgiveness until the second attempt, they are only referring to a case in which one is

---

133 Maimonides, *Mishneh Torah, Hilkhot Ḥovel u-Mazik* 5:10.

134 R. Falk's comments were said in reference to R. Karo's paraphrase of the passage.

135 When the conjunction "ו" (*vav*) means "and," it is referred to as a "copulative *vav*"; when it means "or," it is referred to as a "disjunctive *vav*."

136 Falk, *Sma, Ḥoshen Mishpat* 422:5.

a teacher of Torah whose student has committed an interpersonal offense against him, and the student is now coming to ask for forgiveness.[137] In such a case, it would be permissible to delay the forgiveness until the second time that one is asked; otherwise, one should grant forgiveness the first time that he is asked.[138]

This question of how readily one grants forgiveness is intertwined with the questions of how sincere one's forgiveness must be and what is one supposed to do if he or she simply cannot find it in his or her heart to forgive the other person. The latter two questions, and the debates surrounding them, will be addressed in the section below entitled "How Sincere Must One's Forgiveness Be?"

When One Is and Is Not Obligated to Forgive

The General Rule. Based on the ruling of Maimonides in *Hilkhot Teshuvah* (2:10) that requires one to grant forgiveness and states that "even if he caused him pain and sinned against him to a great extent, he should not take revenge nor bear a grudge" (see p. 338 above), it would appear that, as a general rule, one is obligated to grant forgiveness regardless of the severity of the offense committed. This certainly seems to be the view that is expressed by R. Ezekiel Sarna (1890–1969):

> Anyone who is a descendent of Israel, even if he is not a *tsadik* [a righteous person] or a *ḥasid* [a pious person] his path [in life] must be one of forgiveness, and he is forbidden from doing otherwise, and should he do otherwise he is [considered] cruel. This is applicable [as Maimonides has written] "even if he caused him pain and sinned against

137 The Rabbis viewed the committing of an interpersonal offense against one's teacher of Torah as a particularly grievous sin. See Sirkes, *Bayit Ḥadash, Ḥoshen Mishpat* 422, s.v. *u-mah she katav ela kevan*, and *Oraḥ Ḥayim* 606, s.v. *u-mah she-katav ve-hane mile*.

138 Sirkes, *Bayit Ḥadash, Ḥoshen Mishpat* 422, s.v. *u-mah she katav ela kevan*. For difficulties that have been raised with R. Sirkes's explanation, see Masud Raccah, *Ma'aseh Rokeaḥ*, vol. 4 (Bnei Brak: Shmuel Akiva Yafeh Shlesinger, 1964), *Hilkhot Ḥovel u-Mazik* 5:10, p. 129; and Menaḥem Mendel Horowitz, *Shoshanat Ya'akov* (Zolkiew: Shmuel Pinḥas Shtiller, 1863), *siman* 422, p. 92a.

> him to a great extent"; he should not only not take revenge, but he should also not bear a grudge in his heart; and he should be fully appeased when the one who sinned against him appeases him.[139]

Related to this general rule, the *Ḥafets Ḥayim* writes in reference to someone who commits deliberate and defiant acts against another that "one is required to forgive his friend [who beseeches forgiveness] even if he has acted corruptly towards him in a deliberate and defiant manner."[140]

---

139 Ezekiel Sarna, *Bet Yeḥezkel: Ḥidushim u-Ve'urim be-Inyanim Shonim ba-Shas ve-Gilyonot ha-Rambam* (Jerusalem: Mosad Haskel, 1995), *Gilyonot ha-Rambam, Hilkhot Teshuvah* 2:10, p. 256. One may question R. Sarna's reading of Maimonides in *Hilkhot Teshuvah*. R. Sarna combines and equates what Maimonides wrote about not taking revenge and not bearing a grudge with what Maimonides had written regarding forgiving the other person (see the exact quote from *Hilkhot Teshuvah* above, on p. 338, and compare it with R. Sarna's paraphrase of it). One may argue that there could very well be a difference between not taking revenge and not bearing a grudge, and granting forgiveness to someone. However, one may also put up a strong argument that there is not a significant difference between them, particularly when it comes to not bearing a grudge and granting forgiveness (see Maimonides, *Mishneh Torah, De'ot* 7:8, and Maimonides, *Sefer ha-Mitsvot*, negative commandment 305, in which he defines not bearing a grudge as "eliminating" the offense that was committed against him from his heart and not "remembering" it at all). Germane to this question, there is what appears to be a halakhic debate regarding the relationship between not bearing a grudge and granting forgiveness. For relevant sources, see Weinberger and Heifetz, *Lo Tikom ve-Lo Titor*, 211–16; Zilber, *Derekh Teshuvah*, 242–43; and Cooperman, *Shuvi Nafshi, Hilkhot Teshuvah* 2:10, pp. 95–96. See also R. Aaron of Lunel (thirteenth to fourteenth centuries), who, similar to R. Sarna, paraphrases the passage from *Hilkhot Teshuvah* (2:10) and evidently equates not taking revenge and not bearing a grudge with the granting of forgiveness (i.e., in R. Aaron of Lunel's formulation, what Maimonides had written coalesces into the following: "[one] should forgive him with a whole heart even if he caused him pain to a great extent and sinned against him to a great extent" [Aaron ben Jacob ha-Kohen of Lunel, *Orḥot Ḥayim, Din Erev Yom ha-Kipurim* 10, p. 230]); cf. the quote from *Hilkhot Teshuvah* cited above, p. 338.

140 Ha-Kohen, *Mishnah Berurah, siman* 606, *Sha'ar ha-Tsiyun* 8. The *Ḥafets Ḥayim* adds that if one will forgive his friend who has acted corruptly towards him in a deliberate and defiant manner, then Heaven will certainly forgive one for sins that he committed against God in such a manner. Ibid. (based on *Rosh ha-Shanah* 17a, *Megillah* 28a).

Exceptions to the General Rule—If the Person Continues to Commit the Offense or Shows No Remorse. Halakhic authorities cite a number of important exceptions to the general rule that requires one to grant forgiveness. Probably the two most common exceptions that are of major import are (*a*) if the person who is asking for forgiveness does not regret what he has done or (*b*) if he does not stop[141] the objectionable activity. These two prerequisites are implicitly expressed in Maimonides' formulation cited earlier (p. 340) from *Hilkhot Ḥovel u-Mazik* (5:10):

> [O]nce the person who caused the injury asks of him and entreats him a first and second time and he knows that he [the person who committed the offense] *has repented from his sin and regrets his iniquity*, he should forgive him."[142]

The implication is that if one realizes that the other person has not "repented from his sin" (which apparently means that the other party is continuing to engage in the wrongful behavior; see footnote)[143] or he does not exhibit any remorse,[144] one is not halakhically obligated to

141 See p. 332 n. 106.

142 This ruling also appears in Jacob ben Asher, *Arba'ah Turim, Ḥoshen Mishpat* 422, and Karo, *Shulḥan Arukh, Ḥoshen Mishpat* 422:1.

143 It is difficult to know with certainty the exact intent of the *poskim* (see sources cited in the previous footnote) when they write that the person "has repented from his sin" in this context (which I have explained simply as saying that the person no longer engages in the wrongful behavior); that is, as far as what exactly constitutes "repenting," or the extent of the repentance that is necessary, in this context. (Elsewhere in the *Mishneh Torah*, Maimonides defines what it means to "repent" from a sin: "What is repentance? It is when the sinner abandons his sin, removes it from his thoughts, and resolves in his heart never to do it again . . . ." Maimonides then goes on to state that repentance also requires regret and verbal confession. [Maimonides, *Mishneh Torah, Hilkhot Teshuvah* 2:2]. [*See below, the view of R. Hutner,* p. 345 n. 149.] In reference to cases in which someone repents and stops engaging in a sin but then subsequently backslides into committing the sin again, see Sa'adia ben Joseph, *Ha-Nivhar ba-Emunot uva-De'ot* [New York: Sura, 1970], 5:5, pp. 182–84; and the sources cited in Y[israel] M[enaḥem] Aviad, *Ḥaninat Yisrael: Be-Khamah Inyanim al Seder Moed* [Bnei Brak: n.p., 2014], 374–75; as well as in other sources.)

144 Regarding not exhibiting remorse, see Tsevi Hirsch Sheinberger, "*Perut ha-Ḥet be-Vakashat Meḥilah,*" *Kovets Bet Aharon ve-Yisrael* 18, no. 1 (103) (Tishre-Ḥeshvan

forgive him. It is in reference to this halakhah, as it is cited in the *Shulḥan Arukh*,[145] that R. Mordechai Lichtstein (b. 1865) and R. Yosef Shalom Elyashiv state that if the party who is being asked to forgive knows that the other person is insincere—that "he is only outwardly asking for forgiveness, but this does not reflect what he is actually feeling"—one is not required to forgive him.[146]

Without citing the ruling of Maimonides in *Hilkhot Ḥovel u-Mazik* or its formulation in the *Shulḥan Arukh*, R. Ḥayyim David Halevi asserts that there is no obligation to forgive someone who continues to engage in the wrongful behavior. The rationale that he offers for this is that it is inconceivable for someone to "appease" the person he committed a transgression against unless that someone assures the other party that he will no longer engage in the objectionable activity in the future.[147]

An alternative explanation is offered by R. Jekutiel Halberstam (the Klausenberger Rebbe, 1905–1994). R. Halberstam (who, similar to R. Halevi, does not mention the ruling in *Hilkhot Ḥovel u-Mazik* nor its formulation in the *Shulḥan Arukh*) suggests that the process of asking for forgiveness from one's friend may work similarly to that of asking for forgiveness from God. Therefore, it follows that just as when one repents from a sin and asks God for forgiveness the Halakhah requires that there must be *azivat ha-ḥet*, "abandoning of the sin," and *ḥaratah*, "remorse," so too when asking for forgiveness from a fellow human being for an interpersonal

---

5763 [2002]): 86; Zilber, *Derekh Teshuvah*, 243; and Ya'akov Goldberg, *Devir Kodsho: Mo'adim*, vol. 1 (Jerusalem: n.p., 2008), 116, 119.

145 Karo, *Shulḥan Arukh*, *Ḥoshen Mishpat* 422:1.

146 Mordechai Lichtstein, *Mitsvot ha-Levavot* (Brisk, Lithuania: Avraham Hendler, 1924), *Hilkhot Nekimah u-Netirah*, *sa'if* 31, *Derekh Mitsvotekha* 40, p. 35; and Yosef Shalom Elyashiv, cited in Yosef Yisraelzon, *Kuntres Kitsur Hilkhot ben Adam la-Ḥavero* (Reḥovot: Kolel Avrekhim Reḥovot, 1998), p. 17, *sa'if* 53, n. 63 (R. Yisraelzon uses almost the exact same terminology that appears in R. Lichtstein's work). Similar rulings appear in a number of contemporary works; see, for example, Meir Ḥadash, cited in Cooperman, *Shuvi Nafshi*, *Hilkhot Teshuvah* 2:10, p. 57; David Ari'av, *Le-Re'akha kamokha*, vol. 7 (Jerusalem: Mekhon Le-Re'akha kamokha, 2010), 322; and Yitsḥak Isaac Silver, *Mishpete ha-Shalom: Hilkhot ben Adam la-Ḥavero* (Jerusalem: n.p., 2005), 3:28, pp. 49–50.

147 Halevi, *Aseh lekha Rav*, vol. 6, responsum 42, p. 141.

offense, one must refrain from committing the offense and show remorse for what he has done.[148]

Working along the same lines, of equating the asking of forgiveness from a human being with the asking of forgiveness from God, R. Hutner (who does mention and highlights the ruling in *Hilkhot Ḥovel u-Mazik,* see footnote)[149] points out that just as in regard to the asking of forgiveness from God, the mishnah in *Yoma* (8:9) teaches that "One who says, 'I will sin and repent, I will sin and repent,' he will not be given the opportunity to repent [or if he says] 'I will sin and Yom Kippur will bring atonement,' Yom Kippur will not bring atonement," so too, in an analogous manner, we find a halakhah[150] that states that if someone intends to commit an interpersonal offense against another human being based on the expectation that that person will ultimately forgive him, that person is not required to forgive him.[151]

---

148 R. Halberstam writes this in the context of offering a possible explanation for the wording of Maimonides in *Hilkhot Teshuvah* 2:9. He introduces this explanation only as a possibility (with the words *"ve-ulai efshar hayah lomar,"* "and perhaps it is possible to say"). Jekutiel Jehuda Halberstam, *Sefer Shefa Ḥayim: Mikhteve Torah* (Kiryat Sanz: Igud Ḥaside Tsanz, 1988), *mikhtav* 55, p. 193; cf. the very slight difference in wording in Halberstam, *Divre Yatsiv*, vol. 2, *Oraḥ Ḥayim, siman* 258, p. 521. R. Halberstam's responsum is cited in Shmerler, *Mo'ade Ḥayim*, 207–8, 210. R. Shmerler, apparently, understood R. Halberstam's opinion as I have explained it.

149 According to R. Hutner, the ruling in *Hilkhot Ḥovel u-Mazik* indicates that "a person is not obligated to forgive someone who committed a sin against him unless he is aware that the offender has gone through the [entire] process of *teshuvah* [repentance] in accordance with all of its laws." Hutner, *Paḥad Yitsḥak*, 254–55. After highlighting the ruling in *Ḥovel u-Mazik* and equating the asking of forgiveness from a human being with the asking of forgiveness from God, R. Hutner goes on to propose that, in a certain respect, the requirement to forgive a human being actually requires more from the individual than what a strict comparison to asking forgiveness from God would dictate; see ibid., 255–59.

150 The source for this halakhah is the *"Tefillah Zakkah"* prayer composed by R. Abraham Danzig (1748–1820); Danzig, *Ḥaye Adam*, the end of *kelal* 144, p. 877. At one point in the prayer, one says that he forgives all transgressions that were committed against him except for money that he can rightfully recover in a court of law and cases in which a person said "I will sin against him and he will forgive me" (see *The Complete Artscroll Machzor: Yom Kippur: Nusach Ashkenaz* [Brooklyn: Mesorah Publications, 1986], 41). See also Elyashiv, *Kitsur Hilkhot ben Adam la-Ḥavero*, p. 17, *sa'if* 53; and Ḥayim Pinḥas Scheinberg, *Netivot Ḥayim* (Jerusalem: n.p., 2001), 43. Cf. Shternbukh, *Mo'adim u-Zemanim ha-Shalem*, vol. 8, p. 20.

151 Hutner, *Paḥad Yitsḥak*, 60. See also Lichtstein, *Mitsvot ha-Levavot, Hilkhot Nekimah u-Netirah, sa'if* 31, *Derekh Mitsvotekha* 40, p. 35; and Silver, *Mishpete ha-Shalom*,

Not Forgiving the Person for One's Benefit. In his glosses to the *Shulḥan Arukh*, R. Moses Isserles (c. 1525–1572) rules that one should forgive a person "unless he intends [to withhold forgiveness] for the benefit of the person who is asking for forgiveness."[152] According to the *Ḥafets Ḥayim*, this would mean that it would be permissible not to grant forgiveness if one wishes to "humble the person's uncircumcised heart [so that] he will not become accustomed to doing so";[153] in other words, one may withhold forgiveness to deter the other person from repeating the offense in the future.

Among later halakhic authorities, there is considerable discussion regarding the import of R. Isserles's ruling.[154] R. Elijah Shapira (1660–1712) presents two basic approaches to this ruling—either R. Isserles means to say that (*a*) one can withhold forgiveness *only* if it is for the benefit of the person who asks for forgiveness but *not* for the personal benefit of oneself (i.e., the one who is being asked to forgive), or (*b*) one can withhold forgiveness *even* if it is for the benefit of the person who asks for forgiveness and *certainly* if it is for the personal benefit of oneself.[155] According to R. Shapira, R. Joel Sirkes had understood R. Isserles as saying that one can withhold forgiveness *only* if it is for the benefit of the person who asks for forgiveness, whereas R. Shapira understands R. Isserles as saying that one can withhold forgiveness *even* if it is for the benefit of the person

---

3:28, p. 50, n. 39. See Kohen, *Sefer ha-Teshuvah*, vol. 1, pp. 31, 148, 349–50, who further develops this theme of comparing the asking of forgiveness from a human being to the asking of forgiveness from God.

152 Isserles, *Shulḥan Arukh*, *Oraḥ Ḥayim* 606:1. This is evidently based on the passage in *Yoma* with R. Ḥanina bar Ḥama and Rav (*Yoma* 87b).

153 Ha-Kohen, *Mishnah Berurah*, 606:9. The *Ḥafets Ḥayim* is quoting (and explaining) the words of Ha-Levi, *Ture Zahav*, *Oraḥ Ḥayim* 606:2.

154 See, for example, Sirkes, *Bayit Ḥadash*, *Oraḥ Ḥayim* 606, s.v. *u-mah she-katav ve-hane mile*; Ha-Levi, *Ture Zahav*, *Oraḥ Ḥayim* 606:2; Mordekhai Karmi, *Ma'amar Mordekhai al Shulḥan Arukh Oraḥ Ḥayim*, vol. 4 (Jerusalem: Oz ve-Hadar, 1995), 606:2; Baruch ha-Levi Epstein, *Torah Temimah* (New York: Hebrew Publishing Co., 1928), Gen. 20:17; and Reuben Margulies, *Nefesh Ḥayah* (Lvov: Krenenberg u-Felhendler, 1932), *siman* 606:1.

155 According to R. Shapira, this *a fortiori* is based on the halakhah of *ḥayekha kodmim*, "your life comes before the life of your friend" (see *Bava Metsia* 62a). For an alternative source for deriving this *a fortiori*, see Kluger, *Sefer ha-Ḥayim*, *siman* 606, p. 69a.

who asks for forgiveness.[156] The *Ḥafets Ḥayim* cites R. David ha-Levi (1586–1667), R. Abraham Abele Gombiner, and other *aḥaronim* as permitting one to withhold forgiveness whether it is for the benefit of the person who asks for forgiveness or for one's own personal benefit.[157]

As to the types of cases covered under the ruling that permits one to withhold forgiveness for one's own personal benefit, the *Ḥafets Ḥayim* explains this halakhah as referring to a case in which one "is afraid that he may suffer [some type of] harm if he would grant forgiveness."[158] R. Sirkes and R. Hezekiah da Silva extend the application of this halakhah considerably further than this. According to R. Sirkes, the talmudic passage in *Yoma* (87b), which serves as the source for the ruling, implies that as long as one has some valid reason for withholding forgiveness and is not doing so out of cruelty, one would be permitted to do so.[159] Similarly, R. da Silva contends that R. Isserles himself implies that as long as one is not motivated by cruelty but has some valid reason for withholding forgiveness, not forgiving the other party would be permissible.[160]

As far as practical Halakhah is concerned, some *aḥaronim* placed limitations on R. Isserles's permissive ruling. Regarding not granting forgiveness for the benefit of the person who is asking for forgiveness, R. Jehiel Michal Epstein (1829–1908) writes that only infrequently would one ever encounter such a case.[161] R. Samuel Kolin (1720–1806) maintains that R. Isserles was of the opinion that one may withhold forgiveness for the person's benefit only if one is absolutely certain that it will produce the intended beneficial result, but if there exists a doubt as to whether this will occur, one

156 Elijah Shapira, *Eliyah Rabah* (Jerusalem: Mekor ha-Sefarim, 1999), *Hilkhot Yom Kipur, siman* 606 *sa'if* 1:4, p. 716 (where he writes, "*Ve-gam Rama nireh de-sevira leh de-zeh kol she-ken hu, vede-lo ka-B"Ḥ*"; and see Sirkes, *Bayit Ḥadash, Oraḥ Ḥayim* 606, s.v. *u-mah she-katav ve-hane mile*).

157 Ha-Kohen, *Mishnah Berurah, siman* 606, *Sha'ar ha-Tsiyun* 10.

158 Ha-Kohen, *Mishnah Berurah*, 606:10.

159 Sirkes, *Bayit Ḥadash, Oraḥ Ḥayim* 606, s.v. *ve-da.*

160 Da Silva, *Peri Ḥadash, Oraḥ Ḥayim* 606:1, s.v. *u-mah she-katav im lo.*

161 Epstein, *Arukh ha-Shulḥan, Oraḥ Ḥayim* 606:2.

would be prohibited from doing so.[162] According to the *Ḥafets Ḥayim*, even in those cases when the halakhah would permit one to withhold forgiveness, it appears that internally it is necessary for one to do away with the hatred he is feeling for the other person, seeing that the other person has asked for forgiveness.[163] In regard to the implementation of the halakhah of withholding forgiveness for one's benefit, R. Shmuel Kamenetsky advises that out of the concern for the natural tendency to rationalize one's inappropriate behaviors, which may lead one to unjustifiably withhold forgiveness, one should consult with a qualified halakhic authority before relying on this leniency.[164]

Cases of Motsi Shem Ra. Many *poskim*[165] cite the Jerusalem Talmud that teaches that in cases of *motsi shem ra*, "defamation of character" (literally, "one who brings out an evil name"),[166] "there is never forgiveness for him" (Jer. Tal. *Bava Kamma* 36b), which is understood as teaching that a person is not obligated to forgive someone who committed *motsi shem ra* and is now coming to ask for forgiveness. R. Mordecai Jaffe (1535–1612) offers the following explanation of why a person is not obligated to forgive someone in cases of *motsi shem ra*:

> [This is] because he has impinged upon the person's dignity. He has caused that every single day people will "spill his

162 R. Kolin states that this is how R. Isserles understood the view of Rashi in *Yoma* 87b, s.v. *ḥelma*, which was the source of R. Isserles's opinion. Kolin, *Oraḥ Ḥayim* 606, *sa'if katan* 4.

163 Ha-Kohen, *Mishnah Berurah*, 606:9, *Sha'ar ha-Tsiyun* 9–10. See also R. Moses ibn Ḥabib's interpretation of the talmudic passage in *Yoma* (87b), in which R. Ḥanina withholds forgiveness from Rav. Moses ibn Ḥabib, *Sifre ha-Maharam Ḥabib* (Jerusalem: Mekhon Me'or Harim, 2000), *Sefer Tosafot Yom ha-Kipurim*, *Yoma* 87b, p. 279.

164 Kamenetsky, *Kovets Halakhot*, p. 314, n. 19.

165 For example, Mordecai ben Hillel ha-Kohen, *Mordekhai le-Masekhet Yoma*, *siman* 723; Jacob Weil, *She'elot u-Teshuvot Rabenu Ya'akov Vail*, vol. 1, annotated by Yonatan Shraga Domb (Jerusalem: Mekhon Yerushalayim, 2001), *siman* 191–92, pp. 248, 260; Karo, *Bet Yosef*, *Ḥoshen Mishpat* 420:33; and Isserles, *Shulḥan Arukh*, *Oraḥ Ḥayim* 606:1.

166 For halakhic sources on the topic of *motsi shem ra*, see the commentaries to *Shulḥan Arukh*, *Ḥoshen Mishpat* 420:38.

> blood" [embarrass him][167] when he hears degrading things said about him by others ... [therefore] if he does not want to forgive the [other] person, there is no prohibition in this, and he may bear animosity towards him because of this, for so it is taught in the Jerusalem Talmud. R. Israel Isserlein [1390–1460], of blessed memory, has written that "there is an exceptionally good reason for this, for it is possible that someone has heard the evil rumor about him but has not heard about the person's act of appeasement [and recanting],[168] and therefore he will continue to be suspected of the defamatory thing of which he was accused."[169] Consequently, how can he forgive him ... for how is it possible to forgive him today[170] and tomorrow somebody will come and remind him about the defamatory thing that that person had said about him and he will then be embarrassed[171] [all over again]. How can he not help but recall it and bear enmity regarding this ...[172]

In other words, according to R. Jaffe, due to the severe, constantly recurring, and ineradicable pain of damaging the person's reputation, the Halakhah cannot mandate forgiveness for such an offense.

Even though this ruling seems to have been accepted as the normative halakhah by the *poskim*, a number of them[173] cite the view of R. Solomon Luria (c. 1510–1573), who encourages one to

167 Literally, "spill his blood, since the red will depart and the white will come." The comparison between embarrassing someone and "spilling blood" is based on *Bava Kamma* 58b.

168 See Falk, *Sma, Ḥoshen Mishpat* 422:6.

169 Israel Isserlein, *Sefer Terumat ha-Deshen* (Jerusalem: Shmuel Abitan, 1991), *pesakim u-khetavim* 212, p. 414.

170 Literally, "now."

171 Literally, "and his face will turn pale until the red is gone and the white has come."

172 Mordecai Jaffe, *Sefer Levush ha-Ḥur* (n.p., 2000), *Hilkhot Yom Kipur, siman* 606, p. 569. For an alternative explanation of this halakhah, see Sirkes, *Bayit Ḥadash, Oraḥ Ḥayim* 606, s.v. *katav ha-Semag*.

173 For example, Gombiner, *Magen Avraham, Oraḥ Ḥayim* 606:5; Shneur Zalman of Lyady, *Shulḥan Arukh, Hilkhot Yom ha-Kipurim* 606:4; and Ha-Kohen, *Mishnah Berurah, Oraḥ Ḥayim* 606:11.

overcome one's natural inclination and to forgive even *motsi shem ra*, inasmuch as this would be a sign of humility and piety.[174] R. Jehiel Michal Epstein goes even further than this and maintains that if a person has done everything he can do to publicize that his defamatory remarks were false, one would then be obligated to forgive the person.[175]

How Sincere Must One's Forgiveness Be?

A good starting point in exploring the different opinions regarding the question of the sincerity of one's forgiveness would be to once again look at what Maimonides had written in *Hilkhot Teshuvah* that relates to this topic:

> At the time when one who had committed a sin [against him] asks him for forgiveness, one should forgive him with a *whole heart* and with *a desirous soul*.[176] And even if he caused him pain and sinned against him to a great extent, he should not take revenge nor bear a grudge.[177]

It would appear that according to Maimonides, one's forgiveness should be completely sincere and heartfelt. We shall see that there are later authorities who were of the view that one's forgiveness is supposed to be sincere and heartfelt, and we shall also see

174 Solomon Luria, *Sefer Yam shel Shelomoh* (Jerusalem: Mishnat David, 1995), *Bava Kamma*, chap. 8 *siman* 63, p. 260.

175 Epstein, *Arukh ha-Shulḥan, Oraḥ Ḥayim* 606:2.

176 The phrase "with a whole heart and with a desirous soul" is taken from 1 Chronicles 28:9. It also appears in Maimonides, *Mishneh Torah, Ahavah, Seder Tefilot*, in the section *Nusaḥ ha-Kadish* (near the end of the daily liturgy). As to what is meant by "a desirous soul," see Moshe Shternbukh, *Ha-Derekh li-Teshuvah*, 2nd ed. (n.p.: Agudat Netivot ha-Torah veha-Ḥesed, n.d.), *Hilkhot Teshuvah* 2:10, pp. 27–28.

177 Maimonides, *Mishneh Torah, Hilkhot Teshuvah* 2:10. As I have pointed out previously, Maimonides understands not bearing a grudge as "eliminating" the offense that was committed against him from his heart and not "remembering" it at all (Maimonides, *Mishneh Torah, De'ot* 7:8; and Maimonides, *Sefer ha-Mitsvot*, negative commandment 305). See the discussion of the halakhic parameters of "not bearing a grudge" (pp. 271–91) and the explanations of what it means to not "remember" the offense (p. 268 n. 17, and p. 296 n. 88).

that there are others who expressed the view that this is not an essential element of forgiveness. Being that most of these later authorities did not discuss what Maimonides had written in *Hilkhot Teshuvah* regarding forgiving with a whole heart and a desirous soul,[178] it is impossible to know for sure exactly how they interpreted what he had said. In all likelihood, there were probably those who took what he had written at face value and understood him as saying that one is expected to forgive wholeheartedly, and there were those who had understood him as saying that forgiving with a whole heart and with a desirous soul is an ideal that one should most definitely strive to attain, but it is not an absolute necessity.

Two Basic Opinions. A thorough analysis of the topic of the sincerity of one's forgiveness would necessitate that we differentiate between levels of sincerity (e.g., whether the person who forgives is completely sincere, somewhat sincere, or completely insincere) and, from a halakhic standpoint, that we delineate different levels of requirement (e.g., whether the person who forgives should *le-khatḥilah* [*ab initio*, i.e., ideally] sincerely forgive, but *be-di'avad* [*post factum*, i.e., in retrospect, or not ideally] if he was not sincere in his forgiveness, it would still be acceptable; or is the person absolutely required to sincerely grant forgiveness). In addition to these variables, a thoroughgoing analysis would also necessitate that ambiguities in the primary sources in relation to these and other salient factors be highlighted. So as not to overcomplicate our analysis, having called attention to these issues, this section will skim over them for the most part and only two broad basic views regarding the question of sincerity will be outlined—the view that requires that forgiveness be sincere and heartfelt and the view that does not require this. One should, however, keep in mind that because of the aforementioned issues the topic under discussion is in reality much more complex than it will appear to be.[179]

178 Notable exceptions to this are R. Sarna, R. Halevi, and R. Hutner (see pp. 356–58, and Hutner, *Paḥad Yitsḥak*, 255–57), who do discuss it.

179 Taking all of the aforementioned issues into consideration, the sources and opinions presented could theoretically be divided into a number of subgroups,

Those Who Do Not Require that Forgiveness be Sincere and Heartfelt. In contemporary works, one finds the view that does not require that forgiveness be sincere and heartfelt often associated with the talmudic commentary *Gilyone ha-Shas*, by R. Joseph Engel (1859–1920). In *Gilyone ha-Shas*, R. Engel writes that if one embarrasses another person, or commits a similar offense, and the other person verbally states that he has forgiven the offending party, even though he has not forgiven him in his heart, the halakhic principle of *devarim sheba-lev enam devarim* ("matters of the heart are not matters," see *Kiddushin* 49b–50a)[180] would be applicable to such a case, and from a halakhic standpoint, this would be considered an effectual form of forgiveness. R. Engel cites a ruling of R. Menaḥem of Merseburg (fourteenth century) as an earlier source for this view.[181]

R. Simḥah Zissel Ziv (Broida, 1824–1898) and R. Reuven Grozovsky (1886–1958) are often also cited as subscribing to the view that forgiveness does not have to be sincere and heartfelt. R. Grozovsky writes that he had heard in the name of R. Ziv that it would be acceptable if one says that he has forgiven someone, even if this does not actually reflect what he is feeling in his heart.[182] R. Isaac Blaser (1837–1907), a colleague

are not necessarily mutually exclusive, and could potentially be interpreted in more than one way.

180 For an overview of this principle and rules regarding its application, see *Entsiklopedyah Talmudit*, vol. 7, s.v. "*devarim sheba-lev enam devarim.*" See also footnotes 182 and 185, below.

181 Engel, *Gilyone ha-Shas, Kiddushin* 49b, s.v. *u-devarim*. R. Menaḥem of Merseburg is discussing a case in which someone was involved in a conflict and had come to a compromise with the other party, but "in his heart he had not forgiven him." R. Menaḥem states that the principle of *devarim sheba-lev enam devarim* would be applicable to such a case. Menaḥem of Merseburg, *Nimuke Menaḥem Mirzburk*, in *She'elot u-Teshuvot ve-Hilkhot Sheḥitah u-Vedikah ve-Ḥidushe Dinim*, by Jacob Weil (Jerusalem: Yisrael Wolf, 1959), 173, s.v. *din kevan she-Reuven*. R. Engel and R. Menaḥem of Merseburg are cited in Ari'av, *Le-Re'akha kamokha*, vol. 3, 343 n. 19; Elḥanan Perets, *Ma'aseh ha-Tsedakah* (Jerusalem: Mekhon Merkevet ha-Mishnah, 2005), 271–72; David Breisacher, *Naḥalat Devash* (Israel: Ofarim, 2009), 458–59; and Yitsḥak Zilberstein, *Ḥashuke Ḥemed: Al Masekhet Avodah Zarah* (n.p., 2009), *Avodah Zarah* 71b, p. 497.

182 Refael Reuven Grozovsky, "*Ba-Din Isur Kabalat Lashon Hara*," in *Even Tsiyon: Sefer Zikaron le-Ilui Nishmat Ben Tsiyon ha-Kohen Kahana* (Jerusalem: Yeshivat "Keneset Yisrael"—Ḥevron, 1987), 542. The logic behind this, that is offered by R. Ziv (similar to R. Engel) is that we apply the principle of *devarim sheba-lev enam devarim* to such a case. After citing what he had heard in the name of R. Ziv, R. Grozovsky

of R. Ziv, was evidently also of the same opinion. This was indicated by R. Blaser's yearly practice on the eve of Yom Kippur when he would state that he forgives anyone who had committed an offense against him, even though in his heart he did not forgive the person.[183]

Those Who Do Require that Forgiveness be Sincere and Heartfelt. It was in response to the practice of R. Blaser that R. Abraham Isaiah Karelitz (1878–1953) is quoted as posing the question, "Is that the way one uproots an issue that upsets a person?"[184] The implication of this question being that forgiveness is meant to resolve interpersonal issues and do away with the ill will that accompanies them; therefore, merely saying that one forgives someone when one does not really mean it does not accomplish the intended purpose of forgiveness. Based on the above quote, the view that from a halakhic standpoint forgiveness must be sincere has been attributed to R. Karelitz.[185]

---

goes on to offer his explanation of this view. According to R. Grozovsky, despite the fact that in relation to all areas that pertain to *ḥovot ha-levavot*, "obligations of the heart," that is, *mitsvot* that relate to feelings and emotions, such as love of God, trust in God, love for people, and repentance, the Halakhah is most certainly concerned about what one feels in one's heart, when it comes to the granting of forgiveness for an interpersonal offense this would not be the case. Based on the view expressed by R. Israel Salanter that forgiveness, *meḥilah*, for an interpersonal offense is in a certain sense comparable to the *meḥilah*, "forgoing," or "forgiving," of a financial obligation (see Israel Salanter and Isaac Blaser, *Or Yisrael* [New York: Avraham Yitsḥak Friedman, n.d.], *Netivot Or*, pp. 58a–b, and see above, p. 319), granting forgiveness for an interpersonal offense would work differently than the typical "obligation of the heart," and would only be contingent upon one's spoken word. Ibid. For a possible alternative explanation of R. Salanter's view, according to which R. Salanter would not subscribe to the above, see Shimon Licht, *"Ba-Din Meḥilah i Ba'e ba-Peh o ba-Lev," Torat ha-Adam le-Adam: Kovets Torani ba-Mitsvot she-ben Adam la-Ḥavero* 3 (1999): 35. R. Ziv and R. Grozovsky are cited in Ḥayim Leib ben Dov [Eisenstein], *Peninim mi-Be Midrasha*, vol. 1 (Jerusalem: n.p., 2004), 121; Mordechai Carlebach, *Ḥavatselet ha-Sharon*, vol. 1 (Jerusalem: n.p., 2005), 720; and Ari'av, *Le-Re'akha kamokha*, vol. 3, 343 n. 19.

183 Shlomo Zalman Ulman, quoted in Tzevi Yavrov, *Ma'aseh Ish*, vol. 1 (Bnei Brak: n.p., 1999), 161. R. Blaser's yearly practice was eventually adopted and became an accepted custom in the Ponevezh Yeshivah (ibid.). Also, R. Ḥayim Pinḥas Scheinberg (1910–2012) is cited as subscribing to the view that the rule of *devarim sheba-lev enam devarim* applies to interpersonal forgiveness; see Scheinberg, *Orḥot ha-Rav*, 92.

184 Ulman, *Ma'aseh Ish*, vol. 1, 161.

185 See [Eisenstein], *Peninim mi-Be Midrasha*, vol. 1, 121; and Shemaryahu Yosef Nissim Karelitz, *Sefer Ḥut Shani: Be'urim u-Verure Inyanim ve-Ḥidushe Dinim be-Hilkhot Mezuzah, Inyanim be-Hilkhot Berakhot* (Jerusalem: Ḥ. A. Hokhman, 2012), 345–46,

Aside from R. Karelitz, there are other authorities who have expressed similar views that indicate that forgiveness requires at least some degree of sincerity.[186] One formulation of this view appears in the work *Shulḥan Gevoah* by R. Joseph Molkho (c. 1688–c. 1760). In discussing laws of forgiveness, R. Molkho decries the prevalent custom of his time in which "mediators of peace" would get involved in disputes and coerce the parties to resolve their issues against their

where this view is definitively attributed to R. Karelitz, without any direct reference to R. Blaser's practice. R. Eisenstein, R. Karelitz, and others propose that in contrast to the view that forgiveness does not have to be sincere and heartfelt, which seems to be based on the premise that *meḥilah* for an interpersonal offense is comparable to the *meḥilah* of a financial obligation (and things of a similar nature) and therefore the principle of *devarim sheba-lev enam devarim* would be applicable (see above, p. 353 n. 182), the view that requires sincere and heartfelt forgiveness would maintain that *meḥilah* for an interpersonal offense is a *davar she-talui ba-lev* ("something that is dependent upon the heart"), and therefore the principle of *devarim sheba-lev enam devarim* would not be applicable. [Eisenstein], *Peninim mi-Be Midrasha*, vol. 1, 121; Karelitz, *Sefer Ḥut Shani: Hilkhot Mezuzah*, 345; and the edition of the *Mishnah Berurah* published by Dirshu H' ve-Uzo, *Mishnah Berurah*, vol. 6 (Jerusalem: Dirshu, 2013), *Be'urim u-Musafim, siman* 606:1.

186 Aside from the authorities that I cite in the text, this view has also been attributed to the following: R. Abraham Danzig (1748–1820), R. Eliezer Papo (1786–1827), R. Isaac Hutner (1906–1980); R. Ben Zion Abba Shaul (1924–1998); R. Yosef Shalom Elyashiv (1910–2012), and R. Nissim Karelitz (1926–). See Abraham Danzig, *Bet Avraham* (Vilna: Yosef Reuven Rom, 1847), section 20, p. 11a (R. Danzig mentions wholehearted forgiveness in reference to the one who asks for forgiveness—"[I]t is not enough for him to just ask for forgiveness; [he will] not [fulfill his obligation of seeking forgiveness] until he perceives that he [the other person] has forgiven him wholeheartedly"); Eliezer Papo, *Sefer Orot Elim* (Ashdod: Mekhon Hadrat Ḥen, 2005), *Megillah*, s.v. *Mar Zutra*, p. 55; Papo, *Pele Yo'ets*, s.v. *teshuvah*, p. 652; Hutner, *Paḥad Yitsḥak*, 254–59; Ben Zion Abba Shaul, *Sefer Or le-Tsiyon: Teshuvot*, vol. 2 (Jerusalem: Mekhon Or le-Tsiyon, 1993), *perek* 15, *she'elah* 13; Yosef Shalom Elyashiv, cited in Licht, "*Meḥilah i Ba'e ba-peh,*" 36; and Karelitz, *Ḥut Shani, Hilkhot Rosh ha-Shanah, Yom ha-Kipurim*, 100. It should be noted that there are possible questions that can be posed regarding all of these attributions. See the discussions in Perets, *Ma'aseh ha-Tsedakah*, 271; Perets, *Orḥot ha-Rav*, 93; Licht, "*Meḥilah i Ba'e ba-Peh,*" 36; Michael Yeḥiel Bodenheimer, *Be-Me ha-Torah* (Bnei Brak: n.p., 2009), 361–63; Ari'av, *Le-Re'akha kamokha*, vol. 7, 337 n. 63; Ari'av, *Le-Re'akha kamokha*, vol. 3, 344; Abba Shaul, *Or le-Tsiyon, perek* 15, *she'elah* 13 n. 13; and [Eisenstein], *Peninim mi-Be Midrasha*, vol. 1, 121. Closely related to these views is the view of R. Israel Salanter, that once someone has said that he has forgiven another, he is no longer allowed to walk around with ill will and resentment towards that person; see Salanter and Blaser, *Or Yisrael, Netivot Or*, pp. 58a–b. For a discussion related to the topic of forgiving wholeheartedly, see Feinstein, *Igrot Mosheh, Even ha-Ezer*, vol. 4, *siman* 47:2–3, p.100 (his explanation regarding the requirement of being accompanied by three people).

will. Among the reasons that R. Molkho cites for objecting to this practice is that the one who is granting forgiveness is only "putting on an outward show for the mediators while inwardly is laying a snare against him [the person who committed the offense]"; this is opposed to what should take place, which is that he should "grant forgiveness with heart and soul."[187] From this ruling, it seems evident that R. Molkho would dismiss a completely insincere or merely perfunctory act of granting forgiveness as being ineffectual or, at the very least, highly inadvisable.[188]

From among the authorities who have been cited as proponents of the view that requires sincere and heartfelt forgiveness, R. Shlomo Wolbe (1914–2005) sets forth one of the clearest, and most demanding, formulations. In his work *Ale Shur*, R. Wolbe writes as follows:

> One who has not completely uprooted the feeling of vexation and resentment [towards the other person] from his heart is *prohibited* [emphasis in the original] from saying [to the other person] that he has been forgiven, for this would constitute *genevat da'at* ["theft of the mind," a forbidden form of deceit] ... [and as a result of this] the other person will cease to appease him, since he will rely upon [that which he has been told] that he was forgiven. [In truth] that forgiveness does not qualify as forgiveness, and that appeasement does not qualify as appeasement ... How ludicrous it is that on the day before Yom Kippur people say to anyone who seeks [forgiveness], "I forgive you," without giving any thought to uprooting the ill-will they are feeling ...
>
> True forgiveness is something that one has to work at ... [therefore] one should not be embarrassed to ask from

187 Molkho, *Shulḥan Gevoah, Oraḥ Ḥayim* 606:2, p. 421.

188 Because of a slight ambiguity in R. Molkho's wording, I am not sure if he is saying that coerced forgiveness is ineffectual or just highly inadvisable. It is also possible, based on his wording, that he himself is expressing some doubt as to whether coerced forgiveness is effectual or not. See ibid.

> the one who seeks forgiveness that he [the forgiver] be given time so that he will be able to forgive him with a whole heart.[189]

What Does One Do if One Cannot Find it in One's Heart to Forgive the Other Person? According to the view that requires that forgiveness be sincere and heartfelt, there is an obvious question that has to be addressed—What is one supposed to do if he or she simply cannot find it in his or her heart to forgive the other person? We will discuss three possible approaches to this question. The first will challenge the underlying premise of the question; the second will offer an alternative interpretation of what is meant by forgiving "with a whole heart"; and the third will suggest a basic practical approach to how one goes about forgiving wholeheartedly.

The First Approach. In our discussion of the general rule of when one is and is not obligated to forgive, we had quoted R. Ezekiel Sarna's interpretation of *Hilkhot Teshuvah* 2:10 (see above, p. 341). Within the course of his comments, basing himself on what Maimonides had written, R. Sarna had expressed a view that would apparently take issue with the entire premise that one cannot find it in his/her heart to forgive another person (that is, presumably, under normal circumstances, and excluding cases in which the Halakhah would allow one to withhold forgiveness[190]). To quote R. Sarna once again: "Anyone who is a descendent of Israel, even if he is not a *tsadik* [a righteous person] or a *ḥasid* [a pious person] his path [in life] must be one of forgiveness, and he is forbidden from doing otherwise ... This is applicable [as Maimonides has written] 'even if he caused him pain and sinned against him to a great extent'; he should not only not take revenge, but he should also not bear a grudge in his heart; and he should be *fully* appeased when the one who sinned against him appeases him" (emphasis mine). Based on this quote, it seems that R. Sarna was of the view that (once again, under normal

189 [Shlomo Wolbe], *Ale Shur*, vol. 2 (Jerusalem: Bet ha-Musar a"sh. R' Ḥ. M. Lehman, 1986), 240–41. R. Wolbe cites the anecdote with R. Eliyahu Lopian (see below, p. 359) as support for this view.

190 See, however, the view of the *Ḥafets Ḥayim* cited above on p. 348, n. 163.

circumstances and excluding the halakhic exemptions) one is capable of and obligated to reconcile with and forgive someone in one's heart even when it comes to the most serious offenses.

The Second Approach. R. Ḥayyim David Halevi has a view that appears to be diametrically opposed to R. Sarna's, and to a simple reading of Maimonides.[191] R. Halevi discusses this topic in one of his responsa. He is replying to a query regarding a case in which someone expressed the sentiment that even if he was required by Halakhah to forgive a certain person who had committed an offense against him, on an emotional level he felt that he was incapable of doing so. After quoting what Maimonides had written about granting forgiveness with a whole heart, and postulating that the commandment against bearing a grudge does *not* forbid one from bearing an *emotional* grudge against someone (all that one is prohibited from doing, according to R. Halevi, is to remind the person about his offense at some later date),[192] R. Halevi goes on to respond as follows:

> In truth, it is not within the power of a human being to grant forgiveness to the extent that the past has been totally uprooted. A person is not capable of purifying his heart [and feeling the same towards the person] as before the offense was committed.[193] (Of course, it is understood that we are only discussing a case that involves someone who had committed [a great] evil against his friend and caused him pain to a great extent.) ... The objective of forgiveness among people is the attainment of a state in which conflict and hatred totally cease, and that the offended party will

191 The difference of opinion between R. Halevi and R. Sarna revolves around their respective readings of Maimonides' ruling in *Hilkhot Teshuvah* 2:10.

192 For a discussion of this view, see Weinberger and Heifetz, *Lo Tikom ve-Lo Titor*, 50–54, 63–66.

193 Cf. Moses Cordovero, *Tomer Devorah* (London, n.p., 2003), chap. 1, s.v. *ha-shevi'it yashuv yeraḥamenu*. According to R. Cordovero, "When one sees that his friend [who had committed an offense against him] seeks his love [i.e., he wants to reconcile with him], he should have a level of compassion and love towards him that is much, much more than he had beforehand." Ibid.

> decide that *through his deeds* [he will demonstrate that] he has "forgotten" what has taken place in the past and that it will be as if it had never occurred. The Torah does not obligate the person to forgive on an emotional level since, as was stated [above], this would go against the very nature of a human being. And this is what Maimonides had meant [in the *Mishneh Torah, Hilkhot Teshuvah* 2:10, when he writes that one should forgive him with a whole heart and with a desirous soul and not bear a grudge] ... One should [therefore] treat for all intents and purposes the person who asks for forgiveness as if the offense had never occurred and then, possibly, in the course of time the [negative] effect of what had occurred will be totally uprooted from his heart. And [of course] this is dependent upon the [individual] person and his temperament.[194] (emphasis mine)

R. Halevi is basically saying that when it comes to very serious offenses the average person cannot be expected to literally forgive "with a whole heart," at least not initially. The average person is, however, capable of and can be obligated in the cessation of open and active conflict. Therefore, an alternative interpretation of what is meant by forgiving "with a whole heart" is necessary. The explanation that suggests itself is that when Maimonides writes that one should forgive "with a whole heart and with a desirous soul," all he meant was that a person is supposed to conduct him/herself in a manner *as if* he/she has totally forgiven the other party with a whole heart.

The Third Approach. R. Aharon Leib Steinman (1914–) expresses a view that could be seen as a third, and probably the simplest, approach to the question of what does one do if he/she cannot find it in his/her heart to forgive the other person. In reference to forgiving someone wholeheartedly who had caused great suffering, R. Steinman is quoted as saying, "[Is] everything [that took place between them just] going to be wiped away instantaneously?! That's not the way it goes!

194 Halevi, *Aseh lekha Rav*, vol. 6, responsum 42, pp. 140–46.

A person is not made that way. It takes time until he will be able to erase the matter from his heart."[195] R. Steinman then went on to cite the following anecdote that illustrates this point.

There was a certain individual who had seriously offended R. Eliyahu Lopian (1876–1970). Eventually, that person approached R. Lopian and asked him to forgive him for what he had done. R. Lopian's response was that, owing to the serious nature of the offense, he felt that he was not able to forgive the person wholeheartedly right then and there on the spot. He therefore asked the person who had requested the forgiveness that he give him some time, during which he (R. Lopian) would "work on" himself. Over the next few days, R. Lopian dedicated an extensive amount of time to the study of *musar* (Jewish ethics and character development) pertaining to the issue, until he felt that he was able to find it in his heart to forgive the person wholeheartedly.[196]

Essentially, R. Steinman was saying that sincere and heartfelt forgiveness for serious offenses may very often take time and effort. The anecdote with R. Lopian that he cited, in addition to supporting this idea,[197] also suggests that focusing on pertinent areas of character

---

195 R. Steinman's comments were said in the context of explaining a passage from the Midrash *Esther Rabbah* (in the standard printed edition, *parashah* 7:25) that discusses the biblical episode of Joseph and his brothers (Genesis 37–45). It should be noted that R. Steinman's view (that it may take some time until one can sincerely forgive) is compatible with R. Sarna's opinion. R. Sarna, who expressed the view that one is capable of and obligated in granting forgiveness wholeheartedly, may nevertheless admit that it could very well take some time for one to be able to forgive wholeheartedly.

196 Aharon Yehudah Leib Steinman, quoted in Hillel Cooperman, *Megilat Ester: Im Perush "Haleli Nafshi,"* 2nd ed. (n.p., 2011), 36–37 n. 41. This anecdote also appears in Eliyahu Lopian, *Lev Eliyahu*, vol. 1 (Jerusalem: Ha-Va'ad le-Hotsa'at Kitve Maran Zal, 1972), *Mi-Toldotav*, p. 44. There are different possible ways as to how to explain this anecdote and R. Lopian's conduct. See [Wolbe], *Ale Shur*, vol. 2, 241 (where R. Wolbe understands R. Lopian's conduct as reflecting a halakhic requirement); cf. Perets, *Orḥot ha-Rav*, 93 (where R. Perets refers to what R. Wolbe wrote and asserts that this type of conduct does not reflect a halakhic requirement, but only a righteous character trait); and Ari'av, *Le-Re'akha kamokha*, vol. 3, 344 n. 20.

197 R. Wolbe writes in reference to this anecdote that R. Lopian's conduct indicates that forgiveness is something that is "difficult and complex," and that the story is giving an account of "a *ma'aseh rav* [the conduct of a talmudic scholar that has practical halakhic import], which teaches us that true forgiveness is something that one has to work at" ([Wolbe], *Ale Shur*, vol. 2, 241).

development and "working on" oneself could help one find it in one's heart to eventually forgive another even when it is difficult to do so.

Summary

This chapter has examined laws associated with the asking and granting of forgiveness. I have attempted to elucidate what I considered to be some of the essential features of the practical halakhic discourse on these topics. To facilitate my presentation and analysis, this part of the chapter was divided into two major sections: (1) The Obligations of the One Who Asks for Forgiveness, and (2) The Obligations of the One Who Forgives. These sections presented the primary sources for their respective subtopics, and expounded on those laws that were viewed as having the greatest practical applications, that embody principles of major import, and for which there are significant halakhic discussions.

Among the topics that were discussed in the first section were the following:

- The possible difference that may exist between the obligation of asking for forgiveness on the day before Yom Kippur and the obligation incumbent upon the person year-round.

- The range of interpersonal offenses for which one must seek forgiveness and the question regarding whether one's obligation extends to imagined offenses.

- The debate as to whether one is required to personally go to ask for forgiveness oneself, and what personally going to ask for forgiveness is supposed to accomplish.

- The requirement of specifying the exact offense that was committed, and the possible exception to the rule if by doing so it would be counterproductive and cause further suffering.

- The obligation of asking for forgiveness three times and issues associated with it (e.g., the rationale for asking three times, the question regarding whether one should ask for forgiveness more than three times, and the requirement of being accompanied by three people).

- Maimonides' view as to the three basic requirements that are incumbent upon the one who asks for forgiveness: (1) (financial) restitution, (2) appeasement, and (3) a request to be forgiven.

- The nature of the appeasement of the person who suffered.

In the second section, the following were discussed:

- The various sources for the obligation to forgive.

- The question of how readily one is supposed to forgive.

- Guidelines of when one is and is not obligated to forgive. Cases in which one may not be required to forgive included when the person who committed the offense continues to do so or shows no remorse; if not forgiving will benefit the person; and situations involving defamation of character.

- The concept that rules of asking and granting forgiveness from one's friend are derived from the rules of asking for forgiveness from God.

- The question of how sincere a person's forgiveness must be. We had seen two basic opinions regarding this issue—one that requires that forgiveness be sincere and heartfelt and another that does not require this.

- According to the view that requires that forgiveness be sincere and heartfelt, we addressed the associated question of what does one do if he/she simply cannot find it in his/her heart to forgive the other person.

If I were pressed and had to encapsulate the essential ideas of what was presented in this chapter, I would simply say that there are two basic principles that emerge: (*a*) that there exists a fundamental obligation to ask for forgiveness when one commits an interpersonal transgression against another, and (*b*) that there is a fundamental obligation to grant forgiveness to a person who sincerely apologizes and asks to be forgiven. These two principles of conduct, when put into practice, can serve a major function in the promotion of peace and interpersonal conflict resolution. If for every situation of conflict the parties involved were to make a concerted effort to reflect upon the character of their actions, and if and when they would conclude that their conduct was not in accord with proper standards of behavior, they would then take the initiative to make amends, appease the other party, and ask for forgiveness, and should that other party then feel obligated to readily and sincerely forgive the other, the majority of conflicts could be expeditiously resolved. Such a series of steps would no doubt have a profound impact on interpersonal interactions and relationships and contribute significantly to the promotion of peaceful coexistence among people.

Before proceeding to the next section, I should point out that the material presented in this chapter should not be viewed as in any way coming close to an exhaustive treatment of the topics of the asking and granting of forgiveness in Judaism. There are many aspects of apologies and forgiveness discussed in halakhic literature (and certainly in other genres of traditional Jewish literature) that I have not touched on. These would include such things as discussions of the appropriate timing and setting for the asking of forgiveness;[198] the

198 For discussions related to timing, see *Berakhot* 7a–b (the gemara that states, "We do not appease someone when he is angry"); Joseph Ḥayyim ben Elijah al Ḥakam, *Sefer Benayahu* (Jerusalem: Yitsḥak Bakal, 1965), *Berakhot* 7b, s.v. *minayin*; Yitsḥak Zilberstein, *Ḥashuke Ḥemed: Al Masekhet Berakhot* (n.p., 2005), *Berakhot* 7b, pp.

appropriate manner in which to express that one has forgiven the other person;[199] the granting of forgiveness to someone who has not asked to be forgiven;[200] and innumerable other questions that have been and can be raised regarding apologies and forgiveness.

Similarities and Differences between Contemporary Conflict Resolution and Traditional Jewish Approaches in Respect to Apologies and Forgiveness

In contemporary social-psychological literature, the material that would have the closest correspondence and the most relevance to the subject matter that was discussed in this chapter would be the

---

56–57; Avraham Horowitz, *Orḥot Rabenu: Kan Miktsat me-Orḥot Ḥayav shel Rabenu ha-G. R.Y.Y. Kanevski* (Bnei Brak: Yeshay' ben A. ha-Levi Horvits, 1991), 245; as well as in other sources. Concerning the setting, specifically in regard to asking for forgiveness in public when one has publicly embarrassed the other person, see Bacharach, *Mekor Ḥayim, siman* 606, s.v. *bizahu*; Epstein, *Arukh ha-Shulḥan, Ḥoshen Mishpat* 622:2; and Kamenetsky, *Kovets Halakhot*, 310–11 n. 13.

199 As far as the appropriate manner in which to express forgiveness, see Baḥya ben Asher, *Rabenu Baḥya: Be'ur al ha-Torah* (Jerusalem: Mossad Harav Kook, 2006), Genesis 50:17; Rashi, *Teshuvot Rashi* (Bnei Brak: Yahadut, 1980), *siman* 245, p. 287; Bacharach, *Mekor Ḥayim, siman* 606, s.v. *ve-im hotsi*; Ḥayyim Palache, *Ḥayim be-Yad* (Izmir: Binyamin N. Tsiyon Roditi, 1873), *siman* 57; Ari'av, *Le-Re'akha kamokha*, vol. 3, 344–45, 349; Daniel Roth, *"Masoret Aharon Rodef Shalom ben Ish le-Ish ke-Model Rabani le-Fiyus"* [The Tradition of Aaron Pursuer of Peace between People as a Rabbinic Model of Reconciliation] (PhD diss., Bar-Ilan University, 2012), 116–18; and in other sources as well.

200 See above, p. 315, where this was touched on in relation to the obligation of the one who asks for forgiveness. The question of how the Halakhah views the forgiving of an offender who has not asked to be forgiven, in respect to the forgiver, was never discussed. There are many sources that indicate that this may be something that is meritorious to do, or is considered a "righteous character trait," but it is not obligatory. See Hershel Schachter and Joseph Dov Soloveitchik, *Divre ha-Rav* (Jerusalem: Masorah, 2010), 166–67 (citing *Megillah* 28a, where the Gemara mentions how Mar Zutra before going to sleep at night would forgive anyone who had caused him pain during the day); Hoberman, *Ze'ev Yitrof*, 261–22 (who cites *Megillah* 28a, and contrasts it with *Yoma* 87a, where R. Zeira indicates that he did not want to grant forgiveness unless the other person asks for it); Isaac Blaser, *Netivot Or*, in *Sefer Or Yisrael* [n.p., n.d.], 58a; and Silver, *Mishpete ha-Shalom*, 3:28, p. 50 n. 38. For other relevant sources, see Ha-Kohen, *Mishnah Berurah*, 239:9; Danzig, *Ḥaye Adam*, the end of *kelal* 144, p. 877 (the wording of *Tefillah Zakkah*); the sources cited above, p. 342 n. 139, that discuss whether the commandment to not bear a grudge also requires one to forgive; Maimonides, *Mishneh Torah, Hilkhot De'ot* 6:9; and Zvi H. Weinberger and Baruch A. Heifetz, *Sefer Limud le-Hilkhot ben Adam la-Ḥavero: Lo Tisna et Aḥikha be-Lvavekha* (Safed, Israel: Makhon Torat ha-Adam le-Adam, 1995), 179–82.

material that deals with apologies and forgiveness. Contemporary theories and research related to apologies may be viewed as being analogous and pertinent to concepts discussed in the first section, "The Obligations of the One Who Asks for Forgiveness." Contemporary theories and research related to forgiveness may be viewed as being analogous and pertinent to concepts that were dealt with in the second section, "The Obligations of the One Who Forgives."

The following sections of this chapter will examine a number of the predominant theories and highlights of research on apologies and forgiveness. The focus will be on the elements that contribute to effective apologies and the process of forgiveness, and how they are similar to or differ from concepts of asking and granting forgiveness in traditional Jewish approaches. Subsequently, we will go on to examine the role apologies and forgiveness play in contemporary conflict resolution, and conclude by comparing and contrasting the general approach that is found in contemporary conflict resolution with that of traditional Jewish approaches.

Theories and Research on Apologies

An apology may be defined simply as "a written or spoken expression of one's regret, remorse, or sorrow for having insulted, failed, injured, or wronged another,"[201] or, even a little more simply, "a statement saying that you are sorry about something: an expression of regret for having done or said something wrong."[202] Over the past thirty years, there have been numerous studies done and articles and books written

201 *Random House Unabridged Dictionary*, 2nd ed., s.v. "apology."

202 *Merriam-Webster Dictionary Online*, s.v. "apology," accessed October 7, 2014, http://www.merriam-webster.com/dictionary/apology. Regarding the dictionary definition of the word "apology," see the discussions in Nicholas Tavuchis, *Mea Culpa: A Sociology of Apology and Reconciliation* (Stanford, CA: Stanford University Press, 1991), 15–20; Aaron Lazare, *On Apology* (Oxford: Oxford University Press, 2004); 23–27; and Nick Smith, *I Was Wrong: The Meanings of Apologies* (Cambridge: Cambridge University Press, 2008), 8–9.

about apologies.[203] Many of these have elaborated on the definition of an apology, discussing in detail the different features of an apology and presenting us with numerous alternatives as to what may be considered the fundamental elements that constitute an apology. A considerable number of authors who discuss apologies have also addressed the all-important associated question of why some apologies are effective and accepted, whereas others are ineffective and rejected.

In 2009, Johanna Kirchhoff, Micha Strack, and Uli Jäger conducted a literature review in the fields of jurisprudence, sociolinguistics, sociology, theology, philosophy, and psychology in an attempt to organize and analyze the extremely wide spectrum of views regarding the fundamental components that constitute an apology. In this section, I will present three of the most often-cited views on the topic, the results of Kirchhoff, Strack, and Jäger's analysis, and the results of empirical research on the elements that contribute to effective apologies.

The CCSARP Project. In the 1980s, there was a large-scale research project conducted in the field of sociolinguistics called the Cross-Cultural Speech Act Realization Patterns (CCSARP) project. A total of 1088 subjects in seven countries participated in studies that investigated cross-cultural variations in apologies (and requests). The lead researchers in this project identified five potential strategies, or "semantic formulas," that people employ in apologizing.[204] The CCSARP's findings are often cited in the academic literature that discusses apologies, and for an informed discussion of contemporary views on apologies, it would be worthwhile to be familiar with them.

---

203 For just a small sampling of this material, see Eva Ogiermann, "Bibliography on Apologies," accessed November 4, 2016, https://linguisticpoliteness.wordpress.com/bibliographies/apologies-1/; and Catherine Morris, "Conflict Transformation and Peacebuilding: A Selected Bibliography - Acknowledgement, Apology and Forgiveness," Peacemakers Trust, accessed November 4, 2016, http://www.peacemakers.ca/bibliography/bib44forgivenessapology. html.

204 For a detailed explanation of the project and the research that was done, see Shoshana Blum-Kulka and Elite Olshtain, "Requests and Apologies: A Cross-Cultural Study of Speech Act Realization Patterns (CCSARP)," *Applied Linguistics* 5, no. 3 (1984): 196–213; and Shoshana Blum-Kulka, Juliane House, and Gabriele Kasper, "Investigating Cross-Cultural Pragmatics: An Introductory Overview," in *Cross-Cultural Pragmatics: Requests and Apologies* (Norwood, NJ: Ablex Publishing, 1989), 1–34.

The five apologetic strategies identified by the CCSARP researchers were as follows:

(1) The use of an "illocutionary force indicating device" (IFID),[205] which is a formulaic expression of regret, such as "I'm sorry," "I apologize," "I regret," and may take the form of an explicit request for forgiveness, such as "Excuse me," "Forgive me," or "Pardon me." According to Shoshana Blum-Kulka, Juliane House, and Gabriele Kasper, the IFID "fulfills the function of signaling regret: the speaker asks forgiveness for the violation that motivated the need to apologize, thereby serving to placate the hearer."[206]

(2) The offering of an explanation. Very often, either in lieu of or in addition to the IFID, some type of self-justification for the offense is given. An explanation attributes the objectionable behavior to external factors over which one has very little or no control, which may serve as an apology.[207] An example of this would be when someone comes late to a meeting and explains that his bus was delayed or that he got stuck in heavy traffic.

(3) Accepting responsibility. In apologizing, one may choose to take responsibility for the offense.[208] Such face-threatening recognition of one's fault is intended to appease the person receiving the apology. One may explicitly accept responsibility, for example, by coming straight out and blaming oneself by stating that "it was my fault/

205 The term "illocutionary force indicating device" is taken from John R. Searle, *Speech Acts: An Essay in the Philosophy of Language* (Cambridge: Cambridge University Press, 1969), 33, 54, 57, 62–63.

206 Blum-Kulka, House, and Kasper, "Cross-Cultural Pragmatics," 20.

207 This is in contrast to the understanding of Kirchhoff, Strack, and Jäger; see below, p. 374.

208 According to others, this is something that should be considered an essential element of an apology; see p. 371.

mistake," or one may take responsibility in an indirect manner by expressing some type of self-deficiency, for example, by saying such things as "I was confused," "I wasn't thinking," "I didn't see you," and the like.

(4) An offer of repair. In cases in which there was physical injury or some other type of damage, one may apologize by offering to rectify the situation through financial compensation or some other means.

(5) A promise of forbearance. The apologizer promises that the offense will not reoccur, for example, by promising that "this won't happen again."

Any one of these strategies by itself or in combination with any of the others would constitute an apology according to the CCSARP project.

Aside from the five basic strategies, the CCSARP project also highlighted that apologizers attain "apology intensification" through: (*a*) using an intensifying adverbial expression within the IFID, such as "I'm *very* sorry," or through repetition (or a double intensifier), such as "I'm *terribly, terribly* sorry"; (*b*) expressing concern for the other person, an example of which may be, in a case when one is late, by saying, "Have you been waiting long?"; (*c*) the use of multiple strategies, that is to say, that the apologizer uses more than one IFID and/or one or more of the other four strategies.[209] In one early discussion of the topic, lead researchers of the project also mentioned in passing the vital role that the tone of one's voice plays in the apology.[210]

209 Blum-Kulka, House, and Kasper, "Cross-Cultural Pragmatics," 19–22; see also Blum-Kulka and Olshtain, "Requests and Apologies," 206–9; and Elite Olshtain and Andrew D. Cohen, "Apology: A Speech-Act Set," in *Sociolinguistics and Language Acquisition*, ed. Nessa Wolfson and Elliot Judd (Rowley, MA: Newbury House, 1983), 21–23.

210 Olshtain and Cohen, "Apology," 22, 29.

The Core Elements of an Apology According to Lazare. Aaron Lazare (1936–2015), who was a Professor of Psychiatry at, and former Chancellor and Dean Emeritus of, the University of Massachusetts Medical School, was widely recognized as one of the foremost experts on apologies. Lazare was a prominent lecturer and writer on the topic; his opinion regarding apologies was often sought by major news outlets. His highly acclaimed book, *On Apology*, has sparked considerable discussion in academic circles and has attracted a large popular readership.[211]

In *On Apology*, Lazare asserts that there are four primary components to the apology process:

(1) Acknowledgment of the offense. According to Lazare, the most essential part of an (effective) apology is that the offender acknowledge the offense. Acknowledging the offense entails (*a*) the correct identification of the party responsible for the offense and the party to whom the apology is owed; (*b*) specifying the offending behaviors in adequate detail; (*c*) recognizing the impact these behaviors had on the victim; and (*d*) confirming that the offense was a violation of the "social or moral contract" (i.e., the social rules and moral standards that govern a group or the implicit rules and values of a relationship)[212] that existed between the parties. The apologizer and the recipient of the apology should reach agreement regarding all of these elements. However, their agreement does not need to be explicitly stated; it may just be implicitly understood.

(2) An explanation. Often an offended party will regard an apology as being inadequate if it does not include an explanation of why the offense occurred. Aside from the possible emotional or psychological needs of the offended party that an explanation may fulfill, it may also help to

211 See http://www.umassmed.edu/cme/upcoming-events/on-apology/.

212 See Lazare, *On Apology*, 53–54.

diminish the seriousness of the offense by conveying one or more of the following: (*a*) the offense "was not intentional and therefore not personal," (*b*) "the behavior is not indicative of the 'real self' of the offender," (*c*) "the victim is blameless," and (*d*) similar offenses are unlikely to occur in the future. Most important, an explanation should not "seem dishonest, arrogant, manipulative, or an insult to the intelligence of the victim."

(3) Expression of remorse and various related attitudes and behaviors. The related attitudes and behaviors being: (*a*) forbearance, (*b*) shame, (*c*) humility, and (*d*) sincerity. Remorse is the feeling of "deep, painful regret that is part of the guilt people experience when they have done something wrong." Accompanying remorse there should be forbearance, that is, "a resolve to abstain or refrain from such behavior in the future." Often together with the remorse there is also a complementary expression of shame, either verbally (e.g., by saying, "I feel so ashamed of myself") or nonverbally (e.g., having a bowed head or eye contact avoidance). The apologizer should also exhibit humility (particularly, by avoiding arrogance or hubris within the course of the apology) and, generally speaking, be sincere.

(4) Reparations. For some apologies, reparations, either through financial compensation or some other means, can be the most important feature of the apology. If an offender cannot on his own determine the appropriate reparations, he can ask the offended party, "Is there anything I can do to make it up to you?"[213]

After discussing the four elements mentioned above, Lazare describes an apology as a complex

213 Ibid., 35, 75–133.

> process by which various combinations of acknowledgments, attitudes and behaviors, explanations, and reparations work together to meet the needs of the offended parties ... [the] success or failure [of which] depends on how successfully we can train ourselves to "hear" what is needed and to respond with just the right combination of elements, emphases, and empathy.[214]

On Apology was published in 2004. At a later point in time, in addition to the four elements mentioned in his book, Lazare also listed "forbearance" as a separate fifth element.[215] At that time, he also set forth other important elements of an apology (which were touched on in his book). In what he termed as "A Comprehensive Outline to Healing Mechanisms in Apologies," Lazare discussed issues relating to "principals" (who should be present at the apology), the setting and timing (where and when the apology takes place), catharsis (that the offended party be allowed to verbalize his feelings about the offense and the offender), dialogue (which the offender and offended should engage in), restoration of the offended's dignity and power, restoration of trust, and that the offender should be empathic and understand how the offended party feels.[216]

Smith's "Categorical Apology." In his book *I Was Wrong: The Meanings of Apologies*, Nick Smith, a Professor of Philosophy at the University of New Hampshire, offers a detailed philosophical analysis of the "social meanings" (i.e., the significance, value, and functions) of apologies.[217] In this work, Smith elaborates on the elements of what he calls a "categorical apology." A categorical apology, according to Smith, is the "most robust, painstaking, and

214 Ibid., 133.

215 Aaron Lazare, "Understanding Apology: Mechanisms for Repairing Relationships" (presentation, Annual Meeting of the National Association of College and University Attorneys, June 27–30, 2010); the handout from the presentation is online at http://www-local.legal.uillinois.edu/nacua10/presentations/1E_handout.pdf; pp. 5, 7.

216 Ibid. and Aaron Lazare, "The Apology Dynamic," *AAOS Now*, May 2010, http://www.aaos.org/news/aaosnow/may10/managing5.asp.

217 See Smith, *I Was Wrong*, 18, 21–25.

formal of apologies"; it serves as a benchmark or touchstone against which all other apologies may be compared, and, in practice, is "a rare and burdensome act."[218]

Smith's categorical apology encompasses the following twelve elements:[219]

(1) A "corroborated factual record." There should be mutual agreement between the offender and victim regarding what exactly took place. By having the parties confirm the relevant facts about what transpired, the wrong-doing can then be judged accurately.

(2) Acceptance of blame. The offender accepts causal and moral responsibility for the offense. In accepting blame, the offender admits to causing what happened and that it was wrong (i.e., that there was a moral obligation upon him to do otherwise).

(3) "Possession of Standing." The one who apologizes is the person who is actually responsible for the offense; this is as opposed to delegating the apology to some type of proxy or third party (e.g., an attorney, successor, heir, and so on).

(4) Identification of each harm. The offender should correctly identify, clearly name, and apologize for each offense that was committed against the victim. In other words, he should not apologize for the "wrong wrong," nor should he conflate multiple offenses into one blanket apology.

(5) Identification of the moral principles underlying each harm. The offender identifies and names the moral principles,

218 Ibid., 17, 140, 142, 145.

219 Smith's analysis of these elements is quite lengthy and involved. My presentation is an oversimplified summary of them.

or implicit values, that have been violated in committing the offense. For example, if a person intentionally destroyed a prized possession that belonged to his spouse, beyond, and much more significant than, the visible damage to the possession is the disrespect that is exhibited towards the spouse through the destructive act.

(6) Endorsing the moral principles underlying each harm. After identifying each harm and the underlying moral principles, the apologizer should affirm his commitment to the principles that were violated. He does so by recognizing that he has committed a transgression and denouncing the behavior.

(7) Recognition of the victim as a moral interlocutor. In taking part in an apologetic discourse with the other party and engaging in the elements of a categorical apology, the offender should come to view and treat the other party as his "moral peer," to whom he must justify his actions. This means that, in the eyes of the offender, the victim becomes someone who is of equal worth and deserving of dignity and respect.

(8) Categorical regret. The offender recognizes that his actions constitute a moral failure; he wishes that his transgression could be undone; and he commits to not repeating the behavior.

(9) Performance of the apology. The offender actually communicates words of apology to the other party. This element not only requires that words of apology be conveyed, but it also addresses issues regarding when (i.e., proper timing), where (e.g., whether it is done publicly or in private), and how (e.g., whether it is written or verbal) the apology takes place.

(10) Reform and redress. The apologizer promises to never repeat the offense (see element no. 8), demonstrates commitment to the promise by resisting opportunities and temptations to repeat the offense, accepts sanctions, and provides appropriate compensation.

(11) Intentions for apologizing. The offender should apologize out of a sincere, reflective, and autonomous motivation. He should not be coerced into apologizing or apologize out of a self-serving interest (e.g., if he does not apologize, he will suffer in some way, or he seeks some sort of strategic advantage over the other person).

(12) Emotions. Accompanying the apology, there should be certain feelings on the part of the offender, such as guilt, shame, remorse, sorrow, and empathy. Among the related issues are questions regarding the appropriate degree and duration of the emotions that are felt, if they require a visible manifestation, and what form that visible manifestation should take (e.g., is contrition exhibited through one's tone of voice and gestures).[220]

Ten Recurring Elements in the Literature on Apologies. In their literature review, Kirchhoff, Strack, and Jäger examined 39 studies that were published between 1971 and 2008.[221] The authors of these 39 studies had all expressed their views as to the fundamental components that constitute an apology. Kirchhoff, Strack, and Jäger identified the following ten recurring components that appear in the literature:

(1) The use of an illocutionary force indicating device (IFID), that is, a statement of apology, such as saying,

220 Smith, *I Was Wrong*, 28–107, 140–43.

221 I am indebted to Professor Kirchhoff for sharing with me the list of literature that was reviewed.

"I apologize" (e.g., see CCSARP's element no. 1, and Smith's element no. 9).

(2) Naming the offense(s) for which the apology is given (e.g., see Lazare, element no. 1[b]; and Smith, element no. 4).

(3) Taking responsibility for the offense(s) (e.g., see CCSARP, element no. 3; and Smith, element no. 2).

(4) Attempting to explain the offense. "Trying to explain one's behavior that led to the offense(s) without applying an external attribution" (see footnote).[222]

(5) Conveying emotions. "Revealing emotions such as shame and remorse that one has committed the offense(s)" (e.g., see Lazare, element no. 3; Smith, element no. 12).

(6) Addressing emotions of and/or damage to the other, which were brought about through the offense(s) (e.g., see Lazare, element no. 1[c]).

---

222 In an exchange of emails between me and Professor Kirchhoff, I questioned Kirchhoff, Strack, and Jäger's explanation of what most of the authors in the studies meant by "attempting to explain the offense." Kirchhoff, Strack, and Jäger emphasize that an "explanation," in the context of an apology, does not attribute the offense to something that is external to the person, but only to something that is internal. The very sound logic that they offer for this is that if the person would attribute the offense to something external, it would then by definition be an excuse or justification, and not an apology. Though I grasp what they are saying and find their argument quite compelling, I would still have to question whether this was the understanding of the overwhelming majority of the authors who listed an "explanation" as one of the main features of an apology. For example, it is evident from the CCSARP project's element no. 2, "the offering of an explanation," that the theorists and researchers of that project did not understand an "explanation" as did Kirchhoff, Strack, and Jäger. I believe that most of the other authors who mention an "explanation" as a main element of an apology understood it along similar lines to that of the CCSARP project. I would, however, concede that there are some authors who do include an explanation as a main feature of an apology and imply that it has to be an internal attribution. See, for example, Jeremy C. Anderson, Wolfgang Linden, and Martine E. Habra, "Influence of Apologies and Trait Hostility on Recovery from Anger," *Journal of Behavioral Medicine* 29, no. 4 (2006): 348.

(7) Admitting fault, or norm violation. That one admit that in committing the offense(s) he has violated an explicitly or implicitly agreed-upon rule (e.g., see Lazare, element no. 1[d]).

(8) Promising forbearance. Stating that one plans to refrain from repeating the offense(s) (e.g., see CCSARP, element no. 5; Lazare, element 3[a]; and Smith, element nos. 8 and 10).

(9) Offering reparation. Offering to make up for the harm and/or damages through monetary or symbolic restitution (e.g., see CCSARP, element no. 4; Lazare, element 4; and Smith, element no. 10).

(10) An acceptance request. Stating that one hopes that the apology can be accepted by its receiver (e.g., see CCSARP, element no. 1, in which an IFID takes the form of an explicit request for forgiveness, such as "Forgive me," or "Pardon me"[223]).[224]

Empirical Research on the Elements that Contribute to Effective Apologies. Surprisingly, there have been relatively few empirical studies that investigate the components of apologies and their effects

223 See Manfred Schmitt et al., "Effects of Objective and Subjective Account Components on Forgiving," *The Journal of Social Psychology* 144, no. 5 (2004): 469, which was one of the sources that discusses an acceptance request (cited as a source in Johanna Kirchhoff, Ulrich Wagner, and Micha Strack, "Apologies: Words of Magic? The Role of Verbal Components, Anger Reduction, and Offence Severity," *Peace and Conflict: Journal of Peace Psychology* 18, no. 2 [2012]: 114).

224 Johanna Kirchhoff, Micha Strack, and Uli Jäger, "Apologies: Depending on Offence Severity the Composition of Elements Does Matter" (presentation, International Network of Psychologists for Social Responsibility (INPsySR)—Symposium "Preventing Violent Conflict: Psychological Dimensions," at the 11th European Congress of Psychology, Oslo, Norway, July 9, 2009); Kirchhoff, Wagner, and Strack, "Apologies: Words of Magic," 110–11; and Johanna Kirchhoff, "On the Content of Apologies" (PhD. diss., Philipps-Universität Marburg, 2013), 4–5, http://archiv.ub.uni-marburg.de/diss/z2013/0232/pdf/djk.pdf.

on the acceptance of apologies by the recipients.[225] Taking into consideration all of the primary elements of apologies, their subcategories, and associated features that were enumerated by the CCSARP project, Lazare, Smith, and Kirchhoff, Strack, and Jäger, there is a multiplicity of possible variables that may influence whether an apology will be effective or ineffective,[226] all of which could potentially be the focus of scientific study.

Among the research that has been done and the variables that have been studied are the following: Barry Schlenker and Bruce Darby (1981) did research on the "completeness" of an apology, focusing on five elements—statements of apologetic intent (e.g., saying "I'm sorry"), expressing feelings of remorse, redressing the

---

225 See Ryan Fehr and Michele J. Gelfand, "When Apologies Work: How Matching Apology Components to Victims' Self-Construals Facilitates Forgiveness," *Organizational Behavior and Human Decision Processes* 113, no. 1 (2010): 37; and Kirchhoff, Wagner, and Strack, "Apologies: Words of Magic," 110.

226 Even when similar or equivalent elements that were mentioned in the sources we examined are subsumed under one heading, there are still many possible variables that may influence whether an apology will be effective or ineffective. Some of these would include (1) a statement of apology (e.g., saying "I'm sorry" or "I apologize"); (2) a request for forgiveness, or a request that the apology be accepted; (3) feeling and expressing regret, or remorse; (4) exhibiting shame, guilt, sorrow, and/or humility; (5) that the aforementioned feelings be exhibited appropriately (taking into consideration the manner, extent, and duration that they are exhibited); (6) corroboration of the facts surrounding the offense; (7) specifying the offense (including the underlying principles or values that were violated); (8) taking responsibility for what occurred, or acceptance of blame; (9) promising forbearance; (10) following through with one's promise of forbearance and actually abstaining from the behavior in the future; (11) compensation for the misdeed, whether financially or through some other means; (12) considering when (the proper timing), where (the proper setting), with whom (who should be present) and how (should it be written or verbal) the apology should take place; (13) being sincere; (14) admitting fault or norm violation; (15) offering of some sort of explanation; making it clear (16) that the offense was not intentional and therefore not personal, (17) that the behavior is not indicative of the "real self" of the offender, and (18) that the victim is blameless; (19) restoration of trust; (20) restoration of the person's dignity; (21) engaging in dialogue; and (22) allowing for catharsis. In addition to the elements that I cited in the text, there are other salient factors that may also determine whether an apology is effective or not, such as (23) the severity of the offense (i.e., in a case when someone suffered great pain or loss, he may be less likely to accept an apology), (24) personality traits of the offended party (e.g., if the offended party has a propensity to be angry or is overly sensitive), (25) social, cultural, and other environmental factors, and (26) gender.

situation through an offer of help, self-castigation for what occurred, and an explicit request for forgiveness.[227] Ken-ichi Ohbuchi, Masuyo Kameda, and Nariyuki Agarie (1989) did research on the "desire for" specific components of an apology, focusing on seven elements—saying "excuse me," offering a detailed explanation of the event, accepting responsibility, expressing remorse, "showing consideration for the victim," "begging for forgiveness," and "promising future good deeds."[228] Kirchhoff, Ulrich Wagner, and Strack (2012) did research on how people would rate the importance of specific components of an apology, focusing on the ten recurring elements that Kirchhoff, Strack, and Jäger had identified in their literature review.[229] In each of these three studies, the subjects were being asked to assess the relative importance of the elements that were under consideration in the respective study.

In Schlenker and Darby's study, the subjects were asked to rate the degree to which each of the five elements that they were presented with, as reflected in a specified apologetic statement, matched their idea of what a prototypical apology should be (in a case in which someone bumped into another person). Schlenker and Darby found that an apology that took the form of a request for forgiveness was considered the "most complete," followed by an offer of help, then an expression of remorse, then self-castigation, and the "least complete" of the elements being when one only says "I'm sorry."[230]

---

227 Barry R. Schlenker and Bruce W. Darby, "The Use of Apologies in Social Predicaments," *Social Psychology Quarterly* (1981): 271–78.

228 Ken-ichi Ohbuchi, Masuyo Kameda, and Nariyuki Agarie, "Apology as Aggression Control: Its Role in Mediating Appraisal of and Response to Harm," *Journal of Personality and Social Psychology* 56, no. 2 (1989): 219–27.

229 Kirchhoff, Wagner, and Strack, "Apologies: Words of Magic."

230 Schlenker and Darby, "The Use of Apologies," Table 2. This is in contrast with the results in Table 1 (ibid.), in which the subjects were told to imagine themselves as a character in a scenario in which they had bumped into someone and hurt the other person, and were then asked about the likelihood that they would use each of the elements in an apology they would offer. The results showed that (in conditions of "high responsibility" and "high consequences") they would most likely employ the element of saying "I'm sorry," then, the next-highest-rated element was offering help, followed by expressing remorse, requesting forgiveness, and self-castigation.

In Ohbuchi, Kameda, and Agarie's study, the subjects were presented with a scenario in which someone knocked another person down and as a result that person suffered abrasions on his elbow and knee and his clothes were stained and torn. The subjects were then told to imagine themselves as the one who had suffered the harm and rate how much they would want each one of the seven elements they were presented with to be included in an apology from the other person. The element of saying "excuse me" received the highest rating, followed by accepting responsibility, "showing consideration," expressing remorse, "begging for forgiveness," a detailed explanation, and "promising future good deeds," in that order.[231]

In Kirchhoff, Wagner, and Strack's study, the subjects were asked to rate how important each of the ten recurring elements that appear in the literature on apologies was to them. The element of conveying emotions was ranked most important, followed by admitting guilt, a statement of apology, attempt at explanation, forbearance, addressing emotions of other, taking responsibility, naming of the offense, acceptance request, and offering reparations.[232]

It is important to note that because of certain inherent shortcomings and various technical reasons, the researchers in each of these studies expressly state (as is the standard practice of researchers who conduct empirical studies) that their conclusions have limitations in their generalizability. In the words of Kirchhoff, Wagner, and Strack, "To question or support a set of basic elements of apology ... more studies need to be conducted."[233]

231 Ohbuchi, Kameda, and Agarie, "Apology as Aggression Control," Table 4, under the "no apology made" condition, cf. the "apology condition."

232 Kirchhoff, Wagner, and Strack, "Apologies: Words of Magic," Table 8, Study 1, cf. the results of Study 2.

233 See Schlenker and Darby, "The Use of Apologies," 277; Ohbuchi, Kameda, and Agarie, "Apology as Aggression Control," 226; and Kirchhoff, Wagner, and Strack, "Apologies: Words of Magic," 124–25.

Comparing Contemporary Approaches to Apologies and the Obligations of the One Who Asks for Forgiveness

It is quite evident that there are numerous similarities, and differences, between contemporary approaches to apologies and the obligations of the one who asks for forgiveness that were discussed in this chapter. Certain glaring similarities have been recognized by scholars in the field of apologies, even though they have had a limited amount of primary Jewish source material at their disposal. Lazare himself points out in *On Apology* that "[r]eligious scholars analyze and describe the steps to repentance in virtually the same manner that social scientists describe the apology process."[234] In the case of Judaism, he cites Maimonides' discussions of repentance in the *Mishneh Torah* as an example of this.[235] Smith actually begins his book by referencing Maimonides' *Hilkhot Teshuvah*, which he describes as a "philosophical monograph devoted to apologies," and subsequently cites Maimonides a number of times in the book.[236]

In considering the elements of the halakhic discourse that were presented in the first third of this chapter, there are a number of things that clearly stand out as being comparable to elements that are found in contemporary approaches to apologies. Quoting from *Hilkhot Teshuvah* (2:9), we had seen how Maimonides set forth three basic components to the obligation of asking for forgiveness for an interpersonal offense: a request to be forgiven, "appeasement," and, when called for, (financial) restitution (see above, p. 330). After quoting this halakhah from Maimonides, and proposing that the form of the appeasement should essentially be left up to the good judgment of the party who asks for forgiveness, we had seen that there are apparently three essential components to appeasement: the person asking for forgiveness is supposed to exhibit regret for what he has done, stop engaging in the wrongful behavior, and resolve to never engage in the behavior again. We had also seen that

234 Lazare, *On Apology*, 257.
235 See ibid., 230.
236 Smith, *I Was Wrong*, 1, 8, 81, 86, 116–18, 145, 194.

there is a halakhic requirement to verbally acknowledge the exact offense committed (see pp. 316–19). Every one of these elements—that is, a request to be forgiven, exhibiting regret, forbearance, compensation, and acknowledging the offense—were encountered repeatedly in our discussion of contemporary approaches to apologies, and find very strong support in contemporary theories and research (see footnote).[237] Other elements of the halakhic discourse, such as the questions regarding whether one must personally go to ask for forgiveness oneself or could one use an intermediary, the experiencing of shame, and the involvement of other people (see pp. 312, 314, 324), were also touched on in our discussion of contemporary approaches.[238]

237 A *request to be forgiven* was discussed in the CCSARP project (in reference to IFIDs) and in Ohbuchi, Kameda, and Agarie's study; it was one of the ten recurring elements identified by Kirchhoff, Strack, and Jäger (under the heading of "an acceptance request"); and it was also found to be the "most complete" form of apology in Schlenker and Darby's study. *Exhibiting regret* was part of the basic dictionary definitions of an apology; it was mentioned in the CCSARP project (in explaining the function of an IFID); it was one of the core elements of an apology according to Lazare (element no. 3) and Smith (element no. 8); it was one of Kirchhoff, Strack, and Jäger's recurring elements (under the heading "conveying emotions"); it was rated the third most complete apology in Schlenker and Darby's study, and was found to be the most important element in Kirchhoff, Wagner, and Strack's study (once again, under the heading "conveying emotions"). *Forbearance* was found to be one of the five basic apology strategies that people employ according to the CCSARP project (element no. 5); it was touched on in *On Apology* (element no. 3[a]) by Lazare, who eventually came to view it as a separate core element; it was covered under two of Smith's elements (see elements nos. 10 and 8); it was one of Kirchhoff, Strack, and Jäger's recurring elements; and was rated the fifth most important element in Kirchhoff, Wagner, and Strack's study. *Compensation* was found to be one of the five basic apology strategies according to the CCSARP project (element no. 4); it was one of the core elements according to Lazare (element no. 4, "reparations") and Smith (element no. 10, "reform and redress"); and it was one of Kirchhoff, Strack, and Jäger's recurring elements (element no. 9). *Acknowledging (and specifying) the offense* was seen as the most essential part of an effective apology by Lazare (see element no. 1[b]); it was the focus of two of Smith's elements (elements nos. 4 and 5); and it was one of the recurring elements identified by Kirchhoff, Strack, and Jäger (the element "naming the offense[s]").

238 The question of personally going oneself to ask for forgiveness was addressed by Smith (in element 3); experiencing of shame was mentioned by Lazare (element 3[b]), Smith (element 12), and Kirchhoff, Strack, and Jäger (element 5); and the issue of involving other people was alluded to by Lazare in his "Comprehensive Outline to Healing Mechanisms in Apologies," when he discussed "principals."

As far as differences are concerned, there is one specific category of differences that I would like to address, and that is, the omission of certain elements in the two systems' approaches. In the contemporary approaches to apologies we examined, there were numerous elements mentioned that do not appear in the halakhic sources that we examined. This would include the elements of recognizing the impact that one's behavior had on the victim and exhibiting empathy; admitting that there was some form of norm violation; explaining that the offense was not intentional and therefore not personal, that one's behavior is not indicative of the "real self" of the offender," and that the victim is blameless; allowing for catharsis and dialogue; and other elements. Similarly, there were also elements mentioned in the halakhic sources that we had seen which do not appear in the contemporary approaches that we examined. Two particular elements that, in my mind, stand out are the showing of sensitivity for the other party, by not embarrassing him or causing him unnecessary pain when acknowledging one's offenses, and the need for multiple attempts at apologizing that employ different forms of appeasement (see pp. 319, 334). The omission of these respective elements on the part of traditional Jewish approaches and contemporary approaches could, possibly, reflect that they are not accorded the same degree of importance that they are in the other system's approaches.

I would, however, propose that the omission of all of the aforementioned elements does not actually reflect any real or inherent differences that exist between traditional Jewish approaches and contemporary approaches to apologies. I believe that the omission of these elements can be attributed to the principle, mentioned earlier, that the Halakhah essentially leaves the form of the appeasement up to the good judgment of the person who is asking for forgiveness, and, possibly, to the fact that the material I have presented in this chapter is not an exhaustive treatment of the topics under discussion.

As postulated in the discussion of what does it mean to "appease" someone (see p. 331), classic halakhic sources do not spell out the exact nature of the appeasement that one should engage in, and, evidently, it was felt that this should be left up to the discretion of the person who asks for forgiveness. This would reflect the principle of "everything is in accordance with the time, issue, place, and individual" (see p. 254), which teaches that there are areas in life that are best left up to the discretion and good judgment of each person, who will hopefully do what is called for based on the unique circumstances of the situation, the correct application of Torah values, and good common sense. Asking for forgiveness for a wrong that one committed would certainly qualify as such a case (see Lazare's comments above, p. 370, where he writes that the success of an apology depends on whether one can "hear" what is needed in the particular situation and respond with just the right combination of elements). Therefore, outside a number of basic components, halakhic authorities would not, and could not, establish rigid or exact guidelines for the process of asking for forgiveness. Consequently, the absence in the halakhic discourse of elements that appear in contemporary discussions does not necessarily serve as any type of indication that the Halakhah would not value or would not recommend that these elements be incorporated in the process of asking for forgiveness.

Another factor that is certainly relevant to the issue of omission of elements is that, as I have acknowledged previously, what I have presented in this chapter does not come anywhere near to exhausting all of the traditional Jewish sources that are germane to the asking of forgiveness, nor have I presented all of the contemporary views on the elements that contribute to effective apologies. In respect to the Jewish sources examined, this chapter has only focused on halakhic material, and has not explored the multitude of potential sources that are found in other types of traditional Jewish texts (e.g., biblical, aggadic, philosophical, ethical, and kabbalistic texts). Even in regard to the halakhic material, I have not discussed all of the practical issues related to the asking of forgiveness that appear in halakhic sources (for examples of topics I have omitted, see pp. 362–63). Regarding the contemporary sources on apologies that were discussed, I have only focused on several well-known representative sources, and have not cited the alternative views of others. I therefore believe that the limitations in the scope of my presentation could account for the omission of elements, in that an exploration of other Jewish and contemporary sources may very well reveal that most of the respective omitted elements are valued in both traditional Jewish approaches and contemporary approaches.

Contemporary Models of Forgiveness

The topic of forgiveness started to become a focus of academic interest and research in the 1980s.[239] Since that time, there has been extensive theorizing and research and an overall enormous amount written on the topic.[240] From out of this large body of literature, there have emerged numerous models of forgiveness, which attempt to describe the process of forgiveness and set forth the steps that one should take in order to be able to find it in one's heart to forgive an interpersonal offense when it is difficult to do so. In a research article published in 2004, Donald Walker and Richard Gorsuch analyzed sixteen different models of forgiveness (or reconciliation) and mentioned a number of others that appear in the literature.[241] When one explores the topic of contemporary approaches to forgiveness, it does not take long to ascertain that, in fact, there are many more models of forgiveness in the literature than those that are cited in Walker and Gorsuch's article.[242]

---

239 Michael E. McCullough, Kenneth I. Pargament, and Carl E. Thoresen, eds., *Forgiveness: Theory, Research, and Practice* (New York: Guilford Press, 2001), 3–7; and Célestin Musekura, *An Assessment of Contemporary Models of Forgiveness, American University Studies*, VII, *Theology and Religion*, v. 302 (New York: Peter Lang, 2010), 41.

240 In relation to scientific research alone, only up until 2005, see the 38-page bibliography by Michael Scherer, Kathryn L. Cooke, and Everett L. Worthington, Jr., "Forgiveness Bibliography," in *Handbook of Forgiveness*, ed. Everett L. Worthington, Jr. (New York: Routledge, 2005), 507–45.

241 Donald F. Walker and Richard L Gorsuch, "Dimensions Underlying Sixteen Models of Forgiveness and Reconciliation," *Journal of Psychology and Theology* 32, no. 1 (2004): 13.

242 Examples of models that are not cited in Walker and Gorsuch's article include the well-known models of Fred Luskin, Leslie Greenberg (Greenberg's initial model of forgiveness is referenced, however), and Frederick DiBlasio. For a discussion of Luskin's model, see Fred Luskin, *Forgive for Good: A Proven Prescription for Health and Happiness* (San Francisco: Harper, 2002); for a discussion of Greenberg's model, see

According to Nathaniel Wade and Everett Worthington (a pioneer and highly influential theorist and researcher in the field), there are six core elements that are commonly employed in psychological interventions that try to promote forgiveness:[243]

(1) Defining forgiveness. The purpose of defining forgiveness is to help clarify goals, avoid confusion, and prevent further victimization. Misconceptions about what is meant by forgiveness could potentially be quite problematic, or even dangerous, for someone who is prepared to forgive interpersonal transgressions. By confusing forgiveness with other concepts, such as reconciliation, condoning, or forgetting, one could possibly place oneself in an intolerable or harmful situation by either returning to a bad relationship, allowing the other person to engage in objectionable behaviors, or having an unrealistic perception of the other person. However, when the concept of forgiveness is properly understood, one could very well forgive but not forget what happened, still hold the other person accountable for wrongdoings, and decide not to return to the previous relationship that one had with the offender.

(2) Recalling the hurt. As with most psychotherapeutic approaches, one of the first steps to be taken is that the participants tell their story and discuss the problems that they have been facing. This entails that there are facilitated discussions about the offense, anger, frustration, and hurt that has been experienced, the time spent ruminating on what occurred, and if/how the individual's view of the

---

Leslie Greenberg, Serine Warwar, and Wanda Malcolm, "Emotion-Focused Couples Therapy and the Facilitation of Forgiveness," *Journal of Marital and Family Therapy* 36, no. 1 (2010): 28–42; and for a discussion of DiBlasio's model, see below, p. 392.

243 The interventions that Wade and Worthington refer to were based primarily on the two most popular models of forgiveness, the "Enright model" and the "Worthington model"; see below, pp. 387–92.

world has changed. Recalling the hurt may reduce the impact of the offense and the associated negative emotions through catharsis and by helping the person attain a better understanding of his experiences and himself.

(3) Building empathy. Either through lecturing, stories, discussions, or various exercises, all the interventions that were examined by Wade and Worthington encouraged the party who suffered to try to take the perspective of and empathize with the offender. This component includes discussions about the benefits of perspective taking and the prevalence of attributional errors (see above, p. 214). Special care must be taken in asking victims of repeated offenses or serious crimes to empathize with the offender, which, without the proper timing and sensitivity, could potentially lead to further emotional/psychological harm.

(4) Acknowledging one's own offenses. The party who suffered discusses, records, and/or reflects on times when he committed offenses against others and needed forgiveness. Within this component, there is a strong emphasis on the development of humility. Aside from helping the individual see that he is also fallible and not so different from the offender, acknowledging one's own offenses may also promote forgiveness by reducing the effects of attributional errors. Caution must be exercised in that this element may alienate the party who suffered or, in extreme cases, harm him. Discussions of past offenses should be conducted in a nonjudgmental manner, and connections between the person's past offenses and the offense he is a victim of that would imply blame or causation should be avoided.

(5) Committing to forgiveness. The purpose of this component is to help one set goals for and motivate oneself. The person is encouraged to commit at an early stage in the

process to work towards forgiveness (in accordance with the approach of the "Enright group" model; see the upcoming section) or to commit at a later stage to maintain the forgiveness that has already been achieved (in accordance with the approach of the "Worthington group" model; see upcoming section).

(6) Overcoming "unforgiveness." Most of the interventions that they examined included what Wade and Worthington categorize as attempts to overcome "unforgiveness," that means to say, ways of dealing with negative feelings of resentment, anger, hatred, hostility, desires for revenge, avoidance, and rumination, but not necessarily promoting "forgiveness," which, as understood by Worthington and Wade (and others), relates to positive feelings of goodwill. This component is generally accomplished through discussion. Participants brainstorm ways in which they may effectively deal with unforgiveness; they engage in cognitive reframing (whereby they consider other possible ways of viewing the offense); they reflect on people they are either personally familiar with or famous people in history who have overcome unforgiveness; and they consider potentially positive outcomes from the offense, such as becoming more empathic and sensitive to others' suffering, attaining better self-understanding, or becoming wiser from the experience. This component is particularly useful when the person who suffered does not want to explicitly forgive the other party but would like to move beyond the negative effects of the offense.[244]

In an overview (published in 2014) of interventions that try to promote forgiveness, Worthington, Wade, and William Hoyt present a summary of some of the more prominent models of forgiveness.

244 Nathaniel G. Wade and Everett L. Worthington Jr, "In Search of a Common Core: A Content Analysis of Interventions to Promote Forgiveness," *Psychotherapy: Theory, Research, Practice, Training* 42, no. 2 (2005): 160–77.

In assessing the differences that exist, they assert that "[t]here are more commonalities than differences ... with the major differences being in packaging and in which aspects of experience are emphasized—emotion, cognition, or behavior."[245]

Empirically Supported Models. Most of the interventions that have been studied and found to be helpful in promoting forgiveness are based on one of two models of forgiveness—the twenty-step model developed by Robert Enright or the five-step model developed by Everett Worthington. This is clearly reflected in a meta-analysis of published studies of forgiveness interventions that was conducted by Wade, Hoyt, and Worthington. These researchers examined 64 interventions: 22 were based on Enright's model, 21 were based on Worthington's, and 21 were based on others (e.g., the models of Fred Luskin, Leslie Greenberg, and Frederick DiBlasio).[246] Their analysis indicated that for "serious offenses" Enright's model was the most effective, that for "offenses of moderate severity" Worthington's was just as effective as Enright's, and that other approaches "do not have enough studies investigating their efficacy to merit comparing to Enright's and Worthington's models." Wade, Hoyt, and Worthington also conclude, however, that "the type of forgiveness intervention is much less important than the context [i.e., the nature, or severity, of the offense] and duration of treatment."[247]

The Enright Model of Forgiveness. In 1991, after conducting an extensive review of religious, philosophical, and psychological perspectives on forgiveness, Robert Enright (who, for over twenty-five years, has been one of the leading theorists and researchers in the field) together with the "Human Development

245 Everett L. Worthington Jr., Nathaniel G. Wade, and William T. Hoyt, "Positive Psychological Interventions for Promoting Forgiveness: History, Present Status, and Future Prospects," in *The Wiley Blackwell Handbook of Positive Psychological Interventions*, ed. Acacia C. Parks and Stephen M. Schueller (Chichester, West Sussex: Wiley Blackwell, 2014), 24.

246 See above, p. 383 n. 242.

247 See Worthington, Wade, and Hoyt, "Positive Psychological Interventions," 29–31; and Nathaniel G. Wade et al., "Efficacy of Psychotherapeutic Interventions to Promote Forgiveness: A Meta-analysis," *Journal of Consulting and Clinical Psychology* 82, no. 1 (2014): 154–70.

Study Group" put forth their process-based model of forgiveness. Originally consisting of a series of seventeen "units," or steps, which eventually expanded into twenty (and subsequently came to be referred to as "guideposts") that were subdivided into four "phases," or major headings, this model delineates common psychological variables that are involved in the process of forgiving. Simply put, Enright's model attempts to spell out the steps a person often needs to take to forgive someone when it is difficult to do so.

The four major divisions of the Enright model are referred to as the "Uncovering Phase," the "Decision Phase," the "Work Phase," and the "Outcome [or 'Deepening'] Phase." These headings encompass the following:

> (1) The Uncovering Phase. In the uncovering phase, there are eight units that help the person develop an awareness of the problems he is facing. The individual becomes cognizant of psychological defenses, for example, denial or repression of feelings (unit 1); confronts the anger or hatred he is experiencing (unit 2); recognizes feelings of shame or guilt (if there are any) (unit 3); becomes aware of excessive amounts of emotional energy expended over what took place (unit 4), and whether he is ruminating on and keeps replaying the event in his mind (unit 5); comes to realize that he may be making unhealthy comparisons between himself and the offender (e.g., "He [the offender] is so much better off than I am") (unit 6); faces the reality that he may be permanently and adversely changed as a result of the offense (unit 7); and becomes aware that he may have developed a cynical and pessimistic view of the world (unit 8). The insights into the negative psychological consequences and pain that one is experiencing, which one becomes aware of in this phase, help serve as a motivator to proceed to the next phase in the process.

(2) The Decision Phase. The decision phase encompasses three units: one comes to a realization that previous strategies in dealing with his situation are ineffective (unit 9); he develops an understanding of what it means to forgive someone and comes to consider forgiveness as a viable option (unit 10); and commits to forgive the offender, which at this stage merely entails that the offended party decides to refrain from actively seeking revenge (even in the most subtle forms, such as not speaking ill of the offender to others who do not need to know about the offense), even though he may still be feeling anger and is resentful towards the offender (unit 11).

(3) The Work Phase. The work phase starts off with reframing (i.e., rethinking the situation and seeing it from a fresh perspective). Reframing requires that one engage in perspective taking, and try to understand the offender, his background, and the factors that may have contributed to his committing the offense, without condoning his misdeeds (unit 12). This may foster empathy for the offender which, in turn, may generate compassion for him (unit 13). One "absorbs the pain," not in the sense of repressing his feelings, but by allowing himself to feel and bear the hurt, without passing it on to those around him, for example, his family members (unit 14). The final unit in this phase is the offering of a "gift" to the offender. This means that one should perform some act of kindness, or do something nice, for the offender. There are endless possible forms that this may take, for example, spending time with the offender, sending him a greeting card, expressing concern for his welfare, smiling when you see him, and so on (unit 15).

(4) The "Outcome" or "Deepening" Phase. In this phase, one may come to find meaning in his suffering and realize

> that there is some positive aspect to it; for example, he may have learned valuable lessons from the experience or have become a stronger person because of it (unit 16). He may realize that there were also times that he himself had committed wrongs against others and needed forgiveness. This may help to motivate the person to continue forgiving[248] (unit 17). If he has felt isolated and alone due to what happened, he may come to develop connections with others (e.g., friends, a support group, or a therapist) and find that they are there to help him (unit 18). He may discover a new sense of purpose or direction in life, for example, by helping others who are in a similar situation (unit 19). And, finally, he comes to achieve a decrease in negative emotions and an increase in positive ones, and experiences an internal emotional release (unit 20).[249]

Enright repeatedly emphasizes that his model is by no means invariant or universal. That means to say that the series of units are not carved in stone. They do not necessarily have to be followed in the sequence set forth, nor do they apply to everyone.

The Worthington Model of Forgiveness. Worthington calls his five-step approach the "REACH Forgiveness" model. REACH is an acronym that stands for "**R**ecall the Hurt," "**E**mpathize," "**A**ltruistic Gift of Forgiveness," "**C**ommit to the Emotional Forgiveness that Was Experienced," and "**H**old on to Forgiveness." Before commencing with these five steps, the model first requires that one come to

248 According to Enright, for someone who is ambivalent about forgiving, this should probably take place earlier on in the forgiveness process.

249 Robert D. Enright and the Human Development Study Group, "The Moral Development of Forgiveness," in *Handbook of Moral Behavior and Development: Volume 1: Theory*, ed. William M. Kurtines and Jacob L. Gewirtz (Hillsdale, NJ: Lawrence Erlbaum, 1991), 123–52; Robert D. Enright, Suzanne Freedman, and Julio Rique, "The Psychology of Interpersonal Forgiveness," in *Exploring Forgiveness*, ed. Robert D. Enright and Joanna North (Madison, WI: University of Wisconsin Press, 1998), 52–54; Robert D. Enright and Richard P. Fitzgibbons, *Helping Clients Forgive: An Empirical Guide for Resolving Anger and Restoring Hope* (Washington, DC: American Psychological Association, 2000), 65–88; and Robert D. Enright, *Forgiveness Is a Choice: A Step-by-Step Process for Resolving Anger and Restoring Hope* (Washington, DC: American Psychological Association, 2001), 71–186.

understand what is meant by forgiveness (see above, p. 384). When this has been achieved, the person then should

(1) Recall the Hurt. This entails that one recall the transgression as objectively as possible, without railing against and vilifying the offender or dwelling upon one's own victimization.

(2) Empathize. One should try to understand the offender, see things from his perspective, and identify with him emotionally. In addition to empathy, one should also try to develop other positive emotions towards the offender, such as sympathy, compassion, and even love.

(3) Give an Altruistic Gift of Forgiveness. In combination with empathy, feelings of humility and gratitude that emerge out of recalling times that one hurt others and was forgiven should help inspire the person to forgive the offender.

(4) Commit to the Emotional Forgiveness that Was Experienced. Instead of just forgiving the offender in one's heart, one should make a "public" commitment to the forgiveness that was already achieved in the previous step. This could take many possible forms; for example, one could tell a confidant, put it in writing, or just say it out loud to oneself that one has forgiven the other person. By verbalizing or writing that one has forgiven the offender, the forgiveness will not be as fragile and there will be less of a chance that one will at some later point come to question whether he has really forgiven the person.

(5) Hold on to Forgiveness. One should use various strategies in dealing with unforgiving thoughts, emotions, or behaviors that subsequently surface. For example, one could avoid dwelling on negative thoughts and emotions by

> actively distracting oneself or removing oneself from the situation that triggers them. Alternatively, one could remind oneself of one's commitment to forgive, or repeat the earlier steps in the REACH model.[250]

DiBlasio's Decision-Based Model. In contrast to the "process-based models" that we have been discussing up until this point, there are also "decision-based models" of forgiveness. The basic difference between a process-based model and a decision-based model is that a process-based model views forgiveness as something that is attained through a series of cognitive and affective steps, which can take a considerable amount of time, as opposed to a decision-based model, which views forgiveness as something that revolves around a cognitive decision to forgive, and generally requires a much shorter period of time (for further explanation, see p. 397).

One of the most well-known decision-based models is the one that was developed by Frederick DiBlasio. DiBlasio had been investigating forgiveness in family therapy since 1990. He had found that many clients could forgive serious offenses in much shorter periods of time than those that were indicated by the process-based models. He writes that in many cases "lasting and true forgiveness was granted in a day," or single therapy session. According to DiBlasio, "[w]hen emotions are elevated or the need is critical, people seem to show the capacity to forgive quickly," as can be seen at the bedside of dying patients, where often forgiveness and reconciliation take place within a moment's time.[251]

DiBlasio's model is based on an understanding of forgiveness that sees it as "the cognitive letting go of resentment, bitterness, and

---

250 Everett L. Worthington, Jr., *Five Steps to Forgiveness: The Art and Science of Forgiving* (New York: Crown, 2001), 23–132; Worthington, Wade, and Hoyt, "Positive Psychological Interventions," 25; Everett L. Worthington, Jr., *Forgiveness and Reconciliation: Theory and Application* (New York: Routledge, 2006), 170–71; and Everett L. Worthington, Jr., "Forgiveness Intervention Manuals," http://www.people.vcu.edu/~eworth/.

251 Frederick A. DiBlasio, "The Use of a Decision-Based Forgiveness Intervention within Intergenerational Family Therapy," *Journal of Family Therapy* 20, no. 1 (1998): 78.

need for vengeance," which does not necessarily put an end to the emotional pain, but does often precipitate a significant reduction in the pain. According to DiBlasio, through this approach people become "empowered when they make cognitive choices [to forgive] that promote harmony in their relationships ... [and] healing"; this is as opposed to processed-based models that view forgiveness as a potentially long and ongoing process that can take up to months, or even years, during which a person can become the victim of his own emotional states.[252]

A forgiveness intervention session that employs DiBlasio's model lasts for between two to three hours.[253] The model uses an interpersonal approach, in which the parties involved are given the opportunity to discuss what had occurred and ask and grant forgiveness to each other for past offenses. It consists of thirteen steps that are divided into three sections: steps 1 to 3 prepare the participants for the seeking and granting of forgiveness; steps 4 to 12 encompass the asking and granting of forgiveness; and step 13 completes the session with a ceremonial act that is meant to symbolize the forgiveness. The following elements are included in the 13 steps:

> Step 1—The definition and benefits of decision-based forgiveness are explained and discussed. Among the things that should be highlighted in the first step are the following: forgiveness is a decision to let go of resentment, bitterness, and revengeful thoughts; it is an act of will; it is possible to have emotional pain but also to control revengeful thinking; emotional pain and hurt can be addressed subsequent to the granting of forgiveness; and there are significant personal

252 Ibid.; and Frederick A. DiBlasio, "Decision-Based Forgiveness Treatment in Cases of Marital Infidelity," *Psychotherapy: Theory, Research, Practice, Training* 37, no. 2 (2000): 150–51. According to DiBlasio, his approach is consistent with other cognitive-behavioral approaches to therapy.

253 The two- to three-hour time period refers to an intervention that is being used in the context of couples therapy. This is as opposed to intergenerational family therapy, in which sessions range from between four to six hours. See DiBlasio, "Decision-Based Forgiveness Treatment," 151; and DiBlasio, "Decision-Based Forgiveness Intervention," 81.

and interpersonal benefits in deciding to forgive the other person.

Step 2—It is made clear that the focus will be on seeking forgiveness for what the *offender* deems as wrongful actions. The participants should understand that each one of them will be given the opportunity (but is not required) to seek forgiveness for one's own offenses. The focus will not be on voicing complaints against the other party. Primarily, the session will be a time for personal accountability and to ask for forgiveness for one's own wrongdoings.

Step 3—Introduce the steps that will follow, and the decision to proceed. The participants are given an overview of what will take place in steps 4 to 13. If the participants are willing to proceed, they move on to step 4.

Step 4—The statement of the offense. The offender gives a basic and clear description of a specific offense that was committed against the other party. The statement of the offense should reflect that one understands that there was a wrong committed and that one accepts culpability for what was done.

Step 5—The offender provides an explanation. The offender should summarize the reasons that led him to commit the offense, without presenting them as an excuse or justification for the behavior.

Step 6—Questions and answers about the offense. The offended party is given the opportunity to ask questions about the offense that may help him achieve a better understanding of what took place; the offender should answer the questions truthfully. Questions and answers that would be counterproductive should be avoided.

Step 7—The offended shares emotional reactions. The offended party should give a full description of his feelings related to the offense. All of his pain and hurt should be shared.

Step 8—The offender shows empathy and remorse for what occurred. The offender summarizes the emotional reactions that were shared in step 7. In doing so, he should thoughtfully reflect the emotions and pain that were experienced by the offended party as a result of the offense, showing that he understands and regrets the suffering that he caused.

Step 9—The offender develops a plan to prevent the behavior from reoccurring. The offender should come up with a plan, containing as many strategies as possible, to help him avoid repeating the offense. Where appropriate, the plan may contain some form of restitution for the offense.

Step 10—The offended party shows empathy for the offender. The offended party emotionally identifies with the past suffering of the offender and the regret he has exhibited during the session.

Step 11—Emphasis on choice and commitment to let go. The offended party should be cognizant that if he chooses to grant forgiveness, he is committing himself to not use the offense as a "weapon" against the offender in the future (i.e., he will not berate, harass, or subject the person to suffering because of what happened). This does not mean that the offense will never be discussed again; residual problems and feelings that are still present after the session should be discussed. The offended party may still subsequently experience surges of anger or resentment. If these should occur, they should be dealt with in a constructive manner.[254]

254 DiBlasio suggests that one use a cognitive-oriented approach that helps to regulate unwanted thoughts. (For an explanation of what such a cognitive-oriented approach may entail, see the discussion below, on pp. 440–41.)

> Step 12—A formal request for forgiveness. The offender summarizes elements discussed in previous steps and asks for forgiveness, and the offended party responds by granting forgiveness. To accentuate the formality of the seeking and granting of forgiveness, the person who facilitates the process (i.e., the therapist) serves as a witness to the request and the forgiveness that has been granted. The date and the exact time of the forgiveness should be recorded in writing and kept in some meaningful place.
>
> Step 13—A ceremonial act. The participants come up with some form of ceremonial act that will serve as a symbolic expression that the offense has been formally forgiven (which may assist in reinforcing the commitment to forgive). Examples of ceremonial acts would be when a couple that had a troubled marriage and forgives each other decides to sell their old wedding rings in order to buy new ones, or they decide to renew their weddings vows, or, in a case of forgiveness between parents and children, when the participants decide that they will create a symbolic family album.[255]

DiBlasio has been using some form of this model successfully since the 1980s. As far as empirical support for it is concerned, in addition to incorporating many elements that have been researched in the context of other models and have been found to be effective, DiBlasio's model was the subject of two studies in 2008 in which it was shown that it is effective in achieving forgiveness among married couples.[256]

---

255 DiBlasio, "Decision-Based Forgiveness Intervention," 77–94; DiBlasio, "Decision-Based Forgiveness Treatment," 149–57; and Frederick A. DiBlasio, "Marital Couples and Forgiveness Intervention," in *Evidence-Based Practices for Christian Counseling and Psychotherapy*, ed. Everett L. Worthington Jr., Eric L. Johnson, Joshua N. Hook, and Jamie D. Aten (Downers Grove, IL: InterVarsity Press, 2013), 232–54.

256 Frederick A. DiBlasio and Brent B. Benda, "Forgiveness Intervention with Married Couples: Two Empirical Analyses," *Journal of Psychology and Christianity* 27, no. 2 (2008): 150–58; and Frederick A. DiBlasio, Everett L. Worthington Jr, and David J. Jennings II, "Forgiveness Interventions with Children, Adolescents, and Families," in *Spiritual Interventions in Child and Adolescent Psychotherapy*, ed.

DiBlasio's model differs from those of Worthington's and Enright's in a number of ways. DiBlasio's model utilizes an apology and dialogue between the offender and offended to serve as catalysts for forgiveness; in Worthington's and Enright's models, forgiveness is not dependent on any type of apology or dialogue.[257] According to Thomas Baskin and Enright, there also exists a fundamental philosophical, or definitional, difference between decision-based models, such as DiBlasio's, and those that are process based. Decision-based models view forgiveness as something that is essentially cognitive in nature, the defining moment of which is the decision to forgive and is embodied in the words "I forgive you." When one speaks these words, one is expressing a commitment that, from hereon in, one will not allow any internal resentment control one's actions towards the offender. Enright cites William Neblett's philosophical analysis of forgiveness[258] as representative of this view. This is in contrast to the philosophical, or definitional, approach that underlies process-based models, which view forgiveness as a cognitive-affective process that can take much time and effort, in which forgiveness develops from anger and resentment, through the decision to forgive, into feelings of compassion. The philosophical analysis of forgiveness

---

Donald F. Walker and William L. Hathaway (Washington, DC: American Psychological Association, 2013), 239.

257 In support of an approach that employs an apology, such as DiBlasio's, there is an abundant amount of evidence that a sincere apology helps to facilitate forgiveness (see p. 402 n. 266). Additionally, to quote Lazare, it seems that "[s]ome people will not forgive and even appear psychologically unable to forgive without a prior apology ... a significant portion of the United States and even the world carry grudges over offenses they will not forgive without a prior apology. I regard this phenomenon as a fact of human nature ... The fundamental reason for this demand is that the apology meets the psychological needs of the offended party." Lazare, *On Apology*, 241–42.

258 According to Neblett, saying "I forgive you" can constitute forgiveness, even though one still experiences ill will and negative emotions towards the offender. Doing away with all negative emotions may be a desirable or an ideal feature of forgiveness, but, based on the standard usage of the term, there is a range of other things that also could be categorized as "forgiveness." These would include not berating, harassing, or subjecting the offender to other forms of suffering for his past misdeed, and that one is committed to try to do away with his resentment towards the offender. William R. Neblett, "Forgiveness and Ideals," *Mind* 83, no. 330 (1974): 269–75.

that was set forth by Joanna North[259] is representative of this view and played an important role in the development of Enright's model.[260]

Comparing Contemporary Models of Forgiveness and the Obligations of the One Who Forgives

In this section, I will highlight what I believe to be one major area of similarity and one major area of dissimilarity that exist between contemporary models of forgiveness and the obligations of the one who forgives that were discussed in this chapter. The area of similarity is in relation to the fundamental question of what does it mean to "forgive" someone, and the practical ramifications of the definitions that are used. The area of dissimilarity is in respect to the explicit focus and emphasis on how one goes about forgiving someone when it is difficult to do so.

The Area of Similarity. In our discussion of the obligations of the one who forgives, we saw that there is a debate among rabbinic authorities regarding how sincere or heartfelt one's forgiveness must be. In considering the views of rabbinic authorities in relation to this topic, there emerges what appears to be a fundamental disagreement and difference in practices in traditional Jewish approaches that parallels, to a certain extent, a fundamental disagreement and difference in practices among contemporary approaches to forgiveness.

There were two main groups of rabbinic authorities that were presented in the discussion of how sincere or heartfelt one's forgiveness must be, each of which held an opinion that was in opposition to the other's. One group, which included R. Joseph Engel, R. Simḥah Zissel Ziv, R. Reuven Grozovsky, and R. Isaac Blaser, maintained that

259 Joanna North, "Wrongdoing and Forgiveness," *Philosophy* 62, no. 242 (Oct., 1987): 499–508; and Joanna North, "The Ideal of Forgiveness: A Philosophical Exploration," in *Exploring Forgiveness*, ed. Robert D. Enright and Joanna North (Madison, WI: University of Wisconsin Press, 1998), 15–34.

260 See Thomas W. Baskin and Robert D. Enright, "Intervention Studies on Forgiveness: A Meta-Analysis," *Journal of Counseling and Development* 82, no. 1 (2004): 81–82. For specific concepts that Enright took from North, see Enright and the Human Development Study Group, "The Moral Development of Forgiveness," 126–28, 130, 136, 143.

as long as one verbally states that he has forgiven the offending party, even though he is still feeling ill will towards him and has not forgiven him in his heart, from a halakhic standpoint this would constitute a bona fide act of forgiveness. The other group of authorities, which included R. Abraham Isaiah Karelitz, R. Shlomo Wolbe, and others,[261] were of the opinion that forgiveness has to be sincere and do away with internal feelings of ill will towards the offender, and therefore merely saying that one forgives someone when one does not really mean it, from a halakhic standpoint would not constitute a proper form of forgiveness. Based on the perspective of the latter group, the associated question was raised as to what does one do if he or she has difficulty in uprooting feelings of ill will towards the offender and cannot find it in his or her heart to forgive the other person. It was in response to this question that we saw authorities[262] who expressed the view that forgiveness is something that often requires one to "work on" oneself in order to forgive the other person, which can potentially take a considerable amount of time and effort.

These two opinions exhibit a marked similarity to the two basic trains of thought that were presented in the discussion of the difference between process-based models and those that are decision based. We had seen in that discussion that the underlying difference between process-based and decision-based models is that those that are process based view, or define, forgiveness as something that encompasses various affective components (i.e., doing away with the negative feelings of anger, hatred, hostility, desires for revenge, etc., and having positive feelings take their place), and therefore process-based models incorporate a lengthy series of steps that attempt to address emotions. This is in contrast with models that are decision based, which view, or define, forgiveness as something that is primarily a cognitive decision to not let one's negative emotions affect one's outward behaviors towards the offender and finds

261 Others may include R. Steinman, R. Lopian, and possibly all of the authorities that are listed in footnote 186 on p. 354.

262 See the comments of R. Steinman and R. Wolbe in reference to the anecdote with R. Lopian on pp. 358–59, n. 197.

expression in the statement "I forgive you," and therefore decision-based models can generally achieve forgiveness in a much shorter period of time than those that are process based.

Taking all of the above into consideration, it appears that in both traditional Jewish approaches and in contemporary approaches to forgiveness, one encounters a similar philosophical, or definitional, difference of opinion regarding the meaning of "forgiveness" and similar practical differences that arise from out of the two different opinions regarding the concept. In both traditional Jewish approaches and contemporary approaches, there is a debate as to whether forgiveness has to encompass affective components or not, with one opinion asserting that it does and the other asserting that it does not. The opinion asserting that forgiveness encompasses affective components sees forgiveness as a process that must do away with ill will and negative emotions and therefore often requires a considerable amount of time and effort on the part of the forgiver. The other opinion, which asserts that forgiveness does not have to encompass affective components, sees forgiveness as primarily a decision, expressed through a verbal statement, that one forgives the other person, which does not require that one do away with ill will and negative emotions, and therefore forgiveness will generally take place much faster than it would in contrast to the first approach.

The Area of Dissimilarity. The views in traditional Jewish approaches and contemporary approaches that maintain that forgiveness is a process that must do away with negative emotions inevitably have to address the question of how one is supposed to accomplish this when finding it difficult to do so. Contemporary models offer a variety of methods of how to possibly overcome feelings of anger, resentment, hostility, and other negative emotions that one is experiencing and forgive the other person even on an emotional level. These methods encompass an array of cognitive, affective, and behavioral elements that help deal with the range of negative emotions that are commonly felt towards an offender. In the halakhic sources that we examined in this chapter, the issue of how one does away with negative emotions was hardly ever addressed, at least not explicitly (for how this may have been addressed implicitly, see footnote).[263] When the issue did come up (in the anecdote with R. Lopian that was cited by R. Steinman), the approach that was taken was that one should turn to the study of *musar* (Jewish ethics and character development). The implication is that when it comes to dealing with intense feelings of ill will, anger, animosity, and so forth, it would primarily fall within the province of *musar* to do so and not that of the Halakhah. This is in stark contrast with contemporary models of forgiveness, the explicit focus of which is on the removal of psychological/emotional impediments that stand in the way of forgiveness.

Apologies and Forgiveness in Contemporary Conflict Resolution

There is a prodigious amount of evidence that apologies and forgiveness play a pivotal role in conflict resolution. Studies have shown that apologies help to diffuse anger and hostility,[264] settle disputes,[265]

---

263 There are certainly components of the halakhic requirements that implicitly address emotions and help to facilitate sincere and heartfelt forgiveness. These would include the appeasement of the party who suffered, forbearance, compensation, acknowledging the offense, and the experiencing of remorse on the part of the offender. As we had seen in the section above that discussed contemporary research on apologies, these elements constitute the essential features of an effective apology. Apologies have been shown to be helpful in diffusing negative emotions, such as anger and hostility, and in promoting sincere and heartfelt forgiveness (see the research cited in the next section of the text).

264 See, for example, Anderson, Linden, and Habra, "Influence of Apologies," 347–58; Mark Bennett and Deborah Earwaker, "Victims' Responses to Apologies: The Effects of Offender Responsibility and Offense Severity," *The Journal of Social Psychology* 134, no. 4 (1994): 457–64; and Ohbuchi, Kameda, and Agarie, "Apology as Aggression Control," 219–27.

265 Much has been written about this topic in discussing the advantages of apologies when one is faced with a potential lawsuit. See, for example, Jennifer K. Robbennolt, "Apologies and Legal Settlement: An Empirical Examination," *Michigan Law Review* 102, no. 3 (2003): 460–516; Jonathan R. Cohen, "Advising Clients to Apologize," *Southern California Law Review* 72 (1999): 1009–69; and Deborah L. Levi, "The Role of Apology in Mediation," *New York University Law Review* 72, no. 5 (1997): 1165–210.

promote forgiveness,[266] and restore relationships.[267] Similarly, forgiveness is positively associated with the control of anger,[268] cooperation,[269] constructive communication,[270] the resolution of interpersonal issues,[271] reconciliation, and the maintenance and repair of relationships.[272] In addition to the research-based evidence, leading conflict

266 Julie Juola Exline and Roy F. Baumeister, "Expressing Forgiveness and Repentance: Benefits and Barriers," in *Forgiveness: Theory, Research, and Practice*, ed. Michael E. McCullough, Kenneth I. Pargament, and Carl E. Thoresen (New York: Guilford Press, 2000), 136–37; Guy Foster Bachman and Laura K. Guerrero, "Forgiveness, Apology, and Communicative Responses to Hurtful Events," *Communication Reports* 19, no. 1 (2006): 45–56; and James R. Davis and Gregg J. Gold, "An Examination of Emotional Empathy, Attributions of Stability, and the Link between Perceived Remorse and Forgiveness," *Personality and Individual Differences* 50, no. 3 (2011): 392–97; as well as in many other sources.

267 Holley S. Hodgins and Elizabeth Liebeskind, "Apology versus Defense: Antecedents and Consequences," *Journal of Experimental Social Psychology* 39, no. 4 (2003): 297–316, Study 2. Without going into all of the possible mediating variables, the restoration of relationships by apologies can be simply understood as being brought about through forgiveness. For further elaboration, see Michael E. McCullough et al., "Interpersonal Forgiving in Close Relationships: II. Theoretical Elaboration and Measurement," *Journal of Personality and Social Psychology* 75, no. 6 (1998): 1586–603.

268 See, for example, Kevin S. Seybold et al., "Physiological and Psychological Correlates of Forgiveness," *Journal of Psychology and Christianity* 20, no. 3 (2001): 250–59; Charlotte van Oyen Witvliet, Thomas E. Ludwig, and Kelly L. Vander Laan, "Granting Forgiveness or Harboring Grudges: Implications for Emotion, Physiology, and Health," *Psychological Science* 12, no. 2 (2001): 117–23; and Shih-Tseng Tina Huang and Robert D. Enright, "Forgiveness and Anger-Related Emotions in Taiwan: Implications for Therapy," *Psychotherapy: Theory, Research, Practice, Training* 37, no. 1 (2000): 71–79.

269 Johan C. Karremans and Paul A. M. Van Lange, "Back to Caring after Being Hurt: The Role of Forgiveness," *European Journal of Social Psychology* 34, no. 2 (2004): 207–27.

270 Frank D. Fincham and Steven R. H. Beach, "Forgiveness in Marriage: Implications for Psychological Aggression and Constructive Communication," *Personal Relationships* 9, no. 3 (2002): 239–51.

271 Frank D. Fincham, Steven R. H. Beach, and Joanne Davila, "Forgiveness and Conflict Resolution in Marriage," *Journal of Family Psychology* 18, no. 1 (2004): 72–81; and Frank D. Fincham, Steven R. H. Beach, and Joanne Davila, "Longitudinal Relations between Forgiveness and Conflict Resolution in Marriage," *Journal of Family Psychology* 21, no. 3 (2007): 542–45.

272 Jo-Ann Tsang, Michael E. McCullough, and Frank D. Fincham, "The Longitudinal Association between Forgiveness and Relationship Closeness and Commitment," *Journal of Social and Clinical Psychology* 25, no. 4 (2006): 448–72; Caryl E. Rusbult et al., "Forgiveness and Relational Repair," in *Handbook of Forgiveness*, ed. Everett L. Worthington, Jr. (New York: Routledge, 2005), 187–88, 192, 198–200, 185–205; McCullough et al., "Interpersonal Forgiving in Close Relationships: II"; and in other sources as well.

resolution theorists have also emphasized the importance of apologies and forgiveness.[273] It is therefore somewhat surprising that in certain areas of contemporary conflict resolution, apologies and forgiveness have received only a minimal amount of attention.

There is a perceivable lack of emphasis on apologies and forgiveness in contemporary conflict resolution. Within the field of alternative dispute resolution (ADR), the value of apologies is widely recognized by practitioners; however, due to various factors, such as the concern that an apology may be construed as an admission of legal liability or the inherent psychological/emotional challenges of admitting that one has done something wrong, there is widespread aversion to apologies, and they are often avoided in ADR processes.[274] As far as forgiveness is concerned, the topic receives even less attention in ADR than apologies.[275] Without mentioning ADR or focusing on any other specific subfield within contemporary conflict resolution, Robert Enright has called attention to the fact that, as a general rule, most books that discuss conflict resolution do not emphasize forgiveness.[276]

---

273 See, for example, Morton Deutsch, *The Handbook of Conflict Resolution: Theory and Practice*, ed. Morton Deutsch, Peter T. Coleman, and Eric C. Marcus (San Francisco: Jossey-Bass, 2014), 17, 37, 51 (in reference to apologies), and xxvii, 17, 45, 48–51 (in reference to forgiveness); Dean G. Pruitt and Sung Hee Kim, *Social Conflict: Escalation, Stalemate, and Settlement*, 3rd ed. (New York: McGraw-Hill, 2004), 186, 218, 220–22; Roy J. Lewicki and Edward C. Tomlinson, "Trust, Trust Development, and Trust Repair," in *The Handbook of Conflict Resolution: Theory and Practice*, 120–25, 128. An entire chapter is dedicated to the topic of forgiveness (and apologies) in Wilmot and Hocker's *Interpersonal Conflict*; see Gary W. Hawk, "Forgiveness and Reconciliation," in William Wilmot and Joyce Hocker, *Interpersonal Conflict*, 8th ed. (New York: McGraw Hill, 2011), 296–333.

274 See Levi, "The Role of Apology in Mediation," 1165–1210; Max Bolstad, "Learning from Japan: The Case for Increased Use of Apology in Mediation," *Cleveland State Law Review* 48 (2000): 572, 574–76; and Cohen, "Advising Clients to Apologize," 1023–29.

275 Geraldine Neal, "Alternative Dispute Resolution: Are Apology and Forgiveness Simply Two Sides of the One Coin?" in *A Journey through Forgiveness*, ed. Malika Rebai Maamri, Nehama Verbin, and Everett L. Worthington, Jr. (Oxford, UK: Inter-Disciplinary Press, 2010), 167. For a discussion of the applicability of forgiveness to mediation, see Kenneth Cloke, *Mediating Dangerously: The Frontiers of Conflict Resolution* (San Francisco: Jossey-Bass, 2001), 87–107.

276 Enright, *Forgiveness Is a Choice*, 266–67.

One area in contemporary conflict resolution that I had initially assumed would focus on apologies and forgiveness, but does not, is conflict resolution education. In surveying the major conflict resolution education programs and curricula, I found that they too do not emphasize apologies and forgiveness. It should be understood that there certainly are references to apologies and forgiveness in the educational material that I examined, but these references are relatively scarce. This may very well reflect the trend in the broader field of contemporary conflict resolution, or, possibly, a past prevailing trend in the field of social and emotional learning.[277]

Comparing Contemporary Conflict Resolution and Traditional Jewish Approaches in Respect to Apologies and Forgiveness

Based on my research, I would have to conclude that there is a significant difference between contemporary conflict resolution and traditional Jewish approaches in respect to apologies and forgiveness. As stated above, I have found that even though conflict resolution theorists may emphasize the importance of apologies and forgiveness, in practice some subfields of contemporary conflict resolution do not emphasize these elements. This is in stark contrast to traditional Jewish approaches. We had already seen in Chapter 6 that in the very selfsame halakhah (*De'ot* 6:6) in which Maimonides sets forth the requirement of addressing interpersonal provocations through

277 The major works on social and emotional learning, or emotional intelligence, that I have examined never seem to focus on apologies and forgiveness. At best, they may at some point mention these topics in passing. This trend in social and emotional learning may in turn possibly reflect past prevalent trends in psychology and therapy. See the related discussions, regarding forgiveness, in Kristina Coop Gordon, Donald H. Baucom, and Douglas K. Snyder, "The Use of Forgiveness in Marital Therapy," in *Forgiveness: Theory, Research, and Practice*, ed. Michael E. McCullough, Kenneth I. Pargament, and Carl E. Thoresen, (New York: Guilford Press, 2000), 225; Kristina Coop Gordon, Donald H. Baucom, and Douglas K. Snyder, "Forgiveness in Couples: Divorce, Infidelity, and Couples Therapy," in *Handbook of Forgiveness*, ed. Everett L. Worthington, Jr. (New York: Routledge, 2005), 407; and Varda Konstom et al., "Forgiveness in Practice: What Mental Health Counselors are Telling Us," in *Before Forgiving: Cautionary Views of Forgiveness in Psychotherapy*, ed. Sharon Lamb and Jeffrie G. Murphy (New York: Oxford University Press, 2002), 54–71.

dialogue (i.e., the mitzvah of *tokhaḥah* for interpersonal offenses), he also talks about apologies and forgiveness. Maimonides then goes on to state (in *De'ot* 6:9) that the entire obligation of discussing an interpersonal provocation with the offender hinges upon forgiveness. I believe that this section from Maimonides' *Mishneh Torah* can serve as a good indicative example of how in traditional Jewish approaches forgiveness, apologies, and interpersonal conflict resolution are inextricably connected with each other. Maimonides' formulation is far from being just one isolated example. Taken as a whole, all of the *halakhot* and halakhic debates that were presented in this chapter can serve as more than ample evidence of the strong emphasis that is placed on apologies and forgiveness in traditional Jewish approaches.

Having explored the laws that relate to apologies and forgiveness, this chapter concludes the fourth section, "Basic Commandments and Laws of Interpersonal Conflict Resolution." In the next chapter, we will deal with material that is of a non-halakhic nature and discuss anger, the central emotional component of interpersonal conflict, and approaches to anger management.

PART V

The Affective Component—Anger Management

Chapter 9

Jewish Anger Management

A wrathful man stirs up strife, but he who is slow to anger calms a quarrel.

Proverbs 15:18

The heart is a temple for God's divine presence ... one who becomes angry brings an idol into the temple and drives out the divine presence.

R. Eleazar Azikri, *Sefer Ḥaredim*, 21:17

A study of traditional Jewish perspectives on interpersonal conflict resolution would not be complete if it did not address the affective component of anger. Interspersed throughout the corpus of classic Jewish texts, there is a multitude of sayings and discussions regarding *ka'as*, "anger."[1] Particularly in the *musar* (ethical) literature, amidst discussions of general character development, one usually comes across some discussion or mention of the topic."[2] To the Jewish sages, *ka'as* serves as the force that actuates and impels conflict. It is perceived

1 For talmudic and midrashic sources, see Mosheh David Gross, *Otsar ha-Agadah* (Jerusalem: Mossad Harav Kook, 1993), s.v. *ka'as*.

2 See, for example, Maimonides, *Mishneh Torah, De'ot* 1:4, 2:3; Abraham ben Moses ben Maimon, *Ha-Maspik le-Ovde ha-Shem* (Jerusalem: Salimon Sason, 1965), 43–50; *Orḥot Tsadikim ha-Shalem* (Jerusalem: Feldheim, 1988), chap. 12, *Sha'ar ha-Ka'as;* Zeraḥyah ha-Yevani, *Sefer ha-Yashar* (Bnei Brak: Mishor, 1989), 73–74, 101–2; Elijah ben Moses de Vidas, *Reshit Ḥokhmah ha-Shalem*, vol. 2 (Jerusalem: Or ha-Musar, 1990), *Sha'ar ha-Anavah*, chaps. 2–5, pp. 601–81; Eliezer Papo, *Pele Yo'ets ha-Shalem* (Jerusalem: Mekhon Merav, 1994), s.v. *ka'as;* Jacob Kranz, *Sefer ha-Midot* (Jerusalem: Mekhon Sha'are Yosher, 1993), *Sha'ar ha-Sinah*, 339–41; as well as in many other sources.

as something that is unique in its virulence and potential for spiritual degradation, as is manifest by its ability to impede rational thought, magnify events totally out of proportion, overwhelm deep-seated and naturally good inclinations and habits, eviscerate one's equanimity, and strip away almost every vestige of one's dignity.[3] Based on traditional Jewish sources, a number of contemporary authors have compiled anthologies (some of which also incorporate a considerable amount of original material) on anger. These include R. Avraham Tovolski's *Haser Ka'as mi-Libekha*, R. Shlomo Man's *Dibur be-Naḥat*, R. Eliyahu Porat Teharani's *Alufenu Mesubalim*, and several others.[4] Unquestionably, the two seminal works in this area are R. Abraham Jelen's *Orekh Apayim* and R. Moshe Levinson's *Ma'aneh Rakh*. This chapter will compare and contrast these two works, and thereby highlight some of the major features of their respective approaches to anger management. We will begin with a short introduction to *Orekh Apayim* and *Ma'aneh Rakh* and then proceed to discuss the similarities and differences that exist between them. The chapter will conclude with a discussion of contemporary approaches to anger management and compare and contrast them with the approaches that are delineated in *Orekh Apayim* and *Ma'aneh Rakh*.

---

3 I am basing these assertions on what I perceive as reoccurring themes in the sources cited in footnotes 1 and 2 above and the sources that are cited in the anthological works on anger in the Jewish tradition that I have gone through in preparing this chapter.

4 Avraham Tovolski, *Haser Ka'as mi-Libkha* (Bnei Brak: A. Tovolski, 1978); Shelomoh Man, *Dibur be-Naḥat: Hanhagot ve-Etsot al Inyan ha-Ka'as* (Jerusalem: Sh. Man, Pe'er Binyamin, 1995); Eliyahu Porat Teharani, *Alufenu Mesubalim* (Bnei Brak: Or Elḥanan, 1978). See also Israel Jacob Araten and Avraham Barukh Araten, *Torat ha-Midot*, vol. 2 (Jerusalem: n.p., 1947), *Ka'as*, pp. 207–64; Aryeh Leibish Halberstam, *Aryeh Sha'ag*, vols. 7–8 (Bnei Brak: n.p., 2011), 137–220; Ya'akov Meir Langsner, *Ruaḥ Nakhon* (Lakewood, NJ: Mekhon Be'er ha-Torah, 2007); Zelig Pliskin, *Anger!: The Inner Teacher: A Nine-Step Program to Free Yourself from Anger* (Brooklyn: Mesorah, 1997); Avraham Yitsḥak David Mermelstein, *Be-Naḥat Nishma'im* (in Yiddish) (Brooklyn, NY: A. Y. D. Mermelstein, 1998); Moshe Goldberger, *Guard Your Anger: 32 Pathways to Protecting Your Royal Rights to Greatness* (Southfield, MI: Targum Press, 1999); Chana T. Friedman, *Mastering Patience: Based on Sefer Erech Apayim* (Brooklyn, NY: Hadaf Printing, 2010). There are also a number of works that have been distributed by *Ḥaside Breslav* that deal with anger; see *Sefer Erekh Apayim, Otsar ha-Savlanut* (Jerusalem: Ḥaside Breslev, 1990).

Orekh Apayim and *Ma'aneh Rakh*

How R. Jelen and R. Levinson Describe Their Works

In the introduction to *Orekh Apayim*[5] (*"Slowness to Anger"*), R. Abraham Jelen (pronounced *Yelin*, d. 1934)[6] writes that he has brought together in this work concepts from the Jewish tradition that relate to the character trait of anger, and "there may be found within it great inspiration and many[7] good pieces of advice that have been gleaned from books, critically examined by the intellect, and proven through experience for the correction of this character trait."[8] In the introduction to *Ma'aneh Rakh* (*"A Soft Response"*), R. Moshe Levinson (d. 1911)[9] asserts that there is nothing that is truly original in his work.[10] Rather, all that he has done was to gather together all of the rabbinic sayings and discussions regarding anger that are scattered throughout the classic Jewish sources and explain those that are

---

5 See Proverbs 25:15. The work is often mistakenly referred to as *Erekh Apayim* ("Slow to Anger").

6 R. Jelen is described as being "a shy and retiring person, a talmudic scholar ... who learnt nonstop day and night," "who distinguished himself with his beautiful character traits, and who it was a pleasure to spend time with." Yosef Leschz, "*Reshitah shel ha-Pe'ulah ha-Tsiyonit ha-Datit,*" in *Kehilat Vengrov: Sefer Zikaron* (Tel Aviv: Hotsa'at Yotse Vengrov, 1961), 106; and Shlomo Ziwica, "*Talmide Ḥakhamim,*" in *Kehilat Vengrov: Sefer Zikaron* (Tel Aviv: Hotsa'at Yotse Vengrov, 1961), 102 (for a photograph of R. Jelen, see p. 118). See also the numerous accolades he receives in the twenty-three approbations to *Orekh Apayim* (pp. 3–7).

7 At a later point in the introduction, he writes that the work contains "*all* of the general and specific recommendations" for dealing with anger; Abram. Jelen, *Orekh Apayim* (Brooklyn: Yofi, n.d.), 19 (intro.).

8 Ibid., 9 (intro.).

9 R. Levinson, who was the grandfather of the halakhic authority R. Yosef Shalom Elyashiv, was greatly admired by the Torah sages of his generation and is described as "being renowned during his lifetime for the pureness of his superior character traits and his rare rectitude." See the biographical information and approbations in Mosheh ben Shelomoh El'azar [Levinson, alternatively, Levinzon or Araner], *Ma'aneh Rakh* (Bnei Brak: Sifre Or ha-Ḥayim, 2000).

10 Levinson, *Ma'aneh Rakh*, 11 (intro.). There are no page numbers for any of the front matter in the 2000 edition of *Ma'aneh Rakh*. Therefore, whenever I cite a page number from the introduction of this work, I am designating the first page of the *hakdamah* (introduction) as page 1 and counting onwards from there.

difficult to comprehend.[11] In addition to this, he "put in painstaking effort, toiled, and searched for ... stratagems ... and suggestions" that will help one overcome anger.[12]

R. Jelen and R. Levinson published their works within approximately five years of each other. (*Orekh Apayim* was first published in 1906, and *Ma'aneh Rakh* was first published in 1911.)[13] In their introductions, each author sets forth what he considers to be unique about his work, and in doing so spells out its intended purpose. According to R. Jelen, his *Orekh Apayim* is unique because of its sole focus on anger and its lengthy elaboration (in the first chapter) on the "disgrace of anger and the virtue of forbearance."[14] Aside from offering practical suggestions for controlling one's anger, R. Jelen believes that *Orekh Apayim* will serve a dual purpose: (*a*) it will promote public awareness of the "severity of the prohibition against anger," and (*b*) it will serve as a constant reminder (and a source of inspiration) for those people who are already aware of the seriousness of the prohibition.[15] Even though he admits that there are many Jewish ethical works that discuss anger, R. Jelen feels that these works cannot accomplish what his does. This is because in all other works, the discussions about anger are interspersed among other topics and therefore cannot have the same type of impact on a person as his monograph, with its singular focus on anger.[16]

R. Levinson emphasizes the uniqueness of his work along somewhat similar lines. In addition to the many suggestions that it offers for dealing with anger, he believes that his *Ma'aneh Rakh* is unique because of the potential positive effect it could have on people in controlling their anger.[17] This is because as an anthology on anger

---

11 Ibid., 8–9, 11 (intro.)

12 Ibid., 15 (intro.)

13 *Orekh Apayim* was first published in Piotrków Trybunalski by Ḥ. H. Folman, A. H. 5666 (1906); *Ma'aneh Rakh* was first published in Piotrków Trybunalski by M. Tsederboim, A. H. 5671 (1911).

14 Jelen, *Orekh Apayim*, 12 col. 1, 13 cols. 1–2 (intro.).

15 Ibid., 12–13 (intro.).

16 Ibid., 9–12 (intro.).

17 See Levinson, *Ma'aneh Rakh*, 9 (and 12, intro.), where he writes that he is certain that a person who goes through *Ma'aneh Rakh* two or three times will surely achieve the intended results.

it will "influence a person and leave [a more enduring] impression on his heart" than can be expected when one reads about anger in the classic sources, in which sayings and discussions about anger are interspersed among other topics. Also, by bringing together the concepts that relate to anger from the earlier sources and explaining them in a clear fashion, *Ma'aneh Rakh* has done away with two of the major obstacles that stand in the way of those who are interested in controlling their anger—most people simply do not have the time to adequately research the topic, and they would have great difficulty in grasping the material as it was presented in the original sources.[18]

Some of the Stylistic Differences between Orekh Apayim and Ma'aneh Rakh

Stylistically, there are some very significant differences between R. Jelen's and R. Levinson's works. *Orekh Apayim* primarily offers *etsot*, "pieces of advice," and *ḥeshbonot*, "things to consider and contemplate,"[19] for controlling and overcoming anger. R. Jelen's work is exceptionally well organized. It is neatly divided and subdivided into chapters and subsections; the majority of tangential halakhic discussions, *derashot* (homiletical expositions), and aggadic material are treated in a separate section (called *Va-Yosef Avraham*, "And Abraham Added," which appears on the bottom half of each page in the form of footnotes); sources are meticulously cited; and

18 Ibid., 9, 11 (intro.).

19 Even though one may get the impression when one goes through *Orekh Apayim* and *Ma'aneh Rakh* that R. Levinson puts a *much* greater emphasis on *ḥeshbonot* than does R. Jelen, I do not believe that this is the case. I would argue that one gets this impression only because of the repetitive style of *Ma'aneh Rakh* (R. Levinson often repeats the same *ḥeshbon* a number of times, while R. Jelen, who also repeats certain *ḥeshbonot*, does not do so anywhere near as often as R. Levinson) and because of how these works are organized (R. Jelen, to a great extent, separates between his *etsot* and *ḥeshbonot* by placing a large percentage of his *ḥeshbonot* in the first chapter, "The Disgrace of Anger and the Virtue of Forbearance," whereas R. Levinson's *ḥeshbonot* are rather evenly interspersed throughout his book). I should also point out that the Hebrew term *ḥeshbon* appears repeatedly in *Ma'aneh Rakh*; however, in *Orekh Apayim* there are various different terms that are used to denote the work's cognitive elements.

by and large, when something that was mentioned previously is repeated at a later point, this is acknowledged and a cross-reference is given. Also of great significance is *Orekh Apayim*'s prevalent use of hasidic sources.

R. Levinson's *Ma'aneh Rakh* primarily has a dual focus: (1) it offers *etsot* and *ḥeshbonot* for specifically dealing with anger, and (2) it offers *etsot* and *ḥeshbonot* for dealing with negative character traits that are interrelated with anger (e.g., impetuousness, haughtiness, distain for one's fellow human being, and so on) and the development of their corresponding positive character traits (e.g., deliberativeness, humility, love for one's fellow human being, and so forth). As a result of its dual focus, the constant interpolation of *derashot* and aggadic material, and its somewhat repetitive style,[20] *Ma'aneh Rakh*'s format is complex and makes for a difficult read at times.[21] R. Levinson also often does not cite the exact source for the material he quotes, and he does not cite any hasidic sources.[22]

Significant Similarities between *Orekh Apayim and Ma'aneh Rakh*

Underlying Assumptions and Fundamental Principles

Notwithstanding the stylistic differences, there are a large number of similarities between *Orekh Apayim* and *Ma'aneh Rakh*. Because

20 On a number of occasions, R. Levinson himself states that he has mentioned certain things "a number of times" or "many times"; see Levinson, *Ma'aneh Rakh*, 84 col. 1, 89 col. 2, 98 col. 1, 171 col. 2.

21 This may have just been R. Levinson's writing style (see Mosheh ben Shelomoh El'azar [Levinson], *Sefer Yede Mosheh ve-Torah Or* [Bnei Brak: Sifre Or ha-Ḥayim, 2000]; and idem, *Sefer Ohev Musar* [Bnei Brak: Sifre Or ha-Ḥayim, 2000]). Alternatively, R. Levinson may have purposely chosen to write in such a style because one of his avowed objectives in writing *Ma'aneh Rakh* was to emotionally stir and "inflame" the reader (Levinson, *Ma'aneh Rakh*, 11 [intro]). This being the case, he may therefore have been intent on bombarding and breaking down the reader's "evil inclination" for anger with a plethora of Torah and *musar*.

22 That does not mean to say that R. Levinson does not offer "hasidic Torah." See, for example, *Ma'aneh Rakh*, p. 23 col. 2, where he advances an explanation of a gemara in *Ta'anit*, which is very similar to the interpretation cited in the name of the Ba'al Shem Tov (the founder of Hasidism) in *Orekh Apayim*, 60.

R. Jelen and R. Levinson approached the topic of anger from a rabbinic mindset and based their works (for the most part) on the same primary sources, there are many underlying assumptions and fundamental principles that *Orekh Apayim* and *Ma'aneh Rakh* share. Their approach towards anger, anger management, and overall character development are clearly influenced by the attitudes that are espoused in the *Tanakh* (Hebrew Bible), Talmud, Midrash, Zohar, and a multitude of other traditional Jewish sources. Among some of the most significant underlying assumptions and fundamental principles that they share are the following:

> As a general rule, when one becomes angry and loses his temper, he is committing a sin.[23]
>
> Anger is a natural and normal human emotion, and there is a time and place when anger is called for.[24] (However, according to R. Jelen, even when anger is called for, one is

---

23 See Jelen, *Orekh Apayim*, 1–8, 87–89, 90 col. 2 (throughout the entire work, R. Jelen repeatedly refers to the "prohibition against anger," "serious prohibition against anger," or the "very serious prohibition against anger," passim); Levinson, *Ma'aneh Rakh*, 8 (intro.), 46 col. 1, 49 col. 2, 68 col. 2, 88 col. 1. Among the rabbinic sources that R. Jelen and R. Levinson base this on are *Berakhot* 29b; *Shabbat* 105b; the *Zohar* 1:27b (this is just one of numerous places in the *Zohar* in which a person who becomes angry is compared to an idolater; for other places, see Jelen, *Orekh Apayim*, 3–9; and Levinson, *Ma'aneh Rakh*, 19–20); Maimonides, *Mishneh Torah*, *De'ot* 2:3; Ḥayyim Vital, *Sha'ar ha-Yiḥudim* (Jerusalem: Mekor Ḥayim, 1970), 376; Ḥayyim Vital and Jacob ben Ḥayyim Zemaḥ, *Nagid u-Metsaveh* (Jerusalem: n.p., 1965), 185–86.

24 Jelen, *Orekh Apayim*, 8 (*hashmatot*, cited in the name of Samuel Uceda, *Midrash Shemuel* [Jerusalem: Mekhon ha-Ketav, 1989], chap. 5 mishnah 14, p. 401; Yom Tov Lipman Heller, *Tosafot Yom Tov*, in *Mishnayot Zekher Ḥanokh* [Jerusalem: Ḥ. Vagshal, 1999], *Avot* 5:11, s.v. *kasheh*; and Israel Lipschutz, *Tiferet Yisrael*, in *Mishnayot Zekher Ḥanokh* [Jerusalem: Ḥ. Vagshal, 1999], *Avot* 5:11 n. 87); Levinson, *Ma'aneh Rakh*, 59 col. 1, 168 col. 2, 170–71. Two of the most important rabbinic sources that discuss the positive aspects of anger are Maimonides, *Mishneh Torah*, *De'ot* 1:4; and Jonah ben Abraham Gerondi, *Perushe Rabenu Yonah mi-Gerondi al Masekhet Avot* (Jerusalem: Mekhon Torah Shelemah, 1980), 5:12, pp. 87–88 (this passage does not appear in the standard printed edition found in the Vilna *Shas*).

only permitted to show "anger of the face, but not anger of the heart";[25] see Maimonides, *Mishneh Torah, De'ot* 2:3.[26])

As with all forms of spiritual growth and character development, controlling and overcoming anger is something that can be exceptionally difficult to accomplish.[27]

Despite the great difficulty in controlling and overcoming anger, one who makes a sincere attempt and employs the appropriate means in doing so will achieve his goal.[28]

For one to control and overcome anger, one must be introspective and have an ample amount of self-awareness.[29]

One must employ a combination of sound behavioral and cognitive strategies to control and overcome anger.[30]

---

25 The source for this expression is Moshe Ḥayyim Luzzatto, *Sefer Mesilat Yesharim* (Jerusalem: Mosad Haskel, 1979), chap. 11, p. 100.

26 Jelen, *Orekh Apayim,* 57–65, 82–86. R. Levinson would unquestionably agree that one should always aspire to achieve the level of showing only "anger of the face, but not anger of the heart" (see *Ma'aneh Rakh,* 23, 171 col. 2), but he is also clearly of the opinion that in those instances when one may show anger, it is halakhically permissible to experience genuine anger; see Levinson, *Ma'aneh Rakh,* 12–13 (intro.), 5 col. 2, 27 col. 2, 59 col. 1, 63, 80–81, 84 col. 2 (in regard to a talmudic scholar), 147 col. 2, 170–71.

27 Jelen, *Orekh Apayim,* 16–17 (intro.), 1 (in *Va-Yosef Avraham*), 67 col. 1, 79 col. 1, 80 col. 1; Levinson, *Ma'aneh Rakh,* 45 col. 2, 48 col. 1, 55 col. 1, 95 col. 1, 99 col. 1.

28 Jelen, *Orekh Apayim,* 17 col. 1, 19 (intro., cited in the name of Eleazar Azikri, *Sefer Ḥaredim ha-Shalem* [Jerusalem: n.p., 1990], chap. 8), 65 (see *Va-Yosef Avraham* n. 1), 79 col. 2; Levinson, *Ma'aneh Rakh,* 9 (intro.), 15 col. 1, 24 col. 2, 41–42, 58–59, 80, 95 col. 1, 122 col. 2, 147 col. 2, 171 col. 1. See *Zohar* 2:162b, which is the source for the famous rabbinic saying "There is nothing that can stand in the way of one's will"; and the gemara in *Yoma* 38b–39a, which teaches that "he who comes to purify himself, receives assistance [from Heaven]." Both of these maxims are cited by R. Jelen and R. Levinson.

29 Jelen, *Orekh Apayim,* 67 col. 1, 69; Levinson, *Ma'aneh Rakh,* 10, 14 (intro.), 16 col. 2–17 col. 1, 38 col. 2, 39 col. 2, 128 col. 2, 129 col. 2, 164 col. 1. See the introduction to *Orḥot Tsadikim* (p. 4), which is cited by Levinson; *Ma'aneh Rakh,* 14 (intro.); and Menaḥem Mendel Levin's *Ḥeshbon ha-Nefesh* (trans. Shraga Silverstein [Jerusalem: Feldheim, 1995]) (cited by R. Jelen on p. 79 col. 2 [in reference to a different concept]).

30 *Orekh Apayim* and *Ma'aneh Rakh* are both grounded in this principle, and it is reflected in one way or another on veritably every single page of these works. Among

To be effective, training in anger management should be part of a complete regimen of spiritual growth (i.e., belief and faith in God,[31] the study of Torah,[32] prayer,[33] etc.) and character development (i.e., the cultivation of the entire spectrum of good character traits).[34]

---

the classic rabbinic sources that emphasize this concept are Ha-Yevani, *Sefer ha-Yashar*, 102 (paraphrased by Levinson, *Ma'aneh Rakh*, 142); Maimonides, *Mishneh Torah, De'ot* 1:7 (which only emphasizes the behavioral aspect); Ha-Levi, *Sefer ha-Ḥinukh*, commandment 16 (which also only emphasizes the behavioral aspect and is one of the sources for the famous rabbinic saying "A person develops in accordance with his actions"; neither R. Jelen nor R. Levinson actually quote this saying, but undoubtedly they were both familiar with it). It should also be noted that the emphasis on a behavioral-cognitive-affective approach to character development permeates all of the classic *musar* literature.

31 Jelen, *Orekh Apayim*, 4 (the quote in the name of Shneur Zalman of Lyady, *Likute Amarim: Tanya* [London: Kehot, 1998], *Igeret ha-Kodesh*, chap. 25), 46, 67 col. 2, 83 (in *Va-Yosef Avraham*), 90–93, 104 col. 1 (bot.); Levinson, *Ma'aneh Rakh*, 3–4, 17 col. 1, 55 col. 2, 58 col. 1, 86 col. 1, 133 col. 2 (bot.), 144 col. 1 (bot.), 163 col. 2.

32 Levinson, *Ma'aneh Rakh*, 1, 7–8 (intro.), 38 col. 1, 59 col. 2, 76 col. 1, 81–82, 99 col. 2, 104 col. 1, 112, 114 col. 2, 115, 126 col. 1, 129 col. 2, 136 col. 1. Even though when going through *Orekh Apayim*, one certainly gets the impression that R. Jelen does not put the same type of emphasis on the role that general Torah study plays in anger management as does R. Levinson, I do not believe that this is totally true. See the introduction to *Orekh Apayim* (10–12), in which R. Jelen only downplays the role of Torah study that excludes the study of *musar* and does not focus on what he terms *avodot peratiyot*, "specific tasks" (i.e., specific aspects of character development). Unquestionably, Torah study that incorporates *musar* is a fundamental part of R. Jelen's program for anger management; see Jelen, *Orekh Apayim*, 10–12 (intro.), 78 col. 2–79, 90 col. 1.

33 Jelen, *Orekh Apayim*, 67–68, 86 col. 1, 89 col. 2, 90 col. 1, 97 (in *Va-Yosef Avraham*), 99–100; Levinson, *Ma'aneh Rakh*, 12 col. 2, 42 col. 1, 43 col. 2, 54 col. 1.

34 The need for the cultivation of the entire spectrum of good character traits is actually one of the major themes of *Ma'aneh Rakh*. Among the character traits that R. Levinson sees as having a decided effect on anger are haughtiness/humility (11 col. 1, 20 col. 2–21 col. 1, 55 col. 1, 56 col. 2, 85 col. 1, 94 col. 2, 144 col. 2), love and respect for all humanity (117–20), empathy (138 col. 2), jealousy (40 col. 2), and having a sense of shame/insolence (114 col. 2, and chap. 20). Even though R. Jelen primarily focuses on how anger affects other character traits and not how other character traits affect anger (e.g., see *Orekh Apayim*, 19 col. 1, 23 col. 2, 25–28, 39–40, 45–46, 49 col. 1), R. Jelen is clearly of the opinion that the opposite is equally true; see *Orekh Apayim*, 108 (his explanation for why he concludes his work with a summary of *Tomer Devorah*). Among the character traits that R. Jelen mentions as having an effect on anger are haughtiness/humility (52 col. 2 in parentheses, 80 col. 1, 102), love of one's fellow man (103 col. 1), gratitude (102 col. 2), not being

That one's environment (i.e., family and friends) plays a major role in determining how one will deal with anger.[35]

Changes in one's characteristic inclinations and mode of response to provocations will come very slowly and require that one perseveres and properly paces oneself.[36]

Behavioral and Cognitive Strategies

The systems of anger management that are presented in *Orekh Apayim* and *Ma'aneh Rakh* are primarily composed of behavioral and cognitive strategies[37] in the form of *etsot* and *ḥeshbonot*. A considerable percentage of the *etsot* and *ḥeshbonot* that appear in *Orekh Apayim* also appear in *Ma'aneh Rakh*. The reason for this is that, as mentioned earlier, R. Jelen and R. Levinson utilized the same sources. (One source of particular importance used by both R. Jelen and R. Levinson is the compilation of *etsot* and *ḥeshbonot* for dealing with anger that

---

stingy, that is, the willingness to forego some monetary sum that is rightfully one's due (104), and happiness (69 col. 2, 79 col. 2, 106).

35 Jelen, *Orekh Apayim*, 66 (in *Va-Yosef Avraham*), 72 (where R. Jelen suggests that one inform his family, friends, and acquaintances about his personal resolutions to control anger; see below, p. 424); Levinson, *Ma'aneh Rakh*, 74 col. 2–75, 85 col. 2, 99 col. 2, 126 col. 1, 128 col. 2.

36 Jelen, *Orekh Apayim*, 66–67, 72, 79 col. 1 (bot.)–col. 2, 99 col. 2–100; Levinson, *Ma'aneh Rakh*, 32 col. 1, 37 col. 2, 45 col. 2, 63 col. 1, 95 col. 2. In respect to the importance of proceeding gradually from one level to the next, see Elijah ben Solomon, *Be'ur ha-Gera: Mishle* (Jerusalem: Mossad Harav Kook, 2005), Prov. 19:2.

37 The overwhelming majority of strategies that appear in *Orekh Apayim* and *Ma'aneh Rakh* are either behavioral or cognitive in nature, in that they ask the individual to either act in a certain way or to consider and contemplate certain ideas. The *etsot* and *ḥeshbonot* in these works encompass affective elements as well. Aside from their primary focus of teaching the person how to control and appropriately express his or her emotions, R. Jelen and R. Levinson also, apparently, are trying to help one harness his or her emotions in controlling anger. See, for example, Levinson, *Ma'aneh Rakh*, 11 (intro., in which this is implied); and Jelen, *Orekh Apayim*, 67 cols. 1–2, 94 (in *Va-Yosef Avraham* n. 4, in which he offers *etsot* that require that one be emotionally stirred). See also the related brief summaries of affective strategies for character development that were promulgated by R. Israel Salanter, in Dov Katz, *Tenu'at ha-Musar*, vol. 1 (Jerusalem: Feldheim, 1996), 237–41; and Immanuel Etkes, *Rabbi Israel Salanter and the Mussar Movement* (Philadelphia: Jewish Publication Society, 1993), 101–5.

is found in the ethical-kabbalistic work *Reshit Ḥokhmah* by R. Elijah de Vidas [sixteenth century], which discusses the topic of anger at length.)[38] R. Jelen and R. Levinson basically gathered together the approaches to controlling anger (and general character development) that were found in earlier sources and supplemented and developed them, each one with his own unique insights and approach. Included among the *etsot* that appear in both *Orekh Apayim* and *Ma'aneh Rakh* are the following:

> One should make an effort to simply avoid people and situations that are the source of considerable stress that may lead one to lose his temper.[39]

> When one finds oneself in an anger-producing situation, he should preferably not respond in any way to the provocation.[40]

> When feeling compelled to respond to a provocation, one should wait a period of time in which the anger being experienced may dissipate before responding.[41]

---

38 See de Vidas, *Reshit Ḥokhmah*, vol. 2, *Sha'ar ha-Anavah*, chaps. 2–5, pp. 601–81.

39 Jelen, *Orekh Apayim*, 17 col. 2–18 col. 1 (intro.), 70 col. 2, 82 col. 1, 83 col. 2; Levinson, *Ma'aneh Rakh*, 13 (bot., intro.), 8 col. 1, 21 col. 2, 40 col. 2, 62 col. 2 (because of a slight ambiguity in these sources, I am not totally certain if R. Levinson is actually suggesting that this is a viable *etsah* for dealing with anger).

40 Jelen, *Orekh Apayim*, 18 (intro), 80–84; Levinson, *Ma'aneh Rakh*, 13 (intro.), 3 col. 2, 13, 21 col. 1, 22 col. 2, 48 col. 2, 62 col. 2, 72 col. 1, 85 col. 2–86 col. 1, 92 col. 1, 146 col. 2–147 col. 1, 149 col. 2. It should be noted that the saying "silence at the time of anger is like water for fire," which is used by R. Levinson (*Ma'aneh Rakh*, 3), comes from Papo, *Pele Yo'ets*, s.v. *ka'as*, p. 311.

41 Jelen, *Orekh Apayim*, 18 col. 2 (intro.), 83 col. 1, 85–86 col. 1, 101 col. 1, 104 col. 2; Levinson, *Ma'aneh Rakh*, 29 col. 1, 33 col. 2, 47 col. 2, 53 col. 2, 97 col. 1. When R. Jelen cites this *etsah*, he emphasizes that one should wait until one is certain that the anger has subsided, or, in R. Jelen's words, "has left his heart." R. Jelen also suggests that during the period that one is waiting one should focus on something that will distract his attention from the provocation. Both R. Jelen (*Orekh Apayim*, 85 col. 2) and R. Levinson (*Ma'aneh Rakh*, 29 col. 1) suggest that a person should initially give anger "a night's stay" (i.e., wait until the next day) before acting or responding. This suggestion is based on Judah ben Samuel, *Sefer Ḥasidim*

One should put in the utmost effort to speak softly and with a gentle tone if and when he decides to verbally respond to a provocation.[42] (In addition to speaking softly and with a gentle tone, R. Jelen also stresses the importance of speaking in an "appeasing manner and with love.")[43]

One should employ *tokhaḥah*, "reproof" (see Chapter 6), to openly discuss one's issues with the other person.[44]

One should give the other person the benefit of the doubt, and try to take the other person's perspective.[45]

(Jerusalem: Mossad Harav Kook, 2002), *siman* 83 and 655, and is cited by Jacob Emden, *Migdal Oz* (Jerusalem: Hotsa'at Fisher, 1993), 95; see also Jair Ḥayyim Bacharach, *Sefer She'elot u-Teshuvot Ḥavat Ya'ir* (Ramat Gan: Mekhon Eked Sefarim, 1997), vol. 1, *siman* 65, p. 192; cf. Levi ben Gershom, *Perushe ha-Torah le-Rabenu Levi ben Gershom*, 5 vols. (Jerusalem: Mossad Harav Kook, 1996–2000), vol. 4, Numbers 30, p. 171, s.v. *ha-to'elet ha-sheni*.

42 Jelen, *Orekh Apayim*, 18 col. 2 (intro.), 80 col. 1, 83 col. 1, 104 col. 2–105 col. 1. (There are other places in *Orekh Apayim* in which R. Jelen recommends speaking softly [e.g., 70 col. 2, 72 col. 1, 83 col. 2], but these are referring to a *gader u-seyag* [personal restriction and preventative measure that one accepts upon oneself] to *always* speak softly.) Levinson, *Ma'aneh Rakh*, 1 (intro.), 28 col. 1, 49 col. 2–50 col. 1 (quoting the famous letter ascribed to Naḥmanides, in which it states that "you should always speak in a gentle manner with all people and at all times, and by doing so you will be saved from anger"; Naḥmanides, *Igeret ha-Ramban*, in *Kitve Rabenu Mosheh ben Naḥman*, vol. 1 [Jerusalem: Mossad Harav Kook, 1982], 374).

43 Jelen, *Orekh Apayim*, 18 col. 2 (intro.), 83 col. 1, see also 105 col. 1.

44 Jelen, *Orekh Apayim*, 104 col. 2 (in the name of de Vidas, *Reshit Ḥokhmah*, vol. 2, *Sha'ar ha-Anavah*, chap. 5, pp. 663–64); Levinson, *Ma'aneh Rakh*, 132 col. 2, 157 col. 1, see also 87 col. 1.

45 See *Pirke Avot* 1:6, 2:4; and above, pp. 190–211. Jelen, *Orekh Apayim*, 45 col. 2-46 col. 1 and 102 col. 2 (citing de Vidas, *Reshit Ḥokhmah*, vol. 2, *Sha'ar ha-Anavah*, chap. 5, p. 662, who is quoting the "*Ḥasid Ya'avets*," Joseph Jabez, d. 1507), and see also 80 col. 1; Levinson, *Ma'aneh Rakh*, 13 (intro), 41 col. 1, 49 col. 2, 86 col. 2, 107 col. 1, 116 col. 1 (bot.), 118 col. 2 (bot.), 149 col. 2-150 col. 1, 155 col. 2. (Even though giving the other person the benefit of the doubt and trying to take the other person's perspective are clearly cognitive elements, I have decided to place these under the heading of *etsot* and not under *ḥeshbonot*.)

Among the *ḥeshbonot* that appear in both *Orekh Apayim* and *Ma'aneh Rakh* are the following:

> One should spend time reflecting on the grievousness of the sin of losing one's temper and the great laudability and merit of controlling one's temper.[46]
>
> One should consider all of the possible negative immediate effects and long-term repercussions of anger.[47]
>
> One should put the event, comment, or thought that triggered one's anger into its proper perspective.[48]

---

46 Jelen, *Orekh Apayim*, 13 (intro.), chap. 1 (pp. 1–57), 101; Levinson, *Ma'aneh Rakh*, 10 (intro.), 3 col. 2, 37 col. 2 (bot.), 42 col. 1, 44 col. 1 (bot.)–col. 2 (top), 87 col. 2–88 col. 1, 89 col. 1, 90 col. 2, 99, 125 col. 2, 137 col. 1.

47 Jelen, *Orekh Apayim*, 9–53; Levinson, *Ma'aneh Rakh*, 15 col. 2, 19 col. 1, 24 col. 2, 36 col. 1, 40 col. 1, 52 col. 2–54 col. 1, 76 col. 2, 89 col. 2, 107 col. 2–108 col. 1, 109, 117 col. 1, 149, 156 col. 2–158 col. 1. Aside for the vast assortment of sins that an individual is likely to commit through anger (e.g. , *ḥilul ha-Shem* [profaning God's name], speaking *lashon ha-ra*, embarrassing people, showing disrespect for one's parents, and so on), R. Jelen and R. Levinson also mention the following potential negative outcomes of losing one's temper: one will make oneself miserable and possibly sick, stunt his spiritual growth, exhibit foolish and infantile behavior, cause people to view him in a very negative light, suffer social condemnation, adversely affect his business (i.e., one's career), destroy relationships and lose friends, and may come to commit acts of physical violence. In reference to the immediate effects and long-term repercussions of anger, it should be noted that in contrast to the standard rationalization for losing one's temper that views the strong expression of anger as an effective deterrent to the objectionable behaviors of other people, R. Jelen and R. Levinson (basing themselves on earlier sources, see Eccles. 9:17; *Shabbat* 34a; de Vidas, *Reshit Ḥokhmah*, vol. 2, *Sha'ar ha-Anavah*, chap. 5, p. 678, quoting *Orḥot Tsadikim*, *Sha'ar ha-Ka'as*, pp. 79–80) assert that, generally speaking, this is not the case. According to R. Jelen and R. Levinson, a much more effective approach would be to speak to the other person in a calm and respectful manner. Jelen, *Orekh Apayim*, 44, 53 col. 1, 83 col. 1, 87 col. 2–88 col. 1 (see also chaps. 5 and 6); Levinson, *Ma'aneh Rakh*, 28 col. 1, 167 col. 2.

48 Jelen, *Orekh Apayim*, 83 col. 1, 94–99 col. 1, 103; Levinson, *Ma'aneh Rakh*, 10 (intro.), 28 col. 2–29 col. 1, 30 col. 2, 33 col. 2–34 col. 1, 38 col. 1, 156 col. 2–157 col. 1, 166 col. 2–167 col. 1. Both R. Jelen and R. Levinson emphasize that in order to put things into their proper perspective, a person should focus on the illusionary and transitory nature of things in this world. This incorporates, among other things, that one should bear in mind that with the passage of a relatively short amount of time, whatever it is that is upsetting him at this moment will come to seem very

One should think about the principle of *midah ke-neged midah,* that there exists a correspondence between the rewards and punishments meted out by God and one's good deeds and transgressions. Therefore, if one will be amenable and forgiving towards other people, providence will treat him in a similar manner. Conversely, if he will be harsh and unforgiving, he can expect to encounter experiences in life that will mirror this type of behavior.[49]

One should understand and contemplate that everything in life is brought about through divine providence, even the provocative actions of another human being who possesses free will.[50]

---

insignificant (see *Orekh Apayim,* 97 col. 2–98 col. 1, and *Ma'aneh Rakh,* 34 col. 1). They both also mention the approach of R. Isaac ben Samuel of Acre (1250–1340), that if one desires to overcome anger he should "be 'an intelligent person,'" which entails "that he goes after the essence of the matter." This requires that one seriously take into consideration the possibility that the other person was justified in what he said or did and it was one's own comments or behaviors that were inappropriate; and in instances when the individual determines that the other person was not justified, he should consider the possibility that the other person is "an idiot," and should therefore not take it to heart when that person says something offensive, because "his words are devoid of intelligence and are nothing more than a [meaningless] chirping noise, like the chirping of birds, the barking of a dog, and the braying of an ass." See Jelen, *Orekh Apayim,* 98 col. 2–99 col. 1, 103; Levinson, *Ma'aneh Rakh,* 166 col. 2–167 col. 1; R. Jelen and R. Levinson are quoting Isaac ben Samuel of Acre, who is quoted in de Vidas, *Reshit Ḥokhmah,* vol. 2, *Sha'ar ha-Anavah,* chap. 5, p. 668 (cf. Levinson, *Ma'aneh Rakh,* 33 col. 1).

49 Jelen, *Orekh Apayim,* 54 col. 1, 92 col. 2–93 col. 1; Levinson, *Ma'aneh Rakh,* 45 col. 2, 67 col. 2, 116 col. 2, 136, 158.

50 Jelen, *Orekh Apayim,* 4 col. 1, 33–34 (in *Va-Yosef Avraham*), 46, 83 (in *Va-Yosef Avraham*), 90–93, 104 col. 1; Levinson, *Ma'aneh Rakh,* 4, 17 col. 1, 27 col. 1, 30 col. 2–31 col. 1, 33 col. 2, 34 col. 1, 55 col. 2, 58 col. 1, 86 col. 1, 133 col. 2, 144, 163 col. 2–164 col. 1. Among the essential elements of this *ḥeshbon* is the belief that "a person does not stub his toe below (on earth) unless it is decreed upon him from above (in heaven)" (*Ḥullin* 7b); that "everything the Merciful One does is [ultimately] for the best" (*Berakhot* 60b); that as an expression of love God sends people messages (i.e., that God is letting one know that he should examine his deeds and correct some flaw in his behavior) through adverse experiences (e.g., the disturbing behavior of other people [see II Samuel 16:10–11]); and that if this person would not have caused him the anguish he is experiencing, one would have experienced it in some other way ("There are many messengers that the Omnipresent utilizes," [Rashi, Exodus 16:32, and see also *Ta'anit* 18b]). In regard to the

Significant Differences between *Orekh Apayim* and *Ma'aneh Rakh*

There are numerous minor and not-so-minor differences between *Orekh Apayim* and *Ma'aneh Rakh*. This is true in regard to the different emphases, methodologies, *etsot*, and *ḥeshbonot* that they offer, and in regard to a number of significant secondary aspects. The following sections will highlight some of the prominent differences that exist between the two works.

Unique Features of Orekh Apayim

R. Jelen's Avodah Zemanit and Avodah Temidit. In delineating his program for anger management, R. Jelen begins[51] by describing in detail one of the "paths," or approaches, to general character development that he gleaned from "books" and "scribes" (i.e., scholars) and is "based upon experience." This approach, which R. Jelen applies to the control of anger, requires that one engage in certain tasks on a daily basis (at least once a day) and engage in certain other tasks a number of times each day. The tasks that one engages in on a daily basis R. Jelen designates as *avodah zemanit*, "intermittent [or temporal] work," and the tasks that one engages in a number of times each day he designates as *avodah temidit*, "constant work."

R. Jelen's "intermittent work" encompasses four daily components: (1) "contemplation,"[52] (2) "study," (3) "reflection," and (4) "prayer." Contemplation requires that the person thoughtfully analyze his deeds, recognize his shortcomings, identify the underlying causes for his shortcomings, and come up with strategies for addressing

contradiction between the belief that "everything in life is brought about through divine providence" and the principle that a human being is endowed with free will and is therefore responsible for his actions, see the related discussion above, pp. 271–72.

51 R. Jelen does not really begin to delineate his program for anger management until the third chapter of *Orekh Apayim*; see Jelen, *Orekh Apayim*, chap. 3, p. 67 col. 1.

52 R. Jelen refers to this as *"yishuv ha-da'at,"* which literally translates as "calmness of the mind." This phrase was apparently used in the vernacular in reference to the contemplation of some matter (see Uriel Weinreich, *Modern English–Yiddish, Yiddish–English Dictionary* [New York, YIVO Institute for Jewish Research, 1968], s.v. *"yishuv hada'as"*). See also the next footnote.

the underlying causes.[53] "Study" requires that one review, and read out loud,[54] the behavioral strategies (i.e., the *etsot*) he is supposed to be using for controlling his anger and that one study appropriate Jewish ethical works that will inspire him to correct his behaviors. "Reflection" entails that the person reflect upon the illusionary and transitory nature of things in this world[55] and reflect on the concept that everything in life occurs through divine providence. "Prayer" necessitates that the person sincerely beseech God to help him improve himself.[56]

Similar to intermittent work, "constant work" also incorporates four elements: (1) that the person write down on a small slip of paper, which he should always keep in close proximity to himself,[57] a short phrase or mnemonic that sums up the *etsot* that he has decided to follow,[58] reading it out loud (with emotion)[59] a number of times each day. (2) At various times during the day, one should stop and mentally prepare oneself for any of the foreseeable situations that he will encounter in the next stage of his daily activities that may lead him to lose his temper.[60] (3) Whenever another person causes him anguish or

53 According to R. Jelen, one should only engage in this component when he is not distracted by people or by daily occurrences and can find the clarity of mind to do so. The same holds true for the component of "reflection." Jelen, *Orekh Apayim*, 68 col. 1.

54 In conjunction with reading the behavioral strategies out loud, R. Jelen also requires reading them with emotion, verbally specifying how they are applicable to oneself, contemplating whether one is properly complying with them, and that one (periodically) renew his resolutions to control his anger. Ibid., 67.

55 According to R. Jelen, it is only necessary to focus on the illusionary and transitory nature of things in this world when starting to work on controlling one's anger. Once the person has seen considerable improvement in his ability to control his temper, he should then spend a greater amount of time reflecting and focusing on the majestic nature of God, which helps in developing reverence and love of God. Ibid., 67 col. 2.

56 Ibid., 67–72; in respect to how R. Jelen understands the concept of "prayer," see ibid., 99–100.

57 R. Jelen states that the slip of paper should "always be resting in front of him or in his hand." Ibid., 68 col. 1.

58 See ibid., 68 col. 1, 72.

59 Ibid., 68 (in *Va-Yosef Avraham* n. 5), 69 col. 1, 93 col. 2, 94 (in *Va-Yosef Avraham*).

60 R. Jelen also adds that one should pray for opportunities in which the resolve to control his anger will be tested and that he will be successful in maintaining his composure. This is in order to help develop the character trait of forbearance. Ibid., 68 col. 2. For further elaboration on R. Jelen's view regarding praying for opportunities in which one's resolve will be tested, and how this is consistent with what he had written

insults him, one should repeatedly give thanks to God for providing him with the means of attaining spiritual heights and greatness through something so trifling, inane, and relatively so easy to deal with (such as an insult).[61] (4) One should constantly keep track of how he is progressing by stopping at various times during the day and reviewing in his mind what has taken place and then immediately jotting down in a daily journal any instance in which he has lost his temper.[62]

R. Jelen writes that after one sees progress in his ability to control his temper, one can then slowly cut back on these elements. However, as a bare minimum, to prevent a relapse, one should always continue to employ some element(s) of this *avodah* ("work") at least once or twice each day.[63]

Other Etsot That Are Only Found in Orekh Apayim and Not in Ma'aneh Rakh. After setting forth the approach to anger management that is described above, R. Jelen goes on to offer numerous other *etsot* for controlling anger. Among the *etsot* that appear only in *Orekh Apayim* and not in *Ma'aneh Rakh* are the following:

> One should let his family, friends, and acquaintances know that he is taking it upon himself to control his anger, and he should inform them of the specific resolutions that he has made. This is in order to increase the motivation to fulfill his resolutions (i.e., he will feel impelled to fulfill his resolutions to save face in front of others).[64]
>
> One should designate someone who is often found in one's company to help one fulfill the resolutions he has made by reproving (and encouraging) him whenever he slips up.[65]

---

regarding simply avoiding people and situations that may lead one to lose one's temper, see Abram. Jelen, *Ezor ha-Tsevi* (Warsaw: Y. Edelshtein, 1905), 16–20.

61 R. Jelen writes that one should continually give thanks to God throughout the duration of the adverse experience. Jelen, *Orekh Apayim*, 68 col. 1.

62 Ibid., 67–70. One is supposed to use this journal when involved in the intermittent work of "contemplation" (when contemplating one's deeds; see above, p. 422).

63 Ibid., 66–67.

64 Ibid., 72 col. 2.

65 Ibid., 78.

When insulted, one should respond either with humor[66] or with a very short and assertive response.[67]

One should "fine" oneself (i.e., by doing something that is unenjoyable or causes him some discomfort, e.g., depriving oneself of some food) whenever he does not fulfill a resolution for controlling his temper.[68]

One should employ the *etsot seguliyot,* "mystical [or supernatural] strategies," for controlling anger that are found in kabbalistic and hasidic texts.[69]

If it is feasible, one should consider making a resolution to not react to a provocation in an irritated manner (even when it is permissible to do so; see footnote)[70] until one does three things: study a relevant ethical work, contemplate if there exists some positive alternative to effectively dealing with the situation at hand,[71] and pray for divine assistance so that one will not really become angry.[72]

Other Unique Aspects of Orekh Apayim. Two unique aspects of *Orekh Apayim* that are quite noteworthy are R. Jelen's approach to

66 Ibid., 82 col. 1. R. Jelen suggests that when one is insulted or cursed by one's wife or by another person, one should respond with "a cheery face" and "in a laughable [or cheery] manner" say, "[insult me and] curse me more, and don't hold back at all, [if you could] only just increase the cursing; this gives me so much pleasure and makes me so happy."

67 See ibid., 82 col. 2, quoting Judah ben Samuel, *Sefer Ḥasidim, siman* 72.

68 Jelen, *Orekh Apayim,* 71 col. 2; see also 107 col. 2 (bot.).

69 R. Jelen devotes a complete chapter to *etsot seguliyot;* see ibid., chap. 10, pp. 105–8. One example of a mystical strategy would be to immerse oneself in a *mikveh* (ritual bath) as a means of neutralizing anger. Another example would be to concentrate on certain kabbalistic names of God when praying; ibid., 105–6.

70 R. Jelen is referring to a case in which it is necessary to show anger (e.g., one's children or students are misbehaving) and one is planning to merely feign anger.

71 Together with contemplating if there exists some other alternative, R. Jelen also mentions that one should contemplate whether or not one's motivation is purely "for the sake of heaven" (see above, p. 79).

72 Jelen, *Orekh Apayim,* 86 col. 1.

rearing children and his view on the need for contemporary Jewish works that deal with character development. After advising parents (and teachers) that one should attempt to guide and teach children without losing one's temper,[73] R. Jelen recommends that parents use a decidedly behaviorist approach:

> One should show closeness and greatly compensate him [the child] by taking care of all of his needs with abundant generosity when he is doing what is proper. Conversely, when he is doing what is improper, one should show [a degree of] detachment and withhold [some of] his needs.[74]

A major exception to this rule would be if one's child is "extraordinarily deficient" (i.e., a problem child), who does not respond to the normal forms of rebuke. For such a child, the only feasible means that are available to a parent is to show "extra closeness" to the child and "love him exceedingly."[75]

Also worthy of note is R. Jelen's opinion regarding the need for contemporary Jewish works on character development. In R. Jelen's view, because of the behavioral and dispositional changes that have taken place between "the earlier and later generations," there exists a need for modern works that deal with character development, written by rabbinic scholars.[76] These works would have two major advantages over older rabbinic works—they could surpass the older works by building upon the insights of earlier scholarship, and they could present approaches that are in consonance with the needs of modern times.[77]

---

73 Ibid., 89 col. 2, 60 col. 2–62; cf. Levinson, *Ma'aneh Rakh*, 48 col. 1, 74 col. 2.

74 Jelen, *Orekh Apayim*, 89 col. 2.

75 Ibid., 89 col. 2–90.

76 See ibid., 15 (intro.), where R. Jelen makes it quite clear that he is specifically referring to strictly Orthodox scholars.

77 Ibid., 15 col. 2–16 col. 1 (intro.).

Unique Features of Ma'aneh Rakh

Metinut. Aside from *Ma'aneh Rakh*'s emphasis on the interrelationship between anger and other character traits (see above, pp. 413 and 416 n. 34), one of the most significant aspects that distinguishes *Ma'aneh Rakh* from *Orekh Apayim* is *Ma'aneh Rakh*'s heavy emphasis on *metinut* (lit., "slowness"), namely, the "slowing down" of one's reactions to provocations.[78]

R. Levinson focuses on two distinct aspects of *metinut*—forbearance[79] and deliberativeness.[80] Forbearance requires that one holds oneself back by suppressing emotional knee-jerk reactions to provocations.[81] Deliberativeness requires (among other things) that one develops the habit of thinking before speaking, which entails that when confronted by an insult (or other provocation) the person stops to consider whether to say something back or not, and if he should decide to respond, the person must then consider what to say and how to say it (so that the response will not be counterproductive).[82]

In addition to simply asserting the importance of slowing down one's reactions to provocations, R. Levinson also cites biblical verses (e.g., "Do not hasten in your spirit to be angry" [Eccles. 7:9]),[83] talmudic passages (e.g., *Berakhot* 20a, which relates a story about R. Ada bar Ahavah acting impetuously and concludes with the

78 I do not mean to imply that *Orekh Apayim* does not emphasize this quality; it most certainly does. All I mean to say is that in comparison to *Orekh Apayim*, *Ma'aneh Rakh* puts an *extremely* heavy emphasis on *metinut* and repeatedly discusses it.

79 Levinson, *Ma'aneh Rakh*, 5 col. 2–6 col. 1, 9 col. 2 (quoting the *Vilna Gaon*, R. Elijah ben Solomon), 10 col. 1 (quoting *Malbim*, R. Meir Loeb ben Jehiel Michael Weisser), 12 col. 1, 15 col. 1, 27 col. 2, 45, 47 col. 2, 53 col. 2, 59 col. 1, 76 col. 2, 102 col. 1, 135 col. 1. Even though I have attempted to differentiate between what R. Levinson categorizes as *metinut* and what he categorizes as *savlanut*, "patience," (e.g., see *Ma'aneh Rakh*, 48–49), there may nevertheless be some overlap between the two concepts.

80 Ibid., 15 col. 1, 24 col. 2, 27 col. 2, 45, 53 col. 2, 59 col. 1 (quoting Gerondi, *Perushe Rabenu Yonah al Masekhet Avot*, 2:14), 60, 76, 141 col. 1, 166, 167 col. 2–168 col. 1.

81 See footnote 79 above.

82 Levinson, *Ma'aneh Rakh*, 24 col. 2, 45 col. 1, 53 col. 2, 70 col. 2, 74 col. 1 (accidentally misquoting Rashi, Prov. 16:20), 143 (see also 25 col. 2, 104–5, 165 col. 2–168).

83 Ibid., 59 col. 1, 141 col. 1, 168 col. 2.

statement "slowness is worth four hundred *zuz*"),[84] rabbinic maxims (e.g., "Judge your words before you bring them forth from your mouth" [*Derekh Eretz Zuta* 3]),[85] *derashot*,[86] and classic medieval sayings (e.g., "The fruit of haste is regret" [*Mivḥar ha-Peninim*, 43:27])[87] to support the concept and to drive home its importance.

Principles Adopted from Sefer ha-Yashar. At various points in *Ma'aneh Rakh*, R. Levinson discusses certain fundamental principles of his approach to anger management and general character development. Aside from endorsing a Maimonidean approach to character development, which necessitates that one repeatedly do the exact opposite of what one may be naturally inclined to do[88] (an approach which is also endorsed by R. Jelen),[89] R. Levinson advances a theory of anger management/character development that is based on the view of *Sefer ha-Yashar* ("The Book of the Upright," ascribed to R. Zeraḥyah ha-Yevani, thirteenth century).[90] Paraphrasing *Sefer ha-Yashar*,

84 See Rashi, *Berakhot* 20a, s.v. *d' me'ot*. Levinson, *Ma'aneh Rakh*, 45 col. 2, 168 col. 1.

85 This version of the text appears in *Masekhtot Derekh Erets*, Higger edition, 85; it is cited in the glosses of Judah Bachrach, *Hagahot ha-Grib*, in the standard Vilna edition of the Babylonian Talmud, *Masekhet Derekh Erets Zuta*, chap. 3 n. 60; and it also appears in tractate *Kallah Rabbati*, in the standard Vilna edition of the Babylonian Talmud, chap. 5. R. Levinson quotes a slightly different version of the text; see Levinson, *Ma'aneh Rakh*, 143, 163.

86 See, for example, Levinson, *Ma'aneh Rakh*, 5 col. 2, 45 col. 1, 166 col. 1.

87 Ibid., 24 col. 2, 97 col. 2, 141 col. 1, 168 col. 1 (cf. 166 col. 1), quoting [Solomon ibn Gabirol?], *Sefer Mivḥar ha-Peninim* (Tel Aviv: Sifriyat Po'alim, 1976), *Sha'ar Mitsvat he-Ḥakham li-Vno*, 43:27.

88 See Maimonides, *Mishneh Torah*, *De'ot* 1:7, 2:2; idem, *Shemonah Perakim*, chap. 4; idem, *Perush ha-Mishnayot* (in the standard Vilna edition of the Babylonian Talmud), *Avot* 3:15. As is well known, Maimonides' approach is similar to that of Aristotle's; see Aristotle, *Nicomachean Ethics*, Book II, 1, 2, 9. R. Levinson emphasizes the importance of doing the exact opposite of what one is naturally inclined to do on p. 39 col. 2 (but does not cite this in the name of Maimonides), and he discusses the repetition of behaviors (i.e., the idea of "habit becomes second nature") on pp. 2 col. 2, 10 col. 2, 33 col. 2, 40 col. 2, 95, 147 col. 1.

89 R. Jelen mentions that one should do the exact opposite of what one is naturally inclined to do on p. 70 col. 1, and discusses the repetition of behaviors (the idea of "habit becomes second nature") on pp. 65, 66 (in *Va-Yosef Avraham*), and 83 col. 2 (bot.).

90 See Levinson, *Ma'aneh Rakh*, 97 col. 2, 128 col. 2, 142. There is considerable scholarly debate regarding who the author of *Sefer ha-Yashar* actually was; see Seymour J. Cohen, introduction to *Sefer ha-Yashar: The Book of the Righteous*, by Zerahiah ha-Yevani (New York: Ktav, 1973). Whenever R. Levinson refers to *Sefer*

R. Levinson writes that for one to "cure" anger, one must be well aware of the "[underlying] forces that lead one to become angry and turn them around."[91] Among the factors that lead one to anger are

> a minimal amount of contemplation, the foolishness of the one who becomes angry, a lack of association with wise and intelligent people (who are capable of instructing him to subdue his anger), too much association with foolish and wicked people, and his not recognizing how ugly of a trait anger is and how many good traits are [actualized] in [exhibiting patience] and slowness to anger.[92]

R. Levinson also paraphrases *Sefer ha-Yashar* in emphasizing the need for a cognitive-behavioral approach that starts off with a focus on cognitive elements:

> It is well known that sicknesses of the soul and sicknesses of the body are analogous to each other ... The healing of the soul is dependent upon two things—an action related [i.e., behavioral] component and a thought related [i.e., cognitive] component. One who wishes to heal the soul must first heal the thought related component ... [which is similar to healing sicknesses of the body that are partially internal and partially external, in that] one must first heal the internal component and then the external component (for it would be impossible to heal the disease without treating both), so too it is with the sicknesses of the soul ... [93]

---

ha-Yashar, he ascribes it to *Rabenu Tam* (Jacob ben Meir Tam, c. 1100–1171), as is often done in traditional rabbinic circles. If one would compare *Sefer ha-Yashar*'s overall approach to character development (see Ha-Yevani, *Sefer ha-Yashar*, chaps. 6 and 7 passim) with that of R. Levinson's, one could find many common denominators. It should be noted that *Sefer ha-Yashar* specifically addresses the topic of anger on pp. 73–74, 101–2.

91 Levinson, *Ma'aneh Rakh*, 128 col. 2.

92 Ibid., 128 col. 2, paraphrasing Ha-Yevani, *Sefer ha-Yashar*, 73.

93 Ibid., 142 col. 1; cf. Ha-Yevani, *Sefer ha-Yashar*, 102. Even though R. Levinson is clearly paraphrasing *Sefer ha-Yashar*, he does not cite it as his source. Possibly, the

Even though R. Levinson employs this cognitive-behavioral approach throughout *Ma'aneh Rakh,* at a number of points he emphasizes the need for a threefold approach to character development that focuses on "thought, speech, and actions."[94]

Ascetic Etsot. Another distinctive feature of *Ma'aneh Rakh* is the somewhat ascetic nature of certain of its *etsot.*[95] R. Levinson advises one to abstain from certain everyday activities, which would probably be considered rather extreme by the average person, who may view them as forms of excessive self-deprivation. These would include the avoidance of idle talk[96] and staying away from groups of people who are just standing around and talking among themselves.[97]

Ma'aneh Rakh's Universalistic Emphasis. Another feature of *Ma'aneh Rakh* that certainly deserves to be highlighted is its universalistic emphasis. R. Levinson asserts that one must "take heed not to cause pain to any human being," Jew or Gentile.[98] This is based on the biblical injunction of Leviticus 19:18, "You shall love your neighbor as yourself." According to R. Levinson, the Hebrew word the Torah uses for "neighbor," *re'akha,* is applicable to all people and not only fellow Jews.[99] In support of this view, he cites the

---

reason for this is that R. Levinson is, in certain respects, saying something that is somewhat different from *Sefer ha-Yashar* (e.g., R. Levinson's explanation of the "[underlying] forces that one must first do away with" [Levinson, *Ma'aneh Rakh,* 142 col. 1]; cf. Ha-Yevani [*Sefer ha-Yashar,* 102]), and he was well aware of it.

94 Levinson, *Ma'aneh Rakh,* 50 col. 1, 72–73, 101–3, 128 col. 1.

95 It should be pointed out that R. Levinson was popularly referred to as *der Araner poresh,* "the ascetic of Aran" (Aran [Varėna, Lithuania] is the name of the town where R. Levinson lived). See the biographical information in the beginning of *Ma'aneh Rakh.*

96 Avoidance of idle talk refers to both engaging in and listening to idle talk. Ibid., 63 col. 1, 111 col. 2, 106 col. 2 (see also 50–52, and 69 col. 2, 92 col. 1, 140 col. 2–141 col. 1). See ibid., 38 col. 1 (bot.)–col. 2., in which R. Levinson implies that one should not listen to stories that people tell about others even if the stories do not contain any *lashon ha-ra.*

97 Ibid., 109 col. 1.

98 Ibid., 117 col. 2.

99 It is clear that R. Levinson's source for this is R. Phinehas Elijah Hurwitz's *Sefer ha-Berit;* see Phinehas Elijah Hurwitz, *Sefer ha-Berit ha-Shalem* (Jerusalem: Yarid ha-Sefarim, 1990), section 2 *ma'amar* 13:5; and see pages 118–19 in *Ma'aneh Rakh* (which immediately follow the section that I am paraphrasing in the text), in which R. Levinson cites *Sefer ha-Berit* as the source for the subsequent material that he quotes. For a summary of R. Hurwitz's view, see above, pp. 131–32.

opinions of the midrashic work *Tanna de-Ve Eliyahu,*[100] R. Ḥayyim Vital (1542–1620),[101] R. Yom Tov Lipman Heller (1579–1654, who points out that the mishnah that teaches that "Beloved is man, who is created in the image [of God]" [*Pirke Avot* 3:14] is referring to all human beings),[102] and R. Eleazar Azikri (1533–1600, who points out that the mishnaic teaching "Do not scorn any man" [*Pirke Avot* 4:3] is referring to all human beings).[103]

Summary

In reading through *Orekh Apayim* and *Ma'aneh Rakh,* it is evident that R. Jelen and R. Levinson had formulated well-developed, integrated cognitive-behavioral systems of anger management. Culling from a wide range of traditional Jewish sources, in conjunction with their own personal insights and innovations, R. Jelen and R. Levinson offer a rich array of strategies in the form of *etsot,* "pieces of advice," and *ḥeshbonot,* "things to consider and contemplate," for anger control. Included among the *etsot* that they offer are the following:

> One should make an effort to simply avoid people and situations that may lead one to lose his/her temper.
>
> One should focus on *metinut,* the "slowing down" of emotional knee-jerk reactions to provocations.
>
> When it is necessary to respond to a provocation, a person should wait a period of time in which the anger being experienced may dissipate.

---

100 *Seder Eliyahu Rabah ve-Seder Eliyahu Zuta,* ed. Meir Ish Shalom [Friedmann] (Vienna: Aḥiasaf, 1902), *Seder Eliyahu Rabah,* chap. (15) 16, p. 75; in *Tana de-Ve Eliyahu: Seder Eliyahu Raba ve-Seder Eliyahu Zuta* (Jerusalem: Eshkol, 1991), *Eliyahu Rabah,* chap. 15, sec. 7, p. 157.

101 Ḥayyim Vital, *Sha'are Kedushah* (Jerusalem: R. Fisher, 1967), *ḥelek* 1 *sha'ar* 5, p. 27.

102 Heller, *Tosafot Yom Tov, Avot* 3:14, s.v. *ḥaviv.*

103 Azikri, *Sefer Ḥaredim,* 44:4, 47:17. Levinson, *Ma'aneh Rakh,* 117. See also ibid., 44; cf. 92 col. 2.

> One should put in the utmost effort when responding to an anger-eliciting situation to speak softly and with a gentle tone.
>
> A person should employ *tokhaḥah* in dealing with anger; that is, one should go over to the individual he or she is feeling anger towards and openly discuss the issues at hand in a sensitive and respectful manner.
>
> One should give the other person the benefit of the doubt and try to take the other person's perspective.
>
> One should self-monitor progress in anger control by recording in a daily journal every instance of anger that is experienced during the day.
>
> In attempting to fulfill one's resolutions for controlling anger, a person should elicit the help of family and friends.

Among the *ḥeshbonot* that are offered are the following:

> One should consider all of the possible negative immediate effects and long-term repercussions of anger (e.g., one will make oneself miserable and possibly sick; one will likely exhibit foolish or infantile behavior; one will be viewed by others in a very negative light; one may destroy relationships, lose friends, harm one's career, and so on).
>
> The event, comment, or thought that triggered the person's anger should be placed into its proper perspective (e.g., that with the passage of a relatively short period of time, and from a more objective standpoint, whatever it is that is bothering the person right now will come to seem insignificant; that one should consider the possibility that the other person was actually justified in what he/she said or did; in

those instances when one determines that the other person was not justified, one should consider the possibility that the other person is simply a fool, whose words and actions are meaningless and should not be taken to heart; etc.).

A person should mentally prepare himself for any foreseeable situations that he may encounter during the day that could lead him to lose his temper.

One should work on developing the quality of deliberativeness, which requires that a person gives careful consideration as to how to properly respond to a provocation.

Provocations should be viewed as opportunities for personal growth.

One should engage in self-reflection, whereby he analyzes his deeds, recognizes his shortcomings, identifies the underlying causes for those shortcomings, and comes up with strategies for addressing the underlying causes.

It should be understood that R. Jelen's and R. Levinson's systems are quite complex. Their approaches employ a set of methods reflecting a perspective that sees anger as something that is produced and overcome through an intricate combination of beliefs, attitudes, perceptions, behaviors, and emotions. Also, there are many more *etsot* and *ḥeshbonot* in *Orekh Apayim* and *Ma'aneh Rakh* that may have great practical value that were not touched on at any point in this chapter.[104] Therefore, this chapter should not be viewed as offering

104 One example of an *etsah* that I believe has great practical value, which is cited by both R. Jelen and R. Levinson and was not mentioned at any point in this chapter, is that in conjunction with an ongoing program of studying Jewish ethical works, one should employ a system of "self-talk," in which one verbalizes thoughts and repeats inspiring things to oneself. Levinson, *Ma'aneh Rakh*, 10 (intro.), 55 col. 2–56 col. 1, 74 col. 2 (quoting R. Israel Salanter); Jelen, *Orekh Apayim*, 67 cols.

in any way a complete and systematic analysis of *Orekh Apayim* and *Ma'aneh Rakh*. Rather, all it has done was to simply draw attention to what this author feels are some of the noteworthy features of these works.

Similarities and Differences between Contemporary Conflict Resolution and Traditional Jewish Approaches in Respect to Anger Management

This final section of the chapter will discuss the anger management techniques that are used in the psychotherapeutic treatment of anger and will highlight some of the similarities and differences that exist between them and the approaches that are delineated in *Orekh Apayim* and *Ma'aneh Rakh*. Though there exists an extremely wide range of contemporary techniques that have been suggested for the control of anger, our focus will be on those techniques whose therapeutic efficacies have been assessed and found to have empirical support, and which have found widespread acceptance by experts in the field. At the end of this section, I will present what I believe are the primary elements of anger management that have been adopted by contemporary conflict resolution and how they are similar and differ from those that are found in traditional Jewish approaches.

Foundational Elements of Contemporary Anger Management

Novaco's Anger Control. Raymond Novaco, who coined the term "anger management,"[105] pioneered the modern development (and

---

1–2, 68, 93 col. 2, 94 (in *Va-Yosef Avraham*) (R. Jelen emphasizes that this should be done with intense fervor).

105 Raymond W. Novaco, e-mail message to the author, March 30, 2015; Raymond W. Novaco, "Anger Management," in *The Corsini Encyclopedia of Psychology*, 4th ed., ed. Irving B. Weiner and W. Edward Craighead (Hoboken, NJ: Wiley, 2010), 102; see also *Oxford English Dictionary*, s.v. "anger," Draft Editions May 2001, s.v. "anger management." The *APA Dictionary of Psychology* defines "anger management" as "techniques used by individuals—sometimes in counseling or in therapy—to control their inappropriate reactions to anger-provoking stimuli and to express their feelings

testing) of methods for the regulation of anger with his 1975 landmark book entitled *Anger Control: The Development and Evaluation of an Experimental Treatment.*[106] In this work, Novaco describes in detail how he had adopted principles and techniques from Donald Meichenbaum's "stress inoculation training" for treating anxiety,[107] Albert Ellis's "rational emotive therapy" (also known as "rational emotive behavior therapy")[108] and Edmund Jacobson's "progressive relaxation,"[109] in combination with an array of other techniques (e.g., role-playing, "systematic desensitization,"[110] maintaining a

---

of anger in appropriate ways that are respectful of others." *APA Dictionary of Psychology* (Washington, DC: American Psychological Association, 2007), s.v. "anger management."

106 Raymond W. Novaco, *Anger Control: The Development and Evaluation of an Experimental Treatment* (Lexington, MA: Lexington Books, 1975). Novaco does point out that there were "circumscribed interventions" that were being used prior to the one he developed; see Raymond W. Novaco, "Stress Inoculation: A Cognitive Therapy for Anger and Its Application to a Case of Depression," *Journal of Consulting and Clinical Psychology* 45, no. 4 (1977): 600.

107 See Donald Meichenbaum, *Stress Inoculation Training* (New York: Pergamon Press, 1985). For a summary of Meichenbaum's earlier research and the procedures he employed, which had influenced Novaco, see Donald Meichenbaum and Roy Cameron, "The Clinical Potential of Modifying What Clients Say to Themselves," *Psychotherapy: Theory, Research and Practice* 11, no. 2 (1974): 103–17.

108 Rational emotive therapy focuses on the uncovering, challenging, and replacing of a person's irrational and dysfunctional beliefs. Together with its primary emphasis on cognitive elements, rational emotive therapy employs a wide variety of affective and behavioral elements as well. For a detailed explanation of the approach, which Ellis eventually renamed "rational emotive behavior therapy," see Albert Ellis and Windy Dryden, *The Practice of Rational Emotive Behavior Therapy*, 2nd ed. (New York: Springer, 1997). For a brief summary, see Albert Ellis, "Rational Emotive Behavior Therapy," in *Encyclopedia of Psychotherapy*, vol. 2, ed. Michel Hersen and William H. Sledge (Amsterdam: Academic Press, 2002), 483–87. The work that Novaco references is Albert Ellis, *Humanistic Psychotherapy: The Rational-Emotive Approach* (New York: Julian Press, 1973).

109 See Edmund Jacobson, *Progressive Relaxation: A Physiological and Clinical Investigation of Muscular States and Their Significance in Psychology and Medical Practice* (Chicago: University of Chicago Press, 1929). Jacobson's progressive relaxation employs a lengthy process of muscle relaxation in which one progressively tightens and relaxes groups of muscles. For an explanation of this technique and contemporary variations of it, see Kenneth L. Lichstein, *Clinical Relaxation Strategies* (New York: Wiley, 1988), 4–6, 8, 27–31, 74, 118–23.

110 Systematic desensitization is a procedure in which a patient is gradually exposed to a series of imagined approximations of events/objects that in the past have engendered irrational anxiety (or fear). This is done in conjunction with the use of a shortened form of progressive relaxation. By pairing relaxation with the anxiety-producing stimulus, the patient eventually experiences a decrease in the anxiety that the stimulus has

diary of anger incidents, and the use of problem-solving strategies) and applied them to the treatment of anger.

Anger Control was a revised version of Novaco's doctoral dissertation. For his dissertation, Novaco had developed and tested a treatment program for the self-control of anger. This program consisted of what he at one point describes as "a mélange of ingredients,"[111] the primary components of which were a set of cognitive self-control techniques and relaxation procedures. The cognitive techniques emphasized anger control through self-instructional statements, and the relaxation procedures employed Jacobsonian relaxation, deep breathing, and mental imagery. Novaco hypothesized that together these elements could help regulate the experience and expression of anger in people who are struggling with chronic anger. The following summary is an abridged version of Novaco's treatment program.[112]

Session I. In the first session of Novaco's cognitive self-instruction and relaxation treatment, participants were first asked to share information about the anger problems they were facing and to discuss their anger triggers. The discussion attempted to help participants ascertain the feelings, thoughts, and self-statements they experienced in relation to provocations. This led into Novaco's presentation of the underlying rationale of the therapy to the participants. He explained to them that there is a direct relationship between a person's own internal attitudes, thoughts, and self-statements and the feelings of anger a

---

engendered in the past. See Joseph Wolpe, *Psychotherapy by Reciprocal Inhibition* (Stanford, CA: Stanford University Press, 1958), 139–65; Joseph Wolpe, *The Practice of Behavior Therapy*, 4th ed. (New York: Pergamon Press, 1990), 150–93. See also F. Dudley McGlynn, "Systematic Desensitization," in *Encyclopedia of Behavior Modification and Cognitive Behavior Therapy*, vol. 1, ed. Michel Hersen and Johan Rosqvist (Thousand Oaks, CA: Sage, 2007), 574–82. In the treatment program described in *Anger Control*, Novaco employed the methodology of systematic desensitization but never explicitly refers to it by this name; he merely describes it as a form of counterconditioning.

111 Raymond W. Novaco, "A Treatment Program for the Management of Anger through Cognitive and Relaxation Controls" (PhD diss., Indiana University, 1974), 122; Novaco, *Anger Control*, 51.

112 Novaco's experiment assigned participants to four different treatment conditions: a combined cognitive control (i.e., self-instruction) and relaxation treatment, cognitive control only, relaxation training only, and a control group. I will be summarizing the cognitive control and relaxation treatment.

person will experience. The participants were then informed that they would be learning relaxation techniques that would enable them to reduce anger arousal when provoked. They were also told that they would be required to engage in self-monitoring. This would entail that they start keeping an anger diary in which they would record their anger experiences. As "homework," they were to try to identify their internal, anger-engendering self-statements and had to prepare a hierarchy of seven anger-provoking situations they had dealt with in the past and expected to encounter again in the future (which varied in the degrees of anger experienced, ranging from mild to intense). The session concluded with an introduction to Jacobson's relaxation technique of progressively tensing and relaxing muscle groups, a deep breathing procedure, and guided imagery.

Session II. The second session began with a review of the clients' homework. In discussing the provocations they faced and their self-statements, Novaco explored with the clients certain associated variables—the context of the provocations, the people in their lives who normally elicited their anger, and the clients' coping styles for dealing with anger. Following this, the clients learned about dissecting provocations into a series of four more manageable stages—(*a*) a preparatory stage (i.e., often a person can prepare for the provocation); (*b*) the confrontation; (*c*) coping with the arousal; (*d*) subsequent reflection. The clients then received a sheet listing "anger management principles." Among the principles that they were presented with were the following:[113]

> One is likely to get angry when taking things personally (i.e., perceiving an incident as a personal affront, or a threat to one's ego) even when there is no need to do so.

113 In summarizing the anger management principles that the participants received, I have taken the liberty of rearranging and rewording them. I have done so based on explanations that appear elsewhere in *Anger Control*. See Novaco, *Anger Control*, 4, 8–12, 24, 53–57, 93–94.

> Instead, a much more effective approach, which enables one to control one's anger, would be to remain "task-oriented" when faced with a provocation (i.e., to focus on "what must be done in the situation to get the outcome you want," or what must be done to correct the situation).
>
> By learning and responding in nonantagonistic ways to a provocation (i.e., "expressing negative feelings in ways that lead to a successful resolution of conflict rather than merely escalate a sequence of antagonism"), there is a much greater likelihood that one will be less angry and effectively deal with the situation.
>
> One of the most important things to do in order to "short circuit" the anger process is to "recognize the signs of [anger] arousal as soon as they occur." When the signs of anger arousal are detected, they should be used as a cue to engage in constructive, nonantagonistic strategies.
>
> The use of self-instructional statements is fundamental to controlling one's anger.
>
> Self-congratulatory statements will reinforce the use of nonantagonistic coping strategies and assist in anger regulation.

The session concluded with a relaxation procedure used in conjunction with imaginal exposure to the first item of the clients' provocation hierarchies. During this procedure, when the clients signaled that they were experiencing anger, Novaco instructed them to use deep breathing and a self-statement to cope with the anger.

Sessions III to V. The clients were provided with a list of self-statements that could be used in the regulation of anger.[114] They were,

114 The statements on the list were divided according to the four stages of a provocation, which they had learned about in the previous session. Examples of the self-statements they were presented with include, for the preparatory stage—"I can

however, encouraged not to simply rely on the list but to come up with their own personal self-statements. They then reviewed the anger experiences they had recorded in their diaries and analyzed the associated anger-engendering elements of their self-statements. Any irrational beliefs that were detected were challenged using Ellis's rational-emotive approach. Following this, the clients underwent further training in the use of self-statements and relaxation, and explored the use of problem-solving strategies along with other elements (e.g., cooperation and empathy) in combating anger. Each session concluded with the application of their relaxation techniques and cognitive strategies to the next two items in their provocation hierarchies.[115]

Shortly after the publication of *Anger Control,* Novaco went on to further develop and incorporate additional elements into his approach (e.g., the development of interpersonal skills, such as communication and assertiveness skills, and the use of humor).[116] Novaco's multimodality approach—which incorporates cognitive, affective, and behavioral elements—and the strategies that he

manage this situation. I know how to regulate my anger," "What is it that I have to do?" "Time for a few deep breaths of relaxation"; for the confrontation stage—"Stay calm. Just continue to relax," "There is no point in getting mad," "Don't assume the worst or jump to conclusions. Look for the positives," "For a person to be that irritable, he must be awfully unhappy," "What he says doesn't matter"; for the coping with arousal stage—"My muscles are starting to feel tight. Time to relax and slow things down," "Time to take a deep breath," "Getting upset won't help," "My anger is a signal of what I need to do. Time to talk to myself," "Let's try a cooperative approach. Maybe we are both right"; for the subsequent reflection stage, if the person was successful in handling the situation—"It worked!" "I'm doing better at this all the time," "I guess I've been getting upset for too long when it wasn't even necessary." Novaco, *Anger Control,* 95–96. Examples of self-statements for the subsequent reflection stage if the person was unsuccessful would include "Forget about the aggravation. Thinking about it only makes you upset," "Remember relaxation. It's a lot better than anger," "Don't take it personally. It's probably not so serious." Raymond W. Novaco, "Anger and Coping with Stress," in *Cognitive Behavior Therapy: Research and Application,* ed. John P. Foreyt and Diana P. Rathjen (New York: Plenum Press, 1978), 150.

115 Novaco, *Anger Control,* 22–25.

116 See Novaco, "Stress Inoculation," 601–2; and Novaco, "Anger and Coping with Stress," 148–49, 151.

employed came to serve as the foundational basis for the majority of what constitutes contemporary anger management.

Deffenbacher's Summary. In reviewing the names of those who have made major contributions to the study and development of contemporary anger management since the publication of Novaco's work, one name that stands out is that of Jerry Deffenbacher. Since the 1980s, Deffenbacher has done an enormous amount of research and has written extensively on anger management.[117] In 2006, in a volume written by experts in the field, Deffenbacher offered a brief summary of the five main categories of anger interventions that have the most empirical support. The five categories of interventions he discussed were (1) cognitive, (2) relaxation, (3) behavioral skills, (4) exposure-based, and (5) multicomponent interventions.[118] The following explanations of these categories are based on Deffenbacher's summary.[119]

Cognitive Interventions. Cognitive interventions for treating anger are based on the premise that an individual's personal perceptions, maladaptive thoughts, and beliefs regarding an event play a pivotal role in the development of anger. The primary goals of these interventions are the identification, challenging, and replacement of distorted, irrational, or counterproductive thoughts that engender anger. Early on in a cognitive intervention, a therapist typically helps a client recognize how thoughts and beliefs influence the development of anger. This is often followed by having the client engage in a self-monitoring procedure that helps him develop a greater awareness of his anger triggers and reactions. The client subsequently

117 See Deffenbacher's curriculum vitae, http://psy.psych.colostate.edu/psylist/deffenbacher.pdf.

118 Jerry L. Deffenbacher, "Evidence for Effective Treatment of Anger-Related Disorders," in *Anger-Related Disorders: A Practitioner's Guide to Comparative Treatments*, ed. Eva L. Feindler (New York: Springer, 2006), 51–60.

119 Deffenbacher's summary mirrors the earlier (1995) summary of Raymond Tafrate, which Tafrate had written as part of a meta-analysis of anger treatments. See Raymond Chip Tafrate, "Evaluation of Treatment Strategies for Adult Anger Disorders," in *Anger Disorders: Definition, Diagnosis, and Treatment*, ed. Howard Kassinove (Washington, DC: Taylor & Francis, 1995), 113–25. In my presentation of Deffenbacher's summary, I have omitted numerous elements, reworded certain concepts, and incorporated a considerable amount of material from Tafrate's summary.

evaluates his perceptions, thoughts, and beliefs; identifies those that are anger-engendering; and generates alternative ones that will not lead to anger. The alternative cognitions are then rehearsed in therapy sessions in conjunction with anger-arousing imagery and simulations, and they are then employed in real-life situations.

The self-instructional component of Novaco's treatment is an example of one form of cognitive intervention. Other examples are those of Aaron Beck's "cognitive therapy" (also referred to as "cognitive behavior therapy") and Albert Ellis's "rational emotive behavior therapy," when they are applied to the control of anger.[120] Beck's approach requires a client to critically examine his "automatic thoughts" and correct logical errors in his thinking.[121] Ellis's approach tries to help a client undergo a "philosophic" change about life by challenging irrational and dysfunctional beliefs.[122]

---

120 I am only referring to the cognitive components of Beck's and Ellis's methods.

121 Among the common logical errors in thinking that Beck highlights are "dichotomous thinking" (black-and-white, or all-or-nothing, thinking), "selective abstraction" (i.e., mental filtering, that is, focusing on one negative detail of a situation while ignoring other positive aspects); "mind-reading" (attributing certain thoughts to another person without sufficient evidence), and "magnification/minimization" (unreasonably magnifying the negative and/or minimizing the positive aspects of a situation or person). See Aaron T. Beck and A. John Rush, "Cognitive Therapy," in *Comprehensive Textbook of Psychiatry*, 6th ed., vol. 2, ed. Harold I. Kaplan and Benjamin J. Sadock (Baltimore, MD: Williams & Wilkins, 1995), 1848–49; David J. A. Dozois and Aaron T. Beck, "Cognitive Schemas, Beliefs, and Assumptions," in *Risk Factors in Depression*, ed. Keith S. Dobson and David J. A. Dozois (Amsterdam: Academic Press, 2008), 124; and Judith S. Beck, *Cognitive Behavior Therapy: Basics and Beyond* (New York: Guilford Press, 2011), 137, 181–82.

122 Rational emotive behavioral therapy focuses on challenging irrational and dysfunctional beliefs that, according to Ellis, stem from a philosophy in which the individual dogmatically insists that the world and people must be as the individual wants them to be. Among the beliefs challenged are what Ellis has labeled as "awfulizing" (exaggerating how bad an event is), "musting" (elevating desires and preferences into demands), "damnation" (totally, or near totally, condemning someone for doing or failing to do something), and "I-can't-stand-it-itis" (underestimating one's ability to deal with adversity). See Albert Ellis, *Anger: How to Live with and without It* (New York: Citadel Press, 2003), 17, 26, 28; Albert Ellis and Raymond Chip Tafrate, *How to Control Your Anger before It Controls You* (New York: Citadel Press, 1997), 41–43; Ellis and Dryden, *Rational Emotive Behavior Therapy*, 12, 14–16, 41, 114–15; and Howard Kassinove and Raymond Chip Tafrate, *Anger Management: The Complete Treatment Guidebook for Practitioners* (Atascadero, CA: Impact Publishers, 2002), 214–16.

Relaxation Interventions. Relaxation interventions target the physiological and emotional arousal that is experienced during anger. The objective of these interventions is to enable the client to initiate a feeling of relaxation that will help prevent or reduce anger-related arousal. There are various different types of relaxation techniques that are available. Probably the most popular techniques are shortened forms of Jacobsonian relaxation. There are also much briefer relaxation techniques that are used, such as "cue-controlled relaxation," "breathing-cued relaxation," "relaxation imagery," and "relaxation without tension."[123]

Relaxation protocols call for the training of a client in techniques that will enable him to produce some type of basic relaxation response.[124] At an early stage in the intervention, the client typically engages in self-monitoring activities that help him develop a greater awareness of the physiological sensations that he experiences when he is angry and the situations in which these are normally experienced. A client is then taught one or more relaxation techniques and practices them both in and out of sessions. The relaxation techniques are often used in conjunction with a systematic desensitization procedure (see above, p. 435 n. 110), which should lead to a decrease in reactivity to anger-eliciting stimuli.[125] This requires the client to first develop a hierarchy of anger-producing scenarios. The client then pairs a relaxation technique with the lowest anger-producing scenario in the hierarchy. The pairing of the two normally involves the therapist instructing the client to vividly imagine himself in the scenario

123 For an explanation of these techniques, see Jerry L. Deffenbacher and Matthew McKay, *Overcoming Situational and General Anger: A Protocol for the Treatment of Anger Based on Relaxation, Cognitive Restructuring, and Coping Skills Training* (Oakland, CA: New Harbinger, 2000), 75–81, 88–89.

124 A relaxation response is a state of mental and physiological rest characterized by a decrease in heart and respiration rates, metabolism, and blood pressure; it is viewed as the opposite of the body's fight-or-flight response. See Herbert Benson, *The Relaxation Response* (New York: Morrow, 1975); and Herbert Benson, "The Relaxation Response," in *Mind Body Medicine: How to Use Your Mind for Better Health*, ed. Daniel Goleman and Joel Gurin (Yonkers, NY: Consumer Reports Books, 1993), 233–57.

125 The decrease in reactivity is accomplished either through habituation or counterconditioning. For other possible explanations of the mechanism(s) through which systematic desensitization works, see McGlynn, "Systematic Desensitization," 574–75.

(alternatively, a simulation may be used). As his anger is aroused, he is told to employ relaxation in order to lower the arousal. This will be repeated until the client reports that the scenario no longer produces anger. The client continues to pair relaxation with the other scenarios in his hierarchy in this manner and eventually goes on to utilize his relaxation technique(s) *in vivo* (in real-life situations).

Behavioral Skills Interventions. Behavioral skills interventions are based on the premise that many anger problems stem from deficits in interpersonal skills or other life skills. These deficits often lead to the ineffective handling of interpersonal and daily challenges, which, in turn, contributes to the experience of frustration and anger. The goal of behavioral skills interventions is that the client develop the requisite skills to effectively deal with his interpersonal and daily challenges and thereby avoid problematic, anger-engendering situations.

There are many possible skill deficits that could be targeted in behavioral skills interventions. Among the most commonly targeted are communication skills, assertiveness skills, and conflict resolution skills. Training in these areas generally focuses on the appropriate expression of negative feelings, respectful disagreement, empathic understanding,[126] improving listening skills, assertively expressing one's thoughts and feelings, and learning how to problem solve,[127] negotiate, and compromise. Development of these skills involves modeling, rehearsing, coaching, and feedback in sessions, and the subsequent practice and application of the skills in real-life situations.

Exposure-Based Interventions.[128] Exposure therapy involves exposing a client to anger-engendering situations and having him not engage in typical anger-related responses.[129] Through a process

---

126 Even though empathic understanding would normally be categorized as a cognitive/affective element, Deffenbacher mentions it in his discussion of behavioral skills.

127 Deffenbacher categorizes problem solving as a cognitive intervention; Tafrate places problem solving under the heading of "skills training."

128 In addition to Deffenbacher's and Tafrate's summaries, the following section is also based on Kassinove and Tafrate, *Anger Management*, 177–95.

129 Exposure therapy's primary use is in the treatment of anxiety disorders; see Michael J. Telch, Adam R. Cobb, and Cynthia L. Lancaster, "Exposure Therapy," in *The Wiley*

of holding oneself back from angry responses (which is called "response prevention")[130] and habituation,[131] the angry emotions that are normally experienced in these situations are reduced over time. Exposure-based interventions employ methods that are very similar to those of systematic desensitization (which is often categorized as a form of exposure therapy); however, these methods differ from those of systematic desensitization in that they do not attempt to inhibit angry responses through relaxation.

An example of the use of exposure in the treatment of anger would be when a therapist and a client identify a particular "aversive" statement (e.g., an insult or criticism) that has triggered the client's anger in the past. The therapist repeats the aversive statement to the client, and the client would be required to not respond to the statement in any way. The therapist then asks the client to estimate on a scale from zero to ten how much anger he experienced when he heard the statement (zero being none, and ten being the most anger he has ever experienced). The therapist keeps on repeating the statement until the client indicates that his anger has been reduced to a minimal amount. Subsequently, the therapist repeats this procedure multiple times and progressively increases the intensity of the exposure by changing the tone of his voice to a harsher one, raising the volume of his voice, and using aggressive hand gestures and postures. Once the client has achieved a degree of success in therapy sessions, he then goes on to use exposure and response prevention *in vivo*, by intentionally placing himself in provocative, real-life situations and not responding to them with anger, until he finds that he has significantly reduced his anger reactivity.[132]

Handbook of Anxiety Disorders, ed. Paul Emmelkamp and Thomas Ehring (West Sussex, UK: Wiley Blackwell, 2014), 717–56.

130 Response prevention is a term that is normally used in reference to the treatment of obsessive-compulsive disorder. See Deborah A. Roth, Edna B. Foa, and Martin Franklin, "Response Prevention," in *Cognitive Behavior Therapy: Applying Empirically Supported Techniques in Your Practice*, ed. William O'Donohue, Jane E. Fisher, and Steven C. Hayes (Hoboken, NJ: Wiley, 2003), 341–48.

131 Kassinove and Tafrate, *Anger Management*, 182. This is one explanation of how exposure works; for other explanations, and a general overview of exposure therapy, see Telch, Cobb, and Lancaster, "Exposure Therapy," 717–56.

132 For further clarification, see Kassinove and Tafrate, *Anger Management*, 177–95.

Multicomponent Interventions. There are many anger management programs employing some form of multicomponent approach that incorporates two or more of the aforementioned interventions. The underlying premise of such approaches is that the use of multiple strategies will generally yield much better results than any single strategy. Thus, one often encounters anger management programs that incorporate cognitive, relaxation, behavioral skills, and exposure-based techniques. One example of this type of multicomponent intervention is Novaco's treatment program. Another example is the treatment program that was developed by Howard Kassinove and Raymond Tafrate, which is briefly outlined in the next section.

Additional Elements Included in Kassinove and Tafrate's Anger Management. Kassinove and Tafrate, who are two highly respected and well-known researchers and practitioners in the field, are the authors of a comprehensive anger management manual entitled *Anger Management: The Complete Treatment Guidebook for Practitioners*. This work has been described as "the definitive therapist book on anger control" and their approach as one that "overlooks nothing ... [and] does it all."[133]

Kassinove and Tafrate's multicomponent approach to anger management incorporates all of the cognitive, relaxation, behavioral skills, and exposure-based interventions described above. Among the additional elements that they emphasize are the following: the initial development of the proper motivation to control one's anger;[134] avoidance and escape, which entail that, when called for, one avoids and removes oneself from situations that elicit anger and that one employs such things as "time delays" (i.e., not reacting immediately to a situation, thereby giving oneself time to regain one's composure and respond in a thoughtful manner) and distractions (becoming absorbed in some activity that will take one's mind off the anger-related event);[135] learning how to give and accept criticism and how

133 See the comments of E. Thomas Dowd and Richard Suinn, quoted in Kassinove and Tafrate, *Anger Management*, reviewers' comments section.

134 Kassinove and Tafrate, *Anger Management*, 3, 78–79, 85–97.

135 Ibid., 80, 125–32.

to apologize;[136] considering the short- and long-term consequences of one's actions;[137] forgiveness;[138] and relapse prevention.[139]

Even though Kassinove and Tafrate never explicitly mention it in *Anger Management,* elsewhere Kassinove proposes that by outwardly acting "as if" one were not angry—for example, by talking calmly—a person may reduce feelings of anger.[140] This method of anger control, which is based on the theory that the internal experience of emotions is influenced by their external expression, finds considerable support in contemporary research.[141]

Contemporary Anger Management, Traditional Jewish Approaches, and Contemporary Conflict Resolution

Researchers who have done comparative historical studies of anger management techniques have found many similarities between contemporary approaches and those that have been used down through the ages. In a 1979 study that compared and contrasted methods of anger management that appear in the writings of Greek and Roman philosophers with contemporary approaches, Solomon

136 These elements are discussed in the chapter that deals with behavioral skills; ibid., 151.

137 Ibid., 45–46, 90–91, 163, 255.

138 Ibid., 225–44.

139 Ibid., 245–56.

140 Howard Kassinove and Denis G. Sukhodolsky, "Anger Disorders: Basic Science and Practice Issues," in *Anger Disorders: Definition, Diagnosis, and Treatment,* ed. Howard Kassinove (Washington, DC: Taylor & Francis, 1995), 15–16.

141 See, for example, Aron Wolfe Siegman and Selena Cappell Snow, "The Outward Expression of Anger, the Inward Experience of Anger and CVR: The Role of Vocal Expression," *Journal of Behavioral Medicine* 20, no. 1 (1997): 43; Aron Wolfe Siegman, Robert A. Anderson, and Tal Berger, "The Angry Voice: Its Effects on the Experience of Anger and Cardiovascular Reactivity," *Psychosomatic Medicine* 52, no. 6 (1990): 631–43. See also William James, "What is an Emotion?" *Mind* 9, no. 34 (1884): 197–98; Charles Darwin, *The Expression of the Emotions in Man and Animals* (New York: D. Appleton, 1886), 366–67; John T. Lanzetta, Jeffrey Cartwright-Smith, and Robert E. Kleck, "Effects of Nonverbal Dissimulation on Emotional Experience and Autonomic Arousal," *Journal of Personality and Social Psychology* 33, no. 3 (1976): 354–70; and Leonard Berkowitz, "On the Formation and Regulation of Anger and Aggression: A Cognitive-Neoassociationistic Analysis," *American Psychologist* 45, no. 4 (1990): 500–1.

Schimmel found what he viewed as being relatively little that was truly novel in contemporary approaches.[142] Sixteen years later, in a study that compared and contrasted ancient and medieval methods of anger management with contemporary ones, Simon Kemp and Kenneth Strongman came to a similar conclusion.[143] Though I would question the degree to which Schimmel and Kemp and Strongman have downplayed the innovations of contemporary anger management, I too have found numerous similarities, and differences, between contemporary anger management methods and traditional Jewish approaches.

Similarities and Differences between Contemporary Anger Management and Traditional Jewish Approaches. In going through *Orekh Apayim* and *Ma'aneh Rakh,* I came across many elements that the Jewish approaches to anger management share with contemporary approaches and many elements in which they differ. Some of the noteworthy similarities include the following: both the Jewish and contemporary systems of anger management view the control of anger as being a potentially slow and arduous process;[144] they both heavily emphasize cognitive and behavioral strategies;[145] both stress the development of one's motivation to change;[146] both

142 Schimmel writes that "[a]lthough modern analyses and methods of treatment are in some ways more refined and more quantitatively precise, and are often subjected to validation and modification by empirical-experimental tests, scientific psychology has, to date, contributed relatively little to the understanding and control of anger that is novel except for research on its physiological dimensions." Solomon Schimmel, "Anger and Its Control in Graeco-Roman and Modern Psychology," *Psychiatry* 42, no. 4 (1979): 320.

143 Kemp and Strongman conclude that "our knowledge of anger and its control has developed little in two millennia." Simon Kemp and K. T. Strongman, "Anger Theory and Management: A Historical Analysis," *The American Journal of Psychology* 108, no. 3 (1995): 414.

144 See above, pp. 415 and 417. Though this aspect of contemporary anger management was not highlighted in my summary, it is something that is self-evident or implied in all of the major contemporary works on anger control that I am familiar with.

145 See pp. 412, 415, 417, 429 and pp. 440–46.

146 See p. 445. This aspect of R. Jelen's and R. Levinson's approaches was not clearly highlighted in my summary. However, it is quite evident that R. Jelen was concerned about the development of motivation from his introduction and from his lengthy elaboration on "the disgrace of anger and the virtue of

emphasize the importance of introspection, self-awareness, and the use of self-monitoring;[147] both are of the view that when one exposes oneself to real-life anger-eliciting situations and does not respond with anger (i.e., one acts as if he is not angry, for example, by speaking calmly), this helps in the control of anger through a process of habituation;[148] they both advocate the use of avoidance and escape, time delays, and distractions;[149] both employ core components of their respective systems of conflict resolution (i.e., *tokhaḥah,* giving the person the benefit of the doubt, and perspective taking for the Jewish approaches, and communication skills, empathic understanding [or perspective taking], and problem solving for contemporary anger management);[150] and they are both concerned about the long-term maintenance of what one has achieved through their programs, or "relapse prevention."[151]

As far as differences are concerned, I believe that there are three major areas in which they differ:[152] (1) in regard to differences in the specific concepts that are stressed within their cognitive strategies;[153]

forbearance," which is the first chapter of *Orekh Apayim* and serves as the lead-in to his program for anger management (see above, p. 411, and p. 420). This concern is also evident in the introduction to and throughout *Ma'aneh Rakh* (see above, pp. 411–12, 413 n. 21, and 420).

147 See pp. 415, n. 29, 422–23, 424 and pp. 436–42.

148 See pp. 419, 423 n. 60, 428, nn. 89–90 (the sources that discuss the concept of "habit becomes second nature") and pp. 442 n. 125, 443–44, 446.

149 See p. 418, footnote 41 and p. 445.

150 See p. 419 and pp. 439, 443.

151 See pp. 424 and 446.

152 It should be understood that I could list more than just these three differences between Jewish and contemporary approaches (e.g., contemporary anger management uses psychometric instruments for the assessment of anger, which does not exist in traditional Jewish approaches, or that according to R. Jelen and R. Levinson Jewish anger management involves the cultivation of the entire spectrum of character traits, which, as far as I have been able to determine through my research, does not seem to be the case for contemporary anger management). The three that I have chosen to focus on encompass the majority of what I would consider to be the primary differences between the two systems.

153 For example, R. Jelen and R. Levinson mention that a person should think about the illusionary and transitory nature of things in this world or that with the passage of a short amount of time whatever it is that is upsetting a person right now will come to seem very insignificant, or a person should consider the possibility that the other individual may be justified in what he said or did (see p. 421 n. 48). Though one may possibly find concepts that are analogous to

(2) the use of religious concepts and terminology, which are foundational to the traditional Jewish approaches, and, as a general rule, do not appear in major contemporary works on anger management;[154] and (3) the use of modern relaxation techniques for addressing physical arousal, which play a very prominent role in contemporary approaches and are not found in traditional Jewish approaches.[155]

What Contemporary Conflict Resolution Has Adopted from Contemporary Anger Management. Contemporary conflict resolution has adopted, to varying degrees, many of the elements of contemporary

---

these in contemporary works on anger management, I have not found that these concepts are highlighted in contemporary works (at least not the ones that I am familiar with). Similarly, in examining the list of self-statements provided by Novaco (see p. 438 n. 114) and the concepts that one should focus on according to Beck's and Ellis's approaches (see p. 441 nn. 121 and 122), even though one may possibly find analogous concepts for some of these in *Orekh Apayim* and *Ma'aneh Rakh* (e.g., Novaco suggests that when angered one could say to oneself, "What he [the other person] says doesn't matter," and R. Jelen and R. Levinson suggest that one could simply say to oneself that the other person is "an idiot," which represent the same basic approach of cognitively disregarding the words or actions of another), these types of self-statements and concepts are generally not highlighted in the traditional Jewish texts that deal with anger. I should, however, point out that differences in concepts that are stressed may not necessarily reflect inherent differences that exist between traditional Jewish approaches and contemporary approaches to anger management. (I personally believe that the overwhelming majority of them do not reflect inherent differences.)

154 Examples of religious concepts and terminology would include those that are related to belief and faith in God, divine providence, prayer, and sin.

155 However, it is worth noting that Kenneth Lichstein concludes his historical overview of the development of modern relaxation techniques by suggesting that the next stage in their development may be the emphasis on an "attitude of relaxation" (Lichstein, *Clinical Relaxation Strategies*, 20–21). The development of such an attitude, that is to say, the character trait of *menuḥat ha-nefesh* (literally, "relaxation of the soul," i.e., tranquility and equanimity), which is very much akin to what Lichstein is describing, was cited by some of the *ba'ale ha-musar* (proponents and exemplars of Jewish character development; see Glossary under *musar*) as being helpful in controlling anger. See Jacob Moses Lesin, *Ha-Ma'or sheba-Torah*, vol. 2 (Jerusalem, n.p., 1960), 255–56; and Jeroham Lebovitch, *Da'at Ḥokhmah u-Musar*, 3 vols. (New York: Daas Chochmo U'Mussar Publications, 1966–1972), vol. 3, *ma'amar* 154, p. 169. What R. Lesin and R. Lebovitch had written on the topic was based on the teachings of R. Simḥah Zissel Ziv (Broida, 1824–1898); see Simḥah Zissel Ziv, *Ḥokhmah u-Musar*, vol. 1 (New York: n.p., 1957), 282–83.

anger management that were discussed earlier (see the summary in the introductory essay, on pp. 24–25). What appear to be the primary elements embraced by contemporary conflict resolution are the use of cognitive strategies and the development of behavioral skills. A good indicative example of this is David W. Johnson and Roger T. Johnson's conflict resolution curriculum (which, as I have pointed out previously, is heavily grounded in theory and research and has served as a prototype for other conflict resolution education curricula). In the cognitive realm, Johnson and Johnson's curriculum borrows extensively from Novaco's and Ellis's cognitive techniques,[156] and in the behavioral realm, it emphasizes the development of communication skills for controlling anger.[157] As far as differences between contemporary conflict resolution and contemporary anger management are concerned, probably the two most significant ones that I have come across in my research are that, as a general rule, contemporary conflict resolution curricula do not promote the use of exposure and in their presentation of relaxation techniques the curricula tend to gloss over the inherent limitations of these techniques for anger control[158] (for another significant difference, see the next paragraph).

156 However, Johnson and Johnson never mention Novaco's name, and they mention Ellis's name only once.

157 David W. Johnson and Roger T. Johnson, *Teaching Students to Be Peacemakers*, 4th ed. (Edina, MN: Interaction Book Co., 2005), 6:4–35.

158 Novaco, Lichstein, and Deffenbacher have called attention to a number of the inherent limitations of relaxation techniques. According to Novaco, "It is doubtful that relaxation could actually be counterconditioned to anger stimuli ... The use of relaxation induction as a coping technique would seem to be difficult when the provocation is unexpected ... [I]n many provocation circumstances, it is simply not feasible to engage in muscle relaxation or deep breathing procedures because the demands of the interaction call for continued interpersonal response." Novaco, *Anger Control*, 49–50 (cf. Deffenbacher and McKay, *Overcoming Situational and General Anger*, 86–87). Lichstein points out that "[e]very known method of relaxation exhorts clients to practice regularly ... if the client is obstinately non-compliant in this matter, continued relaxation therapy is futile ... [and] conditioned stimuli such as special words [used in relaxation procedures] will gradually lose their relaxation-evoking properties upon discontinuation of the practiced association between them and deep relaxation"; Lichstein, *Clinical Relaxation Strategies*, 140, 152. Lichstein also points out that briefer relaxation techniques are quite limited in their effectiveness when it comes to dealing with

Similarities and Differences between Contemporary Conflict Resolution and Traditional Jewish Approaches in Respect to Anger Management. Contemporary conflict resolution's and traditional Jewish approaches' respective methods of anger management are certainly fundamentally similar in that they both employ integrated cognitive–behavioral methods of controlling anger. Other similarities include the emphasis on self-awareness, the employment of time delays and distractions, and the utilization of core components of their respective systems of conflict resolution (e.g., constructive communication for contemporary conflict resolution, and *tokhaḥah* and giving the person the benefit of the doubt for traditional Jewish approaches).[159] Contemporary conflict resolution, however, certainly differs from traditional Jewish approaches in respect to the three areas in which contemporary anger management differs from traditional Jewish approaches (i.e., in regard to differences in the concepts that are stressed within their cognitive strategies, the use of religious concepts and terminology, and the use of modern relaxation techniques). One particular difference that stands out between them (and between contemporary anger management and contemporary conflict resolution, which was not pointed out above) is that the approaches to anger management delineated in R. Jelen's and R. Levinson's works (and the approaches taken by contemporary anger management) are highly intensive approaches requiring the individual to put in a substantial amount of time and effort in dealing with anger. This is in contrast to some of the approaches that can be found in contemporary conflict resolution

advanced states of emotional arousal; see ibid., 154–57. Deffenbacher emphasizes that proficiency in relaxation procedures is a skill that requires considerable practice and should be "overlearned." Deffenbacher and McKay, *Overcoming Situational and General Anger*, 86–87, 90. For an example of how relaxation techniques are presented in contemporary conflict resolution curricula, see Johnson and Johnson, *Teaching Students to Be Peacemakers*, 7:5.

159 See the previous paragraph and pp. 447–48.

literature, which employ methods that may be viewed as being somewhat attenuated, or slightly watered down.[160]

To end off, I believe that it would be apropos to cite what Schimmel had concluded in regard to contemporary psychology's approach to anger management. Schimmel writes that "for all its sophistication and accomplishment, however, most of the modern research demonstrates, to its disadvantage, a lack of historical perspective with respect to the analysis and treatment of anger … This attitude has deprived psychology of a rich source of empirical observations, intriguing, testable hypotheses, and ingenious techniques of treatment."[161] Though his tone may be a tad strident,[162] based on my research of traditional Jewish approaches to anger management, I would tend to agree with Schimmel for the most part. The wealth of insights, sage advice, and array of strategies for controlling anger that appear in *Orekh Apayim* and *Ma'aneh Rakh* can all serve as good examples of the sort of observations, hypotheses, and techniques that Schimmel refers to, and from out of which contemporary psychology, and contemporary conflict resolution, could have, and could possibly yet still, benefit.

---

160 In defense of contemporary conflict resolution literature, one has to take into account that anger management is not the major focus of this literature, and the authors are doing their best to present in an encapsulated form a select number of easily implemented and effective methods for controlling anger.

161 Schimmel, "Anger and Its Control," 320.

162 See also above, p. 447 n. 142.

Conclusion

Summary

As explained in the preface, all models of interpersonal conflict resolution consist of five basic components: (1) fundamental, underlying values, (2) fundamental, underlying concepts about conflict, (3) behavioral guidelines and rules of conduct, (4) cognitive elements, and (5) an affective component.[1] The Jewish model of interpersonal conflict resolution that was set forth in this work encompassed all of these components. Fundamental, underlying values and concepts about conflict were discussed in the section entitled "Foundational Values and Concepts." The behavioral guidelines, rules of conduct, and cognitive elements were discussed in the next two sections: "Foundational Commandments and Laws" and "Basic Commandments and Laws of Interpersonal Conflict Resolution." And the affective component was discussed in the section "The Affective Component—Anger Management."

The foundational values (i.e., the core goals and ultimate concerns) of Jewish conflict resolution that were highlighted were (1) the pursuit of peace and (2) the avoidance of destructive conflict. Other values that were touched on include love for one's neighbor, character development, and *kevod ha-beriyot* ("respect for people," or "human dignity").[2]

From within the realm of underlying concepts about conflict, one major area that drew our attention was the rabbinic conceptualization of constructive/destructive conflict. In examining the

1 As I have pointed out previously, these are not totally separate and discrete categories.

2 The values of love for one's neighbor, character development, and *kevod ha-beriyot* were touched on in the section "Foundational Commandments and Laws" (Chapter 4).

mishnah that discusses "a dispute for the sake of Heaven" (*Pirke Avot* 5:17) and its commentaries, we had seen that traditional criteria of constructive conflict include that one engage in dialogue, abstain from hostile/personal attacks, carefully and objectively consider opposing opinions, and willingly retract one's opinion when appropriate.

The behavioral guidelines and rules of conduct for Jewish interpersonal conflict resolution were elaborated on at considerable length. From among the array of *mitsvot* and *halakhot* that relate to the prevention, amelioration, and resolution of interpersonal conflict, the following were discussed:

The general imperative to "seek peace and pursue it" (Psalms 34:15)[3]

The prohibition of "holding on to a quarrel" (i.e., perpetuating a quarrel)[4]

The commandment of "You shall love your neighbor as yourself" (Leviticus 19:18)

The commandment of "You shall not hate your brother in your heart" (Leviticus 19:17)

The prohibition against striking another individual

Three commandments that pertain to verbal abuse, which enjoin one from cursing, embarrassing, or saying hurtful things to another person

The commandments against taking revenge and bearing a grudge

3 This was discussed in the section "Foundational Values and Concepts" (Chapter 2).
4 Ibid.

The halakhic obligation of *tokhaḥah,* which requires that one respond to interpersonal provocations by engaging in open and respectful dialogue

The *halakhot* of asking for forgiveness (i.e., apologizing), and the *halakhot* of granting forgiveness

There were a number of cognitive elements that we focused on. The first chapter of the section "Basic Commandments and Laws of Interpersonal Conflict Resolution" discussed the mitzvah of judging people favorably and how the prescriptive rules of this commandment counter negative judgmental biases. Other cognitive elements that we touched on include the perspective-taking concept of "Do not judge your friend until you are in his place" (*Avot* 2:4) and the concepts that were offered by various authorities to help a person in shaping, or cognitively restructuring, his or her attitude so as not to bear grudges or come to take revenge.[5]

The final chapter, "Jewish Anger Management," dealt with the affective component. This chapter described the various techniques for anger management that have been offered by rabbinic scholars down through the ages, as presented in the two seminal monographs on the topic of anger in the Jewish tradition, *Orekh Apayim* and *Ma'aneh Rakh.*

The Nature of Jewish Conflict Resolution

Gopin's and Steinberg's Characterizations

Marc Gopin and Gerald Steinberg[6] have offered what appear to be diametrically opposed characterizations of Jewish conflict resolution.

5 The concept of "Do not judge your friend until you are in his place" was discussed in Chapter 5, and the concepts that were offered to help a person in shaping his or her attitude so as not to bear grudges or come to take revenge were discussed in Chapter 7.

6 Gopin and Steinberg are two of the pioneers of the modern academic study of Jewish conflict resolution. See Daniel Roth, "*Masoret Aharon Rodef Shalom ben Ish le-Ish ke-Model Rabani le-Fiyus*" (PhD diss., Bar-Ilan University, 2012), 3–7.

In discussing religious approaches to dealing with conflict, including Judaism's, Gopin at one point highlights the very high standards that religious approaches impose, which serve the function of conflict prevention:

> There is a utopian quality to religious ethical constructs, and part of their utopianism is the quite rigorous, almost monastic, demands of piety that, if they are followed, often lead to caring relationships of such intensity and depth that most conflicts are nipped in the bud, or never even arise. The trouble is that they are rigorous and difficult to follow ... It is certainly true that countless religious individuals, past and present, have engaged and lived by these values in many conflictual or violent situations.[7]

This characterization ostensibly stands in stark contrast to that of Steinberg's. Steinberg has described traditional Jewish approaches to conflict management (his preferred term) as being "realistic," or "pragmatic." In his opinion, Jewish approaches are "anchored in a hard-headed 'realist' understanding of human nature," where conflict is something that is simply inevitable. Judaism therefore exhibits a tendency of not trying to eliminate conflict, but rather to rein it in and eliminate its destructive forces.[8]

These seemingly incongruous characterizations also seem to stand in contrast with the characterization that I have offered in this work. I have pointed out repeatedly that traditional Jewish approaches to conflict resolution set very high standards for people, yet, as we have also seen, these standards always try to be reasonable and fall within what Judaism perceives as the functional range of behavior of the average person (i.e., an average person is actually

7 Marc Gopin, *Between Eden and Armageddon: The Future of World Religions, Violence, and Peacemaking* (New York: Oxford University Press, 2000), 176–77.

8 Gerald Steinberg, "Jewish Sources on Conflict Management: Realism and Human Nature," in *Conflict and Conflict Management in Jewish Sources*, ed. Michal Rones (Ramat Gan, Israel: Program on Conflict Management and Negotiation, Bar-Ilan University, 2008), 10–21.

capable of putting them into practice). In essence, what I have been describing is an approach that is both "idealistic" and "realistic."[9] It is idealistic in that it strives for the highest levels of peaceful coexistence, yet, at the same time, it is realistic and fully aware that people have a tendency to interact in a woefully debased manner when embroiled in conflict. Accordingly, one encounters elements of idealism in combination with realism in the Jewish approaches to conflict that we have examined.

Of course, in actuality, there is no real contradiction between the above characterizations. Each of these views of traditional Jewish approaches certainly holds true and has its appropriate applications, but in different domains. Gopin's description of "almost monastic, demands of piety" finds expression in the *midot ḥasidut* (pious character traits) that Judaism hopes that people will strive to attain but are nonobligatory in nature, which I have mentioned on a number of occasions.[10] Steinberg's depiction of an approach that sees conflict as something that is inevitable, in which the focus is on preventing its destructive effects instead of its resolution, is certainly applicable to situations in which a resolution of a conflict is simply not attainable. My delineation of standards that are very high yet fall within the functional range of behavior of the average person is applicable to the realm of practical, or normative, Halakhah. It is in this realm of Halakhah that one finds what Judaism views as the essential basic requirements for the prevention, amelioration, and resolution of interpersonal conflicts, that are well-suited for the normal, average person, and are applicable to the overwhelming majority of times, places, and situations, and which, as previously stated, have been the primary focus of this book.

9 These terms and categories are discussed by Steinberg, ibid.

10 See pp. xxviii–xxix, 196, 415 n. 26. In *Between Eden and Armageddon* (p. 176), Gopin implies that what he characterizes as "almost monastic, demands of piety" could also be applicable to the realm of normative Halakhah as well, which is something that I would take strong issue with. Even the characterization of *midot ḥasidut* as being "almost monastic" is something that is debatable.

Practical Applications for Jewish Education

As far as I have been able to determine based on the discussions that I have had with Jewish educators over the past twenty years, a large percentage of Jewish schools simply do not teach courses in *hilkhot ben adam la-ḥavero* ("laws between man and his fellow man," or laws of interpersonal relations), and, generally speaking, those that do, either do not cover the topics that were the focus of this work, or do so in a relatively superficial manner.[11]

That does not mean to in any way imply that Jewish day schools and *yeshivot* ignore the area of *ben adam la-ḥavero*, "interpersonal relations." That is far, far from the truth. Unquestionably, students' development in the area of *ben adam la-ḥavero* is a major concern and emphasis of Jewish schools. I believe that one could safely say that every Jewish day school and yeshivah stresses, in one way or another, some aspect of *ben adam la-ḥavero, derekh erets, midot tovot, musar,*[12] and/or social and emotional learning. However, one vital component, from a traditional Jewish standpoint, that is often missing from their curricula is the study of the *halakhot* that relate to interpersonal relations and conflict.

The importance of the study of *hilkhot ben adam la-ḥavero*, and not only relying on alternative methods for development in this area, such as the study of *musar* (the primary traditional method for the inculcation of Jewish values and the teaching of Jewish ethics that is used in *yeshivot*), was underscored by such Torah luminaries as R. Abraham Isaiah Karelitz (the *Ḥazon Ish*), R. Israel Meir ha-Kohen (the *Ḥafets Ḥayim*), and R. Israel Lipkin (Salanter, the father of the "*musar* movement"), and others. R. Karelitz stressed this by pointing out that since in Judaism it is the Halakhah that determines what is and what is not

11 This could all be attributed to various possible factors (e.g., curricula overload or budgetary constraints). No doubt one of the major contributing factors is the lack of familiarity on the part of Jewish educators with the wealth of source material that exists in this area of Halakhah.

12 For an explanation of the term *derekh erets*, see p. 133, and p. 174 n. 196; for an explanation of the term *midot tovot*, see p. xxviii; and for an explanation of the term *musar*, see the Glossary.

considered ethical behavior, it follows that one who is not familiar with the relevant *hilkhot ben adam la-ḥavero* will inevitably eventually end up doing what is considered wrong from the perspective of Judaism when interacting with others.[13] The *Ḥafets Ḥayim* emphasized this when he wrote that when people substitute the study of *sifre musar* (ethical works) for the study of halakhic works, they will not come to appreciate the gravity and compulsory nature of the behavior under discussion, but will merely view it as something that is only nice or good to do, as opposed to a religious obligation.[14] And R. Lipkin stressed this concept when he expressed the opinion that the in-depth study of Halakhah could potentially leave a greater impression on the individual than alternative methods (including even the study of *musar*) when it comes to inculcating values and teaching ethics.[15]

For Jewish educators interested in developing and teaching courses in *hilkhot ben adam la-ḥavero* that encompass the topics discussed in this book, I would like to offer them a few suggestions. First, there were certain elements that were only discussed very briefly in this work but nevertheless play a pivotal role in interpersonal relations and the resolution of conflict, and should therefore be emphasized in a well-developed curriculum. For example, it would be important to emphasize empathy,[16] the recognition of the dignity and worth of every human being,[17] the importance of being receptive to constructive

---

13 Abraham Isaiah Karelitz, *Sefer Ḥazon Ish: Emunah u-Vitaḥon* (Tel Aviv: Sifriyati, 1984), 21–22, 28.

14 The *Ḥafets Ḥayim* wrote this in reference to the laws of *lashon ha-ra*. See Israel Meir ha-Kohen, *Kuntres Ma'amar Kevod Shamayim*, in *Kol Kitve Ḥafets Ḥayim ha-Shalem*, vol. 1 (New York: Avraham Yitsḥak Friedman, n.d.), introduction, 2a; cited in Zvi H. Weinberger and Baruch A. Heifetz, *Sefer Limud le-Hilkhot ben Adam la-Ḥavero: Lo Tisna et Aḥikha be-Lvavekha* (Safed, Israel: Makhon Torat ha-Adam le-Adam, 1995), introduction, 19.

15 Israel Salanter, *Or Yisrael* (New York: Avraham Yitsḥak Friedman, n.d.), letter no. 7, p. 54, s.v. *be-khol ha-shanah*, and *Igeret ha-Musar*, pp. 106–8. For further elaboration on the importance of studying *hilkhot ben adam la-ḥavero*, see Avraham Grodzinski, *Torat Avraham* (Bnei Brak: Yeshivat Kolel Avrekhim Torat-Avraham, 1978), 447–55; and Joseph D. Epstein, *Mitsvot ha-Bayit*, vol. 1 (New York: Torat ha-Adam, 1981), 19–74.

16 See pp. 118–19.

17 See pp. 121–32, 171 n. 193.

criticism,[18] and the commandment to emulate God (*imitatio Dei*, which requires that one be compassionate and develop other positive character traits),[19] even though these elements were not major focal points of our discussions. I also believe that it is important to expose students to a wide spectrum of *hilkhot ben adam la-ḥavero* and not only to the ones that I chose to focus on in this book. A Jewish conflict resolution curriculum should be taught in conjunction with all of the other basic commandments and laws that are found in the Jewish tradition for the promotion of harmonious relations among people, for example, the laws of *lashon ha-ra* (i.e., when it is and when it is not halakhically permissible to speak derogatorily of others), the commandments that prohibit stealing (e.g., "You shall not steal" [Lev. 19:11] and "you shall not rob" [Lev. 19:13]) and lying ("You shall distance yourself from falsehood" [Exodus 23:7]), and the concept of "And you shall do that which is right and good" (see Deut. 6:18, with the commentary of Naḥmanides to Deut. 6:18 and Lev. 19:2).[20]

Probably the biggest challenge in implementing a *ben adam la-ḥavero* curriculum, particularly in relation to Jewish conflict resolution, is the creation of a supportive milieu and the modeling of the behaviors being taught. Constant exposure to and prolonged habitual experience with norms that run counter to what you are trying to teach someone transforms the entire endeavor into a daunting challenge. This is the reason why experts in the field of social and emotional learning emphasize the importance of modeling and recommend that educators, to the best of their ability, try to create a social milieu that is permeated with norms that promote what they are trying to teach.[21] In the context of

18 See p. 250 n. 79.

19 See pp. 52, 130–31, 134.

20 When I taught a course based on the material in this book (between 2007 and 2012), I would always start off with a basic overview of the halakhic parameters of approximately fifty *mitsvot ben adam la-ḥavero*. A list of *mitsvot* that may be helpful in this regard, as a good starting point, can be found in Avraham Ehrman, *Sefer Halikhot Olam: Kitsur Dinim ben Adam la-Ḥavero; Ve-Sefer Kodesh Yisrael* (Bnei Brak: n.p., 1996), 4–9.

21 See Maurice J. Elias et al., *Promoting Social and Emotional Learning: Guidelines for Educators* (Alexandria, VA: Association for Supervision and Curriculum Development, 1997), 56, 69, 87–89, 109–10, 119.

Jewish conflict resolution education, this would entail that courses in the laws of interpersonal relations and conflict resolution be offered not only to the school's students but also, if at all possible, to its teachers, administrators, and support staff, and in the communities in which the students live, to their Rabbis, parents, caretakers, and others.[22]

Similarities and Differences between Contemporary Conflict Resolution and Traditional Jewish Approaches

There are many basic similarities and differences that exist between contemporary conflict resolution and the traditional Jewish approaches that have been discussed in this work. Among the basic similarities that were highlighted are the following:

Both systems of conflict resolution obviously share the same fundamental, underlying values of promoting peaceful coexistence and abstaining from destructive conflict.

In both systems, physical violence is unequivocally denounced, proscribed, and potentially punishable by law.

Both systems are concerned about the individual's personal and social development and well-being.

---

22 The "others" I am referring to could include a wide range of other significant people in students' lives with whom they will come in contact on a regular basis and who will very likely have a strong influence on them. I should also point out that it is important that, in conjunction with such a curriculum, an attempt should be made at creating an environment that would nurture certain character traits, such as *savlanut* (patience), *anavah* (humility), *menuḥat ha-nefesh* (equanimity), and so on. One would also be well advised to try to follow the guidelines for social and emotional learning that have been set forth by researchers in the field; see the thirty-nine guidelines for social and emotional learning programs in Elias et al., *Promoting Social and Emotional Learning,* 139–41 (where these guidelines are summarized), and 109–10, 119 (where the key elements are highlighted). In respect to what it takes to effectively implement a conflict resolution program, see Richard J. Bodine and Donna K. Crawford, *The Handbook of Conflict Resolution Education: A Guide to Building Quality Programs in Schools* (San Francisco: Jossey-Bass, 1998), 129–70.

> Both highlight similar elements in their discussions of the characteristic features of constructive conflict.
>
> Both systems' methods of conflict resolution consist of cognitive, behavioral, and affective elements.
>
> Both attempt to counter the negative judgmental biases that contribute to conflict.
>
> In both systems, open and respectful dialogue is the basic method that is used for resolving interpersonal issues.
>
> Both try to prevent retaliatory behaviors and the harboring of grudges.
>
> Both systems employ integrated cognitive–behavioral approaches for the control of anger.

Even though there are many basic similarities between contemporary conflict resolution and traditional Jewish approaches, we also found that there are very significant differences between them as well. Some of the noteworthy differences highlighted include:

> That traditional Jewish approaches seem to put a consistently stronger emphasis on the attainment of certain higher levels of "positive peace" than those that are normally emphasized in contemporary conflict resolution (e.g., traditional Jewish approaches emphasize love for one's neighbor, as opposed to contemporary conflict resolution, which emphasizes cooperation).
>
> Contemporary conflict resolution and traditional Jewish approaches differ in respect to how they define the shared value of character development. Contemporary conflict resolution's understanding of character development reflects

current trends in the field of social and emotional learning, whereas traditional Jewish approaches' understanding of character development is based on classic biblical and rabbinic perspectives.

In regard to the formulation and the imperative nature of their normative elements (i.e., what they ask of the individual), contemporary conflict resolution does not talk in terms of "commandments" (i.e., "*mitsvot*") and "laws" (the English equivalent of "*halakhot*") that dictate one's interpersonal behaviors for the resolution of conflicts. This is in contrast to Judaism, in which binding interpersonal obligations, in the form of *mitsvot* and *halakhot*, with the inherent imperativeness of these types of obligations, are essential concepts.

In regard to the range, or scope, of their normative elements, traditional Jewish approaches often ask more of people and have expectations that are higher than those that typically appear in contemporary conflict resolution (for example, in traditional Jewish approaches, there is the halakhic obligation of *la-khof et yitsro*, "subduing one's inclination [to hate]," which requires one to go against his or her natural inclination to hate someone by being helpful to that person, if the opportunity presents itself;[23] in contemporary conflict resolution, there is no such requirement) (see explanation in the footnote).[24]

---

23 See pp. 143–44.

24 As to differences in the range of their normative elements, regarding which I have repeatedly argued that traditional Jewish approaches apparently set higher standards and ask more of the individual than does contemporary conflict resolution, I would like to offer one possible explanation for this, which I have alluded to on a number of occasions. The differences in standards and expectations between contemporary conflict resolution and traditional Jewish approaches could very well be attributed to divergent views as to what are considered realistic goals for the average person. Contemporary conflict resolution has established goals of conflict resolution in

Though both systems attempt to counter the negative judgmental biases that contribute to conflict, they employ different means in doing so. The prevailing approach that is used in contemporary conflict resolution is perspective taking. In traditional Jewish approaches, in conjunction with perspective taking, an analytic and rule-governed approach is employed that requires one to judge a person's ambiguous and ostensibly negative behaviors based on a critical evaluation of what took place, the person involved, and possible mitigating factors.

The basic form of dialogue that is used in contemporary conflict resolution for resolving conflicts is "cooperative negotiation," which may often encompass a relatively involved process of problem solving. This is in contrast to the basic form of dialogue that is used in traditional Jewish approaches, of *tokhaḥah* for interpersonal offenses, which incorporates a minimal amount of guidelines, that all center around constructive communication.[25]

Conflict resolution theorists may emphasize the importance of apologies and forgiveness, but, generally speaking, in practice these elements are not emphasized. This is in contrast to traditional Jewish approaches, which place an extremely strong emphasis on apologies and forgiveness.

---

accordance with what it deems as being reasonable and attainable by the average person. It would most likely view the emphasis on goals that go beyond these, such as those established by traditional Jewish approaches, as being impractical and an imprudent waste of time and resources, and possibly even counterproductive. Traditional Jewish approaches maintain an alternative perspective on what should be considered reasonable and attainable by the average person. This alternative perspective apparently attributes a greater potential and capacity to ordinary, average people than those which are implied by the normative standards and expectations of contemporary conflict resolution. (This explanation reflects a view that was expressed by R. Henach Leibowitz [1918–2008]; A. Henach Leibowitz, in discussion with the author, c. 2001.)

25 See the discussion on pp. 255–58.

Suggestions for Contemporary Conflict Resolution

A Proposal for Future Research

To conclude, I would like to offer some possible suggestions for contemporary conflict resolution, but before I do, I would first like to put forth a proposal for future research. Even though there are numerous works that explore religious perspectives on conflict, there is still a paucity of scholarly works that offer in-depth, systematic expositions of religious approaches to resolving conflict, particularly interpersonal conflict. This book has attempted to address this issue, in a limited way, in respect to Judaism by explicating a basic paradigm for interpersonal conflict resolution that does not involve any type of third-party intervention. I would suggest as a desideratum for future research an analysis of Jewish perspectives on interpersonal conflict resolution that does involve a third-party intervention (i.e., traditional Jewish perspectives on mediation and/or arbitration).[26] Subsequent to that, a study should be done on Jewish perspectives on intergroup and international conflict resolution. A series of such studies would be of great value to those who are interested in Judaism, religion, peace studies, and conflict resolution, and could be extremely helpful in the development of a wide range of new, and the improvement and revitalization of existent, programs, policies, and interventions.[27]

Some Practical Applications for Contemporary Conflict Resolution

There are many possible applications for contemporary conflict resolution that may emerge from out of the material I have presented

26 An exemplary work of the type of in-depth research that could be done in this area is Roth's "*Masoret Aharon.*"

27 See the related discussion in Gopin, *Between Eden and Armageddon*, 208 (the second recommendation for "Coalescence of Policy Objectives and Prosocial Religious Values") and 209 (the first recommendation under the heading "Vision").

in this work. I would like to offer three very simple, practical recommendations:

(1) Contemporary conflict resolution should, in practice, put a greater emphasis on apologies and forgiveness.[28] The all-important role of apologizing (i.e., the asking of forgiveness) and granting forgiveness, which are essential features of traditional religious approaches to conflict resolution, have found strong support in contemporary research and have been promoted by conflict resolution theorists. There is no valid reason for these elements not receiving much more attention and not being employed to a much greater extent in contemporary conflict resolution.

(2) As suggested at the end of Chapter 5, contemporary conflict resolution should explore the possibility of developing an approach to countering negative judgmental biases that is analogous to traditional Jewish approaches'. In conjunction with perspective taking, such an approach would take into account both overt information and unknowns, and employ a prescriptive, analytic, rule-governed method that considers possible extenuating circumstances and mitigating factors (see pp. 215–22).

(3) Contemporary conflict resolution should consider the possibility of establishing slightly higher goals (even though this may appear to run contrary to what common sense would seem to dictate [see footnote])[29] and raise its expectations and

28 For example, I would recommend that, as a bare minimum, at least one or two units in every conflict resolution education curriculum be dedicated to the study of apologies and forgiveness.

29 One could possibly argue that there are so many people who cannot live up to the standards that are already in place in contemporary conflict resolution, it would just be foolish to set even higher standards, with which we would be setting more people up for failure. My response would be that setting the bar too high is, without a doubt, a very valid concern. However, as psychologists have found in regard to the

> ask more of people. Examples of these may include the placing of greater stress on the enhancement of the parties' relationships and the development of higher levels of positive peace (e.g., feelings of interconnectedness, fraternity, and love for one's family, friends, and neighbors, as well as showing respect and caring concern for all people) in conjunction with the resolution of conflicts, and that when people are engaged in dialogue, they should maintain a heightened awareness of and sensitivity to each other's feelings (e.g., by doing their utmost to avoid saying things that would unnecessarily insult or embarrass the other party).

I have described these recommendations as "simple" (above, p. 466) in the sense that they are easy to understand, but that does not in any way mean to imply that it would be a simple matter to follow through with them and actually put them into practice, which would be far from the truth. Unquestionably, there are formidable challenges that would stand in the way of their implementation, which I am fully aware of. However, I believe that even the mere possibility of achieving the potential benefits that these recommendations may offer—of countering negative judgmental biases and the promotion of forgiveness and peace—is well worth the effort and calls for the serious consideration of these recommendations.

---

engendering of higher levels of functioning and performance from people (e.g., see Edwin A. Locke and Gary P. Latham, "Building a Practically Useful Theory of Goal Setting and Task Motivation: A 35-Year Odyssey," *American Psychologist* 57, no. 9 [2002]: 705–17), and as any experienced teacher would tell you in regard to the education of students, and any effective parent in regard to raising children, if you are attuned to people, and set high, realistic standards or goals, and push them in an appropriate manner, the people you are dealing with will very often be more motivated and productive and accomplish much more than they would if they were only facing lower, and ostensibly more "reasonable," standards or goals.

Glossary

aggadah (Hebrew, "story," "narrative"). Passages in the Talmud and Midrash that are not directly related to halakhah; for example, narrative expansions of biblical stories, stories about the lives of the Rabbis, ethical teachings, theological concepts, and so on.

aggadic. Of or relating to *aggadah*.

aḥaronim (Hebrew, "later ones"). The "later" rabbinic authorities who lived between (circa) the late fifteenth century and the present (cf. *rishonim*).

amora (Aramaic, "speaker," "interpreter"; pl. ***amoraim***). A talmudic sage who lived between the period of the redaction of the Mishnah (c. 200 CE) and the redaction of the Talmud (c. 500 CE).

amoraic. Of or relating to *amoraim*.

Arba'ah Turim (Hebrew, "four rows"). The title of the highly influential codification of Jewish law that was written by R. Jacob ben Asher (c. 1269–c. 1340). The work is divided into four major sections: *Oraḥ Ḥayim* (laws of daily conduct), *Yoreh De'ah* (laws related to a wide spectrum of topics, e.g., dietary laws, Torah study, honoring one's parents, charity, and mourning), *Even ha-Ezer* (laws related to marriage and divorce), and *Ḥoshen Mishpat* (laws related to monetary matters). This quadripartite division of Jewish law was subsequently used by R. Joseph Karo in his *Shulḥan Arukh* and widely adopted by later authorities.

asmakhta (Aramaic, "a support"). A term that denotes the use of a biblical passage to "support" a given law, which, in reality, may have been rabbinic in origin.

baraita (Aramaic, "external teaching"; pl. ***baraitot***). A rabbinic teaching stemming from the tannaic period that was not included in the Mishnah of R. Judah the Prince.

De'ot (Hebrew, "views," "dispositions"). The name of the second section of the first book in Maimonides' *Mishneh Torah*.

derashot (Hebrew, "sermons," "homiletical interpretations"). Homiletical or midrashic style interpretations of a verse.

etsah (Hebrew, "counsel," "advice," "suggestion"; pl. ***etsot***). A piece of advice.

gaon (Hebrew, "genius"; pl. ***geonim***). The title given to the heads of the major rabbinic academies in Babylonia, between the seventh and the eleventh centuries.

Gemara (Aramaic, "completion," "traditional teaching"). **1.** The interpretations of the *amoraim* that are cited in the Talmud. **2.** The Talmud as a whole. **3.** A talmudic passage. (In this book, when the word is used in this third sense, it is not capitalized.)

geonic. Of or relating to the *geonim*.

gezerah shavah. A hermeneutic principle employed by the Rabbis for interpreting Scripture. According to this principle, when two verses in the Bible use similar words, an analogy may be drawn between the two passages.

Ḥafets Ḥayim (Hebrew, "he who desires life"). A popular way of referring to R. Israel Meir ha-Kohen (Kagan, 1838–1933) (when used in this sense, it is preceded by the word "the"), who wrote a book about the prohibition against *lashon ha-ra*, which is entitled *Sefer Ḥafets Ḥayim*. The *Ḥafets Ḥayim*, who was renowned for his piety and scholarship, is accepted as one of the most authoritative *poskim* of the modern era.

halakhah (pl. ***halakhot***). **1.** A particular rule of conduct as prescribed by Jewish law. **2.** A general term for the entire body of Jewish law. (In this book, when the word is used in the latter sense, it is capitalized.)

halakhic. Of or relating to halakhah.

halakhic codes. Systematic codifications of Jewish law, such as R. Jacob ben Asher's *Arba'ah Turim*, Maimonides' *Mishneh Torah*, and R. Joseph Karo's *Shulḥan Arukh*.

ḥeshbon (Hebrew, "reckoning," "calculation," "thoughtful reflection"; pl. ***ḥeshbonot***). Something to consider and contemplate.

Hilkhot Ḥovel u-Mazik (Hebrew, "Laws of One Who Inflicts Physical Harm and Damages"). The name of the fourth section of the eleventh book in Maimonides' *Mishneh Torah*.

Hilkhot Teshuvah (Hebrew, "Laws of Repentance"). The name of the fifth section of the first book in Maimonides' *Mishneh Torah.*

lashon ha-ra. (Hebrew, "evil speech"). Saying something derogatory about another person without a constructive, halakhically sanctioned purpose. (R. Israel Meir ha-Kohen provides a detailed explanation of the laws of *lashon ha-ra* in his work *Sefer Ḥafets Ḥayim.*)

meḥilah. (Hebrew, "pardon," "forgiveness"). **1.** Forgiving an offense. **2.** Relinquishing one's right to collect a monetary sum.

Midrash (Hebrew, "interpretation," "exposition"; pl. **Midrashim**). **1.** An early Jewish interpretation of a biblical passage, clarifying either a point of law or an ethical concept (when used in this sense, in this book, the word is not capitalized). **2.** An anthology of these interpretations.

midrashic. Of or relating to Midrash.

minor tractate. One of the small "extracanonical" texts that are found after tractate *Avodah Zarah* in the Vilna edition of the Babylonian Talmud.

Mishnah (Hebrew, "study" ["repetition"]; pl. ***mishnayot***). **1.** A compilation of oral traditions redacted by Rabbi Judah the Prince (c. 138–c. 217 CE) that forms the foundation of the Talmud. The Mishnah is made up of six major divisions; these major divisions are subdivided into smaller tractates. **2.** A single paragraph from this compilation. (In this book, when the word is used in the second sense, it is not capitalized.)

mishnaic. Of or relating to the Mishnah.

Mishneh Torah (Hebrew, "repetition of the Torah"). The title of the highly influential codification of Jewish law that was written by Maimonides in the twelfth century. The *Mishneh Torah* consists of fourteen books, each of which is divided into several sections. Each of these sections is subdivided into chapters, which are further subdivided into smaller subsections.

mitzvah (Hebrew, "commandment"; pl. ***mitsvot***). A biblical or rabbinic commandment. (In common parlance, the word mitzvah is also used in reference to any "good deed.")

mone ha-mitsvot (Hebrew, "enumerators of commandments"). Rabbinic authorities who composed works enumerating what they considered to be the 613 biblical commandments (which the Talmud refers to in *Makkot* 23b—"613 commandments were told to Moses at Mount Sinai"). Often, in their enumerations, these authorities differentiated between "negative commandments" (commandments that prohibit something, e.g., "You shall not murder" or "You shall not hate your brother in your heart") and "positive commandments" (commandments that require a person to do something, e.g., "You shall surely open your hand [and give charity to the poor]" or "You shall love your neighbor as yourself").

motsi shem ra (Hebrew, "one who brings out an evil name"). Defamation of character.

musar (Hebrew, "reproof," "chastisement," "instruction"). **1**. Ethics. 2. Jewish character development; often specifically referring to the system of character development that was originally promulgated in Lithuania by R. Israel Lipkin (Salanter, 1810–1883) and his students in the nineteenth century.

nekamah. (Hebrew) Revenge.

netirah. (Hebrew) Bearing a grudge.

ona'at devarim (Hebrew, "distress of words"). Causing another person distress through one's words.

Pirke Avot (Hebrew, "Chapters of the Fathers"). A mishnaic tractate that consists chiefly of sayings that relate to ethical principles.

poskim (Hebrew, "decisors"; sing. ***posek***). Rabbinic scholars whose opinions have been accepted as authoritative in deciding practical questions of Jewish law.

Rashi. An acronym that is used when referring to R. Solomon ben Isaac (*Rabbi Shelomoh Yitsḥaki*, 1040–1105). Rashi is the foremost Jewish commentator on the Bible and Talmud.

responsa (sing., **responsum**). The written replies of rabbinic scholars to inquiries that relate to some matter of Jewish law or belief.

rishonim (Hebrew, "first ones"). The "earlier" rabbinic authorities who lived between (circa) the mid-eleventh century and late fifteenth century (cf. *aḥaronim*).

Shulḥan Arukh (Hebrew, "set table"). The title of one of the most influential codifications of Jewish law, which has been dubbed by modern writers as "The Code of Jewish Law." The work is divided into four sections: *Oraḥ Ḥayim, Yoreh De'ah, Even ha-Ezer,* and *Ḥoshen Mishpat* (see *Arba'ah Turim*). Originally compiled by R. Joseph Karo (1488–1575); what is today referred to as the *Shulḥan Arukh* comprises R. Karo's compendium and the glosses of R. Moses Isserles (c. 1520–1572).

Talmud (Hebrew, "instruction," "teaching," or "learning"). The authoritative body of Jewish law, ethics, and theological teachings that incorporates the Mishnah and the Gemara. There are two Talmuds: the Jerusalem (or Palestinian) Talmud, redacted circa end of the fourth century CE; and the Babylonian Talmud, redacted circa end of the fifth century CE.

talmudic. Of or relating to Talmud.

Tanakh. The Hebrew Bible. The word ***TaNaKh*** is an acronym composed of the first letters of the Hebrew names of the three major divisions of the Hebrew Bible: *Torah* (Pentateuch), *Nevi'im* (Prophets), *Ketuvim* (Hagiographa).

tannaim (Aramaic, "teachers"; sing. ***tanna***). The sages of the mishnaic period (c. third century BCE–second century CE [see the discussion in H. L. Strack and Gunter Stemberger, *Introduction to the Talmud and Midrash,* trans. and ed. Markus Bockmuehl (Minneapolis: Fortress Press, 1996), 7]).

tannaic. Of or relating to *tannaim*.

Targum (Hebrew, "translation"). An Aramaic translation of the Bible.

tokhaḥah (Hebrew, "reproof," "rebuke," "admonition," "chastisement"). In rabbinic literature, the word *tokhaḥah* is used in reference to the biblical injunction of Leviticus 19:17, "You shall surely reprove your friend." This commandment is understood by halakhic authorities as incorporating two facets: (1) it establishes a requirement to admonish someone who has committed a sin, and (2) it encompasses a process for resolving interpersonal issues through dialogue.

Torah (Hebrew, "instruction," "law"). **1.** The Pentateuch (the Five Books of Moses). **2.** The entire body of Jewish religious literature.

Tosefta (Aramaic, "addition"). **1**. The "supplement" to the Mishnah. A compilation of *baraitot* that may either elucidate, supplement, or offer parallel/alternative versions to the Mishnah. The questions of when it originated and its relationship to the Mishnah are topics of considerable scholarly debate (see Strack and Stemberger, *Introduction to the Talmud and Midrash*, 149–58). The Tosefta is written in mishnaic Hebrew, and it has traditionally been viewed as originating around the time of the redaction of the Mishnah. **2**. A single paragraph from this compilation.

yeshivah (Hebrew, "sitting"; pl. ***yeshivot***). **1**. A rabbinic academy. **2**. An Orthodox Jewish elementary or secondary school.

Bibliography

Aaron ben Jacob ha-Kohen of Lunel. *Orḥot Ḥayim*. Jerusalem: Y. D. Shtitsberg, 1956.

Aaron ben Meshullam of Lunel. *Teshuvat R. Aharon b.R. Meshulam mi-Lunil leha-Ramah*. In *Sanhedre Gedolah: al Masekhet Sanhedrin*. Vol. 1, 187–88. Jerusalem: Machon Harry Fischel, 1968.

Abba Shaul, Ben Zion. *Sefer Or le-Tsiyon: Teshuvot*. Vol. 2. Jerusalem: Mekhon Or le-Tsiyon, 1993.

Aboab, Isaac. *Sefer Menorat ha-Maor*. Vol. 4. Jerusalem: Mekhon Midrash ha-Mevoar, 1988.

Abraham ben David of Posquières. *Perush ha-Ra'avad*. Commentary on *Sifra de-Ve Rav hu Sefer Torat Kohanim*. Jerusalem: Sifra, 1959.

———. *Perush Rabad al Masekhet Eduyot*. In the standard Vilna edition of the Babylonian Talmud.

Abraham ben Isaac of Narbonne. *Sefer Ha-Eshkol*. Jerusalem: Ḥ. Vagshal, 1980.

Abraham ben Moses ben Maimon. *Ha-Maspik le-Ovde ha-Shem*. Jerusalem: Salimon Śaśon, 1965.

———. *Ma'aseh Nisim*. Paris: L. Guérin, 1866.

Abrahams, Israel. *Studies in Pharisaism and the Gospels: First and Second Series*. New York: Ktav Publishing House, 1967.

Abramson, Shraga. *Inyanut be-Sifrut ha-Ge'onim*. Jerusalem: Mossad Harav Kook, 1974.

Abravanel, Isaac. *Naḥalat Avot*. New York: D. Silberman, 1953.

———. *Perush al ha-Torah: Ḥibro Don Yitsḥak Abravanel*. Vol. 3. Jerusalem: Bene Arabel, 1964.

Abulafia, Meir. *Ḥidushe ha-Ramah al Masekhet Sanhedrin*. Jerusalem: n.p., 1999.

Abu-Nimer, Mohammed. *Nonviolence and Peace Building in Islam: Theory and Practice*. Gainesville, FL: University Press of Florida, 2003.

Aderet, Ofer. "Pioneer of Global Peace Studies Hints at Link between Norway Massacre and Mossad." *Haaretz*, April 30, 2012. http://www.haaretz.com/news/diplomacy-defense/pioneer-of-global-peace-studies-hints-at-link-between-norway-massacre-and-mossad-1.427385.

Aggestam, Karin. "Conflict Prevention: Old Wine in New Bottles?" *International Peacekeeping* 10, no. 1 (2003): 12–23.

Aḥa of Shabḥa. *She'iltot de-Rav Aḥai Gaon*. 5 vols. Annotated by Samuel K. Mirsky. Jerusalem: Institute for Research and Publication, Sura, 1960–1977.

Akra, Abraham ben Solomon. *Me-Harere Nemerim*. Venice: Daniel Zaniti, 1599.

Alashkar, Joseph. *Mirkevet ha-Mishneh*. Lod, Israel: Orot Yahadut ha-Megrab, 1993.

Albeck, Shalom, annot. *Sefer ha-Eshkol*, by Abraham ben Isaac of Narbonne. Jerusalem: Ḥ. Vagshal, 1980.

Albo, Joseph. *Sefer ha-Ikarim ha-Shalem*. 2 vols. Jerusalem: Ḥorev, 1995.

Alexander Susskind ben Moses. *Yesod ve-Shoresh ha-Avodah ha-Shalem*. Bnei Brak: Ḥasde Ḥayim, 1987.

Alfasi, Isaac. *Hilkhot ha-Rif*. In the standard Vilna edition of the Babylonian Talmud.

Algazi, Solomon Nissim. *Yavin Shemuah*. In Jeshua ben Joseph ha-Levi, *Halikhot Olam*. Jerusalem: Mekhon Sha'ar ha-Mishpat, 1996.

Al HaTorah. "Online Rashi Manuscripts—Torah." Accessed September 13, 2016. http://alhatorah.org/Commentators:Online_Rashi_Manuscripts.

Alicke, Mark D. "Culpable Control and the Psychology of Blame." *Psychological Bulletin* 12, no. 4 (2000): 556–74.

Allred, Keith G. "Anger and Retaliation in Conflict: The Role of Attribution." In *The Handbook of Conflict Resolution: Theory and Practice*, edited by Morton Deutsch and Peter T. Coleman, 236–55. San Francisco: Jossey-Bass, 2000.

Almosnino, Moses. *Pirke Mosheh*. Jerusalem: Mekhon Torah Shelemah, 1970.

———. *Pirke Mosheh*. Jerusalem: Haktav Institute, 1995.

Alshekh, Moses. *Torat Mosheh*. Vol. 3. Jerusalem: Mekhon Lev Same'aḥ, 1990.

Alter, Judah Aryeh Leib. *Masekhet Avot im Perush Sefat Emet*. Jerusalem: Y. Y. A. Alter, 2002.

———. *Sefer Sefat Emet*. Jerusalem: Mekhon Hotsa'at Sefarim Mir, 1996.

Altschuler, Jehiel Hillel. *Metsudat David; Metsudat Tsiyon*. In the standard *Mikra'ot Gedolot*.

American Psychiatric Association. *Diagnostic and Statistical Manual of Mental Disorders*. 4th ed., text rev., Washington, DC, 2000.

American School Counselor Association. *The School Counselor* 43, no. 5 (May 1996).

———. *The School Counselor* 44, no. 1 (Sept. 1996).

Amsterdam, Naftali. "*Me-Igrotav shel Maran ha-Gaon he-Ḥasid R. Naftali Amsterdam.*" *Tevunah: Inyane Torah u-Musar* 3, edited by Israel Zisel Dvoretz, *ḥoveret* 7 (Jerusalem, Adar 2, 5703 [1943]): 69–72.

Anav, Jehiel ben Jekuthiel. *Ma'alot ha-Midot*. Jerusalem: Eshkol, 1967.

Anderson, Jeremy C., Wolfgang Linden, and Martine E. Habra. "Influence of Apologies and Trait Hostility on Recovery from Anger." *Journal of Behavioral Medicine* 29, no. 4 (2006): 347–58.

Andreychik, Michael R. "Social Explanatory Style as a Foundation of Social Orientation." Master's thesis, Lehigh University, 2006. Accessed November, 7, 2016. http://preserve.lehigh.edu/cgi/viewcontent.cgi?article=1016&context=cas-campbell-prize.

APA Dictionary of Psychology. Washington, DC: American Psychological Association, 2007.

Appleby, R. Scott. *The Ambivalence of the Sacred: Religion, Violence, and Reconciliation*. Lanham, MD: Rowman and Littlefield, 2000.

Arama, Isaac. *Akedat Yitsḥak*. Pressburg: Victor Kittseer, 1849.

Araten, Israel Jacob, and Avraham Barukh Araten. *Torat ha-Midot*. Vol. 2. Jerusalem: n.p., 1947.

Ardit, Ephraim. *Mateh Efrayim*. Thessaloniki: Mordekhai Naḥman u-Mishnehu David Yisraelig'ah, 1771.

Ari'av, David. *Le-Re'akha kamokha*. 9 vols. Jerusalem: Mekhon Le-Re'akha kamokha, 2000–.

———. "*Ve-Ahavta—le-Re'akha kamokha.*" *Torat ha-Adam le-Adam: Kovets Torani ba-Mitsvot she-ben Adam la-Ḥavero* 4 (2001): 94–117.

Arieli, Yitsḥak. *Enayim la-Mishpat*. Jerusalem: Ha-Ivri, 1971.

Arriaga, Ximena B., and Caryl E. Rusbult. "Standing in My Partner's Shoes: Partner Perspective Taking and Reactions to Accommodative Dilemmas." *Personality and Social Psychology Bulletin* 24, no. 9 (1998): 927–48.

Asher ben Jehiel. *Sefer Rabenu Asher* [*Piske ha-Rosh*]. In the standard Vilna edition of the Babylonian Talmud.

Ashkenazi, Bezalel. *Shitah Mekubetset*. In the standard Vilna edition of the Babylonian Talmud.

———. *Shitah Mekubetset*. Jerusalem: Mekhon Tiferet ha-Torah, 1997.

Ashkenazi, Samuel Jaffe. *Yefeh Mareh*. In *Sefer En Ya'akov*, by Jacob ibn Ḥabib. Vol. 2. New York: Sifre Kodesh, 1971.

———. *Yefeh To'ar*. Commentary to the *Midrash Rabbah*. In the standard Vilna edition of the *Midrash Rabbah*.

Astruc, Solomon. *Midreshe ha-Torah*. Berlin: Tsevi Hirsch Itskovski, 1899.

Aszod, Judah. *Teshuvot Mahari'a: Yehudah Ya'aleh*. New York: Hotsa'at Ḥayim u-Verakhah, 1965.

Attar, Ḥayyim ben Moses. *Or ha-Ḥayim*. In the standard *Mikra'ot Gedolot*.

Attia, Isaac. *Pene ha-Mayim*. Jerusalem: Ha-Sifriyah ha-Sefaradit, 2003.

Auerbach, Shlomo Zalman. *Halikhot Shelomoh*. Vol. 2. Tel Aviv: Yeshivat Halikhot Shelomoh, 2003.

———. *Minḥat Shelomoh: Tinyana*. Jerusalem: n.p., 2000.

———. Quoted in *Mareh Mekomot al ha-Halakhot she-ben Adam la-Ḥavero*, vol. 1 (Jerusalem: Reshet ha-Kolelim Linat ha-Tsedek, 2006), 62.

Aviad, Y[israel] M[enaḥem]. *Ḥaninat Yisrael: Be-Khamah Inyanim al Seder Moed*. Bnei Brak: n.p., 2014.

Aviner, Shlomo. "*Ha-Zekhut li-Teguvah Alimah ve-Ḥovat Hitpayesut.*" *Noam* 25 (5743–5744 [1983–1984]): 202–14.

Avot de-Rabbi Nathan. Solomon Schechter Edition. New York: The Jewish Theological Seminary, 1997.

Avraham, Michael. "*Ha-Im ha-Halakhah hi Pluralistit.*" *Ha-Mayan* 47, no. 2 (2006): 41–56.

Azikri, Eleazar. *Sefer Ḥaredim ha-Shalem*. Jerusalem: n.p., 1990.

Azulai, Abraham. *Pirke Avot im Pe'[rush] me-Etsem Ketav Yad . . . Avraham b. k. h.-R. Mordekhai Azulai*. Jerusalem: Orot Ḥayim, 1987.

Azulai, Ḥayyim Joseph David. *Devarim Aḥadim*. Jerusalem: Yahadut, 1986.

———. *Devash le-Fi*. Jerusalem: Ha-Ma'amin, 1962.

———. *Naḥal Kedumim*. Israel: n.p., 1968.

———. *Sefer Petaḥ Enayim*. Vol. 2. Jerusalem: n.p., 1959.

———. *Shem ha-Gedolim*. New York: Grossman Publishing House, 1960.

Babad, Joseph. *Minḥat Ḥinukh*. Jerusalem: Mekhon Yerushalayim, 1997.

Bacharach, Jair Ḥayyim. *Mekor Ḥayim*. Jerusalem: Mifal Torat Ḥakhme Ashkenaz, 1984.

———. *Sefer She'elot u-Teshuvot Ḥavat Ya'ir*. Ramat Gan: Mekhon Eked Sefarim, 1997.

Bacher, Wilhelm. *Agadot ha-Tana'im*. Jerusalem: Devir, 1922.

Bachman, Guy Foster, and Laura K. Guerrero. "Forgiveness, Apology, and Communicative Responses to Hurtful Events." *Communication Reports* 19, no. 1, (2006): 45–56.

Bachrach, Judah. *Hagahot ha-Grib*. In the standard Vilna edition of the Babylonian Talmud, *Masekhet Derekh Erets Zuta*.

Baḥya ben Asher. *Kad ha-Kemaḥ*. In *Kitve Rabenu Baḥya*. Jerusalem: Mossad Harav Kook, 1970.

———. *Rabenu Baḥya Be'ur al ha-Torah*. Jerusalem: Mossad Harav Kook, 2006.

Bakshi-Doron, Eliyahu. *Sefer Binyan Av: Teshuvot u-Meḥkarim*. Vol. 3. Jerusalem: Mekhon Binyan Av, 2002.

Barash, David P., and Charles P. Webel. *Peace and Conflict Studies*. Thousand Oaks, CA: Sage Publications, 2002.

Bar-Ilan, Naftali Tsevi Yehudah. *Mishtar u-Medinah be-Yisrael al pi ha-Torah*. Vol. 3. Jerusalem: Ariel, 2007.

Bar Shaul, Elimelech. *Mitsvah va-Lev*. Vol. 1. Jerusalem: Or Etsiyon, 1992.

Baskin, Thomas W., and Robert D. Enright. "Intervention Studies on Forgiveness: A Meta-Analysis." *Journal of Counseling and Development* 82, no. 1 (2004): 79–90.

Baumeister, Roy F., Ellen Bratslavsky, Catrin Finkenauer, and Kathleen D. Vohs. "Bad is Stronger Than Good." *Review of General Psychology* 5, no. 4 (2001): 323–70.

Baumeister, Roy F., and Brad J. Bushman. *Social Psychology and Human Nature*. 2nd ed. Belmont, CA: Cengage Learning, 2011.

Bazerman, Max H., and Don A. Moore. *Judgment in Managerial Decision Making*. 7th ed. Hoboken, NJ: Wiley, 2009.

Beck, Aaron T., and A. John Rush. "Cognitive Therapy." In *Comprehensive Textbook of Psychiatry*. 6th ed. Vol. 2, edited by Harold I. Kaplan and Benjamin J. Sadock, 1847–57. Baltimore, MD: Williams & Wilkins, 1995.

Beck, Judith S. *Cognitive Behavior Therapy: Basics and Beyond*. New York: Guilford Press, 2011.

Bediou, Benoit, Christelle Mohri, Jeremy Lack, and David Sander. "Effects of Outcomes and Random Arbitration on Emotions in a Competitive Gambling Task." *Frontiers in Psychology* 2, article 213 (2011): 1–8. doi: 10.3389/fpsyg.2011.00213.

Bekhor Shor, Joseph. *Perushe Rabi Yosef Bekhor Shor al ha-Torah*. Jerusalem: Mossad Harav Kook, 1994.

Ben-Amram, Yosef. *Or ha-Torah*. Vol. 3. Jerusalem: Mekhon Naḥalat Yosef, 2013.

Ben-Menahem, Hanina, Neil Hecht, and Shai Wosner, eds. *Ha-Maḥaloket ba-Halakhah*. 3 vols. Boston: The Institute of Jewish Law, Boston University, 1991–.

Ben-Nayim, Jacob Ḥayyim. *Yeshuot Ya'akov*. Levorno: Avraham Yitsḥak Kastilo, 1784.

Bennett, Mark, and Deborah Earwaker. "Victims' Responses to Apologies: The Effects of Offender Responsibility and Offense Severity." *The Journal of Social Psychology* 134, no. 4 (1994): 457–64.

Benson, Herbert. *The Relaxation Response*. New York: Morrow, 1975.

———. "The Relaxation Response." In *Mind Body Medicine: How to Use Your Mind for Better Health*, edited by Daniel Goleman and Joel Gurin. Yonkers, NY: Consumer Reports Books, 1993.

Benveniste, Ḥayyim. *Dina de-Ḥaye: Be'ur al Sefer ha-Semag*. Jerusalem: Haktav Institute, 1997.

———. *Ḥamra ve-Ḥaye*. Jerusalem: S. L. A., 1988.

———. *Keneset ha-Gedolah*. Vol. 9, *Ḥoshen Mishpat*. Jerusalem: Haktav Institute, 2005.

Ben-Yehuda, Eliezer. *A Complete Dictionary of Ancient and Modern Hebrew*. 8 vols. New York: Yoseloff, 1960.

Berakhah, Eliyahu. *Toldot Noaḥ*. Jerusalem: n.p., 2012.

Berakhah, Yehudah. *Ketsad Mitmodedim*. Vol. 1. Jerusalem: Y. Berakhah, 2006.

Bercovitch, Jacob, Victor Kremenyuk, and I. William Zartman. Introduction to *The SAGE Handbook of Conflict Resolution*, 1–11. Los Angeles: Sage Publications, 2009.

Berghof Foundation, ed. "Conflict Prevention, Management, Resolution." In *Berghof Glossary on Conflict Transformation*, 17–21. Berlin, Germany: Berghof Foundation, 2012.

Berkowitz, Leonard. "On the Formation and Regulation of Anger and Aggression: A Cognitive-Neoassociationistic Analysis." *American Psychologist* 45, no. 4 (1990): 494–503.

Berlin, Isaiah ben Judah Loeb. *Hagahot ha-GRY'P*. In *Shulḥan Arukh ha-Shalem, Oraḥ Ḥayim*. Vol. 9. Jerusalem: Mifal Shulḥan Arukh ha-Shalem, 2002.

Berlin, Naphtali Zevi Judah. *Emek ha-Netsiv*. Vol. 1. Jerusalem: n.p., 1977.

———. *Ha'amek Davar*. Jerusalem: Y. Kuperman, 2009.

———. *Ha'amek She'elah*. Commentary to *She'iltot de-Rav Aḥai Gaon*, by Aḥa of Shabḥa. Vol. 1. Jerusalem: Mossad Harav Kook, 1958.

———. *Hosafot le-Ferush Ha'amek Davar ve-Harḥev Davar*. Jerusalem: Bamberger et Vahrmann, 1928.

———. *Meshiv Davar*. Jerusalem: Yeshivat Voloz'in be-Erets Yisrael, 1993.

Berman, Shemaryahu Yosef. *Sefer Birkat Shai al Masekhet Sanhedrin*. Bnei Brak: Berman, 2002.

Bertinoro, Obadiah. *Perush Rabenu Ovadyah mi-Bartenura*. In *Mishnayot Zekher Ḥanokh*. Jerusalem: Ḥ. Vagshal, 1999.

Bet Yeḥiel: Ḥoshen Mishpat. Vol. 1. Jerusalem: Kolel Bet Yeḥiel, 1999.

Beyer, Gerry W., and Kenneth R. Redden. "Alternative Dispute Resolution." In *Modern Dictionary for the Legal Profession*, edited by Margaret M. Beyer. 2nd ed., 25. Buffalo, NY: William S. Hein & Co., 1996.

Bippus, Amy M., and Stacy L. Young. "Owning Your Emotions: Reactions to Expressions of Self- versus Other-Attributed Positive and Negative Emotions." *Journal of Applied Communication Research* 33, no. 1 (2005): 26–45.

Biton, Daniel. *Shisha Sidre Mishnah im Perush ha-Mishnah leha-Rambam*. Jerusalem: Mekhon ha-Ma'or, 2009.

Blaser, Isaac. "*Netivot Or*." In *Sefer Or Yisrael*, 109–24. N.p., n.d.

Blass, Jonathan. *Minofet Tsuf*. Vol. 2. Neveh Tsuf: Kolel Retson Yehudah, 2006.

Bleich, J. David. "*Ona'at Devarim.*" *Ha-Dorom* 35 (1972): 140–43.

Bloch, Elijah Meyer. "*Ha-Roeh.*" In *Shi'ure Da'at,* vol. 3, by Joseph Leib Bloch, 151–65. Tel Aviv: Netsaḥ, 1956.

Bloi, Ya'akov Yeshayahu. *Pitḥe Ḥoshen.* 8 vols. Jerusalem: Yeshivat Ohel Moshe Diskin, 1982.

Blum-Kulka, Shoshana, Juliane House, and Gabriele Kasper. "Investigating Cross-Cultural Pragmatics: An Introductory Overview." In *Cross-Cultural Pragmatics: Requests and Apologies,* 1–34. Norwood, NJ: Ablex Publishing, 1989.

Blum-Kulka, Shoshana and Elite Olshtain. "Requests and Apologies: A Cross-Cultural Study of Speech Act Realization Patterns (CCSARP)." *Applied Linguistics* 5, no. 3 (1984): 196–213.

Bodenheimer, Michael Yeḥiel. *Be-Me ha-Torah.* Bnei Brak: n.p., 2009.

Bodine, Richard J., and Donna K. Crawford. *The Handbook of Conflict Resolution Education: A Guide to Building Quality Programs in Schools.* San Francisco: Jossey-Bass, 1998.

Bolle, Menachem. *Sefer Va-Yikra* (*Da'at Mikra*). Jerusalem: Mossad Harav Kook, 1992.

Bolstad, Max. "Learning from Japan: The Case for Increased Use of Apology in Mediation." *Cleveland State Law Review* 48 (2000): 545–78.

Boon, Susan. "Revenge." In *Encyclopedia of Human Relationships,* edited by Harry T. Reis and Susan Sprecher, 1378–79. Thousand Oaks, CA: Sage Publications, 2009.

Borisoff, Deborah, and David A. Victor. *Conflict Management: A Communication Skills Approach.* Englewood Cliffs, NJ: Prentice Hall, 1989.

Bornstein, Israel. *Kerem Yisrael.* Piotrków: Ḥanokh H. Folman, 1929.

Borowitz, Eugene B. *Exploring Jewish Ethics: Papers on Covenant Responsibility.* Detroit: Wayne University Press, 1990.

Boskowitz, Benjamin Ze'ev. *Sefer Seder Mishneh.* Jerusalem: Mosdot Ziv ha-Torah, 1991.

Botterweck, G. Johannes, and Helmer Ringgren, eds. *The Theological Dictionary of the Old Testament.* 14 vols. Grand Rapids, MI: William B. Eerdmans, 1974–.

———. *Theologisches Worterbuch zum Alten Testament.* Vol. 7. Stuttgart: W. Kohlhammer, 1993.

Braude, William G., and Israel J. Kaplan. Introduction to *Tanna Debe Eliyahu: The Lore of the School of Elijah*, 3–37. Philadelphia: The Jewish Publication Society of America, 1981.

Braun, Solomon. *She'arim Metsuyanim ba-Halakhah*. Commentary to *Kitsur Shulḥan Arukh*, by Solomon Ganzfried. Jerusalem: Feldheim, 1978.

Breisacher, David. *Naḥalat Devash*. Israel: Ofarim, 2009.

Breslin, William, and Jeffrey Z. Rubin, eds. *Negotiation Theory and Practice*. Cambridge, MA: Program on Negotiation Books, 1991.

Brodianski, Yitsḥak Yeruḥem. "*Be-Ve'ur Torat ha-Bitaḥon*." *Bet Va'ad: Siḥot u-Ma'amre Musar* 1 (Sivan 5757-Iyar 5758 [1997–1998]): 15–28.

Bruk, Eliezer Ben-Zion. *Hegyone Musar*. New York: n.p., 1969.

Bruna, Israel. *She'elot u-Teshuvot Yisrael mi-Bruna*. Jerusalem: n.p., 1973.

Bu'aron, Aharon. "*Be-Geder Kelalah*." *Torat ha-Adam le-Adam: Kovets Torani ba-Mitsvot she-ben Adam la-Ḥavero* 4 (2001): 197–200.

Buber, Solomon, annot. *Midrash Tanḥuma*. Vilna: n.p., n.d.

Bukarat, Abraham ben Solomon ha-Levi. *Sefer ha-Zikaron al Perush Rashi la-Ḥumash*. Petaḥ Tikvah: Mosheh Filip, 1985.

Burgess, Heidi, and Guy M. Burgess, eds. *Encyclopedia of Conflict Resolution*. Santa Barbara, CA: ABC-CLIO, 1997.

Burton, John, ed. *Conflict: Human Needs Theory*. New York: St. Martin's Press, 1990.

———. *Conflict: Resolution and Provention*. New York: St. Martin's Press, 1990.

Bush, Robert A. Baruch, and Joseph P. Folger. *The Promise of Mediation: Responding to Conflict through Empowerment and Recognition*. San Francisco: Jossey-Bass, 1994.

Bush, Robert A. Baruch, and Sally Ganong Pope. "Changing the Quality of Conflict Interaction: The Principles and Practice of Transformative Mediation." *Pepperdine Dispute Resolution Law Journal* 3, no. 1 (2002–2003): 67–96.

Bushman, Brad J. "Does Venting Anger Feed or Extinguish the Flame? Catharsis, Rumination, Distraction, Anger, and Aggressive Responding." *Personality and Social Psychology Bulletin* 28, no. 6 (2002): 724–31.

Capusi, Ḥayyim. *Sefer Be'or ha-Ḥayim*. Jerusalem: Ahavat Shalom, 1989.

Carlebach, Mordechai. *Ḥavatselet ha-Sharon*. Vol. 1. Jerusalem: n.p., 2005.

Carruthers, William L., Barbara J. B. Carruthers, Norma L. Day-Vines, Dee Bostick, and Dwight C. Watson. "Conflict Resolution as Curriculum: A Definition, Description, and Process for Integration in Core Curricula." *The School Counselor* 43, no. 5 (May 1996): 345–73.

Castro, Jacob. *Hagahot ha-Gaon Morenu ha-Rav Ya'akov Kastro.* In the back of the standard printed edition of the *Shulḥan Arukh.*

Castro, Loreta N. "Peace and Peace Education: A Holistic View." In *World Encyclopedia of Peace,* edited by Javier Perez de Cuellar and Young Seek Choue. 2nd ed. Vol. 4, 164–71. Dobbs Ferry, NY: Oceana Publications, 1999.

Catane, Moshe. *"Ha-Le'azim be-Rashi."* In *Da'at Mikra: Shemot.* Vol. 1, 49–53. Jerusalem: Mossad Harav Kook, 1991.

Chajes, Zevi Hirsch. *Mevo ha-Talmud.* In *Kol Sifre Maharits Ḥayot.* Vol. 1. Jerusalem: Divre Ḥakhamim, 1958.

Chappell, David W. *Buddhist Peacework.* Somerville, MA: Wisdom Publications, 1999.

Chmiel, Re'uven. *Sha'ar Re'uven.* Jerusalem: R. Chmiel, 2008.

Cloke, Kenneth. *Mediating Dangerously: The Frontiers of Conflict Resolution.* San Francisco: Jossey-Bass, 2001.

Cohen, Binyamin. *Sefer Ḥafets Ḥayim im Perush Ḥelkat Binyamin.* Brooklyn: n.p., 1993.

Cohen, Jonathan R. "Advising Clients to Apologize." *Southern California Law Review* 72 (1999): 1009–69.

Cohen, Seymour J. Introduction to *Sefer ha-Yashar: The Book of the Righteous,* by Zerahiah ha-Yevani, xi–xx. New York: Ktav, 1973.

Coleman, Peter T. Concluding overview to *The Handbook of Conflict Resolution: Theory and Practice,* 591–600. Edited by Morton Deutsch and Peter T. Coleman. San Francisco: Jossey-Bass, 2000.

Coleman, Peter, and Morton Deutsch. "Introducing Cooperation and Conflict Resolution into Schools: A Systems Approach." In *Peace, Conflict and Violence: Peace Psychology for the 21st Century,* edited by Daniel J. Christie, Richard V. Wagner, and Deborah Du Nann Winter, 223–39. Upper Saddle River, NJ: Prentice Hall, 2001.

Collaborative for Academic, Social, and Emotional Learning. Accessed September 25, 2016. http://casel.org/why-it-matters/what-is-sel.

Colman, Andrew M. *Oxford Dictionary of Psychology*. 3rd ed. Oxford: Oxford University Press, 2009.

The Complete Artscroll Machzor: Yom Kippur: Nusach Ashkenaz. Brooklyn: Mesorah Publications, 1986.

Cooperman, Hillel. *Shuvi Nafshi*. Commentary to Maimonides' *Hilkhot Teshuvah*. Jerusalem: n.p., 2010.

Cordovero, Moses. *Tomer Devorah*. London: n.p., 2003.

Corsini, Raymond J. *The Dictionary of Psychology*. Philadelphia, PA: Brunner/Mazel, 1999.

Coward, Harold, and Gordon S. Smith, eds. *Religion and Peacebuilding*. Albany, NY: State University of New York Press, 2004.

Cowley, A. E., and Adolf Neubauer, eds. *The Original Hebrew of a Portion of Ecclesiasticus*. Oxford, UK: Clarendon Press, 1897.

Crawley, John. *Constructive Conflict Management: Managing to Make a Difference*. San Diego, CA: Pfeiffer and Company, 1994.

da Fano, Menaḥem Azariah. *Sefer Asarah Ma'amarot*. Jerusalem: Mekhon Yismaḥ Lev, 2000.

Daily Prayer Book, Ha-Siddur ha-Shalem. Translated and edited by Phillip Birnbaum. New York: Hebrew Publishing Co., 1949.

Danzig, Abraham. *Bet Avraham*. Vilna: Yosef Reuven Rom, 1847.

———. *Ḥaye Adam*. Jerusalem: Mekhon Me'orot Da'at, 1988.

———. *Kitsur Sefer Ḥaredim*. Jerusalem: Mekhon Me'orot ha-Da'at, 1986.

Darwin, Charles. *The Expression of the Emotions in Man and Animals*. New York: D. Appleton, 1886.

da Silva, Hezekiah. *Peri Ḥadash*. In the standard printed edition of the *Shulḥan Arukh*.

Dauer, Edward A. *Manual of Dispute Resolution: ADR Law and Practice*. 2 vols. Deerfield, IL: Clark, Boardman, Callaghan, 1995.

David ben Abraham Maimuni. *Midrash David al Pirke Avot*. Jerusalem: Siaḥ Yisrael, 1987.

David ben Samuel ha-Levi. *Ture Zahav*. In the standard printed edition of the *Shulḥan Arukh*.

Davis, Albie M. "An Interview with Mary Parker Follet." In *Negotiation Theory and Practice*, edited by J. William Breslin and Jeffrey Z. Rubin, 13–25. Cambridge, MA: Program on Negotiation Books, 1993.

Davis, James R., and Gregg J. Gold. "An Examination of Emotional Empathy, Attributions of Stability, and the Link between Perceived Remorse and Forgiveness." *Personality and Individual Differences* 50, no. 3 (2011): 392–97.

Davis, Mark H. "Measuring Individual Differences in Empathy: Evidence for a Multidimensional Approach." *Journal of Personality and Social Psychology* 44, no. 1 (1983): 113–26.

de Boton, Abraham. *Leḥem Mishneh*. In the standard printed edition of Maimonides' *Mishneh Torah*.

Deffenbacher, Jerry L. "Evidence for Effective Treatment of Anger-Related Disorders." In *Anger-Related Disorders: A Practitioner's Guide to Comparative Treatments*, edited by Eva L. Feindler, 43–69. New York: Springer, 2006.

Deffenbacher, Jerry L., and Matthew McKay. *Overcoming Situational and General Anger: A Protocol for the Treatment of Anger Based on Relaxation, Cognitive Restructuring, and Coping Skills Training*. Oakland, CA: New Harbinger, 2000.

de Medina, Samuel. *She'elot u-Teshuvot Maharashdam*. Lemberg: P. M. Balaban, 1862.

Dessler, Elijah Eliezer. *Mikhtav me-Eliyahu*. 5 vols. Jerusalem: Yotse la-Or al Yede Ḥever Talmidav, 1997.

———. *Mikhtav me-Eliyahu: Divre Ḥokhmah u-Musar ba-Avodat Ḥodesh Elul ve-Yeraḥ ha-Etanim*. 2 vols. Bnei Brak: Sifsei Chachamim, 2008.

———. *Sefer ha-Zikaron le-Va'al Mikhtav me-Eliyahu*. Bnei Brak: Sifte Ḥakhamim, 2004.

Deutsch, Morton. "Cooperation, Competition, and Conflict." In *The Handbook of Conflict Resolution: Theory and Practice*, 3rd ed., edited by Peter T. Coleman, Morton Deutsch, and Eric C. Marcus, 3–28. San Francisco: Jossey-Bass, 2014.

———. "Educating for a Peaceful World." *American Psychologist* 48, no. 5 (1993): 510–17.

———. "Field Theory in Social Psychology." In *The Handbook of Social Psychology*. Vol. 1. 2nd ed., edited by Gardner Lindzey and Elliot Aronson Reading, 412–87. Boston, MA: Addison-Wesley Publishing, 1968.

———. *The Handbook of Conflict Resolution: Theory and Practice*, edited by Morton Deutsch, Peter T. Coleman, and Eric C. Marcus. San Francisco: Jossey-Bass, 2014.

———. Introduction to *The Handbook of Conflict Resolution: Theory and Practice*, 1–17. Edited by Morton Deutsch and Peter T. Coleman. San Francisco: Jossey-Bass, 2000.

———. "A Personal History of Social Interdependence—Theory, Research, and Practice." Accessed November, 7, 2016. http://www.tc.columbia.edu/i/a/document/9450APersonalHistoryofSocialInterdependence_TheoryResearchandPractice.pdf.

———. *The Resolution of Conflict: Constructive and Destructive Processes*. New Haven: Yale University Press, 1973.

———. "Sixty Years of Conflict." *The International Journal of Conflict Management* 1, no. 3 (1990): 237–63.

———. "A Theory of Cooperation and Competition." *Human Relations* 2, no. 2 (1949): 129–152.

Deutsch, Morton, Peter T. Coleman, and Eric C. Marcus, eds. *The Handbook of Conflict Resolution: Theory and Practice*. San Francisco: Jossey-Bass, 2006.

de Vidas, Elijah ben Moses. *Reshit Ḥokhmah ha-Shalem*. Vol. 2. Jerusalem: Or ha-Musar, 1990.

DiBlasio, Frederick A. "Decision-Based Forgiveness Treatment in Cases of Marital Infidelity." *Psychotherapy: Theory, Research, Practice, Training* 37, no. 2 (2000): 149–58.

———. "Marital Couples and Forgiveness Intervention." In *Evidence-Based Practices for Christian Counseling and Psychotherapy*, edited by Everett L. Worthington Jr., Eric L. Johnson, Joshua N. Hook, and Jamie D. Ate, 232–54. Downers Grove, IL: InterVarsity Press, 2013.

———. "The Use of a Decision-Based Forgiveness Intervention within Intergenerational Family Therapy." *Journal of Family Therapy* 20, no. 1 (1998): 77–96.

DiBlasio, Frederick A. and Brent B. Benda. "Forgiveness Intervention with Married Couples: Two Empirical Analyses." *Journal of Psychology and Christianity* 27, no. 2 (2008): 150–58.

DiBlasio, Frederick A., Everett L. Worthington Jr., and David J. Jennings II. "Forgiveness Interventions with Children, Adolescents, and Families." In *Spiritual Interventions in Child and Adolescent Psychotherapy*, edited by Donald F. Walker and William L. Hathaway, 233–58. Washington, DC: American Psychological Association, 2013.

Dimitrovsky, Haim Z. "*Al Derekh ha-Pilpul.*" In *Sefer ha-Yovel le-Khvod Shalom Baron*, 111–81. Jerusalem: American Academy for Jewish Research, 1974.

Dinur, Ben Zion. *Masekhet Avot*. Jerusalem: Mosad Bialik, 1973.

Dirshu H' ve-Uzo. *Mishnah Berurah*. Vol. 6. Jerusalem: Dirshu, 2013.

Diskin, Moses Joshua Judah Leib. *Ḥidushe Maharil Diskin al ha-Torah*. Jerusalem: n.p., 1985.

———. *She'elot u-Teshuvot Maharil Diskin*. Jerusalem: Defus Moriyah, 1911.

Di Trani, Isaiah ben Elijah. Cited in Yehoshua Boaz le-vet Barukh, *Shilte ha-Giborim*. In the standard Vilna edition of the Babylonian Talmud.

Di Trani, Isaiah ben Mali. *Tosafot Rid*. Jerusalem: Machon Harry Fischel, 1962.

Dowd, E. Thomas, and Richard Suinn. Quoted in Howard Kassinove and Raymond Chip Tafrate, *Anger Management: The Complete Treatment Guidebook for Practitioners* (Atascadero, CA: Impact Publishers, 2002), reviewers' comments section.

Dozois, David J. A., and Aaron T. Beck. "Cognitive Schemas, Beliefs, and Assumptions." In *Risk Factors in Depression*, edited by Keith S. Dobson and David J. A. Dozois, 121–43. Amsterdam: Academic Press, 2008.

Duffy, Karen G., James W. Grosch, and Paul V. Olczak, eds. *Community Mediation: A Handbook for Practitioners and Researchers*. New York: Guilford Press, 1991.

Duling, Dennis C. "Matthew 18:15–17: Conflict, Confrontation, and Conflict Resolution in a 'Fictive Kin' Association." *Society of Biblical Literature: Seminar Papers* 37, no. 1 (1998): 253–95.

Dunner, Yosef Tsevi ha-Levi. *Mikdash ha-Levi*. Bnei Brak: n.p., 2009.

Duran, Simeon ben Zemaḥ. *Magen Avot*. Jerusalem: Erez, 2000.

———. *Sefer Milḥemet Mitsvah*. In *Sefer Keshet u-Magen*, 27b–39b. Jerusalem: Mekor, 1970.

———. Commentary to *Avot*. In *Mishnat Re'uven: Masekhet Avot im Perushe ha-Rishonim*. Jerusalem: Mossad Harav Kook, 2005.

Durlak, Joseph A., Roger P. Weissberg, Allison B. Dymnicki, Rebecca D. Taylor, and Kriston B. Schellinger. "The Impact of Enhancing Students' Social and Emotional Learning: A Meta-Analysis of School-Based Universal Interventions." *Child Development* 82, no. 1 (2011): 405–32.

Duschinsky, Joseph Zevi. *Sefer She'elot u-Teshuvot Maharits*. Vol. 2. Jerusalem: J. M. Duschinsky, 1975.

Edels, Samuel. *Halakhot va-Agadot ha-Maharasha*. In the standard Vilna edition of the Babylonian Talmud.

Educators for Social Responsibility. Accessed September 6, 2012. http://esrnational.org/professional-services/elementary-school/prevention/resolving-conflict-creatively-program-rccp/ (site discontinued).

Eger, Azriel Meir. Cited in *Eleh Ezkerah: Osef Toldot Kedoshe 5700–5705*, vol. 5 (New York: Ha-Makhon le-Ḥeker Be'ayot ha-Yahadut ha-Ḥaredit, 1963), 128.

Ehrenberg, Yehoshua Menaḥem Mendel. *Sefer Devar Yehoshua*. Vol. 5. Bnei Brak: Be-Hotsa'at Ḥotne ha-Meḥaber, 1998.

Ehrenraikh, Ḥayim Tsevi. *Ketseh ha-Mateh*. Commentary to *Sefer Mateh Efrayim*, by Ephraim Zalman Margolioth. Brooklyn: Ḥevrah Mefitse Torah mi-Mishpaḥat Kol Aryeh, 2001.

Ehrman, Avraham. *Sefer Halikhot Olam: Kitsur Dinim ben Adam la-Ḥavero; Ve-Sefer Kodesh Yisrael*. Bnei Brak: n.p., 1996.

Eilenburg, Issachar Baer. *Sefer Be'er Sheva*. Jerusalem: n.p., 1969.

Einhorn, Ze'ev Wolf. *Midrash Tanaim*. Lakewood, NJ: Machon Mishnas Rabbi Aaron, 2003.

Eisenblatt, Shmuel D. *Ḥayim shel Shalom: Hilkhot Isure Maḥaloket*. Jerusalem: n.p., 1989.

Eisenstadt, Meir. *Panim Me'irot*. Vol. 1. New York: Kelilat Yofi Publishing, 1962.

[Eisenstein], Ḥayim Leib ben Dov. *Peninim mi-Be Midrasha*. Vol. 1. Jerusalem: n.p., 2004.

Eisenstein, Israel. *Amude Esh*. Lemberg: U. V. Z. Salat, 1880.

Eleazar ben Judah of Worms. *Sefer Moreh Ḥata'im*. In *Kol Bo*. Vol. 4, 201–20. Jerusalem: D. Avraham, 1993.

Eliakim ben Meshullam. *Perush Rabi Elyakim le-Masekhet Yoma*. Jerusalem: Mekitse Nirdamim, 1964.

Elias, Maurice J., and Steven E. Tobias. *Social Problem Solving: Interventions in Schools*. New York: Guilford Press, 1996.

Elias, Maurice J., Joseph E. Zins, Roger P. Weissberg, Karin S. Frey, Mark T. Greenberg, Noris M. Hayes, Rachel Kessler, Mary E. Schwab-Stone, and Timothy P. Shriver. *Promoting Social and Emotional Learning: Guidelines for Educators*. Alexandria, VA: Association for Supervision and Curriculum Development, 1997.

Eliezer ben Nathan. *Masekhet Avot im Perush Rashi ve-im Perush Ra'avan*. Bnei Brak: Mishor, 1992.

Eliezer ben Samuel of Metz. *Sefer Yere'im ha-Shalem*. Israel: n.p., n.d.

Elijah ben Solomon. *Be'ur ha-Gera: Megilat Ester*. Jerusalem: Mossad Harav Kook, 2010.

———. *Be'ur ha-Gera: Mishle*. Jerusalem: Mossad Harav Kook, 2005.

———. *[Be'ure] Ha-Gra al Shulḥan Arukh*. In the standard printed edition of the *Shulḥan Arukh*.

Eliyahu, Mordechai. *Hilkhot Ḥagim*. 2nd ed. Jerusalem: Darkhe Hora'ah, 2003.

Ellis, Albert. *Anger: How to Live with and without It*. New York: Citadel Press, 2003.

———. *Humanistic Psychotherapy: The Rational-Emotive Approach*. New York: Julian Press, 1973.

———. "Rational Emotive Behavior Therapy." In *Encyclopedia of Psychotherapy*. Vol. 2, edited by Michel Hersen and William H. Sledge, 483–87. Amsterdam: Academic Press, 2002.

Ellis, Albert, and Windy Dryden. *The Practice of Rational Emotive Behavior Therapy*. 2nd ed. New York: Springer, 1997.

Ellis, Albert, and Raymond Chip Tafrate. *How to Control Your Anger before It Controls You*. New York: Citadel Press, 1997.

Elon, Menachem. *Jewish Law: History, Sources, Principles*. Philadelphia: The Jewish Publication Society, 1994.

Elyakim, Ḥayim Yosef. *Shem Yosef*. Saloniki: Yuda Kelai and Mordekhai Naḥman, 1769.

Elyashiv, Yosef Shalom. *He'arot be-Masekhet Yoma*. Jerusalem: n.p., 2002.

———. Quoted in Avraham Tsevi Yisraelzon, "*Be-Inyane Yamim Noraim ve-Sukot*," *Kovets Sha'are Hora'ah* 8 (5767 [2007]): 108.

———. Quoted in Moshe Frid, *Va-Yishma Mosheh*, vol. 1 (Jerusalem: n.p., 2010), 196.

———. Cited in Shimon Licht, "*Ba-Din Meḥilah i Ba'e ba-Peh o ba-Lev*," *Torat ha-Adam le-Adam: Kovets Torani ba-Mitsvot she-ben Adam la-Ḥavero* 3 (1999): 36.

———. Quoted in Yitsḥak Zilberstein, *Kav ve-Naki*, vol. 2 (n.p., 2013), 240.

———. Cited in [Yosef Yisraelzon], *Kuntres Kitsur Hilkhot ben Adam la-Ḥavero* (Reḥovot: Kolel Avrekhim Reḥovot, 1998), 8, 9, 17.

Emden, Jacob. *Sefer Migdal Oz*. Jerusalem: Hotsa'at Fisher, 1993.

Engel, Joseph. *Gilyone ha-Shas*. New York: n.p., 1949.

Enright, Robert D. *Forgiveness Is a Choice: A Step-by-Step Process for Resolving Anger and Restoring Hope*. Washington, DC: American Psychological Association, 2001.

Enright, Robert D., and Richard P. Fitzgibbons. *Helping Clients Forgive: An Empirical Guide for Resolving Anger and Restoring Hope*. Washington, DC: American Psychological Association, 2000.

Enright, Robert D., Suzanne Freedman, and Julio Rique. "The Psychology of Interpersonal Forgiveness." In *Exploring Forgiveness*, edited by Robert D. Enright and Joanna North, 46–62. Madison, WI: University of Wisconsin Press, 1998.

Enright, Robert D., and the Human Development Study Group. "The Moral Development of Forgiveness." In *Handbook of Moral Behavior and Development: Volume 1: Theory*, edited by William M. Kurtines and Jacob L. Gewirtz, 123–52. Hillsdale, NJ: Lawrence Erlbaum, 1991.

Ephraim ben Jacob ha-Kohen. *Sha'ar Efrayim*. Jerusalem: n.p., 1981.

Ephraim Solomon ben Aaron of Luntshits. *Sefer Keli Yakar ha-Shalem*. Jerusalem: Orot Ḥayim, 2001.

Epley, Nicholas, Eugene M. Caruso, and Max H. Bazerman. "When Perspective Taking Increases Taking: Reactive Egoism in Social Interaction." *Journal of Personality and Social Psychology* 91, no. 5 (2006): 872–89.

Epstein, Baruch ha-Levi. *Barukh she-Amar: Pirke Avot*. Tel Aviv: Am Olam, n.d.

———. *Torah Temimah*. New York: Hebrew Publishing Co., 1928.

Epstein, Jehiel Michal. *Sefer Arukh ha-Shulḥan*. N.p., n.d.

Epstein, Joseph D. *Mitsvat ha-Etsah*. New York: Torat ha-Adam, 1983.

———. *Mitsvot ha-Bayit*. Vol. 1. New York: Torat ha-Adam, 1981.

———. *Mitsvot ha-Musar*. Vol. 2. New York: Va'ad le-Hotsa'at Sifre Mitsvot ha-Musar, 1948.

———. *Mitzvot ha-Shalom: The Commandments on Peace; a Guide to the Jewish Understanding of Peace and Harmony in Interpersonal and Communal Life in Light of Torah* (in Hebrew). Brooklyn: Torath HaAdam Institute Inc., 1987.

———. *Torat ha-Adam*. Vol. 2. New York: Balshon, 1977.

Escapa, Joseph. *Sefer Rosh Yosef*. Monroe, NY: Yitsḥak Brakh, 1989.

Etkes, Immanuel. *Rabbi Israel Salanter and the Mussar Movement*. Philadelphia: Jewish Publication Society, 1993.

Ettlinger, Jacob. *Arukh la-Ner*. Brooklyn: Mefitse Torah, 1959.

———. *Minḥat Ani*. Vol. 1. Jerusalem: Oz ve-Hadar, 1997.

Even-Shoshan, Abraham, ed. *Ha-Milon he-Ḥadash*. 8th ed. Jerusalem: Kiryat Sefer, 1977.

———. *A New Concordance of the Bible: Thesaurus of the Language of the Bible: Hebrew and Aramaic Roots, Words, Proper Names, Phrases and Synonyms*. Jerusalem: Kiryat Sefer Publishing House, 1993.

Exline, Julie Juola, and Roy F. Baumeister. "Expressing Forgiveness and Repentance: Benefits and Barriers." In *Forgiveness: Theory, Research, and Practice*, edited by Michael E. McCullough, Kenneth I. Pargament, and Carl E. Thoresen, 133–55. New York: Guilford Press, 2000.

Eybeschuetz, Jonathan. *Sefer Ya'arot Devash*. Vol. 2. Jerusalem: Mekhon Even Yisrael, 2000.

Falk, Jacob Joshua. *Pene Yehoshua*. Jerusalem: Or ha-Ḥokhmah, 1998.

Falk, Joshua ben Alexander. *Sefer Me'irat Enayim (Sma)*. In the standard printed edition of the *Shulḥan Arukh, Ḥoshen Mishpat*.

Farissol, Abraham. *Perushe Avraham Faritsol al Masekhet Avot*. Jerusalem: Mekhon Torah Shelemah, 1964.

Fehr, Ryan, and Michele J. Gelfand. "When Apologies Work: How Matching Apology Components to Victims' Self-Construals Facilitates Forgiveness." *Organizational Behavior and Human Decision Processes* 113, no. 1 (2010): 37–50.

Feinstein, Moses. *Igrot Mosheh*. 9 vols. New York: Moriyah, 1959–.

Feldman, Daniel Z. *False Facts and True Rumors: Lashon Hara in Contemporary Culture*. New Milford, CT: Maggid Books, 2015.

———. *The Right and the Good: Halakhah and Human Relations*, expanded edition. Brooklyn: Yashar Books, 2005.

Feldman, David. *Lev David*. London: Defus Feiner, 2000.

Ferguson, John. "Buddhism." In *War and Peace in the World's Religions*, 41–61. NY: Oxford University Press, 1978.

Feshbach, Norma D. and Kiki Roe. "Empathy in Six- and Seven-Year-Olds." *Child Development* 39, no. 1 (March 1968): 133–145.

Feuchtwanger, Asher. *Asher la-Melekh*. Vol. 1. Jerusalem: F. Feuchtwanger, 1988.

Figo, Azariah. *Sefer Binah le-Itim*. Vol. 1. Jerusalem: Hotsa'at Ḥ. Vagshal, 1989.

Fincham, Frank D., and Steven R. H. Beach. "Forgiveness in Marriage: Implications for Psychological Aggression and Constructive Communication." *Personal Relationships* 9, no. 3 (2002): 239–51.

Fincham, Frank D., Steven R. H. Beach, and Joanne Davila. "Forgiveness and Conflict Resolution in Marriage." *Journal of Family Psychology* 18, no. 1 (2004): 72–81.

———. "Longitudinal Relations between Forgiveness and Conflict Resolution in Marriage." *Journal of Family Psychology* 21, no. 3 (2007): 542–45.

Finkel, Nathan Zevi. *Or ha-Tsafun*. Jerusalem: Elḥanan Hoffman and Tsevi Weinreb, 1978.

———. Quoted in Dov Katz, *Tenu'at ha-Musar*, vol. 3 (Jerusalem: Feldheim, 1996), 125.

———. Quoted in Jehiel Jacob Weinberg, *Seride Esh*, vol. 4 (Jerusalem: Mossad Harav Kook, 1977), 312–13.

Finkelman, Shimon, and Yitzchak Berkowitz. *Chofetz Chaim: A Lesson a Day*. Brooklyn: Mesorah Publications, 1998.

Finkelstain, Ariel. *Derekh ha-Melekh*. Netivot: Yeshivat ha-Hesder Ahavat Yisrael, 2010.

First, Mitchell. "What is the Origin of the Word *Meḥilah*?" *Ḥakirah* 18 (Winter 2014): 147–58.

Fish, Ya'akov Ḥizkiyahu. *Titen Emet le-Ya'akov*. Jerusalem: n.p., 2004.

Fisher, Fred. *Building Bridges between Citizens and Local Governments to Work More Effectively Together through Managing Conflict and Differences: Part 1, Concepts and Strategies*. N.p.: United Nations Centre for Human Settlements (Habitat), 2001. Accessed November 7, 2016. http://www.gdrc.org/decision/BuildingBridges.pdf.

Fisher, Roger, William Ury, and Bruce Patton. *Getting to Yes: Negotiating Agreement without Giving In*. 2nd ed. New York: Penguin Books, 1991.

Fiske, Susan T. *Social Beings: A Core Motives Approach to Social Psychology*. Hoboken, NJ: Wiley, 2004.

Florsheim, Yoel. *Rashi la-Mikra be-Ferusho la-Talmud*. Vol. 2. Jerusalem: Rubin Mass, 1984.

Folberg, Jay, and Alison Taylor. *Mediation: A Comprehensive Guide to Resolving Conflicts without Litigation*. San Francisco: Jossey-Bass, 1984.

Follett, Mary Parker. *Dynamic Administration: The Collected Papers of Mary Parker Follett*. Edited by Henry C. Metcalf and L. Urwick. New York: Harper and Brothers, n.d.

Fontaine, Resianne. "Love of One's Neighbour in Pinhas Hurwitz's *Sefer ha-Berit*." In *Studies in Hebrew Literature and Jewish Culture*, edited by Martin F. J. Baasten and Reinier Munk, 271–95. Dordrecht: Springer, 2007.

Fraenkel, David. *Korban ha-Edah*. In the standard printed edition of the Jerusalem Talmud.

Freimann, Aron. *Kuntres ha-Mefaresh ha-Shalem*. New York: American Academy for Jewish Research, 1946.

Fridlander, Ḥayim. *Sifte Ḥayim: Pirke Emunah ve-Hashgaḥah*. Vol. 1. Bnei Brak: Ha-Rabanit Fridlander, 1999.

Friedman, Chana T. *Mastering Patience: Based on Sefer Erech Apayim*. Brooklyn, NY: Hadaf Printing, 2010.

Friedman, Eliyahu Aryeh. *Kuntres ve-Ahavta le-Re'akha kamokha: Ha-Mitsvah ve-Gidreha ba-Halakhah, ba-Maḥshavah, ba-Musar uva-Ḥasidut.* Brooklyn: Moriah, 1994.

Friedman, Shamma, annot. *Perush Yehonatan ha-Kohen mi-Lunel al ha-Mishnah veha-Rif Masekhet Bava Kama.* Jerusalem: Feldheim, 1969.

Fus, Yitsḥak Ḥayim. *"Ha-Mitsvah la-Dun le-Khaf Zekhut veha-Isur la-Ḥshod bi-Khsherim." Torat ha-Adam le-Adam: Kovets Torani ba-Mitsvot she-ben Adam la-Ḥavero* 3 (1999): 124–41.

Gabai, Shaul. *"Be-Geder Ona'at Devarim." Torat ha-Adam le-Adam: Kovets Torani ba-Mitsvot she-ben Adam la-Ḥavero* 4 (2002): 203–5.

Galinsky, Adam D., Debra Gilin, and William W. Maddux. "Using Both Your Head and Your Heart: The Role of Perspective Taking and Empathy in Resolving Social Conflict." In *The Psychology of Social Conflict and Aggression,* edited by Joseph P. Forgas, Arie W. Kruglanski, and Kipling D. Williams, 103–18. New York: Psychology Press, 2011.

Galinsky, Adam D., William W. Maddux, Debra Gilin, and Judith B. White. "Why It Pays to Get Inside the Head of Your Opponent: The Differential Effects of Perspective Taking and Empathy in Negotiations." *Psychological Science* 19, no. 4 (2008): 378–84.

Galinsky, Adam D., Cynthia S. Wang, and Gillian Ku. "Perspective-Takers Behave More Stereotypically." *Journal of Personality and Social Psychology* 95, no. 2 (2008): 404–19.

Galperin, Andrew, and Martie G. Haselton. "Error Management and the Evolution of Cognitive Bias." In *Social Thinking and Interpersonal Behavior,* edited by Joseph P. Forgas, Klaus Fiedler, and Constantine Sedikides, 45–63. New York: Taylor & Francis, 2012.

Galtung, Johan. "Twenty-Five Years of Peace Research: Ten Challenges and Some Responses." *Journal of Peace Research* 22, no. 2 (1985): 141–58.

———. "Violence, Peace, and Peace Research." *Journal of Peace Research* 6, no. 3 (1969): 167–91.

Gantserski, Betsalel Shelomoh. *Darkhe Tsedek: Al ha-Mitsvah la-Dun be-Tsedek.* Tifraḥ: n.p., 2002.

Ganzfried, Solomon. *Kitsur Shulḥan Arukh ha-Shalem.* Vilna: Rozenkrants and Shriftzetser, n.d.

Garner, Bryan A., ed. *Black's Law Dictionary*. 7th ed. St. Paul, MN: West Group, 1999.

———. *A Dictionary of Modern Legal Usage*. New York: Oxford University Press, 1987.

Garrard, Wendy M., and Mark W. Lipsey. "Conflict Resolution Education and Antisocial Behavior in U.S. Schools: A Meta-Analysis." *Conflict Resolution Quarterly* 25, n. 1 (Fall 2007): 9–38.

Gehlbach, Hunter. "A New Perspective on Perspective Taking: A Multidimensional Approach to Conceptualizing an Aptitude." *Educational Psychology Review* 16, no. 3 (2004): 207–34.

[*Genesis Rabbah*] *Midrash Bereshit Rabba*. Edited by J. Theodor and Chanoch Albeck. Jerusalem: Wahrmann Books, 1965.

Gerleman, Gillis. "*Šlm*: to have enough." In *Theological Lexicon of the Old Testament*, edited by Ernst Jenni and Claus Westerman, translated by Mark E. Biddle, 1337–48. Peabody, MA: Hendrickson Publishers, 1997.

Gerondi, Jonah ben Abraham. *Perushe Rabenu Yonah mi-Gerondi al Masekhet Avot*. Jerusalem: Mekhon Torah Shelemah, 1980.

———. *Sefer ha-Yirah im Beur Mekor ha-Yirah*. Jerusalem: Ha-Teḥiyah, 1959.

———. *Sha'are Teshuvah*. Brooklyn: Zundel Berman, 1974.

Gerondi, Nissim ben Reuben. *Derashot ha-Ran*. Jerusalem: Mekhon Shalem, 1974.

———. *Ḥidushe ha-Ran: Masekhet Sanhedrin*. Jerusalem: Mossad Harav Kook, 2008.

———. *Shitah le-Ran le-Rabenu Nisim al Masekhet Ketubot*. Jerusalem: n.p., 1966.

Gershoni, Yehudah. "*Li-Dmuto shel ha-Rav Hertsog*." *Or ha-Mizraḥ* 9, nos. 3–4 (Shevat 5722 [1962]): 6–10.

Ghandi, Rajmohan. "Hinduism and Peacebuilding." In *Religion and Peacebuilding*, edited by Harold Coward and Gordon S. Smith, 45–68. Albany, NY: State University of New York Press, 2004.

Gibianski, Joseph. *Zekhut Avot*. Warsaw: Alexander Ginz, 1876.

Gifter, Mordecai. "*Ha-Halakhah be-Midrash R. Eliezer Beno shel RYH"G.*" *Talpiyot* 1, no. 2 (Tevet-Adar 5704 [1943–1944]): 314–35.

———. *Hirhure Teshuvah: He'arot, He'arot u-Ve'urim ba-Rambam Hilkhot Teshuvah*. Brooklyn, NY: Artscroll/Mesorah, 2007.

Gillan, Joey, ed. *Corporate Counsel's Guide to Alternative Dispute Resolution Techniques* 64, (2002).

Ginsberg, Harold Louis. "Peace." In *Encyclopaedia Judaica*. 1st ed., 194–96.

———. trans. *The Five Megilloth and Jonah: A New Translation*. Philadelphia: The Jewish Publication Society of America, 1969.

Ginsburg, Eliezer. *Sefer ve-Atah be-Raḥamekha ha-Rabim: Al Hilkhot Teshuvah leha-Rambam*. Brooklyn, NY: n.p., 1992.

Girard, Kathryn, and Susan J. Koch. *Conflict Resolution in the Schools: A Manual for Educators*. San Francisco: Jossey-Bass, 1996.

Gold, Avie. *Bircas Kohanim: The Priestly Blessings*. Brooklyn, NY: Mesorah Publications, 1981.

Gold, Shmuel Yehoshua. *Sefer Iyunim be-Rashi: api. 15 Kit. Y. ve-15 Defusim Rishonim*. Bnei Brak: Mekhon Mishnat Rabbi Akiva, 2009.

Goldberg, Rachel, and Brian Blancke. "God in the Process: Is There a Place for Religion in Conflict Resolution?" *Conflict Resolution Quarterly* 28, no. 4 (2011): 377–98.

Goldberg, Stephen B., Frank E. A. Sander, and Nancy H. Rogers. *Dispute Resolution: Negotiation, Mediation, and Other Processes*. 2nd ed. Boston: Little, Brown and Company, 1992.

Goldberg, Ya'akov. *Devir Kodsho: Mo'adim*. Vol. 1. Jerusalem: n.p., 2008.

Goldberg, Zalman Nehemiah. *"Ba-Inyan Ḥiyuv Piyus la-Ḥavero be-Erev YoH'K." Torat ha-Adam le-Adam: Kovets Torani ba-Mitsvot she-ben Adam la-Ḥavero* 3 (1999): 12–15.

Goldberger, Moshe. *Guard Your Anger: 32 Pathways to Protecting Your Royal Rights to Greatness*. Southfield, MI: Targum Press, 1999.

Goldberger, Yonason Binyomin. *Avne Ḥefets*. Vol. 4. Brooklyn, NY: Imre Shafer, 2005.

Goldstein, Arnold P., Barry Glick, and John C. Gibbs. *Aggression Replacement Training: A Comprehensive Intervention for Youth*. Champaign, IL: Research Press, 1998.

Goleman, Daniel. *Emotional Intelligence*. New York: Bantam Books, 1995.

Gombiner, Abraham Abele. *Magen Avraham*. In the standard printed edition of the *Shulḥan Arukh*.

———. *Zayit Ra'anan*. Commentary to *Yalkut Shemoni*. Jerusalem: Mekhon le-Hotsa'at Sefarim ve-Ḥeker Kitve Yad, 1971.

Goodpaster, Gary. *A Guide to Negotiation and Mediation*. Irvington-on-Hudson, NY: Transnational Publishers, 1997.

Gopin, Marc. *Between Eden and Armageddon: The Future of World Religions, Violence, and Peacemaking*. New York: Oxford University Press, 2000.

———. "Conflict Resolution as a Religious Experience: Contemporary Mennonite Peacemaking." In *Between Eden and Armageddon: The Future of World Religions, Violence, and Peacemaking*, 139–66. New York: Oxford University Press, 2000.

Gordon, Kristina Coop, Donald H. Baucom, and Douglas K. Snyder. "Forgiveness in Couples: Divorce, Infidelity, and Couples Therapy." In *Handbook of Forgiveness*, edited by Everett L. Worthington Jr., 407–21. New York: Routledge, 2005.

———. "The Use of Forgiveness in Marital Therapy." In *Forgiveness: Theory, Research, and Practice*, edited by Michael E. McCullough, Kenneth I. Pargament, and Carl E. Thoresen, 203–27. New York: Guilford Press, 2000.

Gordon, L. *Avodat ha-Lev*. In *Otsar ha-Tefilot*. Vol. 2. New York: Avraham Yitsḥak Friedman, n.d.

Goshen-Gottstein, Alon. *"Ha-Maḥaloket ba-Olamam shel Ḥakhamim."* Jerusalem: Hebrew University, 1980.

Gottlieb, Dov Berish. *Yad ha-Ketanah*. Jerusalem: Or ha-Sefer, 1976.

Greenbaum, Aaron. *"Gidre ha-Teshuvah al Pi ha-Gaon Rav Shemuel ben Ḥofni." Sinai* 77 (Nisan-Elul 5735 [1975]): 97–115.

Greenberg, Leslie, Serine Warwar, and Wanda Malcolm. "Emotion Focused Couples Therapy and the Facilitation of Forgiveness." *Journal of Marital and Family Therapy* 36, no. 1 (2010): 28–42.

Grinvald, Ze'ev. *Iture Halakhah: Midot Tovot*. Jerusalem: n.p., 1997.

Grodzinski, Avraham. *Torat Avraham*. Bnei Brak: Yeshivat Kolel Avrekhim Torat Avraham, 1978.

Grodzinski, Ḥayyim Ozer. *Aḥiezer*. Vol. 3. N.p., n.d.

Gross, Mosheh David. *Otsar ha-Agadah*. Jerusalem: Mossad Harav Kook, 1993.

Grozovsky, Refael Reuven. *"Ba-Din Isur Kabalat Lashon Hara."* In *Even Tsiyon: Sefer Zikaron le-Ilui Nishmat Ben Tsiyon ha-Kohen Kahana*, 542–43. Jerusalem: Yeshivat "Keneset Yisrael"—Ḥevron, 1987.

———. *Siḥot Rabi Reuven*. N.p., 2007.

Grünfeld, Simon. *Sefer She'elot u-Teshuvot Maharshag*. Jerusalem: Mordekhai Greenfeld, 1983.

Habermann, Abraham Meir. *Mi-Peri ha-Et veha-Et*. Jerusalem: R. Mas, 1981.

Ḥadash, Meir. Cited in Hillel Cooperman, *Shuvi Nafshi*, commentary to Maimonides' *Hilkhot Teshuvah* (Jerusalem: n.p., 2010), 57.

Hadayah, Ovadiah. *Eved ha-Melekh*. Jerusalem: Y. A. Itaḥ, 1941.

Ha-Entsiklopedyah shel Tanakh. Jerusalem: The Jerusalem Publishing Company, 1987.

Ḥagiz, Moses. *Eleh ha-Mitsvot*. Jerusalem: Ḥorev, 1964.

Ḥakam, Joseph Ḥayyim ben Elijah al-. *Sefer Benayahu*. Jerusalem: Yitsḥak Bakal, 1965.

———. *Sefer Ben Yehoyada*. Jerusalem: Yitsḥak Bakal, 1965.

Ḥakham Kadmon Sefaradi. In *Sifre leha-Tana ha-Elohi Rabi Shimon ben Yoḥai*. Vol. 2. Jerusalem: n.p., 1983.

Ha-Kohen, Israel Meir. *Kol Kitve Ḥafets Ḥayim ha-Shalem*. 3 vols. New York: Avraham Yitsḥak Friedman, n.d.

———. *Kuntres Ahavat Yisrael*. In vol. 1. of *Kol Kitve Ḥafets Ḥayim*.

———. *Kuntres Ma'amar Kevod Shamayim*. In vol. 1. of *Kol Kitve Ḥafets Ḥayim*.

———. *Mishnah Berurah*. 6 vols. Zikhron Ya'akov: Merkaz le-Ḥinukh Torani, 1975.

———. *Sefer Ahavat Ḥesed*. In vol. 2. of *Kol Kitve Ḥafets Ḥayim*.

———. *Sefer Ḥafets Ḥayim*. In vol. 1. of *Kol Kitve Ḥafets Ḥayim*.

———. *Sefer ha-Mitsvot ha-Katsar*. In vol. 1. of *Kol Kitve Ḥafets Ḥayim*.

———. *Shem Olam*. In vol. 2. of *Kol Kitve Ḥafets Ḥayim*.

———. *Shemirat ha-Lashon*. In vol. 1 of *Kol Kitve Ḥafets Ḥayim*.

Halberstam, Aryeh Leibish. *Aryeh Sha'ag*. Vols. 7–8. Bnei Brak: n.p., 2011.

Halberstam, Jekutiel Jehuda. *Sefer She'elot u-Teshuvot Divre Yatsiv*. Vol. 2. Netanya: Mekhon Shefa Ḥayim, 1996.

———. *Sefer Shefa Ḥayim: Mikhteve Torah*. Kiryat Sanz: Igud Ḥaside Tsanz, 1988.

Halevi, Ḥayyim David. *Aseh lekha Rav*. 9 vols. Tel Aviv: Ha-Va'adah le-Hotsa'at Kitve ha-G. R. Ḥ. D. Halevi, 1976–1989.

———. *Mayim Ḥayim*. Vol. 2. Tel Aviv: Ha-Va'adah le-Hotsa'at Kitve ha-G. R. Ḥ. D. Halevi, 1995.

Halevi Even Yuli, Asi. *Shulḥan Arukh ha-Midot*. Vol. 2. Jerusalem: n.p., 2009.

Ha-Levi of Barcelona, [Aaron?]. *Sefer haHinnuch: The Book of (Mitzvah) Education*. Translated by Charles Wengrov. Jerusalem: Feldheim, 1992.

———. *Sefer ha-Ḥinukh*. Netanya, Israel: Mifal Torat Ḥakhme Polin, 1988.

Ḥamishah Ḥumshe Torah, Ariel: Rashi ha-Shalem. Vol. 1. Jerusalem: Ariel, Mif'ale Torah, Yahadut ve-Ḥevrah be-Yisrael, 1986.

Ḥananel ben Ḥushiel. *Otsar ha-Geonim le-Masekhet Sanhedrin*. Jerusalem: Mossad Harav Kook, 1966.

———. *Perushe Rabenu Ḥananel bar Ḥushiel la-Talmud*. Jerusalem: Mekhon Lev Same'aḥ, 1993.

Hansson, Sven Ove. *Decision Theory: A Brief Introduction*. Stockholm: Royal Institute of Technology, 1994. http://home.abe.kth.se/~soh/decisiontheory.pdf.

Ha-Otsar: Otsar ha-Sefarim ha-Yehudi Torah Treasures, version 10 (Jerusalem: Digital Book Systems, 2003), CD-ROM.

Harari, Moshe. *Mikra'e Kodesh: Hilkhot Yom ha-Kipurim*. Jerusalem: Yeshivat Merkaz ha-Rav, n.d.

Harry Fischel Institute. *Halakhah Pesukah*. Vol. 2. Jerusalem: Machon Harry Fischel, 1987.

Harvard Negotiation Project. Accessed November 9, 2016. http://www.pon.harvard.edu/research_projects/harvard-negotiation-project/hnp/.

Har-Zahab, Zevi. "*Ha-Shorashim ha-Mesorasim.*" *Ḥorev* 4, no. 7–8 (Nisan 5697–Tishre 5698 [1937]): 159–70.

Ḥasman, Yehudah Leyb. *Or Yahel*. Vol. 1. Jerusalem: Yitsḥak ha-Kohen Shvadron, 2001.

Ḥatab, Yehudah. *Sefer Mevin Shemu'ah Be'urim al Masekhet Bava Kama*. Jerusalem: Y. Ḥatab, 1998.

Hawk, Gary W. "Forgiveness and Reconciliation." In William Wilmot and Joyce Hocker, *Interpersonal Conflict*. 8th ed., 296–333. New York: McGraw Hill, 2011.

Ha-Yevani, Zeraḥyah. *Sefer ha-Yashar*. Bnei Brak: Mishor, 1989.

Ha-Yitshari, Mattathias. *Perush Masekhet Avot le-Rabi Matityah ha-Yitshari*. Jerusalem: Mekhon Ben-Tsevi, 2006.

Hayner, Priscilla B. "Past Truths, Present Dangers: The Role of Official Truth Seeking in Conflict Resolution and Prevention." In *International Conflict Resolution after the Cold War*, edited by Paul C. Stern and Daniel Druckman, 338–382. Washington, DC: National Academy Press, 2000.

Ḥayyun, Joseph ben Abraham. *Mile de-Avot*. In *Perushe ha-Rishonim le-Maskehet Avot*, edited by Moshe Kasher and Ya'akov Blacherowicz. Jerusalem: Mekhon Torah Shelemah, 1973.

Ḥazan, Yosef. *Sefer She'elot u-Teshuvot Ḥikre Lev*. Vol. 6. Jerusalem: Mekhon ha-Me'or, 1998.

Ḥazan, Samuel b. Kalonymus. "*Perush Shemuel Ḥazan la-Piyut En Tsur Ḥelef*." *Yeshurun* 18 ([Kislev] 5767 [2006]): 118–30.

Heller, Yom Tov Lipman. *Tosafot Yom Tov*. In *Mishnayot Zekher Ḥanokh*. Jerusalem: Ḥ. Vagshal, 1999.

Heller-Wilensky, Sarah. "Isaac Arama on the Creation and Structure of the World." In *Essays in Medieval Jewish and Islamic Philosophy*, edited by Arthur Hyman, 259–78. New York: Ktav, 1977.

Henkin, Yehudah H. *Sefer She'elot u-Teshuvot Bene Vanim*. Vol. 1. Jerusalem: n.p., 1981.

Henkin, Yosef Eliyahu. *Kitve ha-Ga'on Rabi Yosef Eliyahu Henkin*. Vol. 1. New York: Ezras Torah, 1980.

Herford, R. Travers. *Pirke Aboth*. New York: Jewish Institute of Religion, 1945.

Hershman [Ragoler], Shelomoh Zalman. *Bet Avot*. Berlin: Tsvi Itskowitz, 1889.

Hertz, Joseph H. "Leviticus—Additional Notes: 'Thou Shalt Love Thy Neighbor as Thyself.'" In *The Pentateuch and Haftorahs*, 563–64. London: Soncino Press, 1952.

Heschel, Abraham J. "Religion and Law." In *Between God and Man: An Interpretation of Judaism*, edited by Fritz A. Rothschild, 155–61. New York: The Free Press, 1959.

Hezekiah ben Manoah. *Perush ha-Ḥazekuni al ha-Torah*. Annotated by Charles B. Chavel. Jerusalem: Mossad Harav Kook, 1989.

Hibbard, Dawn. "Conflict Resolution and Hinduism." Accessed September 11, 2016. https://www.kettering.edu/news/conflict-resolution-and-hinduism.

Higger, Michael. Introduction to *Masekhtot Kalah*, 11–119. New York: De-Be Rabanan, 1936.

Hildesheimer, Naftali Zevi, ed. "*Hakdamat Sefer Halakhot Gedolot.*" In vol. 3 of *Sefer Halakhot Gedolot,* 1–112. Jerusalem: Ḥevrat Mekitse Nirdamim, 1988.

Hillel ben Eliakim. In *Sifre leha-Tana ha-Elohi Rabi Shimon ben Yoḥai*. Vol. 2. Jerusalem: n.p., 1983.

Hirsch, Samson Raphael. *The Hirsch Chumash*. 6 vols. Translated by Daniel Haberman. Jerusalem: Feldheim, 2000–2009.

———. *The Pentateuch: Translated and Explained by Samson Raphael Hirsch*. Translated by Isaac Levy. Gateshead, England: Judaica Press, 1989.

———. *Pirkei Avot: Chapters of the Fathers*. Jerusalem: Feldheim, 1972.

Hoberman, Ze'ev. *Ze'ev Yitrof: Be-Inyana di-Teshuvah ve-Yom ha-Kipurim*. Lakewood, NJ: Z. Hoberman, 1996.

Hochgelehrter, Yosef ben Ya'akov Yitsḥak. *Mishnat Ḥakhamim*. Jerusalem: Hotsa'at Rashbats, 1996.

Hodges, Sara D., Brian A. M. Clark, and Michael W. Myers. "Better Living through Perspective Taking." In *Positive Psychology as Social Change,* edited by Robert Biswas-Diener, 193–218. Dordrecht: Springer, 2011.

Hodgins, Holley S., and Elizabeth Liebeskind. "Apology versus Defense: Antecedents and Consequences." *Journal of Experimental Social Psychology* 39, no. 4 (2003): 297–316.

Hoffmann, David Zevi. *Ha-Mishnah ha-Rishonah*. Jerusalem: n.p., 1968.

———. *Sefer Va-Yikra Meforash* [*Das Buch Leviticus*]. Translated by Tsevi Har Shefer. Vol. 2. Jerusalem: Mossad Harav Kook, 1954.

The Holy Scriptures: According to the Masoretic Text. Philadelphia: Jewish Publication Society, 1964.

Homolka, Walter, and Albert H. Friedlander. *The Gate to Perfection: The Idea of Peace in Jewish Thought*. Providence, RI: Berghohn Books Inc., 1994.

Horowitz, Avraham. *Orḥot Rabenu: Kan Miktsat me-Orḥot Ḥayav shel Rabenu ha-G. R.Y.Y. Kanevski*. Bnei Brak: Yeshay' ben A. ha-Levi Horvits, 1991.

Horowitz, Isaiah. *Shene Luḥot ha-Berit*. 5 vols. Jerusalem: Oz ve-Hadar, 1993.

Horowitz, Menaḥem Mendel. *Shoshanat Ya'akov*. Zolkiew: Shmuel Pinḥas Shtiller, 1863.

Horowitz, Samuel Shmelke. Quoted in Shalom Mordecai Schwadron, *Tekhelet Mordekhai*, vol. 1 (Brzezany: M. I. Feldmann, 1913), 5b.

Huang, Shih-Tseng Tina, and Robert D. Enright. "Forgiveness and Anger-Related Emotions in Taiwan: Implications for Therapy." *Psychotherapy: Theory, Research, Practice, Training* 37, no. 1 (2000): 71–79.

Huminer, Samuel. *Mitsvat ha-Bitaḥon*. Jerusalem: n.p., 1999.

———. *Sefer Ikre Dinim*. Jerusalem: n.p., 1975.

Hurwitz, Isaac Simḥah. *Yad ha-Levi*. Commentary to Maimonides' *Sefer ha-Mitsvot*. Jerusalem: S. Zuckerman, 1926.

Hurwitz, Phinehas Elijah. *Sefer ha-Berit ha-Shalem*. Jerusalem: Yerid ha-Sefarim, 1990.

Hutner, Isaac. *Paḥad Yitsḥak: Sha'ar Yeraḥ ha-Etanim*. Brooklyn, NY: Ha-Mosad Gur Aryeh, 1974.

———. Letter to Joseph D. Epstein. In Joseph D. Epstein, *Mitzvot ha-Shalom: The Commandments on Peace*, 270–72. Brooklyn, NY: Torath HaAdam Institute Inc., 1987.

Ibn Aknin, Joseph. *Sefer Musar: Perush Mishnat Avot le-Rabi Yosef ben Yehudah*. Berlin: Tsvi Hersh Itskovski, 1910.

Ibn Ezra, Abraham. *Perush Rabenu Avraham ibn Ezra*. In the standard *Mikra'ot Gedolot*.

Ibn Gabirol, Solomon. *Azharot le-Rabenu Shelomoh ben Gavirol*. Jerusalem: n.p., 1987.

[Ibn Gabirol, Solomon?]. *Sefer Mivḥar ha-Peninim*. Tel Aviv: Sifriyat Po'alim, 1976.

Ibn Gaon, Shem Tov ben Abraham. *Migdal Oz*. In the standard printed edition of Maimonides' *Mishneh Torah*.

Ibn Ghiyyat, Isaac. *Hilkhot Ha-Rits Gi'at: Sefer Sha'are Simḥah*. Vol. 1. Brooklyn, NY: Mekhon le-Hotsa'at Sefarim ve-Ḥeker Kitve Yad, 1998.

Ibn Ḥabib, Jacob. *En Ya'akov*. New York: Sifre Kodesh, 1971.

Ibn Ḥabib, Levi. *She'elot u-Teshuvot Maharalbaḥ*. Brooklyn, NY: M. J. Finkelstein, 1962.

Ibn Ḥabib, Moses. *Sifre ha-Maharam Ḥabib*. Jerusalem: Mekhon Me'or Harim, 2000.

Ibn Ḥayyim, Aaron. *Sefer Korban Aharon: Ve-Hu Perush le-Sefer Sifra*. Vol. 2. Jerusalem: n.p., 1969.

Ibn Janaḥ, Jonah. *Sefer ha-Shorashim*. Jerusalem: n.p., 1966.

Ibn Makhir, Moshe. *Seder ha-Yom*. Warsaw: Levenzohn, 1873.

Ibn Pakuda, Baḥya. *Ḥovot ha-Levavot*. Translated by Judah ibn Tibbon. Brooklyn, NY: n.p., 1984.

———. *Sefer Torat Ḥovot ha-Levavot*. Translated by Joseph Kafih. Jerusalem: Ha-Va'ad ha-Kelali li-Yehude Teman, n.d.

———. *Sefer Torat Ḥovot ha-Levavot*. Translated by Shmuel Yerushalmi. Jerusalem: Me'ore Yisrael, 1972.

Ibn Shoshan, Joseph. *Perushe Rabenu Yosef ben Shoshan*. Jerusalem: Mekhon Torah Shelemah, 1968.

Ibn Shu'aib, Judah. *Derashot R. Y. Ibn Shu'aib*. Jerusalem: Mekhon Lev Same'aḥ, 1992.

Isaac ben Abba Mari. *Sefer Ha-Itur*. Vol. 1. Jerusalem: n.p., 1970.

Isaac ben Ḥayyim Volozhiner. *Peh Kadosh ha-Shalem*. Jerusalem: Mekhon Moreshet ha-Yeshivot, 1995.

Isaac ben Joseph of Corbeil. *Sefer Amude Golah-Sefer Mitsvot Katan* (*Semak*). Israel: Mefitse Or, 1959.

Isaac ben Moses of Vienna. *Or Zaru'a*. Vol. 3. Jerusalem: Mekhon Yerushalayim, 2010.

Isaac ben Solomon ben Isaac. *Perushe Yitsḥak b. R. Shelomoh mi-Toledo al Masekhet Avot*. Jerusalem: Mekhon Torah Shelemah, 1965.

Ishbili, Yom-Tob ben Abraham. *Ḥidushe ha-Ritba al ha-Shas*. 21 vols. Jerusalem: Mossad Harav Kook, 2008.

Isserlein, Israel. *Sefer Terumat ha-Deshen*. Jerusalem: Shmuel Abitan, 1991.

Isserles, Moses. *Darkhe Mosheh ha-Shalem al Tur Ḥoshen ha-Mishpat*. Vol. 2. Jerusalem: Mekhon Yerushalayim, 1983.

———. *Shulḥan Arukh, Even ha-Ezer, Hagahot ha-Rama*. 3 vols. Jerusalem: Morashah le-Hanḥil, 2008–.

———. *Shulḥan Arukh ha-Shalem, Oraḥ Ḥayim, Yoreh De'ah, Hagahot ha-Rama*. 17 vols. Jerusalem: Mekhon Yerushalayim, 1994–2006.

———. *Shulḥan Arukh, Ḥoshen Mishpat, Hagahot ha-Rama*. 10 vols. Jerusalem: Morashah le-Hanḥil, 1992–2005.

Jabbour, Elias. *Sulha: Palestinian Traditional Peacemaking Process*. Montreat, NC: House of Hope Publications, 1996.

Jabez, Joseph ben Ḥayyim. *Masekhet Avot im Perush … Yosef Yabe'ts.* Jerusalem: Mekhon Ma'oz ha-Torah, 1990.

Jacob ben Asher. *Arba'ah Turim ha-Shalem.* 21 vols. Israel: Mekhon Yerushalayim, 1993–1994.

———. *Kitsur Piske ha-Rosh mi-Masekhet Yoma.* In the standard Vilna edition of the Babylonian Talmud.

———. *Perush ha-Tur ha-Arokh al ha-Torah.* Jerusalem: Hotsa'at Be-Ferush uve-Remez, 1964.

Jacob ben Jacob Moses of Lissa. *Netivot ha-Mishpat: Ve-Hu Ḥidushim u-Ve'urim al Ḥoshen Mishpat.* Jerusalem: Me'ore Or, 2004.

———. *Sidur Derekh ha-Ḥayim.* Tel Aviv: Sinai, 1954.

Jacob ben Judah Ḥazzan of London. *Ets Ḥayim.* Jerusalem: Mossad Harav Kook, 1962.

Jacob ben Meir (*Rabenu Tam*). Cited in Meir ben Baruch of Rothenburg, *Sifre She'elot u-Teshuvot Piske Dinim u-Minhagim Maharam mi-Rotenburg,* vol. 4, Prague edition (Bnei Brak: Ha-Sifriyah ha-Ḥaredit ha-Olomit, 1999), 159b.

Jacob ben Samson. Commentary to *Avot.* In *Mishnat Re'uven: Masekhet Avot im Perushe ha-Rishonim.* Jerusalem: Mossad Harav Kook, 2005.

[Jacob ben Samson?]. *Maḥzor Vitry.* In *Mishnayot Zekher Ḥanokh.* Jerusalem: Ḥ. Vagshal, 1999.

Jacob Joseph of Polonoye. *Toldot Ya'akov Yosef.* Jerusalem: n.p., 1966.

———. *Toldot Ya'akov Yosef.* Jerusalem: Ha-Mesorah, 2010.

Jacob of Orleans. Quoted in Ḥayyim Paltiel ben Jacob, *Perush ha-Torah le-R' Ḥayim Paltiel* (Jerusalem: Y. S. Langeh, 1981), Leviticus 19:18.

Jacobs, Louis. "Peace." In *Encyclopaedia Judaica.* 1st ed., 196–198.

Jacobson, Edmund. *Progressive Relaxation: A Physiological and Clinical Investigation of Muscular States and Their Significance in Psychology and Medical Practice.* Chicago: University of Chicago Press, 1929.

Jaffe, Mordecai. *Sefer Levush ha-Ḥur.* N.p., 2000.

James, William. "What is an Emotion?" *Mind* 9, no. 34 (1884): 188–205.

Jelen, Abram. *Ezor ha-Tsevi.* Warsaw: Y. Edelshtein, 1905.

———. *Orekh Apayim.* Brooklyn, NY: Yofi, n.d.

Jenni, Ernst, and Claus Westerman, eds. *Theological Lexicon of the Old Testament.* Translated by Mark E. Biddle. 3 vols. Peabody, MA: Hendrickson Publishers, 1997.

Jeong, Ho-Won. *Peace and Conflict Studies: An Introduction*. Burlington, VT: Ashgate Publishing, 2000.

Johnson, B. "*ṣāḏaq*." In *The Theological Dictionary of the Old Testament*. Vol. 12, 239–64. Grand Rapids, MI: William B. Eerdsmans, 2003.

Johnson, David W. "Cooperativeness and Social Perspective Taking." *Journal of Personality and Social Psychology* 31, no. 2 (1975): 241–44.

Johnson, David W., and Roger T. Johnson. *Cooperation and Competition: Theory and Research*. Edina, MN: Interaction Book Co., 1989.

———. "New Developments in Social Interdependence Theory." *Genetic, Social, and General Psychology Monographs* 131, no. 4 (2005): 285–358.

———. *Reducing School Violence through Conflict Resolution*. Alexandria, VA: Association for Supervision and Curriculum Development, 1995.

———. *Teaching Students to Be Peacemakers*. 4th ed. Edina, MN: Interaction Book Co., 2005.

Johnson, David W., Roger T. Johnson, and Dean Tjosvold. "Constructive Controversy: The Value of Intellectual Opposition." In *The Handbook of Conflict Resolution*. 2nd ed., edited by Morton Deutsch, Peter T. Coleman, and Eric C. Marcus, 69–91. San Francisco: Jossey Bass, 2006.

Jonathan ben David ha-Kohen of Lunel. *Perushe Rabenu Yehonatan mi-Lunil al 21 Masekhtot ha-Shas*. Jerusalem: n.p., 1975.

Jones, Tricia S. "Conflict Resolution Education: The Field, the Findings, and the Future." *Conflict Resolution Quarterly* 22, no. 1/2 (Fall/Winter 2004): 233–67.

Judah ben Samuel. *Sefer Ḥasidim*. *Mekitse Nirdamim* ed. Frankfurt am Main: M. A. Wahrmann, 1924.

———. *Sefer Ḥasidim*. Jerusalem: Mossad Harav Kook, 2002.

Judah Loew ben Bezalel. *Derekh Ḥayim: Ve-Hu Perush le-Masekhet Avot*. Vol. 1. Jerusalem: Mekhon Yerushalayim, 2007.

———. *Ḥidushe Agadot Maharal mi-Prag*. Vol. 3. Jerusalem: n.p., 1972.

———. *Netivot Olam*. Vol. 2. Tel Aviv: Mekhon Yad Mordekhai, 1988.

———. *Sefer Gur Aryeh: Be'ur al Pe. Rashi*. Vol. 4. Bnei Brak: n.p., 1972.

———. *Sifre Maharal mi-Prag*. Bnei Brak: Yahadut, 1999.

Kadayifci-Orellana, S. Ayse. "Ethno-Religious Conflicts: Exploring the Role of Religion in Conflict Resolution." In *The SAGE Handbook of*

Conflict Resolution, edited by Jacob Bercovitch, Victor Kremenyuk, and I. William Zartman, 264–84. Los Angeles: Sage Publications, 2009.

Kadushin, Max. *A Conceptual Commentary on Midrash Leviticus Rabbah: Value Concepts in Jewish Thought*. Atlanta, GA: Scholars Press, 1987.

Kafih, Yosef, trans. and annot. *Mishnah im Perush Rabenu Mosheh ben Maimon: Makor ve-Targum, Seder Nezikin*. Jerusalem: Mossad Harav Kook, 1965.

———. trans. and annot. *Ha-Nivḥar ba-Emunot uva-De'ot*, by Sa'adia ben Joseph. New York: Sura, 1970.

Kahane, Kalman. "*Arba'im Ḥaser Aḥat.*" *Ha-Mayan* 10, no. 1 (1970): 18–25.

Kaidanover, Zevi Hirsch. *Sefer Kav ha-Yashar*. 2 vols. Jerusalem: n.p., 1993.

Kalischer, Zevi Hirsch. *Ḥamishah Ḥumshe Torah im ... u-Shene Perushim ... Sefer ha-Berit*. Warsaw: N. Shriftgisser, 1875.

Kamenetsky, Jacob. *Emet le-Ya'akov*. Baltimore: Kisvei Reb Yaakov Publications, 1986.

———. *Emet le-Ya'akov: Sefer Iyunim ba-Mikra al ha-Torah*. 3rd ed. New York: Makhon Emet le-Ya'akov, 2007.

Kamenetsky, Shmuel. *Kovets Halakhot: Yamim Nora'im*. Edited by Daniel Kleinman. Lakewood, NJ: n.p., 2011.

Kaminsky, Howard G. "Traditional Jewish Perspectives on Peace and Interpersonal Conflict Resolution." EdD diss., Teachers College, Columbia University, 2005. ProQuest (document ID 305013218).

Kanevski, Shemaryahu Yosef Ḥayim. *Kiryat Melekh*. 3rd ed. Bnei Brak: n.p., 1983.

———. *Sefer Sha'are Emunah ... al Mas. Pe'ah*. Bnei Brak: Ḥ. Kanevski, 2000.

———. Quoted in Betsalel Shelomoh Gantserski, *Darkhe Tsedek: Al ha-Mitsvah la-Dun be-Tsedek* (Tifraḥ: n.p., 2002), 60.

———. Quoted in David Ari'av, *Le-Re'akha kamokha*, vol. 1 (Jerusalem: Mekhon Le-Re'akha kamokha, 2000–), 348.

———. Quoted in David Ari'av, *Le-Re'akha kamokha*, vol. 8, *Halakhot u-Ve'urim ba-Mitsvah la-Dun le-Khaf Zekhut ve-Isur Sheker* (Jerusalem: Mekhon Le-Re'akha Kamokha, 2012), 486, 490.

Kanevski, Shemaryahu Yosef Ḥayim, Eliyahu Man, and Tsevi Yavrov. *Derekh Siḥah*. Bnei Brak: Sifre Or ha-Ḥayim, 2004.

Kanevski, Ya'akov Yisrael. *Kehilot Ya'akov al Masekhtot Shevuot, Makot*. Bnei Brak: n.p., 1967.

Kanouse, David E. "Explaining Negativity Biases in Evaluation and Choice Behavior: Theory and Research." In *Advances in Consumer Research*, vol. 11, edited by Thomas C. Kinnear, 703–8. Provo, UT: Association for Consumer Research, 1984.

Kanouse, David, and L. Reid Hanson Jr. "Negativity in Evaluations." In *Attribution: Perceiving the Causes of Behavior*, edited by Edward E. Jones, David E. Kanouse, Harold H. Kelley, Richard E. Nisbett, Stuart Valins, and Bernard Weiner, 47–62. Morristown, NJ: General Learning Press, 1972.

Kaplan, Abraham Elijah. *Divre Talmud*. Vol. 1. Jerusalem: Mossad Harav Kook, 1958.

Kaplan, Meir ha-Kohen. *Mitsvat ha-Tokhaḥah*. Jerusalem: Mossad Harav Kook, 1951.

Karelitz, Abraham Isaiah. *Ḥazon Ish: Ḥoshen Mishpat*. Bnei Brak: n.p., 1991.

———. *Kovets Igrot me-et Maran Ba'al Ḥazon Ish*. Vol. 1. Bnei Brak: S. Grainiman, 1990.

———. *Sefer Ḥazon Ish: Emunah u-Vitaḥon*. Tel Aviv: Sifriyati, 1984.

———. Quoted in Tsevi Yavrov, *Ma'aseh Ish*, vol. 2 (Bnei Brak: n.p., 1999), 166.

———. Quoted in Yisrael Shpigel, *She'al Avikha ve-Yagedkha*, vol. 1 (Jerusalem: Mekhon Da'at, 1990), 172.

Karelitz, Shemaryahu Yosef Nissim. *Sefer Ḥut Shani: Be'urim u-Verure Inyanim ve-Ḥidushe Dinim be-Hilkhot Mezuzah, Inyanim be-Hilkhot Berakhot*. Jerusalem: Ḥ. A. Hokhman, 2012.

———. *Sefer Ḥut Shani: Be'urim u-Verure Inyanim ve-Ḥidushe Dinim be-Hilkhot Rosh ha-Shanah, Yom ha-Kipurim, Sukot va-Ḥanukah*. Bnei Brak: n.p., 2010.

Karmi, Mordekhai. *Ma'amar Mordekhai al Shulḥan Arukh Oraḥ Ḥayim*. Vol. 4. Jerusalem: Oz ve-Hadar, 1995.

Karo, Joseph. *Bet Yosef*. In the standard printed edition of Jacob ben Asher's *Arba'ah Turim*.

———. *Kesef Mishneh*. In the standard printed edition of Maimonides' *Mishneh Torah*.

———. *She'elot u-Teshuvot Bet Yosef*. Jerusalem: Tiferet ha-Torah, 1960.

———. *Shulḥan Arukh, Even ha-Ezer*. 3 vols. Jerusalem: Morashah le-Hanḥil, 2008–.

———. *Shulḥan Arukh ha-Shalem, Oraḥ Ḥayim, Yoreh De'ah*. 17 vols. Jerusalem: Mekhon Yerushalayim, 1994–2006.

———. *Shulḥan Arukh, Ḥoshen Mishpat*. 10 vols. Jerusalem: Morashah le-Hanḥil, 1992–2005.

Karremans, Johan C., and Paul A. M. Van Lange. "Back to Caring after Being Hurt: The Role of Forgiveness." *European Journal of Social Psychology* 34, no. 2 (2004): 207–27.

Kasher, Hannah. "*Yisurin le-Lo Avon: Le-Mashma'ut shel ha-Nisayon ba-Moreh Nevukhim*." *Da'at* 26 (*Ḥoref* 5751 [1990–1991]): 35–41.

Kasher, Menaḥem. *Torah Shelemah*. 45 vols. Jerusalem: Hotsa'at Bet Torah Shelemah, 1992.

Kasher, Shimon. *Peshuto shel Mikra*. Jerusalem: Mekhon Torah Shelemah, 1963.

Kasovsky, Chayim Yehoshua. *Otsar Leshon ha-Mishnah*. Vol. 2. Jerusalem: Massadah, 1957.

———. *Otsar Leshon ha-Talmud*. Vol. 14. Jerusalem: Misrad ha-Ḥinukh veha-Tarbut shel Memshelet Yisrael, 1965.

———. *Otsar Leshon ha-Tosefta*. Vol. 3. Jerusalem: n.p., 1942.

Kassinove, Howard, and Denis G. Sukhodolsky. "Anger Disorders: Basic Science and Practice Issues." In *Anger Disorders: Definition, Diagnosis, and Treatment*, edited by Howard Kassinove, 1–26. Washington, DC: Taylor & Francis, 1995.

Kassinove, Howard, and Raymond Chip Tafrate. *Anger Management: The Complete Treatment Guidebook for Practitioners*. Atascadero, CA: Impact Publishers, 2002.

Katz, Dov. *Tenu'at ha-Musar*. Vol. 1. Jerusalem: Feldheim, 1996.

Katz, Tsevi ben Joseph. *Naḥalat Tsevi, Ateret Tsevi*. Vol. 2. Jerusalem: Zikhron Aharon, 2003.

Kaufman, Moshe. *Sefer Ḥafets Ḥayim ... ve-Nilvah alav Ḥibur Netivot Ḥayim*. Bnei Brak: n.p., 2011.

Kayara, Shimon [alternatively, Yehudai ben Naḥman]. *Sefer Halakhot Gedolot*. 3 vols. Jerusalem: Ḥevrat Mekitse Nirdamim, 1988.

Kegley, Charles W., Jr., and Geoffrey G. Kegley. "Global Environment and Peace." In *World Encyclopedia of Peace*, edited by Javier Perez de Cuellar and Young Seek Choue. 2nd ed. Vol. 2, 319–24. Dobbs Ferry, NY: Oceana Publications, 1999.

Kehati, Pinḥas. *Mishnayot Mevoarot*. Vol. 8. Jerusalem: Hekhal Shelomoh, 1966.

Kelman, Herbert C. "Reflections on the History and Status of Peace Research." *Conflict Management and Peace Science* 5, no. 2 (1981): 95–110.

Kemp, Simon, and K. T. Strongman. "Anger Theory and Management: A Historical Analysis." *The American Journal of Psychology* 108, no. 3 (1995): 397–417.

Kenigsberg, David. "*Rekhishat Samkhuyot le-lo Hafalat Koaḥ be-Ḥinukh.*" In *Ha-Madrikh ha-Ishi shelkha*, 240–51. Jerusalem: Darkhe Noam ve-Tiferet Baḥurim-Hatsalat ha-Noar, 2009.

Ketterman, Grace H. *Verbal Abuse: Healing the Hidden Wound*. Ann Arbor, MI: Servant Publications, 1992.

Kharif, Moshe, ed. *Sefer Yalkut Ahavat Yisrael*. Jerusalem: Gamaḥ Ḥamishai, 1999.

Kil, Yehudah. *Sefer Mishle* [*Da'at Mikra*]. Jerusalem: Mossad Harav Kook, 1983.

Kim, Sung, and Richard H. Smith. "Revenge and Conflict Escalation." *Negotiation Journal* 9, no. 1 (1993): 37–43.

Kimḥi, David. *Sefer ha-Shorashim*. Jerusalem: n.p., 1967.

———. *Sefer Mikhlol*. Jerusalem: n.p., 1967.

Kimḥi, Joseph. *Sefer ha-Galui*. Berlin: T. H. Itskovski, 1887.

Kirchhoff, Johanna. "On the Content of Apologies." PhD diss., Philipps-Universität Marburg, 2013. http://archiv.ub.uni-marburg.de/diss/z2013/0232/pdf/djk.pdf.

Kirchhoff, Johanna, Micha Strack, and Uli Jäger. "Apologies: Depending on Offence Severity the Composition of Elements Does Matter." Presentation at the International Network of Psychologists for Social Responsibility (INPsySR)—Symposium "Preventing Violent Conflict: Psychological Dimensions," at the 11th European Congress of Psychology, Oslo, Norway, July 9, 2009.

Kirchhoff, Johanna, Ulrich Wagner, and Micha Strack. "Apologies: Words of Magic? The Role of Verbal Components, Anger Reduction, and Offence Severity." *Peace and Conflict: Journal of Peace Psychology* 18, no. 2 (2012): 109–30.

Klein, Ernest. *A Comprehensive Etymological Dictionary of the Hebrew Language for Readers of English*. New York: Collier Macmillan, 1987.

Klein, Yisrael Yisakhar Dov. *Sefer Ve-Ezer mi-Tsarav: Al Hilkhot Teshuvah leha-Rambam*. Brooklyn, NY: n.p., 2004.

Kluger, Solomon. *Sefer ha-Ḥayim*. New York: Avraham Yitsḥak Friedman, 1968.

Koehler, Ludwig, and Walter Baumgartner. *The Hebrew and Aramaic Lexicon of the Old Testament*. Translated and edited by M. E. J. Richardson. Study ed. Leiden, The Netherlands: Brill, 2001.

Kohen, Jacob ben Eliezer, annot. *Sefer ha-Mada*. Jerusalem: Mossad Harav Kook, 1964.

Kohen, She'ar Yashuv. *Ḥikre Halakhah*. Jerusalem: Va'ad Talmidim, Yedidim ve-Shome Likḥo, 1992.

———. "*Mitsvat Ahavat Yisrael: Be-Halakhah uve-Hagadah*." *Torah shebe-al Peh* 36 (1995): 45–57.

———. *Shai Kohen*. Vol. 1. Jerusalem: Ariel, 1997.

Kohen, Yosef. *Sefer ha-Teshuvah*. Vol. 1. Jerusalem: Machon Harry Fischel, 1989.

Kohut, Alexander. *Arukh ha-Shalem*. Vol. 7. Vienna: Menorah, 1926.

Kolin, Samuel. *Maḥasit ha-Shekel*. In the standard printed edition of the *Shulḥan Arukh, Oraḥ Ḥayim*.

Konstom, Varda, Fern Marx, Jennifer Schurer, Nancy B. Emerson Lambardo, and Anne K. Harrington. "Forgiveness in Practice: What Mental Health Counselors are Telling Us." In *Before Forgiving: Cautionary Views of Forgiveness in Psychotherapy*, edited by Sharon Lamb and Jeffrie G. Murphy, 54–71. New York: Oxford University Press, 2002.

Kook, Abraham Isaac. *Mitsvot Re'iyah*. Jerusalem: Mossad Harav Kook, 1970.

———. *Oraḥ Mishpat*. Jerusalem: Mossad Harav Kook, 1985.

———. *Orot*. Jerusalem: Mossad Harav Kook, 2005.

———. *Orot ha-Kodesh*. 4 vols. Jerusalem: Mossad Harav Kook, 2006

———. *Orot ha-Rambam*. In Ya'akov Filber, *Le-Oro*, 159–234. Jerusalem: Mekhon le-Ḥeker Mishnat ha-Re'iyah, 1995.

Kook, Tzvi Yehuda ha-Kohen. *Siḥot ha-Rav Tsevi Yehudah*. Edited by Shlomo Ḥayim Aviner. Jerusalem: n.p., 1993–2005.

Koraḥ, Shlomo. *Sefat Melekh*. Commentary to *Mishneh Torah, Sefer Mada*. Vol. 2. Bnei Brak: n.p., 1998.

Kosovsky, Biniamin. *Otsar Leshon ha-Tanaim: Mekhilta debe-Rabi Yishmael*. Vol. 2. Jerusalem: The Jewish Theological Seminary, 1965.

———. *Otsar Leshon ha-Tanaim: Sifra*. Vol. 2. Jerusalem: The Jewish Theological Seminary, 1967.

———. *Otsar Leshon ha-Tanaim: Sifre*. Vol. 2. Jerusalem: The Jewish Theological Seminary, 1972.

Kosowsky, Abraham Abba. Letter to Aryeh Leib Poupko, 21 Kislev 5698 (1937). In *Siḥot he-Ḥafets Ḥayim*. In vol. 3 of *Kol Kitve Ḥafets Ḥayim*, 8–10.

Kotler, Aaron. *Mishnat Rabi Aharon al ha-Torah*. Lakewood, NJ: Machon Mishnas Rabbi Aaron, 2001.

Krakovski, Menaḥem. *Avodat ha-Melekh*. Jerusalem: Mossad Harav Kook, 1971.

Kranz, Jacob. *Ohel Ya'akov*. Vienna: Josef Schlesinger, 1863.

———. *Sefer ha-Midot*. Jerusalem: Mekhon Sha'are Yosher, 1993.

Krauss, Robert M., William Apple, Nancy Morency, Charlotte Wenzel, and Ward Winton. "Verbal, Vocal, and Visible Factors in Judgments of Another's Affect." *Journal of Personality and Social Psychology* 40, no. 2 (1981): 312–20.

Krauss, Robert M., and Ezequiel Morsella. "Communication and Conflict." In *The Handbook of Conflict Resolution: Theory and Practice*, edited by Morton Deutsch and Peter T. Coleman, 131–43. San Francisco: Jossey-Bass, 2000.

Kreidler, William J. *Conflict Resolution in the Middle School*. Cambridge, MA: Educators for Social Responsibility, 1997.

———. *Creative Conflict Resolution: More Than 200 Activities for Keeping Peace in the Classroom*. Glenview, IL: Good Year Books, 1984.

Kriesberg, Louis, and Bruce W. Dayton. *Constructive Conflicts: From Escalation to Resolution*. 4th ed. Lanham, MD: Rowman and Littlefield, 2012.

Krizer, Tsevi. *Be'er Tsevi*. Bnei Brak: Ts. Krizer, 2011.

Kronglas, David. *Siḥot Ḥokhmah u-Musar*. Vol. 1. Jerusalem: n.p., 1998.

———. *Siḥot Ḥokhmah u-Musar: Ḥoveret* 3. Jerusalem: Yotse le-Or be-Siyu'a Kevutsat Talmidav, 1982.

Krumbein, Elyakim. "*Nekimah u-Netirah bi-M'kom Tsa'ar ha-Guf*." *Teḥumin* 6 (1985): 292–304.

Kubany, Edward S., David C. Richard, Gordon B. Bauer, and Miles Y. Muraoka. "Verbalized Anger and Accusatory 'You' Messages as Cues for Anger and Antagonism among Adolescents." *Adolescence* 27, no. 107 (1992): 505–16.

Kubin, Barukh Moshe. "*Be-Inyan Ona'at Devarim*." *Torat ha-Adam le-Adam: Kovets Torani ba-Mitsvot she-ben Adam la-Ḥavero* 4 (2002): 206–14.

Kugel, James L. *The Bible as It Was*. Cambridge, MA: The Belknap Press, 1997.

———. "On Hidden Hatred and Open Reproach: Early Exegesis of Leviticus 19:17." *Harvard Theological Review* 80, no. 1 (1987): 43–61.

Landau, Eleazar. *Yad ha-Melekh*. Jerusalem: Mekhon Yerushalayim, 2000.

Landau, Ezekiel. *Derashot ha-Tselaḥ ha-Shalem*. Jerusalem: Mekhon ha-Tselaḥ, 2003.

———. *Noda bi-Yehudah ha-Shalem*. Jerusalem: Mekhon Yerushalayim, 2004.

Langsner, Ya'akov Meir. *Ruaḥ Nakhon*. Lakewood, NJ: Mekhon Be'er ha-Torah, 2007.

Lantieri, Linda, and Janet Patti. *Waging Peace in Our Schools*. New York: Beacon Press, 1996.

Lanzetta, John T., Jeffrey Cartwright-Smith, and Robert E. Kleck. "Effects of Nonverbal Dissimulation on Emotional Experience and Autonomic Arousal." *Journal of Personality and Social Psychology* 33, no. 3 (1976): 354–70.

Larrick, Richard P. "Debiasing." In *Blackwell Handbook of Judgment and Decision Making*, edited by Derek J. Koehler and Nigel Harvey, 316–37. Oxford, UK: Blackwell Publishing, 2004.

The Layman's Parallel Bible. Grand Rapids, MI: Zondervan Bible Publishers, 1973.

Lazare, Aaron. "The Apology Dynamic." *AAOS Now*, May 2010. http://www.aaos.org/news/aaosnow/may10/managing5.asp.

———. *On Apology*. Oxford: Oxford University Press, 2004.

———. "Understanding Apology: Mechanisms for Repairing Relationships." Presentation at the Annual Meeting of the National Association of College and University Attorneys, June 27–30, 2010. http://www-local.legal.uillinois.edu/nacua10/presentations/1E_handout.pdf.

Lebovitch, Jeroham. *Da'at Ḥokhmah u-Musar*. 3 vols. New York: Daas Chochmo U'Mussar Publications, 1966–1972.

———. *Da'at Torah*. Vol. 2. Exodus. Jerusalem: Daas Torah Publications, 2001.

Lederach, John Paul. *Building Peace: Sustainable Reconciliation in Divided Societies*. Washington, DC: United States Institute of Peace Press, 1999.

———. *The Little Book of Conflict Transformation*. Intercourse, PA: Good Books, 2003.

Leibowitz, A. Henach. *Ḥidushe ha-Lev*. Vol. 1. New York: Rabbinical Seminary of America, 2009.

Leibowitz, Nehama. *Studies in Vayikra (Leviticus)*. Translated by Aryeh Newman. Jerusalem: The World Zionist Organization, 1980.

Leizerowski, Baruch. *Sefer She'elot u-Teshuvot Ta'am Barukh*. Philadelphia: n.p., n.d.

Lerma, Judah. *Leḥem Yehudah*. 2nd ed. Brooklyn, NY: Aḥim Goldenberg, 1994.

Leschz, Yosef. "*Reshitah shel ha-Pe'ulah ha-Tsiyonit ha-Datit.*" In *Kehilat Vengrov: Sefer Zikaron*, 105–6. Tel Aviv: Hotsa'at Yotse Vengrov, 1961.

Lesin, Jacob Moses. *Ha-Ma'or sheba-Torah*. Vol. 2. Jerusalem: n.p., 1960.

Levi, Deborah L. "The Role of Apology in Mediation." *New York University Law Review* 72, no. 5 (1997): 1165–210.

Levi, Ḥanan. *Shevile ha-Midot veha-Arakhim*. Vol. 6. Rekhasim: n.p., 2009.

Levi, Moshe. *Mi-shel ha-Avot*. Vol. 3. Bnei Brak: M. Levi, 1992.

Levi, Yehudah. "*Am Yisrael ve-Umot ha-Olam.*" *Ha-Mayan* 24, no. 4 (1984): 10–24.

———. *Mul Etgere ha-Tekufah: Siḥot al ha-Yahadut*. Jerusalem: Olam ha-Sefer ha-Torani, 1993.

Levi ben Gershom. *Perushe ha-Torah le-Rabenu Levi ben Gershom*. 5 vols. Edited by Ya'akov Levi. Jerusalem: Mossad Harav Kook, 1996–2000.

Levin, Avraham Dov, ed. *Piske Din mi-Bet ha-Din le-Dine Mamonot ule-Virur Yahadut shel ha-Rabanut ha-Rashit le-Yerushalayim*. Vol. 5. Jerusalem: Ha-Mo'atsah ha-Datit Yerushalayim, 1998.

Levin (Lefin), Menaḥem Mendel. *Ḥeshbon ha-Nefesh*. Translated by Shraga Silverstein. Jerusalem: Feldheim, 1995.

Levinshtain, Yeḥezkel. *Or Yeḥezkel*. Vol. 4 (*Midot*). Bnei Brak: n.p., 1988.

[Levinson, alternatively, Levinzon or Araner], Mosheh ben Shelomoh El'azar. *Ma'aneh Rakh*. Bnei Brak: Sifre Or ha-Ḥayim, 2000.

———. *Sefer Ohev Musar*. Bnei Brak: Sifre Or ha-Ḥayim, 2000.

———. *Sefer Yede Mosheh ve-Torah Or*. Bnei Brak: Sifre Or ha-Ḥayim, 2000.

Levita, Elijah. *Sefer ha-Tishbi*. New York: Naḥliel, 1951.

Levy, Raphael. *Contribution à la Lexicographie Française selon d'Anciens Textes d'Origine Juive*. Syracuse, NY: Syracuse University Press, 1960.

Levy, Ya'akov, ed. *The Oxford English-Hebrew/Hebrew-English Dictionary*. N.p.: Kenerman Publishing, 1995.

Lewicki, Roy J., David M. Saunders, and John W. Minton. *Essentials of Negotiation*. Boston: Irwin/McGraw-Hill, 1997.

Lewicki, Roy J., and Edward C. Tomlinson. "Trust, Trust Development, and Trust Repair." In *The Handbook of Conflict Resolution: Theory and Practice*, edited by Morton Deutsch, Peter T. Coleman, and Eric C. Marcus, 104–36. San Francisco: Jossey-Bass, 2014.

Lewin, Kurt. *Field Theory in Social Science; Selected Theoretical Papers*. New York: Harper and Row, 1951.

Lichstein, Kenneth L. *Clinical Relaxation Strategies*. New York: Wiley, 1988.

Licht, Shimon. "*Ba-Din Meḥilah i Ba'e ba-Peh o ba-Lev*." *Torat ha-Adam le-Adam: Kovets Torani ba-Mitsvot she-ben Adam la-Ḥavero* 3 (1999): 35–36.

Lichtstein, Mordechai. *Mitsvot ha-Levavot*. Brisk, Lithuania: Avraham Hendler, 1924.

Lickona, Thomas. *Educating for Character*. New York: Bantam Books, 1992.

Lieberman, Saul. *Ha-Yerushalmi ki-Feshuto*. New York: The Jewish Theological Seminary of America, 1995.

———. *Tosefta ki-Feshutah*. Vol. 8. New York: Jewish Theological Seminary of America, 1973.

———. *Yevanit ve-Yavnut be-Erets Yisrael*. Jerusalem: Mosad Bialik, 1962.

Lieberman, Yosef. *Sefer She'elot u-Teshuvot Mishnat Yosef*. Vol. 4. Jerusalem: n.p., 2000.

Liedke, G. "*Rîb*: to quarrel." In *Theological Lexicon of the Old Testament*, edited by Ernst Jenni and Claus Westerman, translated by Mark E. Biddle, 1232–37. Peabody, MA: Hendrickson Publishers, 1997.

Lilienfeld, Scott O., Rachel Ammirati, and Kristin Landfield. "Giving Debiasing Away: Can Psychological Research on Correcting Cognitive Errors Promote Human Welfare?" *Perspectives on Psychological Science* 4, no. 4 (2009): 390–98.

Lipkin, Ḥayim Yitsḥak. *Derekh Teshuvah*. Commentary to *Sha'are Teshuvah*, by Jonah ben Abraham Gerondi. Bnei Brak: Hotsa'at Ḥokhmah u-Musar, 1977.

Lipschutz, Israel. *Tiferet Yisrael: Yakhin u-Voaz*. In *Mishnayot Zekher Ḥanokh*. Jerusalem: Ḥ. Vagshal, 1999.

Litsch-Rosenbaum, Moshe Leib. *Mata di-Yerushalayim*. N.p., 1978.

Litwack, Hillel D. "*Ba-Inyan Geder Benoni*." *Marpe Lashon* 7 (1994): 145–48.

———. *Ḥovat ha-Tokhaḥah*. Brooklyn, NY: n.p., 1991.

———. *Kuntres Sha'are Ona'ah*. Brooklyn, NY: Oraḥ Mesharim, 1979.

———. *Kuntres Yisrael ha-Kedoshim*. New York: n.p., 1978.

———. *Mi-Devar Sheker Tirḥak*. Brooklyn: Simcha Graphic, 1978.

Locke, Edwin A., and Gary P. Latham. "Building a Practically Useful Theory of Goal Setting and Task Motivation: A 35-Year Odyssey." *American Psychologist* 57, no. 9 (2002): 705–17.

Lopian, Eliyahu. *Lev Eliyahu*. Vol. 1. Jerusalem: Ha-Va'ad le-Hotsa'at Kitve Maran Zal, 1972.

Lorints, Shelomoh Zalman. *Milu'e Shelomoh: Berure Sugyot ve-Shu't im Maranan Gedole Torah*. Jerusalem: Feldheim, 2004.

Luban, Ya'akov David. "*Ad she-Yeratseh et Ḥavero*." *Ha-Darom* 64 (Elul 5755 [1995]): 40–53.

Luria, Solomon. *Yam shel Shelomoh*. Jerusalem: Mishnat David, 1995.

Lurya, Mordekhai. *Eleh ha-Mitsvot*. In *Mishneh la-Melekh Aḥaron*. Jerusalem: Shmuel ha-Levi Tsukerman, 1905.

Luskin, Fred. *Forgive for Good: A Proven Prescription for Health and Happiness.* San Francisco: Harper, 2002.

Luzzatto, Moshe Ḥayyim. *Sefer Mesilat Yesharim.* Jerusalem: Mosad Haskel, 1979.

Mader, Avraham. Cited in Shalom Schnitzler, *Kitsur Shulḥan Arukh ve-Nilvu alav Shene Sefarim: Sha'are Shalom, Mevaser Shalom,* vol. 2 (Jerusalem: College for Higher Rabbinical Studies, 1978), *siman* 29, p. 101 n. 27.

Maher, Paul E. *Hebraica Cataloging: A Guide to ALA/LC Romanization and Descriptive Cataloging.* Washington, DC: Cataloging Distribution Service, Library of Congress, 1987.

Maimonides, Moses. *Hakdamah leha-Rambam mi-Seder Zeraim.* In the standard Vilna edition of the Babylonian Talmud.

———. Introduction to the tenth chapter of *Sanhedrin.* In the standard Vilna edition of the Babylonian Talmud.

———. *Masekhet Avot im Perush Rabenu Mosheh ben Maimon.* Translated by Isaac Shailat. Jerusalem: Ma'aliyot, 1994.

———. *Mishnah im Perush Rabenu Mosheh ben Maimon.* Translated by Joseph Kafih. 7 vols. Jerusalem: Mossad Harav Kook, 1963.

———. *Mishneh Torah.* 12 vols. Bnei Brak: Hotsa'at Shabse Frankel, 1975–2007.

———. *Perush ha-Mishnayot leha-Rambam.* In the standard Vilna edition of the Babylonian Talmud.

———. *Sefer ha-Mitsvot.* Translated by Joseph Kafih. Jerusalem: Mossad Harav Kook, 1971.

———. *Sefer ha-Mitsvot.* Edited by Ḥayyim Heller. Jerusalem: Mossad Harav Kook, 1995.

———. *Sefer ha-Mitsvot.* Jerusalem: Hotsa'at Shabse Frankel, 2001.

Makhon Torat ha-Adam le-Adam. *"Kelal Gadol mi-Zeh." Torat ha-Adam le-Adam: Kovets Torani ba-Mitsvot she-ben Adam la-Ḥavero* 4 (Tishre 5762 [2001]): 297–307.

———. *"Likutim ba-Mitsvat 'Ve-Ahavta le-Re'akha kamokha.'" Torat ha-Adam le-Adam: Kovets Torani ba-Mitsvot she-ben Adam la-Ḥavero* 4 (2001): 133–40.

———. *"Ve-Tsarikh Iyun." Torat ha-Adam le-Adam: Kovets Torani ba-Mitsvot she-ben Adam la-Ḥavero* 3 (1999): 217–19.

Malbim, Meir Loeb ben Jehiel Michael. *Sefer ha-Torah veha-Mitsvah*. Israel: Shiloh, n.d.

———. *Sefer Ya'ir Or; Sefer ha-Karmel*. Jerusalem: Mishor, 1982.

Man, Shelomoh. *Dibur be-Naḥat: Hanhagot ve-Etsot al Inyan ha-Ka'as*. Jerusalem: Sh. Man, Pe'er Binyamin, 1995.

Margolioth, Ephraim Zalman. *Mateh Efrayim ha-Shalem*. Jerusalem: G. M. Eisenbach, 1989.

Margolis, Max L. *Notes on the New Translation of the Holy Scriptures*. Philadelphia: Jewish Publication Society, 1921.

Margulies, Reuben. *Margaliyot ha-Yam*. Jerusalem: Mossad Harav Kook, 1958.

———. *Nefesh Ḥayah*. Lvov: Krenenberg u-Felhendler, 1932.

Masekhtot Derekh Erets. Edited by Michael Higger. New York: De-Be Rabanan, 1935.

Masekhtot Kalah. Edited by Michael Higger. New York: De-Be Rabanan, 1936.

Mat, Moses. *Sefer Mateh Mosheh*. Jerusalem: n.p., 1984.

Matsumoto, David, ed. *Cambridge Dictionary of Psychology*. Cambridge: Cambridge University Press, 2009.

McClellan, B. Edward. *Moral Education in America*. New York: Teachers College Press, 1999.

McCullough, Michael E., Kenneth I. Pargament, and Carl E. Thoresen, eds. *Forgiveness: Theory, Research, and Practice*. New York: Guilford Press, 2001.

McCullough, Michael E., K. Chris Rachal, Steven J. Sandage, Everett L. Worthington Jr, Susan Wade Brown, and Terry L. Hight. "Interpersonal Forgiving in Close Relationships: II. Theoretical Elaboration and Measurement." *Journal of Personality and Social Psychology* 75, no. 6 (1998): 1586–603.

McGlynn, F. Dudley. "Systematic Desensitization." In *Encyclopedia of Behavior Modification and Cognitive Behavior Therapy*. Vol. 1, edited by Michel Hersen and Johan Rosqvist, 574–82. Thousand Oaks, CA: Sage, 2007.

Medini, Ḥayyim Hezekiah. *Sede Ḥemed*. 10 vols. Brooklyn: Kehot, 1959.

Meichenbaum, Donald. *Stress Inoculation Training*. New York: Pergamon Press, 1985.

Meichenbaum, Donald, and Roy Cameron. "The Clinical Potential of Modifying What Clients Say to Themselves." *Psychotherapy: Theory, Research and Practice* 11, no. 2 (1974): 103–17.

Meir ben Baruch of Rothenburg. *She'elot u-Teshuvot Maharam BR' Barukh.* Prague-Budapest edition. Budapest: Y. Shternberg, 1895.

———. *Sifre She'elot u-Teshuvot Piske Dinim u-Minhagim Maharam mi-Rotenburg.* Vol. 4, Prague edition. Bnei Brak: Ha-Sifriyah ha-Ḥaredit ha-Olomit, 1999.

Meiri, Menaḥem. *Bet ha-Beḥirah al Masekhet Avot.* Jerusalem: Mekhon ha-Talmud ha-Yisraeli ha-Shalem, 1968.

———. *Bet ha-Beḥirah al Masekhet Avot.* Jerusalem-Cleveland: Mekhon Ofek, 1994.

———. *Bet ha-Beḥirah al Masekhet Bava Kama.* Jerusalem: K. Schlesinger, 1963.

———. *Bet ha-Beḥirah al Masekhet Sanhedrin.* Jerusalem: Kedem, 1965.

———. *Bet ha-Beḥirah al Masekhet Shabat.* Jerusalem: n.p., 1976.

———. *Bet ha-Beḥirah al Masekhet Yoma.* Jerusalem: Mekhon ha-Talmud ha-Yisraeli ha-Shalem, 1970.

———. *Ḥibur ha-Teshuvah.* New York: Talpiyot Yeshivah University, 1950.

———. *Perush ha-Meiri al Sefer Mishle.* Jerusalem: Otsar ha-Posekim, 1969.

Meir Simḥah ha-Kohen of Dvinsk. *Or Same'aḥ.* Jerusalem: n.p., 1973.

Mekhilta de-Rabi Shimon ben Yoḥai. Edited by J. N. Epstein and Ezra Zion Melamed. Jerusalem: Mekitse Nirdamim, 1955.

Mekhilta debe-Rabi Yishmael. Edited by S. Horovitz and I. A. Rabin. Frankfurt am Main: n.p., 1931.

Meklenburg, Jacob Zevi. *Ha-Ketav veha-Kabalah.* Paris: Centre de Recherches des Escrits Sacres, n.d.

Melamed, Ezra Zion. *Iyunim be-Sifrut ha-Talmud.* Jerusalem: Magnes Press, 1986.

Menaḥem of Merseburg. *Nimuke Menaḥem Mirzburk.* In *She'elot u-Teshuvot ve-Hilkhot Sheḥitah u-Vedikah ve-Ḥidushe Dinim,* by Jacob Weil, 167–78. Jerusalem: Yisrael Wolf, 1959.

Mermelstein, Avraham Yitsḥak David. *Be-Naḥat Nishma'im* (in Yiddish). [Brooklyn, NY]: A. Y. D. Mermelstein, 1998.

Meshi Zahav, Avraham. *Dover Shalom.* Jerusalem: Shmuel Dov Eisenblatt, 1980.

Michaelson, Ezekiel Zevi. *Bet Yeḥezkel.* Piotrków: H. Falman, 1924.

Midrash ha-Gadol. Jerusalem: Mossad Harav Kook, 1947.

Midrash le-Olam. In Adolph Jellinek, ed., *Bet ha-Midrash*. Vol. 3, 109–20. Jerusalem: Wahrmann Books, 1967.

Midrash Tanḥuma [the "standard edition"]. With the commentaries *Ets Yosef* and *Anaf Yosef*, by Enoch Zundel ben Joseph. Jerusalem: Levin-Epshtayn, n.d.

Midrash Tanḥuma. Edited by Solomon Buber. Vilna: n.p., n.d.

Midrash Tanaim al Sefer Devarim. Edited by David Zevi Hoffmann. Berlin: Ts. H. Itskovski, 1908.

Midrash Wayyikra Rabbah. Annotated by Mordecai Margulies. New York: Jewish Theological Seminary of America, 1993.

Mikolic, Joseph M., John C. Parker, and Dean G. Pruitt. "Escalation in Response to Persistent Annoyance: Groups Versus Individuals and Gender Effects." *Journal of Personality and Social Psychology* 72, no. 1 (1997): 151–63.

Milgram, Jacob. *The Anchor Bible: Leviticus 17–22, a New Translation with Introduction and Commentary*. New York: Doubleday, 2000.

Mishnat Rabi Eliezer-Midrash Sheloshim u-Shetayim Midot. Annotated by H. G. Enelow. New York: Bloch Publishing, 1933.

Mitnik, Yitzchok, ed. *Avodah Berurah al Masekhet Arakhin*. Vol. 1. Lakewood, NJ: Mekhon Be'er ha-Torah, 2003.

Moellin, Jacob. *Sefer Maharil: Minhagim*. Jerusalem: Mekhon Yerushalayim, 1989.

Molkho, Joseph. *Sefer Shulḥan Gevoah*. Jerusalem: Or va-Derekh, 1992.

Moore, Carey A. *The Anchor Bible: Tobit: A New Translation with Introduction and Commentary*. New York: Doubleday, 1996.

Moore, Christopher W. *The Mediation Process: Practical Strategies for Resolving Conflict*. San Francisco: Jossey-Bass, 1984.

Moore, George Foot. *Judaism in the First Centuries of the Christian Era, the Age of the Tannaim*. Vol. 2. Peabody, MA: Hendrickson Publishers, 1997.

Mordecai ben Hillel ha-Kohen. *Sefer Mordekhai*. In the standard Vilna edition of the Babylonian Talmud.

Morris, Catherine. "Conflict Transformation and Peacebuilding: A Selected Bibliography - Acknowledgement, Apology and Forgiveness." Peacemakers Trust. Accessed November 4, 2016. http://www.peacemakers.ca/bibliography/bib44forgivenessapology.html.

———. "Conflict Transformation and Peacebuilding: A Selected Bibliography - Christian Perspectives on Conflict Transformation, Nonviolence and Reconciliation." Peacemakers Trust. Accessed November 4, 2016. http://www.peacemakers.ca/bibliography/bib40christian.html.

Moses ben Jacob of Coucy. *Sefer Mitsvot Gadol* (*Semag*). Israel: n.p., 1991.

Moshav Zekenim al ha-Torah; Kovets Perushe Rabotenu Ba'ale ha-Tosafot. Jerusalem: Keren Hotsa'at Sifre Rabane Bavel, 1982.

Moskowitz, Gordon B. *Social Cognition: Understanding Self and Others*. New York: Guilford Press, 2005.

Moskowitz, Gordon B., and Michael J. Gill. "Person Perception." In *The Oxford Handbook of Cognitive Psychology*, edited by Daniel Reisberg, 918–42. Oxford, UK: Oxford University Press, 2013.

Moskowitz, Yeḥiel Zvi. *Sefer be-Midbar* (*Da'at Mikra*). Jerusalem: Mossad Harav Kook, 1988.

Movshovits, Mordekhai Shelomoh. *Shalme Mordekhai*. Tel Aviv: Lipa Friedman, 1983.

Mummendey, Amelie, and Sabine Otten. "Aggression: Interaction between Individuals and Social Groups." In *Aggression and Violence: Social Interactionist Perspectives*, edited by Richard B. Felson and James T. Tedeschi, 145–67. Washington, DC: American Psychological Association, 1993.

Musekura, Célestin. *An Assessment of Contemporary Models of Forgiveness, American University Studies*, VII, *Theology and Religion*. V. 302. New York: Peter Lang, 2010.

Musto, Ronald G. *The Catholic Peace Tradition*. New York: Peace Books, 2002.

Naeh, Shlomo. "*Aseh Libkha Ḥadre Ḥaderim: Iyun Nosaf be-Divre Ḥazal al ha-Maḥaloket.*" In *Renewing Jewish Commitment: The Work and Thought of David Hartman*, edited by Avi Sagi and Zvi Zohar. Vol. 2, 851–75. Tel Aviv: Shalom Hartman Institute, 2001.

Naḥman of Bratslav. *Likute Moharan*. Jerusalem: Keren Hadpasah shel Ḥaside Breslav, 1976.

Naḥmanides. *Igeret ha-Ramban*. In *Kitve Rabenu Mosheh ben Naḥman*. Vol. 1, 372–77. Jerusalem: Mossad Harav Kook, 1982.

———. *Perush ha-Ramban al ha-Torah*. Annotated by Charles B. Chavel. Jerusalem: Mossad Harav Kook, 1988.

———. *Sefer ha-Mitsvot leha-Rambam im Hasagot ha-Ramban*. Jerusalem: Mossad Harav Kook, 1981.

———. *Sha'ar ha-Gemul*. In *Kitve Rabenu Mosheh ben Naḥman*. Vol. 2, 264–311. Jerusalem: Mossad Harav Kook, 1964.

Naḥmias, Joseph. *Perushe Rabi Yosef Naḥmi'as al Megilat Esther, Yirmiyahu, Pirke Avot, ve-Seder Avodat Yom ha-Kipurim*. Tel Aviv: n.p., n.d.

Navon, Chaim. *Genesis and Jewish Thought*. New Jersey: Ktav, 2008.

Neal, Geraldine. "Alternative Dispute Resolution: Are Apology and Forgiveness Simply Two Sides of the One Coin?" In *A Journey through Forgiveness*, edited by Malika Rebai Maamri, Nehama Verbin, and Everett L. Worthington Jr., 167–77. Oxford, UK: Inter-Disciplinary Press, 2010.

Nebenzahl, Avigdor. Quoted in Moshe Harari, *Mikra'e Kodesh: Hilkhot Yom ha-Kipurim* (Jerusalem: Yeshivat Merkaz ha-Rav, n.d.), 34–35 n. 4, 38 n. 9.

Neblett, William R. "Forgiveness and Ideals." *Mind* 83, no. 330 (1974): 269–75.

Neudecker, Reinhard. "'And You Shall Love Your Neighbor as Yourself—I Am the Lord' in Jewish Interpretation." *Biblica* 73, no. 4 (1992): 496–517.

Neuman, Yeḥiel. *"Ha-Mitsvah la-Dun le-Khaf Zekhut." Torat ha-Adam le-Adam: Kovets Torani ba-Mitsvot she-ben Adam la-Ḥavero* 5 (2004): 199–214.

———. *"Kuntres 'Lo Titor'." Torat ha-Adam le-Adam: Kovets Torani ba-Mitsvot she-ben Adam la-Ḥavero* 3 (1999): 76–95.

———. *"Ve-Ahavta le-Re'akha kamokha: Berur ha-Shitot." Torat ha-Adam le-Adam: Kovets Torani ba-Mitsvot she-ben Adam la-Ḥavero* 4 (2001): 78–93.

Nhat Hanh, Thich. *Being Peace*. Berkeley, CA: Parallax Press, 1987.

Nolan-Haley, Jacqueline M. *Alternative Dispute Resolution in a Nutshell*. 3rd ed. St. Paul, MN: Thomson/West Publishing, 2008.

North, Joanna. "The Ideal of Forgiveness: A Philosophical Exploration." In *Exploring Forgiveness*, edited by Robert D. Enright and Joanna North, 15–34. Madison, WI: University of Wisconsin Press, 1998.

———. "Wrongdoing and Forgiveness." *Philosophy* 62, no. 242 (Oct., 1987): 499–508.

Norzi, Jedidiah Solomon Raphael. *Minḥat Shai*. In the standard *Mikra'ot Gedolot*.

Novaco, Raymond W. "Anger." In *Encyclopedia of Psychology*. vol. 1, edited by Alan E. Kazdin, 170–74. Washington, DC: American Psychological Association, 2000.

______. "Anger and Coping with Stress." In *Cognitive Behavior Therapy: Research and Application*, edited by John P. Foreyt and Diana P Rathjen, 135–73. New York: Plenum Press, 1978.

———. *Anger Control: The Development and Evaluation of an Experimental Treatment*. Lexington, MA: Lexington Books, 1975.

———. "Anger Management." In *The Corsini Encyclopedia of Psychology*. 4th ed., edited by Irving B. Weiner and W. Edward Craighead, 101–4. Hoboken, NJ: Wiley, 2010.

———. "Stress Inoculation: A Cognitive Therapy for Anger and Its Application to a Case of Depression." *Journal of Consulting and Clinical Psychology* 45, no. 4 (1977): 600–608.

———. "A Treatment Program for the Management of Anger through Cognitive and Relaxation Controls." PhD diss., Indiana University, 1974.

Ogiermann, Eva. "Bibliography on Apologies." Accessed September 22, 2014. https://linguisticpoliteness.wordpress.com/bibliographies/apologies-1.

Ohbuchi, Ken-ichi, Masuyo Kameda, and Nariyuki Agarie. "Apology as Aggression Control: Its Role in Mediating Appraisal of and Response to Harm." *Journal of Personality and Social Psychology* 56, no. 2 (1989): 219–27.

Olshtain, Elite, and Andrew D. Cohen. "Apology: A Speech-Act Set." In *Sociolinguistics and Language Acquisition*, edited by Nessa Wolfson and Elliot Judd, 18–35. Rowley, Mass.: Newbury House, 1983.

Orenstein, Avraham. *Entsiklopedyah le-To'are-Kavod be-Yisrael*. Vol. 1. Tel Aviv: Netsaḥ, 1958.

Orḥot Tsadikim ha-Shalem. Jerusalem: Feldheim, 1988.

Otzar HaHochma. Online database of Jewish books. Ver. 14.0. Accessed September 25, 2016. http://www.otzar.org.

Ouziel, Ben-Zion Meir Ḥai. *Derashot Uziel al Masekhet Avot*. Jerusalem: Ha-Va'ad le-Hotsa'at Kitve ha-Rav, zatsal, 1991.

Palache, Ḥayyim. *Ḥayim be-Yad*. Izmir: Binyamin N. Tsiyon Roditi, 1873.

———. *Sefer le-Ḥayim bi-Yerushalayim*. Jerusalem: Mekhon Shuvi Nafshi, 2000.

Paltiel, Eliezer. "*Ikvotav shel Menaḥem ha-Galili be-Agadat Ḥazal.*" In *Sefer Refa'el: Ma'amarim u-Meḥkarim ba-Torah uve-Mada'e ha-Yahadut le-Zikhro shel Dr. Yitsḥak Refael*, edited by Yosef Movshovitz, 456–67. Jerusalem: Mossad Harav Kook, 2000.

Palvani, Daniel. *Ma'adane Daniyel*. Commentary to *Shulḥan Arukh: Hilkhot Rosh ha-Shanah ve-Yom ha-Kipurim*. Jerusalem: Mosdot Hifkadeti Shomrim, 2013.

Pam, Avraham Ya'akov ha-Kohen. *Atarah la-Melekh*. Brooklyn, NY: Yo.l. a.Y. Talmidav, 1993.

Papo, Eliezer. *Orot Elim*. Ashdod: Mekhon Hadrat Ḥen, 2005.

———. *Pele Yo'ets ha-Shalem*. Jerusalem: Mekhon Merav, 1994.

Pappenheim, Solomon. *Yeri'at Shelomoh*. Vol. 1. Dihrenfurt: Be-Defus Yeḥi'el Mikhal Mai, 1784.

———. *Yeri'at Shelomoh*. Vol. 2. Rodelheim: Wolf Heidenheim, 1831.

Pardo, David. *Maskil le-David*. Jerusalem: Mekhon Even Yisrael, 1986.

Parlamis, Jennifer D. "Venting as Emotion Regulation: The Influence of Venting Responses and Respondent Identity on Anger and Emotional Tone." *International Journal of Conflict Management* 23, no. 1 (2012): 77–96.

Peace and Justice Studies Association and International Peace Research Association Foundation. *Global Directory of Peace Studies and Conflict Resolution Programs*. Accessed January 21, 2012. http://www.peacejusticestudies.org/globaldirectory (site discontinued).

Pedersen, Johannes. *Israel: Its Life and Culture*, vol. 2. London: Oxford University Press, 1926.

Pederson, Paul. "Multicultural Conflict Resolution." In *The Handbook of Conflict Resolution*. 2nd ed., edited by Morton Deutsch, Peter T. Coleman, and Eric C. Marcus, 649–70. San Francisco: Jossey Bass, 2006.

Penso, Ḥayim Daniel. *Shem Ḥadash: ... al Sefer Yere'im*. Vol. 1. Jerusalem: n.p., 1848.

Perets, Elḥanan. *Ma'aseh ha-Tsedakah*. Jerusalem: Mekhon Merkevet ha-Mishnah, 2005.

Perez de Cuellar, Javier, and Young Seek Choue, eds. *World Encyclopedia of Peace*. 2nd ed. 8 vols. Dobbs Ferry, NY: Oceana Publications, 1999.

Perfet, Isaac ben Sheshet. *She'elot u-Teshuvot ha-Rivash*. Jerusalem: n.p., 1968.

———. *She'elot u-Teshuvot Rabenu Yitsḥak bar Sheshet*. Vol. 1. Jerusalem: Mekhon Or ha-Mizraḥ, 1993.

Perla, Jeroham Fishel. Commentary to *Sefer ha-Mitsvot le-Rabenu Sa'adyah: Im Be'ur Meva'er Devarav vi-Yesodotav ve-Shitato*, by Sa'adia ben Joseph. 3 vols. New York: E. Grossman, 1962.

Pesikta de-Rav Kahana. Vol. 1. Edited by Bernard Mandelbaum. New York: Jewish Theological Seminary of America, 1962.

Pesikta Rabati. Edited by Meir Ish Shalom [Friedmann]. Vienna: Yosef Kaizer, 1880.

Philo. *The Works of Philo Judaeus*. Translated by C. D. Yonge. Vol. 3. London: Henry G. Bohn, 1855.

Pliskin, Zelig. *Anger!: The Inner Teacher: A Nine-Step Program to Free Yourself from Anger*. Brooklyn, NY: Mesorah, 1997.

———. *Love Your Neighbor*. Jerusalem: Aish ha-Torah Publications, 1977.

Pomeranchik, Aryeh. *Emek Berakhah*. Tel-Aviv: T. Pomeranchik, 1971.

Poppers, Meir. *Or ha-Yashar*. Jerusalem: H. Y. Valdman, 1981.

Potash, Mordekhai. "*Kuntres Ona'at Devarim*." In *Sefer Darkhe Shalom: Ve-Kuntres Ona'at Devarim*. Jerusalem: n.p., 1993.

Poupko, Aryeh Leib ha-Kohen. *Dugma mi-Darkhe Avi*. In vol. 3 of *Kol Kitve Ḥafets Ḥayim*. New York: Avraham Yitsḥak Friedman, n.d.

Price, Abraham A. *Mishnat Avraham al ha-Semag*. 3 vols. Toronto: Yeshiva Torath Chaim, 1972–1985.

Pronin, Emily, Carolyn Puccio, and Lee Ross. "Understanding Misunderstanding: Social Psychological Perspectives." In *Heuristics and Biases: The Psychology of Intuitive Judgment*, edited by Thomas Gilovich, Dale W. Griffin, and Daniel Kahneman, 636–65. New York: Cambridge University Press, 2002.

Pruitt, Dean G., and Sung Hee Kim. *Social Conflict: Escalation, Stalemate, and Settlement*. 3rd ed. New York: McGraw-Hill, 2004.

Prutzman, Priscilla, Judith M. Johnson, and Susan Fountain. *CCRC's Friendly Classrooms and Communities for Young Children: A Manual for Conflict Resolution Activities and Resources*. Nyack, NY: Creative Response to Conflict Inc., 1998.

Prutzman, Priscilla, Lee Stern, M. Leonard Burger, and Gretchen Bodenhamer. *The Friendly Classroom for a Small Planet: A Handbook on Creative Approaches to Living and Problem Solving for Children*. Gabriola Island, BC, Canada: New Society Publishers, 1988.

Quint, Emanuel B. "An Anthology of Rabbinic Views on the Commandment to Love Your Neighbor." *The Annual Volume of Torah Studies of the Council of Young Israel Rabbis in Israel* 3 (1991): 59–79.

Rabinovitch, Nachum L. *Mishneh Torah: Hu ha-Yad ha-Ḥazakah le-Rabenu Mosheh b. R. Maimon im Perush Yad Peshutah*. 20 vols. Jerusalem: Ma'aliyot, 1997–2011.

Rabinowitz, Chaim Dov. *Da'at Sofrim*. Tel Aviv: Sifriyati, 1958.

Rabinowitz-Teomim, Benjamin. "*Ḥazon ha-Shalom*." *Sinai* 1 nos. 5–6 (Tishre–Ḥeshvan 5698 [1937]): 584–93.

Rabinowitz-Te'omim, Elijah David. *Bene Binyamin*. In the back of the standard printed editions of Maimonides' *Mishneh Torah*.

Raccah, Masud. *Ma'aseh Rokeaḥ*. Vol. 4. Bnei Brak: Shmuel Akiva Yafeh Shlesinger, 1964.

———. *Ma'aseh Rokeaḥ*. Jerusalem: n.p., 1976.

Raday, Zvi, and Chaim Rabin. *Ha-Milon he-Ḥadash la-Tanakh*. Jerusalem: Keter Publishing House, 1989.

Ragoler, Meir ben Elijah. *Derekh Avot*. In *Sifre ha-Gera ve-Talmidav al Masekhet Avot*. Jerusalem: Yerid ha-Sefarim, 2001.

Raines, Susan S. *Conflict Management for Managers: Resolving Workplace, Client, and Policy Disputes*. San Francisco: Jossey-Bass, 2013.

Rakover, Barukh. *Birkat Eliyahu al Be'ure ha-Gera, Ḥoshen Mishpat*. Vol. 1. Jerusalem: Machon Harry Fischel, 1991.

Rakover, Nahum. *Gadol Kevod ha-Beriyot: Kevod ha-Beriyot ke-Erekh Al*. Jerusalem: Moreshet ha-Mishpat be-Yisrael, 1998.

———. *Law and the Noahides: Law as a Universal Value*. Jerusalem: Ministry of Justice, 1998.

———. *Shilton ha-Ḥok be-Yisrael*. Jerusalem: Misrad ha-Mishpatim, 1989.

Ramsbotham, Oliver, Tom Woodhouse, and Hugh Miall. *Contemporary Conflict Resolution*. 3rd ed. Cambridge: Polity Press, 2011.

Rashi [Solomon ben Isaac]. *Sefer ha-Orah*. Jerusalem: n.p., 1967.

———. *Teshuvot Rashi*. Bnei Brak: Yahadut, 1980.

Ratner, Dov Baer. *Ahavat Tsiyon vi-Yerushalayim: Masekhet Yoma*. Jerusalem: n.p., 1967.

Ravitzky, Aviezer. *Al Da'at ha-Makom: Meḥkarim ba-Hagut ha-Yehudit uve-Toldoteha*. Jerusalem: Keter, 1991.

———. "Peace." In *Contemporary Jewish Religious Thought: Original Essays on Critical Concepts, Movements, and Beliefs*, edited by Arthur A. Cohen and Paul Mendes-Flohr, 685–702. New York: The Free Press, 1987.

Razovsky, Baruch. *Sefer Birkat Avot*. Jerusalem: n.p., 1990.

Reardon, Betty A. *Comprehensive Peace Education: Educating for Global Responsibility*. New York: Teachers College Press, 1988.

Reber, Arthur S., Rhianon Allen, and Emily S. Reber. *Penguin Dictionary of Psychology*. London: Penguin Books, 1985.

Recanati, Menaḥem. *Sefer Rekanati*. N.p., n.d.

Reischer, Jacob. *Iyun Ya'akov*. In Jacob ibn Ḥabib, *En Ya'akov*. New York: Sifre Kodesh, 1971.

———. *Masekhet Avot im Perush Iyun Ya'akov*. Brooklyn, NY: Tiferet Baḥurim de-Bobov, 1994.

Richardson, Deborah R., Laura R. Green, and Tania Lago. "The Relationship between Perspective-Taking and Nonaggressive Responding in the Face of an Attack." *Journal of Personality* 66, no. 2 (1998): 235–56.

Richardson, Deborah R., Georgina S. Hammock, Stephen M. Smith, Wendi Gardner, and Manuel Signo. "Empathy as a Cognitive Inhibitor of Interpersonal Aggression." *Aggressive Behavior* 20, no. 4 (1994): 275–89.

Rivkes, Moses. *Be'er ha-Golah*. In the standard printed edition of the *Shulḥan Arukh*.

Rivkin, Ben Zion. "*Ba-Inyan li-Fne Iver Etsel Goy (Hemshekh)*." *Ha-Darom* 58 (Elul 5749 [1988]): 84–90.

Robbennolt, Jennifer K. "Apologies and Legal Settlement: An Empirical Examination." *Michigan Law Review* 102, no. 3 (2003): 460–516.

Rogers, Carl R. "Empathic: An Unappreciated Way of Being." In *A Way of Being*, 137–63. New York: Houghton Mifflin, 1995. http://www.

sageofasheville.com/pub_downloads /EMPATHIC_AN_UNAPPRE CIATED_WAY_OF_BEING.pdf.

Rogers, Carl R., and Richard E. Farson. "Active Listening." http://www.go-get.org/pdf/Rogers _Farson.pdf.

Rogers, Nancy H., and Richard A. Salem. *A Student's Guide to Mediation and the Law*. New York: Matthew Bender, 1987.

Rokeaḥ, Efrayim. "*Hilel ve-Shamai.*" *Shanah be-Shanah* (5756 [1996]): 456–64.

Rosenberg, Abraham J., trans. *Job: A New English Translation*. New York: The Judaica Press, 1995.

Rosenberg, Shalom. "*Ve-Halakhta bi-Drakhav.*" In *Filosofyah Yisre'elit*, edited by Asa Kasher and Moshe Halamish, 72–91. Tel Aviv: Papyrus, 1983.

Rosensweig, Michael. "*Elu va-Elu Divre Elokim Hayyim*: Halakhic Pluralism and Theories of Controversy." *Tradition* 26, no. 3 (1992): 4–23.

Rosmarin, Moshe. *Sefer Devar Mosheh: Al Masekhet Horiyot, Masekhet Pirke Avot, Sugya de-Kiyum Shetarot*. Jerusalem: n.p., 1978.

Ross, Lee. "The Intuitive Psychologist and His Shortcomings: Distortions in the Attribution Process." *Advances in Experimental Social Psychology* 10 (1977): 173–220.

Rossenbaum, Asher. *Binat Asher*. Tel Aviv: n.p., 1968.

Roth, Daniel. "*Masoret Aharon Rodef Shalom ben Ish le-Ish ke-Model Rabani le-Fiyus*" [The Tradition of Aaron Pursuer of Peace between People as a Rabbinic Model of Reconciliation]. PhD diss., Bar-Ilan University, 2012.

Roth, Deborah A., Edna B. Foa, and Martin Franklin. "Response Prevention." In *Cognitive Behavior Therapy: Applying Empirically Supported Techniques in Your Practice*, edited by William O'Donohue, Jane E. Fisher, and Steven C. Hayes, 341–48. Hoboken, NJ: Wiley, 2003.

Rubin, Jeffrey Z., Dean G. Pruitt, and Sung Hee Kim. *Social Conflict: Escalation, Stalemate, and Settlement*. 2nd ed. New York: McGraw Hill, 1994.

Rusbult, Caryl E., Peggy A. Hannon, Shevaun L. Stocker, and Eli J. Finkel. "Forgiveness and Relational Repair." In *Handbook of Forgiveness*, edited by Everett L. Worthington Jr., 185–205. New York: Routledge, 2005.

Ryan, Kevin, and Karen E. Bohlin. *Building Character in Schools.* San Francisco: Jossey-Bass, 1999.

Sa'adia ben Joseph. *Ha-Nivḥar ba-Emunot uva-De'ot.* New York: Sura, 1970.

———. *Mishle im Targum u-Ferush ha-Ga'on Se'adyah ben Yosef Fayumi.* Jerusalem: Ha-Va'ad le-Hotsa'at Sifre Rasag, 1976.

———. *Sefer ha-Emunot veha-De'ot.* Tel Aviv: Sifriyati, 1959.

Sadalla, Gail, Manti Henriquez, Meg Holmberg, and Jim Halligan. *Conflict Resolution: A Middle School and High School Curriculum.* San Francisco: Community Boards, 1998.

Sagi, Avi. *Elu va-Elu: Mashmauto shel ha-Siaḥ ha-Hilkhati: Iyun Be-Sifrut Yisrael.* Tel Aviv: Hakibbutz Hameuchad, 1996.

Said, Abdul Aziz, Nathan C. Funk, and Ayse S. Kadayifci. *Peace and Conflict Resolution in Islam: Precept and Practice.* Lanham, MD: University Press of America, 2001.

Salanter, Israel. *Or Yisrael.* New York: Avraham Yitsḥak Friedman, n.d.

———. Quoted in Dov Katz, *Tenuat ha-Musar,* vol. 1 (Jerusalem: Feldheim, 1996), 285.

Salanter, Israel, and Isaac Blaser. *Or Yisrael.* New York: Avraham Yitsḥak Friedman, n.d.

Salovey, Peter, Christopher K. Hsee, and John D. Mayer. "Emotional Intelligence and the Self-Regulation of Affect." In *Handbook of Mental Control,* edited by Daniel M. Wegner and James W. Pennebaker, 258–77. Englewood Cliffs, NJ: Prentice Hall, 1993.

Samsonovits, Mosheh. *"Kuntres Min ha-Ḥayim Meshisihu." Marpe Lashon* 3 [1984]: 33–97.

Samuel ben Meir. *Perush ha-Rashbam ha-Shalem.* Breslau: Shlomo Shattlander, 1882.

———. Quoted in *Moshav Zekenim al ha-Torah* (Jerusalem: Keren Hotsa'at Sifre Rabane Bavel, 1982), Leviticus 19:18.

Sarna, Ezekiel. *Bet Yeḥezkel: Ḥidushim u-Ve'urim be-Inyanim Shonim ba-Shas ve-Gilyonot ha-Rambam.* Jerusalem: Mosad Haskel, 1995.

———. *Daliyot Yeḥezkel.* Vol. 1. Jerusalem: Mosad Haskel, 1975.

———. Commentary to *Mesilat Yesharim,* by Moses Ḥayyim Luzzatto. Jerusalem: Mosad Haskel, 1979.

Schachter, Hershel, and Joseph Dov Soloveitchik. *Divre ha-Rav.* Jerusalem: Masorah, 2010.

Scheinberg, Ḥayim Pinḥas. *Netivot Ḥayim*. Jerusalem: n.p., 2001.

———. Quoted in G. Alon and Elḥanan Perets, *Orḥot ha-Rav ve-Rosh ha-Yeshivah* (Jerusalem: Mekhon Ḥukat Mishpat, 2012), 93–94.

Schellenberg, James A. *Conflict Resolution: Theory, Research, and Practice*. Albany, NY: State University of New York Press, 1996.

Schepansky, Israel. *Ha-Takanot be-Yisrael*. 4 vols. Jerusalem: Mossad Harav Kook, 1991–1993.

———. "*Takanot Rabenu Gershom Me'or ha-Golah*." *Ha-Dorom* 22 (1966): 103–20.

Scherer, Michael, Kathryn L. Cooke, and Everett L. Worthington Jr. "Forgiveness Bibliography." In *Handbook of Forgiveness*, edited by Everett L. Worthington Jr., 507–45. New York: Routledge, 2005.

Schick, Moses. *Maharam Shik al Taryag Mitsvot*. Brooklyn, NY: Yisrael Brach, 1964.

Schiffman, Lawrence H. "Reproof as a Requisite for Punishment in the Law of the Dead Sea Scrolls." In *Jewish Law Association Studies II: The Jerusalem Conference Volume*, edited by B. S. Jackson, 59–74. Atlanta, GA: Scholars Press, 1986.

Schimmel, Solomon. "Anger and Its Control in Graeco-Roman and Modern Psychology." *Psychiatry* 42, no. 4 (1979): 320–37.

Schlenker, Barry R., and Bruce W. Darby. "The Use of Apologies in Social Predicaments." *Social Psychology Quarterly* (1981): 271–78.

Schmid, H. H. "*Ḥlq*: to divide." In *Theological Lexicon of the Old Testament*, edited by Ernst Jenni and Claus Westerman, translated by Mark E. Biddle. Peabody, MA: Hendrickson Publishers, 1997.

Schmitt, Manfred, Mario Gollwitzer, Nikolai Förster, and Leo Montada. "Effects of Objective and Subjective Account Components on Forgiving." *The Journal of Social Psychology* 144, no. 5 (2004): 465–86.

Schofield, Janet Ward. "Cooperative Learning." In *Encyclopedia of Child Behavior and Development*, edited by Sam Goldstein and Jack A. Naglieri, 415–16. New York: Springer, 2011. doi: 10.1007/978-0-387-79061-9_693.

Schor, Abraham Ḥayyim. *Torat Ḥayim*. Jerusalem: n.p., 1969.

Schotten, Samuel. *Kos ha-Yeshuot*. Podgórze, Poland: M. Traube, 1903.

Schwadron, Shalom Mordecai. *Tekhelet Mordekhai*. Vol. 1. Brzezany: M. I. Feldmann, 1913.

Schwartz, Baruch J. "Selected Chapters of the Holiness Code: A Literary Study of Leviticus 17–19." Ph.D. thesis, Hebrew University, 1987.

[Schwartz, Yoel]. *Or la-Amim*. Jerusalem: Devar Yerushalayim, 1983.

Scimecca, Joseph A. "Self-Reflexivity and Freedom." In *Conflict: Human Needs Theory*, edited by John Burton, 205–18. New York: St. Martin's Press, 1990.

Searle, John R. *Speech Acts: An Essay in the Philosophy of Language*. Cambridge: Cambridge University Press, 1969.

Seder Eliyahu Rabah ve-Seder Eliyahu Zuta. Edited by Meir Ish Shalom [Friedmann]. Vienna: Aḥiasaf, 1902.

Sefer Erekh Apayim, Otsar ha-Savlanut. Jerusalem: Ḥaside Breslev, 1990.

Sefer ha-Mafte'aḥ. In Maimonides, *Mishneh Torah*. Frankel ed. Jerusalem: Hotsa'at Shabse Frankel, 2001.

Sefer ha-Mafteaḥ le-Masekhet Bava Kama, Sefer Shinuye Nusḥa'ot. Bnei Brak: Yeshivat Ohel Yosef, 1996.

Segal, Dan. "*Emunah u-Vitaḥon: Ha-Derekh la-Avor et ha-Ḥayim.*" *Bet Va'ad: Siḥot u-Ma'amre Musar* 3 (Sivan 5759–Iyar 5760 [1999–2000]): 93–104.

Segal, Yehudah Zeraḥyah, "*Yaḥas Torani le-Foshe Yisrael.*" *Shanah be-Shanah* (5754 [1994]): 198–205.

[Seḥayek, Moshe]. *Mi-Zekenim Etbonen*. Vol. 1. 2nd ed. Bnei Brak: Mishpaḥat Seḥayek, 2012.

Sende, Ken. *The Peacemaker: A Biblical Guide to Resolving Personal Conflict*. Grand Rapids, MI: Baker Books, 2004.

Seybold, Kevin S., Peter C. Hill, Joseph K. Neumann, and David S. Chi. "Physiological and Psychological Correlates of Forgiveness." *Journal of Psychology and Christianity* 20, no. 3 (2001): 250–59.

Sforno, Obadiah. *Bet Avot*. Tel Aviv: Nehdar, 1966.

Sha'are Teshuvah: 353 Teshuvot ha-Ge'onim. Leipzig: Leopold Shenois, 1858.

Shabbetai ben Meir ha-Kohen. *Sifte Kohen*. In the standard printed edition of the *Shulḥan Arukh*.

Shailat, Isaac, trans. *Masekhet Avot im Perush Rabenu Mosheh ben Maimon*. Jerusalem: Ma'aliyot, 1994.

Shalom of Neustadt. *Hilkhot u-Minhage Rabenu Shalom mi-Noishtat.* Jerusalem: Mekhon Yerushalayim, 1997.

Shapira, Abraham. Letter to Moshe Harari, 25 Av 5754 (1994). In *Mikra'e Kodesh: Hilkhot Yom ha-Kipurim,* by Moshe Harari, 330–33. Jerusalem: Yeshivat Merkaz ha-Rav, n.d.

Shapira, Elijah. *Eliyah Rabah.* Jerusalem: Mekor ha-Sefarim, 1999.

Shapira, Judah Loeb. *Rekhasim le-Vikah.* In *Moda le-Vinah.* Brooklyn, NY: Moshe Stern, n.d.

Shapira, Moshe Shmuel. "*Ba-Inyan Tokhaḥah.*" *Yeshurun* 18 ([Kislev] 5767 [2006]): 403.

Shapira, Shalom Tsevi. *Meshiv Nefesh: Al ha-Rambam, Hilkhot Teshuvah.* Bnei Brak: n.p., n.d.

Sharan, Shlomo. "Differentiating Methods of Cooperative Learning in Research and Practice." *Asia Pacific Journal of Education* 22, no.1 (2002): 106–16.

Sharkey, William. "Bibliography of Embarrassment Research." Accessed November 11, 2016. www2.hawaii.edu/~sharkey/embarrassment/embarrassment_references.html.

Sharvit, Shimon. *Leshonah ve-Signonah shel Masekhet Avot le-Doroteha.* Be'er-Sheva: Ben-Gurion University of the Negev Press, 2006.

———. *Masekhet Avot le-Doroteha.* Jerusalem: Mosad Bialik, 2004.

Shaviv, Yehuda. *Yodukha Aḥikha.* Alon Shvut: Yeshivat Har Etzion, 2004.

Shealy, Craig N. "The Visions and Values of Conflict Resolution Education: Frontline Achievements and Real-World Aspirations." *Beliefs and Values* 2, no. 2 (2010): 104–10. doi: 10.1891/1942-0617.2.2.104.

Sheinberger, Tsevi Hirsch. "*Perut ha-Ḥet be-Vakashat Meḥilah.*" *Kovets Bet Aharon ve-Yisrael* 18, no. 1 (103) (Tishre-Ḥeshvan 5763 [2002]): 82–86.

Shelomoh Yitsḥak ha-Levi ha-Sefaradi. *Lev Avot.* Salonika: n.p., 1565.

Sherira ben Ḥanina Gaon. Quoted in [Joseph Bonfils ?], *Teshuvot Ge'onim Kadmonim* (Tel Aviv: n.p., 1964), responsum 100.

Shilo, Shmuel, and Menachem Elon. "*Ona'ah,*" in *Encyclopaedia Judaica,* 2nd ed., 423–26.

Shinuye Nusḥa'ot. In the standard "*Yakhin u-Voaz*" [Vilna edition] *Mishnayot.*

Shlozover, Avraham. *Be'er Yehudah.* Brooklyn, NY: Aḥim Goldenberg, 1991.

Shmerler, Ḥayim. *Moade Ḥayim.* Jerusalem: Mekhon Arba, 2002.

Shmuelevitz, Ḥayim Leib. *Siḥot Musar.* Jerusalem: n.p., 1980.

Shneur Zalman of Lyady. *Igrot Kodesh: Admur ha-Zaken, Admur ha-Emtsa'i, Admur ha-Tsemaḥ Tsedek*. Brooklyn, NY: Kehot, 1980.

———. *Likute Amarim: Tanya*. London: Kehot, 1998.

———. *Shulḥan Arukh ha-Rav*. Brooklyn, NY: Kehot, 1968.

Shonholtz, Raymond. "The Promise of Conflict Resolution as a Social Movement." *The Journal of Contemporary Legal Issues* 3 (1989–1990): 59–74.

Shperber, David. *Metsudat David: Al Shishah Sidre Mishnah*. Jerusalem: n.p., 2004.

Shternbukh, Moshe. *Ha-Derekh li-Teshuvah*. 2nd ed. N.p.: Agudat Netivot ha-Torah veha-Ḥesed, n.d.

———. *Mo'adim u-Zemanim ha-Shalem*. 9 vols. Jerusalem: n.p., n.d.

———. *Teshuvot ve-Hanhagot*. vol. 1. Jerusalem: Netivot ha-Torah veha-Ḥesed, 1986.

Shulevits, Eliezer. *Or Eliezer*. Vol. 2. Petaḥ Tikvah: Yeshivat Lomza, n.d.

Siegman, Aron Wolfe, Robert A. Anderson, and Tal Berger. "The Angry Voice: Its Effects on the Experience of Anger and Cardiovascular Reactivity." *Psychosomatic Medicine* 52, no. 6 (1990): 631–43.

Siegman, Aron Wolfe, and Selena Cappell Snow. "The Outward Expression of Anger, the Inward Experience of Anger and CVR: The Role of Vocal Expression." *Journal of Behavioral Medicine* 20, no. 1 (1997): 29–45.

Sifra de-Ve Rav: Hu Sefer Torat ha-Kohanim. Edited by Isaac Hirsch Weiss. Vienna: Ya'akov ha-Kohen Shlosberg, 1862.

Sifre al Sefer Devarim. Edited by Louis Finkelstein. Berlin: Ha-Agudah ha-Tarbutit ha-Yehudim be-Germanyah, 1940.

Sifre de-Ve Rav: Maḥberet Rishonah … al Sefer ba-Midbar. Edited by Saul Horovitz. Leipzig: n.p., 1917.

Sillars, Alan L. "Attributions and Interpersonal Conflict Resolution." In *New Directions in Attribution Research*. Vol. 3, edited by John H. Harvey, William Ickes, and Robert F. Kidd, 279–305. Hillsdale, NJ: Lawrence Erlbaum Associates, 1981.

Silver, Yitsḥak Isaac. *The Code of Jewish Conduct: The Laws of Interpersonal Relationships*. Jerusalem: Center for Jewish Values, 2008.

———. *Mishpete ha-Shalom: Hilkhot ben Adam la-Ḥavero*. Jerusalem: n.p., 2005.

Sirkes, Joel. *Bayit Ḥadash*. In the standard printed edition of Jacob ben Asher's *Arba'ah Turim*.

Slavin, Robert E. *Cooperative Learning: Theory, Research, and Practice*. Englewood Cliffs, NJ: Prentice-Hall, 1990.

Smith, Karl A., David W. Johnson, and Roger T. Johnson. "Can Conflict Be Constructive? Controversy versus Concurrence Seeking in Learning Groups." *Journal of Educational Psychology* 73, no. 5 (1981): 651–63.

Smith, Nick. *I Was Wrong: The Meanings of Apologies*. Cambridge: Cambridge University Press, 2008.

Smith, Richard H. and David Ryan Schurtz. "Resentment." In *Encyclopedia of the Mind*. Vol. 17, edited by Harold Pashler, 658–60. Thousand Oaks, CA: Sage Publications, 2013.

Sofer, Moses. *Ha-Ḥatam Sofer al Masekhet Avot*. N.p., n.d.

———. *Ḥatam Sofer: Derashot*. Vol. 1. New York: The Rabbi Joseph Nehemiah Institute, 1961.

———. *Ḥatam Sofer he-Ḥadash al ha-Torah*. Jerusalem: Mekhon Da'at Sofer, 2000.

Sofer, Shemuel Binyamin. *Divre Sofrim: Kelalim be-Mevo ha-Talmud*. Vol. 1. Jerusalem: Hotsa'at Divre Sofrim, 1956.

Sofer, Ya'akov Ḥayim. *Menuḥat Shalom*. Vol. 9. Jerusalem: n.p., 2002.

Sofer, Ya'akov Shalom. *Sefer Yeshovev Sofer*. Jerusalem: David Sofer, 1976.

Sokoloff, Michael. *A Dictionary of Jewish Babylonian Aramaic of the Talmudic and Geonic Periods*. Ramat Gan, Israel: Bar Ilan University Press, 2002.

Sol and Evelyn Henkind Talmud Text Databank. Accessed September 27, 2016. http://www.lieberman-institute.com/.

Solomon ben Adret. *She'elot u-Teshuvot ha-Rashba*. 8 vols. Jerusalem: Mekhon Or ha-Mizraḥ, Mekhon Yerushalayim, 1997–2001.

Soloveichik, Ahron. *Logic of the Heart, Logic of the Mind*. [Jerusalem]: Genesis Jerusalem Press, 1991.

———. *Paraḥ Mateh Aharon*. Jerusalem: Hotsa'at Targum, 1997.

———. *"Sovlanut ba-Halakhah." Torah shebe-al Peh* 40 (1999): 60–64.

Soloveichik, Ḥayyim. Quoted in Ahron Soloveichik, *Paraḥ Mateh Aharon* (Jerusalem: Hotsa'at Targum, 1997), 189.

Soloveitchik, Joseph B. *The Halakhic Mind: An Essay on Jewish Tradition and Modern Thought*. New York: Seth Press, 1986.

———. "*Kol Dodi Dofek: Listen—My Beloved Knocks.*" Translated by David Z. Gordon. Edited by Jeffrey R. Woolf, 9–55. [New York]: Yeshiva University, 2006.

———. "Korach Rebellion Part 2." Accessed November 11, 2016. http://www.yutorah.org/lectures/lecture.cfm/767863/Rabbi_Joseph_B_Soloveitchik/_Korach_Rebellion_Part _2_#.

———. *Soloveitchik on Repentance: The Thought and Oral Discourses of Rabbi Joseph B. Soloveitchik*. Translated by Pinchas H. Peli. New York: Paulist Press, 1984.

Soloveitchik, Joseph Dov. "*Kol Dodi Dofek.*" In *Divre Hagut ve-Ha'arakhah*. Jerusalem: Ha-Histadrut ha-Tsiyonit ha-Olamit, 1983.

———. "*Mi-Pi ha-Shemu'ah mi-Maran ha-GRY"D Solovets'ik.*" *Mesorah* 2 (Tishre 5750 [1989]): 3–59.

———. *Nora'ot ha-Rav*. Vol. 13. Lectures transcribed by B. David Schreiber. New York: n.p., 2000.

———. *Sefer Harare Kedem*. Lectures summarized by Michal Zalman Shurkin. Jerusalem: n.p., 2000.

———. *Shiure ha-Rav ha-Ga'on Rabi Yosef Dov Solovets'ik, zatsal: Al Pesaḥim, R.H., Yo. ha-Kip., u-Megilah: Mi-Pi ha-Shemu'ah*. Lectures summarized by Hershel Schachter. Jerusalem: n.p., 2002.

———. *Yeme Zikaron*. Jerusalem: Sifriyat Aliner, 1986.

———. Quoted in Hershel Schachter, *Nefesh ha-Rav* (Jerusalem: Reshit Yerushalayim, 1995), 59–71.

Sperber, Daniel. Introduction to *Perek ha-Shalom*. In *Masekhet Derekh Erets Zuta u-Ferek ha-Shalom*, 185–89. Jerusalem: Tsur-Ot, 1994.

Stanovich, Keith E., and Richard F. West. "Individual Differences in Reasoning: Implications for the Rationality Debate." *Behavioral and Brain Sciences* 23, no. 5 (2000): 645–65.

Steif, Jonathan. *Mitsvot Hashem*. Vol. 2. N.p., n.d.

Steinberg, Gerald. "Jewish Sources on Conflict Management: Realism and Human Nature." In *Conflict and Conflict Management in Jewish Sources*, edited by Michal Rones, 10–23. Ramat Gan, Israel: Program on Conflict Management and Negotiation, Bar-Ilan University, 2008.

[Steinman, Aharon Yehudah Leib]. *Yemale Pi Tehilatekha: Iyunim ba-Tefilah.* Bnei Brak: n.p., 2012.

Steinman, Aharon Yehudah Leib. Quoted in Hillel Cooperman, *Megilat Ester: Im Perush "Haleli Nafshi,"* 2nd ed. (n.p., 2011), 36–37 n. 41.

Steinsaltz, Adin. *Talmud Bavli im Kol ha-Mefarshim al ha-Daf im Hosafot Ḥadashot.* Jerusalem: Ha-Mekhon ha-Yisraeli le-Firsumim Talmudiyim, 1998.

Stephens, John B. "'Gender Conflict': Connecting Feminist Theory and Conflict Resolution Theory and Practice." In *Conflict and Gender,* edited by A. Taylor and J. Beinstein Miller, 217–35. Cresskill, NJ: Hampton Press, 1994.

Strack, H. L., and Gunter Stemberger. *Introduction to the Talmud and Midrash.* Translated and edited by Markus Bockmuehl. Minneapolis, MN: Fortress Press, 1996.

Strashun, Samuel. *Ḥidushe ha-Rashash.* In the standard Vilna edition of the *Midrash Rabbah.*

Stuckless, Noreen and Richard Goranson. "A Selected Bibliography of Literature on Revenge." *Psychological Reports* 75, no. 2 (1994): 803–11.

Substance Abuse and Mental Health Services Administration's National Registry of Evidence-Based Programs and Practices. Accessed October 6, 2016. http://legacy.nreppadmin.net/ViewIntervention.aspx?id=64.

Tafrate, Raymond Chip. "Evaluation of Treatment Strategies for Adult Anger Disorders." In *Anger Disorders: Definition, Diagnosis, and Treatment,* edited by Howard Kassinove, 109–29. Washington, DC: Taylor & Francis, 1995.

Taklitor ha-Torani (*The Torah CD-ROM Library*). Jerusalem: Disc Book Systems Ltd, 1999. CD-ROM, ver. 7.5.

Tana de-Ve Eliyahu Raba ve-Zuta: Im Perush . . . Mishpat u-Tsedakah. Jerusalem: n.p., 1959.

Tana de-Ve Eliyahu: Seder Eliyahu Raba ve-Seder Eliyahu Zuta. Jerusalem: Eshkol, 1991.

[*Tanna de-Ve Eliyahu*] *Seder Eliyahu Raba ve-Seder Eliyahu Zuta.* Edited by Meir Ish Shalom [Friedmann]. Vienna: Aḥiasaf, 1902.

Tarika, Jedidiah Samuel. *Sefer Ben Yedid.* Solonika: Sa'adi Ishkenazi [sic], 1806.

Tavuchis, Nicholas. *Mea Culpa: A Sociology of Apology and Reconciliation.* Stanford, CA: Stanford University Press, 1991.

Teharani, Eliyahu Porat. *Alufenu Mesubalim.* Bnei Brak: Or Elḥanan, 1978.

Telch, Michael J., Adam R. Cobb, and Cynthia L. Lancaster. "Exposure Therapy." In *The Wiley Handbook of Anxiety Disorders,* edited by Paul Emmelkamp and Thomas Ehring, 717–56. West Sussex, UK: Wiley Blackwell, 2014.

Teomim, Joseph. *Peri Megadim.* In the standard printed edition of the *Shulḥan Arukh.*

———. *Sefer Matan Sekharan shel Mitsvot.* In *Sifre Ba'al Peri Megadim.* N.p., n.d.

Theodor, J. and Chanoch Albeck. *Midrash Bereshit Raba u-Ferush Minḥat Yehudah.* Vol. 1. Jerusalem: Wahrmann Books, 1965.

Thomas, Kenneth. "Conflict and Conflict Management." In *Handbook of Industrial and Organizational Psychology,* edited by Marvin D. Dennette, 889–935. New York: John Wiley & Sons, 1983.

Thomas, Kenneth W., and Ralph H. Kilmann. *Thomas-Kilmann Conflict Mode Instrument.* Mountain View, CA: CPP, 2007.

Thomas, Kenneth W., and Louis R. Pondy. "Toward an 'Intent' Model of Conflict Management Among Principal Parties." *Human Relations* 30, no. 12 (1977): 1089–102.

Thompson, Leigh, Janice Nadler, and Robert B. Lount Jr. "Judgmental Biases in Conflict Resolution and How to Overcome Them." In *The Handbook of Conflict Resolution: Theory and Practice,* 2nd ed., edited by Morton Deutsch, Peter T. Coleman, and Eric C. Marcus, 243–67. San Francisco, CA: John Wiley and Sons, 2006.

Tidwell, Alan C. *Conflict Resolved: A Critical Assessment of Conflict Resolution.* New York: Pinter, 1999.

Tomasi, Luigi. "Values." In *Encyclopedia of Religion and Society,* edited by William H. Swatos, 537–39. Walnut Creek, CA: AltaMira Press, 1998.

Torczyner, Harry [Naphtali H. Tur-Sinai]. *Die Entstehung des Semitischen Sprachtypus ein Beitrag zum Problem der Entstehung der Sprache.* Wein: R. Löwit, 1916.

Tosefta. Edited by M. S. Zuckermandel. Jerusalem: Wahrmann, 1975.

Tosefta. 5 vols. Edited by Saul Lieberman. New York: Bet ha-Midrash le-Rabanim sheba-Amerikah, 1993–2007.

Toviyahu ben Eliezer. *Midrash Lekaḥ Tov*. Vol. 2. Jerusalem: n.p., 1960.

Tovolski, Avraham. *Haser Ka'as Mi-Libkha*. Bnei Brak: A. Tovolski, 1978.

Trager, Yitsḥak, and Aharon Auerbach. *Orḥot Halakhah*. In *Halikhot Shelomoh*, by Shlomo Zalman Auerbach. Vol. 2. Tel Aviv: Yeshivat Halikhot Shelomoh, 2003.

Trani, Joseph ben Moses. *She'elot u-Teshuvot Maharit*. Vol. 2. Tel Aviv: Sifriyati, 1959.

Trani, Moses ben Joseph. *Igeret Derekh Hashem*. Venice: n.p., 1553.

———. *Kiryat Sefer*. 2 vols. Jerusalem: Hotsa'at Yerid ha-Sefarim, 2002.

———. *She'elot u-Teshuvot Rabenu Moshe bar Yosef mi-Trani*. Jerusalem: Yad ha-Rav Nissim, 1990.

"TRANSCEND International's Statement Concerning the Label of Anti-Semitism against Johan Galtung." Accessed March 3, 2013. https://www.transcend.org/galtung/statement-may-2012.

Treves, Menaḥem. *Oraḥ Mesharim: Shulḥan Arukh le-Midot*. Jerusalem: Meir Kleiman, 1969.

Tsang, Jo-Ann, Michael E. McCullough, and Frank D. Fincham. "The Longitudinal Association between Forgiveness and Relationship Closeness and Commitment." *Journal of Social and Clinical Psychology* 25, no. 4 (2006): 448–72.

Tsuriel, Moshe. "*Ahavah Universalit—Yaḥas Ḥiyuvi le-Umot ha-Olam*." Accessed November 11, 2016. http://www.yeshiva.org.il/midrash/shiur.asp?id=4453.

———. *Otsrot ha-Musar*. Vol.1. Jerusalem: Yerid ha-Sefarim, 2002.

Twersky, Isadore. *Introduction to the Code of Maimonides* (*Mishneh Torah*). New Haven, CT: Yale University Press, 1980.

Uceda, Samuel. *Midrash Shemuel*. Jerusalem: Mekhon ha-Ketav, 1989.

Ulman, Shlomo Zalman. Quoted in Tzevi Yavrov, *Ma'aseh Ish*, vol. 1 (Bnei Brak: n.p., 1999), 161.

Van den Born, Adrianus. *Encyclopedic Dictionary of the Bible*. Translated by Louis F. Hartman. New York: McGraw-Hill, 1963.

Van Kleef, Gerben A. "Don't Worry, Be Angry? Effects of Anger on Feelings, Thoughts, and Actions in Conflict and Negotiation." In *International Handbook of Anger: Constituent and Concomitant Biological, Psychological, and Social Processes*, edited by Michael Potegal,

Gerhard Stemmler, and Charles Spielberger, 545–59. New York: Springer, 2010. doi: 10.1007/978-0-387-89676-2_3.

Vanunu, Shimon. *Sefer ve-Ahavta le-Re'akha kamokha*. Jerusalem: Shimon Ḥen and Mordekhai Ḥen, n.d.

Vidal Yom Tov of Tolosa. *Magid Mishneh*. In *Mishneh Torah*. Jerusalem: Shabse Frankel, 2002.

Vinman, Yisrael. *Mishnat Yisrael: Be-Mitsvot she-ben Adam la-Ḥavero u-Shemirat ha-Lashon*. Jerusalem: n.p., 2009.

Vital, Ḥayyim. *Sefer Sha'are Kedushah*. Jozefow, Poland: S. Y. Vaks, 1842.

———. *Sha'ar ha-Yiḥudim*. Jerusalem: Mekor Ḥayim, 1970.

———. *Sha'are Kedushah*. Jerusalem: R. Fisher, 1967.

Vital, Ḥayyim, and Jacob ben Ḥayyim Zemaḥ. *Nagid u-Metsaveh*. Jerusalem: n.p., 1965.

Vozner, Shemuel. *Shevet ha-Levi*. 3rd ed. 10 vols. N.p., 2002.

Wade, Nathaniel G., William T. Hoyt, Julia E. M. Kidwell, and Everett L. Worthington Jr. "Efficacy of Psychotherapeutic Interventions to Promote Forgiveness: A Meta-analysis." *Journal of Consulting and Clinical Psychology* 82, no. 1 (2014): 154–70.

Wade, Nathaniel G., and Everett L. Worthington Jr. "In Search of a Common Core: A Content Analysis of Interventions to Promote Forgiveness." *Psychotherapy: Theory, Research, Practice, Training* 42, no. 2 (2005): 160–77.

Wald, Marcus. *Shalom: Jewish Teaching on Peace*. New York: Bloch Publishing Company, 1944.

Wald, Stephen G. "Hillel." In *Encyclopaedia Judaica*. 2nd ed., 108–10.

Waldman, Shimon Moshe. *Sefer Naḥalat Shimon: Al Dine Ḥodesh Elul ve-Rosh ha-Shanah, Aseret Yeme Teshuvah ve-Yom Kipur*. Monroe, NY: n.p., 2009.

Walker, Donald F., and Richard L. Gorsuch. "Dimensions Underlying Sixteen Models of Forgiveness and Reconciliation." *Journal of Psychology and Theology* 32, no. 1 (2004): 12–25.

Walkin, Aharon. *Metsaḥ Aharon*. Jerusalem: n.p., 1971.

Wallach, Shlomo Moshe. "*Me-Va'er de-Yesh Shene Dinim ba-Ḥiyuv le-Fayes et Ḥavero ba-Erev Yom ha-Kipurim*." *Reshimot meha-Va'ad* 12 (Shevat 5766 [2006]): 92–94.

Ware, Stephen J. *Alternative Dispute Resolution*. St. Paul, MN: West Group, 2001.

Wasserman, Eleazar Simḥah. *Be'ure Rabi Elḥanan al ha-Torah: Kovets Parshiyot*. Jerusalem: Yeshivat Or Elḥanan, 2012.

Wasserman, Elḥanan Bunim. *Sefer Kovets He'arot le-Masekhet Yevamot*. N.p., n.d.

Weary, Gifford, John A. Edwards, and Shannon Riley. "Attribution." In *Encyclopedia of Human Behavior*, 291–99. San Diego, CA: Academic Press, 1994.

Weil, Jacob. *She'elot u-Teshuvot Rabenu Ya'akov Vail*. Annotated by Yonatan Shraga Domb. Vol. 1. Jerusalem: Mekhon Yerushalayim, 2001.

Weinberger, Zvi H., and Baruch A. Heifetz. *Sefer Limud le-Hilkhot ben Adam la-Ḥavero: Lo Tikom ve-Lo Titor*. Safed, Israel: Makhon Torat ha-Adam le-Adam, 2003.

———. *Sefer Limud le-Hilkhot ben Adam la-Ḥavero: Lo Tisna et Aḥikha be-Lvavekha*. Safed, Israel: Makhon Torat ha-Adam le-Adam, 1995.

[Weinberger, Zvi H. and Baruch A. Heifetz]. "*Yom Yom*." *Torat ha-Adam le-Adam: Kovets Torani ba-Mitsvot she-ben Adam la-Ḥavero* 2 (1998): 136–40.

Weiner, Bernard. "An Attributional Theory of Achievement Motivation and Emotion." *Psychological Review* 92, no. 4 (1985): 548–73.

Weinfeld, Abraham. "*Mitsvat Ahavat ha-Ger le-Da'at ha-Rambam*." *Torat ha-Adam le-Adam: Kovets Torani ba-Mitsvot she-ben Adam la-Ḥavero* 5 (2004): 139–41.

Weinreich, Uriel. *Modern English-Yiddish, Yiddish-English Dictionary*. New York: YIVO Institute for Jewish Research, 1968.

Weinthal, Benjamin. "Swiss Group Suspends 'Anti-Semitic' Norway Scholar." *Jerusalem Post*, August 9, 2012. Accessed September 27, 2016. http://www.jpost.com/International/Article.aspx?id=280726.

Weiss, Asher. *Minḥat Asher: Leket Shiurim ve-Siḥot al Sefer Va-Yikra*. Jerusalem: Mekhon Minḥat Asher, 2003.

Weiss, Isaac Jacob. *Minḥat Yitsḥak*. 10 vols. Jerusalem: Hotsa'at Sefarim Minḥat Yitsḥak, 1989–.

[Wessely, Naphtali Herz]. *Netivot ha-Shalom: Va-Yikra*. Vienna: Adalbert Della Tore, 1861.

Wessely, Naphtali Herz. *Yen Levanon*. Warsaw: Yitsḥak Goldman, 1884.

Wispé, Lauren. "History of the Concept of Empathy." In *Empathy and Its Development*, edited by Nancy Eisenberg and Janet Strayer, 17–37. Cambridge: Cambridge University Press, 1990.

Witvliet, Charlotte van Oyen, Thomas E. Ludwig, and Kelly L. Vander Laan. "Granting Forgiveness or Harboring Grudges: Implications for Emotion, Physiology, and Health." *Psychological Science* 12, no. 2 (2001): 117–23.

[Wolbe, Shlomo]. *Ale Shur*. Vol. 2. Jerusalem: Bet ha-Musar a"sh. R' Ḥ. M. Lehman, 1986.

[Wolfsohn], Yehoshua Falik Ze'ev. *Sefer ha-Midot*. Munkacs: Kahn and Fried, 1906.

Wolpe, Joseph. *The Practice of Behavior Therapy*. 4th ed. New York: Pergamon Press, 1990.

———. *Psychotherapy by Reciprocal Inhibition*. Stanford, CA: Stanford University Press, 1958.

Worthington, Everett L., Jr. *Five Steps to Forgiveness: The Art and Science of Forgiving*. New York: Crown, 2001.

———. *Forgiveness and Reconciliation: Theory and Application*. New York: Routledge, 2006.

———. "Forgiveness Intervention Manuals." Accessed September 27, 2016. http://www.people.vcu.edu/~eworth/.

Worthington, Everett L., Jr., Nathaniel G. Wade, and William T. Hoyt, "Positive Psychological Interventions for Promoting Forgiveness: History, Present Status, and Future Prospects." In *The Wiley Blackwell Handbook of Positive Psychological Interventions*, edited by Acacia C. Parks and Stephen M. Schueller, 20–41. Chichester, West Sussex: Wiley Blackwell, 2014.

Wurzburger, Walter S. "Darkhei Shalom." *Gesher* 6 (1977–1978): 80–86.

———. *Ethics of Responsibility: Pluralistic Approaches to Covenantal Ethics*. Philadelphia: The Jewish Publication Society, 1994.

Yehuda, Zvi A. "*Leumiyut ve-Enoshiyut be-Diyune Ḥakhme Yisrael*." *Ha-Doar* 80, no. 11 (May 4, 2001): 7–9.

Yehudah ben Eliezer. *Rabotenu Ba'ale ha-Tosafot al Ḥamishah Ḥumshe Torah*. Bnei Brak: Ha-Makhon le-Hafatsat Perushe Ba'ale ha-Tosafot al ha-Torah, n.d.

Yellin, Aryeh Loeb. *Yefeh Enayim*. In the standard Vilna edition of the Babylonian Talmud.

Yosef, Ovadia. *Ḥazon Ovadyah: Yamim Noraim*. Jerusalem: n.p., 2005.

———. *Sefer She'elot u-Teshuvot Yeḥaveh Da'at*. Vol. 5. Jerusalem: n.p., 1977.

Zacuto, Abraham. *Sefer Yuḥasin ha-Shalem*. Jerusalem: n.p., 1963.

Zacuto, Moses. *Sefer Kol ha-Remez*. Moshav Bitḥah, Israel: Mekhon Kol Bitḥah, 1999.

Zaichyk, Ḥayim Ephraim. *Va-Ani Tefilah*. Vol. 4. Bnei Brak: Lipa Friedman, 1974.

Zaks, Hillel. *"Ba-Mitsvat be-Tsedek Tishpot ba-Isur Lashon ha-Ra." Marpe Lashon* 3 (1984): 7–9.

———. *"Lashon ha-Ra u-Rekhilut ve-Lav shebe-Khlalot." Kol ha-Torah* 54 (Tishre 5764 [2003]): 58–61.

Zalb, Zvi Chaim. *Gematria ve-Notarikon*. Jerusalem: n.p., 1955.

Zer-Kavod, Mordechai. *Sefer Mishle*. Jerusalem: Mossad Harav Kook, 1992.

Zilber, Binyamin Yehoshua. *Az Nidberu*. 14 vols. Bnei Brak: n.p., 1969–1987.

———. *Derekh Teshuvah*. Jerusalem: n.p., 2009.

[Zilber, Binyamin Yehoshua]. *Sha'are Teshuvah im Beur Zeh ha-Sha'ar*. Bnei Brak: Hotsa'at Ḥokhmah u-Musar, 1977.

[Zilberberg, Tzvi Meir]. *Siḥot Hitḥazkut: She-Ne'emru be-Vet ha-Midrash Naḥalat Ya'akov: Be-Inyene Diyun le-Khaf Zekhut*. Jerusalem: Ḥaverim Makshivim, 2006.

Zilberstein, Yitsḥak. *Ḥashuke Ḥemed: Al Masekhet Avodah Zarah*. N.p., 2009.

———. *Ḥashuke Ḥemed: Al Masekhet Berakhot*. N.p., 2005.

Zillman, Dolf. "Mental Control of Angry Aggression." In *The Handbook of Mental Control*, edited by Daniel M. Wegner and James W. Pennebaker, 370–92. Englewood Cliffs, NJ: Prentice Hall, 1993.

Zinner, Gavriel. *Sefer Nit'e Gavriel: Hilkhot Yom ha-Kipurim*. Jerusalem: n.p., 2001.

Ziv [Broida], Simḥah Zissel. *Bet Kelm*. Vol. 2. Bnei Brak: Sifte Ḥakhamim, 2010.

———. *Ḥokhmah u-Musar*. Vol. 1. New York: n.p., 1957.

Ziwica, Shlomo. *"Talmide Ḥakhamim."* In *Kehilat Vengrov: Sefer Zikaron*, 102. Tel Aviv: Hotsa'at Yotse Vengrov, 1961.

Index

Note. Page numbers followed by "n" denote notes.

A

Aaron ben Jacob of Lunel, 342n139
Aaron ben Meshullam of Lunel, 60n107
Abaye Kashisha, 62
Abba Shaul, Ben Zion, 354n186
Aboab, Isaac, 315n50
Abraham ben David of Posquières (*Rabad* III), 81n18, 124–126, 125n44, 167, 278n39
Abraham ben Isaac of Narbonne, 311, 312n41
Abraham ben Moses ben Maimon, 286, 286n68, 408n2
Abrahams, Israel, 115n16
Abramson, Shraga, 124n39, 125n44
Abravanel, Isaac, 42, 42n17, 42n19, 88n34, 228
Abulafia, Meir, 148n115
Abu-Nimer, Mohammed, xxiin6
active listening, 21
adjudication, definition, 8, 8n16.
affective component of conflict resolution, xxxiii, 31
  basic definition, xxiv
Agarie, Nariyuki, 377, 378, 380n237, 401n264
Aggestam, Karin, xxin5
Aḥa of Shabḥa, 63, 136, 136n77
ahavat ha-beriyot, love for all humanity, 121–134, 171n193
  Abraham Isaac Kook on, 122–123
  its interrelationship with *ahavat Yisrael,* love for one's fellow Jew, 123, 123n38
  sources for the concept
    "And you shall walk in His ways," 130–131
    Ben Azzai's teaching, 124–129
    human beings are created in the image of God, 129–130
    universal common ancestry of humankind (brotherhood of humanity), 126–127, 129
    "You shall love the Lord your God," 130
    "You shall love your neighbor as yourself," 131–132, 430
  as understood by Phinehas Elijah Hurwitz, 131–132, 430n99
Akiva, R., 111, 124, 129, 318
Akra, Abraham ben Solomon, 89, 89n40
Alashkar, Joseph, 82n19, 91–92nn45–46
Alashkar, Moses, 96n60
Albeck, Chanoch, 124n39
Albeck, Shalom, 312n41
Albo, Joseph, 42, 43n20, 118n22, 122n35, 318n61
Alexander Susskind ben Moses, 119n26
Alfasi, Isaac, 47n45, 55n78, 143n102, 318, 329, 334
Algazi, Solomon Nissim, 89n40
Alicke, Mark D., 216n76
Allen, Rhianon, 118n23
Allred, Keith G., 25n61, 215n73, 216n76, 217n78
Almosnino, Moses, 91n43, 96n61, 207n51
Alshekh, Moses, 233n34

Alter, Judah Aryeh Leib, 208n59, 310n32, 324, 328n91
alternative dispute resolution (ADR), 3–4, 6–9, 403
  arbitration, 3, 6, 8–9
  basic definition, 8
  hybrid processes, 9n17
  mediation, 8
  negotiation, 6–7
Altschuler, Jehiel Hillel, 237n48, 336n120
Ammirati, Rachel, 215–216nn74–75, 219n84, 222n89
Amsterdam, Naftali, 321–322
analytic-comparative framework, interpersonal conflict resolution five basic components, 30–34
Anav, Jehiel ben Jekuthiel, 50n59, 254n84
"And he shall not be as Korah and his assembly." *See* holding on to a quarrel, prohibition of
Andreychik, Michael R., 212n66
"And you shall walk in His ways." *See ve-halakhta bi-drakhav*
anger
  control (*see* anger management)
  how it affects conflict, 24, 408
  natural emotion, 414–415
  rabbinic attitudes towards, 408–409, 414
  triggers, 24, 436, 440
anger management, xxiv, xxxiii, 18, 24–25, 31
  comparative historical studies of, 446–447
  contemporary approaches to, 24–25, 434–446
    Deffenbacher's summary of anger interventions, 440–445
    Kassinove and Tafrate's *Anger Management*, 445–446
    Novaco's *Anger Control*, 434–440
    similarities and differences between contemporary and Jewish approaches, 447–449
  definition, *APA Dictionary of Psychology*, 434n105
  traditional Jewish approaches to (*see Ma'aneh Rakh; Orekh Apayim*)
  what contemporary conflict resolution has adopted, 449–450
apologies
  in contemporary conflict resolution, 401–404
  contemporary theories and research on, 364–378
  core elements according to Lazare, 368–370
  Cross-Cultural Speech Act Realization Patterns (CCSARP) project's research on, 365–367
  dictionary definition of, 364
  Kirchhoff, Strack, and Jäger's literature review on, 365, 373–375
  list of elements that may influence whether effective or ineffective, 376n226
  research on elements that contribute to effective apologies, 375–378
  similarities and differences between contemporary approaches to apologies and the Jewish obligations of the one who asks for forgiveness, 379–383
  Smith's "categorical apology," 370–373
  traditional Jewish approaches to, (*see under meḥilah,* "forgiveness," obligations of the one who asks for forgiveness)
appeasement
  the English word appease, 330n99
Appleby, R. Scott, xxiin6
Arama, Isaac, 39–42, 42n17, 66n125, 71
Ardit, Ephraim, 230n20
Ariav, David, 121n31, 158n154, 160, 164n176, 166, 166n187, 199nn32–33, 201n36, 203n40, 205n48, 206n50, 208n57, 234, 235n37, 248n75, 344n146, 352n181, 353n182, 354n186, 359n196, 363n199
Arieli, Yitsḥak, 148n114
Aristotle, 428n88
Arriaga, Ximena B., 217n78

Asher ben Jehiel (*Rosh*), 139n87, 143n102, 150n124, 153, 305, 311, 318, 318n63
Ashkenazi, Bezalel, 159n157, 301n4
Ashkenazi, Samuel Jaffe, 312–314, 339n130
Astruc, Solomon, 233n34
Aszod, Judah, 146n108
Attar, Ḥayyim ben Moses, 141, 228
Attia, Isaac, 278n41
Auerbach, Aharon, 321n72
Auerbach, Shlomo Zalman, 199n33, 205n47, 322
Aviad, Yisrael Menaḥem, 343n143
Aviner, Shlomo, 130n58, 335n117
Avot. See Mishnah, *Avot*
Avraham, Michael, 106n83
Azikri, Eleazar, 52, 53n69, 53n70, 118–119, 134, 141, 205–206, 229n16, 230n21, 245n67, 248, 288, 288n78, 408, 415n27, 431
Azulai, Abraham, 89n37
Azulai, Ḥayyim Joseph David, 39n13, 89n40, 226n8, 233n34, 312n41

B

Babad, Joseph, 145n105, 166n186, 241n58, 246n70
Bacharach, Jair Ḥayyim, 287n74, 308n27, 309, 310n32, 311n35, 363nn198–199, 419n41
Bacher, Wilhelm, 114n12
Bachrach, Judah, 428n85
Baḥya ben Asher, 58, 60n107, 123n36, 255n86, 315n50, 318n61, 363n199
Bakshi-Doron, Eliyahu, 143n100
Barash, David P., 4n3
Barenbaum, Michel, xvii
Bar-Ilan, Naftali Tsevi Yehudah, 90n41
Bar Shaul, Elimelech, 122n32
Baskin, Thomas W., 397
Baucom, Donald H., 404n277
Baumeister, Roy F., 213n68, 215n74, 216n75, 221n88, 402n266
Baumgartner, Walter, 38n5, 57n92, 111n3, 224n4
Beach, Steven R. H., 402nn270–271
Beck, Aaron, 441
Bediou, Benoit, 24n59
behavioral guidelines and rules of conduct, xxiv, xxvii
  of contemporary conflict resolution, 31, 34, 69–70, 72–73, 174–184, 295–296, 403–404
  purpose of, xxvii
  of traditional Jewish approaches, 69–70, 72–73, 170–172, 174–184, 295–296, 298, 403–404, 453–455
Bekhor Shor, Joseph, 143n99, 227n11, 228, 229n17, 248, 249, 279n42
Ben-Amram, Yosef, 277n34
Ben Azzai. *See* Simeon ben Azzai
Benda, Brent B., 396n256
benefit of the doubt, giving a person. *See also* "In righteousness you shall judge your friend"
  recommended by conflict resolution scholars, 221
Ben-Menahem, Hanina, 76n6, 101n72
Ben-Nayim, Jacob Ḥayyim, 247n72
Ben Sira, 45, 85n32, 227
Benson, Herbert, 442n124
Benveniste, Ḥayyim, 146n107, 148n116, 161n165
Ben-Yehuda, Eliezer, 38n6, 38n9, 38n10, 57n93, 57n95
Berakhah, Eliyahu, 133n68
Berakhah, Yehudah, 270n20
Bercovitch, Jacob, xixn2, 10n19
Berkowitz, Yitzchak, 195n17
Berlin, Isaiah ben Judah Loeb, 299n1
Berlin, Naphtali Zevi Judah, 62n111, 65n120, 84n30, 136n78, 167, 168n189, 228, 232
Berman, Shemaryahu Yosef, 147–148nn113–114
Bertinoro, Obadiah, 88n34, 91n43, 94n51, 96n60, 190n2, 202n39
Beyer, Gerry W., 8n16
bias awareness, 15, 18, 18n43, 29–30
Bible. *See Tanakh*
binding arbitration. *See* arbitration
Bippus, Amy M., 21n51
Biton, Daniel, 202n39
Black's Law Dictionary, 6, 9n17, 27n66

Blancke, Brian, xxn2
Blaser, Isaac, 279n43, 279n45, 321–322, 352–353, 354nn185–186, 363n200, 398
Blass, Jonathan, 272n25
Bleich, J. David, 157
Bloch, Elijah Meyer, 208n57
Bloi, Ya'akov Yeshayahu, 147n113, 149n120, 319n65
Blum-Kulka, Shoshana, 365n204, 366, 367n209
Bodenheimer, Michael Yeḥiel, 354n186
Bodine, Richard J., 14n35, 15n37, 16n40, 18n42, 22n55, 32n75, 461n22
Bohlin, Karen E., 33n76
Bolle, Menachem, 192n6
Bolstad, Max, 403n274
Boon, Susan, 261n1
Borisoff, Deborah, 20n49
Bornstein, Israel, 92n47
Borowitz, Eugene B., xxviin14
Boskowitz, Benjamin Ze'ev, 231–232nn27–28
Botterweck, G. Johannes, 57n91, 151n127, 224nn3–4, 262n4
Boulding, Kenneth, 11
Braude, William G., 226n8
Braun, Solomon, 315n51
Breisacher, David, 352n181
Breslin, J. William, 6n10,
Brodianski, Yitsḥak Yeruḥem, 273n26
Bruk, Eliezer Ben-Zion, 92n47, 94n53, 95nn55–56, 99n71
Bruna, Israel, 254n83
Bu'aron, Aharon, 164n176
Buber, Solomon, 48n50, 337n121
Bukarat, Abraham ben Solomon ha-Levi, 57n94, 193n9
Burgess, Heidi and Guy M., 3n1, 11nn20–21, 13n29, 14n33, 20n49
Burton, John, 9n18, 11, 11n25
Bush, Robert A. Baruch, 28–29, 70, 258n90
Bushman, Brad J., 25n61, 215–216nn74–75, 221n88

C

Capusi, Ḥayyim, 233n34
"cardinal sins," 134n73
Carlebach, Mordechai, 353n182
Carruthers, William L., 16n40
Cartwright-Smith, Jeffrey, 446n141
Castro, Jacob, 283n59
Castro, Loreta N., 5n5
Catane, Moshe, 155n144
Chajes, Zevi Hirsch, 48n53, 128n49
Chappell, David W., xxiin6
character development
  in contemporary conflict resolution, 33, 172, 177n201, 181, 184–188, 462
  definition of, 33
  in Judaism, 170–171, 184–188, 359, 401, 408, 414, 415, 416, 416n30, 416n32, 417n37, 418, 422, 426, 428, 449n155, 453, 462–463, 471
Chmiel, Re'uven, 270n20
Choue, Young Seek, 4n3
Cicero, 132n66
Clark, Brian A.M., 217nn77–78
Cloke, Kenneth, 403n275
Cobb, Adam R., 443n129, 444n131
cognitive dissonance, 104, 107, 143n100
cognitive processes, xxiv–xxv, xxx–xxxii, 31, 191, 211, 219, 296–297, 392–393, 397, 399, 412n19, 415, 416n30, 417, 429, 435n108, 436, 440–441, 447, 448, 450, 453, 455, 462
  related to the prohibition against bearing a grudge, xxx–xxxi, 274–227, 296–297
cognitive therapy, 440–441, 441n121
Cohen, Binyamin, 207n36
Cohen, Jonathan R., 401n265, 403n274
Cohen, Seymour J., 428n90
Coleman, Peter T., xixn1, xxivn8, 3n2, 105n83, 218n79
collaborative negotiation. *See* cooperative negotiation

Colman, Andrew M., 212n67, 214nn70–71
commandments. *See mitsvot*
communication, xxin4, 15, 17n41, 18, 20–21, 27, 29, 31, 32, 104, 107, 119, 150–175, 181–182, 185, 214, 217, 221, 225, 228, 235–242, 253, 255–260, 294, 402, 419, 419n42, 420n47, 427, 432, 439, 443, 448, 450, 451, 464
in conflict resolution education, 20–21
differences and similarities between contemporary conflict resolution and traditional Jewish approaches, 255–260
three primary components of, 238n51
in *tokhaḥah*, 235–242
verbal abuse, in Judaism, 150–168
compromise, xxiii, 26, 255
conflict categories
interpersonal and intergroup
definition, xx
similarities and differences, xx–xxin4
conflict management
definition, xxin5
conflict resolution
contributions from other disciplines
American judicial system, 14
civil rights and peace movements, 12–13
international relations, 11–12
organizational psychology, 10
religion, 14–15
social psychology, 12
creating cooperative climate for, 27
definition, xxin5, 3
education, core components, 15–29
affective component, 31
anger management, 24–25, 31
behavioral guidelines and rules of conduct, 31
bias awareness, 29–30
cognitive processes, 31
communication, 20–21, 31
cooperation, 19–20, 31–33
decision making and problem solving, 25–26, 31–32
fundamental underlying values (and sub-values), 31–33
perspective taking, 21–24, 31
"principles of conflict resolution," 26–29, 31, 33
education, empirical research that supports, 185n214
fields of study
alternative dispute resolution (ADR), 6–9
peace studies, 4–5
the three basic fields, 3–4
focus on underlying needs and interests, 11–12, 14, 28
interdisciplinary field, 10
overlap
with ADR, 9
with peace studies, 5
proper timing of, 27
separate the people from the problem, 14, 28
conflict transformation, John Paul Lederach's, 15, 70n134
Confucius, 113n10
"constructive conflict." *see also* "dispute for the sake of Heaven"
according to
John Crawley, 103
Louis Kriesberg, 103
Mary Parker Follet, 10, 103
Morton Deutsch, 103–105
contemporary conflict resolution and traditional Jewish approaches
differences and similarities between the two, in respect to, xxxiii, xxxivn27
anger management, 451–452
apologies and forgiveness, 363–364, 404–405
behavioral guidelines and rules of conduct, 69–70, 72–73, 170–188, 258–260, 293–298
fundamental, underlying concepts about constructive/destructive conflict, 102–108

fundamental values, 68–73, 169–174
judging people favorably, 211–212, 218–222
methods for resolving interpersonal conflict through dialogue, 255–260
retaliation and resentment, 293–298
value of promoting peace, 68–73
possible explanation for differences in behavioral guidelines and rules of conduct, 463n24
support for setting higher behavioral standards, 466n29
Cooke, Kathryn L., 383n240
cooperation, 12, 18, 19–20, 31–33, 72, 172–174, 179, 462
cooperative learning, 19, 20n48
cooperative negotiation, 7, 27–28, 31, 34, 175, 181, 218n81, 255–257, 294, 464
Cooperman, Hillel, 334n110, 342n139
Cordovero, Moses, 131n60, 357n193
corporal punishment, 145n105
Corsini, Raymond J., 214n69
Cowley, A. E., 45n37
Crawford, Donna K., 14n35, 15n37, 16n40, 18n42, 22n55, 32n75, 461n22
Crawley, John, 103

D

da Fano, Menaḥem Azariah, 153n136
Danzig, Abraham, 64n118, 153n135, 335n116, 345n150, 354n186, 363n200
Darby, Bruce W., 376, 377, 378n233, 380n237
darkhe shalom, "paths of peace"
definition, xxvii–xxviii
the entire Torah is for the sake of, xxvii, 48, 69, 110, 170
in relation to idolaters, 133
Darwin, Charles, 446n141
da Silva, Hezekiah, 313, 329, 334, 347
Dauer, Edward A., 6n7, 9n17, 14n33
David ben Abraham Maimuni, 96n60
Davila, Joanne, 402n271
Davis, Albie M., 10n20
Dayton, Bruce W., 103n78
de Boton, Abraham, 145n105, 241n57, 246n70
decision making. *See* conflict resolution, education, decision making and problem solving
decision theory, 25–26
Deffenbacher, Jerry L., 440, 442n123, 443nn126–128, 450n158
de Medina, Samuel, 146n108
derekh erets, 133, 174, 174n196, 458
Dessler, Elijah E., 106n83, 143n100, 208n59, 233n34, 270n20, 323
destructive conflict
contemporary conflicts understanding of, 103–105, 173, 180
Jewish understanding of, xxvi, 74, 77–102, 105–108, 180, 453
mitsvot that prevent, xxix, 110, 168, 191
refraining from, 36–73
Deuteronomy. *See under Tanakh*, Torah
Deuteronomy Rabbah. *See under* Midrash, *Midrash Rabbah*
Deutsch, Morton, xixn1, xxin4, xxivn8, 3n2, 12, 12nn26–28, 20n46, 24n58, 103–104, 106–108, 123n38, 215n73, 218n79, 221n88, 294n86, 403n273
de Vidas, Elijah ben Moses, 239n52, 251n80, 287n72, 408n2, 418, 419nn44–45, 420nn47–48
DiBlasio, Frederick A., 383n242, 387, 392–397
Didache (1:2), 113n10
Dimitrovsky, Haim Z., 90n40
din Torah, xxiii
Dinur, Ben Zion, 93n49
Diskin, Moses Joshua Judah Leib, 121n31, 125n43, 178n203
"dispute for the sake of Heaven," xxvii, 74–108
attributes of Hillel and Shammai, 80–85, 90–93, 99
desire "to establish the truth," 83, 84–85, 86, 90, 91–93
interpretations of *rishonim* and *aḥaronim*, 91–93

the mishnah in *Eduyyot*, 81, 84, 91n45, 92
the Tosefta, 82–84, 86, 91, 97, 100
attributes of Korah and his Group, 80, 85–86, 90–91, 93–97, 98–99
display of acrimony, 94
interpretations of *rishonim* and *aḥaronim*, 90, 93–95
Midrashim, 85, 86, 93–94, 94n52, 95, 101
motivated by an ulterior motive, 85, 86, 91, 93–96, 99
reluctance to engage in dialogue, 95
simple reading of the biblical narrative, 80, 85–86
intellectual integrity, 81–82, 83, 85, 86, 97, 101
mishnah in *Avot*
English translation, 75
literal-primary sense of, 77–87
meaning of *sofah le-hitkayem*, 75n4
not be taken at face value, 78
the proper nouns "Hillel" and "Shammai," 87
rudimentary explanation, 78–80
simple meaning of *le-shem shamayim* and *shelo le-shem shamayim*, 79
the value of argumentation, 74, 87–90
positive relationships, maintaining, 92–93
recognition of ulterior motives, 97–100
seeming volatile nature of, 78n9
di Trani, Isaiah ben Elijah, 48n53
di Trani, Isaiah ben Mali, 145n105
divine providence, 269, 271–273, 421, 423
"do not judge your friend until you are in his place," 207–209, 219, 220n86, 455
Dowd, E. Thomas, 445n133
Duffy, Karen G., 8n15
Duling, Dennis C., 225n6
Dunner, Josef Hirsch, 64
Duran, Simeon ben Zemaḥ, 88n35, 92n46, 96n60, 203n40, 284n63, 288n78
Duschinsky, Joseph Zevi, 284n61

E

Ecclesiasticus, 45n36
Edels, Samuel Eliezer (*Maharsha*), 49n58, 84, 115, 115n17
Edwards, A., 214n70
Eger, Azriel Meir, 208n59
Ehrenberg, Yehoshua Menaḥem Mendel, 315n51
Ehrenraikh, Ḥayim Tsevi, 310n33
Ehrman, Avraham, 194n14, 281n51, 288n78, 460n20
Eilenburg, Issachar Baer, 65n120
Einhorn, Ze'ev Wolf, 302n9
Eisenblatt, Shmuel D., xxvn12, xxix, 110, 176n198, 268n17, 285n66
Eisenstadt, Meir, 317n59
Eisenstein, Ḥayim Leib, 353n182, 353n185, 354n186
Eisenstein, Israel, 74n2
Eleazar ben Azariah, 252, 302
Eleazar ben Judah of Worms, 154
Eleazar ben Matya, 226, 226n9, 231, 237n47
Eleazar ben Simeon, 54
Eliakim ben Meshullam, 280n49
Elias, Maurice J., 17n41, 25n62, 26n64, 460n21, 461n22
Eliezer ben Nathan, 94n51
Eliezer ben Samuel of Metz, 111n4, 123n36, 131n59, 135n76, 146n108, 151n129, 152n132, 159n156, 161n165, 164n177, 225n5, 228, 237n47, 238, 248, 262n6, 283, 283nn54–55, 283nn59
Elijah ben Solomon (Vilna Gaon), xxviiin18, 54n76, 61n110, 149n120, 150n125, 166n187, 204n40, 316n56, 318n61, 329, 329n, 332n106, 334n114, 336n119, 337n122, 417n36, 427n79
Eliyahu, Mordechai, 327
Ellis, Albert, 435, 435n108, 439, 441, 441n122, 450
Elon, Menachem, 49, 177n202, 319n64
elu va-elu divre elohim ḥayim, "these and those are the words of the living God," 106n83
Elyakim, Ḥayim Yosef, 241n56

Elyashiv, Yosef Shalom, 119n26, 245n68, 322, 322n75, 324, 331, 344, 345n150, 354n186, 410n9
embarrassment, 259, 260, 301, 314, 315nn50–51, 319, 321n72, 349, 381, 420n47, 467. *See also under mitsvot,* "You shall not bear sin because of him"
definition, 162n169
prohibition against embarrassing someone, 151, 158–163, 227n11, 236, 237, 240–242
public, 153, 163, 363n198
rabbinic measures to deter people from embarrassing others, 153
Emden, Jacob, 207n53, 419n41
empathy, xxin4, 17n41, 21, 22n52, 23, 24, 31, 118, 118n23, 119, 120, 176–179, 181, 187, 214, 217, 217n77, 220, 370, 373, 381, 385, 386, 389, 390–391, 395, 416n34, 439, 443, 448, 459
Engel, Joseph, 335n117, 352, 398
Enright, Robert D., 387–388, 390, 397–398, 402n268, 403
Ephraim ben Jacob ha-Kohen, 241
Ephraim Solomon of Luntshits, 267n13
Epstein, Baruch ha-Levi, 89n37, 123n36, 131n63, 147n112, 171n193, 346n154
Epstein, Jehiel Michal, 150n123, 161n167, 230n22, 234n36, 304n14, 308n27, 309n31, 320n68, 329n95, 335n116, 347, 350, 363n198
Epstein, Joseph D., xvii, xxvn12, xxviin15, xxvn12, 39n14, 53, 58–59, 65–66, 67, 70, 71, 73, 123n36, 141, 154n141, 154n143, 156n149, 158n154, 229n16, 235n38, 236, 244, 279n44, 459n15
theory of "passive conflict," 65–66
theory of "positive peace," 53–55, 65–67, 70–71, 73
equity, xxiii, 39, 255
Escapa, Joseph, 328n91, 329n96
Etkes, Immanuel, 417n37
Ettlinger, Jacob, 49n58, 233n34, 253n82
Even-Shoshan, Abraham, 37n1, 56n87, 224n2, 299n1
"everything is in accordance with the time, issue, place, and individual," 254, 258, 331n103
exegetical motifs, 87
Exline, Julie Juola, 402n266
Exodus. *See under Tanakh,* Torah
Exodus Rabbah. See under Midrash, *Midrash Rabbah*
exposure therapy, 443–444
Eybeschuetz, Jonathan, 92n47, 94, 99

F

Falk, Jacob Joshua, 335n117
Falk, Joshua ben Alexander (*Sma*), 150n125, 154n142, 166n187, 289, 339n129, 340, 349n168
Farissol, Abraham, 91n43
Farson, Richard E., 21n50
Fehr, Ryan, 376n225
Feinstein, Moses, 74n2, 119n26, 161nn167–168, 309n31, 317n59, 325n84, 354n186
Feldman, Daniel Z., 113n9, 153n135, 154n143, 160n158, 160n162, 194n13, 237n47, 308n28, 316n52, 321n72
Feldman, David, 51n60
Ferguson, John, xxiin6
Feshbach, Norma D., 118n23
Feuchtwanger, Asher, 243–245
Figo, Azariah, 233n34
Fincham, Frank D., 402nn270–272
Finkel, Nathan Zevi (Alter of Slabodka), 64, 125n43, 135n74, 174n196
Finkelman, Shimon, 195n17
Finkelstain, Ariel, 133n68
First, Mitchell, 299n1
Fish, Ya'akov Ḥizkiyahu, 55n79
Fisher, Fred, 103n79
Fisher, Roger, 6n10, 14, 223n1
Fiske, Susan T., 212n66
Florsheim, Yoel, 253n82
Foa, Edna B., 444n130
Folberg, Jay, 8n15
Folger, Joseph P., 28–29, 70, 258n90
Follet, Mary Parker, 10, 103

Fontaine, Resianne, 132n66
forgiveness
  in contemporary conflict resolution,
    401–405
  contemporary models of, 383–398
  DiBlasio's model of, 392–398
  difference between process-based
    and decision-based, 392,
    397–398, 399–400
  Enright's model of, 384n243, 386,
    387–390, 397–398
  similarities and differences between
    contemporary models of
    forgiveness and the Jewish
    obligations of the one who
    forgives, 398–401
  traditional Jewish approaches to (see
    meḥilah)
  Worthington's model of, 384n243,
    386, 387, 390–392
Fraenkel, David, 79n14, 125, 127
Franklin, Martin, 444n130
Freimann, Aron, 89n40
Friedlander, Albert H., 48n49
Friedlander, Ḥayim, 272n24
Friedman, Chana T., 409n4
Friedman, Eliyahu Aryeh, 116n17
Friedman, Shamma, 301n5
fundamental theoretical concepts
  about conflict resolution, xxiv–xxv,
    19, 31, 33–34, 102
fundamental values
  character development, 33,
    170–172, 177n201, 181,
    184–188
  of contemporary conflict resolution,
    31–33, 68–73, 172–174, 177,
    179, 180–181, 184–188, 461,
    462–463
  cooperation, 31–32, 33, 172–174,
    177n201, 179, 181, 187, 462
  definition of, 31
  implicit values, 32
  of Jewish conflict resolution, xxv,
    xxvi, xxix, 68–73, 76, 169–174,
    179, 184–188, 453, 461, 462
  loving one's neighbor, 170–174,
    179, 453

  personal and social development
    and well-being, 33, 185,186,
    188, 461
  problem solving, 32, 33, 172,
    177n201, 181, 258n90
  promoting peace, 32–33, 68–73,
    169–170, 172, 173, 453, 461
Funk, Nathan C., xxiin6
Fus, Yitsḥak Ḥayim, 205n48, 206n49

G
Gabai, Shaul, 156n149
Galinsky, Adam D., 22n52,
  217nn77–78
Galtung, Johan, 5, 13, 13n30, 71
game theory, 12
Gantserski, Betsalel Shelomoh,
  194n14, 195n16, 199n33, 201n36,
  203n40, 206n50
Ganzfried, Solomon (Kitsur Shulḥan
  Arukh), 230n22, 313, 313n46
Garner, Bryan A., 6n8, 8n16, 9n17,
  27n66
Garrard, Wendy M., 185n214
Gehlbach, Hunter, 22n52
Gelfand, Michele J., 376n225
Genesis. See under Tanakh, Torah
Genesis Rabbah. See under Midrash,
  Midrash Rabbah
Gentiles, 116n19, 122, 122n34,
  123n36, 128, 131, 133, 268n15,
  310n33, 338, 430
  love for (see ahavat ha-beriyot)
  righteous, 128, 128n49
Gerleman, Gillis, 37n2, 38, 38n5,
  38n7, 39
Gerondi, Jonah ben Abraham (Rabenu
  Yonah), 64n118, 65n120, 91n43,
  119n26, 135n76, 146n108,
  151n129, 153n134, 155n146,
  159n156, 164n177, 171n193,
  193n10, 197, 198n28, 199nn30–31,
  201–203nn36–40, 207n52, 207n55,
  283, 307n24, 308n28, 315n50,
  318n61, 320, 320n72, 325n84,
  332n106, 414n24, 427n80
Gerondi, Nissim ben Reuben (Ran),
  55n80, 115n15, 165n180

Ghandi, Rajmohan, xxiin6
Gibbs, John C., 25n61
Gibianski, Joseph, 93n49
Gifter, Mordechai, 128n49, 330n100, 332, 332n107
Gilin, Debra, 22n52, 217nn77–78
Gill, Michael J., 212n66
Gillan, Joey, 6n7, 8n14
Ginsberg, Harold Louis, 39n11, 237n48
Ginsburg, Eliezer, 335n117
Girard, Kathryn, 18n42
Glick, Barry, 25n61
Gold, Avie, 47n46
Gold, Shmuel Yehoshua, 60n107
Goldberg, Rachel, xxn2
Goldberg, Stephen B., 6n7, 8n14, 9n17
Goldberg, Ya'akov, 344n144
Goldberg, Zalman Nehemiah, 304n14
Goldberger, Moshe, 409n4
Goldberger, Yonason Binyomin, 62n111
"Golden Rule," negative formulation of, 113n10
Goldstein, Arnold P., 25n61
Goleman, Daniel, 17n41
Gombiner, Abraham Abele (*Magen Avraham*), 137n81, 227n9, 230n22, 234n36, 237n47, 316, 319, 319n63, 322, 329, 334, 347, 349n173
Goodpaster, Gary, 6n10
Gopin, Marc, xix, xx, xxiin6, 15n39, 186n216, 455–457, 465n27
Goranson, Richard, 293n86
Gordon, Aryeh Leib, 229n1
Gordon, Thomas, 21
Gorsuch, Richard L., 383
Goshen-Gottstein, Alon, 82n22
Gottlieb, Dov Berish, 89n37, 92n47, 94n51, 95nn55–56, 96n61, 97n64, 99, 99n71, 119n26, 138, 208n58, 229n17, 268n16, 291n85
Green, Laura R., 22n52
Greenbaum, Aaron, 318n61
Greenberg, Leslie, 383n242, 387
Grinvald, Ze'ev, 277n34
Grodzinski, Avraham, 129n53, 459n15
Grodzinski, Ḥayyim Ozer, 123n36
Grosch, James W., 8n15
Gross, Mosheh David, 408n1
Grozovsky, Refael Reuven, 129n54, 352, 352n182, 398
grudge. *See also under mitsvot,* "You shall not bear a grudge"
  definition of the English word, 261n2
  prohibition against bearing
    practical halakhic discourse on, 277–291
    in relationship to *tokhaḥah,* 290–291
    underlying reasons for, 263–277
Grünfeld, Simon (*Maharshag*), 279n44, 280n49

H

Habermann, Abraham Meir, 123n38
Ḥadash, Meir, 344n146
Hadayah, Ovadiah, 241, 241n56, 246n70
Ḥafets Ḥayim. See Ha-Kohen, Israel Meir
Ḥagiz, Moses, 168
Ḥakam, Joseph Ḥayyim ben Elijah al- (*Ben Ish Ḥai*), 56n80, 147n112, 362n198
Ha-Kohen, Israel Meir, 31n23, 50n59, 52n66, 55n78, 65n120, 110n2, 120n28, 122n32, 137n81, 138n85, 139–140, 154n139, 157, 160, 161n165, 161n167, 162, 162n173, 175, 176n198, 193n10, 197–205, 206n50, 208–209, 220n86, 230n22, 234n36, 254n83, 277n35, 278n39, 278n41, 280n49, 281n51, 283–285, 286–289, 296, 308n27, 309n31, 313, 317, 320, 327, 328n90, 329, 335n116, 342, 346, 347, 348, 349n173, 356n190, 363n200, 458, 459, 469
halakhah (Jewish law)
  definition, 469
  within the functional range of the average person, xxix, 112–113, 118, 141, 187–188, 276, 287, 292, 357–358, 456–457, 463n24

role in Judaism, xxvii, xxviin14, 458–459
Halberstam, Aryeh Leibish, 409n4
Halberstam, Jekutiel Jehuda, 315n51, 344, 345n148
Ha-Levi, David ben Samuel (*Taz*), 150, 329n92, 346nn153–154,
Halevi, Ḥayyim David, 128n49, 268n17, 277n34, 327, 344, 351n178, 357–358
Halevi Even Yuli, Asi, 114n14, 121nn30–31
Ha-Maḥaloket ba-Halakhah (Ben-Menahem, Hecht, and Wosner, editors), 76n6, 101n72
Ḥananel ben Ḥushiel, 148n115, 280n49
Hanh, Thich Nhat, xxiin6
Hanson, L. Reid Jr., 214n70
Hansson, Sven Ove, 26n63
Harari, Moshe, 321n73
Harvard Negotiation Project (HNP), 14
Har-Zahab, Zevi, 299n1
ḥaside umot ha-olam, "righteous Gentiles," 128, 128n49
Ḥasman, Yehuda Leib, 97n64, 98n67
Ḥatab, Yehudah, 301n4
hatred. *See also mitsvot,* "You shall not hate your brother in your heart"
approaches to dealing with hatred, 142–145
contemporary conflict resolution and traditional Jewish approaches' respective approaches towards, 180–183
concealed, why it could be worse than revealed hatred, 138–139
Hebrew noun *sinah,* 139
Rabbis perspective on, 134–135
Hawk, Gary W., 403n273
ḥayekha kodemim, "Your life takes precedence," 114n11, 346n155
Ha-Yevani, Zeraḥyah (*Sefer ha-Yashar*), 408n2, 416n30, 428
Ha-Yitshari, Mattathias, 91n45,
Ḥayyun, Joseph ben Abraham, 58n100, 91n45, 94, 96nn60–61
ḥazakah, legal presumption of, 324
Ḥazan, Samuel b. Kalonymus, 62n110
Ḥazan, Yosef, 136n78, 162n170, 284n65
Hecht, Neil, 76n6, 101n72
Heifetz, Baruch A., xvii, 138, 139n89, 141, 141nn92–93, 226n9, 234, 235nn37–38, 236n39, 245n67, 246, 247n71, 248–250, 268n15, 268n17, 277n34, 277n36, 278n41, 279n44, 280nn46–47, 280n49, 281–282nn51–53, 284n61, 284nn63–64, 285n66, 287n74, 291, 335n117, 342n139, 357n192, 363n200, 459n14
Heller, Ḥayyim, 231n23
Heller, Yom Tov Lipman, 91n45,129n53, 154n143, 272n23, 301n4, 414n24, 431
Heller-Wilensky, Sarah, 42n17
Henkin, Yehudah, 160
Henkin, Yosef Eliyahu, 62n111
Herford, R. Travers, 90n42
Herodotus, 113n10
Hershman (Ragoler), Shelomoh Zalman, 82n19, 83n25, 91n45, 94n51
Hertz, Joseph, 115n16, 128
Heschel, Abraham J., xxviin14
"He shall not add [on]; lest he strike him an additional blow" (the commandment prohibiting physical violence), 145–150
Hezekiah ben Manoah, 227n11, 228, 248,
Hibbard, Dawn, xxiin6
Higger, Michael, 45n36
Hildesheimer, Naftali Zevi, 52n65
hilkhot ben adam la-ḥavero, "laws between man and his fellow man"
being taught in Jewish schools, 458
developing a course or curriculum in, 459–460
importance of studying, 458–459
Hillel ben Eliakim, 143n99
Hirsch, Samson Raphael, 88n34, 192n6, 193n11, 228, 246n70, 247n71, 253n82, 301n4
Ḥisda, R. 323–324, 334

Hoberman, Ze'ev, 308n28, 363n200
Hochgelehrter, Yosef ben Ya'akov Yitsḥak, 246n70, 283n59
Hodges, Sara D., 217nn77–78
Hodgins, Holley S., 402n267
Hoffmann, David Zevi, 79nn13–14, 83–84, 114, 117, 228
holding on to a quarrel, prohibition of, 62–65
Homolka, Walter, 48n49
Horovitz, S., 44n27
Horowitz, Avraham, 363n198
Horowitz, Isaiah (*Shelah*), 51n59, 62, 144n104, 233n34, 251n80
Horowitz, Menaḥem Mendel, 341n138
Horowitz, Samuel Shmelke, 128n50
ḥoshed bi-khsherim, "suspecting 'kosher' people," 205
Hoyt, William T., 386–387, 392n250
Hsee, Christopher, K., 17n41
Huminer, Samuel, 275n29, 321n72
Huna, R., 61, 62, 81, 148, 184
Hurwitz, Isaac Simḥah, 138n83
Hurwitz, Phinehas Elijah, 131–132430n90
Hutner, Isaac, 207n52, 272, 279n44, 305, 307, 321n72, 343n143, 345, 351n178, 354n186

I

Ibn Aknin, Joseph, 90n 91n43, 92n47, 94n51
Ibn Ezra, Abraham, 134n71
Ibn Gabirol, Solomon, 288, 428n87
Ibn Gaon, Shem Tov ben Abraham, 232n28, 246n70
Ibn Ghiyyat, Isaac, 281n50, 283n59
Ibn Ḥabib, Jacob, 312–314, 316
Ibn Ḥabib, Levi, 51
Ibn Ḥabib, Moses, 348n163
Ibn Ḥayyim, Aaron, 156n149, 193n9
Ibn Janaḥ, Jonah, 194n12
Ibn Makhir, Moshe, 208n57
Ibn Pakuda, Baḥya, 271n23, 317n60, 318n61, 333
Ibn Shoshan, Joseph, 94n51
Ibn Shu'aib, Judah, 92n46, 94n51
Ibn Tibbon, Judah, 333n110
Ibn Tibbon, Moses, 231nn23–24
Ibn Tibbon, Samuel, 203n40
imago Dei, human beings are created in the image of God, 125, 126, 127, 129–130, 154, 167–168, 316
  as the source for *kevod ha-beriyot,* "respect for people," or "human dignity," 129n54
  therefore deserving of respect and love, 130
I-messages, 21, 235n37
"In righteousness you shall judge your friend" *(be-tsedek tishpot amitekha)* (the commandment to judge people favorably), 190, 192–195. *See also* judging people favorably
  basic halakhic parameters of, 195–205
  derivation of the commandment from the word *be-tsedek,* 193–195
  related concepts, 205–209
  simple explanation of the verse (the "*peshuto shel mikra*"), 192
  talmudic interpretation, 192–193
  unique cognitive nature of, 191, 211
integrative problem-solving approach, 7, 10, 28, 103. *See also* win-win solutions
interdependence, 4
  positive, 19
  social, 12
International Center for Cooperation and Conflict Resolution (ICCCR), xxiii–xxiv
interpersonal conflict
  definition, xx
  models of resolution, basic components, xxiv
Isaac ben Abba Mari, 98n67
Isaac ben Ḥayyim Volozhiner, 253n82
Isaac ben Joseph of Corbeil (*Semak*), 52, 65n120, 111n4, 131n59, 135n76, 146n108, 151n129, 159n156, 161n165, 164n177, 193n10, 250n79, 263n6
Isaac ben Moses of Vienna, 327n85
Isaac ben Solomon, 94n51, 96n61
Ishbili, Yom-Tob ben Abraham (*Ritba*), 55n80, 75n4, 148n116, 165n180, 284n63

Isocrates, 113n10
Isserlein, Israel, 349
Isserles, Moses, 139n88, 149n118, 149nn120–122, 153n138, 289, 303n14, 304n14, 336n119, 337nn122–123, 346–347, 348n162, 348n165

J

Jabbour, Elias, xxiin6
Jabez, Joseph ben Ḥayyim, 206n49, 207, 419n45
Jacob ben Asher (*Ba'al ha-Turim*), 113, 143n102, 147n11, 150n124, 152n133, 165, 166n187, 228, 303, 304nn14–16, 305, 311, 312, 327, 329, 329n96, 337, 339, 343n142, 468
Jacob ben Ḥayyim Zemaḥ, 414n23
Jacob ben Jacob Moses of Lissa (Lorbeerbaum), 166n187, 304n14
Jacob ben Judah Ḥazzan of London, 235n38, 246
Jacob ben Meir (*Rabenu Tam*), 149n119, 429n90
Jacob ben Samson, 76n7, 90nn42–43, 94n51, 208n58
Jacob Joseph of Polonoye, 147n112, 233n34
Jacob of Orleans, 125, 126
Jacobs, Louis, 39n14, 44n25
Jacobson, Edmund, relaxation technique, 435, 435n109, 436, 437, 442
Jaffe, Mordecai (*Ba'al ha-Levushim*), 348–349
Jäger, Uli, 365, 366n207, 373, 374n222, 375n224, 376, 377, 380nn237–238
James, William, 446n141
Jelen, Abraham, xxxiii, 208n57, 285n66, 409–412, 414, 415nn26–29, 416nn30–34, 417–419, 420–421nn46–50, 422, 423nn53–60, 424–426, 428, 431, 433, 447n146, 448nn152–153, 451. *See also Orekh Apayim*
  biographical information, 410n6
Jenni, Ernst, 224n3
Jeong, Ho-Won, 4n3, 5n5
Johnson, B., 194n12
Johnson, David W., 12nn27–28, 17n42, 19, 22n53, 23, 24n58, 25n61, 105n82, 217n78, 450
Johnson, Judith M., 15n37, 29n70
Johnson, Roger T., 12nn27–28, 17n42, 19, 22n53, 23, 24n58, 25n61, 105n82, 450
Jonathan ben David ha-Kohen of Lunel, 63
Jones, Tricia S., 185n214
Jose bar Ḥanina, R., 324, 328–329, 334
Joseph Ḥayyim ben Elijah. *See* Ḥakam, Joseph Ḥayyim ben Elijah al-
Josephus, 85n32
Judah ben Samuel (*he-Ḥasid*) of Regensburg, xxxin23, 158n154, 206n49, 236, 327n85, 418n41, 425n66
Judah Loew ben Bezalel (*Maharal* of Prague), 36, 58, 60n107, 130, 147n112, 155, 174n196, 315n50
Judaism, xxix, xxvii
  false impressions regarding, 122n35
judging people favorably, 190–222. *See also* "In righteousness you shall judge your friend"
  basic halakhic parameters of the mitzvah, 195–205
  basic *halakhot* are easily and intuitively grasped, 210
  countering negative judgmental biases, 191, 194–195, 215–222
  different categories of actions and people, 195, 197–203
  Ḥafets Ḥayim on, 197–205
  how should one do so, 196, 204–205
  the need to focus on unknowns, 220–221
  "towards the scale of merit" (*le-khaf zekhut*), meaning of the expression, 190
judicial procedures
  Jewish, xxiii

K

kabdehu ve-ḥoshdehu, "respect him and suspect him," 205–206

Kadayifci-Orellana, Ayse S., xixn2, xxiin6
Kadushin, Max, 45, 46n38
Kafih, Joseph, 81n18, 203n40, 231n23, 264n8
Kagan, Israel Meir ha-Kohen. *See* Ha-Kohen, Israel Meir
Kahane, Kalman, 145n105
Kaidanover, Zevi Hirsch, 233n34
Kalischer, Zevi Hirsch, 128n50
Kameda, Masuyo, 377, 378, 380n237, 401n264
Kamenetsky, Jacob, 106n83, 114n12, 117,
Kamenetsky, Shmuel, 327, 328n90, 348, 363n198
Kanievsky, Shemaryahu Yosef Ḥayim, 164n176, 166, 178n203, 199n33, 206n50, 232, 234n36, 237n47, 322, 339n131
Kanievsky, Ya'akov Yisrael, 136n78
Kanouse, David E., 213n68, 214n70
Kaplan, Abraham Elijah, 133n68
Kaplan, Israel J., 226n8
Kaplan, Meir ha-Kohen, 229n16, 230n20
Karelitz, Abraham Isaiah, 78n9, 121n31, 158, 166nn186–187, 259, 315n51, 316n52, 353, 399, 458
Karelitz, Shemaryahu Yosef Nissim, 315n51, 321n72, 353n185, 354n186
Karmi, Mordekhai, 346n154
Karo, Joseph, 137n78, 139n87, 143–144nn102–103, 147n111, 149n122, 150n124, 152n133, 164n179, 165n184, 166n187, 303, 303n13, 305, 309n29, 318nn62–63, 327, 329, 335n117, 336n119, 337, 337n122, 339, 340n134, 343n142, 344n145, 348n165, 468, 472
Karremans, Johan C., 402n269
Kasher, Hannah, 272n25
Kasher, Menaḥem M., 85n32, 86n33, 142n98
Kasher, Shimon, 125n43
Kasovsky, Chayim Yehoshua, 58n96
Kassinove, Howard, 441n122, 443n128, 444nn131–132, 445–446
Katz, Dov, 78n9, 97n65, 125n43, 321n73, 417n37
Katz, Tsevi ben Joseph, 309–310
Kaufman, Moshe, 193n10, 195n17, 201n36, 285n66
Kayara, Shimon, 52n64, 111n4, 130n59, 135n76, 146n108, 151n129, 159n156, 164n177, 224n5, 262n6
Kegley, Charles W. Jr., 5n5
Kegley, Geoffrey G., 5n5
Kehati, Pinḥas, 81n18
Kelman, Herbert C., 11
Kemp, Simon, 447
Kenigsberg, David, 234n35
Ketterman, Grace H., 150n126
kevod ha-beriyot, "respect for people," "human dignity," 129n54, 171, 453
Kharif, Moshe, 234n34
Kil, Yehudah, 275n29
Kilmann, Ralph H., 223n1
Kim, Sung Hee, 24n60, 215n73, 294n86, 403n27
Kimḥi, David, 84n27, 224n2, 325n83
Kimḥi, Joseph, 84n27
Kirchhoff, Johanna, 365, 366n207, 373, 374n222, 375nn223–224, 376, 376n225, 377, 378, 380nn237–238
ki yeḥam levavo, "when his heart is in the heat of anger," 287n74, 289n83
Kleck, Robert E., 446n141
Klein, Ernest, 38n6, 39n10, 57n92, 57n94, 224n4
Klein, Yisrael Yisakhar Dov, 331n102
Kluger, Solomon, 335n117, 346n155
Koch, Susan J., 18n42
Koehler, Ludwig, 38n5, 57n92, 111n3, 224n4
Kohen, Jacob ben Eliezer, 120n28
Kohen, She'ar Yashuv, 113n9, 122n32, 316n55
Kohen, Yosef, 316nn52–53, 317n60, 335n117, 346n151
Kohut, Alexander, 278n38
Kolin, Samuel, 202n39, 318n63, 347
Kook, Abraham Isaac ha-Kohen, 122, 122n35, 136n78, 178n203, 281n52, 285, 285n67, 287n74
Kook, Tzvi Yehuda, 130n58
Koraḥ, Shlomo, 328
Kosovsky, Biniamin, 58n96
Kosowsky, Abraham Abba, 320
Kotler, Aaron, 250n79

Krakowski, Menaḥem, 226n9, 230n20, 231n27, 237n47, 284n63, 336n120
Kranz, Jacob, 233n34, 287n72, 408n2
Krauss, Robert M., 20n49, 238n51
Kreidler, William J., 18n42, 22n53, 26n64, 29n70
Kremenyuk, Victor, 10n19
Kriesberg, Louis, 103, 108
Krizer, Tsevi, 171n193
Kronglas, David, 171n193, 193n11, 210–211
Krumbein, Elyakim, 284n65
Kubany, Edward S., 21n51
Kubin, Barukh Moshe, 156n149
Kugel, James L., 113n10, 225n6, 227

L

Lago, Tania, 22n52
la-khof et yitsro, "subduing one's inclination [to hate]," 142–144, 182, 463
Lancaster, Cynthia L., 443n129, 444n131
Landau, Eleazar, 275
Landau, Ezekiel, 99n70, 125n43
Landfield, Kristin, 215–216nn74–75, 219n84, 222n89
Langsner, Ya'akov Meir, 409n4
Lantieri, Linda, 18n42, 21n51, 22n55, 26nn64–65, 29n70
Lanzetta, John T., 446n141
Larrick, Richard P., 216n74, 222n89
lashon ha-ra, 110n2, 135n75, 176n198, 206, 320, 322, 420, 430, 459, 460, 470
Latham, Gary P., 467n29
Lazare, Aaron, 364n202, 368–370, 374, 375, 376, 379, 380nn237–238, 382, 397n257
Lebovitch, Jeroham, 119n26, 129n54, 154n143, 171n193, 253n82, 316n55, 449n155
Lederach, John Paul, 15, 70n134, 105n82, 258n90
Leibowitz, A. Henach, xvii, 125n43, 464n24
Leibowitz, Nehama, 113n10
Leizerowski, Baruch, 308n28
Lerma, Judah, 75n4
Leschz, Yosef, 410n6
Lesin, Jacob Moses, 449n155
Levi ben Gershom (Gersonides), 228, 287n74, 419n41
Levi, Deborah L., 401n265, 403n274
Levi, Ḥanan, 277n35
Levi, Solomon (II) ben Isaac, 88–89
Levi, Yehudah, 49n54, 268n15
Levin (Lefin), Menaḥem Mendel, 415n29
Levinshtain, Yeḥezkel, 125n43
Levinson, Moshe, xxxiii, 409–414, 415–416nn26–34, 417–418, 419n42, 419nn44–45, 420nn46–48, 421nn49–50, 426n73, 427–431, 433, 447n146, 448nn152–153, 451. *See also Ma'aneh Rakh*
biographical information, 410–411, 430n95
Levita, Elijah, 299n1
Leviticus. *See under Tanakh,* Torah
Leviticus Rabbah. See under Midrash, *Midrash Rabbah*
Levy, Raphael, 155n144
Lewicki, Roy J., 6n10, 403n273
Lewin, Kurt, 12, 12n26
Lichstein, Kenneth L., 435n109, 449n155, 450n158
Licht, Shimon, 353n182, 354n186
Lichtstein, Mordechai, 138n83, 141, 278n39, 283n58, 344, 345n151
Lickona, Thomas, 33n76
Lieberman, Saul, 45n37, 74n2, 83–84
Lieberman, Yosef, 315n50, 316n55, 325n84
Liebeskind, Elizabeth, 402n267
Liedke, G., 56n87, 57n93
Lilienfeld, Scott O., 215–216nn74–75, 219n84, 222n89
Lipkin, Ḥayim Yitsḥak, 320n72
Lipkin (Salanter), Israel, 78n9, 97n65, 320–323, 353n182, 354n186, 417n37, 433n104, 458–459, 471
Lipschutz, Israel, 88n34, 91–92nn45–47, 96, 129n53, 208n58, 335n117, 414n24
Lipsey, Mark W., 185n214

litigation, definition, 6, 8n16
Litsch-Rosenbaum, Moshe Leib, 310n33
Litwack, Hillel D., 55n79, 158n154, 163n174, 199n33, 234n34, 235n38, 268n17
Locke, Edwin A., 467n29
Lopian, Eliyahu, 356n189, 359, 399nn261-262, 401
Lorincz, Shlomo, 244
lo ta'asu agudot agudot, "You shall not create factions," 66
Lount, Robert B. Jr., 221
Luban, Ya'akov David, 308n28
Ludwig, Thomas E., 402n268
Luria, Solomon, 149n121, 349
Lurya, Mordekhai, 268n15
Luskin, Fred, 383n242, 387
Luzzatto, Moshe Ḥayyim, 156n149, 276n31, 287n72, 415n25

M

Ma'aneh Rakh
  intended purpose of, 411-412
  seminal work, xxxiii
  similarities and differences between *Ma'aneh Rakh* and contemporary approaches, 447-449
  similarities to *Orekh Apayim*
    behavioral and cognitive strategies, 417-421, 433n104
    underlying assumptions and fundamental principles, 413-417
  stylistic aspects of, 412-413
  unique features of, 427-431
Maddux, William W., 22n52, 217nn77-78
Mader, Avraham, 209n61
maḥaloket, "conflict"
  the biblical term *riv*, 57
  comparison to fire, 62, 62n111
  escalation, 61
  halakhic obligation of refraining from, 62-66
  the Hebrew term, xxvi, xxvin13, 56-59, 75n3
  intractable nature, 61-62
  other Hebrew terms for conflict, 56
  talmudic and midrashic perspectives, 59-62
Maharal of Prague. *See* Judah Loew ben Bezalel
Maharsha. *See* Edels, Samuel Eliezer
Maher, Paul E., xxxvin29
Maimonides (*Rambam*), 51n60, 52n68, 54n77, 64n119, 66, 76n7, 81n18, 82, 83n23, 88, 90-91nn42-43, 96n61, 111n4, 116, 119-121, 122n33, 123, 127, 128n49, 131, 132-134, 137-138, 143n102, 145n105, 146n108, 147n111, 151, 152nn131-133, 153n135, 154n139, 155, 157, 159n156, 160, 161, 163n175, 164n177, 165, 166n187, 167, 168n191, 170n192, 171n193, 176, 179, 188, 193, 195n17, 197, 198n28, 199nn31-32, 201nn36-37, 202-203nn39-40, 207n55, 224n5, 225, 227n11, 228-231, 232n28, 233-243, 245-246, 247n72, 248-250, 260n92, 262n6, 266-268, 269n18, 271n23, 272, 275, 280n50, 284, 285-286, 290, 291n85, 292, 303, 308n28, 309, 317nn59-60, 318, 324, 325n84, 327, 329, 330-331, 334, 335n117, 336nn119-120, 337-341, 342n139, 343-344, 345n148, 350-351, 356-358, 361, 363n200, 379, 404-405, 408n2, 414nn23-24, 415, 416n30, 428n88, 470
Maimuni, David ben Abraham, 96n60
Makhon Torat ha-Adam le-Adam, 178n203, 308n27, 316n54
Malbim. *See* Weisser, Meir Loeb ben Jehiel Michael
Malcolm, Wanda, 384n242
Man, Shlomo, 409
Marcus, Eric C., 218n79
Margolioth, Ephraim Zalman, 304n14, 308n27, 310n33, 313, 320n68, 335n116
Margolis, Max L., 59n101
Margulies, Reuben, 88n35, 346n154
Maslow, Abraham, 11
Mat, Moses, 312

Matsumoto, David, 214n71
Mayer, John D., 17n41
McClellan, B. Edward, 33n76
McCullough, Michael E., 383n239, 402n267, 402n272
McGlynn, F. Dudley, 436n110, 442n125
Medini, Ḥayyim Hezekiah, 131n63, 145n105
meḥilah, "forgiveness"
  etymology of the word, 299n1
  obligations of the one who asks for forgiveness
    appeasement of the person who has suffered, 330–335
    comparison between the asking of forgiveness from God and the asking of forgiveness from a fellow human being, 314n50, 317–318, 332, 344–345
    experiencing shame in the course of asking, 314–316
    how many attempts one must make at asking, 323–329
    if one must personally go to ask, 312–316
    obligation to ask on the day before Yom Kippur, 303–312
    range of interpersonal offences for which one must seek, 309–312
    similarities and differences between contemporary approaches to apologies and the obligations of the one who asks for forgiveness, 379–383
    the requirement of having other people accompany the one who asks, 302, 323, 324–328
    specifying the offence committed, 316–323
    talmudic sources, 300–303
  obligations of the one who forgives
    how readily must one grant forgiveness, 339–341
    how sincere must one's forgiveness be, 350–360
    primary talmudic and midrashic sources for the basic obligation, 335–337
    similarities and differences between contemporary models of forgiveness and the obligations of the one who forgives, 398–401
    what does one do if he cannot find it in his heart to forgive, 356–360
Meichenbaum, Donald, 435
Meir, R. 50n59
Meir ben Baruch of Rothenburg, 149n119, 154n139
Meiri, Menaḥem, 75n4, 84n29, 91n43, 94, 96nn60–61, 148n115, 203n40, 207n55, 208n58, 275n29, 280n49, 283n59, 301n4, 335n117, 336n119
Meir Simḥah ha-Kohen of Dvinsk, 254n83
Meklenburg, Jacob Zevi, 57, 233n34, 253n82
Melamed, E. Z., 75n3
Menaḥem of Merseburg, 149n118, 149n120, 352
Mermelstein, Avraham Yitsḥak David, 409n4
Meshi Zahav, Avraham, xxvin12, 44n26
Miall, Hugh, xxin5, 11n20
Michaelson, Ezekiel Zevi, 273n26
midah ke-neged midah, 60, 421
midot (character traits)
  of God, 52, 131
  ḥasidut (pious, or righteous, character traits), xxviii–xxix, 200n34, 243, 246, 288, 312, 359n196, 363n200, 457
  tovot (good character traits), xxviii–xxix, 196, 202n38, 203n40, 211, 413, 416, 416n34, 429, 449n155, 458, 460, 461n22
Midrash, xxii, 37n, 470
  Mekhilta debe-Rabi Yishmael
  Amalek (1), 79n11
  Mishpatim (5), 146n107

Mekhilta de-Rabi Shimon ben Yoḥai, 170n192
Midrash Agadah (*Mishpatim* 23:5), 144n104
Midrash ha-Gadol, 338n127
Midrash Lekaḥ Tov, 115n15, 164n179, 165n184
Midrash le-Olam, 339n131
Midrash Rabbah, 37n
Genesis Rabbah (Theodor-Albeck edition), 79n10, 79n12, 124n39, 168n189
Genesis Rabbah (8:5), 56n85
Genesis Rabbah (24:6), 126n45
Genesis Rabbah (24:7), 124n39, 125n44, 127n46, 154n143, 168n189
Genesis Rabbah (28:6), 59n101
Genesis Rabbah (38:6), 48n51, 273n27
Genesis Rabbah (42:8), 79n13
Genesis Rabbah (44:1), xxviin15, 170
Genesis Rabbah (54:3), 223, 231n27, 251n80
Exodus Rabbah (1:31), 64n117
Exodus Rabbah (30:17), 56n84
Exodus Rabbah (33:5), 85n32
Leviticus Rabbah, 46n39
Leviticus Rabbah (9:3), 174n196
Leviticus Rabbah (9:9), 44n28, 44n31, 46n39, 51n61
Numbers Rabbah (8:4), 339n128, 339n130
Numbers Rabbah (11:7), 36, 44n28, 45nn32–34, 59n101
Numbers Rabbah (12:4), 45n34
Numbers Rabbah (18:4), 60n105, 95n54
Numbers Rabbah (18:12), 59n103, 61n108
Numbers Rabbah (18:16), 85n32
Numbers Rabbah (19:27), 51n61
Deuteronomy Rabbah (5:15), 50n59
Esther Rabbah (7:25), 359n195
Midrash Shuvah Yisrael, 305
Midrash Tanaim al Sefer Devarim, 79n13
Midrash Tehilim (99:3), 144n104
Mishnat Rabi Eliezer-Midrash Sheloshim u-Shetayim Midot, 46n39, 47n47
Pesikta de-Rav Kahana (12:14), 47n48
Pesikta Rabati, 305
Pirke de-Rabbi Eliezer, 304–305
Sifra
Kedoshim (3:13), 165n181
Kedoshim (4:4), 193n9
Kedoshim (4:8), 159n155
Kedoshim (4:11), 278
Kedoshim (4:12), 111n6, 124n39, 125n41, 278
Sifre
  Naso (42), 44n27
  Be-Ha'alotekha (104), 232, 233n33
  Pinḥas (136), 79n11
  Devarim (2), 251n80
  Ekev (49), 52n68, 130–131nn59–60
  Shoftim (187), 134
  Shoftim (188), 145n105
  Shoftim (286), 146n107
  Tetse (222), 142n98
  Tetse (225), 142n98
  Tetse (243), 145n105
  Tetse (286), 145n105
  Tetse (293), 148
Tanḥuma
  Mishpatim (1), 144n104
  Tsav (Buber 10), 48n50
  Koraḥ (1; Buber 3), 93–94, 94n52
  Koraḥ (1; Buber 3, *Hosafah le-Farshat Koraḥ* 2), 85n32
  Koraḥ (2; Buber 5), 98n68
  Koraḥ (5; Buber 12), 98–99n68
  Koraḥ (6; Buber 15), 95n57
  Koraḥ (6; Buber 15, 17), 86n33
  Koraḥ (10; Buber 25), 98n68
  Ḥukat (19), 336
  Ḥukat (Buber 46), 337
  Tanna de-Ve Eliyahu, 226–227, 233n33, 431
Yalkut Shemoni
  Shemot (18:273), 47n48
  Kedoshim (613), 226n9
  1 Samuel (85), 147n112

Mikolic, Joseph M., xxin4
Milgram, Jacob, 224n3
Minton, John W., 6n10
Mishnah, xxii, 37n, 470. *See also* Talmud
  Pe'ah (1:1), 50
  Yoma (8:9), 301–302, 345
  Sotah (1:7), 60n106
  Bava Kamma (8:7), 300–301, 306, 336n118, 338
  Sanhedrin (3:5), 139–140
  Eduyyot (1:1–4), 79, 81, 81n18, 84, 91n45
  Eduyyot (1:12–14), 92
  Avot (1:6), 202n39, 419n45
  Avot (1:12), 53
  Avot (1:18), 45
  Avot (2:4), xxxii, 207–209, 419n45, 455
  Avot (3:11), 153n135, 160n164
  Avot (3:14), 129, 431
  Avot (4:3), 431
  Avot (5:7), 255n85
  Avot (5:11), 338
  Avot (5:17), xxvi, 57n96, 74–101, 454
Mitnik, Yitzchok, 247n72
mitsvah kiyumit, 121n31
mitsvot. See also under individual commandments
  613 commandments, xxviin15, xxviii, 51, 64, 110, 470–471
  "He shall not add [on]; lest he strike him an additional blow" (the commandment prohibiting physical violence), 145–150
  "And he shall not be as Korah and his assembly" (*see* holding on to a quarrel, prohibition of)
  "In righteousness you shall judge your friend" (the commandment to judge people favorably), 190–195, 211 (*see also* judging people favorably)
  that people neglect, considered like a *met mitzvah,* xxxin23
  thirty-eight that relate to conflict, xxix, 110
  were given in order to "purify people," 170
  "You shall cut away the barrier of your heart," 250n79
  "You shall love your neighbor as yourself," 52, 111–121, 122, 123, 124, 126–128, 131–132, 134, 137, 169, 171n193, 172, 173, 174, 176, 178, 179, 430
  "You shall no longer stiffen your neck," 250n79
  "You shall not bear a grudge," 137, 262, 263, 266, 267, 268, 274, 277–286, 290–291, 295–296, 399n131, 342n139, 350n177, 357, 363n200
  "You shall not bear sin because of him" (the prohibition against embarrassing someone), 142, 151, 158–163, 175, 226n9, 227n11, 237, 240–242
  "You shall not curse a deaf person" (the prohibition against cursing someone), 164–168, 187–188, 240n54
  "You shall not hate your brother in your heart," 134–142, 175, 182, 226n9, 227, 247n71, 258n90
  "You shall not hurt one another" (the prohibition against saying things that are hurtful), 150–158, 162–163, 259, 287, 288n80
  "You shall not take revenge," 137, 262, 266, 267, 269, 273–274, 277–287, 295–296, 339n131
  "You shall surely reprove your friend," 142, 158–159, 162–163, 224–255, 290, 472
  "And you shall walk in His ways" (*see ve-halakhta bi-drakhav*)
Moellin, Jacob, 334
Molkho, Joseph, 304n14, 328n91, 354–355
Moore, Carey A., 113n10
Moore, Christopher W., 8n15
Moore, Don A., 215n74
Moore, George Foot, 44n26, 115n16
Mordecai ben Hillel ha-Kohen, 149n122, 154n139, 154n142, 303n14, 305, 348n165

Morris, Catherine, xxiin6, 365n203
Morsella, Ezequiel, 20n49
Moses ben Jacob of Coucy, 65n120, 111n4, 115n15, 118n22, 123n36, 131n59, 135n76, 146n108, 151n129, 152n132, 159, 161n166, 164n177, 193n10, 224n5, 228, 234n36, 236, 238n50, 263n6, 283, 329, 334
Moskowitz, Gordon B., 212n66, 213n67
Moskowitz, Yeḥiel Zvi, 80n15
Mummendey, Amelie, xxin4
musar, 97, 131, 286n72, 359, 401, 408, 413n21, 416n30, 416n32, 449n155, 458, 459, 471
Musekura, Célestin, 383n239
Musto, Ronald G., xxin6
Myers, Michael W., 217nn77–78

N

Nadler, Janice, 221
Naeh, Shlomo, 57n96
Naḥmanides (*Ramban*), 112, 113n11, 116n18, 120n26, 164n179, 165n181, 165n183, 170n192, 194n12, 227n11, 228, 229n17, 248, 249n78, 254n83, 255n86, 271n23, 272, 279n42, 284n63, 419n42, 460
Naḥman of Bratslav, 208n59
Naḥmias, Joseph, 91n43, 94n51,
Nathan, R., 54
Nathan ben Abraham, 76n7
Navon, Chaim, 125n43
Neal, Geraldine, 403n275
Nebenzahl, Avigdor, 321n72, 327
Neblett, William R., 397
negative judgmental biases
  adverse effects on conflict, 214–215
  attributional biases, 213–214
  contemporary conflict resolution's approach, 218, 219
  countering, 215–218
  debiasing techniques, 215–217
  fundamental attribution error, 214
  negativity biases, 213
  research on, 212–215
negative peace
  absence of animosity, bickering, strife, etc., 39, 53, 54n76, 55, 70, 72, 73
  absence of physical violence, 13, 38n5, 71
negotiation
  basic definition, 6, 27
  competitive as opposed to cooperative, 7
  cooperative/collaborative (*see* cooperative negotiation)
Neubauer, Adolf, 45n37
Neudecker, Reinhard, 114n13
Neuman, Yeḥiel, 118n22, 195n17, 202n39, 206n49, 291n85
Nhat Hanh, Thich, xxiin6
Noahide commandments, 133n68
Nolan-Haley, Jacqueline M., 6n7, 6n9, 9n17
normative decision theory, 25–26
North, Joanna, 390n249, 398
Norzi, Jedidiah Solomon Raphael, 46n41
Novaco, Raymond W., 24n60, 434–440, 441, 445, 449n153, 450, 450n158
Numbers. *See under Tanakh,* Torah
Numbers Rabbah. See under Midrash, *Midrash Rabbah*

O

Ogiermann, Eva, 365n203
Ohbuchi, Ken-ichi, 377, 378, 380n237, 401n264
Olshtain, Elite, 365n204, 367nn209–210
ona'at devarim, 151, 152n131, 155–158, 162–163, 259, 287, 288n80, 321n72
Orekh Apayim
  intended purpose of, 411
  seminal work, xxxiii
  similarities and differences between *Orekh Apayim* and contemporary approaches, 447–449
  similarities to *Ma'aneh Rakh*
    behavioral and cognitive strategies, 417–421
    underlying assumptions and fundamental principles, 413–417
  stylistic aspects of, 412–413
  unique features of, 422–426
Orenstein, Avraham, 79n14

Orḥot Tsadikim, 229n17, 236n40, 238–239, 408n2, 415n29, 420n47
other religious traditions, xxin6, 14–15
Otten, Sabine, xxin4
Ouziel, Ben-Zion Meir Ḥai, 207n51

P

Palache, Ḥayyim, 313, 363n199
Paltiel, Eliezer, 84n31
Palvani, Daniel, 334n110
Pam, Avraham Ya'akov ha-Kohen, 143n100, 194n14
Papo, Eliezer, 119n26, 138–139, 233n34, 252n80, 275–276, 315n51, 354n186, 408n2, 418n40
Pappenheim, Solomon, 43, 57, 253n82
Pardo, David, 192n7
Pargament, Kenneth I., 383n239, 402n266, 404n277
Parker, John C., xxin4
Parlamis, Jennifer D., 25n61
paths of peace. *See darkhe shalom*
Patti, Janet, 18n42, 21n51, 22n55, 26nn64–65, 29n70
Patton, Bruce, 6n10, 14
peace. *See shalom*, "peace"
"peace ethos," definition, xxv
peace, pursuing, 36–73. *See also shalom*, "peace"
peace studies, 3–5, 32, 69, 70, 465
Pedersen, Johannes, 38n2
Penso, Ḥayim Daniel, 161n165, 238n49, 283n55
Pentateuch. *See Tanakh*, Torah
Perets, Elḥanan, 352n181, 354n186, 359n196
Perez de Cuellar, Javier, 4n3, 5n5
Perfet, Isaac ben Sheshet, 48n53, 280n49
Perla, Jeroham Fishel, 136n78, 160, 161n165, 161n 168, 162, 163n174, 166n186, 284n63, 284n65, 285–286
personal and social development and well-being, 33, 184–188, 461. *See also* character development; values, character development
person perception, 212
perspective taking
  cognitive process, 31, 219
  in cooperative negotiation, 27
  core component of conflict resolution, 18, 21–24, 72, 177n201, 185, 218–220
  core component of social and emotional development, 17n41
  countering biases through, 217–220
  "do not judge your friend until you are in his place," 207–209, 219, 220n86, 455
  in transformative mediation, 29
pesharah (compromise), xxiii, 255
Philo, 48n49
physical violence
  contemporary conflict resolution and traditional Jewish approaches' respective approaches towards, 183–184
  expression of hatred, 136–138
  prohibition against, 145–150
  responding with, when being attacked, 150
  talmudic condemnation of, 146–148
Pirke Avot. See Mishnah, *Avot*
Pliskin, Zelig, 409n4
Pomeranchik, Aryeh, 120n28, 171n193
Pondy, Louis R., 217n76
Pope, Sally Ganong, 29n69, 258n90
Poppers, Meir, 168
positive peace
  absence of structural violence (promulgation of social justice), 13, 70–71
  according to Joseph D. Epstein, 53–55, 65, 67, 70, 71
  as interconnectedness, fraternity, friendship, and love, 53, 70, 72, 73, 467
  in Judaism, 40, 53–55, 67–73
Potash, Mordekhai, 158n154
Poupko, Aryeh Leib, xxxin23
Price, Abraham A., 136n78, 164n176
problem-solving

approach to negotiation/mediation/ conflict resolution, 7–8, 10, 11, 18, 27–28, 72, 103, 255, 257, 464
as an underlying value, 31–33, 172, 177n201, 181
core component of conflict resolution education, 15, 18, 25–26
heuristic for, 25
preoccupation with resolving the specific, immediate issues at hand, 258n90
seems to favor expert problem-solvers, 258n90
progressive relaxation. *See* Jacobson, Edmund, relaxation technique
Pronin, Emily, 215n73
Pruitt, Dean G., xxin4, 24n60, 215n73, 221n88, 294n86, 403n273
Prutzman, Priscilla, 14n36, 15n37, 22n53, 29n70
Puccio, Carolyn, 215n73
pursuit of honor, 94, 96, 107

Q

Quint, Emanuel B., 114n13

R

Rabad III. *See* Abraham ben David of Posquières
rabbinic hyperbole, 48
Rabin, Chaim, 194n12
Rabinovitch, Nachum L., 165n183, 232
Rabinowitz, Chaim Dov, 192n6
Rabinowitz-Teomim, Benjamin, 123n38
Rabinowitz-Te'omim, Elijah David, 227n9, 231n27
Raccah, Masud, 242, 244n62, 245n67, 341n138
Raday, Zvi, 194n12
Ragoler, Meir ben Elijah, 92nn46–47, 94n51
Raines, Susan S., 215n73, 221n88
Rakover, Barukh, 166n187
Rakover, Nahum, 128n49, 129n54, 133n68
Rambam. *See* Maimonides
Ramban. *See* Naḥmanides
Ramsbotham, Oliver, xxin5, 11n20
Rapoport, Anatol, 11
rasha (wicked person), 146, 147n112, 149, 184, 199, 199n33, 200, 202, . *See also resha'im*
Rashi (Solomon ben Isaac), xxviiin15, 49–50n58, 54n73, 60n107, 61n109, 82n20, 84, 90n42, 93n49, 98n68, 115, 144n104, 145n105, 146n110, 147n113, 148n116, 152n132, 155, 161, 165n181, 190n2, 191, 192n7, 196, 204, 205n47, 232n31, 238n49, 253n82, 255n86, 262n5, 279n43, 302nn9–10, 310n34, 311, 312n41, 323, 323nn77–79, 324n83, 325n84, 329, 337n121, 339n129, 348n162, 363n199, 421n50, 427n82, 428n84, 471
rational emotive behavior therapy, 435, 435n108, 439, 441, 441n122
rationalization, defense mechanism of, 98
Ratner, Dov Baer, 327n85
Ravitzky, Aviezer, 43, 43n23, 46n38, 49n56
Razovsky, Baruch, 316n52
Reardon, Betty A., 4n3, 5
Reber, Arthur S., 118n23
Reber, Emily S., 118n23
Recanati, Menaḥem, 283n59
Redden, Kenneth R., 8n16
Reischer, Jacob, 55n80, 92nn46–47, 96n61, 116n17, 336n119
relaxation response, 442, 442n124
religious traditions, other, xxin6, 14–15
repentance (*teshuvah*), 270, 305n19, 315n50, 317–318, 332–333, 340, 343, 343n143, 344, 345n149, 379
"*resha'im*," wicked people, 61, 64, 128n50. *See also rasha*
"resident aliens" (*ger toshav*), 133
respect, showing to people. *See also derekh erets; kevod ha-beriyot*
component of "You shall love your neighbour," and *ahavat ha-beriyot*, 118–119, 171n193, 173

in the course of *tokhaḥah*, 238n49, 257, 432, 455
obligation stems from *imago Dei*, 127, 129–130
response prevention, 444, 444n130
revenge. *See also mitsvot*, "You shall not take revenge"
dealing with the emotional and psychological challenges of not taking, 274–277
definition of the English word, 261n1
practical halakhic discourse on, 277–291
prohibition against, 262–291
underlying reasons for not taking, 263–277
Richardson, Deborah R., 22n52, 217n78
Riley, Shannon, 214n70
Rivkes, Moses, 289n80
Rivkin, Ben Zion, 268n15
Robbennolt, Jennifer K., 401n265
Roe, Kiki, 118n23
Rogers, Carl R., 21n50
Rogers, Nancy H., 6n7, 8n14, 9n17, 21n50
Rokeaḥ, Efrayim, 79n14
role reversal, 22
Rones, Michal, xxn3, 456n8
Rosenberg, Abraham J., 323n78
Rosenberg, Shalom, 111n5
Rosensweig, Michael, 106n83
Rosmarin, Moshe, 160n158
Ross, Lee, 214n72
Rossenbaum, Asher, 92n47
Roth, Daniel, xxin6, xxviiin17, 53n72, 363n199, 455n6, 465n26
Roth, Deborah A., 444n130
Rubin, Jeffrey Z., 6n10, 24n60, 215n73, 221n88, 294n86,
Rusbult, Caryl E., 217n78, 402n272
Ryan, Kevin, 33n76

S

Sa'adia ben Joseph (Sa'adia Gaon), 60n107, 136n78, 165n183, 263–264, 266n11, 271n23, 343n143
Sadalla, Gail, 18n42, 25n61, 29n70
Sagi, Avi, 106n83
Said, Abdul Aziz, xxiin6
Salanter, Israel. *See* Lipkin (Salanter), Israel
Salem, Richard A., 21n50
Salovey, Peter, 17n41
Samsonovits, Mosheh, 202n38
Samuel ben Meir, 124, 125n41, 126, 227, 228n14
Sander, Frank E. A., 6n7, 8n14, 9n17
Sarna, Ezekiel, 92n47, 93, 94n53, 97n64, 99n68, 99n71, 116n17, 341, 342n139, 351n178, 356–357, 359n195
Saunders, David M., 6n10
Schachter, Hershel, 131n60, 306n22, 363n200
Scheinberg, Ḥayim Pinḥas, 328n89, 345n150, 353n183
Schellenberg, James A., 221n88
Schepansky, Israel, 129n53, 149nn117–118
Scherer, Michael, 383n240
Schick, Moses, 114n12
Schiffman, Lawrence H., 225n6
Schimmel, Solomon, 447, 452
Schlenker, Barry R., 376, 377, 378n233, 380n237
Schmid, H. H., 57n94
Schmitt, Manfred, 375n223
Schofield, Janet Ward, 19n44
Schor, Abraham Ḥayyim, 152n131
Schotten, Samuel, 148nn114–115
Schurtz, David Ryan, 294n86
Schwadron, Shalom Mordecai (*Maharsham*), 125, 126n45, 128
Schwartz, Baruch J., 227n13
Schwartz, Yoel, 133n68
Scimecca, Joseph A., 12n25
Searle, John R.,
Sefer ha-Ḥinukh, 111n4, 113n9, 131n59, 135n76, 146n108, 151n129, 154, 155, 157, 159n156, 164n177, 168n191, 193n10, 225n5, 228, 236, 237n47, 248, 249n78, 262n6, 266n10, 269–274, 275–276, 284–289, 416n30
Sefer Halakhot Gedolot, 52, 111n4, 135n76, 146n108, 151n129, 159n156, 164n177, 224n5, 262n6

Sefer ha-Yashar, 408n2, 416n30, 428–430
Segal, Dan, 273n26
Segal, Yehudah Zeraḥyah, 122n32
Seḥayek, Moshe, 277n35
self-awareness, 17n41, 103, 253n82, 415, 448, 451
self-monitoring, 17n41, 20, 432, 437, 440, 442, 448
self-motivation, 17n41
self-regulation of emotion, 17n41, 24, 436
Sende, Ken, xxiin6
Seybold, Kevin S., 402n268
Sforno, Obadiah, 88n34, 91n43, 96n60
Shabbetai ben Meir ha-Kohen (*Shakh*), 98n67, 139n88, 149n120
Shailat, Isaac, 90n42, 96n61, 203n40
shalom, "peace." *See also darkhe shalom*, "paths of peace"
  altering the truth for the sake of, 54–55
  basic, Hebrew "peace terminology," 67
  the biblical term
    according to modern Hebraists, 37–39
    according to traditional rabbinic scholars, 39–43
  earthly and supernal functions, 45–46
  encomiums in praise of, 44–45
  meta-halakhic principle, 49
  normative status, 49
  numinous qualities, 46–47
  occurrence of the Hebrew term, xxvin13, 37
  promoting peace
    the general imperative, 49–53
    nature and extent of the obligation, 49–56
    source in the Torah, 51–53
  "seek peace and pursue it," 49–51
  talmudic and midrashic perspectives, meaning and significance of, 44–49
  as Torah Value, 47–49
Shalom of Neustadt, 316
Shapira, Abraham, 321n72
Shapira, Elijah, 346, 347n156
Shapira, Judah Loeb, 114, 345n155
Shapira, Moshe Shmuel, 238n50, 241n56
Shapira, Shalom Tsevi, 325n84
Sharan, Shlomo, 19n45
Sharkey, William, 162n169
Sharvit, Shimon, 75nn3–5
Shaviv, Yehuda, 64n118
Shealy, Craig N., 32n75
Sheinberger, Tsevi Hirsch, 343n144
Shelomoh ben Yitsḥak ha-Levi ha-Sefaradi (Solomon [II] ben Isaac Levi), 88
Sherira ben Ḥanina Gaon, 139n89, 153
Shilo, Shmuel, 319n64
Shlozover, Avraham, 246n70
Shmerler, Ḥayim, 315n50, 345n148
Shmuelevitz, Ḥayim Leib, 60n107, 93n49, 95nn55–56
Shneur Zalman of Lyady, 51, 78n9, 150n125, 161n165, 161n167, 230n22, 234n36, 246, 317, 320n68, 325n84, 335n116, 349n173, 416n31
Shonholtz, Raymond, 32n75
Shperber, David, 302n9
Shpigel, Yisrael, 78n9
Shternbukh, Moshe, 128n49, 308n28, 315n51, 316n52, 323, 345n150, 350n176,
Shulevits, Eliezer, 131n63
Siegman, Aron Wolfe, 446n141
Sillars, Alan L., 215n73
Silver, Yitsḥak Isaac, xvii, 200, 201n36, 203n40, 207n54, 344n146, 345n151, 363n200
Simeon ben Azzai, 124–129
Simeon ben Lakish, 63, 146, 147n112, 184
sinat ḥinam, "baseless hatred," 134–135, 135n74
sins, verbal confession to God, 307n24, 317–318
Sirkes, Joel (*Bayit Ḥadash*), 150n125, 307, 308n27, 312, 312n42, 316–318, 319, 328, 329, 334, 340, 341nn137–138, 346, 347, 349n172
Slavin, Robert E., 19n45
Smith, Karl A., 23

Smith, Nick, 364n202, 370–371, 373n220, 374, 375, 376, 379, 380nn237–238
Smith, Richard H., 293n86
Snow, Selena Cappell, 446n141
Snyder, Douglas K., 404n277
social and emotional development
essential elements, according to Mayer and Salovey, 17n41
social and emotional learning, 17, 185n214, 186, 404, 460, 461n22, 462
social cognition, 213n67
social interdependence, 12
social psychology, xix, 12, 123n38, 211, 212, 213, 363
Sofer, Moses, 43n22, 206n49, 233n34
Sofer, Shemuel Binyamin, 89n40
Sofer, Ya'akov Ḥayim, 168n190
Sofer, Ya'akov Shalom, 89
Sokoloff, Michael, 61n109
Solomon ben Adret (*Rashba*), 148n116, 149n119, 168n191, 170n192
Solomon ben Isaac. *See Rashi*
Solomon ha-Bavli, 62n110
Soloveichik, Ahron, 129n55, 131, 268n15, 321n72
Soloveichik, Ḥayyim, 310n32
Soloveitchik, Joseph B., xxviin14, 122n35, 129n54, 131n60, 154n143, 171n193, 271, 271n22, 305–307, 317n60, 363n200
Sperber, Daniel, 44, 44n26
Stanovich, Keith E., 216n75
Steif, Jonathan, 131n63
Steinberg, Gerald, xxn3, 455–457
Steinman, Aharon Yehudah Leib, 47n46, 358–359, 399nn261–262, 401
Stemberger, Gunter, 472, 473
Stephens, John B., 3–4, 9, 9n18
Sternbuch, Moshe. *See* Shternbukh, Moshe
Strack, H. L., 472, 473
Strack, Micha, 365, 366n207, 373, 374n222, 375nn223–224, 376, 376n225, 377, 378, 380nn237–238
Strashun, Samuel, 125
Strongman, K. T., 447
structural violence, 5, 13, 71
structured academic controversy, 23
Stuckless, Noreen, 293n86
suffering
attributing to divine providence, including the actions of another human being, 271–272, 421
of innocent children, 60n107
the view that "there is no suffering without sin," 272
Suinn, Richard, 445n133
Sukhodolsky, Denis G., 446n140
systematic desensitization, 435, 435n110, 442, 442n125, 444

T

Tafrate, Raymond Chip, 440n119, 441n122, 443nn127–128, 444nn131–132, 445–446
Talmud, xxii, 37n, 472
Talmud, Babylonian
Berakhot (5a), 271n21
Berakhot (7a–b), 362n198
Berakhot (12b). 315n50
Berakhot (19a) 201n36
Berakhot (20a), 427, 428n84
Berakhot (25b), 276
Berakhot (29b), 414n23
Berakhot (31a–b), 226n7
Berakhot (43b), 153n134, 161n164
Berakhot (55b), 47
Berakhot (60b), 421n50
Shabbat (10a–b), 46n42
Shabbat (14b), 81, 87, 91n45
Shabbat (15a), 81n17
Shabbat (31a), 112n7, 113n10, 115, 115–116n17
Shabbat (34a), 238, 284n62, 420n47
Shabbat (55a), 226n7, 272
Shabbat (88b), 289n81
Shabbat (97a), 205n48
Shabbat (105b), 135n75, 414n23
Shabbat (119a), 98
Shabbat (127 a–b), 191, 202n38, 211
Shabbat (133b), 130n59
Eruvin (13b), 93n49, 106n83
Pesaḥim (113b), 142n96
Yoma (9b), 135, 135n74,

Yoma (19b), 205n48
Yoma (22b–23a), 280nn47–48, 281, 281n53, 286, 289, 289n81, 291n85
Yoma (38b–39a). 415n28
Yoma (85b), 300, 302, 302n8, 306
Yoma (86b), 300, 318
Yoma (87a), 302, 303, 303n11, 310–311, 311n35, 312, 312n42, 323, 324, 324n80, 324n83, 326, 334, 363n200
Yoma (87a–b), 300, 303, 305, 310n32, 311n36, 312, 312n42, 328
Yoma (87b), 329n96, 337, 346n152, 347, 348n163,
Betsah (3b), 284n62
Betsah (16a), 79n11
Betsah (30a), 226n7
Rosh Hashanah (17a), 79n13, 342n140
Ta'anit (18b), 421n50
Ta'anit (20a–b), 338n127
Ta'anit (22a), 56n86
Ta'anit (24a), 79n10
Ta'anit (31a), 79n12
Megillah (11a), 64n116
Megillah (12b), 244
Megillah (28a), 342n140, 363n200
Ḥagigah (3b), 89n39
Ḥagigah (5a), 158n154
Yevamot (14b), 92–93
Yevamot (44a), 56n85
Yevamot (65b), 54, 226n7, 245
Yevamot (79a), 338
Yevamot (109a), 49
Ketubot (16b–17a), 55–56n80
Ketubot (33a), 146n107
Ketubot (67b), 153n134, 161n164
Ketubot (105b), 98
Ketubot (106a), 226n8
Nedarim (64b), 64n117
Sotah (10b), 153n134
Sotah (12a), 79n11
Sotah (14a), 130n59, 131n60
Sotah (47b), 82n21, 84n28
Gittin (6b), 106n83
Gittin (36b), 289n81
Gittin (59b), xxvii, 48n49, 110, 170
Gittin (89b), 90n42
Kiddushin (21b), 142n97
Kiddushin (30b), 97n63
Kiddushin (40a), 50
Kiddushin (49b–50a), 352
Bava Kamma (28a), 148
Bava Kamma (37a), 148n116
Bava Kamma (58b), 349n167
Bava Kamma (81b), 79n11
Bava Kamma (83b), 150
Bava Kamma (84b), 150n123
Bava Kamma (92a), 300–301, 306, 335n117, 336, 336n118, 338
Bava Metsia (31a), 226n7
Bava Metsia (32b), 143n101
Bava Metsia (49a, 52a–b, 75b–76b, 77b, 79a–b), 280
Bava Metsia (51b), 319n65
Bava Metsia (58b), 151, 153n134, 153n137, 156n150, 349n167
Bava Metsia (58b–59a), 161n164
Bava Metsia (59a), 56n86, 152n132
Bava Metsia (62a), 114n11, 346n155
Bava Metsia (71a), 132n66
Bava Metsia (75b), 202n38
Bava Batra (16a), 79n12
Bava Batra (145b), 280
Sanhedrin (3a), 192n8
Sanhedrin (6b), 53n72
Sanhedrin (6b–7a), 61–62
Sanhedrin (14a), 287n75
Sanhedrin (17a), 88
Sanhedrin (19a), 139n88
Sanhedrin (26a), 202n38
Sanhedrin (27b), 139–140, 140n90
Sanhedrin (29a), 139n87
Sanhedrin (32a), 145n105
Sanhedrin (32b), 192n8
Sanhedrin (39b), 79n11
Sanhedrin (40b), 145n105
Sanhedrin (40b–41a), 145n105
Sanhedrin (56a), 133n68
Sanhedrin (58b), 146–148, 146n109
Sanhedrin (66a–b), 164–165, 165n180
Sanhedrin (72b), 145n105
Sanhedrin (74a), 135n73, 150n124
Sanhedrin (81b), 145n105

Sanhedrin (85a), 146n107
Sanhedrin (88b), 82n21, 91n45
Sanhedrin (90a), 60n106
Sanhedrin (99a), 153n135, 161n164
Sanhedrin (110a), xxxn21, 62–65, 85n32, 98n68
Makkot (16a), 145n105
Makkot (22a–22b), 145n105
Makkot (22a–23a), 145n105
Makkot (23b), xxviiin16, 51n63, 110, 471
Shevuot (30a), 190, 192n8, 193n9
Shevuot (36a), 164n179
Shevuot (39a), 226n7
Avodah Zarah (3a), 276
Avodah Zarah (5a), 64n117
Avodah Zarah (7a), 284n62
Avodah Zarah (8a), 79n11
Avodah Zarah (58b), 58
Zevaḥim (116b), 79n11
Ḥullin (7a), 84n28
Ḥullin (7b), 421n50
Ḥullin (89a), 286–287n72
Ḥullin (137b), 58
Arakhin (15b), 135n75
Arakhin (16b), 136, 151, 158–161, 163, 226, 226n7, 227n11, 232n28, 237, 238n50, 247, 247n72, 252n81
Temurah (4a), 164n179
Tamid (28a), 79n12
Niddah (13a–b), 148
Niddah (61a), 206n50
Talmud, Jerusalem
Berakhot (2:9), 79n10
Peah (4a), 51n61
Terumot (5:2), 92
Shabbat (1:4), 74n2
Yoma (8:7), 312n43, 314n48, 325n84, 326, 327
Ḥagigah (2:1), 79n13
Ḥagigah (2:2), 81n16, 82n21
Nedarim, (9:4), 111, 111n6, 118n22, 124, 124n39, 126n45
Gittin (1:4), 79n13
Kiddushin (1:1), 93n48
Kiddushin (4:1), 79n12
Bava Kamma (8:7), 326, 327n85, 335n117
Bava Kamma (36b), 348
Bava Metsia (5:3), 280
Sanhedrin (1:4), 82n21
Talmud, Minor Tractates, 470
Avot de-Rabbi Nathan (12:3), 54n74
Avot de-Rabbi Nathan (12:6), 54n76
Derekh Erets Rabbah (5), 205n47
Derekh Erets Zuta (3), 428n85
Derekh Erets Zuta (9), 58, 58n97, 59n101, 60, 60n104
Derekh Erets Zuta (10), 79n12
Derekh Erets Zuta (*Perek ha-Shalom*), 44, 44n29, 54, 54n73
Kallah Rabbati (3), 45n37, 48n52, 50n59
Kallah Rabbati (4), 79n12, 225n85
Kallah Rabbati (5), 428n85
Kallah Rabbati (9), xxxii, 199n32, 205n47 206n49
Kallah Rabbati (10), 55n80
Tanakh
Torah (Pentateuch)
Genesis (1:27), 125n43
Genesis (5:1), 124, 125, 125n43, 128, 154
Genesis (9:6), 125n43, 129
Genesis (13:7), 56, 56n87
Genesis (13:8), 56n84
Genesis (20:7), 301
Genesis (20:17), 230, 335n117, 336
Genesis (21:25–27), 252n80
Genesis (26:27–31), 252n80
Genesis (33:18), 37n1
Genesis (37–45), 359n195
Genesis (37:14), 41
Genesis (50:17), 324, 334
Exodus (2:13), 146n109
Exodus (22:27), 164–165
Exodus (23:2), 288n78
Exodus (23:4–5), 51, 142, 142 n96
Exodus (23:7), 54, 460
Leviticus (16:30), 302
Leviticus (19:11), 460
Leviticus (19:13), 460
Leviticus (19:14), 164–165
Leviticus (19:15), 190, 192–195, 193n9, 194n15

Leviticus (19:17), 113n9, 134–137, 139–142, 151, 158–159, 224–228, 227n11, 237, 253n82, 290, 454, 472
Leviticus (19:18), 52, 111–121, 115n15, 123, 131, 262, 267, 268, 277–280, 339n131, 430, 454
Leviticus (19:36), 194n15
Leviticus (20:9), 164–165
Leviticus (25:17), 151
Leviticus (26:41), 338n125
Numbers (5:6–7), 317n60
Numbers (12:1–16), 232
Numbers (12:9), 232
Numbers (16:1–17:15), 62–64, 80, 80n15, 85–86, 90–91, 93–95
Numbers (16:3), 85
Numbers (16:8–11), 64, 85
Numbers (16:12–14), 64, 85
Numbers (16:12a), 85
Numbers (16:12b), 86
Number (16:13), 94n53
Numbers (16:19), 85
Numbers (16:25), 63, 64
Numbers (16:27–33), 60
Numbers (17:5), 63
Numbers (21:7), 337, 337n121
Deuteronomy (1:16), 194n15
Deuteronomy (6:5), 113n9, 130
Deuteronomy (6:18), 255, 460
Deuteronomy (10:16), 250n79
Deuteronomy (16:18), 194n15
Deuteronomy (16:20), 194n15
Deuteronomy (19:6), 289n83
Deuteronomy (19:11), 134n72
Deuteronomy (20:10), 52
Deuteronomy (22:6), 51
Deuteronomy (24:21), 51
Deuteronomy (25:1), 56, 56n87
Deuteronomy (25:3), 145–146
Deuteronomy (25:12), 148
Deuteronomy (25:15), 194n15
Deuteronomy (28:9), xxxn21, 52, 130
Nevi'im (Prophets)
Judges (5:31), 282n53, 289
Judges (6:24), 46
1 Samuel (2:12–17), 147
1 Samuel (2:16), 147
1 Samuel (2:17), 147
1 Samuel (2:25), 229n17, 302n9
1 Samuel (10:27–11:13), 281n53
1 Samuel (12:23), 336
2 Samuel (11:7), 41
2 Samuel (13:22), 230
2 Samuel (16:10–11), 421n50
2 Samuel (16:10–12), 272
2 Samuel (16:11), 270
2 Samuel (21), 338
2 Samuel (21:2), 338
1 Kings (2:5), 38n5
1 Kings (2:8–9), 272
Isaiah (5:20), 207
Isaiah (45:7), 42, 53
Isaiah (58:4), 56n83
Isaiah (60:7), 301n6
Jeremiah (9:7), 138
Jeremiah (9:25), 338n125
Jeremiah (15:10), 56n82
Ezekiel (16:42), 43
Ezekiel (44:7), 338n125
Ezekiel (44:9), 338n125
Hosea (10:2), 59n101
Amos (1:11), 338n126
Habakkuk (1:3), 56n82
Zechariah (8:17), 39
Zechariah (8:19), 92
Malachi (2), 128
Malachi (2:6), 53n72
Malachi (2:10), 126
Ketuvim (Hagiographa)
Psalms (19:13), xxxv
Psalms (32:5), 317n60
Psalms (34:15), 49–51, 454
Psalms (37:37), 39
Psalms (38:4), 41
Psalms (39:11), 56n86
Psalms (85:11), 39
Psalms (106:16), 85n32
Psalms (145:9), 133
Proverbs (3:17), 48, 133, 144
Proverbs (3:29), 138n84
Proverbs (6:2–3), 324–325n83
Proverbs (9:8), 245, 250n79
Proverbs (10:12), 134n71

Proverbs (10:18), 138n84
Proverbs (12:18), 154
Proverbs (13:10), 56n83
Proverbs (14:15), 207
Proverbs (15:18), 408
Proverbs (16:2), 98
Proverbs (17:14), 56n82, 61, 62
Proverbs (17:15), 207
Proverbs (17:19), 56n83
Proverbs (19:2), 417n36
Proverbs (20:22), 274, 275n29
Proverbs (21:2), 98n67
Proverbs (21:12), 207
Proverbs (24:29), 274, 285
Proverbs (25:15), 237, 410n5
Proverbs (26:21), 56, 56n87
Proverbs (26:25), 207
Proverbs (26:27), 265
Job (3:18), 43
Job (4:6–7), 156n150
Job (25:2), 46, 53n69
Job (33:27), 323, 326, 334
Ecclesiastes (3:8), 38n5
Ecclesiastes (7:9), 288, 427
Ecclesiastes (9:17), 237, 239, 420n47
1 Chronicles (27:1 ff.), 57, 75n3
1 Chronicles (28:9), 350n176
Targum
definition 472
Targum Onkelos, 194, 194n15, 224n4
Targum Pseudo-Jonathan, 94n53, 115n15, 142n96
Tarika, Jedidiah Samuel, 245
Taylor, Alison, 8n15
Tavuchis, Nicholas,
Teharani, Eliyahu Porat, 409
Telch, Michael J., 443n129, 444n131
Teomim, Joseph, 115n17, 161nn167–168, 299n1, 318n63, 330n100
teshuvah. *See* repentance
Testaments of the Twelve Patriarchs, 227
Theodor, J., 124n39
Thomas, Kenneth W., 217n76, 223n1
Thompson, Leigh, 221
Thoresen, Carl E., 383n239
Tidwell, Alan C., 10n20, 11n24, 13n29
Tjosvold, Dean, 105n82
Tobias, Steven E., 25n62
Tobit (4:15a), 113n10
tokhaḥah, "reproof"
basic concept of, xxx, 225, 229, 472
be-derekh kavod, "in a respectful manner," 238n49
the biblical source, 225–228
compared with cooperative negotiation, 175, 255–257, 257n90, 464
connection with "do not judge your friend until you are in his place," 208–209, 220n86
the dialogic component, 247–250
embarrassing someone in the course of, 158–159, 162–163, 240–242
"everything is in accordance with the time, issue, place, and individual," 254, 258
focus on overt information, 220
forgiving the person instead of, 242–247, 405
fundamental challenges of, 252–253
in a gentle manner, 233n34, 235–239, 240, 241, 242, 253, 259, 260
incorporates two distinct facets, 225, 472
in private, 236–237, 241, 253, 254
Maimonides discussion of the laws of, 228–250
method for dealing with anger, 419, 448, 451
method for dealing with hatred, 142, 227, 229–231, 239, 247n71, 258n90
method for dealing with resentment, 291, 293
ona'at devarim in the course of, 163, 163n174, 259
one should be receptive to and appreciate, 250n79
process of clarification, 253n82
promotes love and peace, 223, 251
in relationship to the prohibition against bearing a grudge, 290–291

sources that may serve as guides to the dialogue of, 254–255
translation of the word, 224
types of issues it encompasses, 229n17, 291n85
Tomasi, Luigi, 31n72
Torczyner, Harry, 38n10
Tosafot, 46n43, 81n17, 145n105, 148n116, 153n134, 153n136, 164n179, 165n180,
Tosefta
Bikkurim (2:15), 79n11
Ḥagigah (2:4), 82n21
Yevamot (1:3), 93n48
Sotah (14:1), 82n21
Sotah (14:10), 84n28
Sanhedrin (7:1), 82n21
Sanhedrin (11), 145n105
Makkot (3:10), 145n105
Toviyahu ben Eliezer, 115n15, 164n179, 165n184
Tovolski, Avraham, 409
Trager, Yitsḥak, 321n72
Trani, Joseph ben Moses, 150n125, 319, 322
Trani, Moses ben Joseph, 119n26, 143n99, 150n125
transformative approach, Bush and Folger, 28–29, 70
Treves, Menaḥem, 246n70, 247n71
tsa'ara de-gufa, "personal suffering," 277, 280–286, 280n49, 292n85
tsa'ar ba'ale ḥayyim, the suffering of a living creature, 144
Tsang, Jo-Ann, 402n272
Tsuriel, Moshe, 130n58, 174n196
Twersky, Isadore, 231n26

U

Uceda, Samuel, 75n4, 89n37, 94n51, 96n60, 414n24
Ulman, Shlomo Zalman, 353nn183–184
Ury, William, 6n10, 14, 223n1

V

van den Born, Adrianus, 38n3
Vander Laan, Kelly L., 402n268
Van Kleef, Gerben A., 24nn59–60
Van Lange, Paul A. M., 402n269
Vanunu, Shimon, 119n26
ve-halakhta bi-drakhav, "And you shall walk in His ways" (*imitatio Dei*), xxxn21, 52, 130–131, 134, 460
venting anger, 25, 25n61, 188n217
verbal abuse
defining, 150n126
prohibitions against, 150–168 (*see also under individual prohibitions*)
rabbinic stance towards, 152–154
Victor, David A., 20n49
Vidal Yom Tov of Tolosa, xxviiin18, 254n83
Vilna Gaon, *see* Elijah ben Solomon
vindicating the wicked, 206–207
Vinman, Yisrael, 321n73
Vital, Ḥayyim, 129n53, 131n63, 144n104, 414n23, 431
Vozner, Shemuel, 155n145

W

Wade, Nathaniel G., 384, 385, 386, 387, 392n250
Wagner, Ulrich, 375nn223–224, 376n225, 377, 378, 380n237
Wald, Marcus, xxvn12, 37n1, 39n11, 39n14, 44n26
Wald, Stephen G., 79n14
Waldman, Shimon Moshe, 334n110
Walker, Donald F., 383
Walkin, Aharon, 95n55, 99n71
Wallach, Shlomo Moshe, 311n38, 311n40
Ware, Stephen J., 6, 7, 8n16, 9n17
Warwar, Serine, 384n242
Wasserman, Eleazar Simḥah, 268n15
Wasserman, Elḥanan Bunim, 163n174
Weary, Gifford, 214n70
Webel, Charles P., 4n3
Weil, Jacob, 149n119, 149n121, 348n165
Weinberg, Jehiel Jacob, 135n74
Weinberger, Zvi H., xxvii, 138, 139n89, 141, 141nn92–93, 226n9, 234, 235nn37–38, 236n39, 245n67, 246, 247n71, 248, 249, 249n78, 250,

268n15, 268n17, 277n34, 277n36, 278n41, 279n44, 280nn46–47, 280n49, 281nn51–52, 282n53, 284nn61, 284nn63–64, 285n66, 287n74, 291, 335n117, 342n139, 357n192, 363n200, 459n14
Weiner, Bernard, 205n46
Weinfeld, Abraham, 121n30
Weinreich, Uriel, 422n52
Weinthal, Benjamin, 13n30
Weiss, Asher, 163n174, 203n40
Weiss, Isaac Hirsch, 111n6
Weiss, Isaac Jacob, 65n120, 246n70
Weisser, Meir Loeb ben Jehiel Michael (*Malbim*), 43, 113n10, 114, 143n99, 193n11, 427n79
Wessely, Naphtali Herz, 75n3, 82n19, 91n45, 92nn46–47, 94n51, 95n55, 112
West, Richard F., 216n75
Westerman, Claus, 224n3
White, Judith B., 22n52, 217n77
win-win solutions, 7, 10, 28, 103, 255, 257
Wisdom of Ben Sira, 45, 227
Wispé, Lauren, 217n77
Witvliet, Charlotte van Oyen, 402n268
Wolbe, Shlomo, 106n83, 253n82, 355, 359nn196–197, 399
Wolfsohn, Yehoshua Falik Ze'ev, 207n51
Wolpe, Joseph, 436n110
Woodhouse, Tom, xxin5, 11n20
Worthington, Everett L. Jr., 383n240, 384, 385, 386, 387, 390, 392n250, 396n256, 397
Wosner, Shai, 76n6, 101n72
Wurzburger, Walter S., 49n54

Y

Yehuda, Zvi A., 130n58
Yehudah ben Eliezer, 116n17
Yehudai ben Naḥman, 52n64, 111n4, 224n5, 262n6
Yellin, Aryeh Loeb, 327n85
Yisrael kasher, "a proper Jew," 128, 128n48
Yonge, C. D., 48n49
Yosef, Ovadia, 313n44, 322
Young, Stacy L., 21n51
"You shall cut away the barrier of your heart," 250n79
"You shall do that which is right and good in the eyes of the Lord," 255, 460
"You shall love your neighbor as yourself." *See also mitsvot,* "You shall love your neighbor as yourself"
  achieved through self-identification, 117–118n22
  centrality of the commandment, 111–112, 134
  in comparison with Ben Azzai's principle, 126–128
  encompasses acts of *ḥesed,* "loving-kindness," 116–117
  encompasses the promotion of peace, 52
  expressed as empathy, 118, 119, 176
  form and degree of love required, 114–121
    centrist position, 116–117, 121n31, 171n193, 176
    maximalist position, 117–121, 176
    minimalist position, 115, 121n31, 176
  negative formulation, 113n10, 115, 116n17
  reasons for rejecting a literal interpretation, 112–114
  in relation to *kevod ha-beriyot,* 171n193
  transgresses this commandment when one exhibits hatred, 137
  as value, as opposed to cooperation, 172–174
  when not applicable, 178n203
  whether it applies to all humankind, 120, 122, 123n36, 131–134, 430 (*see also ahavat ha-beriyot,* love for all humanity)
"You shall not bear a grudge." *see* grudge, prohibition against bearing
"You shall not bear sin because of him" (prohibition against embarrassing someone). *See also* embarrassment; *mitsvot*: "You shall not bear sin because of him"

prohibition against embarrassing someone, 151, 158–163, 227n11, 236, 237, 240–242
"You shall not curse a deaf person" (the prohibition against cursing someone), 164–168, 175, 187–188
basic parameters of, 164
explanations for the prohibition, 167–168
not necessarily a prohibition against "verbal abuse," 164–166
source for the prohibition, 164, 165–166
"You shall not hate your brother in your heart," 134–145, 175, 182.
degree of hatred that is prohibited, 139–141
exceptions to the prohibition, 140–141n92
form of hatred that is prohibited, 135–139
"You shall not hurt one another" (the prohibition against saying things that are hurtful). *See ona'at devarim*
"You shall not take revenge." *see mitsvot*: "You shall not take revenge"; revenge, prohibition against
"You shall surely reprove your friend." *see tokhaḥah*

Z

Zacuto, Abraham, 312n41
Zacuto, Moses, 155, 157
Zaichyk, Ḥayim Ephraim, 324n82
Zaks, Hillel, 193n10, 195n17, 199n33
Zalb, Zvi Chaim, 59n102
Zartman, I. William, 10n19
Zer-Kavod, Mordechai, 325n83
Zilber, Binyamin Yehoshua, 202n38, 283n58, 308n27, 311n38, 315n51, 321n72, 322, 323n76, 325n84, 342n139, 344n144
Zilberberg, Tzvi Meir, 194n14, 195n16
Zilberstein, Yitsḥak, 323n75, 352n181, 362n198
Zillman, Dolf, 217n76
Zinner, Gavriel,
Ziv (Broida), Simḥah Zissel, 97n64, 123n38, 131, 131n62, 209n61, 352–353, 352n182, 398, 449n155
Ziwica, Shlomo, 410n6
Zohar, 44n26, 53n69, 414, 414n23, 415n28

CPSIA information can be obtained
at www.ICGtesting.com
Printed in the USA
JSHW052137111121
20394JS00006B/163

9 781618 118455